THE CRUSADERS' KINGDOM

THE CRUSADERS' KINGDOM

European Colonialism in the Middle Ages

JOSHUA PRAWER

PRAEGER PUBLISHERS

New York · Washington

BOOKS THAT MATTER

Published in the United States of America in 1972
by Praeger Publishers, Inc., 111 Fourth Avenue,
New York, N.Y. 10003

© 1972 by Joshua Prawer

Library of Congress Catalog Card Number: 72-77069

Printed in Israel

CONTENTS

LIST OF ILLUSTRATIONS

Between pages 308 and 309

The refectory of the order of St John, Acre (courtesy Ronald Sheridan, Israel Department of Antiquities).

Aerial view of Acre (courtesy Israel Air Force).

View of Pilgrim's Castle (courtesy Israel Department of Antiquities).

Aerial view of Caesarea (courtesy Israel Air Force).

Remains of St Louis's fortifications in Caesarea (courtesy Israel National Parks Authority).

Façade of the Church of the Holy Sepulchre (courtesy Zodiaque).

Aerial view of the medieval citadel of Jerusalem (courtesy Werner Braun).

The church of the Nunnery of St Anne (courtesy Zodiaque, J. Schweig).

Main nave of the Church of the Nativity (courtesy Ronald Sheridan, Israel Department of Antiquities).

Between pages 436 and 437

A painted glass, probably from Tyre (courtesy British Museum, London).

Capital from Nazareth depicting St Peter raising Tabitha (courtesy J. Schweig, Israel Department of Antiquities).

Capital from Nazareth showing demons threatening the believer (courtesy J. Schweig, Israel Department of Antiquities).

Columns of the portal of the Church of the Holy Sepulchre (courtesy Ronald Sheridan, Israel Department of Antiquities).

Right lintel above entrance to the Church of the Holy Sepulchre (courtesy J. Schweig, Israel Department of Antiquities).

Left lintel above the entrance to the Church of the Holy Sepulchre (courtesy J. Schweig, Israel Department of Antiquities).

Ivory covers of Queen Melissande's Psalter (courtesy British Museum, London).

The trimphal entrance to Jerusalem, from a 12th-century crusader illuminated manuscript (courtesy British Museum, London).

Plan of Belvoir on page 302 (courtesy Israel National Parks Authority).

Reconstruction of Belvoir on page 303 (courtesy M. Ben Dov, R. Gardiner and E. Gilbron).

Plans and elevations of Montfort on page 310 (courtesy Israel National Parks Authority).

Plan and section of Pilgrim's Castle on page 314 (courtesy Israel Department of Antiquities).

Section and plan of the Crusader cathedral at Ramleh on page 420.

Engraving and plan (simplified) of the Church of the Holy Sepulchre during the Crusader period on page 426.

Line representations of the paintings on the columns in the Church of the Nativity, Bethlehem, on page 458 (courtesy British Museum).

Maps on pages 27, 168 and 289 drawn by Carta, Jerusalem.

FOREWORD

This study is not a new history of the Crusades or of the Latin establishments in the Levant, but an attempt to describe and analyse a mediaeval society transplanted to the Eastern Mediterranean, which created its own social and cultural patterns of existence beyond the physical and cultural boundaries of Europe. Though colonization is not a new phenomenon in European history, only since the Crusades is there continuity and filiation between colonial movements. Ever since, colonialism has remained a major factor in European and non-European history. In this sense it is justified to regard the Crusader kingdom as the first European colonial society.

The definition of the Crusades as a colonial movement, though the adjective was not explicitly used, dates back several centuries to a time when this term had no pejorative connotation. Colonialism acquired a deprecatory meaning only in the Age of Enlightenment, becoming condemnatory during the last phase of imperialism before World War I and continuing as such down to our own times.

Although early labelled a colonial movement, the Crusades were seldom – or perhaps never – analysed as such; nor were the crusader establishments studied from that point of view. The accepted usage is to cite the Crusades and the Latin kingdom as the first example of European colonial expansion without stopping to explain their essence. They never merited even the place of a substantial opening chapter in the history of colonialism. Indeed, no author bypasses the Crusades in his introductory remarks on European expansion, colonialism and imperialism, but very few ask what it must have meant to put a colonial movement into motion seven hundred years ago. Neither is there any study of what a twelfth or thirteenth-century 'colony' looked like, how it lived and how it developed as a 'colonial' establishment.

The ideological premises of the movement, the existence of European establishments in the Levant, their organization and achievements are the main subject matter of the following study. We hope thereby to contribute to the view of mediaeval history, as well as to the history of colonial movements.

The plan of this book was conceived after twenty-five years of studying the Crusades and the crusaders. The idea grew out of discussions on several associated problems with a colleague at the Hebrew University, the late Dr Yonina Talmon, a sociologist whose premature death was a great loss to her friends and to the University. The years which passed before the work was completed put my publishers to a severe test, and I would like to thank them for their help and forbearance. Let me also express my thanks to Mr and Mrs R. Sirot, in whose Parisian home the larger part of this study was written. I am also grateful to Mr D. Ben-Ya'akov for the efforts he invested in editing the manuscript for publication.

Last, but not least, I would like to thank my close friends Prof. S. N. Eisenstadt and Prof. J. B. Talmon, who kindly read the typescript and allowed me to profit from their advice and knowledge; Prof. M. Barash, who kindly read the chapter on the Arts; Dr B. Kedar, for many valuable remarks and criticisms; and Miss S. Schein, my assistant, who composed the index. My debt to other historians is amply attested to in the bibliography and footnotes. It is only fitting to acknowledge the special debt to my friends Cl. Cahen of the Sorbonne, J. Richard, Professor of History at Dijon, and H. E. Mayer, Professor at the University of Kiel, whose books and studies opened new vistas of research and facilitated, inter alia, the writing of this book.

Joshua Prawer
The Hebrew University, Jerusalem   *August, 1972*

... *Consider, I pray, and reflect how in our time God has transferred the West into the East. For we who were Occidentals now have been made Orientals. He who was a Roman or a Frank is now a Galilaean, or an inhabitant of Palestine. One who was a citizen of Rheims or of Chartres now has been made a citizen of Tyre or of Antioch. We have already forgotten the places of our birth; already they have become unknown to many of us, or, at least, are unmentioned ... Some have taken wives not merely of their own people, but Syrians, or Armenians, or even Saracens who have received the grace of baptism. Some have with them father-in-law, or daughter-in-law, or son-in-law, or step-son, or step-father. There are here, too, grandchildren and great-grandchildren ... Different languages, now made common, become known to both races, and faith unites those whose forefathers were strangers ... Those who were strangers are now natives; and he who was a sojourner now has become a resident. Our parents and relatives from day to day come to join us, abandoning, even though reluctantly, all that they possess ... You see, therefore, that this a great miracle, and one which must greatly astonish the whole world. Who has ever heard anything like it?'*

Fulk of Chartres
Historia Hierosolymitana, III, 37

I

ON THE EVE OF THE
FIRST CRUSADE

The lands of the Levant extend along the eastern littoral of the Mediterranean in a near-straight line. Their ancient peoples, who settled the plains and hills between the yellow dunes of the western sea and the inhospitable desert to the east, witnessed a long series of conquerors and conquests. Powerful nations of the north from the Fertile Crescent and from the Nile valley in the south staged periodic invasions to round out a border province of their empires, impose hegemony on the constantly feuding rulers of Syria and Canaan or create a buffer zone around the core of their dominions.

These centres of ancient culture, cradles of the two great monotheistic religions – Judaism and Christianity – were absorbed by the ever-widening folds of imperial Rome, and subjected to the unifying and levelling influence of the most dominant force in antiquity. Ultimately, the spiritual forces generated by these subject peoples conquered the empire from within by imposing their religion and code of morals throughout its vast extent.

This birth-place of religion and ethics led its own life under the empire, while greatly contributing to philosophy, theological dispute and religious heterodoxy. From the gnostic heresies in the second century till the end of the seventh, when Christian dogma crystallized, Syria and Palestine often played a decisive role in formulating the creed and elaborating the structure of Christendom.

Whereas the empire as a whole accepted creeds imposed by imperial decree, Syria, Palestine and the lands to the East – removed from immediate control – harboured heterodoxies. The population of basically Semitic stock – Phoenicians and Jews, mingled with Greeks, and Roman settlers – was fragmented by new divisions and sects in the wake of religious controversies.

In the second quarter of the seventh century, Islam spread its banners over this array of conflicting Christian sects – sometimes tolerated, but more often persecuted by the official church of Byzantium – and over the Jewish and Samaritan remnants in the Holy Land. A new power emerged, disrupting the centennial equilibrium on the imperial frontiers, from the Euphrates to the Nile delta. A new empire arose, born on the lances of the horsemen who swept northwards from the Arabian peninsula and, in less than a generation, watered their horses in the rivers of Egypt and Mesopotamia. Two generations later, at the beginning of the eighth century, Arab horses were neighing at the gates of Constantinople while the drums beat a dirge for defeated Christian Spain at Xerez de la Frontera (711). From the Pyrenees, through North Africa, Egypt, Palestine, Syria, Asia Minor – almost to the Indus – the sword of Islam made millions of new believers bow towards Mecca.

At the beginning of the eighth century a new political configuration determined the future destinies of both the Near East and Europe. Three empires converging on the Mediterranean confronted each other. The vigorous and half-barbaric Romano-Germanic empire of the Franks faced Islam on the Ebro in Spain and along the northern shores of the Mediterranean. Byzantium encountered Islam from the coast of the Adriatic to the Taurus mountains above the fertile valleys of Mesopotamia. The Mediterranean – once an inland sea of the Roman empire – became the dangerous frontier of warring rivals. The new Europe was cut off from the cradle of its religion and from its richest and most sophisticated provinces in North Africa and Asia.

Having lost its southern provinces, Byzantium reorganized its remaining forces in the Balkans and Asia Minor. Driven back to the heartland it became more Greek than ever before.

The energies of Islam were devoted to absorbing the vast and newly conquered lands and their heterogeneous populations. The immense Moslem empire did not survive its initial expansion under the Omayyads. By the middle of the eighth century, an

2

autonomous caliphate had risen in Spain, and at the beginning of the tenth, the 'Abbasid caliphate of Baghdad was undermined by the competing and heterodox Shi'ite Fatimids of Cairo. In the wake of disruption the authority of the 'Abbasid caliph weakened. At the beginning of the eleventh century the former spiritual and temporal Ruler of all Believers found himself deprived of political power, even in the vicinity of his capital Baghdad. The conquered provinces – although converted to Islam – regained some of their ethnic and cultural identity by the rise of local dynasties. The latter acknowledged the supremacy of the caliph and evoked his name in the solemn Friday prayer, whilst they achieved a great measure of actual independence within the loose framework of the caliphate.

The disintegration of the 'Abbasid caliphate was halted in the middle of the eleventh century by tribes of relatively new converts to Islam – the Turkish Seljuqs. Surging out of the steppes of Central Asia, they moved into India, Iran and Mesopotamia, infusing new strength into the waning caliphate. In Baghdad they proclaimed themselves to be the strong arm of the caliph, who in 1056 conferred upon their leader – Toghrul Beg – the title of sultan, viz. 'Ruler of the Faithful', in the caliphate and all the territories of future conquests.

The Turks expanded westward, defeated the Byzantines in 1071 at the battle of Malazgerd (Manzikert) and occupied the whole of Asia Minor, almost up to the gates of Constantinople. Turning south, one of their hordes overran Syria and Palestine and crushed the Egyptians, who retained only the coastal cities.

The core of the Turkish conquests remained in Iran and the sultan's residence was fixed at Reyy, near Teheran. But the new empire hardly lasted a generation. The provinces, though proclaiming the caliph of Baghdad as the only true and legitimate 'Commander of the Faithful' and the sultan as their supreme ruler, quickly split into independent principalities. Asia Minor, Syria and Palestine became a mosaic of small and constantly warring emirates. At this moment the armies of the First Crusade reached Asia Minor and, after a victory over the Turks at Dorylaeum (1097), marched into Syria and Palestine.

3

II

THE CRUSADE

Pilgrimage, military expedition, holy war, colonial war, a mighty movement of migration were all applied to the Crusades according to the temper of the historian or publicist and the climate of public opinion at the time of writing. Extolled or vituperated, the Crusades have been represented as a sinister plot of popery, a transparent cloak for material greed, a precursor of imperialism or a frenzied mass psychosis, but also as a gigantic enterprise to realize lofty ideals, the most articulate expression of collective contrition and a Messianic movement which ushers mankind to the Day of Judgement and the approaching Kingdom of Heaven.

Most of these views are not new. As the armies of the First Crusade (1095–9) assembled, German chroniclers expressed their consternation. Fifty years later, during the Second Crusade (1147–50) – especially after its failure – more than one voice was raised in doubt of its divinely inspired plan. The Third Crusade (1187–90) was criticized as being opposed to basic Christian teachings. The Fourth Crusade (1202–4), which ended in the conquest and subjugation of Christian Constantinople, caused a scandal in Christendom. Opposition grew during the thirteenth century, strong protest and scathing criticism coming from such different sides as theologians and pacifist elements, troubadours, statesmen and missionaries, commercial interests or even Franciscan and Dominican monks. An exasperated Dominican, Humbert de Romans (d. 1274), obsessed by the fear of Moslem expansion into Christian Europe (a fear realized two hundred years later with the rise of the Ottoman Empire), angrily answered detractors and opponents that 'the aim of the Church is not to fill the Earth but to replenish Heaven' (with martyrs). Only the papacy never wavered, the originator of the idea and its staunchest supporter for two hundred years.

The why and how of the Crusades are among the most difficult problems of historical research. It seems doubtful that any one man, institution or ideology can be directly credited with its inception. Events in different spheres of life at different periods, and in different countries, prepared Christendom for the First Crusade. Papal policy fused these elements and created a movement defined in aim, space and time.

Certain material pre-conditions made the Crusades feasible. A movement of migration on a scale hitherto unknown in European history since the *Völkerwanderung* would have been unthinkable, had not a reservoir of manpower been available at the end of the eleventh century and in the next two hundred years. Though the causes of the demographic explosion – or at least of unprecedented population growth – during that century have not been satisfactorily explained, there is little doubt of the fact. This vast increase of numbers in rural eleventh-century Europe found an outlet in a great wave of internal colonization. For two hundred years forests were cleared, swamps drained and thousands of new villages founded. Intensive cultivation was accompanied by a redistribution of the family exploitation units (the manse). The 'white mantle of new churches and monasteries' which covered Europe was already noted before the middle of the eleventh century by the Frenchman Raoul Glaber, and attested to the new density of settlement. The new masses facilitated the foundation of cities and the urban revolution in the twelfth century. The surplus rural population furnished the human element and more intensive agriculture fed all who did not draw their living directly from the soil, such as artisans and merchants.

In some areas this movement of colonization served more than purely economic purposes. German colonization in Slavonic lands had political overtones and the economic *Drang nach Osten* prepared the way for future expansion. The same expanding reservoir of European manpower made the Crusades physically possible, although it did not cause them.

The evolution and transformation of the warrior class or nobility in Western Christendom was not connected with this major feature of European development during the eleventh century. Its origins go back to the early Carolingian period, when a new type of social cohesion – the creation of tight and direct links between lord and vassal – stemmed the tide of insecurity which followed the final disappearance of the late Roman administration and the disintegration of the early Germanic tribal constitution. A new social stratification and hierarchy brought about the emergence of a professional class of warriors from the ranks of the common people. It seems that a hereditary class of nobles was created only during the eleventh century. An as yet unwritten code of behavior expressed the ethos of the noble warrior. In the process of evolution this code gained the recognition and sanction of the Church, which marked an important milestone in its development. Opposed to bloodshed in principle, the Church did not grant its blessing until traditional patterns of private warfare had been made to conform to certain ideals. To be worthy of his standing, the soldier (*miles*) had to aspire to a vocation, that of being the soldier of Christ (*miles Christi*). In his new capacity the Germanic-warrior virtues of military skill, bravery and loyalty were united with the biblical precepts of defending the weak and oppressed and the defence of the Church. The ideal of chivalry, or Christian knighthood, was born. The ancient ceremony of knighting through the conferring of arms was henceforth performed in the shadow of the Cross. A vigil of prayers prepared the young squire for his future responsibilities. The arms he received were blessed by a priest, who pronounced a special benediction. The ceremony of knighting became a second baptism, that of a noble adult.

The turbulent warrior caste, whose excesses had earlier been curbed by such popular Church-inspired movements as the 'Truce of God' and the 'Peace of God' (first half of the eleventh century) in the Capetian kingdom, now became a pillar of society. Hopefully, they were expected to be the mainstay of peace and security. Curbed at home, its fratricidal petty wars decried by Church, Crown and public opinion, the energies and traditions of this class found an outlet in the Crusades. The knights and nobles could now fight the Infidel with full religious sanction.

While the European nobility underwent the profound transformation which was to make it the mainstay in the war against Islam, another trend arose in Christendom. Not all its aspects – often connected with the great monastic reform of Cluny and the reformed papacy – are directly relevant to our subject. Nevertheless, the movement as a whole created a climate which favoured the growth of the crusading idea.

The most important expression of the renewed spirituality in the eleventh century – which originated in Cluny – was the penitential pilgrimage. Conceived as a penance in the wake of contrition, the pilgrimage became a meritorious act for the pious or the repentant sinner. The novelty of the eleventh-century revival lay in characterizing pilgrimage as an act of collective expiation. The first millennium of Christianity had ended. Many expected the year 1000, others the year 1033 (a thousand years after the traditional date of the Crucifixion) to herald a new era in the history of the old world. Some expected the Day of Judgement and the Second Coming of Christ. The dates passed without visible change, but the sentiment remained. Mankind felt the burden of sin more deeply. Natural calamities seem to have been more numerous (or the chroniclers of the eleventh century preferred to dwell upon them in detail). Famine, floods and diseases added to a feeling of distress and were interpreted as signs of threatening doom. The dramatic confrontation of papacy and empire during the Investiture conflict was widely regarded as a machination of Antichrist. Many gave up the world and entered monasteries in the hope of personal salvation. Others answered the appeal of wandering preachers to repent and return to evangelical poverty – to the *Vita Apostolica* – the life of the first apostles. In a generation which fearfully expected the Day of Judgement, penance became a general expression of piety. Pilgrimage to holy shrines changed from an act of individual piety to one of collective penance. Hundreds of people from all stations of life – both clergy and laity – assembled for common pilgrimages, some directed to the Holy Land.

These different developments might never have coalesced into a great movement. A political event and the genius of a pope brought them together. Some ten years before the Crusades, the emperor of Byzantium turned to Western Europe for help. Permanently threatened by the invading Seljuqs, Alexius Comnenus sought help from Robert, Count of Flanders. In response, a small contingent of European knights was sent to Constantinople. The experiment must have been successful, for in 1095 the emperor repeated his demand. This time the request was made by his envoys to a church council, presided over by the pope in Piacenza. The ambassadors explained the dangerous position of the Christian Orient and the calamity which might befall the Eastern Church and its Christians if Islam should overrun the empire. Although, objectively speaking, the situation of Byzantium at this date was far more secure than a generation earlier, the envoys – bent on receiving help – must have painted a dark picture.

Pope Urban II welcomed the request. There is no reason to doubt his sincere concern for the Christians in the East, though the papacy had its own axe to grind. A great schism had rent the Western and Eastern churches since the middle of the century. There were minor differences on some questions of dogma, as well as liturgical and religious practice. But the major problem lay in the non-recognition of papal supremacy by the patriarch of Constantinople. The relations between Rome and Constantinople had been interrupted since the pontificate of Leo IX and of the Greek patriarch, Michael Cerularius (1054). Urban II saw the imperial request as a chance to unite the two churches and re-establish the supremacy of the Roman pontiffs. The idea was not entirely new. A generation earlier it had already been advanced by the great Gregory VII. In a famous letter written to the Emperor Henry IV in 1074, the pope had announced his intention of organizing a Western army to move on Constantinople. Moreover, he proposed to command this army himself and reach Santa Sophia. Thus Byzantium would be saved, the schism healed and the pope recognized as the supreme head of Christendom. So prestigious a victory was certain to have repercussions in the West. The traditional task of the Roman emperors – the defence of Christendom – an idea elaborated at the court of Charlemagne and inherited by his imperial successors, would be taken over by the papacy. This spectacular move might possibly tip the balance in the Investiture conflict rending Europe.

With some such ideas in mind the pope left Italy for France, journeying slowly through the southern provinces, and convened the council of Clermont in Burgundy (1095). The main business was to reform the French Church; there was also the thorny problem of King Philip I of France, excommunicated for concubinage.

The pope's journey led him across lands which, for some time, had been in contact with Christian Spain. Consciousness of the Moslem danger and of the need for a Holy War against the Infidel was already astir. The *reconquista* of Spain from Moslem rule found adherents in France, and French knights and nobles, from Provence and Languedoc, had already participated in some expeditions to that country. Is is thus quite possible that Urban II, stimulated by his meeting with the Byzantine envoys at Piacenza, had already formed definite ideas while on his way to Clermont.

The council itself was a rather modest affair, a far cry from that described by the chroniclers after the success of the First Crusade. It was attended by some French prelates and the local nobility. Conspicuous by their absence were the prelates of the Capetian domain whom King Philip I prevented from journeying to Clermont. Only on the last day of the council (27 November) did Urban II raise the problem of the Crusade. It is a historical irony that his epoch-making speech has not been preserved and we are obliged to reconstruct the text from several later versions, some written during the Crusade. Urban II called on Western knighthood, especially that of France, to organize a military expedition to the East. He stressed the Moslem peril and the dangerous position of the Eastern Christians, appealing to the vigorous and warlike West to mobilize for the rescue. But at that point Urban II departed from the Byzantine emperor's request. Constantinople was no longer the principal aim, but rather the liberation of the Holy Land, Jerusalem and the Holy Sepulchre from the yoke of the Infidels. This new purpose became a turning point in European history. An appeal to help Constantinople or the Eastern Christians could have fallen on deaf ears, it would certainly not have engendered the mass response actually achieved by the call of Clermont. Few knew about Constantinople and even fewer were interested. But Jerusalem and the Holy Sepulchre were names which, for a thousand years, had resounded in every chapel, church and monastery. Repeated in every prayer, these names were a living reality. A man might not have known the name of the next province, but Jerusalem, Bethlehem, and Nazareth were part of his religious life and upbringing.

The response was unexpected and overwhelming. Emotional dykes crumbled and a mighty flood of faith gushed into dry souls. Appointed and self-appointed preachers travelled the country and roused the people to liberate the Holy Land. Not only was the Holy Sepulchre to be rescued from the sacrilegious domination of unbelievers, but Christ Himself – captive among the Moslems – was to be rescued and restored to glory.

The call of Clermont penetrated the silence of the cloister, the solemnity of the cathedral, the haughtiness of the castle and even the dumb misery of the peasants. Tens of thousands responded. Reasons differed from man to man and class to class. The warlike noble saw the Crusade as an outlet for his energy and skill. Fighting the Infidel was not only a noble pursuit but also God-willed. The clergy among the nobility felt it was a way of salvation. Urban II promised remission of their temporal punishments for sins to all taking the Cross. The Cross – instrument of Christ's Passion – became the emblem of His soldiers, intent on liberating the Saviour and the scene of His earthly appearance. The march to Jerusalem was an armed pilgrimage – a purifying penance for those who reached their goal or the crowning glory of martyrdom for all who fell on the way. For the malcontent of all classes the Crusade seemed a road to a better future. The nobles dreamt of principalities, castles and manors and the villeins of loot. Moreover, the peasant who joined the armies of the Cross divested himself of serfdom and became a free man.

Religious fervour was not confined to the upper classes, indeed, among the masses Messianic frenzy reached its peak. A year after

Clermont and long before the nobility mobilized for the expedition, amorphous peasant armies sprang up all over France, moving to the Rhine and the Danube valleys. Sometimes they were commanded by local knights, though more often they elected their own leaders. One such host even followed a duck, a mediaeval symbol of witchcraft. Organized leadership was felt to be superfluous. *Deo duce* (under the leadership of God) they moved with wives and children atop wagon loaded with their meagre belongings. Once past their familiar neighbourhood and into unknown provinces, they would ask on approaching each new city if they had finally reached 'Heavenly Jerusalem'.

An ancient faith was revived, that of the Poor of Christ in the original Christian community of Jerusalem. Influenced by ecstatic preachers eager to save souls and reform the world, who like the apostles left the world to live in poverty and in Christ, they reasserted that only the poor would enter the Kingdom of Heaven. Only the poorest were accepted into this community of the elect, with but one prayer: Let Thy Kingdom come.

Lust, adventure, piety and greed – the sublime and the base – all had a part in the movement. When the first hosts assembled and began to move eastward, mass psychosis and social pressures added ever more recruits, swelling small groups into armies. As previously mentioned, the first to move were the peasants. Their march across the Rhine and along the Danube was marked by one of the greatest and most horrible massacres of Jews in European history, unequalled until our time. Jewish communities that had existed in the Rhineland since Roman times – before the Germans ever settled there – were ruthlessly exterminated. Here and there the bishops, through conviction or bribery, protected the Jewish communities, but, with few exceptions this was of no avail. It was only fitting if one wanted to fight the Infidels abroad, to begin by putting one's own house in order! Community after community was offered the choice of apostasy or death. Jews were baptized by force; others, threatened by death, agreed to be sprinkled with holy water; still others chose martyrdom, drawing inspiration from the tale of Anna and her seven sons (II Macc. 7), or from the last heroic stand of Israel against Rome at Masada.

Even our own age, which witnessed the holocaust of millions, cannot fail to be moved on reading contemporary Hebrew chronicles. Fathers killed their wives and children as well as themselves in a ritual sacrifice to escape defilement at the hands of the gentiles. This vast pogrom, which destroyed centres of learning and whole Jewish communities, marked the beginning of a thousand years of tragedy to come. This was the 'Doom of 1096', as it is called in Jewish sources (*Gzeroth Tatnu*), an event never to be forgotten by the nation, perpetrated by those who claimed the Holy Land – basing themselves on the Jewish sacred books, by those who went to liberate the sepulchre of a God of love and peace universal.

This first movement ended in disaster. The unruly hordes ran out of provisions somewhere in Bohemia and began to plunder. They were practically exterminated by local resistance in Hungary and in the Byzantine Balkans. Very few reached the shores of the Bosphorus. The contemporary Bohemian chronicler, Cosmas of Prague (d. 1125), regarded their extinction as God's just wrath and vengeance for the horrible massacre of the Jews.

In the meantime four great armies were assembling in France: the Normans, with the Anglo-Normans under Duke Robert of Normandy and the Flemish under Count Robert of Flanders and Stephen of Blois; the nobility of northern France and western Germany under Godfrey de Bouillon; the Provençals under Raymond de Saint-Gilles, Count of Toulouse; and the Normans of Italy under Bohemond and Tancred. The papal legate, Adhemar of Puy, exercised a sort of supreme command. The northerners followed the overland route of the earlier Popular Crusade; the southerners went via Illyria or crossed the Adriatic into the Balkans. By the spring of 1097, they had reached Constantinople

The arrival of such 'helpers' hardly reassured the Byzantines. At Piacenza Byzantium had asked for a contingent of the famous European cavalry. It received a *grande armée* which plundered the provinces on its way to Constantinople, set fire to the suburbs and displayed an arrogance and lust for spoils that boded no good. Neither could the Byzantines overlook the fact that the host included Italian Normans, who some years earlier had tried to encroach upon their Balkan provinces.

Prolonged negotiations followed between the emperor and the crusaders. If not the supreme command, the emperor wanted at least an assurance that these armies would not be fighting on their own account. His case was strengthened by the fact that the crusader armies needed guides and provisions to cross Asia Minor –a Byzantine province only a generation earlier, now held by the Seljuqs – and thence to Syria and the Holy Land.

After protracted negotiations, the leaders of the hosts finally promised loyalty – some took an oath of fealty, others even doing homage. Thus Byzantine claims to future conquests were assured. On his part, the emperor promised guides and provisions. No one was satisfied and all were distrustful. Under such inauspicious circumstances the armies of the First Crusade were transported across the Bosphorus into Asia Minor. The emperor could breathe freely once more and the crusaders finally came face to face with the Infidel. In one memorable battle, at Dorylaeum (today Eski-Shehir) in July 1097, the Seljuqs were routed and their power reduced. Their newly conquered lands in Asia Minor were now easy prey to the crusaders.

Heavy loss of human life and incredible suffering accompanied the long march through the arid wastes of Asia Minor. The army split after crossing the Taurus mountains and reaching southern Cilicia. One part, under Baldwin, brother of Godfrey de Bouillon, moved swiftly eastward to the Euphrates – where Christian Armenians in and around Edessa invoked their help. The bulk of the army moved southward along the Syrian coast.

The coastal cities closed their gates, but the Crusade met no strong opposition until it reached the capital of Syria, Antioch. A difficult and protracted siege ended in June 1098 with the capture of the city through the treachery of one of its commanders. This was near miraculous because a great Seljuq army was only a few days march away. The besiegers of yesterday found themselves almost immediately besieged in the newly captured city. Their provisions had been eaten away during the former siege; famine and disease held reign. The situation was critical and the Crusade could have found its tomb in Antioch. At a moment of general despair, the Holy Lance, which a thousand years earlier had allegedly pierced the body of the Crucified, was miraculously 'discovered'. Strengthened by this visible sign of the Divine Will, the Franks sallied forth and routed their Seljuq besiegers. The city was freed and there was now no force which could bar the road to Jerusalem.

At this point, all the pent-up jealousies and ambitions got the upper hand – a menace equal to the Moslem danger. Moral bankruptcy and the almost total disintegration of the armies followed. The leaders abandoned Antioch and forayed into enemy country, each trying to carve out a domain for himself. Some succeeded, while many more were frustrated either by friend or enemy. The host, if such there was, temporized in Syria. The Promised Land appeared to have been on the Orontes and not in the mountains of Judea. Gone were the Messianic visions and the hopes of a New Kingdom. The ideals of the Crusade were dismissed and the basest desires held sway. In this spiritual crisis among the leadership a reaction set in from below. The lowest and most needy peasants among the crusader host were more numerous, or at least, more articulate, in the Provençal army. Murmur led to a riot and a popular revolt threatened the leaders: northern Syria was to be abandoned at once and the march to Jerusalem continued, otherwise the walls of Antioch would be razed and the city fired. This was the voice of the original Crusade, in which the earthly and Heavenly Jerusalem were hopelessly confused in the mind of the masses. These wretches were led by a group of fanatics called 'Tafures', who fought on foot without shield or protection, believing their lives to be in the hands of providence. Not only did they kill their Moslem foes mercilessly, but they even ate their flesh. This popular element rekindled the spark of enthusiasm.

The ultimatum sobered the leaders and the army pushed southward, stopping only at Tripoli while vainly hoping for an easy conquest of the Lebanese cities. From there the armies marched on Jerusalem. Bypassing the Egyptian-held coastal cities of the Lebanon and the Holy Land, the army turned inland between Caesarea and Jaffa, halted at Ramleh, abandoned by its Moslem inhabitants, and crossing the mountains in mid-June 1099, appeared before the walls of Jerusalem.

III

CONQUEST AND ESTABLISHMENT

Even before the crusaders set eyes on the walls of Jerusalem a new map of the Near East was being created. Their victorious march through Asia Minor destroyed the Seljuq power which had threatened Constantinople. Following in the wake of the Frankish victories, the Byzantine empire was able to regain its lost territories and expand its frontiers anew to the coast of the Aegean and to the confines of the Taurus mountains.

In the Taurus, Armenian-Christian communities liberated from the Moslem danger eagerly laid the foundations of their future kingdom of lesser Armenia.

Beyond this mountainous barrier, in Syria, the crusaders founded the principality of Antioch. To the east, Baldwin, future king of Jerusalem, founded a Frankish-ruled Armenian principality in Edessa on the Euphrates.

Farther south, on the coast of Lebanon, the crusader army established a bridgehead for the future county of Tripoli. Finally, on 15 July 1099, after a five-week siege, the crusaders captured Jerusalem from its Egyptian garrison. In the ensuing three-day slaughter of the Moslem and Jewish defenders, some twenty or thirty thousand inhabitants perished. Thanksgiving prayers were celebrated in a silent Jerusalem, reeking with the stench of decaying corpses and amidst burned mosques, synagogues and houses.

The capture of Jerusalem ended the three-year epic of the First Crusade. The victorious army had reached its declared goal: it had liberated the Holy Sepulchre from the domination of Islam. The crusaders had a capital, the kingdom was yet to be created. Surrounded on all sides by Moslems, the destinies of the new state were still in the balance. Any concentration of Moslem forces could have put an end to the precarious Latin settlements in the East. At this crucial moment, however, the Moslems were unable to co-ordinate their efforts. Rivalries between Damascus and Cairo paralysed any concerted attack on the Latin settlements, and Iran, the centre of Seljuq power, was too distant to impose effective control on its Syrian vassal emirates.

Profiting from the near-paralysis of Moslem power which followed the shock of conquest, the crusaders succeeded in adding a fully fledged kingdom to their capital in Jerusalem in less than a decade. Jerusalem, in the heart of the Judean mountains, could expect no help from the Latin strongholds to the north, hundreds of miles away. The nascent Frankish colonies at Antioch and Edessa had to fight for their own existence and could spare neither men nor equipment. Jerusalem's survival depended on the capture of the Mediterranean ports and on the establishment of direct contact with Christian fleets and Europe.

On their road to Jerusalem, the crusader armies turned inland from Caesarea, towards Ramleh. Fortunately for the Franks, the Moslems panicked and abandoned Jaffa and Ramleh, which the crusaders seized immediately. Throwing small garrisons into these two strategic places they assured the lines of communication between Jerusalem and the coast. The way to Ramleh from Jaffa, over the fertile plain of Sharon, was to remain insecure for more than a decade, and the road over the mountain passes of Judea, from Ramleh through Nabi Samwil (the crusaders' Montjoye), was impassable without military escort, though there were no Moslem strongholds along this highway. Under escort, merchants and pilgrims could pass to and from Jerusalem. Too late, the Egyptians and Damascenes realized the importance of the road between Jerusalem and Jaffa, and when they did, the opportunity was gone. During the next six years (1099–1105), the almost annual Moslem attacks against Ramleh and the surrounding countryside did little more than devastate the central part of the country. In the meantime, the crusaders continued to receive European reinforcements. They were smaller than expected, but large enough to prevent the annihilation of the Latin establishments.

It would seem that on the eve of the Crusades only the Palestinian coast and its maritime cities were fortified. In addition, some castles guarded the highway from Damascus to Moab and Idumaea, which joined the Hijaz road to Mecca and the desert route across Sinai. The hilly and mountainous Palestinian interior, comprising Judea, Samaria and the Galilee, does not seem to have had any notable strongholds or fortifications.

Realizing that the interior of the country was almost defenceless, Tancred pushed northward, taking Nablus in Samaria and Beisan, where the Jordan River crosses the Valley of Jezreel. Farther north, he captured Tiberias, on the shores of that lake. Thus with one stroke he added a whole new principality to the kingdom, the principality of Galilee. Tancred tried to annex Haifa (then a small port, though boasting a Fatimid shipyard), to serve as a sea-outlet for his newly acquired principality. His ambition was thwarted by Baldwin I, king of Jerusalem, who enfeoffed Haifa to one of his followers in 1100. Frustrated to the west, Tancred sought compensation in the east. The daring Norman from Sicily, commanding hardly more than eighty knights, crossed the Jordan and penetrated into the fertile plateau at the southern tip of the Lebanon ridge. From here, a series of foraging expeditions brought him into the southern granary of Damascus. The defenceless countryside, rich in crops and herds, was systematically pillaged. In the Syrian metropolis, prices of victuals soared and the first signs of scarcity appeared. On this undefended battlefield, Tancred won a major political, if not military, victory. The rulers of Damascus were compelled to recognize that a new power was rising in the Middle East and was determined to stay. They were constrained to negotiate with the Franks and to sanction a strange *modus vivendi*, whereby the Golan, that is the lands to the east of Lake Tiberias and to the south of Damascus, would remain in a kind of *condominium*. Both parties agreed not to fortify the area but to divide its income: a third to Damascus, a third to the Franks and a third to the fellahin, or peasants, tilling the land. This agreement, though broken several times by the Damascenes – who even tried to penetrate and capture Moab and Idumaea to the south – proved to be the most lasting of all Frankish agreements. Damascus learned in times to come that it was safer to have the Franks as a neighbour than a Moslem power which would try to 'save' it from the Infidel, only to become its master. Thus in the second decade of the Frankish kingdom an agreement, accepted under duress, became a cornerstone of Damascene policy. Strangely enough, it remained in force even when Damascus fell to the unification policy of Nur ed-Din in the middle of the century, and up to the great debacle at Hittin in 1187. The foundation of the principality of Galilee was the outcome of an individual's enterprise. It was quickly integrated by Baldwin I when Tancred left the country to assume the task of Regent for his captured kinsman, Bohemond, prince of Antioch.

In the meantime, the crusaders hammered at the bridgeheads along the coast. Jaffa and Haifa were already Frankish at the accession of Baldwin I in 1100. But the coast was studded with cities: some, like Arsuf, were no more than small fishing ports; others, like Caesarea, had lost their ancient glory; while some were first-rate emporia, like Tyre and Acre with its artificial harbour, built under the Tulunids in the ninth century. Acre's natural bay offered secure anchorage in a land notoriously devoid of harbours along its coast. It lay at the meeting point of the coastal road from south to north and the transverse road to the plain of Jezreel and to Galilee and Transjordan.

The conquest of the coast proved a hard task for a kingdom acquired by mounted knights and foot soldiers. It would have been practically impossible to besiege such maritime cities, which could be supplied with provisions and manpower across the sea from Egypt or Tyre, had it not been for help and intervention by the rising and dynamic sea powers of Italy. Some of them, like Amalfi, had long-standing connections with the eastern Mediterranean. Its merchants frequented the port and the *souks* of Alexandria and had even established a Latin church and hospice in Jerusalem in the third quarter of the eleventh century. But Amalfi's power was beginning to wane, particularly since its conquest by the Normans. Younger cities took to the waves, and foremost amongst them were those which up to this time had not been connected with the Levant. Venice, half-ally and half-rival of Constantinople and a familiar visitor to Alexandria, hesitated to get into a risky war which might jeopardize lucrative trade with the Moslem Levant; but Genoa and Pisa, whose ships plied the coasts of western Italy and of southern France, eagerly turned to the East for new markets and sources of supply. Sometimes enterprising individuals equipped ships for the Levant; more often the building and equipping of a fleet was a communal enterprise, commanded by the city's lay or ecclesiastical rulers. Christian sentiment, love of adventure, and the smell of riches launched sizeable fleets, which turned their prows to the Holy Land. Agreements were signed between the Latin kingdom and the Pisans and Genoese, granting the latter spoils and extensive privileges in future conquests. A little later, Venice, which commanded the strongest fleet, threw in her lot with the new crusader states. The city of St Mark was not insensitive to the mark of silver.

The co-operation of the Italian fleets tipped the scales in favour of the crusaders. The Egyptian fleets, which could have successfully fought the Europeans with the advantage of familiar seas, coasts and nearby ports, never seriously entered action. Their sporadic appearances showed lack of determination, and the few naval encounters usually ended in the Egyptians retreating to their base at Ascalon. The failure of the Egyptian fleet to intervene was a major military blunder which cost the Moslems the whole eastern littoral and facilitated the definitive establishment of the Franks.

Year after year, between Easter and late autumn, when the Italian ships arrived from Europe (winter was still felt to be too dangerous for navigation), the Frankish armies took to the field and struck at some port, while the newly arrived Italian ships blockaded it from the sea. A few weeks of vigorous siege usually ended in conquest. The cities were systematically looted and their populations massacred. Only in the second decade of the kingdom was there a notable change in this policy. By then the Frankish nobles, who expected to be enfeoffed with the new conquests, tried to restrain the looting and massacring mob. They obviously preferred to receive cities with their mercantile and artisan population intact rather than heaps of smouldering ruins.

Around 1110, the whole coast, with the exception of two cities, was in Frankish hands. To the north, Tyre, with its excellent harbour, held out until 1124. In the south, the Egyptians turned Ascalon into an impregnable bulwark that constantly threatened Jerusalem, Ramleh and Jaffa. Ascalon remained Moslem until 1153.

Around the middle of the 1120s the crusaders seem to have defined their military aims and strategic policy as expansion and attainment of natural frontiers. Palestinian rivers were not much use as frontiers. Even the Jordan was easily crossed at many shallow fords, and the sun-scorched and almost arid south and south-east of the country had no rivers at all. The natural frontier adopted by the crusaders was the desert. Except in the north-west, where the road between the sea and the mountains of Lebanon linked the Kingdom of Jerusalem with the Frankish county of Tripoli and in the west defended by the sea-wall, the crusaders established their frontiers on the line between inhabited and arable land and the desert. As already mentioned, the lands between Lake Tiberias and Damascus, the biblical Golan and Bashan, remained a demilitarized and non-fortified territory under a strange Franco-Damascene *condominium*. To the south, the crusaders found allies among the local Christians and laid the foundations of a Frankish principality, the lordship of Transjordan. Wisely strengthening ancient sites and building new fortifications in the proximity of springs along the famous road, they made the whole land, from 'Amman to 'Aqaba, a Frankish dominion. Wedged between Damascus and Egypt, it became a serious, if not insurmountable, obstacle, which cut the direct connections between Syria and Egypt. At the same time, the new Frankish castles controlled one of the major arteries of traffic and commerce in the Islamic world.

With the foundation of the lordship of Transjordan the Frankish frontiers moved close to the edge of the desert, preventing the concentration of Moslem troops on the eastern flank. An elaborate system of castles and garrisons, built and organized by the Franks, aimed to secure this frontier against any foe attempting an attack from the East. With time, a curious *modus vivendi* was established in these outlying, open spaces of the east. The Franks had no intention of paralysing either commerce or pilgrimage. They preferred to profit by assuring the passage of Moslem caravans, even furnishing armed escorts against payment of tolls and protection money.

Whereas the expansion and consequent stabilization of the frontiers in the East was relatively easy, since it was not opposed by any real military power, the situation was entirely different on the south-western borders of the country. South of Jaffa, along the coast, the sand dunes had been encroaching inland since the departure of the Byzantines. No settlements of any importance were to be found there. Further south only the ancient cities of Ascalon, Gaza and Raffah continued to exist, drawing a living from the narrow strip of fertile land behind the sand dunes, from coastal commerce and from the caravans passing to and from Egypt via the northern road through Sinai. A month after the conquest of Jerusalem, Ascalon was almost captured by the Franks. Intimidated by the Frankish army and near capitulation, the hesitating Ascalonites gained strength when a quarrel broke out among the crusader leaders. The momentary dissension cost the Franks fifty years of struggle to bring Ascalon to its knees. Ascalon[1] became, for two whole generations, a thorn in the flesh of the kingdom. The Egyptians rightly appreciated its importance : an inhabited and well fortified city across the Sinai desert, it could serve as a bridgehead against the Latin kingdom. Provisions, stores of equipment, a garrison and a detachment of the fleet based in the port of the city made it practically impregnable to the always meagre crusader resources. The Egyptians did their utmost to hold the city. Three or four times yearly they changed the garrison, pouring fresh and eager units within the strong walls. Any child born in the city was put on the army's pay roll, to assure a stable population. Moreover, Egypt provided everyday provisions for Ascalon when constant Frankish harassment made agriculture impracticable. Several Frankish attacks against the city failed, although the Moslems abandoned Gaza and Raffah.

[1] On Ascalon and its importance: J. Prawer, 'Ascalon and the Ascalon Strip in Crusader Politics' (Heb.), *Eretz Israel*, IV (1956), 231–48.

The presence of Moslem Ascalon made itself felt in a most painful manner. Hebron and Bethlehem, in the south, were in constant danger of being overrun. The plain of Ramleh, on the road from Jerusalem to Jaffa, became a yearly battlefield between the Ascalonites and the Franks. The Egyptians could easily risk battle. At worst a defeat meant the loss of an army. For the Franks, every battle engaged almost all their available manpower, leaving an empty and undefended Jerusalem in the hands of clergy, old men and women. A defeat could have meant the loss of the kingdom.

During the struggle for Ascalon the Franks developed a new strategy. Ceaseless Frankish attacks on the city destroyed its agricultural countryside, but neither induced the city to capitulate nor brought the Egyptian army to its knees. Consequently, the Franks elaborated a new stragegy, as original as it was effective. Their first aim was to stop the dangerous Moslem raids against Frankish territory. To achieve that, they systematically blocked all major roads from Ascalon to the north and east. A ring of castles enclosed the city. The site of ancient Eleutheropolis, the Talmudic Beth-Govrin, was chosen as the site of a small castle (c. 1136), which barred the road from Ascalon to Hebron and Bethlehem. Then followed the fortification of Yabneh of Talmudic fame, Ibelin in the French vernacular, in 1141. This new fortress barred the road from Ascalon to the plain of Ramleh and to Jaffa. This was followed in the next year (1142) by the construction of a castle at Tell el-Safi, renamed Blanchegarde (the White Guard), which blocked another road leading from Ascalon in a more northerly direction. The fortified cities of Jaffa, Lydda and Ramleh and the smaller castles of Château Maen (Beit-Dajan) and Château des Plains (Yazur), between Ramleh and Jaffa, safeguarded the kingdom's south-western approaches and tightened the girdle of stone around Ascalon.

However, the building of isolated castles in a desolate country created problems of logistics. The crusaders solved them in an ingenious way by settling Frankish farmers in villages built in the shadow of the new fortifications. The farmers cultivated the land, assuring provisions for the castle garrison; at the same time they performed military duties and were promised a share in any spoils taken from the Moslems. Consequently, these fortified villages became self-contained and self-supporting units, guarding a dangerous frontier while also providing a force ready to invade enemy territory.[2]

The fall of Ascalon now seemed only a question of time. The occasion was furnished by internal dissension in Egypt, which paralysed all attempts to save the city. Ascalon was besieged for eight months and finally capitulated in 1153 on condition of free departure for its garrison and inhabitants. The Egyptian bridgehead had fallen, and now the desert separated the Latin kingdom from Egypt. Even earlier the Franks strengthened the defences of this frontier by building a castle (1149) on the site of the ancient and abandoned city of Gaza, where a Frankish population settled inside the empty walls. Later on, a castle was built (1168) on the edge of the desert at Darum (Deir el-Balah), which became the southern-most outpost of the kingdom. A Frankish garrison and Frankish officials guarded the frontier and levied customs on incoming cara-vans from Egypt. The crusaders even ventured into the desert several times, destroying the oasis village of al-'Arish on the road to Egypt. The village was rebuilt but never fortified, marking the no-man's land between Christendom and Islam. 'La Grande Berrie' (from Arab: *barriah*), 'the great desert', as the Franks called the desert area between Gaza and 'Aqaba, remained the surest guardian of the southern frontiers, as did the desert to the east of 'Pilgrims' Road' in Transjordan.

The conquest of Ascalon and the extension of the south-western frontiers up to the fringe of the desert mark not only the definite end of the period of conquest, but also the zenith of the kingdom's territorial expansion.

Fifty years elapsed between the capture of Jerusalem and the fall of Ascalon (1099–1153). The capture of Ascalon in the middle of the twelfth century, important in itself, was not more than a belated episode, the last stanza in the epic of conquest. The Latin

---

[2] On the military uses of rural colonization, see: J. Prawer, 'Colonization activities in the Latin Kingdom of Jerusalem', *Revue belge de philologie et d'histoire*, 29 (1951), 1063 ff.

establishments in the East were by then strongly anchored in Syrian and Palestinian soil, their social structure firmly defined and their political regime coming to maturity. Baldwin III, fourth king of Jerusalem (1143–62), could look with satisfaction at his frontiers, which coincided with the cultivable area of the Holy Land. Beyond the frontiers was the desert – the safest frontier of all.

But across this desert barrier at the time when the kingdom reached its greatest power, new voices were raised in the Moslem camp. Though mere rumblings in a cloudless sky, the storm which they heralded broke over the kingdom a generation later.

It is not our purpose to tell the story of the Crusades. The following pages outline the main events in the history of the kingdom and serve as a chronological framework for our main aim, the description and analysis of crusader society, economy, institutions and culture.

The kingdom reached its greatest territorial expansion under Baldwin III. At the same time, Moslem unification began to gather momentum in the north and to threaten the frontiers and finally the existence of the Latin establishments in the East.

After two generations of bickering, Moslem unity came about under the banner of the *Jihad*, the holy war proclaimed against the Christian Infidel. Earlier attempts were not lacking – some were sponsored by the caliphs of Baghdad, though most originated with the Seljuq emirs of Mossul. These efforts never fully succeeded in unifying the emirates of Mesopotamia and Syria, and the half-hearted attempts to create a common front of the Moslem north and Fatimid Egypt all ended in failure. Many an emir regarded the expeditions under the call of the holy war more as a danger to his own independence than as a serious attempt to destroy the crusaders.

To make the *Jihad* – in abeyance many generations before the First Crusade – a living reality, Islam needed a pietist revival and an intellectual and spiritual preparation which would make the call effective. Zengi, emir of Mossul, laid the foundations of the movement, but only his successor Nur ed-Din reaped the benefits.

CONQUEST AND ESTABLISHMENT

Zengi (assassinated, 1146) succeeded in dominating some emirates of Upper Mesopotamia by force, cunning or persuasion, and then those of the Syrian plateau, which faced the crusader principalities in the north. Aleppo, Homs, Hims opened their gates and a series of victories pushed the crusaders to the west bank of the Orontes River. Mossul and Aleppo became henceforth the two key positions in the struggle against the crusaders. Yet not the whole of Moslem Syria was ready to fall to Zengi. Damascus thwarted his victorious progress. Jealous of its independence, the great Syrian capital preferred an alliance with the Latin kingdom to 'liberation' by Zengi. Despite threats and intrigues Damascus opposed Zengi for almost a generation (1130–54). This largely prevented a direct confrontation in the south with the Latin kingdom, but did not hinder Zengi from attacking and capturing Edessa in 1144, the first principality created by the Christians in the East, even before the First Crusade reached Jerusalem. An attempt to recapture Edessa (1146) failed and Zengi's successor, Nur el-Din, increased his pressure on the eastern frontiers of Antioch and Tripoli. The so-called Second Crusade (1147–9), led by Louis VII of France and Conrad III of Germany, not only failed to restore the county of Edessa but caused a fateful disruption of the political balance established during the fifty years of the kingdom's existence. A miscalculated attack on Damascus (1148) – the only crusader ally among the Moslems – threw it into the arms of Nur el-Din, who thus consolidated his position from Mesopotamia across Syria to the southern approaches of Lebanon, on the northern frontiers of the Latin kingdom.

Despite territorial reductions and the loss of an extremely important ally, the Latin establishments were not too seriously weakened. The position of the northern principalities became, indeed, more precarious, and intervention by Manuel Comnenus forced them into a short-lived Byzantine dependence, but unexpected possibilities opened in the south. The conquest of Ascalon (1153) meant more than the destruction of the last Egyptian bastion in the Holy Land. Egypt, weakened by civil strife, became a prey to its Christian and Moslem neighbours. On the invitation of a thwarted vizier the crusaders under King Amalric (1163–74) invaded Egypt five times. They never lost a serious battle but they lost the war. Crusader banners floated over Cairo (1164) and Frankish fiscal agents collected tribute and reparations, but the whole enterprise turned into a disaster. Nur ed-Din, called in by a contending Egyptian faction, entered the field after some initial hesitation. Crusader and Syrian, each supported by a political faction, now competed in the 'liberation' of Egypt. The outcome was clear. The crusaders, who could have ruled Egypt temporarily, overplayed their hand when they tried to conquer the country. Even a decisive victory could not have assured permanent Frankish domination of the Nile.

The outcome of the unfortunate attempts to conquer Egypt became a turning point in the history of the Near East. Amalric's Egyptian ventures weakened the Frankish kingdom, which lost its drive, and even the political and military initiative. Moreover, a new political and religious constellation was created in the Near East. The Syrian 'liberators' of Egypt became its masters. Nur el-Din's Kurdish lieutenant, Saladin, put an end to the Shi'ite caliphate of the Fatimids (1171) and Egypt fell under the rule of the Sunnite caliphate of Baghdad. The complete transformation of the political scene was of even greater importance. Saladin bore impatiently the suzerainty of Nur el-Din and the resulting tension explains the inactivity or the half-hearted attempts to attack the kingdom simultaneously from Syria and Egypt. The death of Nur el-Din (1174) prevented an open break between the Syrian overlord and his overmighty Egyptian vassal. Saladin moved from Egypt to Syria and consolidated his power by systematic removal of the relatives or former satellites of the Zengids. After almost ten years the new Ayyubite dynasty controlled Syria. Damascus was acquired as early as 1174, but Aleppo held out until 1183.

Saladin's accession to power in Egypt (1169) was followed by some desultory attempts to attack the crusader kingdom which were apparently more propaganda moves than military enterprises. The Transjordanian castles were besieged briefly and some minor raids were launched against the kingdom. The only serious attack led by Saladin in 1177 ended in his complete defeat at Montgisard (bibl. Gezer), but then Saladin was a mediocre

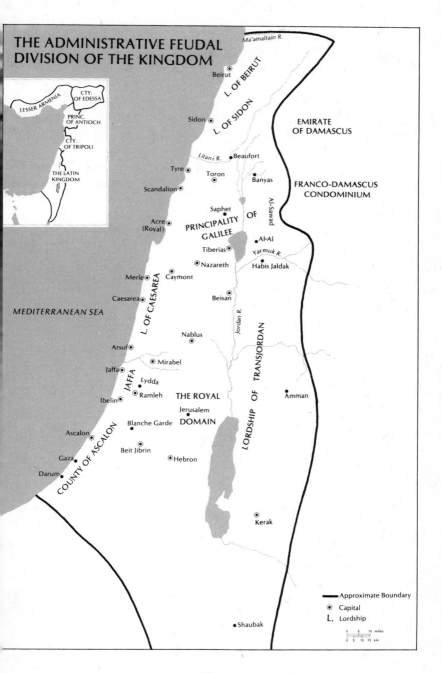

THE ADMINISTRATIVE FEUDAL
DIVISION OF THE KINGDOM

LESSER ARMENIA
CTY. OF EDESSA
PRINC. OF ANTIOCH
CTY. OF TRIPOLI
THE LATIN KINGDOM

Ma'amaltain R.

Beirut

L. OF BEIRUT

L. OF SIDON

EMIRATE
OF DAMASCUS

Sidon

Litani R. Beaufort

Tyre
Toron
Banyas

FRANCO-DAMASCUS
CONDOMINIUM

Scandalion

Al-Sawad

Saphet

PRINCIPALITY OF
GALILEE

Acre
(Royal)

Tiberias

Al-Al

Yarmuk R.

Nazareth
Habis Jaldak

Merle Caymont

Caesarea
L. OF CAESAREA

Beisan

MEDITERRANEAN SEA

Jordan R.

Nablus

LORDSHIP OF TRANSJORDAN

Arsuf

Jaffa Mirabel

JAFFA
Lydda

Ibelin Ramleh

THE ROYAL

Amman

Jerusalem

Blanche Garde DOMAIN

Ascalon

COUNTY OF ASCALON

Beit Jibrin

Gaza
Hebron

Darum

Kerak

Approximate Boundary

Capital

L. Lordship

Shaubak

0   5   10 miles
0 5 10 15 km

27

general. His greatness lay in his command over the hearts and loyalties of men.

Yet time worked in his favour. The stabilization of his rule in parts of Mesopotamia, Syria, Egypt – and even in far away Sudan and Yemen – put at his disposal large armies which from time to time could take the field in rotation. In contrast, immigration slowed down in the Latin kingdom after the Second Crusade, and a demographic halt or even a recession can be assumed. Each military expedition involved the almost total mobilization of available forces and one lost battle could have ended in the loss of the entire army and the destruction of the kingdom.

Nevertheless, the dangers should not be exaggerated. Despite the unqualified support of pietistic circles and of the great masses of the people, Saladin did not fully command the material resources of the Islamic world. Neither were his defences impenetrable. This was amply proven by the successful attempts of the Franks to cross Sinai and invade the eastern frontiers of Egypt or the great, adventurous expeditions of Renaud de Châtillon into the Red Sea (1183), as far as Mecca and Medina. It was internal events in the Latin kingdom which invited intervention. Civil strife and contending factions weakened the central government at a time when (since 1183) Saladin's attacks grew more frequent and pressing, until the fateful battle of Hittin (July 1187).

There was nothsng exceptional in this famous campaign. The troops mustered by Saladin might have been more numerous than usual, but so was the Frankish army led by King Guy de Lusignan. Even the strategy was standard : the crossing of the Jordan and an attack on a central target, in this case Tiberias, with smaller marauding detachments devastating the countryside. The Frankish answer was to manoeuvre their army into a position which would allow frontal attack by the massed striking power of their heavy cavalry, or an extended concentration of their forces until the Moslem armies dissolved or retreated, since none could remain in the field for long. On the eve of Hittin the Franks first decided on the latter tactic, but then – following misguided advice – marched to the relief of Tiberias. On this march the army was trapped into a battle which ended in its annihilation. Some 1,200 knights and 15,000 foot soldiers were killed or captured. The army ceased to exist and with it the kingdom.

Mobilization on the eve of Hittin was so complete that there was literally no one left to defend the cities and castles. When Saladin offered free retreat to Christian-held areas, most opened their gates immediately or after brief resistance. Jerusalem capitulated on 2 October 1187 after eighty-eight years of Christian domination. Small pockets of resistance remained in Galilee, but they gradually disappeared and there was nothing left of the kingdom but Tyre by the end of 1189. In the north Antioch, Tripoli and Margat were the only Frankish islands in a sea of Islam.

The Third Crusade (1189–92) re-established the Latin kingdom. The fall of Jerusalem shocked Europe, which was once again called upon to liberate the Holy Sepulchre. Armies from France, England and Germany, led by Philip II, Richard Coeur de Lion and Frederick I, with smaller contingents from other parts of Europe, landed in Tyre and in the bay of Acre. Their strength was seriously reduced when the German army – marching overland through Asia Minor – accidentally lost its leader, the aged Emperor Frederick I. The arriving contingents joined Guy de Lusignan, who had been released by Saladin, and laid siege to Acre. For three years (1189–91) Acre became an important focus of Near Eastern and, in some measure, of European history. Starved into submission the city capitulated and Richard Coeur de Lion's march to the south, his valour and perseverance regained some parts of the coast for the Franks. Christian and Moslem were ready for peace, ratified by the treaty of Ramleh (2 September 1192). A narrow coastal strip, from Tyre in the north to Jaffa in the south, marked the new and precarious boundaries of the kingdom.

Compared to the tremendous European effort, the results of the Third Crusade were disappointing. Moreover, the expected influx of immigrants to resettle the kingdom seems to have ended in failure. The basic problem of its existence was not that of military strength to defeat an enemy in battle (which the crusaders rarely failed to do), but the total manpower available and the ability to strike roots in newly acquired areas and territories slated for future reconquest. This became virtually impractical in the face of a major change in Moslem strategy. During the Third Crusade Saladin embarked upon a scorched-earth policy which was continued by his Damascene and Egyptian successors. All castles and cities captured from the Franks were systematically destroyed. Money and time were needed to rebuild these defences under the permanent threat of Moslem attack. On the other hand, only renewed mass migration could fill the cities and castles and replace the losses at Hittin and in the Third Crusade. But migration did not depend on the crusaders. It was governed no less by demographic and economic events in Europe than by the spiritual and emotional links which bound Christendom to its offspring in the Holy Land.

Each successive Crusade endeavoured to recover some of the lost lands. Though some of these efforts were reduced to insignificant forays, certain former parts of the kingdom were recovered. Thus the Crusade of 1197 created a link between the southern coast and the county of Tripoli by adding captured Beirut; the Crusade of 1204 added Sidon in the north and assured complete possession of Ramleh and Lydda, which until then were divided between Moslem and Frank.

The inadequate results, coupled with the difficulties of securing a firm foothold in the interior of the country, explain the deviation of later Crusades from the Holy Land and the direct attacks against Egypt, the main Moslem power in the Near East. Twice, in 1218–21 and in the Crusade of St Louis, 1248–50 (he stayed on in the Holy Land until 1254), it seemed that the crusaders would recover the Holy Land and their former kingdom on the battle-fields of Egypt. Twice the bright beginning, crusader victory and Egypt's willingness to cede to the Franks almost the whole of the former kingdom (with the exception of Transjordan), ended in disaster and the evacuation of Egypt.

What was not won in battle was gained by favourable political circumstances : the disintegration of the Ayyubite empire after the death of its founder, Saladin (1193). This was followed by a renewed struggle between the rulers of its former parts, nominally subjected to the sultan of Egypt. By a subtle game of threats and alliances the Latin kingdom twice recovered some of its former possessions, though it never regained its previous frontiers.

The famous Crusade of Frederick II Hohenstaufen – though some denied it this honourable name – ended in the treaty of Tel-'Ajul and Jaffa (1229). Frankish possessions were markedly enlarged by the addition of Nazareth and part of Jerusalem, as well as by two corridors, which connected the coast with the new acquisitions in Galilee and Judea. Jerusalem became Christian again, though not for more than fifteen years (up to 1244) when Khwarizmian troops captured the city, which returned to Egyptian rule.

The Franks were definitely ousted from the Holy City and no Christian power ruled there again until the entry of Allenby after the Turkish retreat in 1917. Thirty years later (1947) half the city became the capital of a resurrected Israel and the other half was occupied by King Abdullah of Transjordan. Twenty years later, in the wake of the Six Day War (1967), the whole of Jerusalem was incorporated by Israel.

The frontiers of the kingdom expanded by Frederick II in 1229 were again enlarged in 1240–41, following the Crusades of Thibaut, Count of Champagne, and then of Richard, Earl of Cornwall, brother to King Henry III of England. The former concluded a treaty with Damascus which badly needed a Christian alliance against Egypt. A treaty of defence and alliance was concluded, which assured the crusaders Sidon and Beaufort, but also a sort of *condominium* in Galilee with its capital Tiberias. These acquisitions were enlarged a year later during Richard of Cornwall's Crusade (1240–1), when a peace treaty with Egypt confirmed former and added new possessions. The whole of Galilee was ceded to the crusaders as well as Jerusalem, Bethlehem and a corridor through Ramleh and Lydda to Jaffa. Moreover, the connecting enclave was now enlarged to include Beth-Jibrin inland and Ascalon on the coast. The new frontiers were the largest the kingdom ever reached in the thirteenth century. Comparing it with the First Kingdom, one notes the loss of Transjordan, Golan, northern Judea and Samaria, which remained under Moslem rule.

These new frontiers could have guaranteed a territorial basis of existence, but favourable frontiers were no longer enough to make the kingdom a viable entity. The future depended on man-power willing and able to strike roots in the newly acquired areas.

Some efforts were certainly made, for example by the military orders, to enter into their former possessions. But one has to read the detailed description of the fortification of Saphet (1240) to realize the sums needed for wholesale restoration. The acquired lands were desolate, their castles destroyed and only steady waves of European migration could have assured a genuine restoration of the kingdom. There was no hope for such a movement. At best, Crusades like those of St Louis or Prince Edward (future King Edward I) of England were launched. But these military expeditions left behind them little if any additional manpower.

The arrival of Khwarizmian troops, invited by the Egyptians (1244), deprived the crusaders of Jerusalem and was the first in a long list of calamities. St Louis, whose great Crusade floundered in the muddy delta of the Nile, drew the logical conclusion : he remained for four years on the crusader coast fortifying or subsidizing the fortification of the cities – the only strongholds which could become starting points of a real *reconquista* should Christian Europe respond to the needs of the East.

The coastal cities and castles were refortified at ease due to the momentary inaction of Egypt, in the throes of a Mameluk takeover from the weakened Ayyubite regime (1250). Moreover, the Mongol invasions – one of the major catastrophes in Asiatic and European history – reached the Near East a generation after Gengis Khan and created a new framework of political relations. The Mongol conquest of Persia and the subsequent threat to Mesopotamia and Syria not only challenged the hegemony of Egypt in the Near East, but even that of Islam.

St Louis as well as the crusaders regarded the new power as a possible ally. There were Christian tribes and Christian commanders among the Mongols, the result of Nestorian missions in Central Asia. The Mongols attacked the caliphate and the hour of a direct clash with the major Moslem power was nearing.

The *Jihad* in the middle of the thirteenth century did not mean war against the Christian remnants, but a holy war against Mongol power. The attempts of the crusaders to create an alliance with the Mongols failed, and during the decisive confrontation the crusaders were mere spectators to the mighty events which decided the future of the Near East. The man who led the *Jihad* and guided the destinies of Islam – Baibars, Mameluk ruler of Egypt – had outstanding abilities and was the dominant figure in the Near East during the third quarter of the thirteenth century. Victor over a Mongol expedition at the battle of 'Ain Jalud (1260) and in subsequent battles against the Mongols in Syria, Baibars (died 1277) also destroyed the crusader establishments in Syria and Palestine. In three years (1263–6) and in the course of as many major expeditions Baibars undermined crusader domination in Galilee and then turned his attacks to the strongly fortified cities and castles on the coast. The captured cities and castles were systematically razed to prevent any re-establishment of crusader domination or any foothold for future European Crusades, still the nightmare of Moslem rulers.

The fall of the remaining crusader strongholds was merely a question of time. In 1291 al-Malik al-Ashraf Halil besieged Acre (5 April–18 May) and the city fell after a heroic defence of forty-four days. Tyre and Sidon were evacuated, so were Beirut and Haifa. On 14 August 1291 the Templars evacuated Château Pèlerin – the last crusader stronghold in the Holy Land – and escaped to Cyprus.

IV

THE KINGDOM
OF JERUSALEM

The modern student may be surprised to learn that when the
First Crusade marched to help oriental Christendom and to liberate
the Holy Sepulchre, nobody – neither pope nor prince – indicated the fate of future conquests. What would happen to the
conquered lands once the Holy Sepulchre was liberated from the
far from oppressive Moslem yoke? It was true that Urban II
had allegedly (we possess no direct testimony) promised incredible riches to those who would go to the East, but this expression attributed to the pope sounds more like spoils than dominions.
It seems that, among the great leaders of the host, only Raymond
de Saint-Gilles, commander of the Provençal contingent, thought
of remaining in the East. Others made arrangements for ruling
their dominions in their absence, as if expecting, sooner or later,
to return to their homelands.

During the three-year march to the East some ideas as to the
future of the conquests began to ripen; unexpected occasions
created *faits accomplis*, which neither plan nor ideology could have
foreseen. The first to realize the new possibilities were the versa-
tile, unscrupulous and rather impecunious Normans of Sicily.
Bohemond aspired to become the Byzantine emperor's representative in the crusading host, and his nephew Tancred tried to
make himself master of the cities in the Cilician plain, even before
the army reached northern Syria. It was again Bohemond who
carved out a dominion for himself, wresting Antioch from Raymond de Saint-Gilles after its capture from the Seljuqs. Close on
his heels came Baldwin, brother of Godfrey de Bouillon, who,
invited by the Armenians of Edessa to protect them against their

34

Moslem neighbours, succeeded in the shortest time in fomenting a revolt against the local Christian ruler and succeeding him as lord of the new county of Edessa.

After the capture of Antioch, the crusaders wrote letters to the pope, imploring him to join the host and take over command of the armies. The history of the Middle East might have been entirely different had the pope followed their request. But no pope ever appeared in the new provinces of Western Christendom (as a matter of fact no pope ever appeared in the cradle of Christianity until our own times), although a number of pontiffs were elected from among the prelates of the Latin East.

Even if sincere, the appeal from Antioch was ephemeral. Never again would the crusaders ask the pope to lead their armies. More-over, as already mentioned, at Antioch the crusaders and their leaders had tried to carve out principalities and lordships for themselves.

The future was as yet undetermined, but the lesson learned at Antioch and Edessa was not forgotten. It was evident that once a city was conquered, a ruler would have to be appointed and some kind of organization set up. The first ideological clash concerning the future of the conquests took place during the siege of Jerusalem. This untimely debate in the shadow of the unconquered walls allows us a glimpse into the political concepts crystallized during the three-year epic of the First Crusade.

The lay leadership of the army, the dukes, counts and nobles who led their hosts from Europe to Jerusalem, rather naturally suggested the immediate election of a ruler. By then, the majority of the crusaders must have made up their minds to return to Europe following the conquest of the city, the liberation of the Holy Sepulchre and the formal fulfilment of their vows at the beginning of the Crusade. These mighty leaders had considerable experience in ruling their own countries. It was clear to them that a lay ruler would have to be elected if the fruits of the Crusade, which cost so many lives and fortunes, were to be preserved. Their difficulty lay in the choice of a suitable ruler, but not in the form of government.

Diametrically opposed was a group which voiced the sentiments of a popular movement that had nearly led to a riot at Antioch. We do not know who their speakers were, but it is possible that members of the lower clergy presented their proposals. Still imbued with the Messianic tension at the birth of the Crusade, they refused to elect or appoint any ruler whatsoever. Interpreting the prophecy in the Book of Daniel rather strangely, they claimed that the Messiah was near and that, with his coming, all anointment would lapse[1]. To those who left Europe with 'Christ is our leader', to those led by a duck, who filled the roads of France and Germany, who asked in every village if they had finally reached Jerusalem, the idea of establishing a natural state with ruler, laws and institutions in the image of things left behind seemed a treacherous perversion of the Crusade. For would not the walls of Jerusalem fall, even like those of biblical Jericho, when a barefooted and repentant army marched around blowing its trumpets? These people felt themselves to be already purified and cleansed from sin, ready for the Kingdom of Heaven. In the circumstances, the idea of an earthly state and ruler seemed preposterous.

The third group, led by some prelates, did not contest the necessity of appointing a lay defender and guardian of the city. They claimed that the election of a patriarch should precede that of the ruler. As things spiritual, they argued, have precedence over things temporal, so should the election of the spiritual head precede that of the temporal. But protocol was not their main problem. The Crusade came into being through a papal appeal; no European king took part in the Crusade. Was it not, therefore, natural that the newly conquered lands should recognize papal supremacy? True that at this stage no plan was voiced demanding the creation of a papal state, a St Peter's dominion in the birth-land of St Peter. But a few months later an aggressive patriarch, the Pisan Daimbert, was to bring Godfrey de Bouillon, Baldwin of Edessa and Bohe-

---

[1] The speaker of this party is the Provençal chronicler Raymond of Aguilers, *RHC, Hist. Occidentaux*, III, 296. He refers to Daniel 9.24: 'Seventy weeks of years are decreed concerning your people and your holy city, to finish the transgression, to put an end to sin, and to atone for iniquity, to bring in everlasting righteousness, to seal both vision and prophet and to anoint the Most Holy (Saint of Saints).'

mond of Antioch, the three rulers of the Latin East, to their knees, swearing homage to the patriarch, Godfrey even promising to abandon the holy city to him.

The clash of opinions was interrupted by that of arms and the thud of stone projectiles against the ramparts. The debate was postponed to be continued after the capture of the city. Only after victory, pillage and massacre – when the entire population of the holy city was exterminated, with a few prisoners spared for ransom – did the leaders meet again in the Church of the Holy Sepulchre. The lay commanders prevailed and, rejecting the candidature of the haughty and powerful Raymond de Saint-Gilles, elected Godfrey de Bouillon as ruler of the city.

A pious legend has it that Godfrey refused the title and the royal crown in the place in which Jesus wore a crown of thorns. He accepted the ambivalent title of 'Advocate of the Holy Sepulchre', usually translated as 'Defender of the Holy Sepulchre', though this is partially misleading. The title of 'advocate' had a definite meaning to the contemporary nobles of France and Germany. An 'advocate' was usually a noble who represented an ecclesiastical establishment (church or monastery) in fulfilling its public duties as a feudal lord. At the same time, the 'advocate' swore homage to the prelate of the church, held land from him as his fief, and theoretically obliged himself to defend the establishment. Godfrey's strange title meant, probably, that he recognized some kind of ecclesiastical suzerainty, even if the practical meaning of this recognition remained vaguely undefined. His homage and promises to the patriarch Daimbert, hardly a year after the conquest of Jerusalem (1100), point in the same direction. [2] But Godfrey was the first and last ruler of Jerusalem who recognized a certain dependence on pope or patriarch. Already Baldwin I, Godfrey's brother and successor to the throne of Jerusalem, had made it entirely clear that his kingship was 'by the grace of God' without dependence

[2] The homage of the three rulers at the end of 1099 is described by Fulk of Chartres, *RHC, Hist. Occidentaux*, III, 446 and *William of Tyre*, IX, 15. The oath of Godfrey de Bouillon during Easter 1100 and his deathbed promise are mentioned in patriarch Daimbert's letter to Bohemond, *William of Tyre*, X, 4. There are some doubts as to the authenticity of this letter.

on any intermediary. It is even possible that the choice of Bethlehem rather than Jerusalem for his coronation was somehow connected with his will to disassociate himself from ecclesiastical claims, though it might also have emphasized his claim as heir to King David, anointed in Bethlehem. The image of the Holy Sepulchre on the kingdom's money and engraved on the royal seals was the only witness of a connection between the kings of Jerusalem and the Holy Sepulchre. But the money and seals also represented the Mosque of Omar (Dome of the Rock), which became the 'Temple of the Lord' of the crusaders, and the Tower of David, i.e. the citadel of the holy city, bearing witness to the non-ecclesiastical character of the kingdom. The Holy Sepulchre was just another landmark, the most famous and most venerated in the city and in the kingdom, but it never represented a claim to suzerainty.

The new kingdom thus became a lay state, ruled by lay kings and nobles. But the force of religious tradition did not vanish entirely and left deep traces in the political structure.

In a glance at the map of the Latin establishments in the East, a long and narrow strip of land from Cilicia to 'Aqaba – some 500 miles in length – or even at the map of the kingdom proper from Beirut to the Red Sea (c. 300 miles), one is struck by the abnormal position of its capital. Surely the geographical centre of these possessions ought to be somewhere around Lebanese Tripoli; in the kingdom proper, Ramleh or Acre would have been more suitable; and yet Jerusalem became the capital. And Jerusalem, at the farthest southern end of the crusader possessions, gave its name to the kingdom. But it is not only the eccentric geopolitical position of the chosen capital which is remarkable. A good number of crusader cities far surpassed Jerusalem in size, population and opulence. Acre and Tyre were certainly more important centres than Jerusalem, while Antioch was the most populous and wealthy of the crusader cities. Jerusalem, an inland city, had no particular commercial attractions, nor was it linked with any main routes of international traffic. Economically as well as strategically, Jerusalem was more of a liability than an asset.

Nevertheless, Jerusalem was chosen as capital and the crusader armies accepted this as a matter of fact, naming their rulers 'Kings of Jerusalem'. The name of the kingdom varied between 'Kingdom of Jerusalem', 'Kingdom of Jerusalemites' and 'Kingdom of David'. These names pointed, more than anything else, to the conscious links with biblical history. In the traditional creed Christendom was the heir, 'according to the Spirit', to the historical, once blessed Israel, which forfeited its privilege as the chosen people by not recognizing Jesus as Christ, the Messiah.

An unwritten rule governs the destinies of Jerusalem. Since David, King of Israel, proclaimed Jerusalem 'Temple of King and capital of Kingdom' (Amos, 7, 13. Heb. original) all nations and races that accepted the Bible as a holy book, or as part of their spiritual heritage, chose Jerusalem as their capital. Thus it was in the time of the kingdoms of Judah and Israel, and again in the time of the Hasmonaean kings and the Second Commonwealth, during the British mandate and in Israel of our own times. Neither Egyptian, Babylonian, Persian, Roman, Byzantine, Arab nor Turk who ruled the country at different periods in the four-thousand-year history of Jerusalem, assigned it a place of honour. Caesarea, Ramleh, Gaza and Safed were the chief cities. Moreover, Jerusalem was a capital only when the Holy Land enjoyed the status of an independent country. Whenever it was a province or satrapy of the East the honours of a capital were denied to it.

Thus, despite all handicaps, Jerusalem was declared the capital of the kingdom. The historical name bore unrivalled prestige, which outweighed the economic and strategic shortcomings of the city.

Since it became the capital of the Latin East, Jerusalem's early rulers had to repopulate the city, for its native inhabitants had been exterminated. In the beginning, not more than one quarter of the city, that nearest to the Holy Sepulchre and the Tower of David, was inhabited, although some mosques in other parts of the city, like the Mosque of Omar on the Temple esplanade, became churches and the Mosque of al-Aqsa, the royal palace. But even this meagre population showed intentions of abandoning the city for the coast, where livelihood was easier. A decree had to be promulgated threatening all absentee landlords with the loss of their property which, at the end of a year, would belong to the tenants. Another decree aimed to make Jerusalem more attractive for settlement, by abolishing tolls on all foodstuffs at the city gates. But, finally, the kings of Jerusalem, who were the overlords of the city, had recourse to systematic repopulation of the capital. In the second decade of the kingdom (c. 1115), they organized an immigration of oriental Christians from Transjordan, granting them the north-eastern and formerly Jewish quarter of the city, still called *Juiverie*. With time, the city rose from its ruins.[3] Because Jews and Moslems were barred from settling in the city,[4] it became entirely populated by European newcomers and oriental Christians. The exiguous commercial possibilities were partially offset by a constant stream of pilgrims. Furthermore, the royal administration and church headquarters, represented by the patriarch, the military orders and numerous churches and monasteries, made Jerusalem a rather prosperous, although typical consumers' city. Its only exports consisted of an unlimited supply of holy relics piously stolen or credulously bought and carried to sanctuaries in the West.

Thanks to the prestigious status of the city, only its ruler bore a royal title. Antioch was a principality, whereas the lords of Edessa and Tripoli bore the title of count. Only at the turn of the twelfth century did the newly consolidated Armenian state in lesser Armenia crown its ruler with a royal diadem. The Lusignans, Frankish rulers of Cyprus, accidentally conquered during the Third Crusade, also took the royal title. But these were later creations not directly linked with the primary impetus of the Crusades.

The royal title as well as the name Kingdom of Jerusalem had a double meaning. These titles implied a general suzerainty exercised by the king of Jerusalem over all Frankish principalities, a position sometimes stressed by princely acts of homage. Moreover, in time of trouble, like vacancies caused by minority, captiv-

---

[3] J. Prawer, 'The Settlement of the Latins in Jerusalem', *Speculum*, 27 (1952), 490–503.

[4] *William of Tyre*, XI, 27, and a number of Hebrew sources. See: J. Prawer, 'The Jews in the Latin Kingdom' (Heb. with Engl. summary), *Zion Quart. Rev.*, XI (1946), 13ff.

ity or death among the lords of the northern principalities, the kings of Jerusalem exercised a tutelary overlordship in their territories. This particular status of the kings of Jerusalem was never a subject of formal legislation but a matter of general consent, largely owing to the fact that the king ruled the city of Jerusalem, the central scene of holy history.

On the other hand, the title 'King of Jerusalem' and the name 'Kingdom of Jerusalem' were used in a more restricted sense to describe the ruler and the southernmost principality among the Latin establishments in the East.[5] At the time of its greatest extent, it bordered on the county of Tripoli in the north. The common frontier ran some miles north of Beirut along the river Nahr el-Mu'amiltain. It was a frontier created more or less accidentally. Beirut happened to be the northernmost city captured in 1110 by the king of Jerusalem, whereas Jubail (ancient Byblos) across the river had already been taken (1103) by Raymond de Saint-Gilles, founder of the Frankish dynasty which ruled the county of Tripoli. With the fall of the city of Tripoli in 1109, the whole area north of the little river came under the rule of the Provençal counts of the city. This was the only common frontier between the Latin kingdom and any other Latin establishment, and it measured but a few miles. More to the east, the frontier reached the mountains of Lebanon, where the borders were hardly ever marked. Immediately to the east of Beirut, in mountainous al-Gharb, the Moslem population enjoyed a good measure of autonomy, although it officially recognized the suzerainty of the Frankish lords of Beirut. A lucky accident has preserved some curious crusader documents, in Arabic, enfeoffing the local sheikhs with villages and lands in this territory.[6] Moreover, this area was inhabited by the Maronites, the native Christians of the Lebanon. The mountain villages with

---

[5] On the geography of the Latin kingdom: R. Dussaud, *Topographie historique de la Syrie antique et médiévale*, Paris, 1922; E. G. Rey, *Les colonies franques en Syrie au XIIe et XIIIe siècles*, Paris, 1883; P. Deschamps, *Les châteaux des Croisés en Terre Sainte*, 2 vols. Paris, 1934-9, and see bibliography to cap. IX: The Lordships – Government at the Local Level.

[6] See Salih ibn Yahya, *Histoire de Beyrouth et des Bohtors émirs d'al-Gharb* (Arab.), ed. L. Cheikho, Beirut, 1902.

their excellent archers usually had friendly relations with the Franks and ultimately recognized the supremacy of the Roman see.

From the ranges of Lebanon the Frankish frontier sloped to the south. Its course seems to have paralleled the Litani on its way from north to south up to its sharp western bend near the castle of Qal'at al-Sheqif, called Beaufort by the crusaders. The great and fertile depression to the east of the Litani, Marj 'Ayun (lit. Plain of the Springs), baptized by the crusaders as 'Val Germain', and the more easterly Wadi al-Taim, which served as pasture for nomadic Bedouin and Turcomans, seem hardly to have belonged to the kingdom. The crusaders quite often invaded these lands and returned driving herds of cattle before them, spoils of a raid. The nomads were compelled to pay protection money to the Franks. Excepting Beaufort, the Franks tried neither to colonize nor fortify these pasture-lands (unless the small fort of Hasbiyah to the east of Wadi al-Taim can be identified with the often mentioned l'Assabèbe of crusader sources).[7]

At the famous sharp turn of the Litani the Frankish frontier turned to the east. It left behind the tip of the Lebanon and, crossing the Jordan sources, reached the southern tip of snow-clad Hermon. On one of the ridges connecting with Mount Hermon stood Qal'at al-Subeibe (today Qal'at Nimrud), which dominated the town of Banyas and marked the most north-eastern Frankish possession.[8] At this point no real or formal frontier divided the Latin kingdom from its northern Moslem neighbour, the great city of Damascus.

The Jordan's sources and the small rivers which further south become the Jordan, were inside the frontiers of the kingdom. But the eastern table land of Gaulanitis (Heb. *Golan;* Arab. *Jaulan*) and the more southerly al-Sawad (crusader *Terre de Sueth*) overlooking Lake Tiberias were no-man's land or, rather, a *condominium* of Franks and Damascenes. The whole area, as far south as the

---

[7] Suggested by J. Richard, 'Les listes de seigneuries dans le livre de Jean d'Ibelin. Recherches sur l'Assabebe et Mimars', *Rev. hist. de droit français et étranger,* 1954, 565–77.

[8] The accepted view that Qal'at al-Subeibe was the citadel of Banyas is erroneous and the history of the place under the crusaders has to be rewritten.

Yarmuk River, although politically dependent on Damascus, paid heavy tribute to the princes of Galilee. Two small fortresses on the eastern side of Lake Tiberias, al-'Al and Qaṣr Bardawil (Castle of Baldwin), seem to have been the only fortifications in the area, and it is not very clear when and by whom these castles were built.[9]

Just across the Yarmuk, on its southern bank, we find a strong fortress, the strange cave-fortress called in Arabic *Habis*, or *Habis Jaldak*, and by the crusaders, *Cave de Sueth* (Fortress of al-Sawad). This was a natural stronghold occupied by the crusaders during the major part of the twelfth century, although it sometimes changed hands and found itself, on occasion, in Damascene possession.

Continuing from *Habis Jaldak* to the sources of the Yarmuk were the great pasture-lands between Muzeirib and Dar'a, called *Maidan*, that is 'the Plain'. The crusaders penetrated this area and became masters of Dar'a which, enfeoffed to a Frankish noble from the vicinity of Paris, was called the 'City of Bernard d'Etampes'. But the crusaders' domination was very shortlived. As a matter of fact, they could hardly master enough manpower to dominate, let alone colonize, these peripheral areas.

More to the east were the cities of Bosra and Salkhad. The commanders of these places were appointed by the rulers of Damascus. But the remoteness from Damascus and the vicinity of the Franks – who during the twelfth century came to be regarded by many a Moslem as a convenient, although hated and intimidating ally – at times provoked rather strange political manoeuvrings. In the middle of the twelfth century an independent Moslem emirate was created in Bostra and Salkhad with the connivance of the Franks. This suited the Franks perfectly as they were not in a position to man far outlying posts, but could profit from the existence of an autonomous buffer state entirely dependent on their goodwill. But the Franks overplayed their hand and the ephemeral, independent emirate disappeared after a short and turbulent existence.

To the south of the Yarmuk the high plateau of ancient Gile'ad

---

[9] The newly conducted archaeological survey of these places (1967/8) did not find any traces of the crusader period.

(Arab. *Jebel 'Awf*) and its southern part, the Jebel 'Ajlun, with the deep Jordan depression, the Ghor, in the west, were never dominated by the Franks, although one of their military expeditions brought them as far as Gerasa (Jerash), which they destroyed. A Moslem castle built near 'Ajlun in the twelfth century, Qal'at al-Rabad,[10] is a lonely witness to Moslem suzerainty in this desolate area.

Frankish domination becomes more tangible in the ancient lands of 'Ammon and Moab to the south of the river Zerza. This spacious area, extending far into the south up to the Red Sea, became the Frankish lordship of *Oultre-Jourdain*, or Transjordan.

The Frankish frontier here contoured the inhabited and cultivable land. To the east was the Transjordanian desert, changing imperceptibly in the south around Ma'an, on the crossroad of the Hejaz and the Sinai peninsula, to the Arabian desert. The Frankish frontier seems to have been based on the great road, which reached the shores of the Red Sea at 'Aqaba. As early as 1115, the Franks descended upon the place from the north and took the fishing village without resistance. They built a small fortress there, which guarded the outlet to the Red Sea and the road that passed through 'Aqaba to Sinai and Egypt in the west and Arabia in the south.

At this point the frontier again disappeared in the sands of the desert. From the period of Byzantine domination the Negev was depopulated and its cities covered by sand. This was 'La Grande Berrie' ('the Great Desert'), as the crusaders called the desert of south-western Palestine. No frontiers were marked in the desert, which extended to the west into Sinai. But for the few oases on the three main roads which cut through Sinai, there was no human settlement. Very early, at the time of the capture of 'Aqaba, Baldwin I reached the monastery of St Catherine at the foot of the traditional Mount Sinai. The Greek monks of the monastery asked him to leave the place so as not to compromise their relations with the Moslems, who were either nomadic Bedouin or Egyptian officials.

---

[10] C. N. Johns, 'Medieval 'Ajlun. The castle – Qal'at ar-Rabad', *Quart. Dept. Antiquit. in Palestine*, I (1931), 21–33.

Only on reaching the Mediterranean coast along the northern-most road linking Egypt to Palestine, the Frankish frontier was again marked by the fortress of Darum, or Deir el-Balah, on the fringe of the desert. From here it continued the safest part of its course along the coast of the Mediterranean.

V

THE CONQUERED LANDS
AND THEIR PEOPLE

During the fifty years (1099–1153) in which the Kingdom of Jerusalem was almost uninterruptedly expanding towards the fringes of the desert on all its frontiers, the nuclei of the other Christian principalities – founded during the First Crusade – also achieved their greatest extent. Ultimately, the Latin establishments on the Syrian coast stretched from the bay of Alexandretta in the north to 'Aqaba on the Red Sea.

Natural features divided the crusader territory, some six hundred miles long, into a western part along the sea and an eastern part bordering the desert. The dividing line was a steep valley, a deep geological depression which cut the mountainous plateau. The lofty ranges of the Taurus which seal the southern approaches of Anatolia, merge towards Syria into the ridge of the Ammanus. At Antioch they are succeeded by the Ansariah mountains to the west and the high plateau of Aleppo in the east, followed by the Lebanon and the Galilean ranges to the west and the high plateaux of Golan and Bashan in the east.

This massif is not impenetrable. The transverse valleys of the al-Aswad, 'Afrin and Orontes rivers cut a passage between the Ammanus and the Ansariah mountains, connecting Aleppo with Antioch. The Buqaia valley links Homs and Tripoli, and the Valley of Jezreel allows free passage between Galilee and Samaria or Judea.

These basic physical features influenced the destinies of the Latin conquests. Having occupied the beaches and their ports, the crusaders tried to enlarge their territories by expanding to the east, but their success was moderate. Only the county of Edessa penetrated

46

the Euphrates and Tigris valleys. All the other principalities, except for very short periods, never really ruled the territories to the east of the great north–south depression. Time and again, crusader armies penetrated deep into Moslem territory. At one moment their sphere of influence even reached the very gates of Aleppo, but the armies retired, the castles changed hands and the tense frontiers were established along the great valley. A singular exception was the most southerly crusader state – the Kingdom of Jerusalem proper – which, for almost a hundred years, ruled the lands east of the Jordan down to the port of 'Aqaba.

The territories occupied by the crusaders thus presented a very long and extremely narrow strip of land between the Mediterranean and the great valley in the east. They emcompassed some of the most famous lands in history and with them, cutting through ancient political, ethnic and religious frontiers, the most variegated populations.

Islam,[1] the official religion of the conquered countries, was split between the two contending caliphates, that of the Sunnites of Baghdad and the Shi'ites of Egypt. This division not only expressed a competition for religious supremacy and legitimacy in Islam, but also two major political powers struggling for hegemony over the believers. Military victories meant as much in the sphere of politics as in that of religious allegiance. The local Moslem population changed its loyalties and, often, its official creed according to the domination of one or the other power. On the eve of the

---

[1] The Moslem population data is based on Islamic sources, foremost the descriptions of Palestine by: Nasir-I-Khusrau (1047), *Diary of Journey through Syria and Palestine*, transl. from Persian by G. Le Strange in *PPTS*, IV; Mukkadasi, *Description of Syria including Palestine*, *PPTS*, III and Aly al-Harevy in *Archives de l'Orient latin*, I, 593 ff. Useful data including the thirteenth-century geographer Yaqut can be found in: G. Le Strange, *Palestine under the Moslems. A description of Syria and the Holy Land*, 650–1500, transl. from the works of medieval Arab geographers, Boston, N. Y., 1890. A.-S. Marmadji, *Textes géographiques arabes sur la Palestine*, Paris, 1951, and in the contemporary Arabic chronicles, published in *RHC, Hist. Orientaux*, 5 vols. Paris, 1854–87. Most illuminating are the contemporary: *Memoirs of Usama ibn Munqidh, an Arab-Syrian Gentleman and Warrior in the Period of the Crusades*, transl. Ph. K. Hitti, N. Y., 1929. See also: R. Hartmann, *Palästina unter den Arabern*, 632–1516, Leipzig, 1916.

establishment of the Latin kingdom, Palestine and Lebanon were – true to their unfortunate historical fate – a contested area between their powerful neighbours in the north and south, the two contesting caliphates. The declining Sunnite 'Abbasids of Baghdad found defenders in the vigourous Turkish Seljuqs. Syria, Lebanon and Palestine were overrun by the Turks while the last remains of Byzantine rule around Antioch were wiped out. The Egyptians were ousted from citadels and strongholds and relegated beyond the Sinai desert. Turkish populations and garrisons occupied the cities, ruling the newly conquered territories. Sometimes, however, the local notables seized the occasion created by political chaos and set up autonomous emirates on the Syrian and Phoenician coast. Egypt, which had lost its Palestinian territories with the Turkish invasion in the last quarter of the eleventh century, still held some of the coastal cities. Several months before the appearance of the Franks, the Egyptians even succeeded in ousting the Turks and recapturing Jerusalem (1098).

The invasions and counter-invasions of Palestine and Syria by Egyptians and Turks had little or no influence on the ethnic composition of its population. The main stock consisted of ancient Semitic peoples, successively Hellenized, Romanized, Christianized and, finally, converted to Islam, although a minority always preserved the religion of its ancestors. The impact of conquests in terms of an influx of new populations was always small. Parts of the different garrisons which at one time or another dominated the country, Ptolemaic and Seleucid, Roman or Romanized Celts and Germans, very often intermarried with the local inhabitants. Nomadic Arab tribes on their wanderings may have left some local traces, but these additions were normally insignificant. The same was true for the new Turkish garrisons in the cities and castles, which were easily absorbed by the local population, the common religion facilitating integration.

At the time of the crusader conquest, the majority of the local population was already Moslem. Sunnites and Shi'ites, they proclaimed in their Friday prayer the name of their caliph (in the 'Khotba'), in a thousand mosques. This was more a political than a religious alignment, since it expressed the allegiance of the local

ruler, who decided on the name to be proclaimed. The local population had little or no say in the matter. The commander of the
Egyptian garrison in a maritime city would proclaim the name of
the Fatimid caliph, whereas the Turkish commander in a neighbouring inland stronghold would do the same for the 'Abbasid
caliph of Baghdad.

At the end of the tenth century, an Arab, Jerusalem-born geographer noted that the overwhelming majority of Moslems in
Syria and Palestine were Sunnites, but in the eastern and northern
parts of the country, in Tiberias and Kadesh (in Galilee), and Nablus
and 'Amman in Transjordan the population belonged to the Shi'a. [2]
On the eve of the Crusades, when the Egyptians held the seacoast,
we can assume the spread of the Shi'a even in the western parts of
the country.

Whereas the bulk of the Moslems lived in cities and villages,
some were, as they still are, nomadic tribes. These were Bedouin, [3]
called by Moslem sources 'Arabs', who, in their constant search for
pastures, moved between the Euphrates and the Nile. The establishment of the Latin kingdom interfered for a short time with their
customary wandering, but the crusaders very quickly came
to recognize their needs and, unexpectedly, established very close
relations with the dwellers of the desert.

The great Bedouin tribe of the Ta'alaba with its two main
branches – the Banu Darma and Banu Ruzaiq on the Egyptian
border – co-operated with the Franks, which did not make them
popular with their fellow Moslems. Their relations from among the
Banu Tayy, called Jarm Quda'ah, had their pastures on the fringes
of the desert, between Gaza and the hilly country of Hebron.
To the south of Gaza, around Darum or Deir el-Balah, were other
branches of the same tribe, the Banu Ghor and Banu Buhaid. Other
tribes moving from oasis to oasis between Egypt and Syria were

---

[2] Mukkadasi in *PPTS*, III, 66 and compare Nasir-I-Khusrau in *PPTS*,
IV, 11–12, 19.

[3] Numerous data are to be found in Qalqashandi, *Subh al-A'sha*, IV, Cairo,
1914, 203–15. See also: A. S. Tritton, 'The Tribes of Syria in the XIVth and XVth
Centuries', *Bulletin of the School of Oriental and African Studies*, 12 (1948), 507–73;
F. G. Peake, *A History of Jordan and its Tribes*, Miami, 1958.

the Banu Sadr, Banu Ha'aid and Banu Ubayy.[4] Often in this area, we find mention of nomadic tribes, known also from Egypt and southern Transjordan, like the warlike Banu Kinana, Banu Haubar and Banu Khaled. In southern Transjordan, around the strongholds of Kerak and Shaubaq (the crusaders' Montreal) were the Banu 'Uqbah and Banu Zuhair – and more to the north around 'Ajlun the Banu 'Awf, who gave their name to the high plain, Jebel 'Awf. To the north, as far as Damascus and the Hauran, was the domain of the great tribe of Banu Rabi'ah, itself a branch of the Banu Tayy. On the eve of the First Crusade they were lords of the capital of the country, Ramleh, a position sanctioned by the Fatimid rulers of Egypt and Palestine. Later on we find them on the north-eastern confines of the Latin kingdom. More to the west in the Wadi al-Taim, a valley connecting southern Lebanon and Palestine, we also find a nomadic population eager to profit from the good pastures of this territory.

Very few nomadic tribes seem to have lived inside the frontiers of the kingdom. Some are known to us in the vicinity of Nablus, where they were paying taxes to the king of Jerusalem, but it seems impossible to say, with certainty, to which tribes they belonged. The Banu 'Amila, an Arab tribe that settled in Galilee following the Moslem conquest in the seventh century, left its Arabic name to the north of Palestine as Jebel 'Amila. They left no other traces in this area, but they might possibly have migrated at an undetermined date to Syria, between Homs and Damascus.

Of different stock, but leading the same life, were the remnants of the Turkish nomads. Whereas the majority became sedentary during the twelfth century, others continued their pastoral wanderings. Arabic as well as crusader sources called these wandering tribes Turkomans, to distinguish them from the sedentary and ruling Seljuqs.

The kings of Jerusalem were overlords of all the nomadic tribes who crossed their frontiers. The tribes were obliged to pay pro-

---

[4] Known as eaters of dead animals. They lived in the al-Jafr and Hisma area, that is the deserts of Sinai and southern Transjordan. See Usama ibn Munqidh, transl. Ph. K. Hitti, 36. The same source mentions also the Banu Fuhayd, *ibid.*, 53.

tection and pasture money for free pasture and the right to wander
in or across the country. Unfortunately, crusader knights were not
always able to restrain themselves, when they saw the magnificent
horses bred by the nomads and, agreements notwithstanding,
attacked their encampments. In a curious charter[5] King Baldwin IV
granted to the Order of St John in Belvoir (Galilee) the privilege
of attracting to their new domain one hundred tents (families) from
among the Bedouin tribes, on condition that they did not formerly
belong to the king of Jerusalem.

Between the Sunnites of the north and the Shi'ites of the south –
hidden in the inaccessible recesses of the Lebanon – were the
Druzes.[6] The sect was organized in the third decade of the eleventh
century following the assassination in 1021 of the half-mad Fatimid
caliph al-Hakim. The belief that al-Hakim was the last 'Incarnation
of the Godhead' spread beyond the frontiers of his Nile kingdom,
into the mountains and valleys of Lebanon. Even earlier, other
heterodox Moslem sects found a refuge here. As some of them believed in incarnation, the preaching of al-Darazi, who gave the
name to the sect, fell on fertile soil. Strangely enough, the real
organizer of the sect, Hamza ibn 'Ali, later proclaimed al-Darazi's
teachings heretical, but the name of the first teacher remained that
of the sect. In all probability, as often happened in this area, the
incarnation teachings were adopted by an ethnic group and became
its official religion near the castles of Qal'at al-Sheqif and Banyas
and the neighbouring pasture lands of Wadi al-Taim. A Moslem
historian[7] described the area as a concentration point of Nusairis,
Druzes, Zoroastrians and other sects.

The earliest description of the Druzes comes from the pen of the
Jewish traveller Benjamin of Tudela. He states that the land of the
Druzes stretched from Mount Hermon to the coast of Sidon. It is
clear that he did not know what to make of them. Near Sidon – he
says[8] – 'some ten miles away there is a nation fighting those of
Sidon (i.e. the Franks). This nation is called the Druzes and they are

5 Delaville le Roulx, *Cartulaire de l'Ordre de Saint Jean*, I, 271–2, no. 398.
6 Ph. K. Hitti, *The Origins of the Druze People and Religion*, N.Y., 1928.
7 Ibn al-Athir in *RHC, Hist. Orientaux*, II, 383.
8 Benjamin of Tudela, ed. and Engl. transl. by Asher, N.Y., 1907, 18.

pagans and have no religion. They inhabit the high mountains and the recesses of the rocks and there is no king or judge over them. And they stretch as far as Mount Hermon, some three days march.' If Benjamin's description is exact, and he is usually a very reliable observer, then it is possible that the sheikhs of Wadi al-Taim to the east of Sidon, often referred to in crusader sources, were Druzes. In the thirteenth century the Frankish lords of Sidon had almost cordial relations with the population in the mountain region to the east of Sidon and Beirut, in the area called al-Gharb and al-Shuf. It is quite possible that the population was of Druze stock.

Benjamin of Tudela was not alone in his inability to classify the Druzes. Two generations later, the bishop of Acre, Jacques de Vitry – a vituperous preacher bent on blotting out all sects and heresies – noted with dismay: 'And there are other Saracens, called of the Occult Religion. They don't reveal their religion but to their sons when they are already grown up.'[9]

On the eve of the Crusades the overwhelming majority of the native population of Syria and Palestine was already Moslem. And yet, not the whole Near East embraced Islam. Christians of autochthonous Semitic stock held out, even under Islam. Large areas of Asia Minor in the Taurus and along its southern slopes were settled by a substantial Armenian population, loyal to their autocephalous church. During the twelfth century its ruling dynasties created a Christian kingdom known as lesser Armenia, reminiscent of 'Great Armenia' around Lake Van, lost in the waves of Moslem conquest.

Whereas the eastern parts to the south of the Taurus barrier were Moslem, the situation differed in the west along the coast to Antioch. Here the population seems to have remained Christian, primarily of the Greek-Orthodox or Byzantine rite. True, Antioch was under Moslem rule for more than three hundred years (636–969). But these were followed by a hundred years of Byzantine domination (969–1084), and Antioch belonged to Byzantium until a generation before the First Crusade. The Moslem conquest of Antioch (1084) some fifteen years before the

[9] *Lettres de Jacques de Vitry*, ed. R. B. C. Huygens, Leiden, 1960, 5.

appearance of the First Crusade (1098) could not have radically changed the ethnic or religious composition of the city. Neither did the Frankish conquest do more than add a ruling class to the ancient capital of Syria. Its population remained, basically, Byzantine and the Basileus of Constantinople looked upon himself as their patron and protector, a task which he exercised with the consent of Moslem authorities everywhere in the Near East before the appearance of the Franks.

Yet the Greeks were not the only Christians in this territory. The *Suriani*, as they were called by Frankish sources, are very often a generic name for all non-Roman sects who looked 'oriental' or 'Syrian' to the non-discerning Franks. Formally, the name should apply to oriental Christians who followed the Byzantine rite and used Greek in their liturgy and Arabic in their everyday life. The term is still often applied to the Jacobites. The origins of the Jacobite church go back to the theological controversy concerning the nature of Christ which rent the Church in the middle of the fifth century. Whereas the orthodox teaching decreed by the Council of Chalcedon in 451 proclaimed two natures (*physis*), a Divine and a Human, in the person of Christ Incarnate, the condemned heterodox dogma accepted one nature, namely the Divine only. The sectarians were thus called 'Monophysites'. During the sixth century, three monophysite churches were founded: the Coptic church of Egypt and Abyssinia, the Armenian national church and the Jacobite church of Syria and Palestine. The name 'Jacobite' is derived from the Syrian organizer of the church in the sixth century, Jacob Baradaeus. The Jacobites had their own patriarch in Antioch, who was not always allowed to live there under Byzantine rule. With the Moslem conquest of the Near East, the Jacobites found themselves in a more favourable position than their persecutors, the Greeks, as the Moslem authorities often suspected the latter, and probably justly so, of pro-Byzantine loyalties. The Jacobites preferred the rule of the Moslem Seljuqs to that of Christian Byzantines, and new Jacobite churches were built in Antioch after its conquest by the Turks. The Jacobites, whose native language was Aramaic, accepted the influence of the new conquerors by adopting Arabic as their native language, but continued to use 'Syriac' – that is the west-Aramaic dialect – in their liturgy. The age-long hatred between Greeks and Jacobites survived all political changes and upheavals. Under Frankish rule in the last quarter of the twelfth century, Michael the Syrian, Jacobite patriarch of Antioch, never missed an occasion to besmirch the Greeks.

The other monophysite churches, those of Armenia and Egypt, were only slightly represented outside their native countries. Yet the attraction of the holy city was so great that each of them had a church or monastery in Jerusalem and even elsewhere in the Holy Land. The Coptic church of Mary Magdalen in Jerusalem was built almost immediately after the conquest of the city by the Turks.

Not very different was the situation of another national church, that of Christian Georgia (called often 'Iberia') in the Caucasus. Its great sanctuary outside its native kingdom was the monastery of the Holy Cross in Jerusalem, the traditional place where the tree for the Cross was cut. The monastery had strong links with the far-away kingdom and lived on the bounty of its princes and kings, among them the famous Queen Tamara.

The Nestorian was another sectarian church that arose from a Christological controversy. Whereas the orthodox teaching of the Council of Ephesus in 431 upheld one person, at once God and Man, in Christ Incarnate, the heterodox dogma accepted two separate persons in Christ Incarnate, one Divine and the other Human. The sectarians consequently opposed St Mary's title 'Mother of God' – *Theotokos*, as it was the Human person which was born from Mary. The main centre of the eastern Nestorians was in Persia, in the county of Edessa and in Iraq, where Baghdad became the seat of the patriarch. From here their famous missions reached and baptized populations in central and eastern Asia. The sect was only slightly represented in the territories occupied by the Franks. Yet a small Nestorian community existed in Jerusalem under Frankish rule.

The last Christian sect to be mentioned here, which played a part in the history of the Latin kingdom while its own destinies were deeply influenced by it, was the Christian inhabitants of the Lebanon, the Maronites. Despite frequent efforts by the Maronites to prove their original and continually sustained orthodoxy, it seems fairly evident that they followed the dogma assigning one will to Christ Incarnate. This theological, 'monothelite', controversy could only have been understood by professional theologians. It became the identifying creed of the Lebanese Christians after the Moslem conquest and the loss of contact with the Byzantine church. The name 'Maronites' is ascribed by its members to John Maro, allegedly patriarch of Antioch at the end of the seventh century. At this date, however, this name is not known among the patriarchs of Antioch. A Maro did live in the fifth century, and a monastery of St Maro on the Orontes in Syria served as a centre of Christian life; but the schism dates from the seventh century. This Christian community, like its neighbours, the Druzes, lived in the mountainous parts of Lebanon and enjoyed a good measure of autonomy under the Moslems. The Maronites were excellent soldiers and archers, which endeared them to the Franks. In 1182, the Frankish patriarch of Antioch, Amalric, succeeded in bringing this nation into communion with the papacy. Forty thousand people, according to the great Frankish historian, William of Tyre, abjured the monothelite creed and accepted that of Rome. With various incidents, following a great effort of the Roman curia in the sixteenth century, this communion continues to exist to our own day.

To the east of Antioch, across the Tigris and Euphrates, there was still a substantial Christian population, mainly Armenians and smaller communities of the Syrian, Jacobite and Nestorian churches. These areas, around Tel Basher and Edessa, which until the middle of the eleventh century belonged to Byzantium, regained their autonomy and Christian identity by establishing under Frankish leadership the new county of Edessa.

Somewhere between Antioch and Tripoli Christian populations became scantier. Southern Syria, Lebanon and Palestine were cut off from the Byzantine empire in the middle of the seventh century and, although a successful Byzantine *reconquista* in the tenth century pushed as far south as the Valley of Jezreel and Caesarea on the Palestinian coast, its gains were merely transient.

During the four hundred years of separation from the Byzantine empire, these territories were thoroughly Islamized. Unfortunately, the lack of sources makes it virtually impossible to describe this process with any measure of accuracy. Still, it may be safely assumed that the conversion to Islam was rather slow, since these territories, and especially Palestine – the most southerly part – were never really settled by the conquering Moslem Arabs and relatively few invading tribes took root in the narrow strip of land along the coast. At the beginning of the eleventh century, however, Islam seems to have been not merely the religion of the rulers, but also of the majority of the population, certainly to the south of the Lebanon. Some areas, however, even in the south, remained predominantly Christian. This was undoubtedly true of the Christian holy places, like Nazareth and Bethlehem, but was also partially true for a city like Jerusalem, which seems to have been still predominantly Christian (according to a Moslem geographer) as late as the end of the tenth century. This situation changed later, but in the middle of the eleventh century the Christians still inhabited one quarter of the city, the north-western quarter around the Holy Sepulchre. An agreement concluded then between the emperor of Byzantium and the Fatimid rulers of Egypt enabled the emperor to rebuild the destroyed Church of the Holy Sepulchre and concentrate all Christians in the quarter around it.

More interesting is the presence of Christian communities in large enclaves outside the cities in the countryside. Christian villages were no exception between Bethlehem and Jerusalem and, then again, between Jerusalem and Ramallah on the main road to Nablus, around Gaza in the south and in the vicinity of Mount Tabor in Galilee in the north.

The survival of Christian rural communities in Palestine after four hundred years of Moslem rule and the continuous Islamization seems rather surprising. As already mentioned, we really know very little about the conversion to Islam and the explanation offered is purely hypothetical.

On the one hand, the proselytizing pressure of Islam was, barring short periods, not very aggressive, facilitating the survival of Christian communities. On the other hand, it must be remembered that the Byzantine Church was a great landowner and remained so despite some Moslem confiscation until the crusader conquest. As such, it intervened between the Moslem officials and the peasantry in its villages. Consequently, in the estates of the Church, there was no direct confrontation between Moslem representatives or landowners and the tillers of the soil, which lessened pressures that might have accompanied such contacts. The process of Islamization must have been far more rapid and penetrating in the cities, where the daily presence of Moslem authorities and the self-evident advantages of belonging to the ruling religion prompted conversions. It was also in the cities that the anti-Christian and anti-Jewish legislation, which imposed specific dress on the members of the 'protected' communities, evidently degraded the non-Moslem and could have ultimately prompted conversion.

Arabic slowly replaced Greek as the official language during the seventh century, but it became the local vernacular only some two hundred years later, around the year 800. It never completely replaced Greek or Aramaic in the north and Hebrew in the south.

Even then, the process was not complete. The first Christian Arabic texts from Syria and Palestine, Bible translations, hagiographic texts and similar literary products, still used the Greek and Aramaic alphabets and the Jews were to continue for ages to write Arabic in their own Hebrew alphabet. Moreover, the native languages continued to exist and flourish as the normal vehicle of communication between scholars. Therefore, whereas the process of Arabization became a significant fact of Near-Eastern history in the ninth century, the process of Islamization was slower and never completely blotted out the earlier religions of the region.

Clinging tenaciously to their ancient homeland, Jewish communities existed in fairly large numbers in Palestine and neighbouring countries.[10] The Moslem conquest of the seventh century meant, for the Jews, liberation from Byzantine persecution and degradation. The Byzantine ban on their presence in Jerusalem was lifted despite the insistence of the patriarch of Jerusalem – who

---

[10] The historical sources regarding the Jews prior to the Crusades are collected in *Sefer ha-Yishuv* (Heb.), vol. 2, ed. S. Assaf and L. A. Mayer, Jerusalem, 1939.

capitulated to the Moslem conquerers – to retain this aspect of existing legislation. A substantial Jewish community settled in Jerusalem after the Moslem conquest, near the ancient Temple area and, later on, in the north-eastern part of the city, to the east of the Christian quarter around the Holy Sepulchre. Far larger Jewish communities existed elsewhere. The most important was Ramleh, the newly erected Moslem capital of southern Palestine, which replaced Tiberias as the centre of Jewish life in the Holy Land.

Jewish communities were also to be found in some maritime cities, but their greatest concentration was in Galilee. Whereas the Jewish communities in Judea and the coastal plain were to be found in cities, Galilee offers a different picture. There the Jewish communities lived in villages, although the latter were probably not exclusively Jewish but of mixed population. Some of these Galilean Jewish communities were probably autochthonous, going back to the Second Temple and the independence of Israel. We know that, after the final Roman victory, Judea suffered most, whereas the situation in Galilee was far more favourable. Jewish literary sources as well as archaeological finds completely bear out the impression of the survival of a dense Jewish population in the north, hundreds of years after the destruction of the Temple.

The major Jewish centre immediately after the Moslem conquest was Tiberias. The academy (*Yeshiva*) and the chief rabbinical court remained there for some generations until circumstances allowed their return to Jerusalem. But in the mountainous country of Galilee there were some two score Jewish villages.

This autochthonous Jewish community in Palestine was strengthened, time and again, by immigration from abroad. Jewish pilgrims and settlers came from neighbouring Mesopotamia and Egypt and even from far away Byzantium, Russia and Christian Europe. The Egyptian domination of Palestine and Syria in the tenth and eleventh centuries favoured the existence of the Jewish communities since their influential co-religionists with access to the court of the Fatimids could intervene on their behalf, curbing the arbitrary excesses of governors and officials.

The movement of immigration to the Holy Land received a strong stimulus in the tenth century from a rather unexpected quarter. It came from a Jewish sect, the Karaites, which split from official or 'rabbinical' Judaism, as it was called, in the eighth century. Some of the Karaite leaders in the Holy Land framed an appeal to their co-religionists to leave their homes in the Diaspora and settle in the Holy Land, especially in Jerusalem. The Karaite communities were not very numerous, but individually they appear to have been rather large and prosperous. The city of Ramleh, the Moslem capital of the country, often witnessed clashes between them and the Jewish community.

In the middle of the eleventh century, both communities reached their zenith, as we learn from the rich correspondence of the period. But a generation later, the Seljuq invasion of the seventies undermined their position.

The wars of the Turkish conquest, followed by quarrels of the local commanders, brought destruction and insecurity in their wake. The leadership of the Jewish community, the Gaonate, the academy and the court moved from Ramleh to Tyre and finally settled in Damascus, whose Turkish overlords ruled the Holy Land with the exception of the maritime cities. At the same time, another part of the community settled in al-Fustat (old Cairo), in Egypt.

The Samaritans, historical brethren of the Jewish community, continued to live in the mountainous region of Nablus, the ancient Sichem. Alternately persecuted and tolerated by the Byzantine rulers, they enjoyed more peaceful days under Islam. The age-long tradition of the ritual sacrifice on Mount Gerizim at Passover testified to the ancient creed dating back several centuries before the destruction of the Hasmonean state. The high priest and the priestly caste ruled the community, and its old annals list the succession of high priests from generation to generation, adding scanty information about persecutions and calamities.

The kaleidoscopic juxtaposition of ethnic groups and religions reminds one of the biblical catalogue of nations. Every ethnic group and every creed known to the civilized world was present in these ancient biblical lands and particularly in Jerusalem. Any nation or creed which had a share in the Jewish biblical heritage made sure that it was represented in the cradle of its religion.

VI

THE CONQUERORS

A   Nobility

The Latin settlements in the East were the first European attempt to found and rule a colonial kingdom. Several mediaeval societies were created by conquest and based on strict segregation between conquerors and conquered, but in hardly one did such a division continue uninterrupted for two hundred years. The crusaders neither tried to expel the autochthonous population nor attempted to integrate it by conversion, since it suited them to keep the native population as their main source of sustenance. The same reasoning hampered a policy of conversion and the consequent liberation of the converted.

Frankish society ruled over an alien and subjugated majority. It perpetuated its own existence and way of life by an almost incessant stream of pilgrims and settlers during the twelfth century and by creating barriers between itself and the native population, which were never bridged or broken. Once conquered, Palestine became the homeland of the invaders and their descendants, destined, according to their designs, to exist as a colonial Christian kingdom on the frontiers of Islam.

Whereas war and conquest were not new phenomena, the administration of a colonial settlement had no antecedents in mediaeval European experience. The shaping of Frankish society, patterns of social stratification, links with homeland and relations with the local inhabitants were all new experiences. Some of the resulting effects were consciously worked out, though most developed under the pressure of circumstances in the East. Certain of the experiences were to be put to use later on, when dealing with similar phenomena in the Mediterranean. Lately it has even been suggested by an eminent scholar that their influence can be traced during the period of the great European expansion to the Canary Islands and North America. [1]

To a European in the middle of the twelfth century, the nobles of the Latin kingdom seemed to embody the highest knightly ideals. Their undoubted bravery, their connection with the Holy Land and their consequent guardianship of the Holy Sepulchre and the defence of Christendom idealized these descendants of the first crusaders and fixed their image in resemblance to the most venerated and popular of all knightly saints, St George. Mail-coated, high on his war-horse killing the monstrous dragon – he is known from a multitude of frescoes, stained-glass windows and sculptures decorating the lintels, tympana and pillars in hundreds of churches.

This idealized image was not always far from reality. The crusaders were rightly famed for bravery, endurance and fighting prowess. But even a fighting society does not live by the sword alone. Though chronic, fighting was not permanent, and these mighty warriors, before whom the Moslem East trembled, enjoyed long spells of peace – rearing their families, managing property and leading the normal life of a colonial ruling class. As warfare is covered in another chapter [2], the following is mainly concerned with Frankish society as such, its foundation, structure and evolution during the two hundred years of its existence.

The hosts of the First Crusade were the foundations upon which all the social classes in the kingdom developed. The knightly and popular masses led by a predominantly French nobility, with some minor additions from Germany and northern Italy, formed the nucleus of the future society. And in a sense, the Crusade itself became a factor in its evolution. The tens or even hundreds of thousands who joined in the march to the East remain anonymous.

[1] Ch. Verlinden, 'Précedents mediévaux de la colonie en Amerique', *Homaje à Jose Marti. Comision Panamericana de Historia*, Mexico, 1954.
[2] See below, cap. XV: Warfare and Fortifications.

No mediaeval chronicler ever bothered to record their origins or social composition. We can identify only the great leaders. Sometimes we get an inkling of some members of their retinue, outstanding knights, whose feats of arms merited honourable mention, but these are merely passing references. The men on horseback and the thousands of marching peasant families who accompanied them on their slow way to the East are hidden in the grey dawn of the past.

The names in the earliest documents which list the holders of the first noble fiefs created in the kingdom, can hardly even be positively connected with a European noble house, even from among the minor nobility, let alone with the great houses of the West. This leads us to conclude that with the exception of a few princely houses (like those of Godfrey de Bouillon, Bohemond of Otranto, his nephew Tancred and Raymond de Saint-Gilles) no princely or noble house contributed to the kingdom's nobility at its formative stage. The fief-holders in the Latin kingdom in the first quarter of the twelfth century are all *homines novi*, new men, who started out on their own and made good in the Holy Land. In their homelands some belonged to the great mass of dependent knights serving in the retinue or household of the local nobility.[3] Others were probably knights living in modest country manors, leading a life not unlike that of the rich peasantry in their villages. They were neither men of position nor substance. For many it was natural to join the contingent of the nearest grand seigneur. A good number enrolled in his retinue and others might have started out independently. But during the long march to the East, their meagre resources dwindled and they in turn became vassals by swearing homage to one of the leaders. Henceforth the latter had to assure their keep and they to fight for his glory and profit.

These territorial contingents represented ethnic and linguistic entities. The followers of Count Robert of Flanders spoke mostly Flemish, though their leaders certainly spoke French ; the Normans under Duke Robert of Normandy were joined by some knights

---

[3] See a thorough study of an early crusader retinue: J. C. Andressohn, *The Ancestry and Life of Godfrey de Bouillon*, Indiana, 1947.

from Norman England; Duke Godfrey of Lorraine had probably a mixed German- and French-speaking host (and is today claimed by both nations although the Belgians count him among their heroes); the Languedoc host included Provençal and perhaps Catalan-speaking knights led by Raymond de Saint-Gilles; and the Franco-Norman conquerors of southern Italy and Sicily were led by Bohemond and Tancred.

This quasi-national division of the host had a decisive influence on the future character of the conquered lands in the East. The leaders of the Crusade, who became rulers of the newly conquered principalities, settled them by granting incomes and then fiefs to their followers. Consequently, the principality of Antioch ruled by Bohemond became Norman in character and custom, the county of Tripoli founded by Raymond de Saint-Gilles became Provençal[4], whereas the Kingdom of Jerusalem proper was nearest to northern France. The county of Edessa differed from the beginning: its largely Armenian (but also Jacobite) native population was not replaced by the conquerors. Indeed there were hardly any Frankish settlements in the principality. Though ruled by the French Bouillons and later the Courteneys, a substantial stratum of the native Armenians and local nobility were preserved.[5]

Whether Norman, French or Provençal, all crusader principalities created their nobility more or less from scratch. The rise of new families was a protracted process in a war-ridden country, where enemy, climate and plague constantly decimated the ranks. The nobility were self-made men whose careers largely depended on their individual prowess.

According to the chroniclers many an impecunious man became rich during the fighting by acquiring property in the captured cities. This was the first real property 'legally' acquired in the Holy Land by the curious 'Law of Conquest' enacted during the Crusade.

---

[4] See the classical studies for Antioch and Tripoli: Cl. Cahen, *La Syrie du Nord à l'époque des Croisades*, Paris, 1940. J. Richard, *Le comté de Tripoli sous la dynastie toulousaine*, Paris, 1945.

[5] There is no basic study of the county of Edessa under the crusaders. See: R.L. Nicholson, *Joscelin I, Prince of Edessa*, Urbana, 1954. Detailed chapters in Grousset, *op. cit.*, and very often in Cl. Cahen, *op. cit.*

Knight and commoner struck economic roots in their new country.[6]

The same law seems to have also been valid with regard to rural property. In the sources many a village in the neighbourhood of Jerusalem is called not by its historical Hebrew, Greek or Arabic name, but by that of the Frankish warrior who became the owner. Villages must simply have been claimed by knights of the early kingdom on the strength of this 'Law of Conquest'.[7]

In some cases this land-grabbing had political consequences. When Tancred captured Nablus, Beisan, Tiberias and Mount Tabor, it was not a simple acquisition of property but aimed at creating an independent principality. Only the appeal of the Antiochenes, who called Tancred to rule their city in the absence of Bohemond, prevented the creation of an additional Latin state in the East. But this was an exceptional case warranted by the Norman's rank and position. The small knights of the Crusade did not think in such terms. They wanted rural estates or city properties to assure their position. We can imagine them hesitantly venturing into the still dangerous countryside around Jerusalem where marauding Turks, Bedouin or infuriated peasants lay in ambush for the hated Franks. The villages were not fortified and their inhabitants would not attack a Frank for fear of retaliation. Certain knights, perhaps with some companions, would occupy a village and claim it as their property.[8] It took some time before the rudimentary royal administration was in a position to organize the subdued countryside. The captured villages claimed by their 'conquerors' would then be officially assigned to them as fiefs or holdings and the new situation sanctioned by taking the double oath of fealty and homage to the king.

[6] The Law of Conquest is explained by Fulk of Chartres I, 1, cap. 29; Raimond of Aguilers, 275B, 292E; Albertus Aquensis, VI, 43; William of Tyre, VIII, 20–1. Cf. Usama ibn Munqidh, transl. Ph. K. Hitti, 178.

[7] R. Röhricht, *Regesta*, no. 205.

[8] An interesting example is that of Christian villages usurped by knights. Abbé Martin, 'Les premiers princes croisés et les Syriens jacobites de Jérusalem', *Journal asiatique*, 133/4 (1888/9), 471–90. F. Nau, 'Le croisé lorrain, Godefroy d'Ascha d'apres deux documents syriaques du XIIe siècle', *ibid.* 155 (1899), 421–31.

But the chief conqueror was the king himself. He organized every military expedition of any importance and signed treaties with the Italian fleets to besiege the coastal cities. The conquered cities were not immediately enfeoffed, neither by Godfrey de Bouillon nor by Baldwin I. Following a very cautious and wise policy, they aimed to create a considerable royal domain before granting fiefs to their followers. The conquered city usually received a royal governor and a garrison. A proportion of the city revenues, such as tolls and customs, was assigned to them as their living. Real seigniorial fiefs were granted by the king to his knights only at the end of the first decade. These enfeoffments of captured villages, requisitioned city property and assigned municipal revenues formed the earliest economic basis of the knightly class. And yet a large number of knights were paid directly by the king and in reality were no more than a class of salaried warriors, although the whole ceremony of knightly homage was performed.

A clearer pattern of administrative organization is discernible at the end of the second decade, which more or less coincided with the total conquest of the country (c. 1120). Although the royal domain was still quite substantial, a good part of the land was already divided into seigniories and fiefs. In all probability the enfeoffment of a seigniory implied that the new lord would enfeoff part of his domain to assure the military services of his vassals. But the new holders of important fiefs from the Crown followed royal policy in that they were not eager to distribute their recently acquired lands. It is characteristic of the feudal system in the kingdom that the fiefs normally granted were just sufficient to maintain a single knight – *fief de son corps* as they were called in Frankish sources, paralleling a 'one knight's fief' in Europe. Only in exceptional cases would a larger fief be granted, enabling the holder to enfeoff dependent knights. Another characteristic was the substitution of city rents or property for land-fiefs. These *fief de besant* were not entirely unknown in Europe, but were certainly an exceptional way to remunerate the services of a vassal. In the Latin East they became extremely common, not only for simple knights, but even for persons of rank and position. There were two main reasons for this particular development. On the one hand, Frankish lordships were comparatively small and the owner could realize no administrative or other profit in dividing large parts of his domain into partially enfeoffed sections. He preferred direct enfeoffment to assure himself of the military feudal services of simple knights without noble or knightly intermediaries. On the other hand, there was the direct influence of local circumstances. The crusaders probably created the only feudal society in a developed money economy. Palestine and Syria, as well as all the neighbouring countries of the Moslem East, never passed through a period of an almost exclusively natural economy, with a very restricted use of money. Gold Arab dinars, Byzantine hyperpera and silver drachmas, minted of almost pure gold and silver alloy, were the normal vehicles of commerce. The crusaders adopted this monetary economy, since no other choice was feasible in the East.

The crusaders thus introduced the use of money even into their feudal system. Gate and market tolls, customs duties, urban taxes on real estate, merchandise and through traffic were paid in cash and it was natural for a Frankish lord to assign some of this revenue to his vassals. As a money economy prevailed, the simple knight found it even more convenient to receive his feudal income in cash rather than payment in land. The rent-fief thus became the dominant type in the Latin kingdom.

This particular development of feudal practice had a far-reaching impact on the structure of Frankish society. Compared with contemporary Europe, the links of vassalage in the Frankish East were simpler, but at the same time brought about a rapid polarization within the nobility. In effect, it split the nobility into a small group of higher nobles and landowners and a great mass of dependent minor knights. The latter were often no more than paid hereditary retainers. Nothing reminds us of the numerous class of European squires. Only a few actually owned villages, and hardly any lived in a country manor. Since they were not in touch with the countryside, they bore the character of a patrician city garrison.

This unique feature of the Frankish nobility was further accentuated by the fact – hardly found elsewhere in Western Christendom – that almost the entire Frankish population was concentrated in the cities. The Holy Land was an urbanized area *par excellence*. The Moslem rulers inherited the Hellenistic, Roman and Byzantine tradition of city-centred administrative units and, settling in cities themselves, saw no reason for change. The crusaders adapted to these realities and tailored their own feudal system to existing conditions. Furthermore, in an unfortified countryside the rulers of the cities were also rulers of the land. Fortification of the countryside was largely a crusader innovation, but newly built castles – even smaller ones – were almost immediately surrounded by quasi-urban agglomerations or fortified suburbs and became citadels[9] of a new city.

This pattern of settlement, found nowhere in contemporary Europe, accentuated the rather pedestrian character of the Frankish knight. He was a vassal, swore homage and fealty, performed the normal duties of 'counsel and aid' to his lord; but the lord's treasury or one of its branches paid his salary, presumptuously called a 'fief'. Payment was in cash, but sometimes partly in kind: with wheat, barley, oil, wine and fodder.[10] This latter practice, although it may have been the result of expediency, was also practised in some Moslem armies. We know, for example, that it was a normal system of payment among the Mameluks in thirteenth-century Egypt. It is, consequently, not impossible that the Franks were influenced by their Moslem neighbours.

We have already stated that the earliest possessors of crusader lordships were relative parvenus. Moreover, for more than a generation, they were a constantly changing element. Lordship after lordship was enfeoffed by the kings of Jerusalem and a few years later escheated again to the Crown, only to be enfeoffed to another tenant-in-chief. This does not mean that the principle of heredity was ever debated. As far as we can see, it existed from the beginning, as such a tradition was already well established in eleventh-century Europe. The frequent escheats were directly

---

[9] J. Prawer, 'Colonization activities in the Latin Kingdom of Jerusalem', *Revue belge de philologie et d'histoire*, 29 (1951), *passim*.

[10] A good example is that of the seigniory of Arsuf. See Delaville le Roulx, *Cartulaire de l'Ordre de Saint Jean*, III, 6–7, no. 2985.

caused by the structure of early crusader society. A good many nobles who joined the Crusade were married, but left their families behind. The great majority were younger people and bachelors and the knightly host included very few women. This is well attested by intermarriage with the local population; crusader popular etymology derived the name *pullani* or *poulains* (colts), given to the Syrian-born Franks, from Apulia in southern Italy.[11] This was said to be the native land of their mothers, brought out for breeding purposes, not unlike the women of la Rochelle and le Havre sent to Canada in the seventeenth century.

The absence of family ties and commitments was mainly responsible for the instability of the upper seigniorial nobility. The death of a noble left his lordship vacant, as there was seldom a son or relative to claim it. The lordship escheated to the Crown, which was free to grant it again in fief, sometimes to a relative of the royal house or to a deserving knightly retainer. But quite often to a newcomer, who had decided to settle in the East.

A generation after the foundation of the kingdom the genealogies of fief-holders become clearer and we can detect regular and hereditary transmission. At this time noble families founded dynasties, those famous *familles d'Outremer*, extolled in future history, legend and literature as paragons of knightly virtue and valour.

Nevertheless, Frankish society was still far from being solid and stable. The main problem was a chronic shortage of suitable manpower, badly needed to defend and expand the kingdom. A whole set of laws promulgated at this early period testifies to a conscious effort to attract European knights. Whereas the earliest fiefs were granted to a man and to his direct heirs only, the new fiefs were granted to a man and all his relatives. This strengthened the dynastic principle and at the same time made settlement more attractive. Daughters were granted the right to inherit fiefs at a time when this was not yet the general practice in Europe. But royal legislation kept a tight rein on the nobles. An early law prevented,

---

[11] Jacques de Vitry, *Historia Orientalis* I, cap. 67, in Bongars, *Gesta Dei per Francos*, 1611, 1086. Cf. Joinville, cap. 84, par. 434.

for example, the concentration of fiefs in one hand. A man who already held a fief would be bypassed in inheritance for the benefit of a more distant but landless relative. Such legislation tended to employ the land and the money resources of the kingdom in the most economical way. It encouraged immigration and settlement by assuring feudal property for prospective immigrants.

This egalitarian trend of early legislation changed drastically in the second quarter of the twelfth century. The lordly dynasties became stronger as the transmission of their seigniories was assured to their families, they also became richer with the political stabilization of the country. The surplus from agriculture, which found new outlets in the newly settled urban centres, and income from commerce – especially in the maritime cities – strengthened that class and created a different tone in the relations between Crown and nobility.

It would be quite justified to describe the second quarter of the twelfth century as the formative period of the higher nobility. The early egalitarian laws against the accumulation of fiefs by one person were abrogated. Henceforth, the strict rule of inheritance and the transmission of fiefs and dowries changed the outlook of the higher nobility and its mode of behaviour. They were becoming an exclusive and excluding caste. A Frankish noble would assure the economic and social standing of his daughters by marrying them off to men of position. This created a closed circle of landed families, connected by ties of marriage or common ancestry. Through repeated intermarriage, their numbers became smaller, while their property grew constantly.

At the end of the First Kingdom no more than half a dozen or ten families belonged to the gilded circle of the higher nobility. Their ambitions and pretensions reached the ultimate pinnacle. They aspired to curb royal intervention in marriage contracts by insisting on their own agreement to the marriage of heiresses, in order to prevent possible *mésalliances* with the king's favourites. At that time they intermarried with the royal house of Jerusalem and eventually wound up marrying into that of Armenia. They even married into the imperial house of Constantinople. Many a noble in the Latin kingdom could look back with satisfaction upon the fortunes of his house, risen from obscure and impecunious knightly immigrants to the East. Two generations later his descendants could count themselves among the most famous families of Christendom. As the glorification of the self-made man was yet unknown, some of them did their best to eradicate the memory of their humble origins. Not everyone could claim descent from a swan like Godfrey de Bouillon, though he could really boast a less avian parentage without being the worse for it, since he was descended on both sides from Charlemagne. Some could at least try to link their families to the European nobility at the time of the First Crusade.

The most remarkable rise of a Frankish noble family is that of the famous Ibelins.[12] Although a later tradition ascribed their descent to a viscount of Chartres, there is a very strong probability that they really came from a Pisan merchant family or, as has been recently argued, from a minor knightly clan of Norman Sicily. At the end of the First and during the Second Kingdom almost all noble families, including the dynasties of Antioch and Tripoli, the royal house of Jerusalem and the royal Lusignans of Cyprus, were connected by marriage with the Ibelins.

The closing of the ranks of this enchanted circle often led to collisions with royal policies and the public interest was not always best served. Whereas the first, and to some extent the second, generation of the Frankish nobility freely welcomed European newcomers, by the middle of the century a definite change had occurred in their attitude. The Frankish nobility now saw the newcomers as intruders and competitors. Thierry of Flanders, who pilgrimaged four times to the Holy Land, created such opposition that the local nobility preferred to negotiate with the besieged Moslems in Shaizar and abandon the siege (1157) rather than see the city handed over to a newcomer.[13]

Such extreme attitudes were occasionally at variance with the heart throbs of some heiress. This was the case of the impecunious

[12] J. Richard, 'Guy d'Ibelin, évêque de Limassol', *Bulletin de correspondance hellénique*, 1950, 98–133. See another hypothesis by W.H. Rüdt-Collenberg, 'Les premiers Ibelins', *Moyen-Age*, 1965, 433–74.

[13] S. Runciman, *History of the Crusades*, II, 349.

knight Renaud de Châtillon (near Paris) who came to the Holy Land in the retinue of Louis VII of France. He decided to stay after the precipitate return of his royal master, who abandoned the unsuccessful siege of Damascus due to unfounded suspicions of treachery by the local Franks and only too-well founded suspicions of his wife's infidelity, the famous Eleanor of Aquitaine.

The handsome and gallant knight stayed on, joining a substantial group of rivals for the hand of the widowed princess of Antioch. His personal charm overcame all competition and won the affections of the princess. But royal consent was still needed for the marriage. Renaud left the siege of the lady for the siege of Ascalon (1153) to find the king of Jerusalem. Fearing rather unsavoury rumours about the flirtatious princess, the latter was happy to give his consent and entrust her to the strong arms of Renaud. The choice was excellent. Renaud defended his principality successfully and made himself feared by his Moslem neighbours. Unfortunately he was ambushed and spent the next fourteen years as a prisoner in Aleppo, where he put the time to good use and learnt Arabic and Turkish. When finally ransomed he found himself a widower and his principality ruled by the son of his wife from an earlier marriage. But a new possession was in the offing. The lord of Transjordan died, leaving an heiress, Eschive de Milly. Renaud received her hand and dowry. Some years later the same Renaud actually tried to capture Mecca and Medina with the help of friendly Bedouin. He built ships in the Transjordanian castle of Montreal, transported them piecemeal to 'Aqaba and launched them on the Red Sea, sowing panic from Cairo to Jedda in an attempt to navigate Bab el-Mandeb in search of the commercial route to the Indies. Appropriately, he met an honourable death at the hands of Saladin himself.[14]

True romances like that of Renaud made the rounds of European castles, stirring the imagination and making young squires dream about the Promised Land. Reality was unfortunately different, the number of available heiresses limited and already monopolized by the local nobility. This nobility favoured the marriage of the

[14] G. Schlumberger, *Renaud de Châtillon*, Paris, 1923.

heiress to the kingdom, Sibylle (after the death of her heroic and childless brother, Baldwin IV) to one of their number, Baldwin of Ramleh. Sibylle offered her hand and the kingdom to a new-comer, William Longsword, and after his death to the brave and handsome Guy de Lusignan (unfortunately lacking political and military insight). The highest prize was thus snatched from the hands of the local nobility and the resentment of one of its most powerful members, Raymond of Tripoli (prince of Galilee by marriage), was partly responsible for the disunity of the kingdom on the eve of Hittin.[15]

This circle of magnates, the *grands lignages*, accumulated lord-ships and Crown offices, monopolized real authority in the king-dom while weakening the royal power, which became a mere shad-ow of its former self. According to mediaeval social theory, not the magnates but every knight belonged to the nobility. Many a knight was certainly poorer than the average merchant in one of the mari-time cities, but class distinctions were clear-cut and almost un-bridgeable. A different upbringing, way of life and different ideals grouped even quite minor and impecunious knights with the nobility. Customary law and royal legislation were always con-cerned with the class of nobles as a whole, and although they made it clear that the class, or rather, the 'estate', is not homogeneous, that it is divided into magnates (*riches homes*), barons and lesser knights (*chevaliers*), they made no distinction as far as law is concerned. All are equal before the law of their own 'estate', that of the nobility.

Despite the shortcomings of the sources, we can get a fairly good picture of the class. The Latin kingdom proper, when mobilized (without military orders and mercenary forces) could raise an army of some six hundred knights.[16] In skirmishes and smaller engage-ments, often described by the chronicles, we seldom come across such a large number of fighting men. Even so great an enterprise as the attack upon Egypt by Amalric I was undertaken (on good,

---

[15] M. W. Baldwin, *Raymond III of Tripoli and the Fall of Jerusalem*, Princeton, 1936.

[16] See below in cap. XV, Warfare and Fortifications: B.

contemporary authority) with some three hundred odd knights.

Lesser knights usually lived in the city, either as members of the standing garrison or in the daily entourage of its ruler. In all probability the knights were employed in rotation on garrison duties in the citadel or in one of the smaller castles which dotted all the major roads of the country. The garrisons of large outpost castles, like those of Transjordan, were probably permanent.

As in all feudal systems a knight was dependent on his immediate lord. But in the Latin kingdom, for reasons already explained, this was usually the overlord of a city – the capital of the seigniory – without any intermediates. This made for stronger cohesion between lord and vassal, but also involved stronger links of dependence. The latter was even more accentuated by the fact that such a knight was under the direct supervision of his lord. Moreover, living on a rent-fief without any agricultural domain of his own, he was hardly typical of the European noble, whom a great historian (Marc Bloch) has defined as possessing 'the right to command'. True that a small group of knights was in a better position. A noble who owed the service of seven knights to the Crown was a man of some standing. A noble 'courtier', like the famous Philip of Novara (who lived in the middle of the thirteenth century), a hanger-on of the Ibelins, became quite influential in the kingdom. His versatility and accomplishments as a writer, rhymester, lawyer, adviser and mediator, made this Italian-born knight a favourite of the Ibelins and the royal family, who paid his debts and assured him a decent income.[17]

But very few knights ever reached such a position. The overwhelming majority were simply salaried warriors. A normal fief, whether in land or money, assured a knight an income of some 450 to 500 gold besants annually. This was thought fairly good and equalled the annual income from an average village. We should keep in mind that the daily expenses of a knight in the middle of the thirteenth century were calculated at one besant a day. This meant that his annual fee was barely sufficient to maintain a high standard

[17] See J. L. La Monte's introduction to the Engl. transl. of Philip of Novara, *The Wars of Frederick II against the Ibelins in Syria and Cyprus*, N. Y., 1936.

of living if he was a married man with a family, which must have been usual. The relatively small income made the Frankish knight very dependent on his immediate lord. Such a feature of feudal relations had deep repercussions on the political system of the country. The emergence of seigniorial dynasties and the predominance of the *lignages* in the political life of the kingdom in the thirteenth century have to be considered within the framework of the kingdom's nobility. The hegemony of seigniorial dynasties prevented direct contact between the Crown and the vassals of the great lords.

Nevertheless, the social position of a knight was enviable. Whatever his economic resources, he was above the rest of the Frankish population, not to mention the native inhabitants of the country. Landed property, whether in cities or in the countryside, once classified as fiefs, could legally belong to knights only. Burgesses, men of the communes, were excluded from this status-giving type of property.[18] The penalty for insulting, wounding or killing a noble (and in this respect there was no difference between magnate and simple knight) bore no comparison with those for injuring a Frankish commoner. A noble's testimony in court was sufficient to convict the accused. No commoner had the right to trial by combat.[19] Moreover, no knight could be imprisoned for debt, although his fief could be sold to pay it.[20] Class consciousness was expressed by extravagant legislation such as that of the 'Assise of Bilbeis' (1168). According to this decree, a knight was not obliged to descend from his horse even when besieging or attacking a besieged city.[21] The horse, symbol of status, was more important than military expediency.

Despite such barriers, intermarriage with the lower classes was not uncommon. Knights had property in the cities, not only as part of their fiefs, but property of specifically burgess origins, held in the so-called burgage tenure. As such tenure was explicitly reserved

---

[18] *Abrégé du Livre des Assises des Bourgeois, Lois* II, ed. Beugnot, 312ff.
[19] *Livre des Assises des Bourgeois* in *Lois* II, 221ff.
[20] Jean d'Ibelin, c. 188, *Lois* I, 300–1.
[21] *Lois* I, 455, n. c.

for commoners, we have to assume that it came into knightly possession by marriage, although the city lord could also have disposed of it by grant to his knights.[22] It should not, however, be concluded that there was a great deal of social mobility in the kingdom. After the middle of the twelfth century we know of no knight who rose from the ranks into the higher nobility. During the thirteenth century this was hardly possible even through marriage, since the female relatives of the magnates and their dowries were well guarded by special privileges. At least in one known case in Tripoli a rich burgess became lord of Butron by marrying the heiress and paying her weight in gold to her guardian, the count of Tripoli. More often, knights intermarried with burgess families, an occurrence facilitated by the proximity of the two classes within the cities.

Exogamous marriages were, on the other hand, rather common among the upper nobility even during the twelfth century, when the limited number of noble families caused intermarriages to be canonically prohibited. A good many demands for divorce were based on the 'discovery' of such prohibited consanguinity. As previously mentioned, the upper nobility often married into Armenian or Byzantine noble families or with European nobility settled in the Levant, Cyprus and Greece, though direct matrimonial relationships with French and other nobilities also occurred.

During the thirteenth century, especially after the departure of Frederick II (1229), the upper nobility became the rulers of the kingdom, *de facto* and *de jure*. The absentee king was virtually replaced by an oligarchy. It is in this context that the kingdom's nobility developed one of their most characteristic features: a passionate and even fanatic interest in law and legality. In no contemporary Christian nobility was knowledge of customary law and procedure and mastery over the intricacies of constitutional law so cultivated and cherished as in the Latin kingdom. This nobility did not produce even one scholar, theologian, or man of letters, excepting William of Tyre. All its intellectual energies

22 J. Prawer, 'The *Assise de Teneure* and the *Assise de Vente*. A Study of Landed Property in the Latin Kingdom', *Econ. Hist. Rev.*, 4 (1951).

appear to have been concentrated in the study of law. This was not restricted, as occurred in Europe, to the descendants of minor knights, such as Glanville, Beaumanoir or Pierre de Fontaine, but applied to members of the highest nobility like Jean d'Ibelin and his family. Legalistic hair-splitting was their favourite pastime. Had this inclination – strange in nobles – been directed to upholding the law and assuring justice, the crusader nobility would truly have embodied the lofty ideals of mediaeval *justitia*. Alas, these intellectual efforts were mainly directed to preserving the privileged social position of its exponents. Legal scholarship sought to render the feudal framework immutable. This proved disastrous for the future of the country, but it endowed Europe with one of the best collections of juridical treatises on the feudal system, regarded as classics up to the end of the *ancien régime* in Europe.

B   Burgesses

Below the nobles, Frankish commoners constituted the ruling class. If the mounted warriors of the First Crusade were the nucleus of the future knightly classes, the foot-soldiers fathered the future non-noble settlers. Heterogeneous in their ethnic composition, they followed the baronial contingents and settled with their leaders.

Crusader usage baptized these commoners with the rather misleading name of 'burgesses' (*burgenses, borjois*). A Frank who was neither noble nor belonged to one of the Italian communes was classified as a 'burgess', a name which penetrated even contemporary Arabic. And yet these people could hardly claim urban origins. There were but few European cities at the end of the eleventh century, limited in size and in the number of their inhabitants. Furthermore, the cities maintained and enlarged their numbers by constantly absorbing the surplus of the relatively overpopulated countryside. This process went on uninterruptedly during the two hundred years of the kingdom's history. With few exceptions, it thus seems unlikely that cities which were not producing a surplus population could serve as a reservoir for overseas emigration.

The overwhelming majority of Frankish commoners were thus of peasant origin, from northern France, Germany, and Italy. Perhaps only in southern France, where some forms of urban life survived the early Middle Ages, urban elements may have participated in the Crusade. This might also have been the case in northern Italy, but the Italians joined the communes and not the 'burgesses'. Later European emigration during the twelfth century does not seem to have changed this basic pattern. The remarkable demographic growth of the peasantry in the eleventh century furnished the bulk of those who settled in the new urban centres, as well as the manpower which facilitated the immense task of clearing forests, draining marshes and the foundation of hundreds of new villages during the twelfth century. The Crusades and the migration to the East were an additional outlet for rural overpopulation in Europe at the time.

A peasant who joined the Crusade left behind not merely his native soil, but also the shackles of servitude. Not even his feudal lord could prevent him from leaving. No manorial obligations existed in the crusader host and no servile duties had to be performed for the commander of the host. By tacit agreement and later by custom, which became law, all participants in a Crusade became free men. It goes without saying that freedom once achieved was not lost at the moment of settlement. The former serf was now on his own and no links bound him to any master. With luck he acquired property in the city or in the surrounding countryside. The less fortunate and the latecomer might become tenants. But the servile links which bound the man to the soil or exact services incompatible with his standing as a free man were never re-established. There were still public obligations. He was bound to military service whenever there was a *levée en masse*. This involved not merely the defence of his city, but participation in military expeditions whenever the kingdom was in danger. On the other hand, not being feudally connected with the overlord of the city, he owed no military service, unless based on a special agreement, for example, to serve as a 'serjant' (*serviens*) for stipulated pay. The change in the juridical and economic status of commoners was enhanced by their position in the newly colonized kingdom.

77

Although below the nobility, they belonged to the conquerors and rulers, far above the mass of conquered natives.

The class designation 'burgesses' is rather baffling. It is hardly possible that this name – which replaces that of 'foot-soldier' at the end of the kingdom's first decade – should have been created for this class in Europe. It was a new name, and in the Latin East designated people who were neither nobles nor serfs. The name *burgensis* admirably described this position. But whereas in Europe the name was derived from *burgus* (suburb, borough), in the new settlements in the East which mushroomed near fortified places, it had no such etymological connection, but simply implied the new and free standing of the settlers. It is not impossible that the typical city land-tenure, the burgage tenure, so popular in the West, might have influenced the use of the word. As a matter of fact the real property of commoners was defined as *borgesie* – burgage-tenure. With nobles and the clergy barred from its holding, it was the exclusive monopoly of the new class. By a significant extension in the use of this right, landed property, or even whole villages, could also be held by burgage tenure, a phenomenon unknown, or at least very exceptional, in the West.[23] The status of the man decided the status of his holdings. Burgage tenure was the nearest the Middle Ages ever came to the notion of full property. Apart from military service, the payment of a nominal rent to the overlord of the city was practically the only public obligation of the burgess. He was free to alienate his property through sale, rent, division or exchange. Some small symbolic payments[24] were due to the lord for the right of alienation, reminiscent of the seigniorial agreement required some generations earlier for the alienation of such property in Europe. Certain archaic limitations for safeguarding the rights of relatives still existed, e.g. the right of pre-emption. At times they must have proved a nuisance in the developed economy of the country. This explains the fact that another survival from the age of limited property

[23] *Abrégé des Assises des Bourgeois*, cap. 21, gives a very concise summary of the problem.
[24] *Ibid.*, 253.

rights, the so-called *retrait lignager*, was singularly abbreviated in the kingdom. In Europe a relative could claim pre-emption rights for a year and a day after the conclusion of a sales contract for landed property, thus voiding the agreement or leaving the status of property uncertain for a long time. In the Latin kingdom such a claim was valid for not more than a week after the public announcement of the sale.[25] General freedom and the impact of economic conditions thus tended towards completely free property.

Almost from the beginning the burgesses were ruled by customary law, applicable to their persons and property. The elaboration of this code is interesting in itself. The participants in the First Crusade, and subsequent waves of immigration, were of heterogeneous origin. Their legal notions were based on the law of their homelands and their social origin. As a rule, this meant northern manorial law. Since the crusaders never adopted the system of personal law, already more or less in abeyance in eleventh-century Europe, the question of formulating a local code common to all burgesses became imperative. The tradition of the manor hardly suited the new social and economic realities. The slow rhythm of manor life could not furnish the legal instruments for a developed urban economy. The local population, Moslem, Christian, and Jewish was used to the Moslem legal system and its Byzantine predecessor. The crusaders apparently adopted the customary code of southern France, where city life had lingered on from late Roman times. There, a form of Roman law, modified by local custom, was in force until the full revival of Roman law in the twelfth century. This code was well suited to the economic realities of the kingdom. Moreover it was not unfamiliar to the Italian communes or to the native population. Unfortunately we do not possess the original code or collection of '*Assises*' of the burgesses. The author of a private, thirteenth-century collection of laws and procedures followed in the court of burgesses (a collection known as *Livre des Assises des Bourgeois*) used a Provençal law book, *Lo Codi*, as its model.[26] Roman Common Law was supplemented

[25] *Livre des Assises des Bourgeois*, cap. 30, *Lois* II, 35.
[26] J. Prawer, 'Étude préliminaire sur les sources et la composition du *Livre des Assies des Bourgeois*', *Rev. hist. de droit francais et étranger*, series 4, 32 (1954), 198ff.

by royal legislation regarding burgesses, some of which is preserved in the aforementioned collection.

The normal type of burgess property was city real estate, a house with its courtyard, well, garden, with a vineyard, orchard and vegetable garden, near the city, or even within the walls. Some burgesses made their fortunes early in the history of the kingdom. The previously mentioned 'Law of Conquest' gave many of them access to substantial possessions. The problem of the kingdom in the earliest phase of its development was not a shortage of city land, but of manpower. Jerusalem, for example, probably had some twenty thousand inhabitants at the time of the crusader conquest, though this dropped in the next few years to several hundred only. Empty houses were to be had for the asking. The danger of living in an isolated city quarter concentrated the new population of Jerusalem in one area, around the Holy Sepulchre.[27] Enterprising burgesses also came into possession of landed property outside the cities, even of entire villages. Such cases are attested near Jerusalem[28] and probably also near Acre. Thus a rising group of rich burgesses was created by the fact of conquest or by early settlement in the country. Others climbed the social ladder by a different route. The long Crusade and the following waves of immigration made for social mobility. Knights whose horses were killed in action or devoured by the starving host, became to all appearances foot-soldiers, and the outward differences between knight and commoner became blurred. The rich spoils of war and its chronic continuation during the whole first decade frequently overcame the barriers of class distinction. Thus we can identify some people of clearly burgess origins who suddenly appear in the documents with the proud title of *milites* – knights.[29]

Slowly a semi-patrician class becomes discernible among the burgesses. Although its members could seldom boast fabulous wealth, an upper class of burgesses did come into being. The most

[27] J. Prawer, 'The Settlement of the Latins in Jerusalem', *Speculum*, 27 (1952), 490–503.
[28] R. Röhricht, *Regesta*, no. 205.
[29] *Ibid.*

lucrative sources of city wealth were taken over by the members of the organized and privileged European communes. Consequently, apart from the acquisition of property, burgesses rose to prominence via royal, seigniorial or church administration. Time and again we find the same burgesses signing royal or ecclesiastical documents, some concerned with everyday matters, others even of political content. Almost imperceptibly the same burgesses slip into jurors' benches, as members of the court of burgesses, the highest position in the hierarchy of that class. This constant familiarity with administration and the dispensing of justice even created a class of burgess jurists, whose reputation was so high that they were consulted on points of feudal law, attended the seigniorial court – or even the royal court, the highest judicial body in the kingdom.[30] This higher and quasi-patrician group was called to special service in times of emergency. Balian d'Ibelin, charged with the defence of Jerusalem besieged by Saladin, chose certain bachelor burgesses whom he knighted.[31] This isolated case may be explained by the imminent danger of Moslem conquest.

But only a select group could have risen to such social heights. For the great majority of burgesses their status was certainly an upgrading compared with their origins. Their stone houses were palaces compared with the peasant hovels of the West. Their diet was different and more varied, and their garments of better cloth, sometimes even silk. Nevertheless, their position in Frankish society as a whole was not prominent.

The burgesses made up the bulk of the city population in the Latin kingdom, although in Tripoli and in Antioch – let alone Edessa – they were outnumbered by the local Christians. They appear in all the usual urban occupations as butchers, shoemakers, tailors, carpenters, smiths, shield-makers, leather craftsmen, bakers, brewers, cooks (a new occupation, very much in demand in cities overflowing with single men and pilgrims), barbers, spice and perfume vendors.[32] A good number were shopkeepers living and

[30] The most famous were the Antiaume family, Raymond at the end of the 12th century and his son Nicolas in the next generation.

[31] *Ernoul*, ed. Mas Latrie, Paris, 1871, 175.

[32] See H. Prutz, *Kulturgeschichte der Kreuzzüge*, 335ff.

working in small rooms which were entered directly from the street. Some owned their shops while others rented them from the landlord, king, church or monastery.[33] In the *souk* of Jerusalem one can still see stalls with the letters *SCA ANNA*, denoting mediaeval property rights of the Church of St Anne, which rented to the Latin burgesses. On the other hand we rarely find great merchants among them. This was a situation peculiar to the Latin kingdom, where large-scale commerce was concentrated in the hands of privileged southern European communes.

People in the administration, domain stewards and accountants, tax receivers, customs officials, market supervisors and city police were also recruited from among the burgesses. The salaried footsoldiers, *serjeants* or *serjeants à cheval* of the seigniorial entourage and military contingent were also recruited from among the burgesses.

Other burgesses, although living in the cities, continued in their old occupations as farmers in the surrounding countryside. This was the case in all the major cities of the kingdom.

As previously mentioned, most of the Frankish population were concentrated in three big cities. Jerusalem, the capital, was the smallest of the three and its population can be estimated at some 20–30,000. Acre was the most important, even during the twelfth century. In the thirteenth century its population probably exceeded 60,000, and next to it came the northern city of Tyre.[34] Other cities, and this includes ports and inland towns, were much smaller. One may have numbered some 5,000 inhabitants, a rather large number by contemporary European standards, but small compared with Near Eastern cities. There were some twenty cities of this size in the kingdom and the burgesses formed the majority of their inhabitants.

A special position among the burgesses was assumed by those who left the cities and settled entirely new Frankish villages. The kings of Jerusalem, and also city lords, military orders and other

---

[33] A good example is furnished by the inventory of city property pertaining to the chapter of the Holy Sepulchre in Jerusalem. E. Rozière, *Cartulaire du Saint Sépulcre*, no. 185.

[34] J. Prawer, 'Étude de quelques problèmes agraires et sociaux d'une seigneurie Croisés au XIIIe siècle', *Byzantion*, 23 (1953), 143ff.

church establishments encouraged the settlement of land which had been partly laid waste during the fighting and massacres in the wake of conquest. The largely Moslem native population partly abandoned the land, preferring to find refuge in Damascus or Egypt than remain at the mercy of unknown conquerors. The burgesses furnished the manpower to restock the abandoned countryside. The lead in colonization was taken by the ecclesiastical establishments and was soon followed by the kings and other lay lords. More often than not, the newly founded villages were built near older settlements on the place of abandoned and depopulated native villages probably located near wells and available buildings or building materials. These new villages were far bigger than their local counterparts. The native Palestinian village hardly numbered more than twenty families, while Frankish villages sometimes reached 150 families which meant about 500 souls. These numbers were warranted by security considerations and almost all Frankish villages were fortified or at least provided with a tower to serve as an observation point or refuge.

A closer look[35] at some of these new villages will give us an idea of their structure and composition. In 1136 King Fulk fortified Beit-Jibrin on the road between Ascalon and Jerusalem and handed it to the Order of St John. A Frankish settlement was founded in the shadow of the order's fortress, and a generation later (c. 1153) the number of families was thirty-two, i.e. some 150 inhabitants. Apart from farmers, we also find a tailor, carpenter and camel-driver. Benjamin of Tudela mentioned three Jewish families living there, in all probability dyers. Two of the settlers came from Jerusalem, one from Edessa, one from Hebron and one from Rama or Ramleh. The others represent a cross-section of the European West: Auvergne, Gascony, Lombardy, Poitou, Catalonia, Burgundy, Flanders and Carcassonne are specifically mentioned. Each settler received two *carrucae*, i.e. some seventy hectares of land. His obligations were the payment of a land rent (*terragium*), a tithe on all crops and fruits except olives, and a percentage of what he got

---

[35] J. Prawer, 'Colonization activities in the Latin Kingdom of Jerusalem', *Revue belge de philologie et d'histoire*, 29 (1951), 1063–1118.

from raiding the Moslems! The settler had the right to alienate his property – safeguarding a pre-emption right by the order and a small payment.

Another example is that of Mahomeria (el-Bira). In the middle of the twelfth century the new village had ninety families and some time later an additional fifty settled around the small castle, bringing the Frankish population to some 500 souls. Again we find people from Auvergne, Provence, Burgundy, Gascony, Limoges, Poitou, Tour, Bourges, Catalonia and Lombardy, in addition to Palestinians from Jerusalem, Nablus, Singil, Nabi Samwil, and Jaffa. Some were *fratres conversi*, Augustinian lay-brothers, but the majority were laymen. Some were craftsmen: a smith, carpenter, shoemaker, gardener and mason are specifically mentioned, but their main occupation was farming and vineyards. The lordship belonged to the canons of the Holy Sepulchre, but the settlers were ruled by a court of burgesses with their own jurors. The canons signed contracts with the settlers regarding the system of cultivation and payments, usually of the *champart* and *complant* type (division of fruit between the contracting parties). The mill and the bakery, both erected by the canons, had monopoly rights, and the farmers were obliged to bring their grain and flour there.

It is impossible to evaluate the extent of this colonizing movement. It was no doubt quite vigorous in the twelfth century, and as a matter of fact we hear of about half a dozen different 'customs of settlement', used by the respective colonizing agents and transferred from one place to another. This proves the vitality of the movement, but does not enable us to appreciate its extent. In any case, the men who made it possible were the burgesses. We know that they came from the poorest stratum of society. One chronicler even remarks that those who settled outside the cities were men unable to make a living in them.[36] Many simply returned to their previous occupations before embarking for the 'Eldorado' in the East.

Whatever his social position and economic standing, the Frankish commoner was always a free burgess. All his duties were

[36] *Eracles* in *RHC, Hist. Occidentaux*, I, 977.

public obligations. In addition, according to his occupation, he might be liable to payments resulting from economic, but not personal, dependence. No manor court had competence over him and he was tried solely by the court of burgesses[37] in his particular settlement by a set of non-arbitrary laws. No wonder a contemporary chronicler in one of the fanciful mediaeval etymologies said that the crusaders are called 'Franks' because they are *franches* – free men.

C   National Communes

A characteristic feature of the kingdom's social stratification and political organization was the existence of a distinctive class of national communes : Italian, Provençal and Spanish. Their juridical status and social position can be regarded as typical of the colonial spirit which pervaded the institutional structure of the Latin East. The name 'commune' was imported from Italy, where it had been used to describe the great urban centres that became politically independent entities between the tenth and twelfth centuries. By extension the term came to denote a collectivity of their nationals who settled in the kingdom. Although European and of the Latin rite, and as such belonging to the ruling conquerors, the members of the communes were not regarded as nobles or burgesses, but formed a class apart, which enjoyed a distinctive status and specific privileges different from both noble and burgess. If the Franks as a group were a conquering minority who founded a colonial kingdom, the communes were the earliest expression of that type of colonial spirit which, some centuries later, established the English, French and Dutch trading companies. But whereas these trading companies were the precursors of conquering colonial powers, the communes in the crusader kingdom were profit-making organizations living on foreign soil which drew their strength from the fact that their members never became citizens of the country. The kingdom's common law did not apply to the communes, and they almost succeeded in creating a state within a state.

[37] See below, cap. IX, The Lordships – Government at the Local Level: B.

Nearly always autonomous political entities, they pursued their own aims and were more closely linked to their countries of origin than to their new homeland. In a sense the nationals of the communes were never permanent settlers. Their population fluctuated, more often than not being composed of people who went to the East with the clear intention to return to the West once they had made enough money. But even those who stayed on never regarded themselves as citizens. If the crusader kingdom can be regarded as a European colony on foreign soil, the nationals of the communes colonized a colony.

They monopolized the kingdom's extensive foreign trade and almost all banking and shipping. Nevertheless, their economic functions did not determine their privileged place. A long list of 'international agreements' between the kings of Jerusalem (and later the individual lords of maritime cities) and the Italian cities defined the social status of their nationals. These privileges were the result of the Italian contribution to the conquest. First Genoa, Pisa and then Venice sent ships to the East, which were of the utmost importance in capturing the whole seaboard. Without their co-operation the conquest of the coastal cities would have taken much longer, or might never have succeeded.

For services rendered, or more exactly for services to be rendered, the three great city-states demanded recompense. Although this sounded a discordant mercenary note, which jarred the chivalrous effort of Christendom, times were hard and the Italian services irreplaceable. The Venetians pompously declared that they came to fight for the liberation of the Holy Land, but this did not prevent the doge who participated in the siege of Tyre (1124) from exacting one-third of the captured city and its territories, plus almost total exemption from tolls and customs and the granting of privileges which made Venice as powerful as the king in this great northern port. Neither the archbishop of Pisa, Daimbert, who commanded the Pisan fleet in Jaffa in 1100, nor the noble Embriaci – one of the great consular families of Genoa who participated in the siege of Jerusalem – omitted to exact political and economic privileges. The crusader leaders were indeed eager to capture the ports and to see the country settled and economically developed, and might have regarded these exorbitant demands as a source of future profit. It was in their interest to attract the Italian merchant, a familiar figure in the European economy, and attach him to the young kingdom. If the privileges so lavishly bestowed on the Italians had actually been exercised in full, very little of the cities would have remained in the hands of the new rulers and settlers. The grant of a quarter in almost full property and autonomy in varying degrees is a constant feature in the privileges accorded to the communes. It is impossible to say whether the implications of such general wording in the charters were overlooked by the grantors, or whether such provisions were a verbal formality. The fact remains that these privileges and their implications remained on the books of the kingdom.

From the point of view of the Italian communes it would seem that their demands were prompted as much by greed as by ignorance. In these early stages it was impossible to know which areas would flourish and be suited for commercial development and which not. It was simpler and more expedient to demand privileges everywhere.

The Italians learnt by experience. An important city like Jerusalem proved to be economically sterile and without real importance. The central administration of kingdom and church, and even the constant flood of pilgrims, still did not make this city an international emporium which needed the type of merchandise handled by the Italians. This was even more so with smaller inland cities like Tiberias or Nablus. Their markets catered to the everyday needs of the local population and offered no advantage to the great merchants. But in some of the maritime cities the Italians really found possibilities for lucrative business. The great port of Acre and the northern port of Tyre became their most important bases in the kingdom proper. Under certain circumstances (usually political) Beirut also played a role in their commerce. In the principalities the capital cities – Tripoli and foremost Antioch – became the main centres of their commercial activity. Ports like Jaffa, the natural outlet for Jerusalem, Haifa, Caesarea and Sidon, captured with Italian help, did not attract their merchants. Although privileges assured them property and customs exemptions, they never settled in these secondary ports.

Whatever the original expectations of the kingdom's rulers and the Italian merchants, a generation after the conquest it became clear that the Holy Land would not oust Constantinople or Alexandria as the chief emporia of Levantine commerce. As commodity markets the great ports of the kingdom were but of secondary importance. And yet, the existence of a friendly Christian state in the Levant brought certain advantages and compensations. Pogroms, expulsion and confiscation – not unknown in Byzantium and Egypt – did not threaten the Italian merchants in Acre. Their autonomous quarters, well-protected from foe and friend, largely influenced the evolution of the Italian settlements. In the earliest period the maritime cities, the autonomous quarters and market-places were no more than temporary bases for economic activities, trading-posts rather than permanent settlements. A small nucleus of more or less permanent inhabitants, people in charge of administering the commune's property and the churches lived in the autonomous quarters, but the average Italian merchant often spent three or six months of the sailing season (from late spring to the end of autumn) aboard ship, visiting Egypt, Contantinople, and neighbouring countries. He exchanged his gold and silver ingots and bought goods to be sold during the voyage or later on in Europe. He stopped and sometimes even wintered in one of the crusader ports, returning to his metropolis with his wares during the earliest spring *passagium*.

This pattern of activity continued during the whole of the twelfth and thirteenth centuries. The Venetian and Genoese inventories of Acre and Tyre record *palazzi* and rooming houses which remained empty for most of the year, but were rented with the coming of the *stolae* (the merchant fleets) for the duration of the season. But gradually the Italian quarter changed its character.

The early period of Italian settlement, which might be called the 'wintering period', slowly gave way to a different pattern. In the second half of the twelfth century, the fluctuating Italian population became more stable and settled down. Sometimes the type of their privileges influenced settlement. Such, for example, was the

case in Tyre. According to the treaty between the patriarch Warmund in 1123 (in the absence of the captured King Baldwin II) and
the doge of Venice, one third of the city and its countryside had to
be ceded to the commune of Venice. This treaty was scrupulously
observed and one third of all villages in the seigniory became
Venetian, as did a quarter in the northern part of the city, near its
port (the southern port of classical fame was by then silted up).
Venice enfeoffed some of the villages to its nationals in return for
feudal services which (an exceptional case) the commune owed
to the kingdom. Thus a landowning group of Venetian settlers
stayed on in Tyre, strengthening the local Italian population. Other
nationals rented from the commune authorities houses, courtyards,
vineyards, market stalls and benches, thus becoming real residents.
They performed the function of regular intermediaries between the
incoming ship owners and merchants and local business interests.
Merchants extended their habit of wintering and settled in the
East. So did agents of great merchant and banking houses, quite
often relatives and partners in the trading companies.

From among the merchants who frequented the maritime cities
of the kingdom the central governments of the respective communes chose representatives for the Levant. Their term of office
was usually short, often not more than a year or two. They bore
the titles of 'consul' or 'vicomte' and ruled their quarters and
respective nationals. But after the fall of the First Kingdom (1187)
and during the restoration, a more centralized system was introduced almost simultaneously (c. 1192) by all major communes.
Henceforth a *bailli général* in Acre represented the Venetians, with
authority over all other *baillis* in the Latin Levant. At the same time
the Genoese appointed a 'consul general' for Syria, whereas Pisa,
which in the beginning nominated two 'consuls general', reduced
their number to one who had authority over the local officials.

In the earlier period the officials were appointed from among the
local merchants, and probably with their participation; later they
seem to have been sent directly from the metropolis. It was,
however, convenient and logical that the appointees should have a
knowledge of the Levant and they were therefore quite often
chosen from among the Levantine merchants.

Thus a kind of local Italian patriciate which united wealth and political power began to evolve in the crusader kingdom, since the officials were naturally chosen from among the wealthier merchants whose power was often augmented by the presence of relatives in the Italian metropolis. Members of this wealthy group stayed on in the Levant. Very often their sons went back to Italy to find suitable brides, whose dowries were paid in merchandise or investments, and then returned to Acre or other ports of the kingdom. Thus Levantine extensions of Venice, Pisa and Genoa were founded, transferring Italian dialects, customs and churches to the East. During the thirteenth century members of Genoese consular families, the highest nobility of the city, settled in the East. Likewise every high Venetian name – families who had supplied their city with doges, captains, counsellors and senators – was found in the East. We can follow the history of some of them for three generations in the Latin kingdom. [38]

The commune's privileges were hereditary. For generations the members would claim exemptions and privileges conceded more than a hundred years earlier, at the time of the First Crusade. It was worthwhile to keep one's national identity. Their autonomy and commercial privileges assured Italian nationals overwhelming advantages over all local Frankish merchants. It was only natural that as early as the middle of the twelfth century the kings of Jerusalem tried to curb these excessive privileges. They were only partially successful. Even the Holy See, pressed by the *Serenissima* or the *Superba*, as Venice and Genoa were called respectively, would call the kings to order. Genoa even tactlessly erected a gilded monument in the Holy Sepulchre listing its privileges! The merchants were thus hardly expelled from the Temple. Yet sometimes the kings got the better of the Italians, using political or security reasons to curtail their privileges. For example, Henry of Champagne fixed at thirty the number of Pisan families allowed

---

[38] Among the Genoese families active in Levantine commerce the so-called 'consular' family of da Volta predominates. Among the Venetians we note members of the patrician families of Michiel, Falier, Contarini, Dandolo, Morosini. See bibl. cap. XVIII: B. Colonizing the Colonists – The Italian Experiment.

to stay in Acre. On the other hand, in times of danger the old privileges were renewed and even extended. Thus Conrad of Montferrat, besieged in Tyre in 1190, confirmed and enlarged old privileges to the communes and the unfortunate Guy de Lusignan confirmed the same *verbatim*. When a new political star was in the ascendancy – as happened with the arrival of St Louis – the communes copied their privileges *en gros* and asked for renewed royal confirmation.

The Crown could neither abolish the privileges nor master the communes, but tried hard to prevent the most extreme abuses. Although their nationals were barred by law from holding feudal fiefs and burgage tenures, it often happened that by accident of marriage, inheritance or commercial transactions the nationals of the commune acquired land or homes belonging to classified property outside their quarters. A large number of Venetians, Genoese and Pisans thus had the best of both worlds. They acquired local, non-commune property and at the same time enjoyed the exemptions of commune nationals. The general vagueness of property rights in the Middle Ages, their involvement with personal status, and, in this case, with the political and economic standing of the communes created an incredible imbroglio. This often led to clashes, not only with the kingdom's authorities, but between contending communes. Some cases which were brought to court or arbitration and whose protocols are extant, show that the lawyers had a field day in debating the finer points of jurisprudence. Whatever the case, such complications meant that city taxes or feudal dues could escape the seigneur, whether city lord or king. The latter, following a Byzantine precedent of the middle of the twelfth century, insisted that they should forgo their new property, pay the customary taxes, or relinquish their national privileges and become citizens. The problem was never satisfactorily solved, and as late as the fourteenth century, after the loss of the kingdom, the crusader kings of Cyprus were still wrestling with this thorny problem.

Around the big three – Venice, Genoa and Pisa – clustered a large number of other Italians. Eager to enjoy Pisan privileges, merchants from all over Tuscany tended to declare themselves as

Pisans and, being recognized as such by the head of the colony, the consul of Pisa, they could then enjoy the commune's prerogative. The Tuscan merchants would in turn recognize Pisa's rights of jurisdiction over them and their property, as long as they stayed in the East. Naturally such proceedings were not exclusively limited to Pisa.

But in the meantime new participants in the Levant trade appeared. One of them was Marseilles, whose citizens were joined by those of Montpellier and other towns of Provence. The privileges they gained were few and far from the exorbitant demands of the Italians. By then the kingdom had already learned its lesson and became much more circumspect in granting privileges. The merchants of Marseilles tried to extend their power by the device of falsifying a privilege and back-dating it, rather clumsily, to the middle of the twelfth century. Other communes which later came on the scene, headed by the Catalan city of Barcelona, gained for the most part only commercial privileges and did not attempt to create national quarters. The communes of Marseilles and Barcelona were never of great importance. The famous maritime statutes of Marseilles, compiled in the middle of the thirteenth century, show a rather primitively organized Eastern colony, reminiscent of the Italian colonies a hundred years earlier. The *fondaco* of Marseilles was little more than a halting place and an outpost for merchants trafficking in the East.

It is impossible to evaluate the number of nationals in the communes in the Latin kingdom. If topographical indices and inventories of property can be relied upon, their number were usually small, several hundreds at the most. But their strength did not lie in mere numbers, particularly with regard to their economic position. The Eastern colonies were backed by the power of their great mother cities. The metropolis sent its fleets, merchant ships in times of peace, and armed galleys in times of war. Conversely, the communes of the East often became battlefields where Italian powers fought out their mainland and colonial struggles. Rivalries in Corsica, competition in Constantinople, clashes in the Aegean came to a head in the middle of the thirteenth century, to make Acre a bloody battlefield of Italian jealousies. The local Italians took part in the battles, their numbers strengthened by sailors and soldiers arriving from Europe. The quarters occupied by each of the communes were fortified, dividing Acre into miniature republics surrounded by walls and towers, fighting their neighbours and destroying the city. The leaders of the communes had by this time emerged as independent rulers, who hardly recognized the existence of the kingdom.

VII

THE CROWN

The First Kingdom (1099–1187) was blessed with five kings called Baldwin, a name to which the Franks of the East seemed rather partial. Modern numismatists and sigillographers consequently find it nearly impossible to assign with any accuracy coins or royal seals to individual Baldwins of Jerusalem. For the twelfth century, only the coins and seals of Amalric can be identified with certainty. The designs on coins and seals do not differ perceptibly from each other. They generally represent one or more of the three major buildings in the capital. On some of the better-engraved and more elegant seals (in themselves a sign of growing prosperity) the design combines the three major landmarks of the city: a square tower, with nail-studded double gates topped by battlements and two cupolas on slim turrets represents the citadel, the so-called 'Tower of David'. In its shadow the royal palace was later built. A conical roof with a round aperture at the top, resting on pillars and a small square construction represents the Church of the Holy Sepulchre. And, finally, a beautiful dome topped by an enormous cross, represents the 'Temple of the Lord', the former Mosque of Omar. The obverse of these coins usually shows a cross encircled by the name of the king. The obverse of seals regularly depicts a king of Jerusalem, usually wearing a round or a polygonal crown, sometimes with a round lower band. Pendants, presumably adorned with precious stones, appear on both sides of the head. He wears a kind of loose tunic with wide lapels, with an orb in one hand and a cross or sceptre in the other. [1]

[1] Two major studies cover the sigillography and numismatics of the Latin kingdom: G. Schlumberger, *Numismatique de l'Orient latin*, Paris, 1878 and

Nothing in this representation distinguishes the king of Jerusalem from a ruler of Western Christendom. Perhaps because the seal engravers were Europeans they followed traditional patterns, or these Levantine kings may actually have wanted to be portrayed in the fashion of their Western contemporaries.

Everywhere in Christendom, the coronation that inaugurated a new reign fused temporal and spiritual elements. It expressed the standing of the king as the legitimate heir or the elected ruler – as well as the 'Lord's anointed' – ruling a Christian kingdom by Divine grace. But anointment and coronation in the city of David (the only exception during the First Kingdom was the coronation of Baldwin I in Bethlehem) were charged with historical and spiritual associations unparalleled in Christendom. It is therefore all the more remarkable that the worldly elements in the coronation ceremony contrasted so strongly with the religious in their exceedingly sober and over-legal character. Their main purpose was not merely to establish legitimacy but also to renew a covenant between the king and his warrior electors – as was allegedly done at the end of the First Crusade.

As in almost every twelfth-century kingdom, succession to the Crown wavered between election and heredity. Even the Plantagenets and Capetians, although hereditary for all practical purposes, still preserved traces of ancient elective elements. One of them, the consent of the ruled, which had long lost its real importance, was symbolically expressed in an acclamation by the nobles present. Only in a crisis, as in the absence of direct descendants, was the ancient electoral prerogative of the nobility exercised to select a king from among the members of the dynasty.

The Latin kingdom still preserved many traces of the ancient electoral practices when heredity was already a well-rooted and accepted principle.[2] Several factors converged to preserve this

---

Supplément 1882; G. Schlumberger, F. Chalandon, A. Blanchet, *Sigillographie de l'Orient latin*, Paris, 1943. Both have excellent reproductions of seals and money. See also bibliography of cap. XVI.

[2] The elective and hereditary elements in the rights of the Crown of Jerusalem were exhaustively studied by J. L. La Monte, *op. cit.*, 1–85.

peculiarity. The most important precedent was the election of Godfrey de Bouillon. The whole history of the kingdom began with the election of the 'Advocate of the Holy Sepulchre'. The legend around the election of the 'modest' Godfrey was known to all. Hereditary claims to the Crown of Baldwin I (1100–18) and Baldwin II (1118–31), second and third rulers of the kingdom, barely existed. The nobles were primarily responsible for their accession to the throne and, in the case of Baldwin II, they actually overruled the herditary claim by Eustace of Boulogne, brother and legitimate heir of Baldwin I. The memories of real elections were simply too recent to be relegated into oblivion. Consequently, the purely hereditary principle was not established in practice until 1131, when Queen Melissande succeeded her father.

But the significance of the electoral principle in the coronation ceremony was not merely due to tradition, but in the formulation and introduction of a formal oath, which not only obliged the king to rule justly, but also submit to the common and other law of the kingdom. It is difficult to assign a precise date to the introduction of this elaborate oath into the coronation ceremony, which created a 'covenant' or 'social contract'. The earliest extant record connected with the coronation, that of a Baldwin (possibly Baldwin I),[3] contains the usual vague formulation that the king will rule with justice, and safeguard the rights of the Church. But after the middle of the twelfth century, in the time of King Amalric (1162–74), when the magnates were striving to become the equals of the king in governing the realm, a stricter formula was introduced.

By then, the mass of legislation promulgated over half a century and the accumulated precedents began to play the role of a gospel in the political theory and practice of the kingdom. The respective positions of king and nobles, in terms of the sacrosanct privileges of the nobility – at the expense of the Crown – were increasingly defined. The 'liberties and franchises', as the European nobility fondly described their privileges, became the corner-stone of

---

[3] Preserved in the cartulary of the Holy Sepulchre, see E. de Rozière, *Cartulaire du Saint-Sépulcre*, no. 122.

political thought, so that the preservation of these prerogatives was elevated from its original role to become the *raison d'être* of the kingdom. At this time the legend of Godfrey de Bouillon as the 'law-giver' came into being. Godfrey was elected by his fellow nobles of the First Crusade to be their ruler and established the laws of the kingdom. This dual aspect of the first coronation established the idea of a *contrat social* by the two parties: the kings of Jerusalem would henceforth give an unqualified confirmation of existing customs and liberties as a prerequisite for their acceptance and subsequent coronation. It seems likely that under Amalric, when the nobility were strong enough to force the king to divorce his wife before recognizing his claim to the throne, such strict formulations became possible. It is also significant that the later coronation oath of the kings of Jerusalem explicitly mentioned the royal obligation to observe the 'Laws of King Amalric and his son Baldwin', i.e. Baldwin IV (1174–85), indicating that the nobility set great store by constitutional practice and theory elaborated during that period. Thus the Crown of Jerusalem bore, at least from the middle of the twelfth century, two liabilities or mortgages, legally expressed in the coronation ceremony: the special standing of the patriarchs of Jerusalem and the royal obligations to the nobility. The great day of the coronation started with preparations in the main buildings of the capital: the royal palace adjacent to the citadel (Tower of David), the Church of the Holy Sepulchre, the 'Temple of the Lord' and in the Templars' headquarters ('Temple of Solomon' – the Mosque of al-Aqsa). The streets through which the royal procession was to pass were gaily decorated; the balconies of the flat-roofed houses were resplendent with oriental rugs, and an air of festivity pervaded the city. Knights and nobles from all parts of the kingdom participated in the solemnities. On these occasions the grand officers of state performed duties dating back to their Carolingian origins. The four grand officers of the kingdom, the seneschal, constable, marshal and chamberlain – each in charge of a different part of the ceremony – symbolically enacted both their humble beginnings and their fully-developed functions of state.

The busiest[4] man in the city on coronation day was the seneschal, who performed his erstwhile functions as the royal major-domo. His was the responsibility for the ceremony as a whole, and he was charged with the supervision of his colleagues and of the numerous retainers and scribes.

The future king donned his coronation robes in the palace. In dressing, he was assisted by the chamberlain, the ancient *camerarius*, or household officer responsible for the king's chamber or *camera*. Once attired, he left his apartments and, surrounded by members of his family and officials, appeared before the royal palace. Here he was joined by the marshal and the constable who waited with the royal standard. This was a square of white cloth with a red cross at each corner and a fifth cross in the centre, recalling the altar with its five crosses representing the wounds of Christ. The king mounted his horse, bedecked for the occasion, and the festive procession led off, headed by the chamberlain, who pointed the way with the royal sword in his charge. Close behind came the seneschal carrying the sceptre, followed by the constable, the ancient *comes stabuli*, or 'Master of the Stable'. He bore the royal standard until the *cortège* reached the Holy Sepulchre. Here the king dismounted and the constable seized the bridle and handed the royal standard to the marshal. It seems that the king did not ride into the precinct of the sanctuary, but walked the last part of the way. Before the magnificent portals of the Holy Sepulchre the king was received by the patriarch of Jerusalem, the prelates and the numerous Latin and oriental clergy.

The king, who wore the traditional deacon's vestments – a richly embroidered dalmatic and perhaps even a stole – knelt, as did the grand officers, before the patriarch, who led the prayers. This was the prelude to the coronation proper.

At the request of the patriarch, the king took the coronation oath.[5] Its first part did not differ essentially from similar oaths taken

[4] The relevant texts regarding the ceremony are connected with the grand officers of the Crown. Jean d'Ibelin, cap. 256 ff.

[5] In addition to the already mentioned coronation formula for one of the earliest Baldwins (Rozière, no. 122) we have a full Latin text (Rozière, no. 154) for King Aimery from 1199, which is substantially the same as given in French

by European sovereigns. The king promised to guard the possessions and rights of the Church and the privileges of the clergy, and
further swore to protect widows and orphans. In addition, the
king took an extraordinary oath to the patriarch : 'I shall be from
this day henceforth your faithful helper and defender of your
person against all men living in the Kingdom of Jerusalem.'[6] This
was an affirmation of the ancient church mortgage. Although not
an oath of homage, it did sound like a vassal swearing fealty.
Though anachronistic by the middle of the twelfth century, this
oath preserved an ancient memory, Godfrey de Bouillon's recognition of sovereignty claimed by the patriarch.

This first part of the oath was not taken to the community as a
whole, but specifically to the patriarch and Church. This was followed by what may justly be called a renewal of the covenant.
Whereas a general promise to guard the rights, possessions and
privileges of the people can be found in the coronation oaths of all
European monarchs, none had such pointed phrasing as that of the
kings of Jerusalem :

> I shall guard the *Assises* of the Kingdom and those of the Kings, my
> predecessors of blessed memory, and the *Assises* of King Amalric and
> his son, King Baldwin, and the ancient customs and *Assises* of the
> Kingdom of Jerusalem.

Not merely its tenor rendered this oath far more stringent than its
European counterparts, but also the way in which it was administered. When Hugh III de Lusignan was accepted (1269) as king
of Jerusalem:

> Jacques Vidal – speaker for the 'community of the realm' – presented
> to him a writing which contained the text of the oath, which he said
> that the lords of that kingdom used to take and are obliged to take
> and the king swore it so as it was in that writing. And immediately

by Jean d'Ibelin, cap. 7 (another edited in *ROL.*, VIII, 443). In addition, a
summary in *Livre des Assises des Bourgeois*, cap. 26. See now H. E. Mayer, 'Das
Pontifikat von Tyrus und die Krönung der lateinischen Könige von Jerusalem',
Dumbarton Oaks Papers, no. 21, 194.

[6] Jean d'Ibelin, cap. 7.

after he had done it, the liegemen of the Kingdom of Jerusalem who were present made homage to him. [7]

This made the coronation oath a bilateral contract between the king and his nobility.

Following the oath-taking, the patriarch raised the king and, holding his right hand, promised 'to maintain and defend the Crown justly put on his head, saving the rights of the Church of Rome' (or of the monastic order if the patriarch was a monk). Then the patriarch kissed the king and turning to the assembled knights, clergymen and burgesses, called on them to affirm, *viva voce*, that this man was lawful heir to the Crown. After three exhortations the assembled populace shouted : '*Oill*' – 'Yes'.

The population assembled in the courtyard heard the oath taken by the king and acclaimed him as their legal lord, then joined the choir in singing *Te Deum laudamus*. The treasury of the Holy Sepulchre, to which the Hospitallers and Templars possessed the keys, was opened and the royal crowns (for both the king and queen) were borne by the great barons. The king remained at a stall near the altar while the *Te Deum* still reverberated throughout the cathedral. At the conclusion of the prayers by the patriarch, the king was enthroned facing the Holy Sepulchre. Mass was said, and after reading the 'epistle and sequence', the king was led back to his stall before the altar. The patriarch then announced '*Benedicimus*', and proceeded with the anointment. A vase or a horn-like receptacle (shown in all contemporary representations) contained the consecrated oil with which the patriarch anointed the king's head and shoulders. He then put a ring, a symbol of loyalty, on the king's finger and girded him with a sword, the emblem of justice and the defence of the faith. Finally, he placed the crown on his head and the sceptre in his right hand – symbol of temporal punishment for malefactors, and the orb into his other hand, which signified dominion. After announcing three times in Latin, 'Long live the king in prosperity', the king kissed the prelates, went back to his throne, and the mass ended with Gospels, and the

[7] *Documents relatifs à la successibilité au trône et à la régence*, cap. 17 in *Lois* II, 418 ff.

preface. The king took communion, and the whole ceremony ended with the patriarch blessing the royal standard, which the king then returned to the constable.

The royal procession left the Church of the Holy Sepulchre and made its way through the narrow streets to the 'Temple of the Lord'[8] where the king placed his crown on the altar, symbolically commemorating the presentation of Jesus to Simeon in the Temple. From here the royal suite made its way to the 'Temple of Solomon' (the al-Aqsa Mosque) for the coronation banquet, which may have been held there, since the 'Temple of Solomon' had once served as a royal palace.

The banquet was served as a special duty and privilege, by the burgesses of Jerusalem,[9] under the direction of the seneschal. The dishes and drinking-cups used became his property. The king's horse with its sumptuous trappings became the property of the constable, and his cup that of the chamberlain. During this banquet the sceptre was held before the king.

Only seven of the nine crusader rulers over the First Kingdom were actually crowned in Jerusalem, then capital of the country. Godfrey de Bouillon was never crowned and Baldwin I was crowned in Bethlehem. Only one ruler of the Second Kingdom took the Crown in Jerusalem. Frederick II Hohenstaufen, excommunicated by pope and patriarch, took the crown from the altar of the Holy Sepulchre and put it on his head (1229). All the other rulers were crowned in Tyre, second city of the realm. In the absence of the patriarch, the archbishop (second in rank to the patriarch of Jerusalem) performed the ceremony. But even if the coronation were held in Tyre, the main celebrations naturally would take place in Acre, the real capital of the Second Kingdom.

Observance of the law, by king and nobility alike, was the constitutional corner-stone of the realm. The power of the kings of Jerusalem, like that of almost all mediaval rulers had its sovereign and feudal aspects and, more often than not, the second aspect

---

[8] One of the first acts of Saladin after the capture of the city was to remove the cross from the Temple.

[9] Jean d'Ibelin, cap. 7.

constituted the king's real power. It is significant that whereas, in all their official documents, the kings used the title *rex* or *rei* (French-written acts appear from 1211), juridical treatises normally use the term *chief seigneur*. This was in no way derogatory, but simply stated the fact that in the everyday business of ruling the king exercised his standing and prerogative as the apex of the feudal pyramid. The mesh of feudal links and dependencies formed the framework of state and society, and the right of the ruler to dominate that structure was his real power.

Thus the exercise of power was neither absolute nor arbitrary. It depended on the possibility of bringing into harmony the naturally opposed interests of the king and his vassals. The institutional instrument that could either bring about this co-operation or jeopardize the king's policies was the meeting of the king and his direct vassals – the great tenants-in-chief – in the king's court, the *Curia regis* (called by the crusaders *Haute Cour*). Each new reign was inaugurated by a meeting of the *Haute Cour*. The links of feudal vassalage, which, according to law, had lapsed with the disappearance of one of the contracting parties (in this case the deceased king), were re-established by taking an oath of fealty and by the act of homage. In exceptional cases of a disputed accession to the Crown, the *Haute Cour* would meet and deliberate before the coronation, as it had ultimately to declare the legitimacy of any claim.

The actual beginning of a reign was marked by the feudal oaths taken after the coronation. The nobles, ordered by rank, knelt before the king, swearing homage and fealty. Each noble declared himself to be the king's man and was confirmed in the possession of his fief. Then followed the actual oath of fealty. At the end of the thirteenth century, the differences between the two were vague. The oath of fealty was sworn on the Gospels and did not include a reciprocal promise by the king, as was the case in the oath of homage. The former oath had a more general character and its obligations were unilateral.

The oath of vassalage that immediately followed the coronation was taken only by officers of state, nobles, tenants-in-chief and knights of the royal domain. But the following customary period of forty days kept the king quite busy. Since the last quarter of the twelfth century *all* fief-holders (barring cases of *force majeure*) had to take the oath and be confirmed in their possessions during these forty days, otherwise they would lose them. Under King Amalric and his famous *Assise sur la ligece* (*c.* 1170), not only tenants-in-chief, but every single fief-holder in the realm and rear-vassals of all degrees had to take the oath of homage. This must have meant at least six hundred oaths (the total number of knights obliged to give military service) and possibly far more. The seneschal may have replaced the king in the tedious duty of receiving oaths from simple knights.

In some cases, when the king was in doubt about the loyalty of some of his nobles, he could even demand an additional oath from the inhabitants of the cities within their lordships. [10] As it is hardly conceivable that the inhabitants took individual oaths, the jurors in the court of burgesses may have taken the oath to the king or to his representative, to affirm the fidelity of all citizens.

Later, during the second half of the thirteenth century, the solemn meeting of the *Haute Cour* was enlarged by the attendance of the high prelates and the masters of the military orders, the heads of the Italian communes and, finally, by the new bodies, the confraternities of burgesses, which came into prominence during the anarchic period following the Crusade of Frederick II. In time, these discarded their passive role and directly took an oath of fealty to the new ruler. At a time when feudal links were weakened and the framework of state and society was tending to disintegrate, such an oath might even have been of some practical value. But it also heralded the decline of the feudal system. [11]

The two hundred-year-old Crown of Jerusalem went through several distinct phases of evolution. Compared with contemporary European developments, the position of the Crown seems to have

[10] Philip de Novara, cap. 51 and parallel Jean d'Ibelin, cap. 140 and 199; ·Jacques d'Ibelin, cap. 10.

[11] J. Prawer, 'Estates, Communities and the Constitution of the Latin Kingdom', *Proc. Israel Academy of Sciences and Humanities*, II (1966), No. 6.

THE CROWN

followed a course in the opposite direction. European monarchs on the eve of the First Crusade were only just beginning to lay the foundations of their future power. Louis VI of France even experienced difficulties travelling within the narrow boundaries of his Île de France. The kings of Jerusalem possessed far more power, both in theory and practice. Conversely, by the middle of the thirteenth century, when Western Europe was dominated by such powerful rulers as Frederick II, St Louis and Edward I, the Crown of Jerusalem was but a shadow.

Although the first ruler of Jerusalem was humbly titled 'Advocate of the Holy Sepulchre', no hint of weakness reduced the royal power during the earliest period of the kingdom. The social composition of the warrior class which remained after the First Crusade favoured the existence of a strong monarchy. For more than a generation the royal house remained unopposed by any rival, since no noble could boast a sufficiently illustrious origin or the independent power to challenge the Crown. Since the fate of the warrior class depended on royal bounty, their allegiance was assured. Nevertheless, not only the absence of a strong aristocracy favoured the position of the kings of Jerusalem. Above all, the new state needed a strong ruler to survive. It has been said of the centralized English feudal regime that its strength was based on two conquests, that of Normandy by Rollo (911) and that of England by William the Conqueror (1066). In a sense this was also true of the Latin kingdom. For ten years after the conquest of Jerusalem the realm was in a chronic state of war, and the king was first and foremost leader of the host. All his other duties and competences were subservient to this main function. In these circumstances there was simply no place for divided authority. Moreover, during the crystallization of the feudal structure the kings of Jerusalem pursued an extremely cautious internal policy, partially expressed in their reluctance to enfeoff lands and lordships. Godfrey de Bouillon assigned city-incomes rather than fiefs to his faithful warriors and Baldwin I pursued the same policy.[12] As no higher nobility could claim a peer's share in the spoils of conquest, such a policy did not

[12] See cap. IX, The Lordships – Government at the Local Level: A.

104

raise any opposition. But the lack of an administrative infrastructure that could assure effective local government finally led to enfeoffments and the creation of seigniories.

During the first half of the twelfth century, the royal domain was very considerable. Almost the whole of ancient Judea and Samaria, as well as the coast from Jaffa to Ascalon – often used as an appanage for royal scions – formed part of the royal domain. The main ports of the country, Acre and Tyre, also belonged to it and scattered possessions and castles rounded out the Crown lands. For five consecutive reigns, from Godfrey de Bouillon to Baldwin III, the Crown's possessions were larger and far richer than all the enfeoffed seigniories together. Furthermore, for a generation after the conquest, the enfeoffed nobles rarely transmitted their fiefs to their descendants, which reverted to the Crown on their death.

This well-entrenched position of the Crown slowly began to change in the second quarter of the century. Some of the enfeoffed nobles established hereditary baronial dynasties. Moreover, the administration of far-away possessions, like the great lordship of Transjordan (created by conquest in 1115 and enfeoffed c. 1140), changed the balance between feudal holdings and Crown property. But even during this period of change, the royal power and prerogative remained strong indeed. An *Assise*, which probably goes back to the time of Baldwin III (1143–62), who hardly made innovations in this field, assured the king the right to confiscate fiefs from his great tenants-in-chief without trial for a variety of reasons. Some, such as fomenting an uprising of peasants against the king, or attacking the king's family or person, would have been admitted as just in any feudal court. But other offences listed prove the extent of royal power in the middle of the twelfth century. Opening a maritime port, establishing a commercial route to Moslem countries, striking coins or falsifying the royal coinage were liable to the same punishment without a court decision.[13] These were royal prerogatives and monopolies which, despite the

[13] J. Prawer, 'Étude sur le droit des *Assises de Jérusalem*: Droit de confiscation et droit d'exhérédition', *Rev. hist. de droit français et étranger*, 1961, 520–51; 1962, 29–42.

existence of independent seigniories, the Crown of Jerusalem succeeded in retaining. Moreover, until very late in the twelfth century the Crown guarded its rights to supervise the different lordships. Though especially true of intervention in the sphere of justice, this also applied to other aspects, where the seigniories were not entirely free of royal tutelage. This was tangibly expressed by the fact that the presence of the king in any seigniory or seigniorial court made it instantly 'royal'. The preponderance of the royal power explains why agreements with the Italian communes, even regarding cities located in the seigniories, were concluded by the Crown.

The royal hold also extended in great measure to the church. Early attempts to turn the kingdom into an ecclesiastical state failed, and even the claims of the patriarch to temporal lordship in Jerusalem and Jaffa – although conceded by Godfrey de Bouillon – were never put into practice. The same claim renewed under Baldwin I did not meet with greater success. The only trace of these claims may have been the patriarch's quarter in Jerusalem around the Holy Sepulchre. Paradoxically enough, the Church never achieved any political standing in the 'kingdom of the Cross'. The Investiture conflict which rocked European Christendom, was unknown. As a matter of fact, despite appeals to Rome in contested elections or disputes involving simony, the king of Jerusalem had a decisive influence in episcopal elections. The custom recorded in the middle of the twelfth century allowed him to choose a bishop from among three candidates proposed by the chapter. [14] Moreover, on many occasions the king directly influenced the choice of candidates, pressing his favourites on the electors.

Around the middle of the twelfth century the nobility gained ground at the expense of the Crown. This soon became apparent in new legislation, which favoured the growth of the baronies and

[14] The procedure of election is described by *Ernoul*, ed. Mas Latrie, p. 84, cf. p. 166, no. 2. This was, it seems, abrogated in 1191 by a bull of Celestine III, *Rev. d'hist. ecclésiastique*, 50 (1955), 430, n. 38. It was proved recently by H.E. Mayer (above n. 5) that the kings of Jerusalem were canons of the Holy Sepulchre, yet this does not seem to have had any bearing on their standing in patriarchal elections.

strengthened their autonomy. A disputed accession when Baldwin III came of age led to a short civil war (1152) against the power-hungry Queen Dowager Melissande. This struggle strongly compromised the standing of the Crown, as both parties needed the help of the nobility. A generation later another disputed succession upon the death of the brave leper, King Baldwin IV (1185), brought a new crisis. A court party, led by another dowager queen, Agnes of Courtenay, her daughter – the much-married Sibylle – and the Lusignans, was opposed by the local nobility, led by Raymond III of Tripoli, prince of Galilee by marriage. Although the royal party won, the new king, Guy de Lusignan (1186–90) – husband to Sibylle and successor to the child-king Baldwin V (1185–6)–never commanded the respect of his nobles and never regained the lost prestige of the Crown.

This period, immediately before the disaster of Hittin, witnessed a new trend in relations between the Crown and the nobles. Two of the great magnates, Renaud de Châtillon, lord of Transjordan and Raymond III of Tripoli, prince of Galilee, behaved like independent rulers, each pursuing a distinct foreign policy.[15] Thus Renaud de Châtillon broke the peace treaty which guaranteed the rights of passage for caravans from Egypt to Damascus and Raymond consented to a Moslem raid into the kingdom across his Galilean territory. The fatal battle of Hittin (1187) set seal on the weakness of the Crown, and the power void was filled by crusader magnates.

Nothing better exemplifies the situation than the fact that the leaders of the Third Crusade, Richard Coeur de Lion and Philip II Augustus, agreed to divide their future conquests, as if no political and legitimate power existed in the realm. The brisk business of offering the Crown of Jerusalem consecutively to Conrad of Montferrat (1190–2) and Henry, Count of Champagne (1192–7) by the European kings, is another example of the crown's helplessness.

With the accession of Jean de Brienne (1210–25), it seemed that the kingdom, now cut to a fifth of its former territory, might finally

---

[15] M. W. Baldwin, *Raymond III of Tripoli and the Fall of Jerusalem, 1140–1187*, Princeton, 1936, and G. Schlumberger, *Renaud de Châtillon*, Paris, 1898.

enter a period of stability. But, before long, a Crusade moved against Damietta and the papal legate, Pelagius, was contending that the lands captured in Egypt did not belong to the Latin kingdom. [16] Jean had to convince the pope – following the failure of the Crusade – to safeguard the rights of the kingdom against any anticipated conquest by a future Crusade.

The accession of Frederick II Hohenstaufen (1225–43) to the throne marks the final decline of royal power. Among the many crowns and titles he bore – 'Emperor of the Romans', 'King of the Germans', 'King of Sicily' – the title of 'King of Jerusalem' was glorious, but not profitable. The pragmatic Hohenstaufen was always ready to use his privileges as a crusader, but never took his subsequent duties too seriously. Once his German and Italian patrimonies were at stake, the Holy Land no longer figured in his schemes. His famous Crusade, his incredibly brilliant success, the scandal to Christendom of an excommunicated crusader who crowned himself in the Holy Sepulchre while Jerusalem was laid under interdict – all these events hardly strengthened the position of the Crown in a disintegrating state. Frederick's departure from the Holy Land in 1229 created a fictitious royalty which terminated in the absentee kingship of his son, Conrad (1243–54), who never visited the Holy Land. Central power disappeared entirely and the nobility as well as the great corporate bodies, the military orders, and the Italian communes took the lead. The farce of the acceptance of the claims of Princess Alice (granddaughter of King Amalric) and her husband Raoul de Soissons in 1243 as regents, left the claimants with a vague title and no power. The nobles argued that this was done in the name of legitimacy to safeguard the rights of Conrad, son of a Frankish princess, Isabelle (daughter of Jean de Brienne), and the haughty Frederick II. A sad epilogue to a line of heroic kings.

The last three monarchs, the Lusignan Kings of Cyprus, became, through an accident of inheritance, kings of Jerusalem. The efforts of Hugh III (1268–84), Jean I (1284–5) and Henri II (1285–91; died in 1324) to preserve the mainland kingdom, which at that time

[16] J. P. Donovan, *Pelagius and the Fifth Crusade*, Philadelphia, 1950.

included no more than a number of cities on the coast, were pathetic and futile. They involved a financial and military burden for Cyprus, with no hope of serious European intervention and recovery of the lost territories. The spectacle of the Crown of Jerusalem being sold in 1277 to Charles I of Anjou (a sale sanctioned by Rome) was far from edifying. The absentee claimant ousted the Cypriot Lusignans for a time, but never ruled the country. On the other hand, the Lusignans, who finally established their right to the throne, ruled by the grace of the military orders and communes, who defied the Crown whenever it suited their immediate purpose. When Acre sustained its last siege (1291), the king of Cyprus and Jerusalem courageously appeared in the city and defended it until all hope was lost. Then he escaped from the last Christian bulwark in the Holy Land to his island kingdom of Cyprus.

VIII

THE MACHINERY
OF GOVERNMENT

The royal court of Jerusalem had undergone a good many changes since the half-starved warriors of the First Crusade elected their first ruler in the Church of the Holy Sepulchre. The growing prosperity of the kingdom in the twelfth century, contact with the Orient and the example of the fabulous oriental courts – climate, food, dress – all influenced the Frankish court in the East. A mission from the Latin kingdom to the courts of the West at the end of the twelfth century impressed the prosperous Westerners as effeminate, overdressed, over-perfumed and over-jewelled. [1] This embassy was composed of churchmen who came begging for financial help from the West ! It can be assumed that the royal court was hardly less glittering than its ecclesiastical ambassadors.

The first palace of the kings of Jerusalem was in the magnificent al-Aqsa Mosque. Here the original Temple precincts meet the southern walls of Jerusalem. The royal palace overlooked the ancient city of David, with the valley of Kedron below and the Mount of Olives beyond. The splendours of the mosque were greatly diminished when captured by Tancred during the conquest of the city; he hoisted his banner on the dome and made away with its golden lamps and treasures. But to the hardened warriors of France it must still have seemed like a fable of the marvellous East come true.

This was the palace inhabited by Godfrey de Bouillon, Baldwin I and Baldwin II. It seems that under Baldwin II the royal palace

---

[1] Ralph Niger, 'De re militari et triplici via peregrinationis Jerosolimitanae', ed. G. B. Flahiff, 'Deus non vult', *Mediaeval Studies*, 9 (1947), 179.

moved from the splendid mosque (whose disadvantage was its isolated position in a scantily populated city) to the western part of the capital. It is not clear if a new building was actually erected or whether an old one, possibly the former residence of the Fatimid commander, became the royal palace. What we do know is that the palace was next to the citadel, the so-called 'Tower of David', and was certainly connected to it. To the north lay the citadel, while on the west the palace overlooked the deep ditch which cut off the city from the surrounding plain, which extended to the cemetery of Mamillah. This was the traditional burial place of the city and under the crusaders became the cemetery for the clergy of the Holy Sepulchre. On the east, facing the city within the walls, it overlooked the Greek monastery of St Sabas and the Armenian monastery of St James.

What the palace was like we do not know, as no contemporary descriptions survive and no excavations, like those in the neighbouring 'Tower of David', have unearthed its former glories. On a twelfth-century map of Jerusalem[2] the palace is represented as a building three or four storeys high, surrounded by a wall and flanked by two round corner towers. The lower storeys are invisible, hidden behind a wall, but the upper storey is represented as a gallery opening through a range of arcades towards the city. The roof is not of the flat oriental type, but Western and gabled, covered by tiles or strips of lead with a decorative pattern.

Outside Jerusalem there were royal palaces in Acre and Tyre. The palace in Acre was in the citadel and stood at the centre of the outer northern wall, in all probability at the weakest point of its defences. Later it partly lost its martial character, since a new suburb was fortified during the thirteenth century by a strong

---

[2] The new palace is well represented as *Curia regis* in a twelfth-century map of Jerusalem preserved at Cambrai. Reproduced by R. Röhricht, 'Karten und Pläne zur Palästinakunde', *Zeit. d. deut. Palästinavereins*, 14 (1891), pl. 4. The newest excavations of the area (1971) by M. Broshi discovered vaulted silos and wells in what seems to be the basement of the palace. An excellent sculptured double cross ('Cross of Anjou') was preserved on one of the walls. See below cap. X, n. 30. The neighbouring churches are described by the Russian pilgrim Daniel. See below in cap. XII: The Oriental Churches.

girdle of walls. Consequently, the citadel and the palace were now almost at the centre of the capital.[3] Normally, the castle served as the residence of the castellan, but during the king's visit and later during his permanent stay in Acre, it was the royal residence.

As everywhere else in Western Christendom the *Curia regis* formed the centre of the government. The model was probably French, a fact easily explained by the origin of the ruling dynasty and warrior class of the kingdom. It is true that by the turn of the eleventh century the differences between the royal courts of Europe were not great. The court of Jerusalem resembled that of Norman England, Capetian France or the dukes of Normandy. Like the latter, it had considerable real power. Its conservative nature characterized the court of Jerusalem. Starting from similar conditions, during the twelfth century European courts had developed a machinery which was easily adapted to the centralizing tendencies of the Crown, and to the new realities of economic development. Through a process of differentiation, the European *Curia regis* became the cradle of the great divisions in governmental machinery: administration, jurisdiction and legislation. This did not happen in the Latin kingdom. The central machinery of government fossilized at the stage it had reached somewhere around 1125, that is, a generation after the conquest, and remained fundamentally unchanged until the fall of the kingdom in 1291. At the end of the First Kingdom (1187) this machinery was already anachronistic and during the Second Kingdom it proved completely obsolete.

It is not easy to explain the awkwardness of this development or, rather, non-development. Three major factors seem to have converged and determined this pattern. In the first place the chronic state of war during the first generation after the conquest subordinated all government business to the supreme tasks of war, expansion and defence. The workings of a central government, let alone the systematic development of administrative machinery, were certainly of minor concern at this stage. The accent was on

[3] The *castellum* is marked on all contemporary maps of crusader Acre. See J. Prawer, 'Historical Maps of Acre', *Eretz Israel*, II (1952), 175 ff.

military needs and on effective government at the local level, to supply king and nobles with the means of existence. Their co-ordination was a matter of expediency. The Crown and its vassals lived from hand to mouth.

The second factor which accounts for the particular development of the Latin kingdom is related to the evolution of crusader feudalism as a system of government. Its point of departure was a strong monarchy and a subservient nobility. But whereas during the twelfth century Western Europe witnessed the growing strength of the Crown, the curbing of centrifugal feudal tendencies and, finally, the integration or even absorption of autonomous entities into the body of the realm, the Latin kingdom developed in the opposite direction. [4] Just after the middle of the twelfth century, the nobility, or more exactly the great magnates, became the dominant element in the government of the country. Royal prerogatives were tacitly abrogated and effective government was exercised at the local level. As the main functions of government were thus exercised within the feudal subdivisions, hostile to central intervention and strong enough to oppose it successfully, this left little scope for the development of a central administration.

Finally we can discern a corollary to the foregoing development and in a sense a different aspect of the same thing, which might be regarded as a third factor influencing the development of the Latin kingdom. This was the evolution of the 'High Court', the *Haute Cour*, essentially, the traditional meeting-place of the king and his tenants-in-chief and the institutionalized expression of the feudal system, with its patriarchal pattern of familial consultation and the giving of mutual 'aid and counsel'. But in the Latin kingdom the vassal's duty to give 'aid and counsel' to his lord became a privilege, which quickly turned into a set of rules ultimately compelling the king not merely to ask for counsel, but also to follow it. By imperceptible degrees the legitimacy of royal decisions became dependent on the agreement of the *Haute Cour*,

---

[4] J. Richard, *Le royaume latin de Jérusalem*, Paris, 1953, 61–92; J. Prawer, 'La noblesse et le régime feodal du royaume latin de Jérusalem', *Le Moyen Âge*, 1959, 41–74.

which could thus paralyse the king's plans and policies. The *Haute Cour* became the central wheel of the government's machinery, with little room for true royal government and the development of specialized institutions.

In consequence the royal machinery of government developed but slightly beyond its point of departure. The mainstay remained the state offices, which historically date back to the Carolingian tradition of household government over a royal patrimony. At a time when European monarchies were busy abolishing some of these offices or transforming them to honorary sinecures, the Latin kingdom perpetuated them as the only central executive organs throughout the two hundred years of its existence.

More than any other institution the development of the *Haute Cour* characterizes the Latin kingdom. In Latin it was called *Curia generalis* and in the French vernacular sometimes *Parlement*.[5] Only the treatises of the jurists refer to it as the *Haute Cour*. From the twelfth century to the middle of the thirteenth its composition was almost exclusively feudal. It was then enlarged to include some non-feudal elements. In the *Haute Cour* the king met those of his tenants-in-chief who received their fiefs (whether seigniories or simple landed or money fiefs) directly from him. Enfeoffment by the king and the swearing of homage and fealty by the enfeoffed constituted the legal link between the king and his direct vassals. In theory, the meetings of the *Haute Cour* were attended by two types of nobles: the great lords invested with baronies and the direct vassals of the royal domain – usually simple knights of the king's retinue who held their fiefs against military service direct from the king. Among the latter we may also count the household knights of the royal palace. In practice, only the presence of the great lords mattered, the 'magnates' of the kingdom. In the 'undemocratic' and practical Middle Ages votes were weighed rather than counted. The presence and opinion of minor vassals, if they were not royal *familiares* or favourites, was purely decorative.

The meetings of the *Haute Cour* may have been attended by some two score nobles (this was approximately the number of the great

---

[5] Cf. the meeting of 1166 in Nablus. *Eracles*, XIX, 13.

tenants-in-chief), but usually less. Legally, the king and three tenants-in-chief constituted a quorum, but expediency and experience indicated the number and quality of participants required for an effective session of the court.

The composition of the High Court underwent a major theoretical change under King Amalric, around 1162. A famous act[6] known as the *Assise sur la ligece* ('Assize on liege homage'), whose influence was soon to be felt in almost every branch of public life, decreed that henceforth all fief-holders in the kingdom (tenants-in-chief and rear-vassals) were to take a direct and primary oath of homage to the king ('liege homage'). Thus they became peers of each other and were all linked directly to the king. As such, they had a right to participate in the sessions of the *Haute Cour*. This could have significantly enlarged the number of participants since there were more than six hundred fief-holders in the kingdom. However, in practice simple fief-holders only attended when a session of the High Court coincided with a military expedition or another extraordinary event, and we know of several such cases. It is quite possible that a session in Jerusalem or Acre would be attended by the local knights, which would hardly change the character of the session or influence the decisions. The magnates ultimately always dominated the *Haute Cour*.

The composition of the *Haute Cour* changed again[7] around 1232, when a revolutionary movement led by the powerful and noble Ibelins against Frederick II Hohenstaufen created a new institution, which ousted the *Haute Cour* and took over its functions for some twelve years. This was the so-called 'Commune of Acre', in reality a meeting of estates which represented the 'Community of

---

[6] See above, n. 4.

[7] Our study, 'Estates, Communities and the Constitution of the Latin Kingdom', *Proc. Israel Academy*, II, No. 6 started a fruitful discussion of the communes and fraternities. H. E. Mayer, 'On the Beginnings of the Communal Movement in the Holy Land: The Commune of Tyre', *Traditio*, 24 (1968), 443–57. Cf. also H.E. Maxer, 'Zwei Kommunen in Akkon?', *Deut. Archiv für Erforschung d. Mittelalters*, XXV (1970), 434–53. J. Riley-Smith, 'The assise sur la ligece and the commune of Acre', *Traditio*, 27, 1971, 179–204; *Id.*, 'A Note on Confraternities in the Latin Kingdom', *Bull. of the Inst. of Hist. Research*, 44, 1971, 301–8. The conclusions of the paper in *Traditio* are not acceptable to me.

the Realm' of Jerusalem. Using the framework of a confraternity, a religious welfare association dedicated to St Andrew, this assembly constituted itself as a legal revolutionary body. Anxious to assure itself of solid public backing, the commune opened its doors to the knights and nobles who, together with the burgesses of the city, swore an oath of mutual security and elected the officers of the 'Commune'.

The experiment was short-lived and with the disappearance of the Hohenstaufen danger, which allegedly threatened the constitution (that is the body of franchises and privileges), the 'Commune' was dissolved and the *Haute Cour* regained its former position. But this incident left tangible traces. There was, for example, an attempt to change the judiciary procedure of the *Haute Cour*, making written testimony – in this case an official register of deliberations and decisions – obligatory and valid as against the earlier and only admissible 'record', the memory of the court. This attempt of 1250, made during St Louis's stay in the Holy Land, was decided in a common meeting of the *Haute Cour* and the court of burgesses, the latter apparently representing the estate of burgesses.[8] The proposed reform failed, but the procedure of common deliberations is in itself remarkable. Later on, although there were no common meetings of the two courts, some of the meetings of the *Haute Cour* changed in a singular way. As early as the twelfth century the heads of the military orders, though not vassals of the king in the usual meaning of the word, participated in the meetings of the *Haute Cour*. Although their presence could have been justified by the large fiefs in their possession, the true reason was the fact that they were a major, if not the principal, military mainstay of the kingdom. The presence of the higher clergy, though possibly justified as they were fief-holders, in reality reflected their traditional position in Christian society. Nobles, prelates, and the heads of the military orders were joined by new elements, perhaps by the end of the twelfth century, who reflected the new political constellation in the country. The most important of these were certainly the autonomous Italian com-

---

[8] *Abrégé des Assises de la Cour des Bourgeois*, caps. 13–18, *Lois* II, 246ff.

munes. They could also have been legally regarded as tenants-in-chief, but again, their naval power, wealth and military forces assured them a place. Thus representatives of Venice, Genoa and Pisa participated in all important sessions of the *Haute Cour*.

The inclusion of the Italian communes was followed, after the middle of the thirteenth century, by that of the heads of the burgesses' confraternities. It is purely conjecture whether the mayors or captains of the confraternities participated in the meetings of the *Haute Cour* because of a new custom – namely an oath of fealty to their suzerain – or if they took this oath by virtue of participating in a basically feudal assembly. The fact remains that in the second half of the thirteenth century they participated in the deliberations of the *Haute Cour*.

Thus the purely feudal *Curia regis* of the first half of the twelfth century slowly changed, integrating other elements. But it never became a parliament or an *États Généraux*, neither did any representative principle develop. At the end of the thirteenth century the *Haute Cour* was a meeting-place for the different power factors in society, an assembly of those who really counted. A longer lease of life could have brought the institution into line with the contemporary evolution towards a representative system, although this would have necessitated profound changes in the entire structure of the kingdom.

The changes in composition were accompanied by an evolution in the competences of the *Haute Cour*. This was strenuously denied by the thirteenth-century jurists of the kingdom, who insisted on recognizing nothing but the 'immutable' institutions allegedly established by the venerated Godfrey de Bouillon. Their reasoning was completely in character with the mediaeval horror of 'innovation'. Nevertheless, a marked development advanced the *Haute Cour* from a consultative position to that of the *de facto* governing power in the country. Though a list of its competences might prove difficult to draw up, the *Haute Cour* participated as a decisive factor in all aspects of government exercised by the Crown. In addition, the *Haute Cour* was the instrument through which – together with the grand officers of state – the Crown exercised its competence as the official head of the feudal pyramid. The distinction between sovereign or suzerain power was perhaps not always clear in the minds of contemporaries. Nevertheless, such a distinction existed and the *Haute Cour* had a different standing in these matters.

As head of state and commander of the armies, the king decided questions of policy, including international relations, treaties, the declaration of war and the conclusion of peace. In all these matters, the royal decisions were hardly ever arbitrary. Following custom and expediency, such weighty decisions were taken, after due deliberation, with the advice of the *Haute Cour*. Owing to the structure and technique of international relations, many a royal marriage – which usually meant a political alliance – also became an object of debate and decision. We often hear about divided counsel (opposition within the *Haute Cour*), which proves that these consultations were real. In one case, for example, which involved the difficult decision of whether to besiege Ascalon or Tyre (1123), recourse was taken to Divine judgment by letting a boy draw one of the two names written on parchment. But what was characteristic of these deliberations of the *Haute Cour* was the fact that its members were giving advice only. The final decision was in the hands of the king. Although one can generally presume harmonious co-operation, his decision was final.

Even in the first half of the twelfth century, the *Curia regis* greatly surpassed the functions of an advisory body. This was the case, as we have seen, in problems of royal succession, when hereditary right created a claim but did not yet constitute a title. The *domus* Godefridi called in Baldwin I to succeed his brother, despite the opposition of Tancred and the patriarch (1100); the *Curia regis* also called in the cousin of Baldwin I, the future Baldwin II, from Edessa, despite a legal claim by the absent brother, Eustace of Boulogne. The *Haute Cour* constrained Amalric to divorce his wife (1162) before he was accepted as the lawful successor to his brother, Baldwin III. Thus in all matters of succession the *Haute Cour*, acting as a formally constituted body or an informal meeting of magnates, had a decisive role greatly surpassing that of a consultative body. Nevertheless, as late as 1176 Baldwin IV could override baronial opposition and agree to the marriage of his sister and presumptive heir, Sibylle, to William Longsword and in 1180 to Guy de Lusignan.

The situation was different in matters of peace, war and international agreements. Although the king's voice was decisive, expediency demanded the co-operation of the barons and knights, and their opinions were heard and considered. In moments of crisis the *Haute Cour* could act with energy. In a famous agreement concluded by the patriarch Warmund with the Venetians (1123) during the captivity of Baldwin II, we find with some astonishment that the nobles agree to force the king to abide by the agreement upon his release, otherwise they will not recognize him as their lawful ruler. [9]

It is difficult to decide if other royal competences pertain to the sovereign or suzerain aspects of government. We could regard the baronial deliberations on the marriage of royal princesses as stemming from their duty as vassals to counsel their lord. Such procedures were common in every feudal court where the family affairs of the lord were discussed by his vassals. A marriage within the royal family involved more than a family affair or the future of a manor and castle. A great marriage of state nearly always implied political alliance, often with substantial economic or military aspects. When deliberating matters of such consequence, the *Haute Cour* was in reality discussing the foreign policy of the kingdom.

The imposition of non-feudal taxes can also be classified among the competences derived from the sovereign standing of the king. As long as the royal revenue was derived from purely feudal sources there was no need for special decisions or agreements, since all followed the customary pattern. However, this did not apply to an extraordinary tax levy. Thus in 1166, before one of the campaigns against Egypt, King Amalric convened the *Haute Cour* in Nablus, which decided (it seems with the co-operation of burgesses) that a tithe should be imposed on all movables in the kingdom. [10]

---

[9] G. Tafel – G.M. Thomas, *op. cit.*, I, 88.

[10] William of Tyre, XIX, 13. The French text of *Eracles* gives the impression that the tax was a kind of scutage due from those who did not participate in the campaign.

Another and later non-feudal tax, that of 1183, was decreed by the *Haute Cour* meeting in Jerusalem, and imposed on all real property and movables belonging to every inhabitant of the country without distinction of sex or religion. The extraordinary character of this tax necessitated the agreement of those concerned, or of those who represented the community, i.e. the *Haute Cour*. [11]

Important as these competences were, most of the business transacted by or before the *Haute Cour* derived from its standing as the meeting place for the king and his vassals. One of the specific meanings of *curia* was that of an organ for dispensing justice. In this capacity the *Haute Cour*, or its legal quorum (three liegemen and the king), was in permanent session. Justice, or rather jurisdiction, had a wider scope than in the modern world. It covered all cases between the vassals of the king, *ratione personae*, and all cases relating to their fief-holding, *ratione materiae*. Criminal as well as civil jurisdiction in such cases was within its exclusive competence. Murder, rape, assault and high treason – which could be regarded as feudal infractions or as crimes of *lèse-majesté* – were judged by the king in the *Haute Cour*. On the other hand, all cases regarding feudal tenure, inheritance, wardships, obligations deriving from the oath of homage (i.e. feudal service) also came under its jurisdiction. Moreover, any alienation, sale, lease or renting of fiefs could only be transacted before it. In the latter case the decision of the court was not merely binding, but the 'record'. i.e. the memory of its members as to the transaction guaranteed the possessory rights of the parties. The written act of sale or alienation was no more than an *aide-mémoire* and not a valid proof.

The competences of the *Haute Cour* not merely included the right to sit in judgment over the king's vassals, but over the king himself. This was the theory of pure feudalism as proclaimed by the crusader jurists. In reality, we find no such instance in the kingdom's history. Indeed, the claim by the monastery of St Mary of Josaphat against the Crown was decided by Queen Melissande in a session of the *Haute Cour*. Unfortunately, the extant royal charter is not explicit as to whether this was a decision of the court

[11] William of Tyre, XXII, 23.

or an agreement reached between queen and the monks and then recorded (as was the case for land alienation) by the court.[12]

At the end of the twelfth century, when almost all royal courts in the West had developed specialized institutions and personnel to deal with the different cases which came before them, the Latin kingdom alone perpetuated a non-differentiated court. No change occurred in the structure of the court during the two hundred years of its existence.

Jurisdiction led to legislation. The known mediaeval abhorrence for innovation often produced the fiction of an 'old law' or the notion of 'discovering the law'. Nothing was ever an innovation, and the existing law had simply to be interpreted or restated. Nevertheless, in this respect, the crusaders were less conservative than their European contemporaries. The fact that a new kingdom had actually been created broke with the traditional theory of legislation. New laws, explicitly described as such, were enacted, although the bulk of the customary law was case-law. The decisions of the court created precedents and valid law; adjudication was legislation. Thus the *Haute Cour* sitting as a court of justice was also the legislature of the government.

Although the great bulk of customary law and rules of procedure, as reproduced in the middle of the thirteenth century by Philip of Novara and, with embellishments, by the great jurist Jean d'Ibelin, lord of Jaffa, was case-law, legislation also took another direction. There was a conscious effort to legislate on the part of the Crown and the nobility, since there were new needs which customary law could not meet. Administrative ordinances could have been simply decreed by the king and imposed under the penalty of the *ban*. But even in this case there was some opposition e.g. in the grotesque case when one of the Baldwins ordered the streets of the capital[13] to be cleaned on penalty of a fine. The court of burgesses was apparently reluctant to enforce this salutary decree, since the decision was taken without the consent of the court. On

---

[12] Ch. Delaborde, *Chartes de Terre Sainte de l'abbaye de N.-D. de Josaphat*, no. 26.

[13] *Livre des Assises des Bourgeois* in *Lois* II, 225.

the other hand, important legislation could only be passed by the *Haute Cour*. If we can believe a late thirteenth-century tradition, the Crown established in the early years of the kingdom a committee of codification, which, after inquiries in other lands and after due deliberation, proposed a code of laws for the kingdom.[14] This somewhat excessively efficient and enlightened policy from the beginning of the twelfth century seems suspect and is singularly reminiscent of the legends associated with the great Greek and Roman law-givers. On the other hand, there is no doubt that laws were proposed in the king's court, debated and drawn up in the approved form, with copies being then deposited as 'Letters of the Holy Sepulchre' in the kingdom's great sanctuary. These laws are called '*Assises*', with the same meaning as their namesakes in Normandy and England. There was quite a body of such laws, which determined criminal, feudal and civil jurisprudence, as well as many points of procedure. Such legislative activity was extensive in the twelfth century, but seems to have diminished during the thirteenth.[15] Twelfth-century legislation and the accumulated precedent of a hundred years could have been sufficient for the needs of the country, but we venture to suggest that the courage to innovate waned with the growing attachment of the nobility to the 'old law', which became sacrosanct. The laws promulgated by the *Haute Cour* and its judicial decision were the law of the land. But although it could innovate, the court also regarded itself as the repository and defender of ancient laws, customs and franchises.

The paramount importance of the crusaders' *Haute Cour* as the dominant factor in government explains the subsidiary role of the executive machinery, namely the grand offices and officers of the kingdom. Many royal competences were taken over by the *Haute Cour*, while others was absorbed by the growing autonomy of the lordships. This did not leave much scope for a royal administration and could explain the fact that we do not know of any attempts by the *Haute Cour* to control the grand officers, as was done,

[14] Jean d'Ibelin, cap. 1–5.

[15] M. Grandclaude, 'Liste d'Assises remontant au premier royaume de Jérusalem', *Mélanges Paul Fournier*, Paris, 1929, 329 ff. There is no parallel study for later legislation.

for example, in England in the so-called Paper Constitution of 1244 or in the Provisions of Oxford in 1258. Their relative unimportance did not attract the attentions of the usually power-hungry *Haute Cour*. For the same reason, the local nobility never claimed the grand offices as hereditary privileges. Thus we find the great noble families of the kingdom furnishing grand officers in each generation, but this was probably regarded as the normal *cursus* of a nobleman whose main interests lay elsewhere, in the *Haute Cour* and in the administration of his own possessions. Consequently, royalty had a free hand to distribute some of the offices as favours, even to nobles not native to the kingdom.

In these circumstances, the grand offices of the kingdom did not parallel those of the contemporary West. At the point when the office of seneschal became a real power in the West, Philip II Augustus of France left it vacant and contributed to its ultimate decadence. Nothing of the kind happened in the Kingdom of Jerusalem.

Here the constable was a more important figure, although the seneschal had a kind of honorific precedence. The main reason for this difference as compared with the West is the fact that as commander of the armies the constable not only performed a major function in a war-ridden country, but exercised his power in the only sphere where the standing of the king was never challenged. The seneschal might preside over the *Haute Cour* in the absence of the king (exclusive of criminal justice or cases regarding fiefs, if they were not initiated under the king's presidency) and had precedence, but his power was no greater than the king's, who was no more than *primus inter pares* when presiding over the *Haute Cour*.

The seneschal, as the king's personal representative, could preside over the sessions of the *Haute Cour* in times of peace. Usually he commanded the king's *bataille* in war. For the rest, the seneschal also exercised the management of the kingdom's finances. The treasury and department of finance never reached the level of the Norman exchequer, but the administration of the *Secrète* (as the department was called in the Kingdom

[16] See below, p. 144, n. 17.

and in Cypriote sources) was an important function of the seneschal. This included the appointment and control of scribes, clerks and stewards (*baillis*), as well as the collection of royal revenue or its farming out to the highest bidder. Because of his control over finance, the seneschal was also responsible for the maintenance of the royal castles – provisions and garrisons – though not for the command of the royal castellans or to intervene in military matters.

The 'department of war' was, as already mentioned, the domain of the constable or his second-in-command, the marshal. There was a special, rather curious link between the two and the marshal owed homage for his office to the constable. This seems to have been a peculiarity of the Latin kingdom. The practice could have been derived from the fact that the constable held from the king a fief for his office and enfeoffed part of it to the marshal as his chief aid. The constable's main business was the army itself and this included the supervision of troops and equipment, as well as actual command functions. The constable checked the quotas of military service owed by the tenants-in-chief and he was responsible for their equipment. During expeditions he became the judge of the army under martial law, although the actual judgment was carried out by liegemen. This was always a tricky problem with an army composed of haughty nobles, and custom did in fact limit his power as far as the nobles were concerned. But the feudal host was only a part of the army. In times of danger or emergency, king and noble alike hired knights, sergeants and squires. The constable was directly responsible for their welfare and especially for their pay. He represented their demands and on occasions their claims before the court. It seems that in such cases he even presided over the court in the king's absence. The marshal had as his special domain the control of the horses and the division of spoils, especially horses. Horses killed in battle were replaced by him. The office never attained any real importance.

The chamberlain remained more personally connected with the king than the other grand officers, and his office preserved more of its former household character. The office, at least in the twelfth century, carried with it a fief of five villages and was valued at 7500 besants. [17] This brought to the incumbent an income of some 1000 besants a year (revenue calculated at 15% of the capital) that is, the income of two knights' fiefs. The chamberlain administered the oath of homage to the royal liegemen and was responsible for the royal household expenses and for the servants.

The fossilized state of the central machinery is nowhere more evident than in the non-development of the chancery. When royal chanceries all over Europe became key offices, adapting their functions and scope to the unprecedented increase of monarchical power, the chancery of Jerusalem stagnated. Although the chancellor's office was always in the hands of a prelate and sometimes even an important one, it does not seem that he ever influenced royal policies. Neither did a great chancery secretariat develop. More often than not the chancellor himself wrote the charters or dictated them, or sometimes another prelate deputized for him. The type of charters issued were grants only (although this might be a mere impression created by extant charters). The chancery never developed judiciary functions, did not co-ordinate other offices and essentially remained in charge of the royal correspondence and perhaps records. [18]

We have already mentioned the causes which prevented the development of a central machinery of government. Due to the progressive autonomy of the baronies we must seek the complement for the embryonic institutions of central government on the local level. From this aspect, the royal domain can and should be regarded as one of the seigniories, or rather as a collection of different lordships belonging to the Crown.

---

[17] L. de Mas Latrie, 'Le fief de la Chamberlaine et les Chambellans de Jérusalem', *Bibl. de l'École des Chartes*, 43 (1882), 647–52.

[18] New light will be thrown on the problem with the publication of the original royal charters by H.E. Mayer. Cf. R. Hiestand, 'Zwei unbekannte Diplome der Lateinischen Könige von Jerusalem'. *Quellen u. Forsch. aus Ital. Arch.*, 50, 1971, 1–57. The office of 'butler' (*buticularius*) existed in the kingdom, at least in the twelfth century, but nothing is known about its functions.

IX

THE LORDSHIPS –
GOVERNMENT AT THE LOCAL
LEVEL

A   The Lordships and the Feudal Map
of the Kingdom

Nature and politics have a horror of vacuums. Wherever royal
prerogatives were curtailed and wherever central power lost its
grip, the nobility moved in. Thus, when central rule became less
effective in the second half of the twelfth century, government
proceeded at the local level, in the seigniories.

The historical development of the lordships is obscure and not
always easy to follow. We have already mentioned that at least
under the first two kings, Godfrey de Bouillon and his brother
Baldwin I, there was a marked reluctance on the part of the Crown
to grant baronies to their companions in arms.[1] Perhaps the poverty
of the kingdom, or, more probably, a justified fear of creating a
landed nobility liable to compete with the Crown, commended a
policy almost unknown in Europe. To compensate for services
rendered and to assure their future performance, the Crown of
Jerusalem assigned its nobles revenues instead of landed property.
This was naturally all the more feasible as the kingdom, even
after its Frankish conquest, continued the local Near Eastern
tradition of a money economy. The first fiefs were consequently
money fiefs, although not of the type which became common
later, known as *fiefs de besant*. At the beginning total income was

---

[1] J. Prawer, 'The *Assise de Teneure* and the *Assise de Vente:* A Study of the
Landed Property in the Latin Kingdom', *Economic History Review*, 4 (1950),
77–87.

enfeoffed, and not a fixed sum from a given source. For example, the total income from a city or a royal monopoly.

If systematically pursued this policy would have created a quasi-feudal state with a salaried nobility, functioning as a bureaucracy, or, it might have followed an evolution similar to that of the neighbouring Moslem countries. There, the *iqta'* (portion, or *fief*) followed, to begin with at least, a comparable line of development. The Moslem aristocracy were compensated and their livelihood and loyalty assured by assigning them revenues from the treasury. [2]

However, the policy of not creating lordships did not survive the first two reigns. Under Godfrey de Bouillon there was already an exception, hardly desired by the ruler, when the principality of Galilee, with its capital in Tiberias, emerged as a great lordship. The holder, Tancred, probably did not intend to rule a fief dependent on the Crown of Jerusalem, but rather carve out an independent state in the north of the country. The projected state was supposed to include Tiberias, with Lake Galilee as its geographical centre, and to encompass all the lands across the Jordan up to the confines of Damascus in the east and north and the Yarmuk river in the south, while its western boundary up to the Mediterranean would comprise the whole of Galilee. The city of Haifa, claimed by Tancred as promised to him by the dying Godfrey de Bouillon (1100), was destined to serve as the sea outlet. Tancred took the title of *princeps*, which was not that of a royal vassal, but rather (as with the similar title of 'prince of Antioch') of an independent ruler. Historical circumstances forced Tancred to leave for Antioch, thus enabling Baldwin I to integrate the would-be state into the framework of the kingdom. This large area, later limited to Galilee, was then enfeoffed as a lordship to one of the nobles of the kingdom. The ruler of Galilee (and he was the only one among the kingdom's vassals to do it) adopted the title of 'prince', thereby commemorating the ambitions of Tancred.

[2] Cl. Cahen, 'Les liens de dépendance et les sociétés en Europe orientale, á Byzance et en pays musulmans', *Rapports du IXe Congrès internat. des Sciences historiques*, Paris, 1950, 464 ff.; Id. 'L'évolution de l'iqta du IXe au XIIIe siècle', *Annales. Economie, sociétés, civilisations*, 8, 25–52. See now *Encyclopedia of Islam, s.v.* Ikta'.

The creation of the great lordship of Galilee was an exception in more than one sense. As a rule, the main period in which lordships were created was the first quarter of the twelfth century. In the last years of Baldwin I and during the reign of his successor, Baldwin II (1118–31), the broad outlines of the feudal map were drawn, although the process continued sporadically into the third quarter of the century.

The major factor in the creation of lordships was the inability, inherent in all feudal systems, to administer large areas effectively and to carry out public functions, the foremost of which was military service. In Europe, reduced by the barbarian invasions to a natural economy, the early mediaeval kingdoms split into relatively small and quasi-independent units, whose survival was assured by the only available source of wealth, landed property. This was not the case in the Latin kingdom. A money economy was well established in the area before the crusader conquest and in the newly created Latin establishments the use of currency was never abandoned. This could have created a government based on a salaried army and bureaucracy. The nature of the state which ultimately arose was thus not governed by economic conditions, such as the predominance of a rural barter economy. The feudal system was introduced in the crusader states, partly because of their military character, but mainly due to the mentality of the European nobles and knights who clung to traditional patterns of social cohesion and prestige. Feudal practice was the only code known to Europeans and this fact determined the wholesale transfer of the system to the new kingdom.

Whereas the introduction of the system can be explained on the basis of earlier experience and expediency, its unchanging rigidity emphasizes the 'colonial spirit' of the kingdom – in this case, a blind clinging to the past, which not only became glorified, but even sanctified. Thus the spirit of eleventh-century France lived on in the Latin kingdom until the end of the thirteenth century, long after the motherland changed beyond recognition.

The attempt to limit the process of creating lordships gave way to the patterns of the homeland. The companions of Godfrey de Bouillon and Baldwin I, and those newly arrived knights who took service under Baldwin II and later, all expected to be provided with a noble or knightly fief that would assure them a standing in society and a means of livelihood. Their claims did not displease or necessarily weaken the Crown. No mediaeval ruler wanted to be a king of beggars or salaried retainers. Moreover, a policy of effective settlement and colonization, as much as of effective government, postulated the creation of fiefs for the knightly warrior class.

Our sources leave us in the dark as to the nature of early enfeoff-ments. We do not know why some fiefs became independent lordships, whereas others remained simple fiefs in the royal domain. Perhaps the size of a fief and the rank of the noble or his proximity to the king somehow defined its standing in the feudal hierarchy. Presumably this was the early procedure in the kingdom, but the existence of lordships, with two or three vassals (and many were of this type) hardly proves the point. Whatever the explanation, it must be assumed that the original enfeoffment specified the future feudal status as a lordship or fief, stated orally in the act of homage and fealty. Some land-grants, which were in the beginning no more than simple fiefs, later became lordships. This often happened in places where a castle or city was the centre of the fief. It is not too rash to suppose that cases of gradual usurpation were not unknown even in this most legalistically minded feudal state of Christendom.

A lordship carried with it a degree of autonomy which a simple fief never achieved. Later crusader jurisprudence defined a seign-iory or lordship as having the rights of *cour, coins, justice*,[3] i.e. its lord had the right to a feudal court, to a seal and to low and high justice. His feudal court, we are told, was composed of the vassals of his lordship, and three vassals constituted a quorum.[4] If the lordship did not have even that number of vassals, the overlord was obliged to supply them from his own retinue. The second privilege of a lordship was the right to a lead (as distinct from common wax) seal for validating documents. The third one was that of jurisdiction

[3] F. Chandon de Briailles, 'Le droit des "coins" dans le Royaume de Jérusalem', *Syria*, 23 (1942/3), 244–57. A list of these lordships is given by Jean d'Ibelin, cap. 270.

[4] Jean d'Ibelin, cap. 253.

over the inhabitants, that is a court of burgesses in cities and what were essentially manorial courts in rural areas.

Once a lordship was created it could never be abolished as an entity. Its lords might change, the ruling dynasty might become extinct, it might be joined to another lordship belonging to the same lord through marriage, inheritance or acquisition, but through all these changes a seigniory still preserved its identity. The Frankish baron who held several lordships – even if they were contiguous – had to rule and administer each as an independent unit. The feudal court could be held only in the seigniory. Thus, the notion of feudal *lignage*, including members of a family and its vassals, was strengthened by institutionalized administration. What was true for the feudal court of the lordship also applied to its court of burgesses, which probably followed the pattern of a feudal institution. The court of burgesses in any city of the lordship had no links with, let alone dependence upon, any other.[5]

Crusader lordships were not created according to a master plan. Indeed, they were hardly ever planned at all. The notion of Godfrey de Bouillon or of Baldwin I dividing the kingdom into lordships, like a mediaeval Moses distributing the Promised Land to the tribes of Israel, should be relegated to the realm of legends, one of the many created by thirteenth-century crusader jurists.[6]

The fortunes of war and conquest, the pressure of nobles and knights and the strategic needs of defence drew the boundaries of the lordships.[7] Typical, for example, is the case of the principality of Galilee. The grandiose plan of Tancred came to nothing. But what happened to the lordship? Haifa (captured in 1100), the intended port, became a small independent seigniory. The whole western part of the former principality was divided into independent seigniories. Some were directly created by the Crown, others

---

[5] *Livre des Assises des Bourgeois*, cap. 22 ff.

[6] J. Prawer, 'Les premiers temps de la féodalité dans le royaume latin de Jérusalem—une reconsideration', *Rev. d'histoire du droit*, 22 (1954), 401–24.

[7] The vicissitudes of the different lordships, their creation, composition and further evolution is based on the studies of the historical geography of the crusader kingdom.

began their careers as fiefs of the principality of Galilee, but very quickly became independent and direct vassals of the Crown. This movement to bypass their immediate lord may even have been favoured by the Crown, which was not unhappy to see the great feudal baronies lose territory, while it acquired direct vassals at their expense. Thus, for example, the two castles built by the princes of Galilee, Toron (Tibnin) and Chastel Neuf (Hunin), became independent and direct tenants-in-chief of the Crown. On the other hand, as some of the fiefs in the royal domain became independent, the Crown itself lost seigniories. Thus to the south of the royal city of Tyre, the small seigniory of Scandalion (Iskanderune) was created out of Crown lands.

The most important lordships of the kingdom were the principality of Galilee and the lordship of 'Oultre-Jourdain' (Transjordan). The principality of Galilee, as finally constituted in the second quarter of the twelfth century, did not cover more than the mountain and hill region of that area. In the east it included Lake Tiberias and laid claim to a *condominium* with Damascus over the Gaulan (the Syrian high plateau) extending to the confines of Damascus. Since, by tacit agreement, the Gaulan was not fortified by either of the contracting parties, the claim – politically speaking – was often nominal. Nevertheless, the princes of Galilee derived a substantial income from these extensive territories until the disaster of Hittin. In the west the principality lost its projected seaboard which was split up into Crown land and independent lordships.

The great lordship of Transjordan extended from the Yarmuk (or possibly the Zerqa River, the biblical 'Yaboq') in the north to the crusader port of 'Aqaba on the Red Sea. Its strategic position as a crusader wedge between Moslem Egypt and Syria was of paramount importance in the defence of the kingdom. This vast area, around the two mighty castles of Montreal and Crac (Shaubaq), built in 1116 and 1142, respectively, belonged to the Crown of Jerusalem. But it became an independent lordship around 1161. Hence the main burden of defence in a very exposed border fief rested on the shoulders of its holders. They were the de Milly family and, later on, the legendary Renaud de Châtillon. No other seigniory could in any way compare in extent with these two.

A survey of other lordships will suffice to clarify the feudal structure of the kingdom. On the coast in the north-west, by the small river of al-Mu'amaltain, lay the lordship of Beirut. The river formed the kingdom's frontier and across it to the north was the county of Tripoli. Beirut was enfeoffed after the conquest in 1110 to the Flemish family of de Guines, relatives of Baldwin I. It was later acquired under Amalric I by the Crown, and ended up as a fief of one of the branches of the Ibelins. To the south was the lordship of Sidon. From its Arabic name, 'Saida', the crusaders called it 'Saietta' or 'Sagitta' and the heraldic emblem of the city was an arrow (L. *sagitta*). The lordship belonged to one of the two branches of the Grenier family, one of the oldest families in the kingdom (the other branch were lords of Caesarea). To the east of Sidon was the lordship of Banyas (ancient Paneas) – called by the crusaders 'Belinas' – which belonged to the English de Bruce family and later to the lords of Toron. From 1157 half of it was shared with the Order of St John and it was lost to the Moslems in 1164. Two smaller lordships in this area were those of Maron and Toron (Tibnin). The latter centred round a castle built by the princes of Galilee against Moslem Tyre. It became an independent lordship around 1107 and gave rise to one of the famous noble dynasties in the kingdom. The lordship of Scandalion (Iskanderune), opposite Moslem Tyre, directly depended on the Crown.

Following the coast, to the south of royal Acre and the small independent lordships of Haifa and Caymont (Caymun or Yoqna'am), was the rich lordship of Caesarea belonging to the Grenier family. It was confined in the south by the lordship of Arsuf (ancient Apollonia), which at some point, near the middle of the twelfth century, became autonomous and at the beginning of the thirteenth century came through marriage into the hands of the famous Jean d'Ibelin, lord of Beirut. In 1261 it was sold to the Order of St John, only to fall four years later (1265) into the hands of Baibars. To the south was the royal county of Jaffa-Ascalon. Finally, on the coast south of Ascalon were the Templar lordship of Gaza and the kingdom's frontier town and fortress of Darum.

Between the lordships of the coast and the Crown lands in the Judean and Samaritan mountains lay small seigniories destined to play a decisive role in the life of the kingdom. In 1141 King Fulk of Anjou ordered the erection of a small fortress to the south-east of Jaffa to contain the incessant harassing of Frankish possessions from Egyptian-held Ascalon (captured eventually in 1153). The castle was erected on the ancient city mound of Yabneh (in Arabic 'Yibne'), which, a thousand years earlier, had figured in Jewish history as the spiritual centre of the nation after the destruction of the Second Commonwealth. The castle, dependent on the count of Jaffa, was handed over to a certain Balian, who took from it his family name, d'Ibelin. A series of successful acquisitions, mainly through marriage, made the fortune of the family. By the middle of the century, the lordship of Ramleh was already joined to that of Ibelin. In this way the founder of a great noble clan established the territorial base for the future power of his family. By good fortune, his able sons married wealthy heiresses and brought to the Ibelins many lordships and fiefs. Ultimately they became the chief family of the realm, a clan of statesmen and king-makers.

The central coastal plain belonged to the royal county of Jaffa-Ascalon and was flanked in the south by Gaza (reconstructed in 1149/50) of Philistine fame. This also belonged to the Crown, but as a fortress was held by the Templars. The latter also held the castle of Darum on the edge of the Sinai desert. More inland, the small castle of Blanchegarde (Tel al-Safi), erected by the king in 1142, was later joined to the county of Jaffa, when the future King Amalric received Jaffa as an apanage. After his accession to the throne, it became an independent lordship and was enfeoffed to Gautier, lord of Beirut. Two additional lordships, Nazareth and Lydda, are worth noting as the only ecclesiastical seigniories in the kingdom. [8]

Balancing the large number of greater and smaller lordships was the royal domain. Two generations after the conquest, by the middle of the twelfth century, the extent of the Crown lands was still considerable. Their nucleus was formed by an important concentration of territories around Jerusalem. Roughly speaking, it extended over the whole mountain region, from around Hebron

---

[8] See cap. X, The Church: A.

and Bethlehem in the south, through Judea, with Jerusalem at its centre, into Samaria, with Nablus (ancient Sichem) and Sebaste (the ancient city of Samaria) in the north. But around 1174 Samaria was bestowed by King Amalric as a dowry on his wife Maria Comnena. With the marriage of the widow, Balian II of the Ibelins came onto the scene. Hebron, in the southern part of the Crown domain had earlier become an autonomous seigniory and was joined around 1161 to the great lordship of Transjordan.

These vast territories in the interior of the country were, in all probability, of lesser economic importance than some of the coastal regions which belonged to the Crown. Here the royal domain comprised the central and southern coastal plain, with the port of Jaffa. The lordship of Jaffa originally included, in addition to the maritime city, a part of the coast plus the eastern, fertile hinterland, which comprised Mirabel (Majdal Yaba) in the north, Ramleh and Lydda at its centre, Blanchegarde and Ibelin in the south. For a short time, the lordship of Jaffa was detached from the Crown and, from 1120, belonged to the de Puiset family. Following a revolt fomented by a de Puiset against the king (1131), the lordship was confiscated and reverted to the Crown. A generation later in 1151 it became an apanage of Amalric, brother of King Baldwin III, who also received the newly captured city of Ascalon. Thus the county of Jaffa-Ascalon came into being, extending along the coast to the newly rebuilt city of Gaza (1150). With the accession of Amalric to the throne the county reverted to the Crown, only to be reconstituted as the dowry of Sibylle, the king's daughter. With the accession of her second husband – Guy de Lusignan (1186) – to the throne, the country reverted to the Crown.

More to the north, the two great ports of the kingdom, Acre and Tyre, belonged to the Crown. The first remained a royal city and in the thirteenth century served as the capital of the kingdom. Tyre, on the other hand, the only city never captured by the Moslems up to the loss of the kingdom, became, in the second half of the thirteenth century, an independent lordship of the de Montfort family, though it did not entirely leave the royal domain.

No description of the feudal map of the kingdom would be complete without taking into account the position of the military

orders. Around the middle of the twelfth century a new phenomenon came into being, the lordships of the military orders.[9] Under
conditions of endemic warfare and poor finances, it was not surprising that the military orders should take over the burden of
defence. Frontier fortresses or outlying castles had been handed
over to them even before the middle of the century. In time, large
tracts of landed property, whole territorial complexes, came into
their possession. The legal position of these territories is not always
clear ; this is partially due to the fact that the orders acquired lands
on different terms (leases, fiefs). Moreover, the fact that the orders
were ecclesiastical establishments tended to create confusion between the status of their land and the extra-territorial position
of the holders. It is interesting that, in time, a kind of lordship
of these orders was created, a practice which would later determine
the foundation of Prussia as an independent state of the Teutonic
Knights. The culmination of this practice in the Near East was
reached in the county of Tripoli, where, as early as 1142, the possessions of the Order of St John formed an almost independent principality. As such, the order commanded the services of the county's
vassals and acquired the rights of baronial jurisdiction. It seems that
nowhere in the Latin kingdom did the orders achieve a similar
position, although great areas came into their possession. Thus,
for example, the Teutonic Knights created around the fiefs of
Château du Roi (M'ilyah) and Monfort (Qal'at Qurein) in Galilee a
complex of more than fifteen villages (between 1218 and 1220). But
it does not appear that the order also acquired feudal jurisdiction
and the rights of a regular lordship. Another case was that of Arsuf,
acquired by the Hospitallers (c. 1261). There it seems that the order
stepped into the position of the former lord of the place and, as such,
became for a very short time a direct tenant-in-chief of the Crown.

It would be futile to follow the fortunes of the different lordships
during the thirteenth century. The great Crusades of that century
which tried to revive the Crusader kingdom after the disaster
of Hittin never really succeeded in doing more than establish
effective crusader rule in the narrow coastal plain. Certainly in 1240

[9] See cap. XIV: The Military Orders.

(during the Crusade of Richard of Cornwall), the kingdom succeeded in playing off Egypt against Damascus, and received back
large parts of Judea and Galilee. The restoration was shortlived,
as was crusader domination of Jerusalem (1229–44), and a generation later the kingdom shrivelled again to the narrow coastal
plain. In the last quarter of the century even this part of the country
was hardly under effective crusader rule.

The repercussions of the growth in the power of the nobility,
which has been discussed in another context, were also felt in the
general position of the lordships within the kingdom. If we compare them at the beginning and at the end of the twelfth century,
some notable changes are obvious. For example, it is remarkable
that whereas as late as 1120 (the time of the Council of Nablus), the
Crown was still strong enough to preserve for itself the right to
intervene in the jurisdiction of the feudal courts, such a procedure
would have been unthinkable and certainly decried as illegal three
generations later. The king was barred from local feudal jurisdiction, in which his writ did not run. This was an important step
on the road which led the lordships to become autonomous entities.
  Another development tended in the same direction. The early
agreements with the Italian communes according them privileges,
primarily financial and juridical, were concluded and signed by the
rulers of the kingdom. This was the outcome of the existing situation, namely, that the privileges were usually accorded to woo the
Italian communes and to assure them profits in cities to be conquered. Consequently, the conquered places when later enfeoffed
to the crusader nobility were burdened with a mortgage of privileges to the communes. In time, the situation changed. The kings
no longer accorded privileges and signed agreements and their
place was taken by the tenants-in-chief, the lords of the cities. This
change occurred roughly in the period following the disaster of
Hittin. The restoration of the royal power in the thirteenth century
did not put a stop to this ursurpation, which by then had become
customary and lasted until the fall of the kingdom.[10] It strength-

[10] A convenient list of privileges accorded to the communes is in J.L. La
Monte, *Feudal Monarchy in the Latin Kingdom of Jerusalem*, Appendix D.

ened the position of the individual barons, who could now accord privileges and sign treaties with foreign powers as if they were independent rulers.[11]

Another symptom of growing strength and independence in the lordships is the appearance of baronial mints and coinages. A royal *Assise*, which may be assigned to Baldwin II but, more probably, to Baldwin III (1143–62), still declared mints and the striking of coin a royal prerogative and monopoly. Its infringement was punishable by confiscation of the vassal's fief. Nevertheless, archaeology has produced evidence of baronial mints and coinage. No *Assise* records legislation which could have abolished the earlier royal monopoly. Even the juridical treatises written by the nobles of the kingdom, which carefully enumerated their privileges, make no mention of a change in the law. The barons must simply have usurped the royal prerogative. There was no doubt some profit in it, but the material importance should not be exaggerated. Large-scale international business used gold pieces which were struck by the Crown, and the local circulation of coins involved such a variety of royal and Moslem coins that baronial money, limited to small areas, could not have carried much profit. It would seem that the striking of baronial money was more like a declaration of independence by the baron and his lordship.

The curtailing of royal jurisdiction and the infringement on royal prerogative illustrate, at a local level, the emergence of baronial autonomy. This found more spectacular expression in the changing balance of power between Crown and nobility on the constitutional level.

[11] E.g. in 1221 Jean d'Ibelin of Beirut grants privileges to the Venetians in his city. The same grants privileges there to the Genoese. *Regesta*, nos. 950–1.

B   Local Government in Action

In the crusader kingdom, as everywhere else in mediaeval Christendom, the lordship was the basic unit of political and social organization. In feudal Europe, however, the fief, even the simple fief, sometimes played a parallel role in social cohesion. Whereas the lordship embraced first and foremost the collective of vassals, the European village community found its political and social cohesion in the manor. In both cases, in the lordship as well as in the manor, there was a collectivity which belonged to the same type of culture and to the same religion. Rarely did heterogeneous or extraneous elements interfere with the basically monolithic structure of these entities.

The Latin kingdom represents politically, but even more so socially, a different structure of society. The lordship not only comprised the collectivity of vassals, but also represented a collectivity of conquerors, culturally, linguistically and religiously different from those who did not belong. On the level of the manor there was almost no contact between squire and his peasants, because crusader manorial structure did not necessitate squire-villein contacts, neither did they ever belong to or integrate one society.

The purpose of the lordship was to rule its subjects, as that of the manor was to ensure the physical maintenance of the Franks – both were parts of a colonial machinery of government for ruling a conquered land and an alien population.

There was nothing in the earlier crusader experience (which means eleventh-century European experience) which could have prepared them for the task or guided them in the establishment of their own framework of organization. European wars and conquests took place on Christian soil, with a homogeneous population. The Normans of Sicily alone might have had an inkling of the problem and perhaps also the Spaniards, but Norman precedence was not followed in Jerusalem (though it was in the Norman principality of Antioch) and not many Spaniards took part in the First Crusade. The crusaders thus created an original type of organization. There were very few legislative acts of establishment, rather an empirical process which lasted until a uniform system was elaborated and stablized.

There were three underlying principles which guided the crusaders and all reflect a specific attitude by the conquerors, which we could define as 'colonial'. The first was the absolute separation of conquerors and conquered; the second was the recreation of a homeland tradition on foreign soil, although the conquered country offered new and different possibilities; the third was the adoption of existing native institutions with almost no interference from the conquerors.

The lord and his vassals and the lord and his Frankish burgesses formed the closed group of conquerors. Neither merit nor position enabled a non-Frank to enter this community. The political institutions of the lordship, embodied in the feudal court and the court of burgesses, are not only a part of the administrative machinery of the kingdom and the lordship, but at the same time an institutional symbol of class status. The fact of belonging to the jurisdiction of the feudal court or the court of burgesses is the privilege of the class. This tenet was so strong that it even overcame ancient concepts, like the degrading status of certain professions. A Frank, for example, who is a peasant does not belong to the class of villeins; he is a burgess, the lowest grade conceived by the Franks for free men of European origin.

The imitation and re-creation of the homeland's institutions is another remarkable and characteristic feature of this colonial society. Though its economic framework enabled the creation, if not of a bureaucratic state, at least of a state which could make full use of salaried officials and paid armies (such as those which came into being at the end of the thirteenth century in Europe), the crusader kingdom perpetuated traditions brought over from the homeland, preponderantly France. Feudalism, for example, as a system of government – from the high officers of the Crown, through tenants-in-chief and vassalage to the court of burgesses as a court of the lordship (not of the city), down to the manorial system –was a copy of eleventh-century France. Nothing could be more illuminating than the fact that a salaried knight called his salary 'wage-fief' (*fief de soudée*). Some differences, like the former strong position of the Crown and a manorial system without direct demesner, were the only deviations affected by specific conditions.

Outside the realm of these properly Frankish institutions lay the task of ruling the conquered and the task of ensuring the maintenance of the conquerors. The Franks followed the line of least resistance. Institutionally speaking nothing new was created : the conquered population was left to its own devices. Denominational courts, which had already existed under the Moslem domination, were left to continue functioning as the main legal institutions of the conquered. Only in the sphere of unavoidable contacts between conqueror and conquered did the crusaders intervene. Mixed cases would come before a mixed court, whereas the accuser had to bring witnesses of the defendant's party. The adjustment of the two sets of institutions was also expressed in the fact that criminal cases involving life and limb, and civil cases involving more than a certain amount of money, were judged before a Frankish court. For the rest, the conquered were a world apart, valued for profit, while always suspected as a potential threat.

The different political institutions were not an organic growth of the country, but composed of parts different in origin, each with a past, fused into one framework by the fact of conquest and necessity. Experience proved that the machinery worked smoothly and was well adapted to its task. Its shortcomings were not in performance, but lay in their concentration on the immediate task without consideration for a larger whole : the kingdom.

The size of an average crusader lordship was modest or even extremely small. An average seigniory would have measured some fifty square miles. The principality of Galilee was an exception, whereas the great lordship of Transjordan and the county of Jaffa-Ascalon were divided into smaller seigniories (not necessarily enfeoffed), which served as independent administrative units. The modest size of the lordship made it manageable for the crusader administration despite all its shortcomings. At the local level crusader administration was at its best, even when confronted by complex social stratification and minute legal distinctions.

Royal and noble administration at the local level were similar or rather identical. This was partially because some lordships were royal before they were enfeoffed to the nobles and partly due to the fact that the noble lordships imitated the royal example.

The overwhelming majority of crusader lordships and, certainly, the important ones, had as their capital a city or a fortified urban agglomeration. Only in small lordships or frontier areas did a castle serve as the centre of the fief. In such cases, the castle was more than a fortress and often served as the residence of the lord and the centre of administration.[12] This aspect marked at the beginning of the twelfth century a significant difference between Europe and the Holy Land. In the latter, local conditions, the existence of cities and their traditional place in state organization prescribed the structure of crusader lordships.

The three types of habitation, city, castle and village, because of the heterogeneity of their inhabitants, set varied and difficult tasks to baronial administration. Again, local conditions before and after the conquest created a situation which, though not unknown, was certainly not common in Europe. There was no direct relation between the type of habitation and the social or legal standing of its inhabitants. The administration of urban capitals had to cope as much with the Frankish nobles, knights and burgesses as with the non-Frankish city population. The rural areas had to deal mainly with Moslem villeins but also with oriental-Christian peasants. At the same time some villages were settled by Franks who enjoyed burgess status.

The chief organ of administration was the lord's court, a replica of the royal *Haute Cour*. The lord's feudal court was composed of his vassals. This meant all fief-holders, whether of land or revenue or – as was often the case – combined land and revenue fiefs.[13] To

[12] R.C. Smail, 'Crusader Castles in the Twelfth Century', *Cambridge Hist. Journal*, 10 (1951), 133–54.

[13] The lordship of Arsuf (1261) had as vassals 6 knights and 21 'sergeants'. Only one fief is a land-possession. All other vassals receive money and agricultural products as their fiefs. The total expenses of the lordship were: 2,448 besants, 137 measures of wheat, 145 of barley, 22 of vegetables, 127 litres of oil. See J. Prawer in *Byzantion*, 22 (1952), 23 ff.

judge by the military services owed by the different lordships to the Crown, the number of vassals ranged from seventy or eighty in the lordships of Galilee, Jaffa-Ascalon and Sidon, to seven, five or even less in very small seigniories. The court could be legally convened with three members. This was not just a principle of law (*tres faciunt collegium*), but a reality, as the overlord was obliged to supply the missing members of the court if the legal quota was not filled.[14] Jean d'Ibelin counts twenty-two feudal courts of the lordships.[15]

Some of the lordships, because of their size, instituted high offices paralleling those of the royal court. In the smaller ones, there was no reason for an elaborate administration, although some kind of chancery, possibly manned by the chaplain of the lord, was, no doubt, always available. While the competences of the royal *Haute Cour* are known in detail from the treatises written by crusader jurists, we are, strangely enough, left in the dark by the same sources with regard to the feudal courts. It is an axiomatic assumption of the jurists that the feudal court parallels in all aspects the *Haute Cour* of the kingdom. Nevertheless, the objective limitations are so obvious that we can hardly accept this constitutional assumption to be more than a declaration of legal principle.

Actually, things were probably different, because the standing of a simple knight only faintly resembled that of a mighty tenant-in-chief. On the other hand, the lord's authoritarian inclinations were tempered by the patriarchal relations which, generally speaking, permeated the whole feudal system and were more potent in smaller social units than in the royal court.

We do not know if there were any fixed sessions of the feudal court. They could have coincided with the great holidays of the Christian calendar, but even this seems doubtful. On such occasions, the lord would normally attend, with other tenants-in-chief,

[14] A detailed list of services is preserved by Jean d'Ibelin, cap. 270–2. This list came from a royal archive and consequently gives details of lordships which belonged to the royal domain and only a summary of services due by the lordships of the tenants-in-chief. However there is no reason to think that there was any marked difference between the royal domain and the particular lordships.

[15] Jean d'Ibelin, cap. 253.

the meetings of the royal court in Jerusalem, thereby fulfilling his feudal duties as well as participating in the religious celebrations. The relative smallness of the country gave the lord no excuse not to attend the royal court as in Europe, where he stayed at home, holding his own court. Thus, one may assume there were rather sporadic meetings of the feudal court, in accordance with specific needs.

On solemn occasions, the court would be convened to give formal recognition to a new lord. The vassals would then take an oath of homage and fealty to him. On such occasions, even burgesses of the different cities might be present and required to give their oath of fealty to the new ruler. Thus a legal community of the Franks would be duly instituted, or its existence perpetuated in the framework of the lordship. At the same time, a more intimate community, that of the feudal *lignage*, would come into being based on the strong cohesion of the lord and his men, according to the ethos of the feudal age.

The court of the lordship would also be, theoretically at least, the forum in which the vassals would have their say with regard to the marriage of the lord's daughters or his family alliances. But we doubt if, in Palestinian circumstances, such a procedure was practised. Naturally, this depended in great measure on the personality of the lord, but one must remember that the lord belonged to a very small group of magnates headed by the king, where such problems as his own family alliances would more probably be decided. Some of the obligations deriving from the feudal structure would also call for a meeting of the court. Such was the case when the High Court decreed mobilization or taxation or when the lord was captured by enemies and his vassals were obliged to collect a ransom.

Such weighty problems were an exception. Normally the court would deal with prosaic matters, which contemporaries might have regarded as exciting. The main bulk of business derived from the sacrosanct rule that any question regarding feudal property or relations between lord and vassal should and could be dealt in the lordship's feudal court only. Thus, a grant of a fief of any nature by the lord had to be done and 'recorded', that is witnessed, by the presence of the lord's court. The oath of homage and fealty was taken before the court and the lord's sealed grant would then be witnessed by the signatures of some of the members of the court. On other occasions the court was called to acknowledge the claims of a son or the nearest relative to a fief, and the lord invested him with its possession in the presence of the court.

As a record office, and a court of justice, the lordship's court also witnessed all transactions in feudal property inside the boundaries of the lordship. All types of alienations, sale, partition, mortgage and exchange needed the court's presence for their validity. Since an agreement of the lord was required in most of these cases, recording and agreement were done on the same occasion. Both contracting parties were interested in making their agreement public. No registers of proceedings existed, even in the High Court, up to the middle of the thirteenth century, [16] and it is extremely doubtful if, even by then, they were established in the lordship's court. Living witnesses were thought to be the best guarantees of transactions.

Some records of transaction, more particularly dealing with landed property, were kept on the books of the treasury, called *Secrète*. As far as we can tell each lordship had a *Secrète* of its own and its documents were consulted in cases of dispute. [17]

As a court of justice, the court dealt as much with civil as with criminal cases. Law and procedure were those of the kingdom, and as a rule it does not seem that there were, in the lordships, individual codes of law. [18] In both cases, civil and criminal, the lordship's court was supreme and there was no appeal from it to any other court in the kingdom. The nearest we come to an appeal is that of a vassal accusing his lord of illegal action, that is action without the

[16] Registers of the High Court and court of burgesses of Acre were established on the initiative of Jean d'Ibelin, Lord of Arsuf, in February 1250 at a common meeting of the two courts. *Abrégé du Livre des Assises des Bourgeois*, cap. 13 ff. *Lois* II, 246 ff.

[17] J. L. La Monte, *op. cit.*, 167, n. 2 presumed the existence of the *Secrète* in the Latin kingdom, but did not find any proof of its existence before 14th-century Cyprus. But a crusader document of 1243 proves beyond doubt the existence of the *Secrète* in Tyre and Acre. Ch. Kohler, 'Chartes de N.-D. de Josaphat', *Rev. de l'Orient latin*, VII (1899), no. 71.

[18] Yet *assisiae et consuetudines civitatis Tyrensis* are mentioned in 1277. Tafel-Thomas, III, 154.

judgment of court, or accusing him of *défaut de droit*, that is, prevention of his case being heard in court. In the first case, the vassal had the right to make his accusation before the High Court according to the *Assise sur la ligece* of King Amalric by 'conjuring his peers'. In the second case, he could appeal to his lord's overlord that justice be done. But once the lordship's court pronounced judgment, there was no appeal from it. The only possibility open to the vassal was the not very wise accusation of *la cour faussez* – the direct accusation that his judges deliberately biased justice.[19] Such an accusation opened the way for the fantastic procedure of fighting, individually, every member of the court who sat in judgment.

The administrative business of the lordship was also transacted in the court. The appointment of officials, like the officers of the *scribanagium* and *drugemanagium* (usually held in fief), was done in court, and this was also doubtless true of the appointment of all other officials of the lordship, whether feudal or not.

The feudal court of the lordship was thus the supreme judicial and administrative institution of this basic territorial unit. The serious matters of the lordship, as well as everyday problems of its Frankish knightly population, were decided before it. Yet, the social position and the prestige of the institution had little to do with the amount of business it handled. Compared with a few score of knightly families, there were thousands of Frankish burgesses living in the cities and townships of the lordships.

The Frankish burgesses were judged, and in some measure, administered, by a special court, called the court of burgesses (*Cour des bourgeois*), later on (since the middle of the thirteenth century, but perhaps even earlier) called the 'Low Court' (*Cour Basse*). Evidently this last name was coined in a royal city, probably in Acre, as it corresponds to the High Court of the nobles (no feudal court of a lordship is ever called *Haute Cour*). The competences of the court of burgesses were limited to the burgesses of a given city or township. Thus, every city or township with a Frankish popula-

---

[19] Jean d'Ibelin, cap. 110.

tion had its own court of burgesses. There were no links between these courts, and it goes without saying that there was no legal hierarchy. The crusader jurists go so far as to indicate that evidence given and 'recorded' in one court is not acceptable (or at least not necessarily so) in another, even in the same lordship.[20] Whereas, then, the feudal court served as a focus for the whole knightly population of a given lordship, no such central institution existed for the burgesses. The competence of the individual courts of burgesses covered a subdivision of the lordship. The court exercised governmental functions at the local level and had jurisdiction over a legally defined class and its special type of property.

The twenty-two lordships listed by Jean d'Ibelin towards the end of the twelfth century had thirty-seven courts of burgesses.[21] But, their actual number was greater. Contemporary documents enable us to trace forty-two courts of this type and there may have been more.[22] In addition, courts of burgesses not listed by Jean d'Ibelin existed, for example, in villages settled by the crusaders. It is difficult to be certain of the number of such burgess settlements, but at least a dozen are known to us by name. Legally speaking, such village courts could, perhaps, be regarded as manorial courts. If this were really the case, jurisdiction would be in the hands of the possessor of the village, who might be a vassal of the lord or of an ecclesiastical institution, and not necessarily in the hands of the lord. As a matter of fact, we have proof that this was so in several instances.[23] Nevertheless, one can hardly classify such a court as manorial. Its assessors and subjects were Frankish burgesses, and

[20] *Livre des Assises des Bourgeois*, cap. 224 and 226.

[21] Jean d'Ibelin, cap. 270.

[22] The following is the list furnished by Jean d'Ibelin: Jerusalem, Nablus, Acre, Dacron, Jaffa, Ascalon, Ramleh, Ibelin, Tiberias, Saphet, Sidon, Beufort (= Qal'at Shaqif), Caesarea, Beisan, Montréal, Crac (of Moab), Hebron, Bethlehem, Jericho, Beit-Jibrin, Gaza, Lydda, Sebaste, Merle (= Tanturah), Chastel Pelerin (= 'Athlith), Haifa, Caymont, Nazareth, Château du Roi (= M'ilyah), Scandalion, Tyr, Toron, Banyas, Subeibe, Châteauneuf, Beirut. Additionally we know of 'vicomtes' presumably presiding over courts of burgesses in other places. Cf. J. Richard, *Royaume latin de Jérusalem*, 119, n.2.

[23] J. Prawer, 'Colonization Activities in the Latin Kingdom of Jerusalem', *Rev. belge de phil. et d'histoire*, 29 (1951), 1063 ff.

the customary law it followed was that of the kingdom's cities. It may be said that, in this case, the Frankish settler, although outside city walls, carried with him the status and the privileges of his urban class.

The court of burgesses was composed of twelve jurors and a chairman, all appointed by the lord of the city. The chairman's title was *vicecomes* – 'viscount'. [24] The office never became hereditary, and the viscount remained a salaried official of the city lord, appointed usually for a period of several years from among the knights of the lordship. An appropriate term that conveys some idea of the function of the the viscount would be that of governor of the city. He represented the city lord in all his dealings with the non-noble Frankish population and quite often in his relations with the non-Frankish population of the city. He was the chief of the local police and had at his disposal a detachment of 'serjants'. At their head, he made the rounds of the night watch, alternating in this capacity with his second in command, known by his Arabic name of *mathesep* (originally, 'market supervisor'). The safety of the townspeople as well as that of their pockets was in his hands. He supervised the markets, weights and measures, and, to some extent, market prices. At the same time, he collected the lord's revenues in the city, whether rents, sales taxes or income from the lord's monopolies. As head of the court of burgesses, he also collected the judicial fines and duty payments imposed by the court. In this latter capacity, the viscount had under his command the officials of the court and its administration.

Whereas, as city governor, he was responsible for the preservation of the peace and well-being of the city as a whole, his special responsibility was the Frankish population. His most important function was to preside at the meetings of the court of burgesses, direct its proceedings and, once the verdict was pronounced, he was responsible for its execution.

The origins of the title and functions of this important member of the lord's administration are a little enigmatic. The former

---

[24] See *Assises des Bourgeois*, cap. 3 ff., and in a systematic way *Abrégé du Livre des Assises des Bourgeois*, cap. 3 ff.

position of viscounts under the Carolingians, when they were in charge of a sub-district of the *comitatus* or county could only have been a dim memory by the eleventh century. By the twelfth century viscounts were, almost everywhere, hereditary, and viscounties were hardly thought of as subdivisions of a county. The viscount was usually a grand seigneur, a direct vassal of the territorial prince or of the king. Only in Normandy (and hence in England where the Anglo-Saxon sheriff took the new title of *vicecomes*) and in Flanders (with the *castellani*), traces of the earlier institution seem to have been preserved. This makes plausible the assumption that the crusader viscount and his court of jurors derived from these northern prototypes, although a good part of the burgess population, as well as their code of law, had originated in southern France. This in itself is not very surprising, if we bear in mind that the ruling class and the royal dynasty came from northern France.

The court of burgesses was composed of jurors (*iurati* or *jurés*) who derived their name from the oath they took at the time of their appointment by the lord of the city. The court was always a court of the lord of the city and never became an organ of city autonomy, which was unknown in the kingdom. And yet, precisely because the court of burgesses was the only administrative city institution it could, at times, represent the Frankish urban population vis-à-vis their lord. Thus crusader juridical treatises advise the lord to consult the inhabitants of the city concerning the appointment of the viscount. We also hear that some city ordinances were proclaimed after consultation with the jurors.

The twelve jurors of the court of burgesses sat in judgment three days a week – Mondays, Wednesdays, and Fridays, excluding feast days – from sunrise to sunset and dealt with all cases concerning the burgesses of the city and their property. The latter was, generally speaking, land held by burgage tenure. If circumstances (marriage or inheritance) brought burgage tenures into the hands of nobles, the land remained under the jurisdiction of the court of burgesses and not the feudal court of the lordship. Besides its competences in all civil suits, the court of burgesses had supreme criminal jurisdiction over all city inhabitants, with the exception of nobles.

The court of burgesses of every city was as autonomous as any feudal court and, in a sense, even more so, as there was no burgess institution to correspond to the central and noble *Haute Cour*. Its verdicts were final and no appeal was possible, except the accusation of consciously biased judgment, which cast doubts on the honour of the court and its members. Such an accusation cost the accuser his head, unless the lord of the city showed grace by settling for his severed tongue. [25]

It was a pious and venerated tradition that the first ruler, Godfrey de Bouillon, established the two major judicial divisions, one for his knights and nobles and one for his Frankish commoners. Yet we have to wait almost a whole generation, until the second quarter of the twelfth century, to find the formal appearance of the court of burgesses. [26] This in itself would not invalidate the tradition of their establishment. But considering Godfrey's brief rule and the constant warfare which filled his reign, it seems improbable that Godfrey could have established a special court of burgesses. The evolution of the different jurisdictions probably followed a more ordinary course and might already have developed under Baldwin I, when the acquisition of property emphasized the class distinctions between nobles and non-nobles among the conquerors. It was in the nature of feudal society that landed property in the newly conquered countryside was constituted into fiefs, that is, noble holdings. The situation in the conquered cities was less clear. The conquerors, who usually expelled the local population, became, overnight, masters of land and buildings inside the city walls. The overlordship naturally belonged to the lord of the city, but the type of legal claim a man had to his city property was not, generally, and certainly not immediately, defined. Quite often, the social standing of a man decided the status of his holding, whether feudal or burgage tenure. With time, feudal tenures inside the cities became an exception and, often, a special favour, granted by the city lord to

---

[25] There is no adequate study of the procedure and law of the court of burgesses, but for the old introduction of Comte Beugnot to his edition of the *Assises*.

[26] See below, n. 28 and n. 29.

one of his vassals. It was burgage tenure that became the rule in all city land. Moreover, crusader legislation that barred burgesses from holding fiefs associated this largest class among the Frankish population almost exclusively with burgage tenure.[27]

Class stratification as well as legal distinctions in property found their expression in the institutional structure of the kingdom. They already must have manifested themselves in the royal court of the early kings of Jerusalem. As the meeting place of the retinues of Godfrey de Bouillon and Baldwin I, it became the feudal court of the nobility. Later, responding to the developing needs of the Frankish non-noble settlers of Jerusalem, a new institution came into being, the court of burgesses.

The feudal court, coping with noble and knight, was no innovation, but there was less experience to draw on when dealing with men who were neither noble nor villein nor serf. Autonomous urban settlements were still exceptional at the end of the eleventh century, and their courts could hardly have served as an example to the crusaders. Yet the crusaders brought with them, from Europe, some basic principles of law and procedure that could lay foundations for new developments. Essentially they were two : trial by peers and the necessity of witnesses to any transaction or act of sale. Although witnesses were not necessarily peers of the contracting parties, it was usual, and certainly convenient, for this normally to be the case. Hence it is not surprising that the first mention of 'burgesses' in crusader documents is connected with witnessing a deed of sale.[28] Soon after, we find burgesses witnessing transactions with additional titles, such as 'legitimate witnesses' and 'witnesses of His Majesty the King'; later they appear with the title 'jurors' (*iurati*) and, finally, as a *Curia*.[29] The comparison of names proves that, in all these documents, we deal with the same group of people, and it is a fair guess that, although the apellation

[27] J. Prawer in *Economic Historical Review*, 4 (1951), 77 ff.

[28] Rozière, *Cartulaire du Saint Sépulcre*, no. 103.

[29] Cf. Rozière, no. 45; no. 103; Delaville le Roulx, *Cartulaire de l'Ordre de Saint Jean*, no. 116; Rozière, nos 107, 65, 115; Delaville le Roulx, *op. cit.*, no. 464; Rozière, no. 108; Delaville le Roulx, no. 184. The full title of the court of burgesses appears for the first time in 1149 in Jerusalem. Rozière, no. 112.

'court' appears rather late, the burgesses already witnessed the transactions as members of a court, a court of record. This form remained a typical feature of the court of burgesses. Jurisdiction, which might have been very summary in the early period of the kingdom, was later institutionalized. Following the rule of trial by peers, it was vested in a group of jurors of burgess origin presided over by the viscount, himself a vassal, and therefore a knight, of the lord of the city.

The evolution which presumably originated in Jerusalem was later imitated in the other cities of the kingdom. This may have been partly due to the fact that almost all the urban centres of the kingdom were captured from the Moslems by the kings of Jerusalem. Normally they would have established an administration in the newly conquered city on the pattern of Jerusalem. With the enfeoffment of the city to one of the nobles, the institutions would continue as they were, as the transition from royal to seigniorial rule did not necessitate any transformation or adjustment.

The administration of burgess settlement in the newly established villages was based on acquired experience. It was the status of a class that conditioned its institutional establishments. In a sense, the court of burgesses was an expression of the corporateness of the body of settlers of burgess origin outside the city walls.

Had the crusader cities been homogeneous in their ethnic structure, the feudal and burgesses' court would have largely sufficed for judicial and administrative purposes. But this was never the case. But for Jerusalem, which from the day of conquest barred its gates to Moslems and Jews, almost all cities had a mixed population. The remnants of expelled Jewish and Moslem communities settled once again in the cities, and, almost everywhere, there were communities of oriental Christians, mainly Syrians and Jacobites. These communities had a long tradition of self-government, developed during the four hundred years of Moslem domination. Shunning the intervention of any external and, by definition, enemy influence, the communities evolved their own institutions, which were concerned as much with religion as with charity and jurisdiction. The latter also developed as the natural outcome of the fact that civil law, especially family and succession law practised by the communities, derived from ancient Roman and Byzantine legislation and thus diverged from the law of the Moslem conquerors. Deprived of statehood, the Christian community (as the Jewish community had done) substituted its religious establishments for that of the state. The ecclesiastical hierarchy organized communal life and dispensed justice. [30] In cases between members of the same community, the contending parties had recourse to their own courts and their own laws. The penalty of anathema threatened by the clergy was a powerful weapon, which could involve ostracizing a man and cutting him off from his own community and usually from his sources of living as well. In the name of the security and well being of the community, its members were called upon not to ask for the intervention of the state. In fact the Moslem state was as a rule happy to leave self-government in the hands of the autonomous communities. Still, cases of Moslem intervention were not unknown. Strangely enough, they often took place in contended elections for the higher posts of the ecclesiastical hierarchy. Sometimes local authorities intervened in the administration of church property.

Whereas communal jurisdiction in civil cases became a characteristic feature of government under Moslem domination, we do not know much about criminal jurisdiction. Was it in the hands of the community or was it entirely in the hands of the government? Neither do we know what the normal procedure was in 'mixed' cases between members of the different non-Moslem communities. It may, perhaps, be presumed that when arbitration failed, the parties had recourse to government jurisdiction.

The crusader conquest did not bring about much change in the traditional sectarian organization of the Christian minorities. Crusader tradition had it that the 'Syrians', that is, the native Christian population, requested the new rulers to grant them their own courts and the right to have their own laws and customs. That request, we are told, was granted. [31] This can only mean that the

---

[30] See below in cap. XII.
[31] Jean d'Ibelin, cap. 4.

status quo ante was maintained. What was true for the native Christians was also true for the Jewish community; deeds written in its own courts in the Latin kingdom[32] have been preserved.

The native courts took care of the local population in the cities of the lordship, as well as in its villages, on a sectarian basis. In civil cases where marriage, wills, and the like were involved, the competent authority was the ecclesiastical court of the community. In other cases, we hear about a lay head of the community, called a *reis* (from the Arabic : head), who presided over a native court. One cannot classify ecclesiastical authority as being part of the lordship's administration, but it did fill an important gap in its working. The ecclesiastical authority, and the lay-courts of the native Christians, were a part of the machinery which, at a local level, assured government and justice to the non-Frankish population.

It is quite possible that the pattern of ruling the native Christians was first established in the capital and then imitated in the other cities and rural areas of the kingdom. The fact that the kings of Jerusalem settled (*c.* 1115) a large community of oriental Christians, whom they brought from Transjordan, in the capital makes such a conclusion more than plausible. It would be normal to suppose that such immigration *en masse* prompted an institutional development or, at least, served as a catalyst in its evolution.

It is in connection with the native courts that a remarkable change took place at an unspecified date during the twelfth century. Our sources are, unfortunately, not explicit enough to account for it, and we must be satisfied with conjecture. The change that took place was an amalgamation of two different divisions of the judiciary of the lordships, that of the courts of the oriental Christians and that of a special court that existed in every larger urban settlement, the so-called *Cour de la Fonde*, that is, the 'Court of the Market'. *Fonde* or *funda*, which sometimes denoted landed property in general, acquired among the crusaders the meaning of a market-place or an area (square or street) of commercial activity. One of the viscount's subordinates, the *mathesep*, was specifically charged to supervise these teeming and bustling urban centres. Naturally

---

[32] See below in cap. XIII.

enough, a special kind of jurisdiction evolved for the market-place, as the use of the ponderous and formalistic machinery of the court of burgesses for decisions on petty quarrels and transgressions would have hindered more than helped. We do not know the original composition of the 'Court of the Market', but it seems that from its beginnings it was formed by a mixed body of Frankish and Syrian jurors. This would correspond in the main to the general rule of trial by peers, if not in letter, at least in spirit. We have to imagine the most frequent market dealings to be between native producers, peasants, craftsmen and small merchants and their Frankish customers, and less frequently the other way round. It was thus more likely that the defendant would be a native and the plaintiff a Frank. This was fairly well reflected in the composition of the court : four native jurors and two Franks. The president of the court was, naturally, a Frank who bore the title of bailiff (*bailli*). Criminal jurisdiction involving loss of life and limb was excluded from the competences of this court and only civil suits to the amount of one mark silver could be tried before it.[33] Cases transcending these limitations came before the court of burgesses even when the parties did not belong to the same legal class or community.

With time, the 'Court of the Market' enlarged its competences and swallowed the native courts of the *reis*. One wonders whether this was a deliberate step taken by the Franks or if, somehow, things evolved in this direction. It was possibly a combination of both and, in all probability, it did not much change matters. Mixed cases (involving Syrians and Franks) could never have come before the purely 'Syrian' court of the *reis*. The amalgamation of courts thus changed little in the existing situation. The problem was that of cases between Syrians themselves. As long as an autonomous jurisdiction existed, their cases came before the native court presided over by the *reis*; from then, the mixed 'Court of the Market' was the relevant authority. Still, this evolution was probably, in practice, a less definite step, unfavourable to the native

---

[33] In the beginning of the 14th century one mark silver was evaluated at 25 Cypriot besants.

population as it might appear in theory. By analogy with the status of Jewish communities in Islam and Christendom, the new competences of the 'Court of the Market' may not have abolished the earlier, autonomous native institutions. They could probably be used if necessary, depending on the wishes of the contending parties. The preservation of native institutions largely depended henceforth on the overall cohesion of the various communities. Bearing in mind the urge of minority groups to maintain their rights and institutions we can envisage that the courts of the *reis* did not entirely lose their standing or, at least, did not disappear. Moreover, we should always remember that jurisdiction in matrimonial and related matters remained, as before, in the hands of the native clergy.

Thus, both the courts of the *reis* and the 'Court of the Market' dispensed justice at the local level. Still, their scope was limited by the amount of money involved and by the exclusion of criminal cases. The same is also true with regard to landed property of the natives, which, being city land, was under the jurisdiction of the court of burgesses. Yet the court of burgesses was not a court of appeal. The court of the *reis*, as well as the 'Court of the Market', were autonomous courts in the framework of their jurisdiction.

Let us now look at the other towns of the kingdom, where particular needs and special classes brought about the creation of special judicial institutions. In the ports of the kingdom there existed, probably from the second quarter of the twelfth century, a special court to deal with details of maritime law. It took its name from the chain which was strung between two towers on the jetties, and closed the harbour entrance each night, as well as during sieges, when it barred enemy fleets from the city. The 'Court of the Chain' (*Curia catenae*)[34] was composed of sea merchants familiar with mercantile law. More important cases were heard here and then handed over to the court of burgesses. In this latter case we may detect the function of a fact-finding bureau, whose reports were sent to a higher court for a verdict. As in almost all judicial divi-

---

[34] R. B. Patterson, 'The Early Existence of the *Funda* and *Catena* in the 12th-century Latin Kingdom of Jerusalem', *Speculum*, 39 (1964), 474–7.

sions, finance and justice were closely involved, and the 'Court of the Chain' was charged not only with collecting fines but also with collecting anchorage duties and other charges connected with the port. In the thirteenth century we hear about a *vicomte du port*, who probably presided over the court and was responsible for the administration of the port. The 'Court of the Chain' was the only court to handle not a specific legal class but a specific type of case. Nothing of this kind developed in other branches of the crusader administration.

The royal or baronial administration of the major cities (all maritime cities) was complicated, or one might say complemented, by the autonomous administrations of the European communes. Their competences, on the one hand, paralleled those of the feudal court or the court of burgesses in that they were competent instances for the members of the communes. On the other hand, all major communes, though in varying degrees, held lordships. Some of them only had quarters in the city, while others also had important land around the cities. In both cases, the communes had rights of jurisdiction over the inhabitants of their quarters and their villages. Naturally, knights, already linked by a feudal nexus to their lord, were excluded, but burgesses (though there was a lot of litigation on this point), members of other communes and natives, whether Christians, Jews or Moslems, were sometimes under the jurisdiction and administration of the commune.

Outside the city walls local government was dispensed by a court of burgesses in the villages founded by the Franks, and by the native courts in other villages. Not much is known about the working of these native institutions. We do know, however, that in some places under the crusaders there were mosques[35] and Moslem dignitaries, who must have dispensed justice among the Moslems of their district. Local native clergy, whether Greek or Jacobite, must have done the same for the Christian inhabitants of villages. The traditional jurisdiction of the native village also continued

---

[35] Mosques in Acre and Tyre, of Ibn Jubair, *RHC. Hist. Or.*, III, 450–2; in villages near Nablus, Cf. E. Sivan, *Rev. Etud. Islam*, 1967, p. 138.

to exist. It may have been vested in the authority of the village elders, who continued to exercise voluntary justice, or it may have been the head of the family with whom authority rested. That these traditional institutions continued to exist is well attested by the fact that, when a Frankish lord took over a village, he used to receive a kind of native homage from the elders or the heads of families of the village.[36] These were the local *reis* who continued to function under the new rule as they had done for hundreds of years in the same villages, whatever the origin of the landlord and ruler.

The administration of the village was of the simplest type. As there were virtually no manors, properly speaking, and no demesne land, the lord's interest in the village was purely fiscal. His representative, whatever his title, *drugeman* or *scriba* or *gastaldio*, was responsible for the lord's revenue. He would appear in the village at harvest time to see that one third or one fourth of the crop was put aside for the lord and transported into his granary, and the same procedure would be followed when fruit or olives were gathered, or when the time came for the customary *xenia*, euphemistic 'gifts', of wax, honey and such to be paid to the overlord.[37]

Matters were somewhat different in villages that belonged to ecclesiastical institutions. There a monastery or a church would often have a *cella*, which was probably a cottage where a monk, specially delegated to the task, would live (perhaps during the harvest season only) and supervise his monastery's dues. In the military orders a central institution would then supervise the collection of revenues from the different estates belonging to the orders.

Dealing with relatively small territorial units, whether urban or rural, the feudal administration of the crusader kingdom could cope quite well with its problems. Applying feudal machinery to lordships was certainly far more efficient than using it to run a kingdom. The fact that crusader lordships were very small meant that direct

---

[36] A detailed description is furnished by a Hospitaller's document of 1255. Delaville le Roulx, *Cartulaire*, no. 2747.

[37] See below cap. XVI, Economic Life and Commerce: A.

personal knowledge and contacts were strong enough to make the simple machinery run smoothly. This was, perhaps, one of the reasons why crusader administration never developed beyond the stage of the European feudal system of the eleventh century. There was neither a challenge nor an urgent need for change. Changes were needed in the machinery of the kingdom as a whole. But when the need became obvious, some time after the middle of the twelfth century, the power of the Crown was already declining and the pressure of the nobility had already begun to hem it in and prevent any attempt at reform.

X

THE CHURCH

A Position and Organization

One of the more debatable questions of crusader history is whether or not Urban II conceived the conquest of the Holy Land as a preliminary to the establishment of a theocratic state, another 'Patrimony of St Peter' in the East.[1] It is clear, however, that a strong ecclesiastical faction in the armies of the First Crusade took a firm stand following the conquest of Jerusalem, when they contested the election of the first ruler of the kingdom. The prelates demanded that the election of the patriarch of Jerusalem should precede that of a lay ruler for the city and country. This demand reflected the spirit of the First Crusade and suited the mediaeval concept of the superiority of things spiritual over things temporal.

But Jerusalem was conquered four years after the crusade had started, and many an ideal had gone overboard on the long march to the East. The spiritual nature of the movement, but for the rare occasions of ecstatic upsurge, had been lost on the roads of Asia Minor. Moreover, with the death of the papal legate Adhémar of Puy[2] in Antioch, the formal claims of the hierarchy died as well. Even more important, the military leaders of the armies, at least those who decided to stay on in the East, envisaged their future as rulers of lay dominions.

---

[1] M. Spinka, 'Latin Church of the Early Crusades', *Church History*, 8 (1939), 113–31.

[2] Adhémar de Monteuil recently became an object of controversy. See H. E. Mayer in *Deutsches Archiv*, 16 (1960), 547 ff. summing up the studies of J. Brundage and Hill; additionally cf. J. Richard in *Journal des Savants*, 1961, 49 ff.

Nevertheless, some of the earlier spiritual fire still smouldered. The undefined claims of the Holy See and regard for the ecclesiastical hierarchy were decisive in the choice of a title for Godfrey de Bouillon as 'Advocate of the Holy Sepulchre'. For a short time the future character of the kingdom was in the balance, and Godfrey, as well as the princes of Antioch and Edessa, took an oath of fealty and homage to the newly elected patriarch, the Pisan Daimbert, declaring themselves to be vassals of the Holy Sepulchre. Moreover, the 'Advocate of the Holy Sepulchre' promised to relinquish to the patriarch the cities of Jerusalem and Jaffa as soon as the kingdom enlarged its boundaries. This was the climax of ecclesiastical demands. Less than a year later (1100), Godfrey's brother and successor, Baldwin I, was crowned as king and the title 'Advocate' was relegated to oblivion. The propitious moment was gone and when some years later a patriarch (Stephen, 1128–30) renewed these claims, his unrealistic demand was simply ignored. Some bickering between kings and patriarchs accompanied the subsequent history of the kingdom, but, on the whole, the great prelates remained remarkably docile subjects.

Thus in the Latin kingdom, largely established and maintained by the Holy See, the ecclesiastical hierarchy did not play any decisive role. Whereas contemporary European monarchs were desperately fighting for the right to intervene in episcopal elections, the Crown of Jerusalem had an unopposed and decisive voice in appointing its bishops. This was true as much for the episcopate as for the patriarchate. It was customary to allow the chapter of the Holy Sepulchre (later on, the concourse of bishops) to present its candidates to the patriarchal office. The presentation was made to the king, who finally chose the man to be consecrated.[3] The royal court often intervened even in the selection of the candidates by cathedral chapters. This developed during the period when the papacy in Europe engaged all its strength to fight emperor and king to ensure free ecclesiastical elections. Europe would have branded crusader practice as pure simony. Despite the pious declaration by Jean d'Ibelin, lord of Jaffa and author of the famous *Assises de*

[3] *Ernoul*, cap. 8.

Jérusalem (middle of thirteenth century), that the Kingdom of Jerusalem had two 'chief seignors', one spiritual and the other temporal – patriarch and king – the reality was very different. [4]

It is in the light of such relations that we must regard another peculiarity of the Latin kingdom. As everywhere in Christendom, the Church exercised jurisdiction over its own clergy and over laymen in cases regarding marriage, legitimacy, succession, religious heterodoxy and sexual deviations. On the other hand, nothing like the great and numerous European ecclesiastical lordships or principalities ever existed in the kingdom. There were, in all, four tiny ecclesiastical lordships, which had shrunk to three by the second quarter of the twelfth century. The patriarch's claim to the city of Jerusalem seems to have resulted in a compromise, whereby one quarter of the city, that of the Holy Sepulchre or the 'patriarch's quarter', as it was called, became an ecclesiastical seigniory inside the capital, which was itself a royal lordship. Crusader tradition had it that the quarter of the Holy Sepulchre was relinquished to the Christians in the middle of the eleventh century by the Fatimids of Egypt, in an agreement with the Byzantine emperor to pay for the restoration of the city walls adjoining the quarter. Whether the independence of this quarter really goes back to the eleventh century, or whether it owed its existence to a more recent crusader arrangement, is difficult to ascertain. Whatever the case, the quarter had its own patriarchal administration and jurisdiction over the inhabitants. Whether the Crown claimed suzerainty over the ecclesiastical part of the city is not clear and seems doubtful. Security arrangements, which were entirely in the hands of the Crown, probably brought about a *de facto* dependence. [5]

Another ecclesiastical lordship was that of Lydda, the reputed birthplace of St George, the Christian warrior martyr. This seigniory had already been established on the march of the First Crusade prior to the siege of Jerusalem. The army had rested in the neighbouring city of Ramleh, abandoned by its Moslem popula-

[4] Jean d'Ibelin, cap. 260.
[5] The legal position of the patriarchal quarter in Jerusalem was never studied. We hope to publish a study of the problem in the near future.

tion, and vowed the town to God in gratitude for their victories. This was the first Latin bishopric in the Holy Land and also the first lordship. The new bishop's diocese included Ramleh and the adjacent Lydda. But, soon enough (*c.* 1119) we find Ramleh in the hands of a lay lord, while the bishop's see and rule were restricted to the small township of Lydda.

Nazareth was a third ecclesiastical seigniory and purely a crusader creation, for the original bishopric lay in the desolated Beisan. The crusaders transferred it to Nazareth in Galilee and the bishop became lord of the city. The same happened in the small township of Bethlehem, which was elevated to the rank of a bishopric with its bishop as lord of the place.[6]

As we have seen, the territorial power of the Church, as distinct from its economic resources, was extremely small, and certainly contributed to the relative unimportance of the clergy as a political factor.

The exiguity of the political power wielded by the clergy within the feudal framework was also apparent in the kingdom's legislation, which barred ecclesiastical establishments from holding fiefs. This is more or less formally stated in the various treatises of crusader jurisprudence;[7] nevertheless, a perusal of crusader documents shows hundreds of land donations to ecclesiastical establishments. From the legal point of view, donations from the king could technically have been regarded as non-feudal tenures, in this case 'tenures by free alms' (*elemosina*). However, this point of law could hardly be stretched so as to classify all donations given to the clergy by lay lords, vassals or rear vassals of the Crown. The latter were held (with the exception of some small allodial properties) by feudal tenure, and donations to the church were certainly alienations of feudal property which, in the hands of the church became exempted from customary feudal duties. The ban on alienation of feudal possessions to the Church was even extended to city property, to burgage tenure. Crusader jurists explicitly record this

---

[6] P. Riant, *Études sur l'église de Bethleem*, 2 vols., Genève, 1889; Paris, 1896.
[7] *Livre au Roi*, cap. 45; in a more liberal way Philip de Novara, cap. 56 and Jean d'Ibelin, cap. 234 and 249.

prohibition, but church records reveal that large amounts of city property were given to and retained by the Church. Only later in the kingdom of Cyprus was a real attempt made to effect such legal limitations.

Church possessions were not entirely exempt from state obligations. A record of military services in the kingdom composed in the last quarter of the twelfth century[8] contains a list of contingents owed by ecclesiastical establishments to the Crown. They are peculiar in that the Church did not render knightly service, but put at the disposal of the Crown the services of 'serjants', on foot or mounted. These contingents were sometimes considerable and Church property thus contributed to the defence of the kingdom.[9] It would be futile, however, to attempt any evaluation of the relation between Church income and state expenditure.

The formal organization of the Latin Church in the East was a thorny problem which never found a satisfactory solution. The main difficulty lay in the incompatibility of the ancient Byzantine traditions and the new pattern of crusader settlement. The Latin conquest meant a rupture with the Byzantine past, although the Latins had reasons even beyond the theological aspect to regard their newly established rite as the legitimate successor of the former regime. They were thus obliged to adapt existing tradition to new exigencies.

The major change in the organization of the Church in the Holy Land was more the result of political than of pastoral needs. This was the shifting of the traditional boundary between the two eastern patriarchates of Antioch and of Jerusalem. The patriarchate of Antioch had included from antiquity the large archbishopric of Tyre, stretching from Acre in the south to Tortosa in the north with seven suffragan bishops. Here ecclesiastical tradition found itself at variance with the new political framework, since the kingdom included the city of Tyre. Under pressure by the kings of Jerusalem – who could not acquiesce in seeing a part of their

[8] Jean d'Ibelin, cap. 271–2. *Gestes des Chiprois*, 520–1. Another list in Marino Sanudo, III, 7, 1.
[9] See cap. XV, Warfare and Fortifications: B.

kingdom, including its two greatest ports, Acre and Tyre, governed by a patriarch resident in Antioch – the Holy See ruled that the boundaries of the patriarchates should coincide with those of the state.[10] Thus the metropolitan see of Tyre was included in the patriarchate of Jerusalem but lost in the process its suffragan bishoprics outside the boundaries of the kingdom. It became official policy at Rome that any new conquest by the kings of Jerusalem should be subject to the jurisdiction of the patriarch of Jerusalem. Nevertheless, age-old traditions were not so easily eradicated. The claims of Antioch were often renewed, the metropolitans of Tyre vacillated in their loyalties, and the problem was definitely settled in favour of Jerusalem only a hundred years after the conquest of the Holy Land, in 1206.

Another aspect of church organization concerned metropolitan sees and bishoprics. At the beginning of the thirteenth century Jacques de Vitry wrote:

There are also many other cities in the Promised Land, albeit before the time of the Latins they may have had Bishops of their own of the Syrian and Greek churches, yet on account of their number and their poverty the Latins have subjected many churches and many cities to one cathedral city, lest the dignity of a Bishop should be made cheap.[11]

Thus Nazareth, the place of the sanctuary of the Annunciation, became a bishopric (1109) replacing Beisan (Scythopolis) and thwarting the monastery of Mount Tabor, which attempted to lay claim to the see. Bethlehem, with its sanctuary of the Nativity, followed suit in 1110. It is rather strange that the Greeks did not maintain these places as bishoprics, although both had a large Christian population and certainly did not lack dignity. Perhaps, influenced by proximity, they evaluated the importance of the holy places differently. Whatever the case, it was inevitable that

[10] J. G. Rowe, 'Paschal II and the relations between the Spiritual and Temporal Powers in the Kingdom of Jerusalem', *Speculum*, 32 (1957), 471 ff.; *Id.*, 'The Papacy and the ecclesiastical province of Tyre, 1110–1187', *Bull. John Rylands Library*, 43 (1960), 160–89.

[11] Jacques de Vitry, *PPTS*, XI, cap. 58.

Western newcomers in the Holy Land would attach themselves to such places as Bethlehem and Nazareth. The Westerner felt it incongruous that the great shrines of Christendom should be bypassed in the ecclesiastical hierarchy.

Despite these changes, some prompted by political and others by spiritual needs, it can hardly be said that crusader church organization ever really reflected the priorities of the kingdom. An important city like Jaffa never became a bishopric, nor did its counterpart, Nablus. On the other hand, the small township of Hebron was raised to a bishopric, whereas the greatest crusader city, Acre, never became a metropolitan see.

Such phenomena were naturally not unknown in Europe, where claims of old and venerated localities often prevented new and greater centres from taking their place in the ecclesiastical hierarchy. Nevertheless, there is a basic difference between Europe and the Latin kingdom. Mediaeval Europe which emerged from the barbarian invasions developed in a traditional pattern without notable interruption. The crusaders, though not entirely free from earlier Byzantine influence, did make some changes in the organizational framework. The weight of tradition and temporal interests prevented a thorough adaptation of the ecclesiastical establishment to the demographic realities of the country.

The Kingdom of Jerusalem proper was composed of four ecclesiastical divisions: the diocese of Jerusalem headed by the patriarch and four archbishoprics, Caesarea (*maritima*), Nazareth, Tyre and Transjordanian Petra (from 1168). In addition to the metropolitan sees, the patriarch had direct suffragans in the bishops of St George (Lydda-Ramleh), Bethlehem and Hebron.

The history of the two latter bishoprics is interesting. After the conquest, Bethlehem became a priory of the canons of the Holy Sepulchre and Ascalon was intended as a bishopric. But Ascalon was not captured until 1153, and the crusaders felt that Bethlehem, with its sanctuary, should rank higher than a simple priory. Thus the city received its own bishop in 1110 as a direct suffragan of the patriarch. Ascalon, a latecomer in the kingdom, never received a bishop and depended on the bishop of Bethlehem. There was similar development in Hebron. In 1119 the 'discovery' of the tombs of the patriarchs gave it sufficient lustre to raise its status from a priory to that of a bishopric. It is of interest to note that Jaffa never received a bishop and depended directly on the canons of the Holy Sepulchre. This may have been due to the fact that Jaffa had once been promised together with Jerusalem as patrimony to the first patriarch.

To complete the picture of the diocese of Jerusalem, let us note that the abbots of the Temple, of Mount Zion and of the Mount of Olives were also direct suffragans of the patriarch of Jerusalem. From the geographical point of view the direct jurisdiction of the patriarch thus extended over the whole of ancient Philistia and Judea up to the ranges of Samaria.

The archbishopric of Caesarea, squeezed between the patriarchate of Jerusalem and the metropolitan see of Nazareth, had but one suffragan, the bishop of Sebaste (Samaria). Strangely enough, Haifa, next to Acre, also depended on Caesarea. To the north lay the archbishopric of Nazareth, which proudly proclaimed itself the metropolitan see for all of Galilee. It was created in 1108 to replace old Beisan-Scythopolis, which under the crusaders ranked only as a small township. As already mentioned, Nazareth had to contend for the title with the monastery on Mount Tabor. When ultimately triumphant, Nazareth had to surrender half the ecclesiastical revenues of the diocese to the Monastery of the Transfiguration on Mount Tabor. The metropolitan had the bishop of Tiberias as a suffragan. This town was the capital of Galilee, although it did not become its ecclesiastical centre.

The metropolitan of Tyre had as suffragans the bishops of Beirut, Sidon, Banyas (ancient *Caesarea Philippi*) and the youngest crusader creation, the bishopric of Acre.

The last archbishopric was that of Petra in Transjordan. Theoretically its suffragan was the Greek abbot of St Catherine in Sinai. But this was only a fiction since the crusaders' sway rarely controlled the peninsula.

The actual smallness of the dioceses is remarkable. Apparently, the large number of sees reflected ancient tradition (one list of bishops mentions more than a hundred sees in the lands captured by the crusaders), but also mirrored the new society. The pastoral duties of the Latin clergy seldom extended beyond the cities and castles, since the overwhelming majority of the western population lived within walls. The formal boundaries of the dioceses were thus hardly important. In the main, the duties of the clergy were concentrated in the cities and the size of the latter together with the numbers of its Latin population really determined the importance of a see. Outlying rural districts with Moslems and oriental Christians were of secondary importance. Thus the size of a diocese was no real indication of the social or economic position of the Latin prelates. Their main income was derived from parish churches, gifts from a constant stream of pilgrims and, above all, city property and landed possessions, the *casalia* given to them by the bounty of princes and nobles. It is possible that these revenues were actually more important than the rural tithes paid by the Frankish lords.

The metropolitans and bishops resided in the cathedral churches of their cities. The revenue of each church was divided between bishop and chapter and, very often – as in the Holy Sepulchre – according to a drawn up agreement. In 1114, when the controversial patriarch Arnulf imposed the Rule of St Augustine on the canons of the Holy Sepulchre, it was agreed that:

> From all the oblations coming to the Sepulchre of the Lord you will have a half; from other parts of the Church (i.e. sanctuaries connected with it like Calvary, etc.) two parts will go for illumination, the other third to the patriarch; from the Cross of the Lord which is guarded by canons, they will have all the oblations, but for Good Friday or when the patriarch takes it with him in times of need. I also accord to them (the canons) the tithes of the entire holy city of Jerusalem and of the adjacent places except those of the market (*funda*) which are the patriarch's.[12]

The larger cities had a considerable number of churches besides their cathedrals, but frequently these were not parish churches in the accepted sense of the word. A good part of parish duties was tak-

---

[12] E. de Rozière, *Cartulaire du Saint Sépulcre*, 46/7.

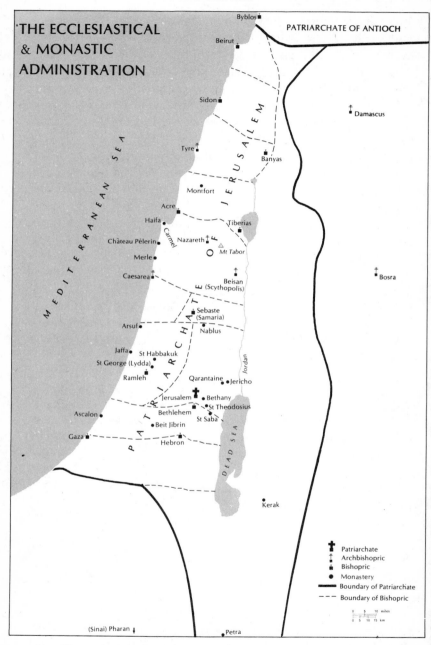

THE ECCLESIASTICAL
& MONASTIC
ADMINISTRATION

PATRIARCHATE OF ANTIOCH

MEDITERRANEAN SEA

Byblos

Beirut

Sidon

Tyre

Banyas

Damascus

Montfort

Acre

Haifa

Château Pèlerin

Nazareth

Mt Tabor

Merle

Caesarea

Beisan
(Scythopolis)

Bosra

Sebaste
(Samaria)

Arsuf

Nablus

Jaffa

St Habbakuk

St George (Lydda)

Ramleh

Qarantaine

Jericho

Jerusalem

Bethany

Bethlehem

St Theodosius

St Saba

Ascalon

Beit Jibrin

Gaza

Hebron

Kerak

JERUSALEM

PATRIARCHATE OF

Carmel

Jordan

DEAD SEA

Tiberias

✝ Patriarchate
† Archbishopric
■ Bishopric
● Monastery
▬ Boundary of Patriarchate
- - - Boundary of Bishopric

0   5   10 miles
0 5 10 15 km

(Sinai) Pharan

Petra

168

en over by monasteries and by the churches of the military orders or belonged to the exempted Italian communes. [13]

It will suffice to review the churches of a city like Acre to visualize the situation. The major church was the cathedral of the Holy Cross, the seat of the bishop of Acre and later of the patriarch of Jerusalem. The Order of St John, the Templars, the Teutonic Knights, the Orders of St Lazarus, Montjoye and of St Thomas – all had their own churches, which often competed with the parish churches. Three major churches, St Mark, St Peter and St Laurent belonged to Venetians, Pisans and Genoese, respectively. St Martin belonged, in the thirteenth century, to a colony of Bretons and a church of St Mary to the Provençals. [14] These churches, almost all exempted from the jurisdiction of the local authorities, caused considerable damage and much chagrin to the local clergy. This explains the sharp words of the bishop of Acre, Jacques de Vitry, on the regular clergy, which, according to him 'after they have been poisoned by riches and grew beyond measure having acquired great possessions, they despise their superiors, break the chains uniting hearts and throw away their yoke'.

For a more complete picture of the ecclesiastical structure we shall now turn to the monastic establishments.

B   Monasteries

The secular clergy with their churches and parochial duties represented one aspect of ecclesiastical institutions. The complement to the regular clergy, as everywhere in Christendom, were the monastic establishments. Monastic life in the Holy Land goes back to antiquity, and only Egypt could boast even older communities. Traces or survivals of this monastic tradition could still be found

---

[13] Typical cases: the agreement with the Pisan Church of St Peter in Acre (1200). *Regesta*, no. 775; a similar case: the agreement (1260) of the bishop of Acre and the priest of the Venetian church of St. Marc. Tafel – Thomas, III, 31–8.

[14] There are 40 churches mentioned in crusader documents for the city of Acre in the 13th century. Some of them are parts of monasteries. See R. Röhricht, *Regesta*, s.v. Acre.

in the Greek *laurae* and monasteries, which existed precariously on the eve of the Frankish conquest, and in the solitary hermits who continued to inhabit places hallowed since antiquity, for example, the caves of Mount Carmel or those in the Valley of Josaphat (Valley of Hinom) and on the slopes of the Mount of Olives. Some of these hermits were Westerners who went on pilgrimage and settled in the Holy Land in the period of Moslem domination. This type of hermit continued to exist under the crusaders and never really disappeared, thus adding to the colourful human scene in the Holy Land. Devotion or individual inclination would draw men to the Orient, intent on following the examples of a St Pachomius or St Hilarion of ancient fame. Only with the arrival of the crusaders did Western monasteries take root in the country. Though some of the new monasteries claimed earlier origin, there is no evidence to connect them even with the establishments founded by Charlemagne, let alone with Gregory I or even earlier foundations. Only memories survived, but these proved sufficiently fertile to create a host of foundation legends.[15] The only Latin establishments that can be traced to the period before the crusader conquest are two Benedictine monasteries, built in the Christian quarter of Jerusalem just across from the Holy Sepulchre. These were the monastery of Sta Maria Latina and its nunnery Sta Maria la Grande, founded by Amalfi merchants after the middle of the eleventh century and connected with the church of Notre Dame, and their hospice for pilgrims dedicated to St John. With the Crusades a new chapter in the monastic history of the Holy Land began.[16]

The earliest monastic foundations were formed from among the monks and clergymen in the armies of the First Crusade, especially

---

[15] D. U. Berlière, 'Les anciens monastères bénédictins de Terre Sainte', *Revue bénédictine*, 5 (1888), 437–46, 502–12, 546–62; L. White, 'A Forged Letter Concerning the Existence of Latin Monks at St Mary's Jehosaphat before the First Crusade', *Speculum*, 9 (1934), 404–7.

[16] On merchant churches see: V. Slessarev, '*Ecclesia mercatorum* and the Rise of Merchant Colonies', *Business Hist. Rev.*, 41 (1967), 177–97; H. Vincent and F. M. Abel, *Jérusalem nouvelle*, II, 646 ff.; H. Vincent, 'L'église Ste Marie latine la Petite', *Rev. biblique*, 10 (1901), 100–6.

from the followers of Godfrey de Bouillon. Almost immediately after the capture of the city, three old sanctuaries, partially destroyed by the Moslems and apparently abandoned by their Greek clergy, were taken over by the Latins. This was the origin of the Benedictine monastery of St Mary in the Valley of Josaphat, rebuilt above the traditional tomb of the Virgin, of the monastery and church of the Ascension on the Mount of Olives and the monastery of Mount Zion.[17] In the élan of conquest and the general spirit of fraternity, the abbots of these new monasteries apparently recognized their direct dependence on the patriarch of Jerusalem, as well as upon the prior and canons of the Holy Sepulchre. This dependence proved to be closer than usual, since the local hierarchy also claimed special rights to celebrate festivities in the churches of the monasteries.

Whereas the above-mentioned monasteries were established in places hallowed by tradition and succeeded the former Greek establishments, new monasteries were also founded in the capital. One of them was the abbey of the Temple of the Lord (*Templum Domini*) on the northern side of the former Mosque of Omar, which should not be confused with the Order of the Templars and its convent established in the nearby Mosque of al-Aqsa. Another, just outside the city walls, facing the Damascus gate, was the monastery of St Stephen. The stoning-place of the proto-martyr was shown at different periods in different places in Jerusalem, but was finally located here.

Parallel to the establishment of convents which, like the canons of the Holy Sepulchre, followed the rule of St Augustine, several nunneries were founded. The most ancient was the Italian nunnery of Sta Maria la Grande in the Amalfi compound near the Holy Sepulchre. However, later establishments became more famous, enjoying royal protection and favour, such as the convent of St Anne. Built in the Syrian quarter, near the gate of Josaphat, the lovely Romanesque church of the convent still recalls the glories of crusader architecture. The place was traditionally connected

[17] For the history of the different monasteries see the monumental work of H. Vincent and F. M. Abel, above n. 16.

with the *Piscina Probatica* of the New Testament, over which a small chapel (*moustier*) was built on splendid Byzantine foundations.[18] More important, the house of St Anne and Joachim and the birthplace of the Virgin were located here. Wives and daughters, members of the royal house, entered, or sometimes were forced to enter, this nunnery. Another famous nunnery was built in Bethany, the traditional site of the resurrection of Lazarus. The second abbess was Yvette, daughter of King Baldwin II.

The overwhelming majority of the monasteries followed the rule of St Benedict, and it is remarkable that very few offspring of the great monastic movements at the beginning of the twelfth century ever sent their representatives to the Latin kingdom. Symptomatic, for example, is the attitude of the Cistercians. Despite the insistence and efforts of King Baldwin I, who generously offered money to build a monastery in Nabi Samwil, the Cistercians refused to establish themselves in the Holy Land, but recommended the Order of the Premonstratensians. The latter built the great church, later turned into a mosque, which overlooks Jerusalem today. The crusaders called it Montjoye (*Mons Gaudii*), since here the hosts of the First Crusade as well as later pilgrims coming from the coast first saw the holy city. In the tradition of the three monotheistic religions it was linked with the prophet Samuel (the place was identified as the biblical Mitzpa or Rama). The explanation given by St Bernard for the refusal of the Cistercians to settle there 'because of the invasions of the pagans and the difficulties of the climate'[19] casts some doubts upon the real motives of refusal. It seems more probable that the Cistercians never accepted whole-heartedly the physical domination of the Holy Land as a religious value. The Premonstratensians who were already established in Jinis or Kenise near Lydda in the

[18] The results of the excavations, conducted here by the *Pères blancs* during the last decade, which discovered the Byzantine church, are not yet published. A short summary was given by P. Benoit, 'Découvertes archéologiques autour de la Piscine de Béthesda', *Jerusalem through the Ages*, 25th Archaeological Convention, Jerusalem, 1968, 48–57.

[19] *S. Bernardi Epistolae* in *PL*, vol. 184, no. 253; *Gaufredi Vita St. Benedicti III*, no. 2.

monastery of Saints Joseph and Abacuc de Cansie – a double dedication which is not easily explained – also settled in Montjoye.[20]

The Cluniacs, so intimately connected with the crusader movement, seldom appeared in the Holy Land. We hear only of a small Benedictine monastery in the crusader village of Palmarea (near Haifa) that was transferred to them (*c.* 1170) when the former establishment showed signs of failing.

Special mention is merited by the great Benedictine monastery on Mount Tabor, on the site of an earlier Greek establishment. For a time it claimed the see of Galilee. Richly endowed, Mount Tabor resembled a small ecclesiastical seigniory. Although the original crusader foundation dating back to the conquest under Tancred was destroyed by a Moslem invasion in 1113, it was rebuilt under Cluny's leadership, which gathered the former monks. As a convent and fortress it often suffered, especially during the thirteenth century, when it almost stood on the frontier of the shrinking kingdom. In these circumstances the monks sold out to the rather unwilling Order of St John, which had to assume the duties of defence and security.[21]

Even a cursory description of the monasteries cannot bypass the only monastic order originally created in the Holy Land under the crusaders, the Carmelites. The first associations of the Carmelites ruled by St Berthold seem to go back to the middle of the twelfth century. Their organization proper did not start before the beginning of the thirteenth century, when a number of monks living on the slopes of the Carmel asked and were granted their first rule by the patriarch Albert (1204–16), later confirmed by Pope Honorius III. The Carmelites, who later settled in Acre as well, never became important in the Holy Land, but they brought to Europe their biblical name and associations with the Holy Land.[22]

---

[20] Roziére, *Cartulaire*, no. 64. The thirteenth century 'Pelrinages et Pardouns de Acre says: 'la (á Iaphet–Jaffa) est un peron qe wn apele le *Peroun Seint Iak*, e une chapele où seint Abakuc soleint meindre.' *Itinéraires de Jérusalem*, ed. Michelant et Raynaud, Paris, 1882, 229.

[21] On Palmarea see: R. Röhricht, *Regesta*, 484; On Mount Tabor: R. Röhricht, *Regesta*, 1230.

[22] A. of St Mary, *The Order of Our Lady of Mount Carmel*, Bruges, 1913.

The development of the monastic movement was not hampered by the fall of the kingdom. On the contrary, there seems to have been a revival in the thirteenth century, though this might be an impression created by the surviving sources. There is no doubt that the loss of the kingdom meant the destruction of the economic basis of monastic life. Land and village, serf and peasant, pilgrims and oblations were no more than memories of the past. Only in the coastal cities did church establishments survive, though often with greatly limited incomes. Among the coastal towns Acre naturally held precedence. Even earlier, in the twelfth century, some of the archbishops, bishops and abbots had their houses there. It must have been convenient to have a house in the great port of the kingdom, not only for financial reasons, but also because state business was enacted there. When the kingdom was lost at Hittin (1187) and restored after the Third Crusade the escaping religious communities fled to Acre. Temporary abode changed to permanent residence and its inhabitants lived in the hope of a *reconquista*, which never materialized. Others left representatives in Acre, but began moving to their possessions in Europe, granted them long ago by virtue of their position as guardians of the holy shrines in Palestine.

The large number of churches and monasteries marked on a thirteenth-century map of Acre is striking. Even more significant is the fact that beside old establishments, branches of new European monastic orders settled in the disappearing kingdom. The most important were naturally the Franciscans and Dominicans, who came rather early (*c.* 1230) and rapidly contributed a large contingent to the Palestinian upper hierarchy. Often their houses became the starting points of missions.[23] With the Franciscans came the sisters of St Clare.[24] The newer congregations included that of the Holy Spirit and of the Holy Trinity (a military congregation, as distinguished from a homonymous hospital). An interesting congregation was that of St Mary Magdalene, which worked

[23] G. Golubovich, *Biblioteca Bio-bibliografica della Terra Santa e del'Oriente Francescano*, I, Quaracchi, 1906; M. Roncaglia, *Storia della Provincia di Terra Santa*, I: *I Francescani in Oriente durante le Crociate*, Cairo, 1954.

[24] H. Lemmens, *Die Franziskaner im Heiligen Lande, I: 1335–1552*, Münster, 1925.

among fallen and repentant women of this cosmopolitan city. The convents of all the ancient military orders, Hospitallers, Templars, Teutonic Knights, were represented, as were the Leper Knights of St Lazarus and the nuns of St Lazarus, possibly connected with the same order, or a branch of the convent at Bethany. In addition, there were the English Order of St Thomas of Canterbury, and a new knightly order of St Lawrence (perhaps connected with Genoa).[25]

It is easily understandable that new and old orders and congregations thought it almost obligatory to have their representatives in the Holy Land. For example, the Dominicans, possibly following an earlier custom of the military orders, decided (at Metz in 1251) that their European houses would send a fixed contingent of brothers to the Holy Land.[26] Some congregations viewed the crusader kingdom as a field for work and propaganda, others were attracted by the climate of spiritual contemplation, and others again felt it imperative to have an establishment in the holy places of the rapidly disintegrating kingdom. These establishments existed until the fall of Acre, which also marked the end of the kingdom. In the mountainous part of the country, those crusader churches and shrines already lost in 1187 returned to their former possessors, the Greeks and Syrians. Some places became mosques thus preserving a continuity of religious function and a living memory to a crusader world which had disappeared.

The Franciscans, relative latecomers to the Holy Land, first adapted themselves to the new situation. As the official 'Custodians of the Holy Land', since the beginning of the fourteenth century, they assured the Latin presence in Palestine, until more favourable conditions in the nineteenth and twentieth centuries witnessed a European revival (Catholic and Protestant) of the Latin foundations in and around the holy places.

[25] The names of churches and monasteries of 13th-century Acre are indicated in contemporary maps of the city. See: J. Prawer, 'Historical maps of Acre' (Heb.), *Eretz Israel*, II, Jerusalem, 1953, 175–85.

[26] F.M. Abel, 'Le Couvent des Frères Prêcheurs à Saint-Jean d'Acre', *Rev. biblique*, 43 (1934), 265–84.

C Church Festivities and Religious Life in the Kingdom

Apart from the holy shrines, the festivities of the Christian calendar were the greatest attraction for pilgrims from abroad. Once the 'Holy Geography' of Jerusalem [27] was established, the festivities were not merely celebrated, but the events of the evangelical narrative enacted in their historical setting. Processions led by the prelates to the different churches of the city and its surroundings vividly demonstrated to the believers the majesty of their faith and the drama of salvation.

Beside [28] the great feast days common to the Holy Land and to Christendom at large, some were particular to the city of Jerusalem. On 15 July of each year, the capital celebrated two memorable events: the capture of the holy city by the crusaders in 1099 and the consecration of the Holy Sepulchre fifty years later in 1149.

The conquest of the city was celebrated by a solemn procession. [29] Led by the patriarch very early in the morning, this passed from the Church of the Holy Sepulchre to the *Templum Domini*, the Mosque of Omar. Here a halt was made and prayers recited at the southern entrance, in that part of the Temple esplanade which faces the Mosque of al-Aqsa. From here, the procession wound its way across the esplanade to the burial place beyond the walls of those who fell in the conquest. Crossing the street of Josaphat it then

[27] See cap. XI: Pilgrims, Pilgrimages and the 'Holy Geography' of the Holy Land.

[28] The following is based on: 'Un Rituel et un Bréviaire du Saint-Sépulcre de Jérusalem (XIIe–XIIIe siècle)', ed. Ch. Kohler in *Mélanges pour servir à l'histoire de l'Orient et des Croisades*, fasc. II, Paris, 1906, 286–404. Cf. A. Schönfelder, 'Die Prozessionen der Lateiner in Jerusalem zur Zeit der Kreuzzüge', *Historisches Jahrbuch*, 32 (1911), 584–6. Several of the feasts are described by pilgrims, so e.g. the feast of Easter eve. The most detailed is that of the Russian pilgrim Daniel, *PPTS*, IV, 70–1.

[29] For the topography of crusader Jerusalem see the excellent map of F. M. Abel, 'L'état de la cité de Jérusalem au XIIe siècle', *Jerusalem 1920–22*, London, 1924.

proceeded to the northern part of the city walls. Here, not far from its north-eastern angle, a cross marked the spot where the knights of Godfrey first penetrated the city.[30] At this place a sermon was pronounced by the patriarch to the assembled clergy and populace, and thanksgiving prayers commemorated the establishment of the crusaders in the Holy Land.

Jerusalem celebrated the great events of the liturgical year in common with all Christendom. These festivities must have had a most moving effect on the participants, crusaders and pilgrims alike. The processions started from the Holy Sepulchre and ended at the traditional locations of the events commemorated. It is true that religious pageantry was sometimes marred by quarrels, since the different congregations did not always mingle harmoniously.

A nearby church would ring its bells to hamper a celebrant of preacher in his celebrations. This happened, for example, to the disgust of the populace, when the Hospitallers decided one day to disrupt prayers in the Church of the Holy Sepulchre. Sometimes a prior or abbot of one of the Jerusalem convents would attempt to be the official celebrant without yielding to the prior or canons of the Holy Sepulchre or the patriarch. Such quarrels were often decided by an ecclesiastical court or arbitration of the high prelates. Christmas was naturally celebrated by the patriarch in the church of the Nativity at Bethlehem.

On Ash Wednesday, the patriarch met the canons and lay brothers of the congregation in the chapter hall. By noon, one of the great bells summoned the people to the chapel of Calvary. From the steps of this exquisite monument, the patriarch preached to the assembled in the *parvis* of the Holy Sepulchre. After confession, absolution and benediction, ashes were strewn over the heads of the believers.

The feast of the 'Purification of the Blessed Virgin' and the

---

[30] The cross is marked on a 12th-century map of the city preserved in Ms. Cambrai. See R. Röhricht, 'Karten und Pläne zur Palästinakunde aus dem 7 bis 16 Jahrhundert', *ZDPV*, 14 (1891), Tafel 4. Cf. now L. H. Heydenreich, 'Ein Jerusalem-Plan aus der Zeit Kreuzfahrer', *Fest. für H. Schnitzler*, Düsseldorf, 1965, 83–90, pl. 62–5. The special liturgy of the day in John of Würzburg, *PPTS*, V, 70–1.

'Presentation of the Lord in the Temple' was appropriately celebrated by a procession with candles, incense and crosses from the
Holy Sepulchre to the 'Temple of the Lord'.

Palm Sunday was celebrated with the greatest pomp. Before
sunrise, just after matins, the clergy of the churches of Jerusalem, the
patriarch, the priors of Mount Zion and the Mount of Olives, as
well as the abbot of St Mary in the Valley of Josaphat, went to
Bethany. The treasurer of the Holy Sepulchre brought the holiest
of all relics, the Holy Cross. In the meantime, the population of the
city assembled in the precinct of the *Templum Domini* together with
the canons of the church of the Resurrection, the convents of St
John, Santa Maria Latina and Mount Zion. In the esplanade of
the Temple one of the prelates blessed the palm and olive branches
borne by the people and led the procession through the gate of
Josaphat to the valley of the same name just below the city walls.
Here they met the procession from Bethany with the patriarch
bearing the Holy Cross. The procession then climbed the steep hill
overlooking the valley and marched into the Temple area through
the 'Golden Gate' (especially opened on this occasion), traditionally
associated with the triumphal entrance of Jesus. After circling the
Templars' compound in the 'Temple of Solomon' (Mosque of
al-Aqsa) the procession ended with prayers in the precinct of the
Templum Domini. Thus an episode of the New Testament, commemorated in thousands of paintings and sculptures all over
Christendom, was enacted *in situ*.

The ceremony of the feet-washing on the eve of Good Friday
was celebrated in the convent of St Mary on Mount Zion. The
twelfth-century author of the *Ritual of the Holy Sepulchre*, whom
we follow in our description, wanted to be sure that the feet of the
invited poor were washed before the celebration, as a precaution
against leprous or cancered feet during the ceremony. Preceding
the ceremony proper, the patriarch preached, and then consecrated
the blessed oil, which was distributed to the different congregations.
Following that, the prior and canons of the Holy Sepulchre came
with basins and towels, washed the heads and feet of the poor,
kissed their hands and distributed clothes and shoes. The following
Friday was the day when the Holy Cross was brought from the

treasury of the Holy Sepulchre and exhibited in the chapel of
Calvary. The convent of the Holy Sepulchre prayed barefooted
and was called to offices not by the ringing of bells, but Eastern-
wise by wooden clappers.

Renowned as these festivities were, the most famous ceremony,
unique to Jerusalem, was that of the 'Holy Fire'. Apparently going
back to remote antiquity (but not attested before the ninth century)
Easter eve, as celebrated in the Holy Sepulchre by the Greeks, was
taken over without compunction by the Franks. At the beginning
the celebrations bore some trace of their Byzantine origin, which
later disappeared. The Greek-Orthodox *hegumen* from Russia,
Daniel, who visited Jerusalem in 1105, though not anti-Frankish,
still took pleasure in noting the participation of Greek monks from
St Sabas in the celebration. He remarked with satisfaction that the
lamps placed on the Holy Sepulchre by the Greeks shone with a different and brighter light than those of the Franks.[31] Later the celebration became purely Frankish, and the *Ritual of the Holy Sepulchre* does not mention any but the Frankish community.

The massed clergy and populace overflowed the great basilica
into the forecourt. The king and his escort had to clear a way
through the small western entrance to their places opposite the
tomb. The incredible pressures (which often ended up with several
suffocated participants) and the expectation of a miracle all created
an atmosphere of quasi-Messianic tension. To contemporary
Christians, Jerusalem was the only place in the world where year
after year, at the appointed time, God's presence became tangible
and the miracle a certainty. There were always doubters, and the
anonymous author of the *Ritual* advises the patriarch 'to choose
three or four people, also from among the pilgrims if such were
present, known for their honesty and piety, whom he may estimate
to be worthy to participate in such a mystery, to refute the reservations of the doubtful and strengthen the faith. These should be sent
to the place where the Holy Cross is guarded'.[32] The Holy Cross
was then brought in procession by four barefooted emissaries, who

[31] Daniel in *PPTS*, IV, 74–82.
[32] Kohler, *Mélanges*, II, 324.

circled the tomb topped by a large silver statue of Christ, beneath
the open cupola of the Anastasis:

> The masses of people assembled there from all nations are pouring out
> loud prayers in plaintive voices, incessantly appealing to God that
> He should be placated by the prayers and tears of his servants and
> deign to gladden his people by sending the Heavenly Fire.

Six or seven times the Holy Cross was born around the tomb to the
accompaniment of a crescendo of prayers and invocations. Finally
a light was seen miraculously kindled in one of the lamps over the
tomb. The man who bore the Cross then went into the cubicle and
with tremor and reverence lit a candle at the miraculous fire. This
was brought to the patriarch, who sent it to the king and his escort
present at the celebration. Then two great bells of the church pealed
out, and thousands of candles were lit from the original one to the
sound of *Te Deum laudamus*. This celebration, more than any other,
struck the imagination of the Frankish inhabitants as well as that
of the pilgrims. But the pious fraud could not continue indefinitely
and the 'miracle' worked only as long as the First Kingdom existed.
With the loss of Jerusalem a sober awakening called the celebration
to task and in 1238 a bull by Pope Gregory ix put an end to the
Latin ceremony (Jerusalem was then for a short time Frankish).
The oriental churches continued the ceremony. Reading a description of the ceremony by Lord Curzon in the mid-nineteenth
century conveys a feeling of being present at similar celebrations
seven hundred years earlier.[33]

Easter was celebrated with the greatest pomp. The central part
of the festivity was the 'Visit of the Holy Sepulchre', a ceremony
which spread in antiquity from Jerusalem and returned with the
crusaders in its European form. It is well known that this ceremony
gave rise to the dramatization of the solemn Easter liturgy. In time,
it contributed to the development of religious drama in the Middle
Ages.[34] One would expect Jerusalem to take the lead in this
development, since the historical locations were available. Such

---

[33] R. Curzon, *Visits to Monasteries in the Levant*, London, 1849.
[34] K. Young, *The Drama of the Medieval Church*, I, Oxford, 1933, 201 ff.

was indeed the case, but at a later and unknown date these beginnings were nipped in the bud. Let us hear the ancient *Ritual of the
Holy Sepulchre*. Once matins are sung:

> three young clerics are dressed up as women behind the altar accord-
> ing to the custom of the ancients . . . and they proceed therefrom,
> preceded by candles and incense, each bearing in his hands a golden
> or silvery vessel with some ointment, singing '*O Deus, quis revolvet?*'
> (= God, who shall roll us away the stone from the door of the
> Sepulchre. Mark 16, 3), and when they near the gates of the Glorious
> Sepulchre, two other clerics standing before the portals or nearby,
> holding candles in their hands and hoods (amice) over their heads,
> answer singing: '*Quem queritis*' (= Whom do you look for). And the
> women answer: '*Jhesum Nazarenum*'. Then the two answer: '*Non
> est hic, surrexit*' (= He is not here, He is risen. Matt. 28, 6). They are
> still singing when the women enter the Tomb and, after a short prayer
> therein, come out to stand in the middle of the choir. Singing loud
> they announce: '*Alleluia. Resurrexit Dominus*'.

The author of the *Ritual* interrupts his description of the dressing up
of clerics as women by the remark: 'but this is no longer done
because of the great number of bystanding pilgrims'. The remark is
perplexing if taken literally, namely, that the pressure of the
assembled population prevented the change of dress. We are rather
inclined to think that the pilgrims (our author does not stress the
populace in general but the pilgrims) found such a performance
(though common in Europe) somehow frivolous or inappropriate
to holy Jerusalem. This was not the only case when Europeans
would be more tolerant toward their own countries than to the
Holy Land which they were visiting.

Ascension Day was naturally celebrated by a procession to the
Mount of Olives, where, after a prayer in the church of *Pater Noster*,
the procession made its way to the church of Ascension (*Ascensio
Domini*), where the imprints of His feet were shown.

The 'Finding of the Holy Cross', a feast which originated
in Jerusalem to commemorate the miraculous discovery (3 May
326) of the Empress Helena, mother of Constantine the Great, was
celebrated inside the church, in the chapel of the Finding of the
Cross.

Although the *Ritual* does not point out the details, we may presume that Pentecost and the 'Descent of the Holy Ghost' was connected with the sanctuary on Mount Zion. Here, too, was celebrated the Feast of the Assumption of the Blessed Virgin, when the participants proceeded to the church of St Saviour and then to that of St Mary of the Valley of Josaphat.

Nothing comparable to the *Ritual of the Holy Sepulchre* is preserved for places outside Jerusalem. Naturally, none could compare in sanctity and the number of memorable places with the capital. Nevertheless, Nazareth, Bethlehem, Mount Tabor, St John in the Mountains ('Ain Karem) and the church of the Visitation as well as the ford of the Jordan (the place of Baptism) were not only places of pilgrimage but important centres of celebrations at the appropriate dates in the liturgical calendar. All year round the narrative of the Gospels was enacted for the pious and curious, an edifying spectacle for native and pilgrim alike.

'Come on you old Infidel, show me where you keep your most precious relics. If you don't, look forward to death !' This is not a phrase from a blood and thunder story, nor even an edifying tale of monkish miracles. The quotation comes from the biography of the Cistercian abbot, Martin of Pairis, written by the monk Gunther, and describes the plunder of Constantinople (1204) by the crusaders. The biographer tells how, during the sack of the city, when every crusader was busy looking for spoils, the good abbot burst into a Byzantine church, the burial place of the mother of the Emperor Manuel Comnenus (the church of the *Pantocrator* in all probability) and piously robbed it of its relics.[35] The last chapter of this vivid biography contains a full list of relics which, once brought to Europe, became the great treasure of the monastery of Pairis in Alsace. The biographer, blessed with a sense of humour, summarizes the great deeds of his abbot in a succinct expression: '*sacrum sacrilegium*' – a holy sacrilege !

The cult of relics, a thorny problem in the first centuries of Christianity, became the most popular expression of mass piety

[35] *PL*, 212, 222 ff., cap. 19.

in the early Middle Ages. The simple man did not wait for the
fathers and schoolmen to work out a theory of sanctity regarding
the remains of martyrs, as an earthly Temple which sheltered the
Holy Ghost. The belief in the miraculous property of relics was one
of the most common religious practices in the West. Sometimes
miraculously, but quite often in ways far from edifying, holy relics
were brought from the legendary East. Not all *Translationes*
(transfers), as this robbery was euphemistically termed, were as
famous as that concerning the body of St Mark, brought from
Alexandria in triumph to Venice, and only a few could boast
supernatural transportation like the body of St James that arrived
in Compostella. Churches and monasteries hankered for 'authentic' relics of any kind in order to enhance their sanctity and status.
In these circumstances the Holy Land and some adjacent countries,
like Egypt and Syria, became a mine for the pious and a boon for the
enterprising. Constantinople, which had hoarded relics since
antiquity, remained the greatest source of supply for the pious needs
of Christian Europe, until the sack of the city during the Fourth
Crusade (1204). This event flooded Europe with holy relics from
the Byzantine capital. Nevertheless, the Holy Land had almost
inexhaustible resources. The shrines of Palestine, especially those
of Jerusalem, Bethlehem and Nazareth, offered to pilgrims many a
possibility of acquiring relics, or at least holy mementoes, which
were then piously treasured in the churches or convents of their
home cities.

It would be tedious to enumerate the many places from which
tangible particles of holiness were brought to Europe.[36] The Holy
Sepulchre, the Rock of Calvary, the Columns of the Flagellation,
oil from the lamps over the Tomb are only a few. Strictly speaking, such fragments of rock or earth impregnated with oil were
not 'relics', but are classified today as 'holy objects', which enjoy some kind of sanctity as having touched the holy places or
relics proper. 'Authentic' relics were naturally fewer; hair, teeth,

---

[36] See: B. Bagatti, 'Eulogie Palestinesi', *Orientalia Christiana Periodica*, 15
(1948), 126–66. See also: G. Schreiber, 'Christlicher Orient und mittelalterliches
Abendland', *Oriens Christians*, 38 (1954), 96 ff.

and bones of saints were among the most appreciated, but none could compare with the fragments of the true Cross, the greatest prize among all the sanctified remains of Christ. Some pieces were sent to Europe, like that sent by Anselm to Paris and venerated for hundreds of years until the French Revolution.[37] Sometimes a collection of relics with a fragment of the true Cross became the vehicle for crusader propaganda abroad. Often an object would be sent from Europe, like the ring of King Louis VII of France, which was sent back to France after touching the different holy places.[38]

It is impossible to say how far this cult of relics was part of the popular religion of the crusaders themselves. Whatever we know is connected with pilgrims or ecclesiastical establishments in Europe. People living in constant contact with shrines may have had a different attitude to relics and sanctified objects than those who came from afar in quest of such objects. If the crusaders did indeed take a more sober view, this was certainly not due to greater sophistication, but simply because of 'familiarization' with the holy. What we know of crusader practice in the realm of beliefs precludes any conclusions as to their sophistication.

Crusader superstitions matched those of their European contemporaries and very often even those of the oriental Christians and Moslems. The belief that earth from Mamre near Hebron (from which Adam was created) was a potent medicine was widely accepted. The same went for the healing properties of immediate sexual intercourse against snake bite.[39] The 'milk of the Virgin' (that is a piece of white rock from the 'Cave of Milk' from Bethlehem), which was carried to the battle of Ascalon (1123) by the bishop of Bethlehem, Anschetinus, assured victory. An arrow which penetrated armour deviated on touching an inscription bearing the name of God.[40] A long list of such superstitions could be drawn from crusader sources. This is not peculiar to the Holy Land and any collection of European sources would yield a similar

[37] J. Richard, 'Quelques textes sur les premiers temps de l'église latine de Jérusalem', *Rec. des travaux offert à M. Clovis Brunel*, Paris, 1955, 423 ff.
[38] R. Röhricht, *Regesta*, nos 317 and 398.
[39] Albertus Aquensis, V, 40.
[40] *Ambroise*, vv. 3571–82, ed. G. Paris, Paris, 1897.

harvest. On the other hand, heavenly apparitions (so common during the First Crusade), knights in resplendent armour leading the hosts of God against the Infidels, silent and mysterious hermits advising the leaders on military tactics diminish with each Crusade. Indeed, one can hardly find any examples in the chronicles of the kingdom proper. This would not by itself prove that the crusaders were more sober or less inclined to the supernatural, but, rather that messianic ecstasy was required to conjure imagined heavenly intervention. In everyday life the inhabitants of the kingdom invoked God's help but relied on their own resources, even if the Moslem was an apprentice of Satan.

A phenomenon peculiar to the crusaders was the veneration of places that enjoyed sanctity among all religions. The tombs of the Patriarchs in Hebron with their Herodian buildings were venerated by Jew, Moslem and crusader. The latter even 'rediscovered' the tombs in 1118. Since the first century the tradition of the tomb of King David was moved from its place (near the Pool of Siloe to Mount Zion (where it remains today) and was venerated by all three religions. The famous Jewish traveller, Benjamin of Tudela, told the story of the Christians who tried to penetrate the tomb and were cruelly afflicted by God's vengeance. The 'Cave of the Lion' just across the Jaffa gate in the cemetery of the canons of the Holy Sepulchre (Mamillah) was pointed out as the place where Christian martyrs who, consigned to the flames by the Persians, were guarded by the miraculous intervention of a lion. In the thirteenth century, alas, a pupil of the great Nahmanides, tells the same story, substituting Jews for Christians and Christians for Persians ! The place outside Acre where Adam tilled the soil near the 'Source of the Oxen' ('Ain Baqar) was held in respect by all three religions. The 'Green Mosque' – al Khadra – in Ascalon became Sta Maria Cathara. The 'Cave of Elijah' on Mount Carmel was renowned among Christians, Moslems and Jews. It goes without saying that the Temple esplanade with its sanctuaries as well as the Mount of Olives were held in greatest respect by all.

These examples, although only a few among many, cannot be taken to prove the existence of syncretist inclinations or religious tolerance. Such practices simply reflect the tortuous history of a country which happened to be the cradle of Judaism and Christianity. Under their combined influence they became fixed even in the religious framework of Islam. Sanctuaries changed hands. Christianity expelled Judaism from its birth-place, building its own churches and monasteries. These became mosques under Islam and were reconverted to churches by the crusaders. The Moslems destroyed sculptures, icons, crosses and mosaics and, like Saladin after the capture of Jerusalem, purified the vileness of Christianity with rose water. Christians closed the *mihrab* in the southern wall of the mosque and built an altar in its east, casting captured metal into bells. The places hallowed by one religion remained so when a new religion achieved predominance. New believers took over the holy scriptures of an earlier religion and continued to pray at the same places with those who looked upon them as their rightful heritage, praying and hoping for ultimate redemption.

Even with all our detailed knowledge of church organization it is not easy to sum up the role of the ecclesiastical hierarchy and the importance of religious life in the kingdom. There is an apparent dichotomy between the official and the actual position of the clergy in state and society. Though the treatises of crusader jurisprudence might call the patriarch one of the two overlords of the kingdom – its 'spiritual lord' – in fact, no prelate ever truly influenced its policies or played a major role in its history. The patriarch, as everywhere in Europe, has precedence on the lists of those present at state councils and ceremonies, as he is the first among the signatories to international treaties. But this is a gesture ingrained in every Christian country, reflecting general concepts of the social order and is no proof of an actual position in the kingdom.

The Latin Church in the East was from the beginning far more likely to achieve a preponderance in the kingdom than the Church ever could in Europe. Nevertheless, in a kingdom largely created by the initiative of the papacy, which remained its mainstay and support for the two hundred years of its existence, the Church never became an influential factor, never represented a party, ideology or even a pressure group to rival the Crown or nobility. It is tempting to conclude that crusader society was therefore more lay-minded or less religious than contemporary European societies. This could be buttressed by a host of pilgrims' impressions and topped in proof by the vituperations of Jacques de Vitry, bishop of Acre.[41] However, sober analysis of his writings can hardly prove or disprove the point. It was not the religiosity or the lack of it which ultimately determined the place of the Church in crusader society, but more likely the type of prelate who governed and represented it.

With one exception, William, archbishop of Tyre, there was never an outstanding personality among the Palestinian clergy. Compared with England, France, Germany or Italy during the same period, the Palestinian clergy never produced the great statesmen, thinkers, scholars or spiritual leaders typical of Europe in the twelfth and thirteenth centuries. This could, in part, be explained by unfavourable conditions in the kingdom, such as the state of almost permanent warfare. Nevertheless, this seems to be an inadequate answer.

A different approach, may perhaps point to a solution. None of the high prelates (again with the exception of William, archbishop of Tyre) was a native of the Holy Land. The higher echelons of the crusader hierarchy were recruited entirely from among Europeans. Some papal legates became patriarchs and visiting clergymen were often elected to bishoprics or became abbots. The land did not produce its own spiritual leadership.

This clerical dependence on Europe is a characteristic feature of the kingdom. In all probability, the crusaders were so accustomed or even conditioned to look to Europe for help and guidance that they accepted as natural and self-evident a clergy always imported from abroad. Perhaps a feeling of inferiority dictated reliance on Europe. There was neither lack of opportunities, nor interest. The many churches and monasteries, the shrines and the attraction of the Holy Land in general coupled with the wealth of the ecclesiastical establishments were all favourable factors, somehow never properly used. Here and there we hear of a master teaching clerics in the Holy Sepulchre, and on another occasion

---

[41] Jacobus de Vitriaco, 'Historia Orientalis', *Gesta Dei per Francos*, ed. Bongars, 1087 ff.

about a master of theology practising in Acre. Such references are very few and so far spaced in time that they cannot be regarded as more than curious exceptions. Schools, which certainly existed in churches and convents, catered only to the lower levels of the clergy and never became real 'schools' in the mediaeval sense of the word. If a man was gifted and wanted an education, he followed William of Tyre, who left the kingdom and for twenty years studied in France and Italy. The kingdom itself provided no intellectual opportunities and no school ever acquired renown. On the periphery of European development the crusader state remained a colonial enterprise, dependent on the mother continent for the innermost aspects of spiritual life.

The obvious mediocrity of local culture and the fact that the kingdom produced neither school nor clergymen go far to explain the relative unimportance of Church and clergy. This contrasts significantly with the wealth of the Church. Hundreds of villages, houses, vineyards, market-stalls, ovens, baths are listed in their inventories. Tithes by the feudal lords from revenues of every kind, rich gifts from abroad and oblations of pilgrims filled the church treasuries.

Turning from clergy to institutions and organisation, we again face a dichotomy. On the one hand, the clergy was certainly opulent, and some of its representatives led a life which was a far cry from the austerity of the First Crusade, let alone any attempt to imitate the apostolic life which had flourished here a thousand years earlier. It is almost superflous to mention a patriarch who had a married woman as an official mistress. The latter even received from the Jerusalemites the title of 'Madam Patriarch'.[42] Even discounting the exaggerations of an acute observer like the Englishman Ralph Niger, it is impossible not to recall his description of the patriarch Heraclius who, on the eve of the destruction of the First Kingdom, came begging for material help from the West:

> I saw the patriarch of the Jerusalemites when he came to the West looking for help. He came with such a pomp of golden and silver equipment that it was sickening to hear his request because of the

[42] *Ernoul*, 86.

constant jangle. Add to it the many and different aromatics and spices which they drank and of which even their attire reeked and it made your head turn. I saw his chapel and the like I never saw in my life, certainly not a more costly one. To sum it up: no patriarch in the Western world ever appeared with such pomp. If we have to judge other luxuries of that land (Palestine) according to what we saw, we can safely presume that there is a great deal which is odious to God. And those who came from this land are telling even stronger tales.[43]

Naturally these were extremes, but the picture as a whole was not wholesome.

Even when discounting a good part of what was said by Jacques de Vitry, bishop of Acre (a man with a permanent holier-than-thou attitude), one is inclined to accept his description of the riches of the Church, for which we have ample documentary proof:

'And when almost the whole world,' wrote the bishop of Acre, 'became tributary to the prelates of the Church and to the regular clergy through alms, donations and different gifts, the shepherd looked for the wool and milk of his sheep (Ezek. 34, 8), feasting himself but relinquishing the care of their souls. They even transmitted the the examples of treachery to their flocks. They became cows fattening on the mountains of Samaria; they became rich from the poverty of Christ, from His humility they became haughty, from his ignomy – opulent; overbearing and expanding they became from his patrimony. And this when God said to St Peter: "Feed my sheep" (John 21, 17) and we never found him saying "Fleece my sheep".'

Some of these prelates were court favourites and they reached the highest ranks of the clergy by royal choice; others, still, pious as they may have been, some learned, some uneducated – their list is not encouraging. In the best of cases, they were mediocre men and mediocre churchmen. They were a type of colonial clergy, men who arrived in the Holy Land and whom special social conditions and the renown of its shrines elevated to positions which they could hardly have reached through their own merits.

[43] 'De re militari et triplici via peregrinationis Jerosolimitanae', ed. G. B. Flahiff in *Mediaeval Studies*, 9 (1947), 181.

In church organization we again face a dichotomy : on the one hand, the new Latin Church is flourishing and expanding on an unprecedented scale. We are overwhelmed by the number of churches and monasteries built in the small area of the Holy Land in the two or three generations after the conquest. Even the hypercritical Jacques de Vitry, who has his greatest flights of lyrical élan when being nasty (which is more often than not), cannot but be impressed by the achievements of the Latin Church in the East :

> Old churches were repaired, and new ones built by the bounty of princes and the alms of the faithful, monasteries of regular monks were built in fitting places, parish priests and all things appertaining to the service and worship of God were properly and suitably established everywhere. [44]

But the same great impetus of individuals and institutions to find a foothold in the Holy Land brought about a very strong process of non-integration. Language differences led to ethnic groupings around particular churches. One could participate in the liturgy with little or no knowledge of Latin, but one could not be asked to follow sermons in an unknown language. Then there were local and deeply-ingrained traditions brought over *in toto* from Europe. Venetian, Pisan and Genoese, if not actually at war were hardly on speaking terms. They brought their own clergy and built their own parish churches dependent on their own cathedrals. Finally, the monasteries and the military orders usurped parish duties and privileges. Officially or semi-officially they were exempted from the local hierarchy and did not decline parish rivalry with the local clergy. They opened their churches for baptism when a city was under interdict; they did not refuse – though certainly for a consideration – Christian burial in times of interdict, nor to those barred from it by the local clergy. Clandestine marriages were celebrated and illegitimate unions, often prohibited by canon law, were performed. The upper hierarchy, lacking forceful personalities, was in no position to oppose these centrifugal powers, stemming from the heterogeneity of immigrant origin.

[44] *PPTS*, XI, 26.

Thus relations within the framework of ecclesiastical organization represent the same centrifugal tendencies which in politics were represented by the immunities and enclaves of the Italian communes and the military orders. As a whole they reflect and are symptomatic of the realities of a colonial state which never surmounted the problem of overlapping and competing institutions. The state failed to integrate its heterogeneous population, who tended to perpetuate its customs and divergencies even within the only common denominator, official religion.

XI

PILGRIMS, PILGRIMAGES AND THE 'HOLY GEOGRAPHY' OF THE HOLY LAND

It is a well known and baffling fact that Latin, the main language of the mediaeval sources, has no corresponding term for 'Crusade'. A crusader is *crucesignatus*, the man signed by a cross or the man who took the Cross, but the action of going on a Crusade and the Crusade itself are described in terms taken from a different set of religious experiences. The Crusade is normally *via Hierosolymitana* – the road to Jerusalem, or *peregrinatio* – pilgrimage. This strange phenomenon of semantics caused a good number of scholars to envisage the Crusades as an expansion of the pilgrimages, mainly differing from them by being armed. However, an armed pilgrims' caravan does not become a Crusade and the substitution of a lance for a staff does not turn a pilgrim into a crusader. Despite many features that Crusades and pilgrimages have in common, especially in the religious sphere, the Crusades did not develop organically out of pilgrimages, although the latter contributed to their formation. When Crusades tended to become armed pilgrimages or just pilgrimages (and as such they were hailed by Bernard of Clairvaux in the middle of the twelfth century), they undermined their raison d'être. Although we do not subscribe to the view that the Crusades were a special type of pilgrimage, there is no doubt that among the thousands who left home to join the great hosts, many regarded the Crusade as a collective armed pilgrimage and as an act which harboured the promise of individual and collective salvation. There will be pilgrimages as long as men believe in a sphere of contact between the divine and the human, and that all places being equal in the perspective of the eternal, some enjoy special grace because of events which occurred there or because they evoke memories which sublimate human thought, confirm faith and lead to a spiritual rebirth.

Even though the relation between Crusade and pilgrimage remains a subject for dispute among scholars, it is generally agreed that during the two hundred years of the Crusades, pilgrimages became one of the most apparent expressions of Christian religious practice, basically different in character from the great military expeditions. Great centres of pilgrimage existed before the Crusades and as a religious practice on the eve of the great movement the pilgrimage already had a millenial Christian tradition. Nevertheless the Crusades gave a new impetus to the practice and made the Holy Land the most desired aim of all pilgrimages, if not the most frequented.

Rome and the tombs of the Apostles, Santiago de Compostella (whose fortunes rose steeply in the twelfth century), Constantinople – each guarded jealously its precious relics and took pride in its sacred traditions, saints and well-attested miracles. Each country, province, and almost every church and monastery aspired to become a centre of pilgrimage, often by way of pious frauds, the manufacture of legends or even the body-snatching of saints and martyrs. The translation of Saint Mark from Alexandria to Venice counted as one of the most glorious feats ever performed by the 'queen of the Adriatic', immortalized by the beautiful mosaic in the tympanum of her cathedral.

The Holy Land, and more specifically Jerusalem, had the oldest tradition of pilgrimage, dating back to when Christianity split from Judaism and connected to the early traditions of ancient Israel. Among Jews the pilgrimage to Jerusalem remained a religious duty as long as the Temple stood. Christianity never raised pilgrimage to such importance as the *Haj* to Mecca and Medina, the holy cities of Islam, but in the course of time it did become an integral part of Christian practice.

Jewish tradition was still very much alive in the first centuries of Christianity, and there was a great deal of scholarly curiosity and nostalgia, which drew some of the early Christian fathers to the Holy Land. But pilgrimages became fashionable only in the fourth century, when Christianity became the official religion of the empire and following the example given by the Empress Helena, mother of Constantine the Great.

The fall of the Western empire and the Moslem invasions in the East did not interrupt pilgrimages. They not only continued, but a new concept of pilgrimage was shaped by factors seemingly far removed from religious life and experience. This new impetus was the practice of exiling offenders, apparently first introduced at the end of the ninth century in Ireland. Exile from the place of offence was normally an alternative to restitution or payment of damages. In time, exile abroad became imbued with new ideas. Wandering tended towards asceticism, since an exile was often forced to lead a life of rigorous austerity. In addition, current beliefs regarding direct intercession by saints or martyrs and the greater weight of prayers in places endowed with special grace began (in the ninth century) to change the *peregrinatio* – wandering in a foreign land – into a 'pilgrimage', which involved a specific geographical aim as well as a spiritual purpose. Part of this change could be attributed to the crimes committed by aimless vagabonds which led temporal and ecclesiastical authorities to legislate against their misdeeds and excesses. But the concept of pilgrimage as a penance was more important. An offender undertook a pilgrimage to a holy shrine in order to redeem his sins. The pilgrimage was thus a temporal punishment and a spiritual preparation, since fervent prayer would invoke saintly intercession. But often, especially in later periods, a pilgrimage was imposed as part of the compensation the offender owed to his victim. Pilgrimage and prayer, like almsgiving and mass, were performed to save the soul of the victim.

Although the introduction of pilgrimage into the codes of criminal law during the early Middle Ages could have propagated the practice, other factors were also at work. Current belief held a pilgrimage to be a meritorious act of faith. As previously stated, this was based on the belief that prayer at given places sanctified by tradition and enriched with holy relics was more efficacious and had a better chance of reaching heaven. This concept was never entirely accepted by the doctors of the Church. Among the fathers there was even criticism of the practice. Consequently, an ambivalent attitude developed, as in the case of St Jerome, who settled in the Holy Land. A more spiritual or Pauline interpretation of Christianity endeavoured to control the deeply human need of common men and simple believers to approach and touch the earthly vestiges of holiness. But popular belief finally had its way.

Among all sites of pilgrimages, Jerusalem had the place of honour and the pilgrimage of the Empress Helena decisively influenced what was later to become the 'Holy Geography' of the Holy Land. Localities connected with the Old Testament were fairly well known at the time of the empress, as we can easily perceive from Eusebius's *Onomasticon*. The traditions of the New Testament were in the process of formation. Eventually not only cities and villages were identified, but actual streets and houses connected with the life of Jesus in Jerusalem, Bethlehem and Nazareth and their surroundings were 'placed' on the holy map. From the site of the Annunciation to the Crucifixion and Resurrection, it was possible to trace a topographic sequence. Sanctuaries were soon built to commemorate these events and offer consolation to the pious.

The desire to visualize the sacred events embodied in this process ultimately led to the 'identification' of sites even for the Apocrypha. By the time of the Crusades the whole land had been mapped accordingly. With the establishment of the Latin kingdom and the opening of regular lines of communication with the West, the Holy Land became the focal point of pilgrimage.[1]

Twice yearly, around Easter and then again in midsummer, numerous fleets gathered in the ports of southern Europe before setting sail for the Levant. Many a ship steered towards Moslem Alexandria, the greatest emporium in the Mediterranean, and then continued to Acre, Antioch and even farther to Constantinople before returning. Other ships would sail directly to the Holy Land, although they might continue from there to Egypt, Cyprus and the Byzantine empire on their homeward journey. These ships were basically commercial vessels and almost all carried a type of merchandise new since the Crusades – pilgrims.

[1] An exhaustive list of pilgrims in antiquity and in the Middle Ages was drawn up by the H. Leclercq in *Dict. de l'archéologie et de la liturgie chrétienne*, s.v. *Pèlerinage*.

Pilgrims in such numbers, moved by considerations remote from gain and earthly riches, marked a new departure in the history of passenger traffic and commerce in Europe. From the purely economic point of view the presence of pilgrims aboard the ships was of the utmost importance in the twelfth century, since ships going to the East had little cargo, whereas those returning from the Levant needed space for their imports. The pilgrims thus played the role of live ballast on the way East and made shipping more lucrative and commercially viable. Instead of a few merchants taking precious metals to the Levant, hundreds and thousands of passengers embarked for the Holy Land. The famous Catalan code of maritime customs – the *Consulado del mar* – uses the Spanish word *pelegri* as synonymous with 'passenger', a reflection of the revolution which had taken place in European commerce.

The distinction between pilgrim and merchant was sharp and no pilgrim was allowed to bring aboard anything but his personal belongings. Naturally, a merchant might turn pilgrim and visit the holy places once his business was transacted. But as commerce with the Levant became more and more specialized, with the same merchants making the trip again and again, few would repeat a pilgrimage.

Although the major 'season' of commerce and pilgrimage began around Easter,[2] the skippers – often themselves shipowners – started hiring their crews in December. Signing on sailors was often a problem. Large ships needed around a hundred or more sailors and craftsmen and the number of vessels going to the Levant was constantly growing. As the usual contract covered only one round trip, each voyage meant a new effort at recruiting. The demand for sailors was constantly growing, while the supply was not easily forthcoming. Wages were not low but a sailor's life was hard. From the moment of signing on for a round trip – usually for not less than half a year – the sailor became almost a serf to his ship and master. Iron discipline was the rule during the voyage, sentences against misconduct were summary, cutting off ears and hands,

---

[2] On maritime commerce, see cap. XVI, Economic Life and Commerce: C.

keelhaulings and brutal floggings were normal. Food was scanty and often abominable. The danger of being captured by Moslem or Christian pirates and sold into slavery was always present, not to mention the hazards of the sea itself.

One of the reasons for joining a crew, beside a basic love of adventure, was the officially accepted practice of combining sailing with commerce. As a rule, sailors were allowed to bring with them a given amount of merchandise without transport charges and there was always a chance that a lucky deal would bring in enough capital to become a merchant. Naturally, only a few did well for themselves. The overwhelming majority would join when young and go to the Levant as long as they had the strength to endure. They would marry and leave their wives and children at home hoping one day to strike it rich or at least to rise in the ship's hierarchy. At this time a sailor's profession was still honourable; it was only in later centuries that convicts and slaves were chained to the oars.

The main departure points for the East were Marseilles, Genoa, Pisa and Venice. Other ports, like Barcelona and some towns in Provence and southern Italy, also shipped to the Levant, although the big maritime powers did their best to monopolize the lucrative transport business. During the twelfth century Genoa virtually forbade the transport of pilgrims from the cities of Languedoc. For a short time Pisa succeeded in overtaking Genoa and assumed the leading role. But in the thirteenth century Montpellier, Marseilles, Saint-Gilles (and from the middle of that century the newly built royal port of Aigues Mortes) competed among themselves and against the Italian maritime powers. The commune of Marseilles formally requested from foreign ships which put into its harbour a solemn oath not to transport any pilgrim along the coast as far as Monaco ! A similar policy was pursued by other cities, with more proclamations and oaths than results. The passenger business was too lucrative to avoid hectic competition. The European cities went so far as to limit the number of pilgrims' ships equipped by crusader bodies. The Templars and the Hospitallers for example were allowed only one yearly shipment of pilgrims from Marseilles to the Holy Land.

Braving the late snows and the rains of early spring, the roads leading south from England, France and Germany filled with pilgrims on their way to the Holy Land. Scandinavians going to Jerusalem – the *Yorsalafari* – sometimes took the overland road to Rome and embarked at one of the Italian ports, but others would take the land route via the immense plains of Russia to Kiev, the Black Sea and Constantinople, continuing from there to the Holy Land.

Nothing was more socially heterogeneous than a crowd of pilgrims. Chaucer's pilgrims seem a select body by comparison. A nobleman accompanied by two young squires with pack horses would head a train, followed by monks and priests or wealthy burgess, all on the road to purification. Some carried money, jealously hidden and guarded ; the wealthier used a credit system and transmitted their funds to one of the banking houses in Italy or deposited money with the local priory of the Templars or Hospitallers, to be refunded on reaching their destination. But others deliberately refused to provide themselves for the road, begging all along the way in accordance with the precepts of Jesus to his apostles. The *pera et baculum* (the scrip and the staff) coming down from the late classical antiquity were the outward signs of a pilgrim, usually given to him by the local priest in the manor, village or home parish before departure. Some inveterate pilgrims wore shells or tiny leaden figures sewn on their cloaks or hats, signs of former pilgrimages to Santiago de Compostella or Rome. All had red crosses sewn onto their hats, tunics or even between their shoulders on their backs. Some pilgrims led a life of utmost asceticism, wearing hair shirts and iron chains around their bodies (made from swords in cases of homicide). The long flowing beard, curly uncut hair and dirty body proclaimed the wandering penitent.

In the port of embarkation the pilgrim would often find himself in the company of people from his own country. If fortunate he would lodge with his compatriots in a local hospice built by the bounty of Christian princes, or more often (as hospices were never numerous) in a local tavern. These port taverns were notorious and could often hardly be distinguished from bawdy houses. The common sleeping quarters, and the normal habit of sleeping two or more to a bed did not contribute greatly to the elevation of morals. Unaccompanied women were forbidden to go on a pilgrimage, but this prohibition was often evaded and even male company could not assure adequate protection. A German proverb has it: 'Departing as a pilgrim, returning as a whore'.

The signing on for transportation to the East was done amidst the noise and hustle of the public square. In Venice the pilgrim was greeted by a forest of ships' flags in the Piazza San Marco overlooking the entrance of the *Canale Grande*. Under each pole the ship's scribe and captain stood soliciting prospective passengers. They proclaimed the merits of individual ships – some significantly called 'The Holy Spirit', 'The Paradise' and the like – the captain's skill, the crew's experience and the excellence of the food. This would finally induce a pilgrim to choose his vessel. After signing the passage contract the captain would invite his new passengers to a dinner aboard ship, serving a huge meal the like of which they were not destined to taste until their homecoming. The pilgrim was at last persuaded – as any modern tourist – that he had the better of the bargain and the spicy meal with its sweet wines so delectable to the northern palate put him into a state of euphoric anticipation of the spiritual and earthly delights of the Orient.[3]

As cheating was an inseparable part of business, the city authorities had to intervene, if not to save the pilgrim, at least to save the good name of the city and assure the continuance of live cargo for the twice yearly *passagia* to the Levant. A copy of the passage agreement contracted between the captain and the pilgrim had to be deposited with the city authorities and could be used for litigation. The contracts listed the cost of passage, the obligations of the captain, the amount of space reserved for the pilgrim, the food

---

[3] Transportation contracts were very often the object of special legislation and were detailed in the maritime codes or communal codes of the period. J.M. Pardessus, *Collections des lois maritimes antérieures au XVIIIe siècle*, Paris, 1828. See also W. Ashburner, *The Rhodian Sea-Law*, Oxford, 1909, introduction. A first-hand description of the procedure is furnished by the 15th-century German pilgrim Felix Fabri, *Evagatorium*, Eng. transl. in *PPTS*, VII-X. Cf. E. Wohlaupter, 'Beiträge zum Recht der Personenbeförderung über See im Mittelalter, *Historisches Jahrbuch d. Görergesellschaft*, 57 (1937).

furnished by the ship's kitchen and the food allowed to be taken by the pilgrim, the time to be spent in the Holy Land, sometimes (especially in a later period) the captain's obligation to care for lodgings and organize the tour of the Holy Land. Last but not least, the pilgrim would stipulate the details of his eventual funeral in case of death during the voyage.

The *stola* or convoy going to the East was normally composed of merchant ships, but occasionally escorted by oar-driven swift war galleys.[4] Some of the transports which carried fodder and horses resembled modern landing craft. Below water their hulls were converted to stables and a kind of drawbridge at the stern facilitated the embarkation and debarkation of the animals. The different maritime codes of the period made it obligatory to have the commune's supervisors on board and sometimes an official, called 'consul' would be in charge of the whole convoy, with powers over the passengers, merchants and crews. Foreign pilgrims were often requested to swear an oath of allegiance and obedience to the city of embarkation for the duration of the voyage.

The Mediterranean ship – heir to the Roman tradition, but influenced by Byzantium and Islam – was remarkably well designed for its purpose. There was little comfort, but this was hardly expected by a pilgrim resolved on penance. The largest ships might be 110 feet long, but most were only half that size. The larger ships measured 41 feet across at the widest point and were 39 feet deep; they could actually transport more than 1,000 people, in addition to 100 or 150 sailors and had a displacement of 500 to 600 tons.

Most pilgrims' ships and large transports were sail driven. The fighting ships or smaller merchant vessels also used oars. A long row of benches on both sides was constructed for the rowers and a bench for two or three rowers was stepped so as to allow free movement, each rower pulling an oar of different length. Some-

---

[4] On ships see the still classical A. Jal, *Glossaire nautique*, Paris, 1848, and *Archéologie navale*, 2 vols. Paris, 1839. See also the very important study by E. H. Byrne, *Genoese Shipping in the Twelfth and Thirteenth Centuries*, Cambridge Mass., 1930, and recently M. Mollet, 'Problèmes navales de l'histoire des Croisades', *Cahiers de civilisation médiévale*, 10 (1967), 345–59.

times two to five rowers would work a single heavy oar some 40 feet long.

The main propulsive power was the wind. A large mast planted amidship was crossed by a beam near its top, the *antenna*, which held the main sail. This was usually a triangle of cotton or stronger canvas. In the twelfth century a single mast was the rule, but later two- and three-masters developed. Steering was by double rudders (the *timons*), two large oars on both sides of the ship often handled by several men. Later the rudders moved to the stern, which greatly improved control of the ship.

When loading and embarkation of the passengers were completed the ship was started on its voyage by a solemn prayer and sometimes a procession. A pilgrims' song, like the German 'In Gottes Namen fahren wir' raised the spirits of passengers faced – perhaps for the first time in their lives – with the immense expanse of the sea. Many a pilgrim must have made a silent vow and addressed a special prayer to St Peter or St Nicholas – patron of seamen – whose remains were guarded at Bari.

A modern reader can hardly visualize the difficulties of a mediaeval sea voyage. The average pilgrim was allocated a 'place' below deck some 6 feet in length and just a little more than 2 feet in width in an unventilated and confined hold running the length of the ship. On this reserved space (often marked with chalk), jealously guarded against trespassers, the pilgrim would deposit his chest and mattress. In theory, the pilgrim would be on deck all day and at night people asleep do not or should not move anyway.

The long row of mattresses along both sides of the hold extended from the 'castle', a defensive superstructure at the prow, to the 'castle' at the stern, where more space could be had by better-paying merchants. The mattresses, often put on the oblong chests of the pilgrims (which also served as coffins in case of death) were arranged in parallel lines, the feet of the sleeping pilgrims in one line almost touching the heads of the next. A narrow passage was supposed to remain free between the lines of mattresses, but this was normally encumbered by baggage.

Where there were ships there were rats. The Catalan *Consulat de la mar* made it obligatory for a ship's captain to keep cats on board if he wanted to avoid paying for goods destroyed by the rats. But rats were not the greatest nuisance. Some travellers – ascetic pilgrims – vowed not to cut their hair or wash during the whole voyage. Their state of cleanliness must have been already appalling when they came aboard after a month or two of travelling on land, and the sea voyage could only have aggravated this condition. Dirt was not restricted to ascetics. The Catalan code ordered that no sailor had the right to undress during the whole voyage except when the ship was in harbour. If the sailor presumed to undress he would be forcefully plunged several times into the sea or might lose his wages !

If the morning found a good number of pilgrims pale and seasick it spared them at least the notorious ship's fare. A glance at a sailor's menu in a well-organized fleet (proposed by Marino Sanudo at the beginning of the fourteenth century for the *reconquista* of the Holy Land) gives us some idea about the roughness of life aboard ship. [5] The *pièce de résistance* was the sailor's bread, the *biscoctum*, of which he received a daily ration of $1\frac{1}{2}$ pounds. This he could soak in sweet wine (served daily in these coffee- and tea-less ages), the first morning drink and nourishment. One ounce of cheese per day and a pittance of vegetables, mostly beans or other leguminous plants, were also shared out daily. Meat – salt pork – amounted to a meagre $3\frac{1}{4}$ pounds per month. These rations cooked with vegetables were served every second day, Sunday being naturally the day of meat dishes. On alternate days a kind of vegetable soup was the main dish. These standard rations were sometimes varied by fresh vegetables, fruit and water from the numerous ports of call during the six-to eight-week voyage. In these circumstances it was really left to the pilgrim to take care of himself. He was allowed to bring aboard vegetables, fruit, wine and most important of all, live chickens. Special cages held these live provisions and the transport contract stipulated his right to use the ship's kitchen. A new profession grew up in the ports of embarkation, that of the *cargator*, a kind of caterer who supplied ship and pilgrim according to specifica-

---

[5] A sailor's menu is described in detail by Marino Sanudo, *Liber secretorum fidelium crucis*, in Bongars, *Gesta Dei per Francos*, Hanover, 1611.

tions. To prevent cheating and restrictive practices, relatives of ships' captains were barred. With all these new facilities it is clear that a pilgrim's voyage to the Holy Land was far from a pleasure cruise. More than one pilgrim was thus accomplishing a real penance, perhaps more than was imposed on him, or more than he bargained for.

The heterogeneous crowd of pilgrims included an unholy sprinkling of knaves and prostitutes. In a voyage of six weeks this could undermine the most stubborn spirits. The municipality of Marseilles was not alone in seeking to curb prostitution in the city, or at least relegate its practice to certain quarters. Women of easy virtue were fined if they wore good clothes and conspicuously expensive dresses, thereby causing many a good man to mistake them for real ladies. The municipality instructed its consuls aboard ships sailing to the Holy Land to prevent the transportation of prostitutes and more especially to prohibit their taking up residence in the commune's houses or quarters overseas.[6] We do not know how far these regulations were obeyed. In the middle of the thirteenth century the pope had to write a strongly worded letter to the clergy of Acre about renting church property to prostitutes. The temptation was strong, since prostitutes readily paid the highest rents.

In the twelfth century ships usually sailed close to the land and hopped from island to island, but in the thirteenth they ventured onto the high seas. A small remnant of factual knowledge – some culled from Greek and Roman writings – floated in a pool of folklore from which sailors would spin endless yarns to frighten landlubbers. The tales of assorted sea monsters made the singing sirens innocent playmates. Graceful and harmless dolphins were, by legand turned into wicked giants who could freeze any man who dared look them in the eye. And what tales would not be told about the occasional misguided whale who found his way into the Mediterranean !

The sighting of another ship was no occasion for rejoicing. One

[6] *Les Statuts municipaux de Marseille*, ed. R. Pernoud, Paris-Monaco, 1949, spec. *Liber Quartus*, pp. 145–64.

never knew what to expect, even when recognizing the flag, since piracy was not restricted to professionals. When the 'War of the Communes' ravaged Acre in the middle of the thirteenth century and alliances were as quickly concluded as hostilities developed (accompanied by hoisting and lowering the flags of friend and foe) no ship was safe from assault, even when transporting pilgrims. Acts of piracy were common on the high seas, in Christian ports and not least in Acre, capital of the kingdom. Danger from man was as great as from the elements.

When, after six or eight weeks, the sandy beaches of the Holy Land were sighted, the joy of the pilgrims knew no end. The captain would skilfully manoeuvre his vessel along the rocky ridge which runs parallel to the coast west of Acre. Coming into the bay he would turn slowly to the west and then north, leaving behind Mount Carmel, and head into port by using the church of St Andrew for his bearings. Prayers of thanksgiving were intoned for the happy conclusion and deliverance, mixed with the ringing of bells in the city which signalled the arrival of a fleet.

During the season of the great *passagia*, larger ships must have anchored outside, since the harbour of Acre was relatively small. But unloading and customs formalities were completed in the port. The ship passed between strong twin towers at the edge of the jetties, each flanked by a wall joining the mainland fortifications. A strong iron chain stretched between these towers and was lowered during the day to permit entrance. Where the jetties joined the land a vaulted structure seems to have connected the city and the jetty walls.

Unloading was performed by stevedores or by pushing chests and bales along planks from the ship to the jetty. Once on the mainland and out of reach of the customs officials, our happy and weary pilgrim would arrange for lodgings and make his way to the cathedral church of Acre, the Holy Cross or to the church of his own nation in the city quarter where he could probably be lodged.

Starting from Acre the Christian pilgrim could choose one of the two most frequented routes in the Holy Land. One led to Lake Tiberias and then continued through Samaria and Judea to Jerusalem; another led from Acre due south along the coast and inland to Jerusalem. When much of the country became definitely Moslem, the latter road was more frequented, since it led through Christian territory. Around the middle of the thirteenth century holy and legendary geography of the Holy Land was minutely fixed until modern research played havoc with this charming canvas of credulity. The 'Pilgrims' Guide' of the thirteenth century offers an insight into a world where history and geography rub shoulders with mediaeval biblical exegesis, folklore and the most improbable identification of sites.[7]

From Acre the pilgrim made his way along the bay bearing the name of the city, a crescent of yellow sand here and there broken by a palm grove where the Na'aman or Belus river empties its lazy waters into the sea. Just across the bay rose the green gentle slopes of Mount Carmel, enclosing the southern tip of the bay. This was the prophet Elijah's mountain with his famous cave venerated even today by Jews and Moslems alike, and no less popular under the crusaders. It was also the birth-place of the Carmelite Order, organized in the middle of the twelth century by St Berthold, who brought together pious hermits living in the numerous caves of the mountain. Here they built their church dedicated to the Virgin, the cradle of the 'Order of Our Lady of Mount Carmel'.

Nearby was the Greek monastery of St Margaret, and between the Latin and Greek monastery a place (no longer identifiable) called 'Anne', claimed the sad honour of being the site where the nails of the Crucifixion were forged.

Strangely enough, St Denis, patron saint of Gaul, found his way to the mountain. In a small crusader village called 'Franchevilla', which may be identical with Palmarea (settled in the middle of the twelfth century at the initiative of the lord of Haifa), the pilgrim was assured that he was at the birth-place of the saint and was shown a well dug by his own hands. This puzzling localization of St Denis's birth-place probably rested on his erroneous identification with Dionysius Aeropagita, allegedly a Syrian. At the same time it

---

[7] The most complete enumeration of the holy places is to be found in a text known as 'Pèlrinages et Pardouns de Acre' written c. 1280, publ. in Itinéraires a Jérusalem, 229–36.

justified the name of the settlement, 'village of the Franks' (in reality 'village of liberties').

Descending from Mount Carmel the pilgrim went along the coast passing on his right ancient Shiqmona, which for some bizarre reason was known to Christians and Jews alike as 'Capharnaum', an identification rightly doubted by the more learned.

Some distance to the south our pilgrim would stop at the little village of Tira, whose church dedicated to St John belonged to the Greeks. Consequently the whole village was called St John of Tyre (or Tyr). Continuing south through the fertile plain of Sharon, flanked on the left (i.e. east) by the lower ranges of Mount Carmel and on the right by dunes rising to a ridge of small hills used for ages as stone quarries, the pilgrim found a small chapel called *Peroun*, a station where Jesus had allegedly rested. Here a narrow passage in the ridge opened to the promontory on which the mighty Chastel Pèlerin stood. This place, ancient 'Athlit or 'Castle of the Son of God' as it was originally called, belonged to the Templars. Since the fortress was only built in 1218 nobody would expect it to be connected with holy traditions. Nevertheless, not more than a decade later it was pointed out as the resting place of St Euphemia![8] How the virgin of Chalcedon martyred under Diocletian ever came to rest here baffles the imagination.

Returning to the main road the pilgrim would continue due south. Here a small fortress overlooked the calm bay where Dor of classical fame once stood. Called by the crusaders *Merle*, the blackbird, a creature more common on Mount Carmel than in the plain, it claimed to be the birth-place of St Andrew and a cave in the vicinity was pointed out as a hiding-place of Mary and Jesus.

The dunes and hillocks of the coast changed to marsh land some four miles southward. Mary – who had found temporary refuge in *Merle* – had also rested here, and a chapel of 'Notre Dame of the Marshes' commemorated this legendary event.

By now the pilgrim could perceive the splendid fortifications of Caesarea recently rebuilt by St Louis (1251). All around the crusader city – less than a tenth the size of the glorious Herodian

[8] *Ibid.*, p. 229.

capital – columns, capitals and marble slabs were strewn over the plain. Just outside the crusader city a chapel appropriately harboured the body of the centurion Cornelius, the Gentile who was baptized by St Peter in Caesarea.

The ancient Herodian hippodrome and the huge obelisk which served as a marker for chariot races fascinated the mediaeval pilgrim as it does the modern tourist. To find a 'holy' connotation for this monument was natural and it became in due course the 'Table of Jesus Christ', the two smaller conical pillars being the 'Candles of the Lord'. These wonders were supplemented by the tomb of the daughters of the apostle Philip, who baptized the eunuch. True that his daughters – celebrated for their prophetic powers – went to Assyria, but it seems that they returned to preach in Caesarea and were buried there.

To the south the pilgrim encountered marshy land near the Crocodile river. A chapel dedicated to Mary enjoyed some celebrity as a popular place of pilgrimage from Caesarea. There was also a village with the baffling name '*Peine Perdue*' or '*Pain Perdu*', also called the 'Tower of Saint Lazarus'.

The road then led to the ancient Semitic city of Rishpon – the Greek 'Apollonia' – 'Arsuf' in Arabic, often misnamed 'Assur' by the crusaders. The vicinity was dangerous for a lone pilgrim. A passage cut in the rock, called *Roche taillé* (an ancient drainage tunnel for the sluggish water of the Faliq river) was notorious as an ambush point of local robbers.

From here the pilgrim reached Jaffa and its unsafe harbour. The city of Jaffa was connected with the prophet Jonah, and also had a church of St Peter near the castle, which dominated the port. The city claimed the further glory of possessing the '*Perron Saint Jacques*', whence the body of St James was miraculously transported to Spain, where it made the fortune of Santiago de Compostella.

Further south the pilgrim entered land barren of holy associations. Ascalon with its ancient 'Green Mosque', which became a Christian church, offered neither relics nor indulgences. Gaza could boast memories of Samson, but had no special attractions for the pious traveller.

Usually the pilgrim turned from Jaffa or Caesarea towards

Ramleh on the crossroads to Jerusalem. In nearby Lydda with its magnificent Byzantine basilica and in Ramleh (where a plain but pure Romanesque cathedral was built by the crusaders) the pilgrim was shown the burial place of St George – patron saint of European knighthood. No other saint appeared more often to help the crusaders against their enemies. No wonder that Lydda, sometimes even Ramleh (built in the eighth century), was called the city of St George.

From here the pilgrim reached Beit Nuba, unless he chose the more southerly and picturesque – but very dangerous – road to *Toron des Chevaliers* (Latrun) identified with the *Spelunca Latronum*. A road through the Judean hills ultimately brought the pilgrim to a mountain-top overlooking Jerusalem from the north, Nabi Samwil or St Samuel. Venerated by the faithful of all three religions, the tomb of the prophet was called 'Montjoye' by the Franks, since from here the pilgrim first beheld the holy city.

Jerusalem, the goal of the Crusades and the ultimate aim of all pilgrims, stirred the deepest emotions. The Christian pilgrim knelt upon Montjoye and thanked God for having brought him within sight of his quest. The Jewish pilgrim beholding Jerusalem from Nabi Samwil (identified with the biblical Ramathaim) or from the Mount of Olives – if he came from the west or south – would tear his garments and recite a prayer for the deliverance of captive Zion from Christian and Moslem rule and for its re-establishment as the glorious 'City of David'. Under the crusaders neither Jew nor Moslem was allowed to settle in Jerusalem. After Saladin's conquest of the city some Jews settled in what later became the Jewish quarter, which continued to exist until its destruction by the Arab Legion after the 1948 war.[9]

The greatest sanctuary in Jerusalem was naturally the Holy Sepulchre. The church rebuilt in the first half of the twelfth century (consecrated in 1149) enclosed the remains of several Byzantine shrines partially restored at the end of the previous century. The small marble cubicle of the Sepulchre beneath the great dome of

[9] The Jewish quarter is now (since 1968) being rebuilt and resettled by the Israeli authorities.

the church was the holy of holies, and every Christian sect tried to secure some space in its vicinity and a fixed time for divine service.

The Calvary, the chapel of St Helena and a great number of smaller chapels – some in the possession of Greeks, Armenians, Jacobites and Copts – were visited commemorating the last hours of Jesus, his Crucifixion and Resurrection. Here also the curious pilgrims were shown 'the navel' (the centre of the world), a mediaeval belief based on a whimsical exegesis of some biblical passages. Mediaeval cartographers drew their maps accordingly, with Jerusalem as the central meeting point of Europe, Asia and Africa.

Upon leaving the Church of the Holy Sepulchre, the pilgrim passed the oldest Latin monastery and hospice of the city, antedating the Crusades – St Mary of the Latins – and nearby the new palace of the Order of St John, which continued to serve as a hospital under Moslem rule (after 1189). The street led across the teeming bazaars to the magnificent *Templum Domini*, as the Mosque of Omar was baptized by the Latins. Crossing the esplanade the pilgrim could visit the Templars' headquarters – the Mosque of al-Aqsa or the 'Temple of Solomon' – as it was called by the Christians ('Solomon's Academy' to the Jews).

The alleged 'Tomb of King David' and the chapel of the 'Descent of the Holy Spirit' and the 'Last Supper' on Mount Zion were also visited. Piety went so far as to localize the place where the crowing cock witnessed Peter's hesitation. A church of St Peter in *Gallicantu* (in the vernacular French, '*in Galicie*') graced the slopes of the hill.

Descending from here the pilgrim would visit the '*Hakel Dema*', '*Acheldema*' as it was called, i.e. the 'bloody field', the place of the betrayal of Jesus and now the poor pilgrims' cemetery. He would wind up his pious tour of Jerusalem by visiting the citadel, still called the 'Tower of David'. Then, further on, he reached the Latin cemetery around the Mamillah pool, which Christians and Jews alike claimed as the burial place of their martyrs, miraculously prevented by a ferocious lion from falling into impious hands. Mamillah ultimately became a Moslem cemetery (as it is today) uniting in death those who had fought in life for possession of the city.

Continuing westward the pilgrim reached the picturesque 'Valley of the Cross' with its ancient Georgian monastery and church. Here was the traditional place where the tree for the Cross was cut.

Every event in the Gospels, indeed, almost every step taken by Jesus was localized and a Christian sanctuary erected on the site. The '*Via Dolorosa*' with the pool of Bethesda, church of St Anne, Pilate's House, the 'Arch of *Ecce Homo*' (the latest addition) and the 'Stations of the Cross' are further examples of the effort to map 'holy history'.[10] But the complete pilgrims' tour led beyond the city, to the sanctuaries of Gethsemane, the Mount of Olives and St Lazarus's village of Bethany.

After Jerusalem the pilgrim made preparations to go east. This was rough country and pilgrims usually arranged for an escort before venturing towards the Jordan. The first station was the palm-studded oasis at Jericho, from which one of the most famous sites – the traditional place of Jesus' baptism in the Jordan – was within easy reach. Here amidst special celebrations the pilgrim would bathe in the Jordan, one of the highlights of every pilgrimage. From here he would also bring back the leaf or branch of a palm tree. In Europe these objects earned a returning pilgrim the title of 'Palmer'. He would then fill his flat flask with Jordan water. Later this could cause trouble with the ship's crew, since it was a common belief that the presence of Jordan water had a vast influence on the weather. In the event of a violent storm the pilgrim would be forced to part with his treasure and throw it into the sea.

Very few pilgrims dared actually to visit Mount Sinai and the tomb of St Catherine, the virgin martyr of Alexandria. The fabulous monastery built by Justinian in the heart of the desert remained in the hands of Greek monks who centuries before had succeeded in finding a *modus vivendi* with the Egyptian authorities and the local Bedouin. The crusaders reached the place around 1115, but left almost immediately so as not to endanger the helpless

[10] The elaboration of the Stations was a prolonged process. Some were added as late as the eighteenth century.

monks. The desert monastery was famous and the pilgrim would certainly have heard and later repeat or even incorporate in his tale the miracle of the transparent marble tomb and the miraculous oil which healed the sick and fed the ferocious beasts of the desert.

From the Jordan pilgrims usually returned to Jerusalem and visited the resplendent Byzantine church of the Nativity in Bethlehem, which the emperors continued to embellish even under crusader rule. The road passed the tomb of Rachel, venerated by all three religions, though naturally with greater fervour by the Jews. Bethlehem and its vicinity recalled the most human and popular narrative of the New Testament: the 'pit' where the guiding star of the Three Kings fell, the place where the Innocents were massacred at the orders of Herod, the place where the Angel announced the birth of Jesus to the shepherds and finally the site of the Nativity itself.

From Bethlehem a pilgrim sometimes ventured to Hebron, city of the patriarchs, with its famous 'Double Cave', miraculously rediscovered under Frankish rule in the second decade of the twelfth century. This place was also revered by all three religions and later endowed by the Moslem authorities with a famous *waqf* (an earlier one was created shortly after the conquest of the country by the Arabs in the seventh century). This was a pious foundation which supplied weary pilgrims with food and refreshment. The Christian pilgrim could admire not far from here a very old tree where Abraham received the three angels, which in the Christian exegesis presaged the Holy Trinity.

Some pilgrims continued their journey to the north, returning to Jerusalem and then striking out through the mountainous country on the east to Samaria. In Nablus they would be shown the place where Jesus spoke to the Samaritan woman and in the beautiful basilica at Sebaste they would be shown the place where St John was decapitated. From here they continued via Mount Tabor to Galilee.

In the thirteenth century pilgrims would usually forgo visiting Samaria and use Acre as a base for their travels. The road passed by a small Frankish castle at Shafr'am, renamed 'Safran' by the crusaders. A very recent tradition connected the place with St James and St John, but another located the church of St Saffroun at this spot. This is undoubtedly composed of the place name and perhaps that of St Sophronius, patriarch of Jerusalem, who witnessed the fall of his capital into Moslem hands (638). From here, past the alleged tomb of St Nicholas, the pilgrim reached Saphorie, with its small castle on the hill and a lovely Romanesque church in the valley, another alleged birth-place of St Anne. From a nearby fountain the Frankish host started on the fatal march to the battle-field of Hittin.

Nazareth with its memories of the childhood and youth of Jesus was another important pilgrim centre. The main site was the church of the Annunciation, but there was also the carpenter's workshop of St Joseph, and the well of Mary on the outskirts of the city. The most dramatic place was the '*Saltus Domini*', an abrupt rock over-looking the main road which led from the plains to hilly Nazareth. From Nazareth the pilgrim would turn to Cana in Galilee, where he would be shown the traces of the two jars used at the famous marriage.

The road led now through Naim, where Jesus resuscitated the son of the widow, to Lake Tiberias and its associations with the apostles and the miracles of Jesus. The birth-place of St Peter and St Andrew would be shown, as also Capharnaum and the *Mensa Christi*, the spot where the multitude was fed with five fishes and two loaves. Even the place where Jesus was arrested and imprisoned until St Peter caught a fish and opening it found a *denarius* to pay the toll was duly identified and shown. The very waters of the lake and its fish were venerated.

Returning from Tiberias through the mountains of Galilee the pilgrim beheld high on a hill top the tremendous castle of Saphet, rebuilt in the middle of the thirteenth century at the initiative of Benedict d'Alignan, bishop of Marseilles. The place was un-known in antiquity, but acquired a holy genealogy under Frankish rule by locating there the burial cave of Tobias.

On his way back the pilgrim could still visit majestic Mount Tabor, which dominated the Valley of Jezreel, a mountain de-scribed in modern times as an altar erected to the glory of God. A tortuous road led to the summit, but the pilgrim was rewarded by praying in the place of the Transfiguration and the Sermon on the Mount (claimed also by a hill near Tiberias).

Finally the pilgrim would reach Acre again. Though the biblical associations of the town were nil, this only spurred pious invention. 'Acco or 'Acca was erroneously identified with the biblical 'Ekron. The city thus received sacred credentials and its name was mispronounced (and used in this form all over the world) as Acre. From here it was only a step to identifying the main tower at the port's entrance with the 'Tower of Flies', the *Ba'al Zebub* of biblical 'Ekron. Here the pagans were believed to have offered their sacrifices and the flies were attracted to the blood of the freshly slaughtered animals, which gave the name to the tower.

Nevertheless, Acre never acquired much in the way of holy associations. What it lacked in biblical memories was offset by the profusion of indulgences accorded to visiting pilgrims. Nearly every church and monastery offered some to the praying pilgrim. Even the seashore assured four years and forty days of indulgences. A list from the late thirteenth century totals more than three hundred years of indulgences!

XII

THE ORIENTAL
CHURCHES

The main theme of Urban's famous speech at Clermont was an appeal to succour the Christians of the East, threatened by Moslem invasions. It is therefore with some astonishment that we read a letter sent to the pope on 11 September 1098 by the leaders of the First Crusade after the capture of Antioch:

> We conquered the Turks and pagans, but we could not defeat the heretics, the Greeks and Armenians, Syrians and Jacobites. We request then and repeat our request, our beloved father, that . . . you should come . . . and you, who are the vicar of St Peter, should sit in his see (that is in Antioch), and will have us, your sons, obedient to do the right things and all the heresies whatever they might be, you will eradicate and destroy by your authority and our valour. [1]

A strange proclamation indeed coming from an army bent on saving oriental Christendom! Whereas the Monophysite sects were officially heretical, this hardly applied to the Greek-Orthodox Church of Byzantium. Although relations between Rome and Constantinople had been broken off since the middle of the eleventh century and never re-established, the Byzantine Church was not regarded as heretical.

With the foundation of the Latin kingdom, one of the major problems which faced the conquerors was the policy to be adopted towards the local Christians. In all countries under Moslem domination, the Church (like the synagogue) was the focus not merely of religion, but also of community life. The clergy ruled

[1] *Die Kreuzzugsbriefe aus den Jahren 1088–1100*, ed. H. Hagenmayer, Innsbruck, 1901, Ep. 16, p. 164.

the community and officially represented it. Ecclesiastical policy thus meant in reality general policy towards oriental Christendom.

On the eve of the crusader conquest the basic division of rulers and ruled in the Holy Land was expressed in terms of the unbridgeable chasm which separated Islam from Christianity. 'Islam' or the 'Law of the Saracens' were the two terms used by crusader propaganda to stir the West. This also played up the horrifying idea of the Holy Sepulchre held captive by the Infidel.

The encounter with the Christian East beyond the walls of Constantinople must have caused the crusaders considerable bewilderment. 'Oriental Christendom' proved to be an abbreviation for an extremely complex phenomenon, and covered half a dozen communities divided by a common religion.

The swift rumours which preceded the approaching armies of the First Crusade created a climate of tense expectation in the East. A contemporary Hebrew letter from the Balkans reveals that there was even a Christian Messianic movement in the peninsula.[2] In oriental Christian literature the Turks were often represented as Gog and Magog, and the crusaders as the Divine host soon to participate in smiting Satan on the battlefield of Armageddon. The Armenian Matthew of Edessa saw the crusader movement as the fulfilment of a prophecy by the venerable Armenian patriarch Narses :

It was by employing the arm of the Franks that God wanted to combat the Persians (= Turks). . . They came to break the chains of the Christians, to liberate the holy city of Jerusalem from the yoke of the Infidels and to take by force from the hands of the Moslems the venerated tomb which received God.[3]

The Jacobite, Michael the Syrian, recorded the following piece of wishful thinking :

The Franks who crossed the sea, assembled and promised to the Lord, that if they were granted to enter Jerusalem, they will live in peace

---

[2] The letter was published several times. Best edition by J. Mann, 'Messianic Movements during the Early Crusades' (Heb.), *Hatekufa*, 23, 253 ff.

[3] Matthieu d'Edesse in E. Delaurier, *Bibl. hist. armén.*, 212–13.

with all Christian confessions and will bestow churches and convents on all nations which confessed Christ. [4]

The word 'liberation' comes often from the pen of oriental Christian writers but to whatever they may have referred, it was certainly not to any notion of a free Christian statehood. Whereas the Greeks of Antioch could still dream about the return of the Byzantine empire – which would restore their former position as rulers in the Syrian capital – and the Armenians of the Taurus and Cilicia could have envisaged political autonomy without Greek or Turkish encroachment, such visions were obviously out of the question for the Jacobites, Nestorians, Syrians and Copts. The first three could not look back to any traditions of statehood or independence. Their religions had at no time been identified with a territory or with an ethnic group. It was somewhat different for the Egyptian Copts, but whatever their feelings, their Moslem neighbours did not regard them as anything more than '*dhimmis*', protected clients of a Moslem state. The only exception was the Lebanese Maronites, who evolved from a territorial and, possibly, ethnic group and found cohesion in their faith, though they were scorned by Greeks and Monophysites alike.

For the oriental Christian sects 'freedom' meant – in the best of cases – freedom of worship, and this had never been associated with Christian domination. Moslem rulers rather than Christians liberally granted freedom of worship. 'They did not' wrote Michael the Syrian 'inquire about the profession or faith, nor did they persecute anybody because of his profession as did the Greeks, a heretic and wicked nation. [5] The sons of Magog, as he calls the Turks, 'ruled with God's permission', and this put the heretic persecutors [Greeks] into a state of anxiety. Thus they [the Turks] did not force the orthodox [that is the Jacobites], as is their [the Greeks'] cruel custom, to convert themselves to their heresy. [6]

Fear and hatred of the 'Chalcedonian' – the Greek-Byzantine Church – is the permanent *Leitmotif* in the great historical narrative

4 Michel le Syrien, III, 183.
5 *Ibid.* 222.
6 *Ibid.* 221.

of Michael the Syrian (twelfth century). And the same sentiments are reflected in the sources from which he drew his information on earlier periods. This also applies to a thirteenth-century man of letters, the famous Abu 'l Faraj ibn 'Ibri (Bar Hebraeus), a Jacobite and son of converted Jews. Fear of the Greeks is never forgotten by the Armenians of Asia Minor, or by the Copts of Egypt.

This historical experience of Armenian, Jacobite and Copt, could partly explain the hesitant welcome extended to the armies of the First Crusade in the oriental Christian sources. The Alexandrain Copt Sawirus ibn al-Mukaffa' has only a short paragraph to describe the events:

> In the days of Abba Michael (the Coptic patriarch of Alexandria) armies of the Romans (al-Rum) and the Franks arrived from Rome and from the lands of the Franks in Syria in great multitudes, and they gained the possession of Antioch and its district and most of Upper Syria . . . Then they gained the possession of the noble city of Jerusalem (al-Quds al-Sharif) . . . We, the community of the Christians, the Jacobites and the Copts did not join in the pilgrimage (al-Haj) to Jerusalem.[7]

Since freedom of worship was the great dream of all Christian sects, the Christian East set its attitude to the Frankish newcomers by this criterion.

Seen from this perspective, the liberation of Jerusalem from the Moslems did not mean as much to the orientals. They could hardly have expected that the holy places would be handed over to them by the crusaders; at best they might gain something at the expense of the Greek Church. There was also a chance to be free from extortions, often a substitute for taxes in Moslem states.

Moreover, the shrines of the Holy Land must have been viewed differently by the oriental sects. There were certainly Eastern pilgrimages to Jerusalem and to the Holy Sepulchre. The feast of the 'Holy Fire' was common to all orientals, but Jerusalem is

---

[7] *History of the Patriarchs*, pp. 398–9. The Coptic historian employs the expression 'al-Haj'–'pilgrimage' for the Crusade. This parallels the European 'peregrinatio' or 'via Hierosolymitana'.

conspicuously absent from the copious writings of Jacobites, Copts and Armenians. Jerusalem became the goal of European ambitions and the Franks felt that they were coming into a legitimate heritage, calling the state 'Kingdom of David'. Nothing of this feeling is found among oriental Christians. Michael the Syrian writes in the shadow of his great Jacobite saint – Bar Sauma – and not of the Holy Sepulchre. Neither Copt, Jacobite nor Armenian ever elevated Jerusalem to the rank of a patriarchate, rarely even a bishopric. Material factors, such as the absence of a large community, certainly contributed to this attitude, but in themselves they are hardly a sufficient explanation. A different perspective and a different religious focus was decisive.

Jerusalem is called by the Copts and by the Moslems *al-Sharif* – 'the Noble'; the Jacobite and Copt will even consecrate bishops destined for other places in the holy city, or a new patriarch will make his first appointment to the see of Jerusalem,[8] piously quoting Luke (24, 27 – Syrian version): 'All begins in Jerusalem', but their interests are elsewhere. One has to compare their attitude with that of the Jews in a not dissimilar political situation, to visualize this difference in the oriental Christians' view of the Holy Land and its shrines.

Whatever the expectations of the Eastern sects, reality proved to be grim indeed. Crusader rule was from the beginning ruthless, and the years of conquest were a period of wholesale suffering. The fact that oriental Christians spoke Arabic, wore beards and dressed in the Moslem fashion made them very often the victims of war and spoliation. But even later, when the Franks learned to distinguish between them and the Moslems, the 'Syrians' always remained suspect.

But the main test was in the sphere of worship and religion. In the sanctuaries the crusaders lost their first encounter with Eastern Christendom, and though some wrongs were later righted, the earliest events were not forgotten. Nothing could be more illuminating than the record of the Armenian historian Matthew of

[8] Michel le Syrien, III, 480. n. 26.

Edessa who, like many of his compatriots, favoured the Franks. In 1102, he affirms, God had to intervene directly to threaten the Franks. The 'Holy Fire' on the tomb of Christ did not descend on Saturday and only the prayers of the true believers (that is the Monophysites) made it appear at all, although a day later. And all that because 'the Franks expelled from the monasteries the Armenians, the Greeks, the Syrians and the Georgians.' After the miracle, though, the Franks repented and 're-established each nation in what belonged to it'.[9] The Copt chronicler Sawirus ibn al-Mukaffa' says explicitly that after the capture of Jerusalem, the Copts did not continue their customary pilgrimage to the holy city 'on account of what is known of their [the Franks'] hatred of us, as also, their false beliefs concerning us and their charge against us of impiety.'[10]

The crusaders missed the right hour or the right occasion and the oriental Christians never became their allies. At times, a local community might favour their domination, but as a whole they evaded involvement. The crusaders never put them on a par with the immigrant Latin population; normally, they were perhaps better treated than the Moslems but not conspicuously so. Were we to draw conclusions only from the legal treatises of the kingdom, we would hardly find much difference in the attitude of the crusaders to the various Christian sects and, strangely enough, even to non-Christians: they were equal before the law, enjoyed internal autonomy and were guaranteed safety of life and possessions. Although there were differences of legal status, this does not seem to have been connected with religious or ethnic groupings. There were Moslem as well as Christian (Syrian and Greek) villeins, some bound to the soil, some not. At the same time, members of all sects (including Moslems and Jews) inhabited cities, paying a poll-tax (*capitatio*), but had freedom of movement, although they were naturally not burgesses. Some oriental Christians even made careers in the army, or as royal retainers. Nevertheless, though certainly not worse off than their co-religionists under

[9] Matthieu d'Edesse in E. Delaurier, *Bibl. hist. armén.*, 233–4.
[10] *History of the Patriarchs*, 399.

Moslem domination, the sympathies of the local Christians were seldom more than superficial. An event like the fall of Jerusalem or Tripoli into the hands of the Moslems would cause an oriental prelate to write a mournful dirge, but its main theme was the profanation of a Christian sanctuary, not its loss by the crusaders.

The egalitarian trend in policy towards all oriental sects and even Jews and Moslems, did not extend to the ecclesiastical sphere. The former was established by laymen who had to contend with realities, the latter was more influenced by the Church, where theology, as well as material interests and often the policy of the Holy See were decisive.

Most affected by the crusader conquest was the Greek-Orthodox Church. In the northern principalities a large number of its adherents were of Byzantine origin, but to the south in the Latin kingdom, its main adherents were the Syrians. These were natives of the Holy Land or neighbouring countries who spoke Arabic but followed the Greek rite. The Syrian Greeks could look back on a thousand years of history with periods of glory, as under the Late Roman Empire, and some gloomy interludes under Islam. But the position of the Greek Church was strong, its property extensive and there was always the possibility of Byzantine intervention, a weighty argument in the policy of Islamic rulers. This changed overnight with the crusader conquest. Partly caused by bad relations with the Byzantine emperor and the ensuing suspicions of adherents of the Greek Church, this change was mainly due to theological differences.

Unlike the Jacobites and Nestorians, the Greek Church was not heretical. Though the Greek-Orthodox were temporarily not in communion with Rome, both churches were different parts of the same body. Consequently, so argued the crusaders, there was no place for a double hierarchy and that of the Greeks had to be abolished and replaced by Latins. The Greek Church thus lost its upper hierarchy and their clergy remained only at the lowest level, obviously under higher Latin control.

The first part of the tragedy was enacted in Jerusalem. The Greek patriarch, Simeon, was expelled by the Moslems or escaped at the approach of the crusader armies, and the conquerors did not hesitate to elect a Latin to his post immediately after the capture of the city. Simeon spent the remaining years of his life (d. 1116) wandering from Cyprus to Constantinople, and from there to Jerusalem. His efforts to regain his see failed, and the old man gave vent to his feelings by writing theological treatises against the use of unleavened bread in the Latin rite. [11]

The same happened in the other patriarchate, at Antioch. The Greek patriarch, Johannes, left his see two years after the capture of the city by the crusaders and retired to Constantinople. The crusaders then enthroned a Latin prelate. As local resistance seemed impossible, the Byzantine Church retaliated by continuing to appoint nominal patriarchs of Jerusalem and Antioch, who resided as exiles in Constantinople.

The difference between the two sees should not be overlooked. Whereas the population of Jerusalem under crusader rule was overwhelmingly composed of Western immigrants, the situation in Antioch was entirely different. Here the majority of the population remained as it had been previously, namely local Greeks and Jacobites. This explains in a large measure the pressure and continuous efforts of the Byzantine emperors to re-establish a Greek patriarch in Antioch. Often, when political circumstances were propitious, their efforts were crowned by success and at one time the prince of Antioch actually accepted a Greek. It goes without saying that at such times the city was laid under interdict by the Latin hierarchy, unconditionally supported by Rome. [12]

The substitution of Latin clergy went hand in hand with stripping the Eastern churches of their possessions. Legitimacy was preserved to the letter since this spoliation was not officially announced. The Latin clergy simply took over earlier Byzantine property. Thus when Godfrey de Bouillon and Baldwin I accorded to the canons of the Holy Sepulchre some thirty villages in the

[11] B. Leib, 'Deux inédits byzantins sur les Azymes au debut du XIIe siècle,' *Orientalia Christiana*, no. 9, Rome, 1924.

[12] F. Chalandon, *Les Comnènes*, II, Paris, 1912, 132, 445, 449, 470, 531; C. Karalevskij, *Antioche*, col. 61 ff. Cl. Cahen, 'Un document concernant les Melkites et les Latins d'Antioche au temps de Croisades', *Rev. des études byzantines*, 1972 (in press).

vicinity of Jerusalem, or when Tancred endowed the monks of Mount Tabor with extensive possessions on both sides of the Jordan, they were simply confirming to new Latin establishments the possessions of their Greek predecessors.[13] When mediaeval travellers and modern historians point out Greek possessions under crusader rule, they are really enumerating remnants of earlier riches.

In the process of conquest many possessions of the native Christian communities were also confiscated by laymen from among the conquerors. Frankish barons were not punctilious as to their rights and treated native Christians as a conquered population. It needed much patience, and very often bribery and the goodwill of the kings of Jerusalem, to restore such property to their legitimate owners. This is what happened, for example, to a Jacobite community near Jerusalem. Its lands were usurped by a Frankish knight and it took a whole generation of litigation until they were restored, and even then not by a process of law, but through the intervention of Queen Melissande, the daughter of the Armenian princess Morfia, who had a soft spot for the Monophysites.[14]

Though crusader legislation made no distinction between the Greek-Orthodox and Jacobite communities, there seems to have been more discrimination against the former. Generally speaking the Jacobite and Armenian communities were far better treated than the Greeks. The crusader conquest brought about a notable rise in the standing of the hierarchy in these two Churches. This was more marked in the northern principalities, which until shortly before had been ruled by the empire (Edessa, Antioch, Tripoli), than in the south. In the former, official Byzantine policy relentlessly persecuted the non-Greek Christian minorities and the crusader conquest, which undermined the position of the Greek Church, was felt as a liberation. In the Latin kingdom the change

[13] Tancred states explicitly that he accords to Mt Tabor what it possessed from antiquity. *Regesta*, no. 36 (AD 1100). Godfrey's donation is known from Baldwin I's confirmation of 1114. *Regesta*, no. 74.

[14] J. P. Martin, 'Les premiers princes croisés et les Jacobites de Jérusalem', *Journal asiatique*, 12 (1888), 471–91; 13 (1889), 33–80. F. Nau, 'Les Croisés lorrain Godefroy de Ascha', *ibid.*, 14 (1899), 421–31.

was not so radical, but the situation in the north certainly influenced the kingdom proper.

The point of weakness was also one of strength. The Greeks could always expect political and financial support from Byzantium. In times of good relations between Constantinople and Jerusalem, the Byzantine emperor even took it upon himself to repair churches and monasteries. Thus Manuel Comnenus repaired and embellished the church of the Nativity in Bethlehem at the time of King Amalric and repaired the Greek *laurae*, i.e. the Anchorite communities in the wilderness of Judea and on the banks of the Jordan (*c.* 1169). In Bethlehem traces of this work can still be seen. The fading, but once resplendent mosaics in the upper part of the main nave depict ecumenical and provincial church church councils, with inscriptions in Latin and Greek.[15] However, such co-operation was rare, and contrasted with the permanent tension between the two parts of Christendom.

Though many churches were taken over by the Latins, the ecclesiastical establishments of the local Christians did not entirely disappear. As a rule the great sanctuaries and city churches changed their clergy. The churches and monasteries in villages where oriental Christians continued to live were staffed by local clergy, though subject to Latin supervision.

Even in the great sanctuaries the local clergy held on, backed by the populace and their traditional Greek or Syriac liturgy. Thus services in the Church of the Holy Sepulchre, as well as in some of its chapels and altars were reserved for non-Latins. The same applied to the church of the Nativity in Bethlehem. Elsewhere the Greeks managed to maintain themselves despite Frankish spoliation. Thus opposite the new Benedictine monastery on Mount Tabor the Greeks retained the monastery of St Elias.[16]

---

[15] R.H. Hamilton, *Guide to Bethlehem*, Jerusalem, 1939. B. Bagatti, *Gli antichi edifici sacri di Betlemme*, Jerusalem, 1952. Manuel Comnenus also covered with golden ornaments the Holy Tomb in Jerusalem. Phocas in *PPTS*, V, 19. About the Emperor's restorations of monasteries, see below.

[16] The Russian pilgrim Daniel in 1106/7 (ed. B. de Khitrovo, 67) does not mention the Greek monastery on Mt Tabor. He found lodgings in the Benedictine monastery. Phocas in 1185 mentions both monasteries. *PPTS*, V, 14.

From a strictly theological point of view we should not expect Greek bishops in the Holy Land. But we hear of one Melethos, who bears the title 'archbishop of the Greeks and Syrians in Gaza and Beit-Jibrin' (1164). These 'Syrians' denote the native Arabic-speaking Christians who used Greek in their liturgy and were ruled by Greek clergy. At the same time we hear of a Greek chapter in the Holy Sepulchre (the church of the Anastasis). Its members bear the titles of *heiereus* (abbot), *deuterarius* (prior), *protodecanos* (archdeacon), *decanos* (deacon). [17] In Jerusalem again we know that the Greek monastery of St Sabbas served as a hospice (*metochion*) and was in good grace with Queen Melissande. [18] In the capital there was another Greek hospice, that of St Moses (1217), [19] which belonged to the abbot of Mount Sinai. [20]

The crusader port of Acre also had Greek monasteries and churches. That of St Catherine is mentioned by name (1217), but there must certainly have been others for the many Syrians in this great city.

Outside Jerusalem in the village and later Hospitaller fortress of Beit-Jibrin there was a Greek monastery of St George. The great sanctuary of this saint's birth-place, in Lydda, was usurped by a Latin bishop, and Greek folk myth took vengeance by reciting

[17] *Regesta*, no. 502 (AD 1173).

[18] In 1164 Queen Melissande donated property to the abbot of St Sabbas. *Regesta*, no. 409.

[19] *Regesta*, no. 897 (AD 1217).

[20] Another proof of the continued existence of the non-Frankish churches is the literary production preserved in the Library of the Greek Patriarchate of Jerusalem (though we are not sure the books were written in the Holy Land). Fourteen volumina can be assigned to the 12th century and one bears the date 1182. The collection of Hagios Stavros has 11 volumina of the 12th century, three bearing dates of 1122, 1167 and 1202 respectively. To this may be added an Evangelion of 1152 from Naos Anastaseos and four volumina from Photios. Interesting are four volumina from the treasury written in Arabic (two of them lexica) with dates 1201, 1207, 1227, that is, already under Moslem rule, and there are three in Syriac of 1251, 1261 and 1289. On the mss of St Sabba and Georgian mss see below. The above data are collected from K. W. Clark, *Checklist of Manuscripts in the Library of the Greek and Armenian Patriarchates in Jerusalem*, Washington, 1953.

the terrible fate of Franks who tried to enter his tomb.[21] Neither did the Greeks succeed in maintaining their position in Nazareth, which became a Latin see. But in Sebaste, where the sanctuary of St John became the Latin bishop's residence, the Greeks re-established themselves and built a monastery higher up, where they claimed the head of St John was brought to Herod.

Outside the greater cities we can only conjecture that Christian villages, or villages with a mixed Christian and Moslem population, had their own churches. Unfortunately it is impossible to ascertain to which rite their inhabitants adhered. Crusader sources often confuse Syrians, who, properly speaking, belonged to the Greek rite, with their sworn enemies, the Jacobites. Thus a good number of villages around Jerusalem, Bethlehem and near Ramleh, Lydda, Birah (Ramallah), Beit-Jibrin, Gaza, Nazareth, Tiberias and in Transjordan, had Christian populations – but we do not know if they were Syrian or Jacobite.[22]

We are better informed about monasteries. Around Jerusalem, Jericho and on the banks of the Jordan, Greek monasteries survived Moslem domination and crusader conquest.[23] Some of them

[21] Phocas in *PPTS*, V, 34.

[22] Syrians, whom we do not know belonged to the Greek or Jacobite rite, are mentioned in the following places (besides in main cities and monasteries) in the kingdom: Casale album near Acre in 1149, *Reg.* 256; Bethlehem in 1150, *Reg.* 258, in 1151, *Reg.* 269; Calandria near Jerusalem in 1151, *Reg.* 207, in 1152, *Reg.* 278, in 1100, *Reg.* 253; Ramathes near Jerusalem in 1182, *Reg.* 278, in 1160, *Reg.* 253, in *c.* 1160 (Jacobites), *Reg.* 365; Montréal in Transjordan in 1152, *Reg.* 279, in 1161, *Reg.* 366; Crac in Transjordan in 1161, *Reg.* 366; Bethelgal near Jerusalem in 1160, *Reg.* 353; Aithara near Jerusalem in 1160, *Reg.* 353; Bethsuri near Jerusalem in 1163, *Reg.* 353; in *c.* 1160, *Reg.* 365; Hadessae near Jerusalem *c.* 1160 (Jacobites), *Reg.* 365; Kafarrus, Vetus Bethoron, Deirfres. near Jerusalem in 1164 (Jacobites), *Reg.* 403; Turchum in 1171, *Reg.* 488; Ramleh in 1175, *Reg.* 533; Château Neuf (M'ilya) in Galilee in 1183, *Reg.* 625; Jish (Giscala) in Galilee in 1183, *Reg.* 627; Manueth in Galilee in 1231, *Reg.* 1077; Cabesie near Tyre, 1239, *Reg.* 1068. A Greek sanctuary of St John existed in al-Tira south of Haifa. In all probability the inhabitants of the Galilean villages St George (Labaena) and Bethlehem were Christians who organized a Syrian fraternity in Acre in the 13th century, recently studied by J. Richard, 'La confrérie des Mosserins d'Acre et les marchands de Mossoul au XIIIe siecle', *L'Orient Syrien*, XI (1966), 451–60.

[23] The following description is based on the 'Itneraries' of the Russian

claimed great antiquity, often going back to the earliest phases of monastic life. Strangely enough, Frankish sources rarely mention them and they seem to have been outside their immediate interest. On the road from Jerusalem to Bethlehem stood the Greek monastery of St Elijah (Mar Elyas), destroyed by an earthquake, but rebuilt by the bounty of Manuel Comnenus. Beyond Bethlehem and towards Jericho were the monasteries of St Theodosius (Deir Dosi), St Euthymius and the famous monastery of St Sabas (Mar Sabba). [24] Here also stood the monastery of St Chariton and in its vicinity a village with a mixed Moslem-Christian population (perhaps 'Anathot) whose sheik escorted the pilgrims on their way to the Jordan. The body of the saint was kept in Jerusalem. [25] The monastery of Calamon marked a legendary resting place of Mary. The awe-inspiring monastery of Khoziba in a deep gorge of the wadi Qelt and St Gerasimus (Qasr Hajla) are mentioned, as is the monastery of St John the Baptist, on the banks of the Jordan (Qasr al-Yahud), where multitudes came to immerse themselves in the river and oriental Christians baptized their children. This monastery, which fell into ruin, was also restored by Manuel Comnenus. Almost all these monasteries – as we learn from the Greek pilgrim Phocas (1185) – were fortified, as their isolated positions were extremely dangerous. Some of them had productive communities and have left manuscripts copied in the crusader period, and scattered today in many libraries. [26] As a rule the Greek

hegumen (abbot) Daniel who visited the Holy Land in 1106–7 (Fr. transl. by Khitrovo; Engl. transl. in PPTS, IV), and the Greek pilgrim Johannes Phocas who visited the Holy Land in 1185. Eng. transl. in PPTS, V. See a list of these monasteries now in O. Meinardus, 'Wall paintings in the Monastic Churches of Judaea', Oriens Christianus, 50 (1966), 46 ff.

[24] The Library of the Greek Patriarchate in Jerusalem possesses the ancient library of St Sabbas. Thirty-one volumina were classified as belonging to the 12th century, i.e. to the crusader period. An Evangelion is dated 1184; a Typicon – 1201. See K. W. Clark, above end of n. 20, and below, n. 26.

[25] John of Würzburg, PPTS, V, 48, 55 and the description of Daniel, ed. Khitrovo, 49.

[26] For example, a 12th-century Greek Gospel written in the monastery of St. Chrysostomus, today in Bibl. San Marco in Venice. See Ch. Kohler, Mélanges II, 289 n.

monastic communities lived according to the ancient 'Rule of St Basil'. We would like to know more about their history, but our sources are unfortunately too meagre to draw many conclusions.

Relations between the three Monophysite churches, the Armenians, Copts and Jacobites were generally very friendly. Newly elected patriarchs of one of these churches normally announced this event to their colleagues. They co-operated in the permanent polemic against the Greeks and sometimes we can even witness theological interventions by a patriarch in the realm of his ecclesiastical colleague. These churches were more favoured by the conquerors than those of the Greeks or Syrians and their attitude towards the crusaders is thus all the more interesting.

In the Holy Land proper the Jacobites represented the Monophysite community, though their main concentration lay between Antioch and Edessa. How little crusader conquest meant to the orientals can be gauged from the fact that the Jacobite patriarch of Antioch never resided in the capital of the principality from which he derived his title (the only exception was Ignace II, 1222–52). Different monasteries and cities (frequently 'Amida) served as his place of residence. True that in the middle of the eleventh century, under Byzantine rule, the Jacobite patriarch was expelled by the Greeks from their city; but things changed under the crusaders and he could have easily settled in the Christian capital, yet he preferred Moslem territory. The fact that the overwhelming majority of his community lived in Moslem lands certainly must have influenced his decision, but the ease with which the Jacobite patriarchs moved between crusaders and Moslems does indicate their reluctance to dwell exclusively among the former. The Syrian 'nation' remained what it had been before the coming of the crusaders, a community dispersed from the Taurus to Jerusalem and from the Mediterranean to Mesopotamia, ruled by the patriarch and in its eastern part by his lieutenant, the *maphrian*. The Jacobites did not migrate to settle among the crusaders, though their relations were almost cordial. The crusaders on their part did nothing to make an oriental Christian a full citizen or partner in their kingdom.

The main Jacobite centre in the Latin kingdom, beside the

various Jacobite villages, was Jerusalem. Here in the Syrian quarter – between the Damascus gate and the Josaphat gate – stood their church, monastery and hospice, dedicated to Mary Magdalene. The church seems to have been founded by a Copt, Macarius of Nabruwah, under the patriarch of Alexandria, Abba Ya'aqub (810–30). The monastery then became Jacobite and was rebuilt under the benevolent rule of the Seljuqs, with the help of a Jacobite in their service, Mansur al-Balbayi (the reading of the name is not clear). The consecration took place in 1092 in the presence of the envoys of the Coptic patriarch, Cyril II.[27] Jacobite tradition regarded the building as the house of Simon the leper and appropriately enough some of the hair of Saint Mary Magdalene was exhibited in the place.[28] Jacobite monks lived in what was also the residence of their bishop in Jerusalem (we have a full list of bishops since 1090), which on occasions also served as the residence of a visiting patriarch. In addition to the bishops of Jerusalem we occasionally hear in the thirteenth century of Jacobite bishops in Acre and Tripoli.[29]

Though relations with the Armenian and Coptic Monophysites were generally friendly, there were periods of polemics and tension. One of the more memorable events was the quarrel between Jacobites and Copts regarding Jerusalem. As previously mentioned, the holy city did not rank as a patriarchate with any of the Monophysite churches. The oasis of al-'Arish in Sinai marked the frontier of the patriarchate of Antioch (to which the bishop of Jerusalem belonged) and Alexandria. After Saladin's conquest of Jerusalem, Egyptian Christians – who often visited Palestine and Syria – de-

---

[27] *Patrologia Orientalis*, X, 461; Sawirus ibn al-Mukaffa', *History of the Patriarchs*, 364–5.

[28] John of Würzburg (1160–70), *PPTS*, V, 23. It must have been through some kind of confusion with the nearby *Piscina Probatica*, that the Moslem traveller 'Ali al-Harawi was shown here (1173/4) a fountain where Jesus made his ablutions, ed. Schefer, 607. A list of Jacobite bishops of Jerusalem is to be found at the end of the chronicle of Michael the Syrian, 476 ff. Recent excavations near Damascus Gate brought to light rests of a native church, probably of St Abraham, known from contemporary maps of the city. J. B. Henessy, 'Preliminary Report on the Excavations at the Damascus Gate, 1964–6', *Levant*, 2 (1970), 22–7.

[29] Bar Hebraeus, I, 681, 708.

manded a Coptic bishop of their own in the holy city. Cyril III
of Alexandria appointed a bishop (1237) whom he consecrated
himself, though this should have been done by the patriarch of
Antioch. The first Coptic bishop was excommunicated by Ignace
II, patriarch of Antioch, but the Franks, who for some fifteen
years ruled Jerusalem after the Crusade of Frederick II, accepted the
new bishop despite Jacobite protestations. The Jacobite patriarch
took vengeance by consecrating a Negro as bishop of Abyssinia, a
right always reserved to the patriarch of Alexandria.[30]

The relations between the Jacobites and the Franks were usually
friendly, but there was a fair amount of condescension if not contempt on part of the Franks. Officially the Jacobite and Armenian
bishops of Jerusalem were suffragans of the Latin patriarch. Inter-
ference by the latter in Jacobite affairs was not unknown and
bribery often played a sordid role in these dealings.[31] Moreover
interference was not restricted to ecclesiastical superiors. The
crusaders took over the Moslem custom of confirming the elections
of oriental patriarchs and bishops. In the twelfth century it was no
longer the caliph who issued letters of appointment, but the
emirs, that is the individual rulers of cities and principalities. The
custom was continued by the crusaders, and Amalric I confirmed a
Jacobite patriarch as did Baldwin IV.[32] This created possibilities
of intervention, which must, however, be regarded as normal, since
rights were reserved to the Crown even in the Latin church.

The Armenians, Georgians and Nestorians were less numerous
than Syrians and Jacobites. The Nestorians were still important
in Mesopotamia and in the eastern provinces of the caliphate. Small
communities of Nestorians survived in the crusader states and it was
customary for the Nestorian 'Katholicos', who resided in Baghdad,
to have a representative in Jerusalem. The Armenians and Georgians represented religious, ethnic and political entities. Their links
with Jerusalem went back to the late Roman Empire, and in the
seventh century Armenian churches and monasteries were very

---

[30] Id., II, 656–64.
[31] E.g. a Jacobite monk Bar Wahbun bribes the patriarch of Jerusalem to
receive the monastery of Mary Magdalene. Michel le Syrien, III, 385/6.
[32] *Ibid.*, p. 379.

numerous in the Holy Land. It seems that under crusader rule Armenian communities existed only in Jerusalem and Acre, though individual Armenians were found among the vassals of the kingdom. Their major sanctuary was that of St James in the street of the Armenians, between the Tower of David and the Zion gate. The Armenian patriarch regarded himself as successor of the apostle James, in whose honour a magnificent cathedral was built around 1165.[33]

The Georgians, often called 'Iberians' (which caused some modern historians to confuse them with Spaniards), had their great sanctuary in the monastery of the Holy Cross outside the walls of Jerusalem. As representatives of a Christian kingdom in faraway Caucasus, they enjoyed favour with the Latins and support by their pious kings. Under Queen Tamara (1184–1211), the greatest poet of the nation – Shotha Rustavili – was sent here and wrote the great Georgian national epic, the *Vapkiss Takossani* ('The Man in the Panther's Skin'). A recent Georgian mission (1964) discovered fifteenth-century frescoes of the poet and his patrons in the once magnificent church.[34]

If the crucial test of human endeavour is the comparison of aims and results, the policy of the crusaders towards oriental Christendom was a total failure. An ethnic group from the Lebanese mountains which had been estranged for centuries from the great current of religious development, the Maronites, was united to Rome (1182). Unification was realized on the terms of Rome, and

---

[33] Abel, *Jérusalem nouvelle*, II, 522. K. J. Basmadijan, 'Chronol. de l'hist. de l'Arménie', *Rev. de l'Orient Chrétien*, 19 (1914), 369. Armenians are mentioned: *Reg.* 590 (and near Jerusalem); *Reg.* 1010 (AD 1229 – Jerusalem); hospital in Acre, *Reg.* 696; there is a confusion among Western pilgrims as to the Armenians in Jerusalem. John of Würzburg, *PPTS*, V, 45, assigns to the Armenians erroneously the monastery of St Sabbas, which belonged to the Greeks. Again the pilgrim Theodorich, *PPTS*, V, 43, assigns to the Armenians the monastery of St Chariton in Jerusalem, which really belonged to the Jacobites. The new catalogue (not yet finished) of the library of the Armenian patriarchate in Jerusalem as well as the thorough studies of my colleague M. Stone did not uncover any ms connected with Jerusalem prior to the fourteenth century.

[34] See in gen. bibl. of this chapter.

the Maronites had to recognize the supremacy of the pope and the Latin hierarchy. We should not underestimate the importance of this act of unification, which left a permanent imprint on the Near East in politics and culture. Nevertheless, this lay in the future, since the Maronites did not become a bridge to Eastern Christendom, neither did they integrate with the ruling crusaders.

If this was the case with oriental Christians who had recognized the supremacy of Rome, it certainly held good for the Greeks, Syrians and Jacobites. Though self-described as 'nations', these Christians never aspired to any freedom, apart from that of worship. They had no feeling of exile, since they were the auto-chthonous inhabitants of the land. Consequently, they never aspired to a 'return'. The feeling of sectarian unity owed its strength as much to permanent intersectarian polemic and competition, as to the surrounding sea of Islam. The scaffolding of the 'nation' was its ecclesiastical hierarchy, spread over the lands between the Mediterranean and the mountains of Persia. The appearance of the crusaders did nothing to change this situation, though it could on occasion add a new element to polemics. The Monophysites and Chalcedonians who had pre-viously composed theological treatises to point out each other's errors now made Latin Christianity the target of their polemics. To them Palestine was thus not a land whose liberation from Moslem rule would sound the trumpets of salvation.

The crusaders on their part did nothing to change the permanent framework of Eastern Christendom, though there were sporadic and mild attempts at conversion. These originated with the Church, or rather with some zealous prelates, and one hesitates to describe them as a religious programme, even less as a policy. Moreover, the state was conspicuously uninvolved in all such endeavours. If we remember that in thirteenth-century Spain the Church mobilized the state to force non-Christians to attend proselytizing sermons, the apathy of the crusader lay-power becomes more meaningful in comparison.

This alone would have sufficed to make it clear that Church and state did not approach the native Christian problem in the same way. Nevertheless the indifference of the state should not be regarded as conscious liberalism or tolerance. There was a practical tolerance in the sense that the state took cognizance of and tolerated heterodox communities; there was liberalism in the fact that each community could pursue its own customs and rites, but the motives of this policy did not arise from tolerance. This was simply the easiest way to handle a complex situation by perpetuating the existing order. All non-Franks were accorded the same position in law, none achieved citizenship. The former *dhimmis* – non-Moslem clients of the Moslem state – now became *dhimmis* of the crusader kingdom.

The official Latin policy of not recognizing the Greek hierarchy and subordinating the other denominations to Latin prelates has its origins in the theological position of Rome. The attitude of the state is explained by colonial pragmatism, which overruled all other possible approaches and recognized a caste of native inferiors. The local Christian was a native and viewed as such by the alien conqueror. His faith did not mitigate the situation, and he enjoyed as much religious freedom as the Jew, Samaritan or Moslem. As much, but no more.

In modern terms this solution seems rather democratic and liberal. One could even say that this was the supreme test of tolerance: to accord to all non-Latins the same status and liberty. This view is naturally misleading, since it ignores the fact that the entire population was split into a ruling caste of citizens and a lower caste of non-citizens, regardless of whether they regarded themselves as 'liberated' or conquered.

The problem of liberalism and tolerance simply does not arise and it would be absurd to project such notions into twelfth-century European society. A true test would have been the readiness to accept and integrate the Christian minorities into one body politic, which was never done or envisaged. The crusaders came as conquerors and remained as such in the Holy Land. All the heterogeneous components were cast into one mould and their isolation strengthened by religious divergence.

The first colonial enterprise started out with different notions, but ended by formulating the classical rule of colonialism: never mix with the natives.

XIII

THE JEWS

Barred from Frankish society and outside the communities of native Christians and Moslems, the Jews led their own secluded lives, precariously clinging to their historical homeland. Neither economic conditions nor social advantages can explain the survival of the community and its determination to live in a country where making a living was notoriously difficult and where Christian or Moslem fanaticism, easily kindled in the vicinity of the holy places, made life a dangerous experience. Despite the enticements of more prosperous countries, such as Egypt or Iraq, the Jewish community never abandoned the Holy Land.

Some Jewish communities of the early Middle Ages were in all probability autochthonous and antedated Roman, Byzantine or Moslem domination. Impoverished remnants of the Jewish population, they had survived Titus, Hadrian and the Byzantine persecutions. Such were, possibly, the Jewish villages in Galilee. Other communities were of more recent origin, for example, the Jews in Jerusalem, who only returned when the Moslem conquest in the seventh century (638) put an end to Byzantine persecution and Christian discriminations.

A remarkable feature of the Jewish community in the Holy Land was the unceasing current of pilgrimage and migration, which, for generation after generation, assured the continuity of the Jewish presence in the Holy Land. Jewish communities might often disappear because of persecution or impoverishment, but some generations later a new community would be created through the settlement of a few families, which would attract more pilgrims who might ultimately decide to remain.

Many places once abandoned were never settled again, but there is no period in Palestinian history without its Jewish community. The Jews seem to have kept alive their unique claim to the country by assuring a continued physical presence. Their daily prayers and the study of the Torah preserved the memory of the Divine promise given to their forefathers.

By the middle of the eleventh century, two generations before the crusader conquest, the most important Jewish centre in the Holy Land was the Egyptian-held capital of the country – Ramleh – in the plain, midway between Jaffa and Jerusalem. At Ramleh also the Jewish sect of the Karaites, permanently quarrelling with the 'Rabbinites' as the Jews were nicknamed, had its most important centre. Both communities maintained a lively correspondence with the spiritual centre in Jerusalem and preserved close relations with their opulent and influential brothers in Cairo, Damascus, Aleppo and Baghdad. Smaller Jewish communities existed in some thirty other localities. The Seljuq invasion a generation before the crusaders, the ensuing wars, depredations and the general state of insecurity probably affected non-Moslems more. However, once the conquest was over, the new Seljuq rulers made a deliberate effort to bring back security to the devastated country. But the period of restoration lasted less than a generation.

Rumours preceded the march of the First Crusade to the East, followed by reports of the monstrous massacres of 1096, perpetrated by the 'Peasants' Crusade' in France and Germany, that threw the Eastern Jewish communities into a state of turmoil and fear. Messianic movements, a phenomenon inherent in Jewish history, agitated the Diaspora. In the Balkans, Christians and Jews alike saw in the movement one of the signs of the approaching Day of Judgement. Whereas the former expected the coming of Antichrist, the latter perceived the rumblings of Gog and Magog,[1] until now shut in beyond the 'Mountains of Darkness'. On their heels would come the Messiah 'Son of Joseph', the Forerunner of

[1] See J. Mann, 'Messianic movements during the early Crusades' (Heb.), *Hatekufa*, 23–4.

the Messiah, 'Son of David'. Some time later the crusader armies appeared before Constantinople and, after crossing Asia Minor and Syria, entered the Holy Land.

The appearance of the crusaders on the coast of Lebanon (1099) brought in its wake the renewed terrors of war. From a small township, Raffah near Gaza, comes a contemporary letter in which an inhabitant of the place implores news from his Jewish co-religionists in Jerusalem so as to be able to escape to neighbouring and fortified Ascalon.[2] Even before the actual crusader conquest, many places were abandoned by their Moslem, Jewish and even Christian inhabitants. This happened in Jaffa and Ramleh, and there is no doubt that the Jewish inhabitants participated in the general flight of the population.

The march of the crusader armies across the Holy Land was not opposed until they reached their goal, Jerusalem. The Seljuqs had already been ousted by the Egyptians. The citadel was defended by an Egyptian and Sudanese garrison, and the walls manned by the mobilized city population. The inhabitants of each quarter were responsible for the defence of their section of the walls. Jews and Moslems (the oriental Christians were regarded as potential traitors) manned the walls, the former defending their own quarter (the section between the Damascus gate in the north and the so-called 'Tower of the Storks' in the north-eastern corner of the city), known even in crusader times as the *Juiverie*.[3] This was the weakest point in the city defences, because no natural valley cut off the city here from the surrounding land and the defence depended entirely on the strength of the walls.

Looking down from the battlements, the Jews could observe the army of Godfrey de Bouillon across the walls and ditches. This section of the walls was finally (after five weeks of siege) chosen by the crusaders as the principal point of attack. On 15 July the walls near the Jewish quarter were forced and the host of Godfrey

[2] See S. D. Goitein, 'Contemporary letters on the capture of Jerusalem by the crusaders', *Journal of Jewish Studies*, III (1952), 162–77.

[3] J. Prawer, 'The Vicissitudes of the Jewish Quarter in Jerusalem in the Arabic period' (Heb.), *Zion Quart. Rev.*, XII (1947), 136–48.

poured into the city, followed by the troops of Tancred in the north-west and Raymond de Saint-Gilles from Mount Zion in the south.

The defenders were pushed back towards the Temple area. Fury and fanatical zeal covered the way of the conquerors with thousands of corpses and looted houses set afire. The Jews, despairing of resistance, sought refuge in their synagogues, where they were mercilessly burned alive. Few escaped the holocaust and those captured by Tancred were sold into slavery in Italy. 'Thirty for a piece of silver' says with glee a Christian chronicler[4] – an expiation for the treason of Judas Iscariot. Others were brought by Raymond de Saint-Gilles with the Egyptian citadel commander to Ascalon and ransomed by the local community with the help of the Egyptian Jews. None remained alive in Jerusalem.

The disappearance of the communities of Jaffa and Ramleh and the massacres in Jerusalem were followed by the annihilation of other communities. Once again we hear of Jews and Moslems jointly defending their city against the Christian foe during the siege of Haifa (1100), where a Jewish community was earlier granted special privileges by the Fatimid rulers of Egypt. The city was blockaded by the Venetians from the sea and besieged by the Franks on land. Tancred was on the point of abandoning the siege, but the patriarch of Jerusalem spurred him to perseverance by pointing out the blemish which would be attached to his name if he were defeated by the resisting Jews.[5] Haifa fell and with it its Moslem and Jewish inhabitants.

During the next ten years of conquest (1100–10) the Moslems and Jews were exterminated in all conquered cities,[6] and crusader domination resembled a return of Titus.

This situation changed in the second decade of the twelfth century. The same crusaders who had marked their passage across Europe with streams of Jewish blood pursued a different policy

[4] Baldricus Dolensis, *RHC, Historiens Occidentaux*, IV, 103.

[5] Albertus Aquensis in *RHC, Historiens Occidentaux*, IV, 521.

[6] See now E. Sivan, 'Réfugiés Syro-Palestiniens au temps des Croisades', *Revue des études islamiques*, 1967, 135–47.

once settled in the Latin kingdom. No pogroms are known during the crusader domination of the Holy Land, and this at a time when every new Crusade was accompanied by repeated massacres of the Jews in Europe.

However, there was no specific Jewish policy of the Frankish rulers. Having once established a general policy towards the native population as a whole, they followed the rules in all their ramifications. A point of judicial procedure preserved in the *Livre des Assises des Bourgeois* may well illustrate this practice:

> If a Greek claims against a Jew and the latter denies – the law stipulates that the Greek should bring Jewish witnesses and these witnesses should take an oath according to their law that there is truth in the claim and that they saw the defendant perpetrate the transgression or heard him saying the insult.

If there are no witnesses the defendant goes free. The Jew took an oath on the Old Testament, the Samaritan on the Pentateuch and the Greek on the Bible.[7] This and similar rules proclaim the general policy towards all non-Franks. The demarcation, obvious in the inventory of criminal penalties, is between those 'who obey Rome and "nations" which do not obey Rome'. The *Wergeld* of the non-Frank is precisely half that of a Frank. The situation was summarized in the following phrase from a crusader law treatise:

> Because, should the people be Syrians, Greeks, Jews, Samaritans, Nestorians or Saracens, they are still men like the Franks and they are obliged to pay and to give whatever will be adjudicated by the court of burgesses.

This was official policy, but as in the case of the oriental Christians, powerful factors in the kingdom only half-heartedly subscribed to it. William, archbishop of Tyre (*c.* 1180), fulminates against Christian princes who prefer Jewish physicians;[8] a poem written in all probability in Jerusalem close to the time of the Third Crusade calls upon Christians to expel the Jews from their coun-

---

[7] *Livre des Assises des Bourgeois*, cap. 241, *Lois* II, 171–3. Here also the following quotation.

[8] William of Tyre, XVIII, 34.

tries.[9] And it goes without saying that Jacques, bishop of Acre (*c.* 1220), who pours fire and brimstone on everything and everybody, wrote a short dissertation about the Jews. He begins by repeating the official church teaching which forbade the forceful conversion and killing of the Jews, because they were 'Witnesses of the Truth', but condemned them to the fate of Cain, the 'Eternal Wanderer', with the sign of murder on his head. Then the bishop of Acre adds on his own :

> The Saracens among whom they live despise and hate them. At the time that the greed of our Christian princes allows them to enslave Christians and rob them through their inhuman usury, among the Saracens they labour with their own hands in the roughest and most despised kind of work. They are enslaved among the Infidels who tolerate them on the lowest level of life only.

The above could hardly have applied to Palestinian Jewry, since usury was firmly in the hands of the Italian merchants and military orders without much fear of Jewish competition. Despite such literary attacks, the general situation was good enough to facilitate Jewish pilgrimages to the Holy Land followed by a renewal and even a brief flourishing of the Jewish community.

Under crusader rule Jewish pilgrimages became far more frequent than before. Not only did Jews of the Near East travel to Jerusalem.[11] but Jews from far-away Byzantium, Spain, France and Germany[12] visited the holy places. This was partly due to the ease and frequency of the new communications which now linked Christendom with the Holy Land. The growing dimensions of the pilgrim movement can best be illustrated by the fact that the rabbinical authorities of the period, the so-called 'Tossafists',[13]

[9] *Archives de l'Orient latin*, II B, 580, vv. 70–4.

[10] Jacques de Vitry, cap. 81, in Bongars, *Gesta Dei per Francos*, 1611.

[11] *Responsa of Maimonides*, ed. H. Freimann, par. 180, 372.

[12] The famous Jewish traveller, Benjamin of Tudela came from Spain. He met in Jerusalem one Abraham al-Konstantini (from Constantinople). Another famous Jewish pilgrim and traveller was the German Jew, Rabbi Petahya of Regensburg. Benjamin of Tudela names a Jew from Carcassonne as the head of the Jewish community in Tyre.

[13] '*Tossafists*', lit. those who add, that is to say, the Exegetical School of the Mishna and Talmud in 11th–13th-century France and Germany.

were induced to change some rules regarding marital law. Talmudic law obliged a wife, under sanction of divorce and loss of
dowry, to follow her husband if he decided to migrate and settle
in the Holy Land. The 'Tossafists' suspended this ruling, deeming
in the beginning the crusader kingdom to be too dangerous to be
inhabited. This rule was reversed to its Talmudic position by the
end of the twelfth century.[14]

The new movement of pilgrimage rejuvenated the older Jewish
centres and some communities might have even been newly created
under crusader rule. Naturally enough, Jews settled together and
crusader documents mention the 'Houses [or House] of the Jews'
(*domus Judaeorum*) and 'street of the Jews' (*rua Judaeorum*) in
several cities of the kingdom.[15] As far as we know Jews were free
to settle wherever they chose, with one exception, the city of
Jerusalem. The crusaders, we are told, felt it sacrilegious that Jews
and Moslems should inhabit the holy city! This enactment, which
must have been promulgated almost immediately after conquest,
was already relaxed by Baldwin II (*c.* 1120), who allowed Moslems
to bring food into the city. Later (*c.* 1174) Benjamin of Tudela
found in Jerusalem some Jewish dyers' families who lived opposite
the royal 'Tower of David'. But a sizeable Jewish community was
not established in Jerusalem before Moslem rule, in the closing
years of the twelfth century.

The largest Jewish communities were in Ascalon, Tyre and Acre.
The first two were apparently the only city communities not
annihilated during the conquest, since both cities capitulated and
were not taken by force. The Jewish community in Ascalon continued to exist under crusader rule to 1191, when the city was razed
on orders of Saladin during the Third Crusade. The Jews abandoned the place as did its other inhabitants, but moved and settled
as a group in Jerusalem.[16]

---

[14] H.J. Zimmels, 'Erez Israel in der Responsenliteratur des Mittelalters',
Monatschrift für die Geschichte und Wissenschaft des Judentums, 1930, 44, n. 2, 52.

[15] E. Strehlke, *Tabulae Ordinis Theutonici*, p. 33.

[16] They were thus called 'Ascalonites' by the Spanish-Jewish poet and philosopher al-Harizi, who pilgrimaged to Jerusalem in 1216. *Tahkemoni*, cap. 25.

Far more important was the Jewish community in Tyre. To the older group of oriental Jews, headed (*c.* 1174) by Rabbi Ephraim 'the Egyptian', was added a new community of European origin. Benjamin of Tudela met here with Rabbi Meir of Carcassonne and Rabbi Hiyyah, the 'Head of the Community' (*Rosh ha-Qahal*). Contemporary documents witness to the direct contacts between the community and Maimonides, who then lived in Cairo. Maimonides even addressed one of the spiritual leaders of the community:

> You are one of the wise among the Sages of Israel, and I always say to the inhabitants of Eretz-Israel and neighbouring countries, that it is because of your dwelling in this place, that God assures us a Redeemer even today.[17]

A sizeable Jewish community already existed in Acre in the twelfth century. From Maimonides' correspondence we learn that it followed the traditional pattern of organization, with a 'Head of the Community' and a rabbinical court.

We can assume that the capture of Acre by Saladin in 1187 hardly influenced the fate of the Jewish community. In any case the community reappears almost immediately after the conquest of the city by the hosts of the Third Crusade (1191), and shortly it became the most important Jewish centre in the country. A crusader ordinance, probably from the early period after the recapture of the city, decreed that non-Franks would not be allowed to live in the Old (that is the twelfth-century) City, where the former crusader inhabitants received back their houses.[18] The Jewish community was thus relegated to the new quarter of Montmusard.

The rabbinical court of Acre not only judged cases brought before it, but also had the right to legislate for the community. Such ordinances (*Taqqanoth*) became law and though, strictly speaking, valid for the local community only, were often accepted

---

[17] Benjamin of Tudela, ed. W. Adler, 20; *Responsa of Maimonides*, ed. H. Freimann, par. 105, 138, 75.

[18] *Assises des Bourgeois*, cap. 243. See J. Prawer, 'L'établissement des coutumes du marché à St. Jean d'Acre', *Rev. hist. de droit français et étranger*, 29 (1951), 329 ff. On this point see below cap. XVI, n. 144.

by all Jewish communities in the Holy Land. We have a good example of such legislation from 1233–4. Some Jewish families alleged their descent from the fourth-century *Nesiim*, that is heads of Palestinian Jewry under the late Roman Empire and claimed accordingly a privileged position, including rights of jurisdiction, and anathema. This claim met with strong opposition. Thirteenth-century Jewish communities were not ruled by traditional families, but by their own elected bodies, where learning and social standing in the community were decisive factors in election. The Egyptian community was first to decree that contemporary *Nesiim* had no special privileges and that the imposition of or absolution from anathema (*Herem*), should be done by the important people of the community in each city. The community of Acre followed suit by repeating the same ordinance. [19]

One of the characteristics of the Jewish community in crusader Acre was its heterogeneous composition. We not merely find a distinction between oriental and Western Jews, but among the latter also between Spanish-Provençal and Franco-German Jewry. This division represented two major trends in thirteenth-century Judaism. On the one hand Spanish-Provençal Jewry, open to its Moslem-Christian surrounding, inclined to philosophy, religious and profane poetry, while simultaneously delving into the new mysticism, the *Kabbala*, which arose in south-western Europe. The more traditional Franco-German Jewry concentrated on study of the Law (*Halakha*) and the exegesis of the Talmud.

The encounter of these two trends of Judaism in Acre was not a happy one. Jews of different origin perpetuated their identities by building separate synagogues, where they could follow their local liturgies and customs. Almost all synagogues had their own Talmudic colleges or academies (*Beit Midrash*), where the adolescent received his education, but which were also frequented by all members of the community whatever their standing and occupation. Such colleges pursued their own ways of learning and exegesis, thus perpetuating the schools and systems brought over

[19] *Responsa of R. Abraham son of Maimonides*, ed. A. H. Freimann, addenda to par. 8, 10. The 'Ordinance of the Sages of Acco', in *Aluma*, 1926, 29 ff.

from the places of their origin. One such academy was founded in Acre by Rabbi Yehiel of Paris, the great spiritual leader of French Jewry, who settled in the Holy Land in the middle of the thirteenth century. The renown of the new academy of the 'Sages of Acre' was so great that Rabbi Shlomo ben Adrath in distant Spain wrote:

> It is a custom among the Sages of the Holy Land and of Babylon, that if a question should be asked nobody answers, but they say: 'Let us be guided by the Sages of Acre.'[20]

In the nature of things this meeting of the different trends of Judaism created friction. A French rabbi, Salomon le Petit, brought tension to a head by renewing the old polemic on the philosophical writings of Maimonides. Salomon le Petit suspected their rationalizing tendencies and worried about their possible influence on youth. Consequently, he proscribed the use and study of Maimonides' writings, as was done fifty years earlier in sone European centres. Certain rabbinical authorities in Germany and Italy gave their support to this interdict and Salomon le Petit openly proclaimed the prohibition. A reaction followed immediately. The Jewish leaders of Damascus, Mossul and Baghdad officially anathematized Rabbi Salomon le Petit and his supporters and an expiatory pilgrimage of Jews was organized to the tomb of Maimonides in Tiberias.

Acre was divided in its opinion. The heterogeneous Jewish community did not rally whole-heartedly to the defence of Maimonides and only one group of rabbis joined the proclamation of anathema. This sad controversy split the community up to the capture of Acre by the Mameluks in 1291.

Outside Tyre and Acre smaller Jewish communities existed in Beirut, Sidon, Caesarea, Lydda, Bethlehem, Beith Nuba, Zar'in and Beit-Jibrin. The Jewish communities in Galilee are of special interest. There was a community in Tiberias and one of its members, Rabbi Nahorai, claimed to be descendant of Rabbi Yehuda ha-Nassi (second century), the codifier of the Mishna. At the beginning of the thirteenth century there was also a com-

---

[20] *Responsa of R. Shlomo ben Adrath* (known as *Rashba*), part 6, par. 89.

munity in Safed. One of its members claimed the title *Rosh Yeshivath Gaon Ya'aqov*, the Head of the Academy which had existed in the Holy Land during the eleventh century, but disappeared with the migration of the academy first to Tyre and then to Damascus. Around these two urban centres in Galilee we find Jews in purely rural areas. They are mentioned in Giscala (Gush Halav), 'Almah, probably also in Bar'am, 'Amuqa, Kefer Hananya, Kefar Tanhum, Meron, Dalatha, Bira, al-'Awiyah and Banyas.[21]

Many of these villages are known from the earlier Arab period and this makes it plausible to assume that these Jewish villages did not suffer much during the crusader conquest. Crusader battles and conquests centred around cities and the rural areas were not directly affected. Moreover, it was in the interest of the crusaders to restore normal conditions in the villages as quickly as possible, because their own material existence depended on their well-being.

There is hardly a period in Jewish history which does not reveal the names of those who travelled to the Holy Land and were subsequently called '*Yerushalmi*' – 'Jerusalemite'. By the beginning of the twelfth century (possibly under Christian influence) a new literary genre developed, 'Itineraries' (*masa'oth*) and inventories of holy tombs ('*Qivrei Avoth*', lit. tombs of ancestors). Christian preachers used *excitatoria*, letters whose aim was to stir public opinion for participation in the Crusades. Among the Jews messengers from Palestine (*shlihim*) would visit European and oriental communities, bearing their lists of shrines and collecting money for the support of Jewish communities in the Holy Land.

Pilgrimage to Jerusalem on the occasion of three great feasts (Passover, Pentecost and Tabernacles) was a religious precept which disappeared with the destruction of the Temple. But the custom continued uninterruptedly for centuries. Even Roman and Byzantine legislation which banned the Jews from living in Jerusalem was unable to withstand their ardent faith ; barred from the city, they pilgrimaged and contemplated the Temple area and the ruins of the sanctuary from the Mount of Olives. If Jerusalem was inaccessible

[21] Many mentioned by Benjamin of Tudela, ed. Adler, pp. 19, 21, 26, 28, 29; additional material in A. Ya'ari's sources. See in gen. bibl. of this chapter.

and if one lived in the Diaspora, there was still the hope to be buried in the Holy Land. One need only visit the newly excavated catacombs of Beit-She'arim, dating back to the late Roman period, to visualize the stream of Jews who came to the Holy Land from Mesopotamia, Egypt, Italy and Spain. Some brought with them the bodies of their deceased relatives, who had expressed the wish to be buried in the Land of Israel, like Joseph.

At the end of the First and the beginning of the Second Kingdom created by the Third Crusade, a remarkable change took place in the life of the Jewish communities and in the attitude of Diaspora Jewry to the Holy Land. With the exception of the sixteenth century (following the expulsion of the Jews from Spain) and in our times, Jewish immigration into the Holy Land never reached such dimensions as during the thirteenth century. Contemporary documents convey the impression that all the long-repressed yearning of the nation for the Holy Land – kept alive by persecution, faith and daily prayer – suddenly found an outlet in a movement of return. Neither pilgrimage nor migration were new, but in the thirteenth century they acquired a particular character, which differed from the foregoing as much in scope and composition as in its aims and motivation.

During the thirteenth century new factors appeared which changed the character of pilgrimage and migration, and ultimately the character of Jewish settlement in the Holy Land. The change may already have started at the time of Saladin's conquest. Although less liberal than later legend made him out to be,[22] Saladin endeared himself to Jewish memory as a ruler who appealed to the Jews to settle in the holy city after its liberation from the crusaders. The famous Spanish-Jewish poet al-Harizi, who travelled to Jerusalem in 1216 relates the following:

> And Saladin ordered to proclaim in every city, to let it be known to old and young: 'Speak ye to the heart of Jerusalem, let anybody who wants from the seed of Ephraim come to her.'[23]

[22] E. Ashtor-Strauss, 'Saladin and the Jews', Heb. Union College Annual, 27 (1956), 305–26.
[23] Tahkemoni, cap. 28.

According to our poet, the date of this solemn proclamation is 1189–90, i.e., two or three years after the conquest of the city by the Moslems. Saladin, presented here as a second Cyrus, permits and even solemnly proclaims the 'Return of the Exiles'. In fact, many centuries were to pass before such a declaration was actually published by Napoleon, during his campaign in Egypt and Syria. There is, however, no doubt that with the Moslem capture of Jerusalem, the former crusader prohibition fell into abeyance and Jews once again lived in the holy city. Entire communities settled there. The 'Ascalonites' came after the destruction of their city by Saladin ; the Jews from the Maghreb, fleeing the persecutions of al-Mansur or his son al-Naser, came around 1198, as did a wave of Jewish migrants from France in 1210–11.

Contemporaneously with the re-establishment of the Jewish community in Jerusalem, there occurred an extraordinary revival of the Jewish link with its ancient homeland. Saladin's victory over the crusaders could have activated this movement, but a more weighty factor was the Jewish view of the Latin kingdom. The First, Second and Third Crusades and the Crusade of St Louis brought in their wake persecutions and sufferings and their corollary : Messianic movements and the expectation of the Day of Judgement. This was a pattern of behaviour unique in the history of mankind. A nation which never lost its identity or the collective memory of former glory reacted this way to a hostile environment and to the incomprehensible decisions of providence. In times of massacres and tragedy, the nostalgia for the homeland, the assurance of deliverance from the blood-stained hands of persecutors and the undaunted belief in salvation and redemption brought forth innumerable martyrs who refused apostasy. The tribulations continued, but great events did, indeed, occur in the cradle of the nation. Moslem and Christian confronted each other and fought for domination of the Holy Land. The Jewish Diaspora advanced its own claim and lacking state and armies, it relied on prophecy and providence. Tens of thousands of Europeans had streamed to their doom in the East, fortunes were squandered and a land completely ruined since Saladin inaugurated his 'scorched-earth' policy by destroying cities after their capture, to prevent any future crusader restoration. The Christian Crusades were a glaring failure and the Latin establishments were doomed. As early as the First Crusade, the Jews tried to explain to themselves the strange ways of providence. In a letter written from the Balkans at the approach of the Christian host, we find the curious explanation that providence had ordered an exodus from Europe, to gather all persecutors in the Holy Land and would then command, repeating the words of the Prophet: 'Stand up and thresh O daughter of Zion'.[24] But the First Crusade succeeded and Christians ruled for a hundred years in the Holy Land. The moderate results of the Third Crusade and the thirteenth-century failures stimulated a new concept of these great historical events. Their foremost exponent was the great luminary of Judaism in the middle of the thirteenth century, Rabbi Moses ben Nahman, the Spaniard Nahmanides. After participating in a religious disputation against the convert Pablo Christiani before the Court of Barcelona in 1263, Nahmanides decided to leave his native Catalonia and migrate to the Holy Land. He settled in Jerusalem (1267), where students flocked to him and it is here that he finished composing his commentary on the Pentateuch. In this work he expounded, *inter alia*, his views on contemporary events and drew conclusions as to their relevance concerning the destinies of the Holy Land. His writings and commentaries reflect a new approach when speaking of the Holy Land and they have an original ring, even when incorporating ancient traditions.

Whereas traditional exegesis mainly confined itself to elucidating the *halakhic*, that is legal content of the Scriptures, Nahmanides' interpretations are redolent of the sights and the scents in the homeland. Expounding the verse in Exodus 3,8: 'A good land and a large, unto a land flowing with milk and honey', he ponders:

> The air is good and wholesome for human beings, and all that is good is found there. . . . It has breadth: lowland, valley and plain are large and fair . . . a land for cattle with good pastures, and there is good water, and the milk increases in the cows. . . . Its fruit is so fat and sweet that it is as if honey issues from the land.

[24] Mica 4, 13. The letter was published by J. Mann in *Hatekufa*, 23, 253 ff.

Deuteronomy 8, 9, reads: 'A land whose stones are iron and out of whose hill thou mayest dig copper.' Nahmanides muses:

> There can also be found quarries of large stones, precious stones, hewn stones to build houses, city walls and towers. And one can find there mines of copper and iron, which supply a great need of the inhabitants of the land. Indeed, thou shalt not lack any thing in it.

No more visions of 'Heavenly Jerusalem' and a royal palace descending from heaven on the Day of Judgement but an image of reality, of farming and building, of crafts and industry, in a land waiting for its settlers. This new realism mirrors the change that had taken place in Jewry's attitude towards the homeland during previous generations.

While Christendom pondered the significance of defeat and theologians were at pains to explain the inexplicable, in their despair reaching the conclusion that the signs and portents may have been misunderstood – or resorting to the traditional Jewish interpretation that their tribulations were due to the sins of mankind – the Jews were also assessing this Christian setback. Nahmanides summed up the great historical experience. Commenting upon Leviticus 26, 32, he says:

> 'And I will bring the land into desolation and your enemies which dwell therein shall be astonished at it.' This is the message of glad tiding throughout the countries of the Exile, that our land does not accept our foes. It is also a decisive proof and a promise to us for in all the inhabited world there is no land so fair and large, settled from time immemorial and which is as desolate as it is now. For ever since we departed from it, it had not accepted a single nation. They all try to settle it but it is beyond their power.

Thus runs the new explanation – the Jewish explanation – of the Crusades: they were a prodigious attempt to wrest the country of the Jews from the Jews (and not from Islam). Rejoicing at the victories of Saladin or Baibars is only incidental. What is of paramount importance is the proof they furnish that no nation can hold the land for long, since it is divinely destined for the Jewish people. Even its desolation is pre-ordained for it prevents others from taking possession. The land awaits the coming of the Jews for 'great is the desolation of the fertile and spacious land for they are not worthy of thee, and thou, too, are not fit for them'.

For Nahmanides the return of the Jewish people is a historical necessity. This is how he interprets Deuteronomy 12, 5:

> 'But the place which the Lord your God shall choose out of all of your tribes to put his name there, even unto his habitation shall ye seek, and hitherto shalt thou come.' That you shall go to Him from a distant land and ask which is the way to the Lord's house and you shall say unto each other, 'Come ye and let us go up to the mountain of the Lord, to the house of the God of Jacob,' as it is written (Jeremiah 50, 5): 'They shall ask the way to Zion with their faces thitherward.' And in *Sifre:* 'Shall ye seek': seek by means of a prophet. You may infer from this that you should tarry until a prophet bids you go. But the Holy Writ says: 'Even unto his habitation shall *ye* seek and thither shalt *thou* come.' Seek and *you* will find and then the prophet will bid you.

In his criticism of Maimonides' *Book of Precepts* he writes:

> We were enjoined to inherit the land given by God – may He be exalted – to our forefathers, Abraham, Isaac, and Jacob and we shall never leave it to any of the nations, neither shall we leave it in desolation, for as Holy Scripture says: 'And ye shall dispossess the inhabitants of the land and dwell therein' (Numbers 33, 53) . . . which means that in all generations were we enjoined to conquer (the land); and I say, that the precept to which the Sages ascribe such great importance, namely to dwell in the Land of Israel . . . all of it is a positive precept, that we are commanded to inherit the land and dwell therein. Consequently this is a positive precept incumbent on *each* generation, binding upon *every* one of us even in time of exile.

Then he goes on to say:

> 'To inherit the land': We shall not leave it in the hands of others or (abandon it) to desolation. . . . And do not be mistakenly led into thinking that this precept applies to the holy war against the Seven Nations (inhabiting the country of Canaan at the time of the Hebrew conquest) . . . this is not so, for we were enjoined to destroy those nations if they make war upon us. But if they wish to make peace, we shall make peace with them and let them stay on upon certain terms. But we shall not leave the land in their hands or those of any other nation at any time whatsoever!

In reaching the conclusion that settlement of the land was a positive precept applying in his own generation, he reverted to the idea expressed in the Midrashic book (*Sifre*) and made it a watch-word : 'Residence in Eretz-Israel equals all other precepts of the Torah.'

This dictum of Nahmanides marks the principal change in the attitude of thirteenth-century Jewry to the Land of Israel. It was no longer a matter of pious pilgrimage, a meritorious act by an individual, nor a prayer for 'restoration of our days of old', but a resolution to strike roots in the land.

Views like those expressed by Nahmanides explain the character and dimensions of the thirteenth-century Jewish migration to the Holy Land. As early as 1209 and again in 1211 two large groups of Jews migrated from Europe. From Provence and Languedoc they came under the leadership of Rabbi Jonathan ha-Cohen, a famous admirer of Maimonides from Lunel. From Normandy and, probably, also from England they were led by the two brothers, Baruh and Meir of Clisson. The outstanding figure in this migration was Rabbi Samson of Sens, one of the most important 'Tossafists' of his age. Two generations later, Rabbi Yehiel of Paris, the leader of French Jewry and hero of another religious disputation (Paris 1240) against the convert Donin, decided to leave France and settle in the Holy Land. According to a local tradition preserved by the first modern student of Palestinology, Eshtori ha-Parhi (beginning of the fourteenth century), he intended to renew in Jerusalem the ritual offering of sacrifices, a clear sign of the belief that the restoration of the Temple was nigh. Yehiel of Paris reached the Holy Land in 1258, but settled in Acre. Here he established the 'Academy of Paris' (*Yeshiva de-Paris*), whose messengers, equipped with a slim volume titled *The Tombs of the Ancestors*, roamed Jewish communities in Europe collecting contributions for the sustenance of their *Yeshiva*. But not only Western Jewry was caught up in this movement.

On 6 December 1286, an edict was issued severely affecting the Jews of the royal domain in the German empire. On coming to the throne, Rudolf von Habsburg ordered the confiscation of property from all Jews leaving Germany. The order in question specifically mentions their destination – *Ultramare* (overseas), a term which in contemporary usage referred to the crusader kingdom. The edict, dealing first with the imperial domain, lists several major Jewish centres: Speyer, Worms, Mainz, Oppenheim and Wetterau – the great Jewish communities on the Rhine.

Six months previously, in the summer of 1286, an exodus from Germany to the Holy Land had begun, headed by the acknowledged leader of German Jewry, Rabbi Meir of Rothenburg. Like his predecessor Nahmanides, Rabbi Meir was moved by the dramatic failure of the Crusades. In a *responsum* he writes:

> It is written: 'And your enemies that dwell therein shall be astonished at it' which means that the gentile nations that are there do not flourish because they are sinful. Therefore the Land of Israel is now desolate and has no walled cities, nor is it settled like other countries.

He urged settlement of the land and cautioned against the immigration of irresponsible people, who regard the religious commandments lightly. Rabbi Meir practised what he preached. Our source – 'Book of Customs of the Community of Worms' (*Pinqas Minhagei Worms*) – gives an eloquent description of his odyssey and sufferings:

> Our teacher, R. Meir of Rothenburg, of blessed memory, set out on a journey across the sea, he and his household, his daughters, son-in-law and all that he had. He came to a certain town amidst tall mountains, known as the '*Lombardische Gebirge*' in German, to wait there until all those who wished to journey with him, arrived. Suddenly the wicked bishop of Basle rode from Rome through that same city accompanied by an apostate Knipse – may his name and memory be blotted out – who recognized our teacher and reported the matter to the bishop and caused Count Meinhardt of Goerts, the lord of that city, to seize him on the fourth of Tammuz in the year of the Creation 5046 and hand him over to King Rudolf...

Here we have a terse, first-hand account of an organized, clandestine flight from Germany led by Rabbi Meir of Rothenburg. Rabbi Meir's party had eluded the vigilance of the authorities and succeeded in making its way as far as Lombardy where they were to meet other groups, heading for the same destination – the

Holy Land. Emperor Rudolf had Rabbi Meir incarcerated in a fortress until he died seven years later. His body was ransomed and interred in Worms.

In this context we can more readily understand a statement by an anonymous disciple of Nahmanides reflecting his master's thinking. Living in Acre shortly before its fall in 1291, he wrote : 'Let no man think that the King Messiah will appear in an impure land; and let him not be deluded either into imagining that he will appear in the Land of Israel among the gentiles'. And he draws the seemingly natural conclusion that the settlement of the Land by the Jews is a prerequisite for the advent of the Messiah, and concludes:

Now many are rising up and willingly going to the Land of Israel. And many hold that the coming of the Redeemer is at hand, when they behold how the gentiles have made their yoke heavy upon Israel in most places, as well as other well-known signs that have been revealed to the Chosen.

XIV

THE MILITARY ORDERS

Few institutions created in the Latin kingdom can claim originality. The kingdom drew its inspirations from European experience and seldom ventured to innovate, unless forced to by local conditions. The mental disposition to perpetuate the customs of the homeland almost precluded any attempts at originality. There was no lack of talent or opportunity, but the social and intellectual climate of crusader society stunted the new and original.

There were two notable exceptions to this general rule, in which the crusaders gave free rein to their particular genius: the military orders, warfare and fortifications. The fact that the crusaders found in religious knighthood and warfare a field for innovation is significant and illuminating. The former expressed a new ethos markedly influenced by the movement and ideology of the Crusades; the latter proved the faculty of learning and adaptation to the most vital of all problems, that of physical existence. The first expressed an institutionalized ideology, whereas the second can be regarded as a practical lesson learned by a minority ruling a kingdom in a permanent state of war, or at the least under active or latent siege from within and without.

The earliest military order in the Holy Land was that of St John. The date of foundation is not decisive in establishing a claim to priority in ideology and organization. In its earliest phase the order of St John devoted itself to the care of sick and needy pilgrims. As such, it filled an important role in the life of the early kingdom, but hardly constituted an innovation, since such institutions existed along the pilgrim routes of Europe hundreds of years earlier. But even at this stage the congregation of St John in

Jerusalem differed, and not by coincidence, from similar European institutions. The originality consisted of linking charity in its most humble aspect – hospital care – to members drawn from a haughty class of hereditary rulers and warriors. Though charity was written large in the code of Christian ethics and social circumstances made it incumbent on the rich and mighty, these biblical sentiments were never embodied in an aristocratic institution. Charity by the mighty meant a condescending distribution of alms. A quite different view was held by the small group of knights which gathered around the saintly Gerard almost immediately after the crusader conquest of Jerusalem. They proclaimed charity as their primary task and obligation. Thus, knighthood entered a hitherto almost exclusively monastic and ecclesiastical sphere.

It is futile to speculate how this important innovation would have influenced mediaeval social attitudes, and its impact on the Holy Land and upon European nobility. The organic evolution of the original Hospitaller ideology was interrupted a generation later, when a new association of knights laid the foundations of the Order of the Temple. The Templars created a new ideology. Its appeal, and consequently its competitive force, was so strong that the older order had to adopt the new ideology while continuing to pursue its original ideals. Thus the Order of St John finally embodied in its rules ideas derived from two different and unrelated premises: a knightly-hospitallery and a newer knightly-monastic ideology. Time proved their incompatibility and brought about a functional differentiation, which ultimately expressed social distinctions within the order. The care of the sick remained an obligation of the order. But in everyday life – though acknowledged very late in the official rule – military aims and its noble brethren-in-arms became the dominant factor of evolution.

The new Templar ideology (tentatively formulated *c.* 1128) fused two current ideals of mediaeval society, knighthood and monasticism, into a code for a community of warrior-monks, a phenomenon new in European history, but not unknown to other cultures.

A thousand years of Christian tradition opposed warfare and bloodshed on principle, though sometimes forced to bow to human nature and reality. Ethical doctrines proclaimed by the Church hardly changed society. Nevertheless, this influence should not be minimized. The warrior lived with a sense of guilt, and his social class, though admittedly necessary for the existence and stability of society, was not accepted without qualifications by the ethical spokesmen of Christendom. Hence the penitences of nobles, recurrent 'conversions' on the death-bed and the taking of a monk's habit with the *viaticum*. The Crusades marked the first breakthrough towards ethical acceptance of the warrior class. This made the idea of a military order legitimate and feasible.

The Crusades and the crusaders' oath sanctioned by the Church, marked a compromise with traditional teaching. The Church legitimized the profession of arms by a definition of its aims. The class of warriors were now justified before God and society. Henceforth, they were endowed with a socially legitimate function in a God-willed society and became an *ordo*.

In mediaeval usage *ordo* meant far more than an organization or corporate body, since it included the idea of a social and public function. Men who belonged to an *ordo* not merely followed their personal destiny, but filled a place in a Christian polity. The warriors as a class were now an *ordo* with an *officium*. This idea is stressed in the short introduction to the early Rule of the Temple. Knighthood, it says, deviated from its aims. 'It despised the love of justice, which pertained to its *office* and did not do what it should, that is – defend the poor, widows, orphans and the Church, but instead competed to rape, spoil and kill.'[1] It is therefore the first aim of the new institution to restore the 'Order of Chivalry' to its purity. This is the meaning of the Templars' claim, that 'in this "Religion" [i.e. the new military association] the Order of Chivalry flourished and was resuscitated'[2] and for this purpose they appealed to those 'who led the life of "secular chivalry" in which Jesus Christ was not the cause and embraced it for human favours, to follow those whom God in his mercy elected from the mass of perdition and ordained for the defence of the holy Church'.[3]

[1] *Règle du Temple*, ed. H. Curson, par. 2.
[2] *Ibid.*
[3] *Ibid.*, par. 1.

An ideal of 'pure' chivalry was then thought to have once existed, though corrupted by time, and the Templars were bent on restoring its pristine purity.

The close relation between the Rule of the Temple and Bernard of Clairvaux is well known and some of the ideas met with here will be repeated by him in a famous treatise called 'On the Praise of the New Knighthood' (*De laude novae militiae*) and propagated twenty years later when preaching the Second Crusade.[4] Similar ideas, however, were already quite current a few years after the capture of Jerusalem. Two non-participant chroniclers of the First Crusade saw this occasion as a God-willed opportunity to restore knighthood to its ideal functions. Guibert de Nogent attributes the following statement to Urban II at Clermont:

> Until now you fought undue (or unjust) wars; you shot poisoned arrows in mutual carnage solely motivated by cupidity and haughtiness. These merited you doom and certain damnation. Now we propose to you wars which carry with them the reward of glorious martyrdom, wars which assure the title to temporal and eternal glory.[5]

Even more outspoken is Baldric, bishop of Dole (*c.* 1110), coining a succinct expression, later propagated (but not invented) by Bernard of Clairvaux. According to his version of the speech at Clermont, the pope said:

> It is not a knighthood of Christ which devours the sheep of the Saviour. Holy Church reserved for her defence knighthood (*militia*), but you depraved it into malice (*malitia*) . . . If you want to save your souls, either throw away the belt of this knighthood or proceed boldly as knights of Christ and go speedily to the defence of the oriental Church.[6]

The pursuit of a chivalrous ideal, which made the worldly warrior into a knight of Christ represented one aspect of Templar ideology. This ideal and the 'conversion' to a new way of life will save man

---

[4] See the study of G. Constable, 'The Second Crusade as seen by Contemporaries', *Traditio*, 9 (1953), 213–79.

[5] Guibert de Nogent in *RHC, Hist. Occidentaux*, IV, 138.

[6] Baldricus episcopus Dolensis in *RHC. Hist. Occidentaux*, IV, 14. The much used *dictum* is *malitia non militia*.

and enable him to escape from the great mass of those predestined to perdition.

Whereas the Rule of the Temple explains the meaning of Christ's knighthood it does not explain that of the monastic community. The latter is accepted as common knowledge and the Rule is more concerned with ordering the life of the members in the new association than in propounding principles. It simply says: 'If any "secular" [of the world] knight, or anybody else, wants to leave the mass of perdition and abandon the world and choose communal life', [7] and again: 'You who renounce your individual wills and others who will serve the Sovereign King for a determined time mounted and with arms for the salvation of your souls.' [8] The meaning was clear to all contemporaries. The monastic vows joined to the precepts of chivalry do not, as is often argued, change the essence of knighthood. Chivalry becomes Christian knighthood not because of monasticism, but by restoration to its proper ideals. The role of the monastic vow is to institutionalize Christian knighthood, and by the triple vow of poverty, chastity and obedience impose a way of life upon knightly existence. The Western genius of organization furnished the element of association, just as six hundred years earlier Benedict of Nursia changed hermitism to monasticism. A warrior's deeds honoured his name, but those of a knight of Christ were to the glory of God. Individual anonymity exalts the community, the Order of the Temple.

Once the ecclesiastical prohibition of bloodshed ceased to be an obstacle, knighthood and monasticism became complementary, as bluntly expressed in the Rule of the Temple: 'This new type of religion' came into being 'so that knighthood should be admitted to religion and thus religion armed by knighthood should progress and kill the enemy without guilt.' [9]

The rise of the Templars from a small group headed by Hugh de Payens around 1118 to a great military order was spectacular.

---

[7] *Règle du Temple*, par. 2, transl. from the French version. The Latin text differs slightly. *Chevalier seculier* is simply *miles; eslire la vostre communal vie* is *vestram communionem et vitam elegerit.*

[8] *Ibid.*, par. 9. *Volentés* is *voluptates* in Latin.

[9] *Ibid.*, par. 57.

Their original task as an armed escort for Christian pilgrims on their way from the coast to Jerusalem and from the capital to the holy places on the banks of the Jordan, soon became obsolete and was replaced by major military responsibilities. The original purpose became unimportant with growing internal security and policing hardly suited a sizeable knightly community. Defence has rarely been a virtue with military establishments and things were not different with the Templars. Protection and defence of pilgrims was metamorphosed into protection and defence of the kingdom. After all, all the crusaders were 'pilgrims'.

Although the military orders were not created by state or Church, no other establishment contributed more to their strength and position. Though they absorbed the military orders into their structures and became strengthened in the process, simultaneous ferment threatened their authority at times. The military orders supported the Church, but were at odds with the local hierarchy; they vastly contributed to the power of the state but not always to that of its institutions.

A long list of papal bulls[10] steadily extended the privileges of the orders. Their exemption from diocesan jurisdiction and their direct dependence on the Holy See went so far as to make them immune to anathema by the local bishops. Finally, they were even allowed to open their churches on specific days when the city was under interdict. The local hierarchy was thus deprived of any disciplinary means against the military orders.

The orders also competed with ecclesiastical organization on the local level. Despite strong opposition, some of the orders' chapels and churches arrogated parish prerogatives, depriving the local churches of their parishioners and income. The cemeteries of the Order of St John competed with those of the local churches and brought substantial legacies to the order's treasury. At the same time, the growing land-holdings of the orders often diminished regular church revenues. The Christian inhabitants of the country

---

[10] The earliest ecclesiastical privilege of the Hospitallers was accorded by the bull of Paschal II: *Pie postulatio voluntatis* in 1113; of the Templars by Innocent II in 1139: *Omne datum optimum.*

were probably obliged to pay tithes since the establishment of the Latin kingdom, but certainly since the Council of Nablus in 1120. These included tithes on landed property and even on the spoils of war. The tithe was paid by the Christian peasantry and by the Frankish landowners, who deducted it from their agricultural rents and duties. The landed properties of the order thus created a particular problem. At this point, the local clergy had the upper hand and the orders were not exempted from payment of the tithe, unless specifically freed by the local authorities.[11] Otherwise formal agreements had to be concluded, sometimes splitting the tithe between the contending parties. A papal privilege[12] which freed the orders from tithe payments on their demesne (financially important as this was in the orders' European possessions) missed the mark entirely in the Latin kingdom. As explained elsewhere,[13] the peculiarity of the crusaders' rural regime was the lack of a proper manorial system, i.e. the absence of demesne lands. Consequently, the orders could only partially profit from the papal privilege. This was used to exempt vineyards, olive groves and sugar-cane plantations, which were directly cultivated for the use of the orders, from tithe payments. Moreover, the orders tried to circumvent the tithe by converting corn-growing properties into tithe-exempt plantations, which often aggravated quarrels with the local clergy, followed by complicated agreements to settle the difference.

When reviewing the different privileges, the aggressiveness of the orders and their almost permanent attempts to exploit their privileges to the point of abuse stand out. This seems to be a feature of many corporate bodies, less easily checked than individuals. The orders even tried to extend their privileges to affiliated laymen (as *confratres*). Since such affiliations included a good number of the local nobility – always the main benefactors of the Church – this could have proved ruinous. At this point the com-

---

[11] The earliest example are the privileges granted by the patriarch of Jerusalem and the archbishop of Caesarea to the Hospitallers in 1112. Delaville le Roulx, I, no. 25 and no. 29.

[12] See details in J. Riley-Smith, *op. cit.*, 380 ff.

[13] See below, cap. XVI, Economic Life and Commerce: A.

plaints of the local clergy once again limited the voracious appetite of the orders.

The unceasing complaints and quarrels recorded in scores of documents prove that the military orders, despite their obvious services to the kingdom, never endeared themselves to the local hierarchy. Even the patriarch of Jerusalem, who gave his blessings to the primitive Templar association and thought of making the military orders a mainstay of his own position,[14] was sorely disappointed when they refused him any but the most theoretical obedience. All these difficulties on the local level stand in glaring contrast to the relations with the Roman curia.

The curia observed the evolution of the military orders with utmost benevolence and solicitude. In the Iberian peninsula and in the Latin establishments of the East, the military orders already played a major role in the defence and expansion of Christendom during the twelfth century. The papacy was not slow to appreciate the possibilities of an international, well-disciplined movement, whose unqualified obedience made every house an effective instrument in the hands of the master and chapter, direct servant of the Holy See. Long before the mendicant orders and the Jesuits, the ramified network of the military orders could be and was at the service of the papacy. The Roman curia was not parsimonious in granting privileges to and in defence of the orders. This drew heavy criticism during the Third Lateran Council, when a flood of complaints demanded a stop to the progressive exemptions of the orders. Some half-hearted attempts to limit the military orders followed, but by then the major privileges had already been granted and they were not abrogated.

It is historical irony that finally, the international character of the orders, their privileges, exemptions and their direct dependence on Rome allowed the pope (hard pressed by the king of France) to dissolve the mighty Order of the Temple and bring its master and his companions to the burning stake.

Although the local hierarchy had reason enough to see an aggressive and encroaching factor in the military orders, critics – even

[14] H. Prutz, 'Die Autonomie des Templer-Ordens', *Sitzungsberichte d. phil. -philolog. und. hist. Klasse d. Bayrischen Akad. d. Wissenschaften* 1905, 7 ff.

from among the clergy – could not but acknowledge their magnificent contribution to the security and strength of the Latin East. Both military orders enjoyed roughly the same ecclesiastical exemptions and privileges, but there was a marked divergence in their political and economic positions in the different crusader principalities.

In the Latin kingdom proper the Hospitallers acquired far more landed possessions than the Templars. Indeed, they had a start of almost a generation on the Templars.[15] This might have influenced the difference in landownership to some extent, but an additional factor should be sought for in the fact that donations to the orders were regarded primarily as acts of charity. The connection of the Hospitallers with welfare might have had more appeal to potential donors. It was charitable to grant an estate to an order which cared for the sick and needy and such aims tallied well with a specific type of donation, the so-called 'grant in alms' (*eleemosina*), involving no counter-services or duties by the recipient, apart from prayers on behalf of the benefactor.

The landed possessions of the orders grew considerably during the twelfth century. With the establishment of the Teutonic Knights as an independent body during the Third Crusade, the orders became an economic power in the country. Their true importance though was not financial since their standing was ultimately determined by their role as the military mainstay of the country.

Several factors combined to create this situation. With the exception of Spain,[16] very few contemporary states were engaged in such constant warfare as the Latin kingdom. Even during the rare years without major military expeditions frontier forays continued, aggravated by permanently insecure roads in the Moslem countryside. This involved a tremendous burden of military readiness. As in European states, the main force of the kingdom was the feudal levy. The crusader host was probably more efficient and easier to mobilize than its European counterpart,

[15] H. Prutz, *Die geistl. Ritterorden*, 49 ff.
[16] See E. Lourie, 'A Society Organized for War: Medieval Spain', *Past and Present*, 1966, 54–76.

but its small size constituted a chronic weakness. The military effectives based on feudal service did not exceed some 670 knights and several thousand foot soldiers. Part of this force was permanently immobilized by garrison duty in citadels or castles, further reducing the numbers which could take the field. This explains the major role of the military orders in the defence of the kingdom.

The orders could raise an army almost as numerous as that of the kingdom. Though exact numbers are not available, it seems plausible that each order kept some three hundred brethren-at-arms in the kingdom. The combined force of the Hospitallers and Templars thus equalled the entire feudal levy.

Numbers were not the sole criterion. The contingents of the military orders lived in a state of permanent mobilization whereas the forces of the kingdom had to be specially mobilized in times of danger. The military orders were always ready, since their existence was based on the premise of war. Fighting or guard duty was the normal pattern of life, and war their normal obligation. Nothing could be blunter than the following quotation from the Rule of the Temple:

> O venerable brothers, God is with you, because you promised to despise the treacherous world for the eternal love of God and to despise the yearnings of your body. Replenished and sanctified with the flesh of God, wise and strengthened by the precepts of the Lord, after the end of the Divine service, be not afraid to go to battle, but be ready for the crown of martyrdom. [17]

The rules of the orders thus not merely facilitated instant mobilization, but also assured the permanence of the effectives. The orders were pan-Christian organizations almost from their inception. Headquarters were naturally located in the Holy Land, but they recruited in Europe, which put at their disposal the means to fulfil their tasks in the Holy Land. The spread of the military orders in Europe remained unparalleled until the rise of the Mendicant Friars a hundred years later. Created in the Holy Land in response

---

[17] *Règle du Temple*, par. 9.

to a local challenge, their success in Europe can be only partially attributed to this limited challenge. The preservation of the liberated Holy Sepulchre and the defence of Christendom against the Infidel were indeed a mighty factor in recruiting the European nobility, but their spiritual and social message to a warrior class in search of identity and ideals proved even more potent.

By 1113 the Hospitallers already owned property and houses at Saint-Gilles (France) and in Asti, Pisa, Bari, Otranto and Messina in Italy.[18] In 1134 Alphonse I of Aragon and Navarre willed his whole kingdom to be equally divided between the Hospitallers, Templars and the Holy Sepulchre.[19] To describe the immense wealth of the orders in Europe exceeds our purpose. Thirteenth-century chroniclers allege that the Hospitallers alone possessed some nineteen thousand manors in Europe![20] These data can hardly be verified, but they reflect the impression made by this wealth on their contemporaries. We are concerned with the fact that year after year one third of the Hospitallers' revenue was transferred to their headquarters in the Holy Land.[21] These were the famous *responsiones* or accountabilities imposed on all houses of the order wherever they might be. Sometimes special needs of the Holy Land would make a given house or province responsible for supplying the mother house with certain items. For example, in 1182 the general chapter of the Hospitallers decreed that the prior of France should send 100 pieces and the prior of Saint-Gilles another 100 pieces of cotton for bed-covers; Antioch had to send 2,000 ells of cotton; the priors of Italy and those of Pisa and Venice 2,000 ells each of fustian in different colours; Constantinople 200 felts; whereas sugar was supplied from the order's estates in Tripoli and Tiberias.[22] The associated costs were to be covered by local revenue or collected in local alms. In addition, the Order of St John

[18] All enumerated in a confirmation of Pope Paschal II. Delaville le Roulx, I, no. 30.
[19] The Latin establishments later on relinquished their parts of the kingdom to the reigning dynasty.
[20] Matthew Paris, *Chronica maiora*, IV, 291.
[21] See details, J. Riley-Smith, *op. cit.*, esp. 334, 344 ff and 362 ff.
[22] Delaville le Roulx, I, 426–7.

had its own ships for transporting supplies collected in Europe to the Holy Land. At times they even competed with the maritime cities in conveying pilgrims and merchandise, thus creating further sources of income.[23]

The same held true for the Templars. In addition to vast European possessions, they became one of the great bankers of the period. With houses all over Europe, inspiring confidence because of their religious standing and the permanent presence of armed guardians, the Templars were quick to enter the field of high finance. Deposits, transfers, the movement and exchange of money, issuance of credit instruments and, finally, money lending, must all have included, dissimulated and decried usury. By the thirteenth century the Templars were familiar figures among the fiscal advisers of Western royalty, as they had long been in the financial councils of the papacy. Their economic activities embraced the whole of western Europe and the traffic between Europe and the Levant. But we also find the Templars and Hospitallers lending money to crusader rulers. It was not unknown for the orders to become landowners and even feudal lords when the mortgaged local nobility were unable to pay their debts. Nevertheless, in the Holy Land the orders seem to have been rather lenient creditors.

There is obviously a deep abyss between those professing to be 'the Custodians and Serfs of our Lords the Poor' or the 'Poor Fellow Soldiers of Christ and of the Temple of Solomon' and their actual position as landowners, lords of castles, rulers of provinces and bankers. This does not imply that the orders used the cloak of sanctity to cover their earthly gains. The *responsiones* of the Hospitallers from Europe were first brought to the ward of the sick and poor,[24] and only then transferred to the order's treasury. This was more than a memory of ideals now relegated to the realm of symbols, or a hypocritical gesture to conceal base instincts. The military orders did not escape a pattern of behaviour met in communities

[23] The contention by Prutz that the Order of St John regulated or even dominated the pilgrim traffic is untenable, even for the early period of the 12th century.

[24] See e.g. in the Rules of Margat (1204–6) in Delaville le Roulx, II, 39 (no. 1193).

vowed to personal, but not collective poverty. Even the more spiritual mendicant orders could not escape this evolution, neither did their most idealistic, poverty-vowed, modern counterparts. It is not our task to pass judgement on the greed or riches of the military orders, but to appreciate the use they made of their resources within the framework of their declared ideals.

Their contribution to welfare, care of the sick and to the defence of the kingdom is hardly open to doubt. The hospital of the Order of St John in Jerusalem is said to have cared for some 2,000 sick any day of the year, the great quantities of food, clothing and the vast alms expended in Jerusalem and Acre drew exclamations of wonder from Christian and Jewish pilgrims, otherwise prone to censoriousness. Nothing on such a scale was known in their native Europe, though the Byzantine empire and the waqf establishments of the Moslem East could have furnished examples for comparison, as they probably did for emulation.

From about 1130 up to the fall of the kingdom, hardly a major military expedition took place without the active participation of the military orders. Their bravery was proverbial, though characteristic of every warrior-class. The knights of the orders were distinguished from the normal run of noble fighters by their obedience and discipline. Every written and unwritten code of feudalism or chivalry made desertion of the lord during battle a monstrous and unpardonable offence. But strategy and tactics were ultimately dependent upon obedience to orders and discipline and these qualities never loomed large in feudal armies, basically composed of unbridled individuals. Nearly every battle tended to dissolve into mounted duels between a knight and his opponent. Only absolute obedience and perfect discipline made the contingents of the orders such a formidable foe to the Moslem armies.[25] In addition, training formed part of their daily schedule and the continuity of their existence turned them into a repository of military tradition and experience. No European host on a

---

[25] The conduct of the Templars when acting as rearguard to the hosts of the Second Crusade at the battle of Mt Cadmos gained them fame and general admiration.

Crusade could dispense with the advice of the orders. They knew the East and the Moslem foe, with all his strengths and weaknesses.

Hesitatingly in the first half of the twelfth century, but with ever-growing alacrity in its second half and in the thirteenth century, the Templars, Hospitallers and finally also the Teutonic Knights manned the bulwarks of Latin domination in the East – the mammoth frontier castles and the strongholds inland. When, under Moslem pressure, the frontiers moved westward and inland castles became border fortresses and when, finally, the walls of the coastal cities became the last frontiers of the kingdom the military orders took over their defence.

Strangely enough, the first order to garrison castles was not the Templars, but the Hospitallers. As early as 1137 the Order of St John received from Fulk, king of Jerusalem, the castle of Beit-Jibrin (*Gibelin*) and began its military career. In 1152 the city of Gaza was handed over to the Templars, and with it the defence of the Egyptian frontier and its main bulwark – Ascalon. Five years later, in 1157, the Hospitallers again participated in the defence of the soon-to-be-lost frontier city and castles of Banyas and Chastel Neuf on the Damascene frontier. It was recently estimated that until 1160 the Order of St John acquired some 7 or 8 castles; with an additional 11 or 12 castles plus certain rights over 6 others by around 1160. By 1180 the order held 25 castles and 29 in 1244.[26] At one time or another the Order of St John held some 56 fortresses in Palestine and Syria.[27] The Templars never held so many castles or fortified places in the East and the Teutonic Knights – relative newcomers – even less. The total number of castles garrisoned by the orders greatly exceeded those held by any ruler, not excluding the king. There was much truth in the remark ascribed to King Thoros of Armenia who visited the Latin kingdom in the middle of the twelfth century: 'When I came into your land' – he said to the king of Jerusalem – 'and asked about the castles, some said to me: "this belongs to the Temple"; others said

---

[26] This last number is far more impressive than is apparent. By 1244 less than one quarter of the former territories belonged to the crusader states.

[27] J. Riley-Smith, *op. cit.*, 69 ff and 136 ff.

that they belonged to the Hospital and others to the abbey of Mount Zion. Thus I could not find any castles, cities or towns which belonged to you, except three. But all belong to the religious orders.'[28]

In the twelfth century, castles handed over to the orders were usually royal, but even then some nobles (like the lord of Banyas) who were unable to maintain and defend their castles were willing to share the responsibility with the military orders in a kind of *pariage*. This situation became acute in the thirteenth century, when the loss of the eastern hinterland in the wake of Hittin, left the Palestinian nobility with very limited resources. Like one of the Ibelins, lord of Beirut, they often spent their revenue from Cyprus to hold their possessions on the mainland. The outcome was a wholesale handing over of castles and even cities to the military orders. The Hospitallers took over Arsuf around 1260 and the Templars the northern cities of Beirut and Sidon in 1278. Estates and very often whole baronies naturally went with the castles and cities.[29]

The poverty of the kingdom explains why all new major fortifications erected in the thirteenth century belonged neither to king nor noble, but to the military orders. Thus the largest of all castles in the Latin East, Chastel Pèlerin ('Athlit – begun 1218) as well as Saphet (beg. 1240) were handed over to the Templars and Monfort (in later tradition 'Starkenberg' – Qal'at Qurein) to the Teutonic Knights. When in the middle of the thirteenth century Mount Tabor became the march, the Hospitallers took over

Despite the decisive role of the military orders in the Latin kingdom, they never achieved in the south the position which they acquired in the northern principalities, the county of Tripoli and the principality of Antioch. As early as 1144 the Order of St John received from Raymond II a large, almost compact territory on the frontier of the county of Tripoli. The gigantic Crac des Chevalier its defence.

[28] *Ernoul*, ed. P. Paris, 26–7.

[29] See G. Beyer, 'Die Verschiebungen der Grundbesitzverhältnisse in Palästina während der Kreuzfahrerzeit', *Palästina-Jahrbuch*, 32 (1936), 101–10.

(*Hisn al-Akrad* – 'Castle of the Kurds') rose later in this area. In 1168, Bohemond III of Antioch handed over the defence of his eastern march with Apamea (Famiyah – Moslem since 1149) to the Order of St John. Though the two grants differ in many details, they have one thing in common. The Order of St John is recognized not only as a tenant-in-chief of the county and principality, but also as an almost independent entity in a loose federation.[30] In both cases the order was recognized as liege lord of its territories and not only allowed to pursue an independent foreign policy in regard to its Moslem neighbours, but both the count and the prince agreed to follow the Hospitallers' advice in regard to their own policy. In the case of Antioch, it was even agreed that the Hospitallers need not abide by treaties contracted by the prince without their consent!

None of the military orders ever reached a similar position of independence in the Latin kingdom proper. The reason might be sought in the fact that during the twelfth century the kingdom was far more secure than its northern crusader neighbours. The defence of the kingdom's marches was based on the castles of Transjordan and on the fortifications in the narrow strip around Gaza. In both areas, the expanse of the desert reduced the danger of sudden incursions, which allowed the royal or seigniorial garrisons to undertake the normal defence of the castles. In addition, the kings of Jerusalem had more prestige than the crusader rulers of the north and the creation of a quasi-independent state in the Holy Land was psychologically less feasible.

Whatever the reason, the military orders did not achieve independent status, nor even the privileges enjoyed by the Venetians in Tyre. There is nothing to prove that the military orders were sovereign lords even in their own quarters. In the capital, Jerusalem, a relatively large quarter, just across the southern entrance of the Holy Sepulchre, belonged to the Hospitallers and corresponded roughly to the present 'Muristan' (Pers. hospital),

---

[30] Delaville le Roulx, *Cartulaire*, nos. 144 and 391. The territories in the principality of Antioch were later enlarged with the acquisition of Margat (Markab) and Valenia (Bulunyas) in 1186. *Cartulaire*, no. 783.

which became a market-place at the turn of this century.[31] But there is no evidence that the Hospitallers held jurisdiction over the inhabitants of the quarter. The same held true for the Templars' area where the Mosques of Omar and al-Aqsa stand. In contrast, the patriarch had rights of jurisdiction in his quarter of Jerusalem. In Acre, three extensive quarters belonged to the great military orders in the old city, in addition to quarters in the new suburb of Mont Musard. In the thirteenth century the latter was enclosed by walls and formed self-sufficient boroughs. Again we have no proof of seigniorial jurisdiction in the quarters. It thus seems plausible to suggest that only members of the orders or the closely affiliated lived or were allowed to live in these quarters. The question of jurisdiction over *all* inhabitants thus never arose, since the orders had absolute jurisdiction over their own members.

On the other hand, there is no question as to the seigniorial jurisdiction of the orders in their rural possessions, or their rights of jurisdiction over burgesses in villages and cities acquired by them. This is specifically stated in some cases as for Beit-Jibrin or Arsuf (in the latter case even baronial jurisdiction) at the time of transfer.

The acquisition of manorial and lordly holdings created military and legal problems. If a lordship was acquired by a military order, it might be stipulated that the military services owed to the Crown should be rendered by the new lord. This could have meant that the contingent of knights raised in the lordship should be furnished by the order. In some cases this was effected by the former hereditary vassals; in others the order could probably supply a contingent of its own. In any case the total numbers were not reduced, though the strength of the feudal levy as such lost in importance.

The legal aspect of the orders' property was more significant. The acquisition of a lordship ousted theoretically a former lay tenant-in-chief from the Crown's counsel and from his position as a member of the High Court. Did this imply that the order would

[31] Cf. C. Schick, 'The ancient churches in the *Muristan*', *Quart. Statement of the Pal. Expl. Fund*, 1902, 50–3. The area is the property of the Greek-Orthodox Patriarchate and as such the carved letters T-Ph (Taphou) on the gate mark it as belonging to the Holy Sepulchre.

take his place and become formal tenant-in-chief to the Crown? As far as we know this was never the case. The orders never legally entered into vassalage with the Crown. Even in the case of Arsuf, where it is formally stipulated that the Order of St John will perform the duties owed by its former lord to the Crown, *service de corps* (which means the personal service owed by the lord 'with his body' to the Crown) was explicitly excepted. It cannot even be proven that the grand masters of the orders ever performed an act of homage for acquired feudal possessions, though an investiture certainly took place and an oath of fealty may have been taken. The orders were not, in the ordinary meaning of the term, vassals of the Crown and their masters were not 'men of their Lord the King'.

Even the ancient oath of obedience to the patriarch of Jerusalem once taken by the Templars fell into abeyance, and no special oath to the king on behalf of the orders was formally taken. There were no formal or legal links between the state and the order. This should not be construed as denoting any kind of tension in their relations. The military orders powerfully contributed to the existence and evolution of the kingdom; their particular legal position only stresses one of the kingdom's characteristics, its loose framework of organization and the juxtaposition of establishments never integrated into one whole.

The position of the two great orders – the Hospitallers and the Templars – is emphasized when compared with the third military order created in the Holy Land, the Teutonic Knights (or the Order of St Mary of Teutons).[32]

The earliest attempt to create a Teutonic association within crusader society harks back to the First Kingdom and is symptomatic of the kingdom's attitude to a linguistic and partly cultural

---

[32] For sources see gen. bibl. Special studies of the Teutonic Order in the Holy Land: H. Prutz, *Die Besitzungen des Deutschen Ordens im Heiligen Lande*, Leipzig, 1877; M. Oehler, *Geschichte des Deutschen Ritterordens*, 2 vols, Elbing, 1908–12; M. Tumler, *Der Deutsche Orden im Werden, Wachsen und Wirken bis 1400*, Wien, 1955 (very apologetic but uses primary sources; excellent bibliography); W. Hubatsch, *Monfort und die Bildung des Deutschordensstaates im Heiligen Lande*, Göttingen, 1966 (title misleading).

minority, unable and perhaps unwilling to be absorbed by the dominant French culture of the conquerors.

The Teutonic Knights were not founded and recognized as a military order before the Third Crusade. A pious fraud, perpetuated by the order itself, alleged an earlier origin by connecting the Teutonic Knights with a hospital founded by Franks of German origin in the city of Jerusalem, during the first half of the twelfth century.[33] As early as the time of Baldwin I (d. 1118) a German hospital, hospice and chapel seem to have been erected for pilgrims of German origin. Such ethnic foundations were not exceptional among the Franks. For example, a Hungarian hospice existed in Jerusalem at the same period, not to mention hospices for oriental Christians, where language and rites defined the establishment and its clientele.

The services of the new establishment were most welcome to pilgrims from central and eastern Europe who did not speak French, the common language of the city. The relations of this establishment with the Order of St John are not very clear.

The great Hospitaller order of St John may have given a helping hand or the new establishment could have looked for such help. Some kind of affiliation seems to have been created, if we can accept as genuine a letter by Pope Celestine II in 1143. This letter mentions an attempt by the German establishment to assure its independence. The pope granted limited autonomy, expressed by the existence of a special prior, within the framework of the older order.[34]

The German establishment in Jerusalem was located in one of the streets which lead from the south-western gate of the city on Mount Zion to the Temple esplanade, just below the Armenian quarter. During the Mameluk period this became the Jewish quarter. Recent excavations (1968) among the ruins of this quarter

[33] A good summary in M. Tumler, *op. cit.* The recent study by W. Hubatsch accepts obvious forgeries to stress the connections between the old German association and the new order.

[34] Delaville le Roulx, I, nos 154 and 155. The bull of Celestine II was renewed by Gregory IX when the Teutonic Order gave its support to the excommunicated Frederick II. R. Röhricht, *Regesta Regni Hierosolymitani*, no. 214 note.

brought to light the remains of a small Romanesque church, which can be safely identified as the church of St Mary of the Teutons. German pilgrims stressed the inadequacy and poverty of the establishment, since it had to rely on the support of German-speaking pilgrims only and Germany never became a centre of crusader activity or migration.

It is impossible to say how this early German establishment would have developed, because the battle of Hittin and the subsequent capture of the holy city by Saladin put an end to its existence. However, the German hospice met a real need of crusader society, which became more acute during the Third Crusade. Despite the fact that Emperor Frederick I died before reaching the siege of Acre, important contingents led by German princes landed in the bay of the city. The need of a hospital for German-speaking soldiers became obvious. According to a venerated and picturesque tradition, a field hospital was erected by crusaders from Bremen and Lübeck, who used planks and ship-sails for its construction. The favour of German princes, especially Frederick of Schwaben and that of his royal brother, Henry VI, brought prompt confirmation by Pope Clement III (1191) and additional privileges from Celestine III (1196). A year later, when a large German contingent tarried in the Holy Land, vainly expecting Emperor Henry VI, the new association was transformed into a full-fledged military order. There is a charming description of this event in the earliest chronicle of the order – written some years later – the so-called 'Narrative of the Origins of the Teutonic Order'.[35]

> To many of the German princes (writes the chronicler) it seemed useful and noble to bestow on the above-mentioned hospital the Rule of the Templars. For this purpose the German prelates, princes and nobles assembled in the house of the Templars (in Acre) and invited to such a salutary gathering some of the available prelates and barons of the Holy Land. One and all decided unanimously that the hospital should follow in regard to the poor and the sick the Rule of the Hospital of St John of Jerusalem as it had done until now; whereas in regard to clergy, knights and other brothers, it should follow

[35] M. Perlbach, *Die Statuten des Deutschen Ordens*, 159 ff. M. Tumler, *op. cit.*, 579 ff.

henceforth the Rule of the Templars .... After this decision was taken the prelates and the masters of the Templars presented the new house with the Rule of the Temple and then they elected there a brother of the house, Henry surnamed Walpoto, as master. ... The master of the Temple handed to him the written Rule of the Knights of the Temple which henceforth had to be followed in the house.

By February 1199 Pope Innocent III accorded to the new military order ecclesiastical sanction and approval.

The connection of the new order with the foregoing German establishment in Jerusalem has been hotly debated.[36] To the many arguments in favour of an entirely new foundation one may add the curious fact that for more than twenty years the order was not connected in crusader documents with the city of Jerusalem. Only in 1220, a generation after its recognition as a military order, we find the name 'The Hospital of St Mary of the House of the Teutons in Jerusalem'.[37] Until then the title varies: 'The Hospital of the Alemans which is in Acre'; 'The House of the Hospital of the Teutons'; 'The Church of the Alemans which is in Acre'; 'house of the Alemans in Acre'.[38] Henceforth, the name of Jerusalem will never disappear from its title. By 1229 the grand master of the new order, Herman von Salza – one of the outstanding personalities of his time – could even claim and receive from Emperor Frederick II the property of the earlier German establishment in Jerusalem.[39] Connecting the new order with the older German foundation, which enjoyed the prestigious name of Jerusalem,

[36] Good summary in M. Tumler, *op. cit*, 583 ff.

[37] Significantly the connection with Jerusalem is stressed outside the kingdom a whole generation before it appears in the kingdom's documents. Jerusalem is mentioned in the privileges of Clement III of 1191 and Celestine III in 1196. Rome was far away without knowledge of local circumstances. The name of Jerusalem appears in crusader documents for the first time in a sale deed of Otto, Count of Henneberg (1220): '*hospitale Sanctae Mariae domus Theutonicorum in Ierusalem*', Strehlke, no. 52.

[38] Strehlke, nos 26, 29, 31; 28, 30, 32. It is on this basis that three obvious forgeries, the acts of Kings Amalric (1173 and 1177) and Guy de Lusignan (1186) should be assigned to the period before 1220. Strehlke, nos 6, 8, 20.

[39] Strehlke, no. 69.

was so obvious a step that one wonders why it was not done earlier. By 1220 the remnants of the generation which survived the catastrophe of Hittin were already disappearing and with them the memory of actual events.

The progress of the new order was relatively rapid, since by the beginning of the thirteenth century ecclesiastical privileges were regularly granted to orders. However, the Teutonic Knights did not develop on the lines of their predecessors. Though the possessions which they acquired outside the Holy Land were scattered all over Europe, the special connection with Germany was there from the beginning. This ultimately shaped the order as a major instrument of German expansion and penetration into the lands of its Slavonic neighbours. In a sense, the evolution of the Teutonic Knights may be regarded as a fulfilment of latent aspirations by all military orders. The Templars and Hospitallers initiated this development in the northern principalities of the crusader establishments, by creating semi-independent states in Antioch and Tripoli. Unable to rule as independent lords of Spain, the Templars toyed for a short time with the idea of becoming overlords of Cyprus. [40] Less than a generation later (1211) the Teutonic Knights tried to carve out an independent state in the Burzenland of Hungary. Initial success brought their expulsion (1225) by the king and local aristocracy. Six years later (1231) Conrad of Masovia opened the northern marches of Poland to the order and the state of the Teutonic Knights was founded on the shores of the Baltic, the future Prussia.

That such aspirations were not alien to the military orders – even in the crusader establishments of the East – is proven by the examples of the county of Tripoli, the principality of Antioch and Cyprus. If the results were not encouraging this was not due to lack of will, but to political circumstances. Whenever and wherever the latter were propitious, the inherent dynamics came into play and found their expression in the foundation of an independent

---

[40] The island was accidentally captured by Richard Lionheart from the Byzantines during the Third Crusade. He handed it to the Templars, who later relinquished it to the Lusignans.

state. The Templars did not reach this stage because their existence was interrupted by the political stragagems of Philip the Fair.

Despite untroubled establishment, recognition and acceptance of the Hospitaller and Templar Rules, the progress of the Teutonic Knights in the kingdom was relatively slow. The possessions of this order were substantial, but hardly matched those of the older orders. Even its main castle, Monfort (Qal'at Qurein), though picturesque, cut a poor figure compared with such giants as Pilgrim's Castle or Saphet of the Templars. One reason for this retarded evolution was probably the sheer smallness of the thirteenth-century kingdom. Even areas recovered by the crusaders – like Galilee – did not remain in their power for more than a generation. Moreover, these were not no-man's land. Earlier possessors – including the older military orders – had well founded claims. This is only a partial explanation and a further reason can be deduced from the detailed inventories of the order. Compared with the Hospitallers and Templars, it is obvious that the new order enjoyed very little popularity in the kingdom. Almost all its rural possessions were bought and very little came through donations. Here and there we find royal donations, but they are mainly city property. When it comes to villages and acreage the order is always buying. Almost all of the sixty villages belonging to the order were bought for cash and an indemnity was even paid to the king of Jerusalem. Moreover the funds available to the order did not come from the kingdom itself, but mainly from pilgrims of German origin or from moneys collected in the Germanic areas of Christendom. The sums involved are large and one has a feeling that the Teutonic Knights got adequate support,[41] though from a limited area of Europe. The Papacy intervened quite often in its favour, sometimes even exaggerating the importance of the Teutonic enterprise, as in the case of Monfort. The Emperors Henry vi and even more so Frederick ii Hohenstaufen were always its staunch supporters, but both emperors hardly represented the idea of a Christian *Imperium*. Their intervention derived first and foremost from their standing as German rulers

[41] Cf., e.g., Strehlke, no. 52.

with German interests. Pure coincidence, a political marriage engineered by the pope, brought the Kingdom of Jerusalem as a dowry to Frederick II. As king of Jerusalem he bountifully endowed the Teutonic Knights,[42] but under his aegis the knights also began their careers as the bearers of Germanization and Christianity along the Baltic shore.

Despite their early establishment in Prussia the Teutonic Knights did not abandon the Holy Land until the final fall of the kingdom. We find the order participating in all major military and political events of the thirteenth century. Smaller and poorer than their comrades-in-arms, the Teutonic Knights never played as important a part in the history of the kingdom. They never became involved in local politics, strategic orientations and aristocratic intrigues as did the Hospitallers and Templars.

This late offspring of the military orders can be compared with the Italian communes, insofar as they tried to preserve their cultural and linguistic identity. Here all similarity ends, because the Italian merchants never created an ideal, nor did their oath-bound organization transcend the customary aims of communal association. The Teutonic Knights represented an attempt by a cultural minority to survive as such while simultaneously integrating into the working machinery of state and society. Their failure proved that the notion of a pluralistic society was so far removed from mediaeval realities that even in a colonial state – which by definition represented the common effort of mediaeval Christianity – they could not find their proper place. The common denominator of religion was not strong enough to integrate an association which, though it accepted the establishment unreservedly, represented an alien element.

Imitating the great military orders, less important associations grew up in the Holy Land during the twelfth and thirteenth centuries. Their military or political importance was negligible, but they are interesting as expressions of the same social and spiritual urges which gave rise to the great orders.

The most curious among the smaller orders was the 'Order of the

[42] Strehlke, nos 58, 59, 60.

Leper Knights' or 'Order of St Lazarus'. We assume that it was founded in Jerusalem during the second decade of the twelfth century, though the first traceable privilege dates from a generation later (1130–45). [43] The association started as a hospitaller institution caring for the most wretched of outcasts, the lepers. Their central establishment was the 'House of lepers' (*Domus leprosorum*) in the northern wall of Jerusalem, near a little postern to which they gave their name. The Middle Ages had no cure for leprosy and the aim of the institution was to assure their isolation from society. A seal of the establishment shows a leper, his countenance ravaged by the sickness, wearing an open-necked tunic with his head covered by a bonnet. One of his hands is hidden in the tunic and the other holds a clapper. Whenever they left their asylum they were obliged to warn people of their presence by noisily agitating their clappers.

The 'House of lepers' soon had its own church and convent (1142) and by the middle of the century (1147) we hear about 'Leper Brothers of Jerusalem'. [44] A little later (1155) a *magister* of the institution existed. By then the establishment already had houses in Tiberias and Ascalon and later in Acre – and possibly in Caesarea – (where they also held the church of St Lawrence in nearby '*Pain Perdu*') and at Beirut. It seems that by the middle of the twelfth century the early hospitaller establishment became a military order with commensurate duties. It is said that the master of the order had to be a leper himself as were the brethren-at-arms. We know that the Leper Brothers participated with the great military orders in the disastrous battle of Forbie (Hirbia) in 1244, where they suffered heavy losses. In Acre, the new capital of the kingdom, the order had its 'Tower of St Lazarus' in the northern suburb of Montmusard, and was responsible for its defence. Its house was near the sea at the northern tip of the city, and a leper nunnery appears on a contemporary map of the city near the cathedral. In 1253 the order made an ill-fated foray against the Moslems in Ramleh and was saved from utter destruction by the timely intervention of St Louis.

[43] It is a donation of a cistern confirmed by the patriarch William. *Archives de l'Orient latin*, II, 123.

[44] *Ibid.*, nos 2, 4.

Other orders are less known, e.g. the 'Order of the Trinity', the 'Order of the Sword' (*Militia Spatae*), the 'Order of the Holy Spirit' (*Militia Sancti Spiritus*), 'St Lawrence of the Knights (*Sanctus Laurentius de Militibus*), which appear during the final siege of Acre in 1291 or on contemporary maps of the city.[45] The 'Order of the Holy Spirit' might have developed from a fraternity of the same name and constituted itself as a military order. The 'Order of St Lawrence of the Knights' might have been a special order of knights from Genoa whose patron saint was St Lawrence. In this case we may assume linguistic and quasi-national motives in its foundation, similar to that of the Teutonic Knights, thd English Order of St Thomas of Canterbury, or the Spanish Order of St James. Some of these orders had their own hospitals and cemeteries but none ever came to prominence.

Since the military orders were international associations primarily interested in maintaining the crusader presence in the East, they were certainly more concerned with the Holy Land – on which they lavished lives and fortunes – than the Italian communes. After the first flush of crusader zeal had passed in the first quarter of the twelfth century, the latter often regarded the Holy Land as a commercial station where political conditions were highly propitious. The headquarters and governments of the communes were in Europe, the clergy came from the homeland and their churches depended on the cathedrals of the metropolis. In contrast, all the houses and provinces of the military orders in Christian Europe looked to and served their headquarters in the Holy Land. Nothing is more significant than the vocabulary used by the orders: the expression *Outremer* (overseas), which during the twelfth and thirteenth centuries everywhere meant the Holy Land, denotes Europe in their 'Rules' and statutes. This expressed their perspective, a Jerusalem-centred ideology.

The military orders were a means to mobilize the resources and manpower of Europe for the Latin East, complementing the papal proclamations of Crusades and the ordinary and extraordinary ecclesiastical taxation associated therewith. Their international status represented a brotherhood in arms and the universal nature of Christendom. If the Latin kingdom came into being by a common effort of Europe and if the recurrent Crusades were a formalized prolongation of that effort, the military orders represented the institutionalized permanence of a concomitant ideology.

Despite institutionalization this ideology did not withstand the combined pressures of time and society. The primary ideals of charity and a war of defence performed by the same group of men, noble in origin, was very early interpreted so as to make the double task incumbent upon the order as a whole, but not on each of its members. Thus the military orders adapted to the social structure and its current divisions. Everyday care of the sick became the normal task of the non-noble and warfare that of the knight. The war of protection and defence went the way of all pious intentions. By manning their castles, the orders were indeed protecting the Faith and the kingdom, but then as today, protection cannot remain defensive when frontiers are permanently tense and the country in a state of perpetual siege.

The commanders of the orders in the Holy Land – without exception – did not belong to the higher European nobility, though of noble origin. This tallies well with what we know about crusader nobility in its formative stage. The military orders, like early crusader society, opened careers for scions of the minor European nobility and thus became an instrument of social mobility. This was naturally limited by the rules of celibacy, since it did not create noble houses nor pave the way for relatives. As in the monastic orders, an individual could climb from mediocre or obscure origins to the commanding ranks of the order.

Surprising and not less significant is the absence of crusader nobility proper among the higher ranks of the orders. Here were rich and important establishments, bearers of the chivalrous ideal, which should have attracted the local nobility. Yet the latter are conspicuously absent from the higher ranks.[45] We must therefore conclude that the military orders – despite their unquestionable

---

[45] The only exceptions we found are the master of the Templars, Philip de Milly (c. 1169) and the master of the Hospitallers (c. 1190) Garnier de Nablus. It is interesting to note that the de Milly family also came from Nablus.

merits – were regarded as a foreign factor by the native aristocracy. Their fame, power and code of knightly behaviour were a sufficient incentive to bring many a local noble into limited affiliation. But these factors were not strong enough to make them enter whole-heartedly into the orders, regard them as a vocation and rise to their ruling echelons.

One result of this phenomenon was the non-involvement of the military orders in local politics, with one famous exception – the implacable hatred of the master of the Templars, Gérard de Ridefort, for Raymond of Tripoli – which played a notable role on the eve of Hittin. Their interests lay in international politics, where they represented different and opposing orientations; in local politics they were mediators rather than partisans. Their aloofness and detachment placed them in latent opposition to the faction-ridden local aristocracy. Without family ties to the ruling class – when such relations and their feudal consequences were one of the main power factors in state and society – they remained outside the tightly knit coteries of crusader nobility.[46]

---

[46] As this book was in press, a paper appeared by J. Riley-Smith, 'A Note on Confraternities in the Latin Kingdom of Jerusalem', *Bullet. of the Inst. of Hist. Research*, 1971, 301–8, which draws attention to 13th century *confréries* with crusader obligations.

XV

WARFARE AND FORTIFICATIONS

Up to the resurrection of Israel the trimillenial history of Palestine knows no other period in which the pace of frantic building could compare with that of the Latin kingdom. The crusader military establishment relied on two factors: fortifications and the army. The first represented the static element of defence and rule, the second tactical mobility and expansion. The military architecture of the crusaders is probably their most original and impressive achievement in the East and in this field European genius found its best expression. In the realm of fortifications traditionalist attitudes – with their rejection of the native and local – were overcome. The crusaders were ready to learn from Byzantine and Moslem alike.

Crusader fortifications cannot be viewed as a mere branch of architecture, nor regarded solely from the aspect of warfare. The nature of crusader domination assigned to their fortresses functions far beyond the military. From the beginning, these castles not merely defended the frontiers, but also dominated a conquered country and served as the administrative centres of crusader rule. This was in line with European tradition on the eve of the crusades: castles became administrative centres in the period of insecurity which followed the dislocation of the Carolingian empire.

However, the position of crusader castles and their place in the framework of defence, rule and administration were not determined by the disintegration of a central government, but conditioned by two factors: actual or latent war and the need to dominate a permanently hostile population. The failure of the Latin establishments to populate their dominions placed them in the position of a permanent minority and the castle became the tangible symbol of crusader presence and rule. When dealing with fortifications the demographic weakness of the kingdom makes it imperative to include, not only fortresses or castles proper, but also cities, villages and even churches and monasteries. When the European Romanesque church and monastery were shedding their squat fortress character for more light and elegance, the ecclesiastical buildings of the crusaders – even inside cities – largely followed the earlier pattern. This applied *a fortiori* outside the main inhabited area.

Military security was the guiding motive of Frankish life overseas. A minority at the time of conquest, the crusaders remained a minority during the two hundred years of their existence. Thus the Latin kingdom was bound to concentrate its greatest efforts on security. One aspect of this all-pervading imperative was the pattern of Frankish settlement. As minorities always do, the Franks tended to concentrate in a few places. This shortened their lines of defence and enabled a massive display of their military potential. Thus the overwhelming majority of the Frankish population lived in strongly fortified cities and castles. Even in the countryside their villages were fortified.

At the time of the conquest, Palestine had some fortified cities, almost all along the seaboard, and very few inland castles. The crusaders used existing facilities, but in response to their own needs they embarked on a tremendous task of making their kingdom impregnable. In a country where shortage of manpower was a constant feature of existence, stone walls had to replace warriors in the permanent and arduous task of defence. From among some twelve hundred inhabited places in Palestine the crusaders probably fortified no less than a hundred.

A   Fortifications

I   *The Geo-Political Framework of Fortifications*

Crusader[1] fortifications were not created according to a preconceived master-plan, but grew gradually as a function of expan-

---

[1] To facilitate identifications the names in italics, if not otherwise stated, are of crusader origin.

sion before they ever came to mark and secure the frontiers. Castles were built and places fortified in response to immediate challenges. Thus the castles and fortified settlements built in the second quarter of the twelfth century around the Egyptian-held outpost of Ascalon aimed to neutralize this city by a girdle of fortifications. This prevented the Egyptians from invading the crusader-held corridor extending from Hebron, through Bethlehem, Jerusalem and Latrun (*Toron des Chevaliers*), to Ramleh and Jaffa. Three castles: *Ibelin* (ancient Yabneh), Tel el-Safi (*Blanchegarde*) and Beit-Jibrin (*Gibelin*) barred the way east and north, whereas the restored and newly fortified ancient city of Gaza (1149–50) cut off Ascalon from overland connections with Egypt. A similar situation in the northern part of the kingdom gave rise to a cluster of fortresses around Moslem-held Tyre. The small castles of Hunin (*c.* 1106–7 – *Chastel Neuf*), Tibnin (*Toron*[2]) and Akhziv (*c.* 1123–*Casal Imbert*) surrounded the city from east and south.

Other castles marked the rhythm of crusader expansion and rule in newly conquered territory. Thus the foundation of the two great castles, *Montréal* (1115 – Shaubak) and Kerak (1142 – bibl. Qir Moab), on a sector of the pilgrims' road (Darb al-Haj) to Mecca and Medina, marked crusader penetration into Moab down to the Red Sea at 'Aqaba (captured *c.* 1116) and to the northern approaches of the Hijaz. The three strongholds in these large open spaces could more or less control the traffic of the great caravans – always in need of watering places for men and beast – and Bedouin forays, though less effectively. However, they could hardly prevent the invasion of a regular army, either Egyptian or Damascene. To consolidate their rule the crusaders proceeded to build a number of smaller castles along the main highway. Ultimately, seven castles were strung from north to south: Kerak on a hill topping the high plateau, whose fire signals were visible in Jerusalem; Tafilé, some 25 miles to the south, followed (22 miles) by Montréal; and then (15 miles) by Hurmuz (and very near each

---

[2] The date of the construction of Hunin and Toron, according to Ibn Furat, is 1106–7 and this tallies well with the dates assigned to fortifications by Hugh de Saint Omer, Lord of Galilee.

other) Sela', and *Vaux Moïse*[3] (Nabi Musa or al-Wu'aira) some 60 miles from 'Aqaba. Though the area was too large to be effectively policed or defended, the sparse population of the region and the lack of water prescribed the movement of enemy troops. Thus the frontier fortresses were at least redoubtable obstacles.

In view of the conscious effort to fortify the south-east of the kingdom, one would assume a parallel development in the north. All the more, since the principal reservoir of Moslem power lay in nearby Damascus, whereas the south-east was hardly exposed to Syrian invasion and the main enemy – Egypt – was almost two weeks march away across the Sinai desert and Moab. Surprisingly, the eastern area from the sources of the Jordan to the southern tip of the Dead Sea was almost demilitarized. This is an example of a direct and visible link between politics and defence. Early in the history of the kingdom – following incessant incursions on the frontiers of Damascus – a famous agreement (formal since 1108) was reached between crusader Jerusalem and Moslem Damascus, creating a sort of *condominium* in this area. Though occasionally violated by Moslem and Christian alike, the agreement – unbelievable as it sounds – remained in force for three generations, almost to the eve of Hittin. Accordingly, neither side tried to entrench itself in the area by erecting fortifications. The crusaders attempted to circumvent the agreement and toyed with the idea of creating an independent Moslem emirate in Basra and Salkhad to the east of the Yarmuk sources, a kind of buffer state on the south-eastern flank of Damascus. But the enterprise (1147) ended in failure. Other half-hearted attempts to dominate the area by establishing bridgeheads in strategical positions did not fare better. Thus Dar'a on the Yarmuk was for some time in crusader hands, however, their domination was very short-lived (*c.* 1118–29) and only the Crusader name of the place, *Cité Bernard d'Étampes*, preserved the memory of the ephemeral ruler, a native of Étampes near Paris. Something similar happened at Jerash (anc. *Gerasa*) in Gilead (Arab. Jebel 'Awf) which the crusaders captured *c.* 1119.

[3] See recently Ph. C. Hammond, 'The Crusader Fort of El-Habis at Petra', Middle East Center, Univ. of Utah, monograph 2, 1970.

The crusader chronicler's[4] remark, namely that the place was destroyed after its capture because the Christians lacked manpower to hold the outlying area, too far removed from their centres, is noteworthy. The main crusader weakness, their chronic lack of manpower, is proved by the fact that the few fortresses captured or constructed in this area never remained in their possession for long.

The major crusader bulwark against Damascus was the fortified city of Banyas. Rich in water from the Jordan sources, it dominated the major road from Damascus on the eastern flank and southern extension of Mount Hermon.[5] More to the south lay a small crusader fortress, Qasr Bardawil, 'Castle of Baldwin', near the village of al-'Al, whose Arabic name recalls its crusader founder or ruler. The place lay on the most frequent route of invasion from Damascus. These forces usually concentrated south of Damascus at the source of Ras al-Ma and marched to Khisfin and Fiq on the high plateau of the Gaulan (al-Sawad) and the valley of *Puteiha* (al-Batiha) on the eastern shore of Lake Tiberias.[6] Another place worth mentioning here was the curious rock-fortress of Habis Jaldak near the Yarmuk and the commercially important plain of Maidan (near Muzeirib). Its fortunes did not differ from those of the other fortresses in this area.[7]

---

[4] Eracles, XII, 16.

[5] Banyas was handed over to the crusaders in 1129 by a commander of the Isma'iliya sect, against a promise of protection from Damascus. In 1132 the castle was lost to the ruler of Damascus, but in 1140 the crusaders received it back from their new ally Unur of Damascus who courted their help against Zengi. The city and castle were finally lost in 1164 to Nur-al-Din. As to Subeibé (Qal'at Nimrud), usually regarded as the castle of Banyas, we have serious reservations as to its links with the Crusaders. Cf. A. Grabois, 'La cité de Baniyas et le chateau de Suibeibé pendant les croisades', *Cahiers de civilisation médiévale*, 13 (1970), 43 ff.

[6] So, for example, in June 1187, before the battle of Hittin. Similarly, the Crusade of 1217 crossed the Jordan and continued through Fiq and Khisfin.

[7] The place was captured by the crusaders in the first decade of the kingdom. In 1111 it was retaken by the Damascenes, but the crusaders conquered the place in 1118. It remained in their hands until 1182, when it was captured by Farukh Shah. But at the end of the same year the crusaders recaptured it, and probably held it until their defeat at Hittin.

A map of the crusader kingdom can convey the impression that the ten fortresses from Mount Hermon to 'Aqaba served as an outer line of defence. As already explained, they were not the result of overall planning and their construction was caused by specific political circumstances. Furthermore, their military importance in an age of mobile cavalry should not be exaggerated.

Behind the fortresses on the main thoroughfare of Transjordan – roughly corresponding to a line separating the desert from the cultivated lands – lie the Jordan river, the Dead Sea and the great southern desert, *La Grande Berrie*. This served as a second line of security. The Jordan can be crossed at many places, but only fords connected with roads going from east to west are important. There were three main fords on the river in the north. Invading armies could cross near the sources of the Jordan around Banyas, at the entrance to Wadi al-Taim and over the more difficult pass on the Litani river. More to the south a historical ford crosses the Jordan south of the now drained Lake Huleh by the 'Bridge of the Daughters of Jacob' (Jisr Banat Ya'aqub). Then came the ford at the southern outlet of Lake Tiberias at Sinn el-Nabra, from which the roads to Tiberias and Nazareth branch off. Less important fords are now marked by bridges at al-Ma'ajami, Hussein bridge, Damiya and the hallowed ford of St John. The latter, the traditional place of Jesus' Baptism, was guarded by a small fortress of the Templars and the 'Bridge of the Daughters of Jacob' was guarded by the belatedly (1178) fortified *Chastellet* (Qasr al-'Atra), also of the Templars. All other fords were undefended. However, a line of powerful fortresses in excellent strategic locations stretched on the west bank of the Jordan along the edge of the Galilean mountains.

The northern approaches were guarded by the castle of Banyas and its capture by the Moslems (1164) was a serious blow to the kingdom's security. The Wadi al-Taim and Marj 'Ayun valleys were blocked in the south by Hunin and guarded by the picturesque castle of *Beaufort* (Qal'at al-Shaqif) at the sharp western bend of the Litani. The important crossing of Sinn al-Nabra, where the crusaders suffered a memorable defeat in 1113 against a coalition of Moslem forces, was overlooked by the Hospitaller castle of *Belvoir* (Kaukab al-Hawa). The whole Jordan valley, from the southern tip of Lake Tiberias up to the entrance of the Beisan valley, was in full view from this point and no other castle ever enjoyed a better strategic location.

The defences along the middle and lower Jordan were far weaker. The danger was relatively small, since the river was faced by the plateau of Gilead, then very thinly populated. Jerash, as mentioned, was destroyed by the crusaders (c. 1119). Until the construction of 'Ajlun by one of Saladin's emirs in 1184, there was no foothold for local enemies or troops from far away Damascus. Moreover, the area around Beisan was marshy and seldom used by invading troops. This goes also for the Valley of Jezreel, which assumed military significance in the history of the kingdom only at its intersection with the roads from Tiberias and Galilee, near the sources of 'Ain Jalud (bibl. 'Ain Harod). [8] However, a small fort, more a place of refuge than a proper castle, [9] was built in Beisan.

The other fords of the Jordan, Jisr Damiya and St John, were strategically even less important than Beisan. The area across the Jordan, Gilead and Balqa (bibl. 'Ammon) represented no military threat to the kingdom. Located some 180 miles from Damascus it was not a practical assembly area for an invasion. There were many monasteries in and around Jericho – mainly Greek-Orthodox – and often inaccessible by the choice of their founders. Although fortified to withstand robbers and Bedouin forays none could hold up an invading Moslem army. In the south, the Sinai desert and its north-eastern prolongation – empty for some four hundred years since the Arab conquest – served as an excellent bulwark against possible Egyptian invasion.

East and west of the Jordan, two lines of castles created a chess-board pattern of frontier defence backed by a heavily fortified interior. Crusader genius is amply proven by the strategic location of their castles. The country was not a *tabula rasa* at the time of crusader conquest, and three thousand years of history had left

[8] Site of the famous battle between the invading Mongols and the Mameluks of Egypt in 1260.

[9] The place was attacked in 1182 and is described as a small fort surrounded by marshy land. William of Tyre, XXII, 16.

tangible traces. Arab fortifications were mainly in the coastal area, where the crusaders took over what the Arabs had built or restored. The situation was different in the generally non-fortified interior and on the eastern frontier. The crusader network of fortifications followed here the pattern of Byzantium and ancient Israel.

Crusader fortifications in the interior were largely intended to assure internal rule and security, but as the Moslem danger grew some became frontier stations. In addition, a large number of fortified observation points clustered around the important and heavily fortified coastal cities. They served as places of refuge for the local population in case of sudden attack and sounded the alarm at the approach of enemy troops.

The northern coastal cities had fewer such fortifications. Cities like Beirut and Sidon are difficult to attack directly from Damascus, and their northern approaches were defended by the crusader country of Tripoli. Outlying forts near these northern cities which rate mention are: Deir Qal'a (*Mont Glavien*) in the mountains of el-Gharb east of Beirut (the Moslem or Druze population recognized the sovereignty of the crusaders[10] and enjoyed semi-autonomous status); another small fortress, A'amid (*Ahmid*), to the south-east of the former on the Damur river (*Rivière Damor*); and again the small fort of Abu al-Hazem, baptized by the crusaders *Belhacem*, to the north of Sidon. These places had probably been fortified by the Moslems and were put to the same use by the crusaders.

More important, and certainly more curious, was the rock-and-cave fortress at Tirun el-Niha, called by the crusaders *Cave de Tyron*, midway between Sidon and the Litani. Hard to find in a mountain fold, its patrols could observe or place well-hidden ambushes, to endanger the rear of a Moslem detachment venturing against Sidon. It was a small fort with a limited garrison, difficult to enter or leave without danger.

Fortifications were more numerous in the more densely settled south, where a better road-system facilitated communications.

---

[10] Sàlih ben Yahya, *Histoire de Beyrouth et des Bohtors émirs du Gharb*, publ. L. Cheikho, Beyrut, 1902, and Clermont-Ganneau, in *Rec. Arch. Or.*, VI, 1–30.

The most important transverse road was the ancient highway from Damascus to Tyre. To the south of snow-clad Mount Hermon and Lebanon it joined the road from the Jordan valley and its branches in Wadi el-Taim and Beirut. The aforementioned castles of Banyas and Hunin near the sources of the Jordan were complemented by Tibnin (*Toron*), midway between Banyas and Tyre.

Further south two roads lead from Damascus in the direction of Acre to the north and south of Lake Tiberias. The northern road was guarded at the Jordan crossing by the short-lived *Chastellet* and bypassed Saphet (probably built in 1102, but certainly by 1142). Already important in the second half of the twelfth century, Saphet later became (rebuilt after 1240) one of the greatest and strongest castles ever built by the crusaders.

The southern branch of the road crossed the Jordan at the bridge of *Senabra*, where the marshy ground of the valley prevented effective fortifications. The transverse roads of lower Galilee were guarded by a large number of towers and small forts. The only exception was Mount Tabor. The fortified monastery on the hill became an important stronghold in the thirteenth century, when the whole mountain-top was circled by new double walls and an artificial ditch, adding to the natural defences of the steep slope. The little crusader village of Daburia (*Buria*) at the foot of Mount Tabor, the fortified church of the Annunciation in Nazareth, the small tower which guarded the precious water sources at Saffurya (*Sephorie*) and, more to the west, a Templars' tower in Shfar'am (*le Saffran*) were of secondary importance. The same is true of the tower of al-Fula (*La Fève*) amidst the Valley of Jezreel, which had not yet acquired or regained its importance as the main transverse highway of the Holy Land. Its eastern approaches were guarded by the small forts of Bel'ame (*Castellum Beleismum*) and places of biblical and post-biblical fame like Jenin (*Gerin*), Zar'in (*Le Grand Gerin*) and to the west by 'Ar'ara (*Castellum Arearum*).

The Jordan crossing at Jisr Damya and the road which leads across Samaria to Caesarea on the coast was almost without defences, except for the cities of Nablus and Sebaste themselves. *Munitio Malve* (Khirbet el-Neiraba) was an unimportant outpost,

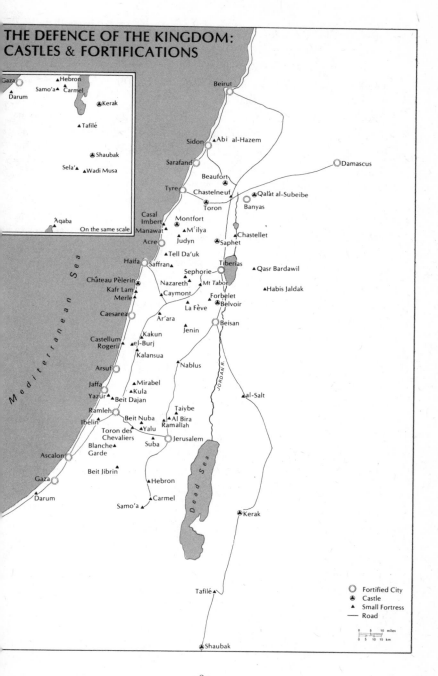

THE DEFENCE OF THE KINGDOM: CASTLES & FORTIFICATIONS

Gaza○
Darum▲   Samo'a▲▲ Carmel   ▲Hebron

⊛Kerak

▲Tafilé

⊛Shaubak

Sela'▲ ▲Wadi Musa

'Aqaba

On the same scale

Beirut○

Sidon○ ▲Abi al-Hazem

Sarafand▲   ○Damascus

Beaufort⊛

Tyre○   Chastelneuf⊛   ⊛Qalât al-Subeibe
      Toron⊛   Banyas○

Casal
Imbert⊛   Montfort
Manawat▲   ⊛M'ilya   ⊛Chastellet
Acre○   Judyn▲   ⊛Saphet
     ▲Tell Da'uk

Haifa○   Tiberias○
   Saffran▲   Sephorie▲   ▲Qasr Bardawil
Château Pèlerin⊛   Nazareth▲ ▲Mt Tabor
Kafr Lam▲   ▲Habis Jaldak
Merle▲   ▲Caymont   Forbelet▲
      La Fève▲   ⊛Belvoir
Caesarea○
   Ar'ara▲   Beisan○
      Jenin▲
Castellum   ▲Kakun
Rogerii▲   ⊛el-Burj
    Kalansua▲
         ▲Nablus
Arsuf○
Jaffa○   ▲Mirabel
Yazur▲ ▲Kula
   ▲Beit Dajan   al-Salt○
Ramleh○   Taiybe▲
Ibelin○   Beit Nuba▲ ▲Al Bira
       ▲Yalu   Ramallah▲
Toron des
Chevaliers⊛   ▲
Blanche▲   Suba▲   Jerusalem○
Ascalon○ Garde
Gaza○
Darum▲   Beit Jibrin▲
        ▲Hebron
   Samo'a▲ ▲Carmel

⊛Kerak

Tafilé▲

⊛Shaubak

○ Fortified City
⊛ Castle
▲ Small Fortress
— Road

Mediterranean Sea

Dead Sea

JORDAN R.

0   5   10 miles
0   5   10   15 km

289

but Kakun (*Caco*) at the crossroads near Caesarea played some role in the military history (1271) of the country.

Generally speaking, Judea and Philistia in the south were more densely covered by fortifications than the north. Yet it would be erroneous to conclude that the south was therefore in greater danger. Here the military threat came from Egypt, ten to fourteen days away. An invasion from that quarter involved costly preparations and burdensome logistics. The dense mesh of fortifications becomes more intelligible if seen not as great bulwarks or military depots, but as small forts to secure the highways, administrative centres and estates. The fact that these fortresses were strung along roads, some of which led to Transjordan, does not invalidate this explanation. The routes of armies were also those of commerce and administration, and it was only natural that the forts should oversee local traffic.

Some of these many forts were so insignificant that their crusader names are unknown and only archaeology can reveal their origin. For example, el-Burj ('Fortress') near the village of Sinjil (Saint-Gilles) at the northern entrance of a narrow valley on the plateau of Samaria and Burj Bardawil ('Fortress of Baldwin') at its exit. Nearby were the small forts of Tayibe (*Effraon*)[11] and Beitin (Bethel). This valley was known to the crusaders as *Vallis de Cursu*, which probably means the 'valley of raids', which corresponds to the more emphatic Arabic name, Wadi al-Haramein – the 'wadi of robbers'! On the same road, nearer Jerusalem, two small forts at al-Bira (*Magna Mahomeria*) and Ramalla (*Ramelie*) guarded the possessions of the canons of the Holy Sepulchre and the crusader villages recently established in the place.[12]

A line of fortified churches and monasteries surrounded Jerusalem, though less picturesque and less fortified than the Greek monasteries near Jericho and the Dead Sea. The monasteries of St

---

[11] Biblical names connected with the root '*Afr*' (like '*Ofra*' in the tribe of Benjamin) were changed by the Arabs because '*Afr*' means bad omen. The places were usually called *Taiybe*, meaning the good. Cf. F. M. Abel, 'Afrabala-Forbelet et l'Ophra de Guédéon', *JPOS*, XVII (1937), 318.

[12] Cf. J. Prawer, in *Rev. belge de phil. et d'hist.*, XXIX (1951), 1096 ff. B. Bagatti, *I Monumenti di Emmaus*, 1947.

George of Khoziba, *Quarantene* near Jericho and St Sabbas in the Qedron valley near the Dead Sea are reminiscent of true crusader fortresses or the inaccessible monasteries of remote Mount Athos.

On the road from Jericho to Jerusalem one passed a small fortress in an excellent location at the tortuous ascent of Ma'ale ha-Adumim (Tal'at al-Dam; *Maldoim* or *Castrum Dumi*), on the way to the small fort of Bethany near the Latin nunnery, before coming to the strongly fortified city of Jerusalem. To the north of the city, on the most frequented road from the coast, lay the monastery and perhaps a fort[13] of Nabi Samwil (*Montjoie*). In the immediate vicinity of the capital stood the Georgian fortress-monastery of the Holy Cross.

From Jerusalem a road led to the most southern barony of the kingdom (excepting distant 'Aqaba), Hebron (*St Abraham*), a fortified township. The road passed by the fortress Church of the Nativity in Bethlehem, a sort of police post at Burj el-Sur (*Bethsura*) and similar fortifications at Kurmul (*Carmel*), where the ancient water reservoir of biblical times was still functioning,[14] and at Samo'a, leading to the Segor (*Palmarea*) oasis at the southern tip of the Dead Sea and hence to Transjordan.

Security and rule were also the purpose of almost all fortresses on the two main parallel roads from Jerusalem to Ramleh-Lydda and hence to the *via maris* near Jaffa. The upper, northern road, *via Montjoie*, was guarded by fortified towers at el-Qubeiba (*Parva Mahomeria*), settled by the crusaders and further on by a small castle at Yalu (*Chastel Hernaut*). The latter is specifically mentioned as having been built to protect pilgrims travelling from the coast to Jerusalem.[15] Finally we reach the biblical Nob of the priests, that is Beit Nuba (*Bethnoble*), el-Burj and the fortified cathedral at Lydda (*St George*). On the southern road there were two small forts, excellent observation points at the Qastel (*Belvoir*) and Suba (*Belmont*) on the first heights at the western approaches

[13] Cf. J. Delaville le Roulx, '*L'Ordre de Montjoie*', *ROL*, I (1893), 52, privilege of Pope Alexander III. Cf. A. J. Foray, 'The Order of Mountjoy', *Speculum*, 46 (1971), 250–67.

[14] Cf. II Chronicles, XXVI, 10 and William of Tyre, XX, 28.

[15] William of Tyre, XIV, 8.

to Jerusalem. There followed two crusader settlements at Iqbala (*Aqua Bella*), a semi-fortified nunnery or manor house, and at *Fontenoid* (today Abu Gosh), which seems not to have been fortified. [16] And finally the Templars' castle of Latrun (*Toron des Chevaliers*). The latter stood on the crossroads running from south to north and from Judea to the coast. Since it also guarded the entrance from the plain into the mountains, it may have had a more strategic function.

The Shefela itself, bound in the east by hills which rise into the mountain ranges of Judea and Samaria and on the west by coastal dunes, was traversed by the ancient highway from Egypt to the north. Movement was easier here than on the shifting dunes and marshy lands along the coast. Some seven miles from this highway ran the coastal road proper. These parallel roads continued up to where the Valley of Jezreel meets the bay of Acre. Further north there was only one coastal road.

All coastal cities were fortified and their defences were more Arab in origin than Byzantine or Herodian. Wherever the more ancient fortifications can be traced, they encompassed a larger area than those of the crusader period. This is due to the economic and demographic decline after the Arab overthrow of Byzantine rule. Some coastal places were newly built by the crusaders, almost always at sites of earlier fortifications.

The ancient cities of the coast captured by the crusaders included some of the most famous names in history – Phoenician, Hebrew and Philistine. Once settled, the crusaders proceeded to restore these cities and often strengthened their fortifications. The three main cities in the north were Beirut, Sidon and Tyre. Sidon profited in the middle of the thirteenth century from the presence of St Louis, who built the 'Castle of the Sea' and the bridge which linked it to the fortifications on the mainland. Tyre with its triple girdle of walls to the land-side, double walls along the sea and a narrow isthmus (which, since Alexander the Great, links the island to the mainland), had an outlying stronghold on the road from Tibnin amidst the famous orchards of the city, the tower of the Hospitallers (Burj el-Shemali, *La Tor de l'Opital*).

[16] The place is called *Castellum Emmaus*, following Luke, XXIV, 13. Biblical Emmaus was also identified with Latrun and Qubeiba.

On the narrow coastal road between Ras Abyad (*Caput Blancum*) and Ras el-Naqura (*Passe Poulain*) lay the castle of Iskanderune (*Scandalion*). Primarily built (1116) to contain the danger of Tyre, it controlled the important coast-road and played a role in the military history of the kingdom (1232) during the fratricidal 'War of the Lombards'.

The cluster of castles on the northern and north-eastern approaches to Acre was not, contrary to appearances, built for the defence of the great crusader city. Akhziv (*Casel Imbert*) on the coast, Manawat (*Manueth*) inland, Qilat el-Rahib (*Raheb*), Judyn (*Iudin*) and M'ilya (*Chastiau dou Roi*) had nothing or very little to do with defence. These places were no more than fortified seigniorial residences, centres of taxation and administration. Their proximity to Acre (in a radius of some 9 miles) allowed some crusader nobles, ordinarily city dwellers, to spend part of their time at their country manors.

In the same vicinity (12 miles north-east in a straight line) lay the thirteenth-century castle of Qal'at Qurein – *Monfort*. It is a common error to assign it strategic importance.[17] Though Pope Gregory IX described it as a frontier bulwark of Christendom,[18] one has but to bear in mind that the Pope's expression is coupled with an appeal to Western Christendom to raise money for the construction of the castle. Not only is the castle too small to be of military importance, its location – away from any highway or road – is such that it is more of a retreat and hiding place than a strategic outpost. This picturesque castle is hidden until one of the higher surrounding ridges has been crossed. Little can be seen from the castle, apart from an enchanting panorama of deep wadis and the steep surrounding slopes covered with dense vegetation. Monfort could have been a place of retreat for the master and chapter of the Teutonic Knights, or perhaps as a safe place for archives and treasure outside turbulent and intrigue-ridden Acre, but certainly not a major military establishment.

[17] See above, p. 269, n. 32.
[18] Cf. The letter of Gregory IX to Christendom in July 1230. Strehlke, *op. cit.*, no. 72.

The strength of Acre lay in its tremendous fortifications. The port was fortified, but the city was without walls on the sea-side, [19] where reefs and protruding rocks mark the coast and make any approach not only dangerous but impossible, even when the sea is calm. In the thirteenth century a second line of walls was added, which encompassed the northern suburb of Montmusard. Constantly repaired and strengthened by St Louis and other European princes almost to the date of its fall, Acre was the best-fortified city of the Latin East.

The coast line from Acre to the south and the immediate ridges of the hill country to the east had many fortified places. Fortified cities like Haifa (*Caifas*), Caesarea, Arsuf, Jaffa, Ascalon and Gaza. Fortified seigniorial habitations like el-Kenise, strangely enough identified by Christian and Jew as *Capharnaum*, Kafr Lam (*Cafarlet*), el-Burj (*Merle*), Khirbet el-Shumariya (*Castellum Feniculi*), Umm Khalid (*Castellum Rogerii Longobardi*) between Haifa and Jaffa on the coast and in a parallel line to the east: Kaimun (*Caymont*), Kakun (*Caco*), Khirbet el-Burj (*Tour Rouge*), Kalansua (*Calansue*), Majdal Yaba (*Mirabel*) and Qula (*Cola*).

Amidst these small and very small forts there was one exception: the mighty Pilgrim's Castle ('Athlit, *Chastel Pèlerin*). Its construction represents a specific phase in the history of the kingdom. A small observation point which overlooked the main road was known in the twelfth century as *Casel Destreiz* (*Districtum*). It was built on a ridge where a narrow way passes through to the coast. The place belonged to the Templars and commanded a good view into one of the valley entrances of Mount Carmel, often said to harbour robbers. As long as the frontiers of the kingdom were across the Jordan there was no need for additional fortifications. Things changed after the Third Crusade, when a rump kingdom was created along the coast. In these circumstances 'Pilgrim's Castle' was built. An exceedingly strong fortress arose (begun 1218) just across from *Casel Destreiz* on a small promontory

---

[19] It is a common error to assign sea-walls to crusader Acre. The detailed description of Marino Sanudo, as well as contemporary maps of the city, do not leave any doubts in this regard.

jutting into the sea and in its shadow a small fortified village or city developed. The proud Templar castle withstood all attacks and was never taken by force. After the fall of Acre (1291) the Templars evacuated the place and escaped to Cyprus.[20]

South of Jaffa there were only two strongly fortified cities, Ascalon and Gaza. The small fortified places like Minat al-Qal'a (*Castellum Beroardi*) – whose dilapidated ruins among the dunes look like a ghost castle – and Deir el-Balah (*Darum*) on the road to Egypt, were respectively a seigniorial seat and a sort of fortified customs post on the way to no-man's land and the desert oasis of el-'Arish.

2 Crusader Castles

The geographical location and setting of crusader fortifications point to the fact that nothing like a 'standard' castle could ever have existed in the kingdom. Castles were not built by contractors in accordance with a general plan, but each presented a particular problem, had a specific function and rose under the influence of time and space. Yet all had a common ancestry: Western tradition modified by techniques acquired in the Byzantine and Moslem East.

Some of the scholarly problems connected with crusader castles, such as the degree of oriental influence, will probably never be solved to everyone's satisfaction, since the written sources are not sufficiently explicit. Modern historiography is reluctant to follow nineteenth-century scholars, who regarded the Near East as a school where Westerners acquired the rudiments of military architecture. We know that in the second half of the eleventh century – one or two generations before the crusader conquest – Europe witnessed a rapid development in the art of fortification. Thus the crusaders, even at the beginning of the twelfth century, knew more than the 'motte and bailey castle' constructed of earth and timber. On the other hand, the crusaders came into direct contact with Arab fortifications, often originally Byzantine, maintained,

[20] See detailed description below.

strengthened and adapted by the Moslems, as early as the First Crusade. This must have influenced and enriched crusader planning. It is impossible to gauge the relative importance of the two factors. Often the apparently 'oriental' is revealed as the outcome of the physical conditions of the site, whereas the conspicuous absence of some 'Western' features might be due to local circumstances. For example, the large water reservoirs in the great castles, the *berquile* (from Arab. birket, 'pool') were determined by climatological conditions in the Holy Land, though their construction is certainly based on local models. On the other hand, the dry fosse surrounding many fortresses is the direct result of the fact that the Holy Land, though blessed with milk and honey, never had enough water to spare for a flooded moat. The same is also true of the shape of walls and towers. Some scholars tried to find a pattern of development indicating the degree of Eastern influence in the round and square towers of crusader castles. This proved to be as misleading as the theory that the double enceinte was a late loan from the Orient. In both cases the lie of the land determined a square or round design as it did the building of a single or double enceinte.

It seems safe to suppose that even the first crusaders brought with them a good deal of knowledge of the art of fortification. In the two hundred years of the kingdom's existence military architecture flourished in Europe and in the Orient. The crusader architects were thus in an excellent position to draw from both sources in accordance with their specific needs, while contributing their own experience in the process.

Quantitatively, the 'tower' (*turris, tour*) was the most common and simplest type of structure.[21] Usually a small and square building, it guarded the roads and housed a small garrison, as much a police force as an administrative arm of king or seigneur. Though it could have been used to shelter the local population fleeing from an approaching enemy, it was certainly too small to hold the possessions or livestock of the peasants and could not withstand

[21] Cf., e.g., the description of the vicinity of Jericho by Phocas in 1185. *PTTS*, V, 26.

a siege. Its functions were purely defensive, a temporary shelter, until a swift raiding party out for easy spoils retreated. Such small towers could not be too choosy as to their location. An available eminence would naturally have been used, but often flat ground would do. In the plain a two-storied building was an excellent observation point and in the clear air of Palestine the man on the lookout could scan a radius of miles. The tower would be defended by fire from the loopholes or battlements, adequate to repel a raid of mounted archers, but insufficient if the enemy decided to storm the place or starve out the garrison. It is futile to speculate where the crusaders picked up this type of fortification. A simplified Western keep could have been the prototype or the many small Moslem *burj*, probably harking back – etymologically and functionally – to the Byzantine *pyrgos*, which formerly dotted the countryside and the *limes*.

The small castles built around the middle of the twelfth century to mark the crusader frontier and defend the exposed countryside from Moslem raids were in a different category. Although geared mainly to defence and protection, they had permanent garrisons and could have been used as starting points for crusader raids into Moslem territory.[22] In time these isolated castles became centres of colonization and part of the crusader environment. The towers became citadels of villages or cities established in their shadow.[23]

This type of small castle was common in the south of the country, and although a detailed description is impossible because of the poor surviving remnants, contemporary accounts provide a fair outline of their shape and structure. The earliest, that of Beit-Jibrin (*c.* 1136), is described as 'a strong fortress surrounded by an impregnable wall with towers, outer walls and a ditch'.[24] A more

---

[22] This double task is explicitly stated by William of Tyre, XIV, 22 and again XV, 25.

[23] So, e.g., the village of Bira near Ramalla had a '*turris*', Fulco Carnot., III, 33, which later became a '*castrum*', Delaborde, *op. cit.*, p. 30. Cf. the village Buria (1182) at the foot of Mt Tabor: '*turris quae suburbio praeerat*', William of Tyre, XIX, 14.

[24] William of Tyre, XIV, 22: '*praesidium aedificantes muro insuperabili, antemuralibus et vallo, turribus quoque munitissimum*'. One should pay attention to

detailed description is that of the castle of Ibelin, where the earlier buildings of Talmudic Yabneh provided building stones and ancient wells furnished water. 'They built' – says the chronicler – 'very strongly a fortress with four towers on the above-said hill, having laid very deep the foundations.'[25] Finally Tel al-Saphi, that is Blanchegarde, was a 'stronghold of hewn stone, resting on solid foundations equipped with four towers of suitable height'.[26]

These developments can best be studied in the crusader fortress at the site of ancient Gaza. The first fort of 1149 was very small. 'It was located' – says the chronicler – 'on a slightly raised hill, and enclosed a rather large space within its walls. Our people, seeing that their energies would not suffice for the present to rebuild the entire area, occupied part of the hill only; and after they had laid the foundations to a suitable depth they built the structure with a wall and towers'.[27] Some years later a small city sprang up there. 'As we said, the castle could not occupy the whole hill on which the city was founded, but people who gathered there to settle the place, so that they should stay in more security, tried to fortify the rest of the hill with gates and a wall, though weaker and more modest.'[28]

A similar picture is conveyed by Darum built in 1170. First came a typical square fort, 'a stone's throw in length' says a contemporary historian. The castle had towers at its angles, but had neither ditch nor outer wall. One of the towers was more massive and better fortified than the rest.[29] Around this erstwhile castle a settlement sprang up with its own church. A generation later, during the

the French version: '*forz murs i firent et hauz, torneles grosses près a près, fossez parfons, barbaquannes bonnes et forz devant les portes*'.

[25] *Id.*, XV, 24: '*in praefato colle, firmissimo opere, jactis in altum fundamentis, aedificant praesidium cum turribus quatuor*'.

[26] *Ibid.*, 25.

[27] *Id.*, XVII, 12. The French version goes into more details: '*la giterent leur fondemenz, et firent tors grosses et forz, les murs hanz et espès, les fossez lez et parfonz; moult fu bien fez cil chastiaux*'.

[28] *Id.*, XX, 20.

[29] *Ibid.*, 19: '*castrum modicae quantiatis, vix tantum spatium intra se continens, quantum est jactus lapidis, formae quadrae, quatuor turres habens angulares, quarum una grossior et munitior erat aliis, sed tamen absque vallo erat et sine antemurali*'.

Third Crusade, the settlement was already fortified and if we can believe the Anglo-Norman troubadour Ambroise, 'it has seventeen towers and turrets, beautiful and strong; one of which is more solid and rises above the others. On the outside it is surrounded by a deep ditch revetted with stone on one side and on the other natural rock.'[30]

Unfortunately, so little remains of all these places that we are reduced to conjecture. Apparently there were two types: square, small castles with towers at their angles (Ibelin, Tel al-Saphi, erstwhile Gaza) with a variant (Darum) of one tower being stronger than the others; tower-like castles with an additional line of walls and a revetted ditch (Beit-Jibrin and Darum). In the latter case the castle proper acts as the *donjon* or keep, the most characteristic element in European castles of the eleventh and twelfth century.

In the second half of the twelfth century, a different type of fortification appears, which could be described as a fortified seigniorial seat. Some of these ruins still dot the countryside: *Manueth* (Arab. Manawat) not far from Acre, Judyn and Summeyrieh in the same vicinity, the picturesque Kafr Lam near Caesarea and *Castrum Beroardi* (Minat al-Qal'a) in the dunes between Ashdod and Ascalon.[31] All these castles are small and rectangular. In some, stone and structure testify to an effort at elegance. Outside the castle with angle towers, as in Kafr Lam, there is a small walled courtyard with vaulted store-rooms and an elegant gate in the low outer wall. In others, like *Castrum Beroardi*, there is only the rectangular building and corner towers. Its location in the dune wastes of the coast indicates a small garrison outpost rather than a manor house. In Kafr Lam and *Castrum Beroardi* the unexpected and charming appearance of round towers at the corners is rather striking. In the latter they have round,

---

[30] *L'Estoire de la Guerre Sainte par Ambroise*, ed. G. Paris, Paris, 1897, vv. 9223–9. Cf. *Itinerarium Ricardi, I*, ed. W. Stubbs, London, 1864, v. 39.

[31] M. Benvenisti, *op. cit.*, 233–9 adds to this list several buildings of Crusader origin almost unknown from literary sources. This opens a new field of archaeological studies. See the detailed study of J. Meyer, 'Es-Samariya – ein Kreuzfahrersitz in Westgaliläa', *Jahrb. des röm.–german. Zentralmuseums Mainz*, XI (1964), 198–202.

sloping *glacis*-like bases. This cannot be assigned to a later date in the thirteenth century, because although Kafr Lam remained in crusader hands during the Second Kingdom, the southern *Castrum Beroardi* was definitely lost at the time of Saladin.

The twelfth century already witnessed the erection of large castles, whose recent excavation has changed our views on the evolution of crusader concepts and techniques in military architecture. The most notable castles constructed in the twelfth century were: Crac of Moab in Transjordan, Chastellet (Qasr al-'Atra) and Belvoir in Galilee; in the thirteenth century: Monfort and Saphet in Galilee and 'Pilgrim's Castle' on the coast. The chronological sequence does not necessarily represent two distinct periods and seems to have little importance in the evolution of crusader military architecture. So the most recent excavations (1964–8) at Belvoir – a castle which can be precisely dated (1168–87) – reveal a perfection of planning and execution as well as the existence of architectural elements, which some scholars would prefer to regard as thirteenth-century innovations.

The framework of this study cannot encompass all the crusader military monuments in the Holy Land. We will thus concentrate on the best examples in existence, which also happen to represent different types of military architecture.

BELVOIR

The castle of Belvoir (Aramaic and Heb. Kokhava, hence Arab. Kaukab al-Hawa and crusader *Coquetum*), built in the second half of the twelfth century, is one of the greatest crusader achievements.[32] Smaller than the gigantic *Crac des Chevaliers* in Syria (6.5 acres) or the huge castle of Saphet (10 acres), Belvoir measures *c.* 3 acres (112m × 100m). It is not merely a magnificent castle, but unique in the sense that its architect had a free hand, more than

---

[32] See J. Prawer, 'History of the Crusader castle Kaukab al-Hawa' (Heb.), *Israel Exploration Journal*, XXXI (1967), 236–49. The author served as scientific adviser to the excavations directed by Mr M. Ben-Dov. The plan as well as a preliminary report of the excavations was published in *Qadmonioth*, (Heb.), II, 1969, 22–47.

elsewhere. Once it was decided to build a castle on the edge of the Galilean plateau above the Jordan valley and to use a natural wadi as its northern border, the planners were left to decide the overall dimensions. Free in his choice, the anonymous architect could realize his ideas as to the best possible shape and size, limited only by labour and money (and it seems that he was not short of either). Though some scholars doubt the use of concentric fortifications as early as the twelfth century, it is absolutely clear that in Belvoir the defensive system included a double *enceinte* from the beginning.

The plan of the castle is based on three distinct units, each with its own particular functions. The three basic units are: the inner castle; the outer wall-curtain and fosse; the great eastern tower. The innermost part of the fortification is an almost regular (*c.* 50m × *c.* 50m) quadrangle. Four solid and identical towers (10m × 10m) stand at each angle, whereas the western wall has an additional fortified tower at its centre to defend the main gate, which led to the outer bailey. There is only one more opening in this compact quadrangle, a narrow and low postern in the eastern wall, closed from above by a huge slab of stone. The square corner towers are built on an impressively solid but not high (*c.* 2m) *glacis*, revetted by beautifully drafted stones of the 'rustic boss' type, that is, a bevelled frame and a protruding, levelled-off centre. Above the *glacis* rose the square towers, almost certainly two storeys high. In each tower an interior staircase led to the upper floors. The purpose of the salient towers was less to strengthen the walls (this was an additional advantage) than to create independent units of defence. Salient and at a short distance from each other (*c.* 35m), they could create effective flanking fire against an enemy attacking the inner castle. Though it seems doubtful if the square roofs of the towers (4m × 4m) offered enough space for the crusaders' heavy artillery.

The thick (3m) walls of the central castle enclosed a square inner bailey (22m × 22m). Even time could not destroy its charming and idyllic serenity. We are reminded of the fact that the inhabitants of the place did not wear armour twenty-four hours a day. The bailey opens on the north and south, through three gates on each side, into the inner rooms of the castle. The space enclosed by the

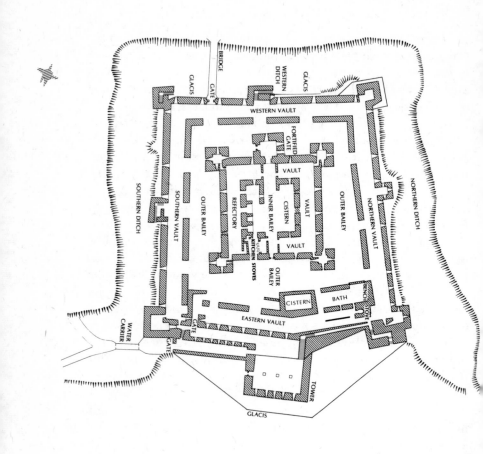

Floor plan and reconstruction of the castle of Belvoir in Galilee

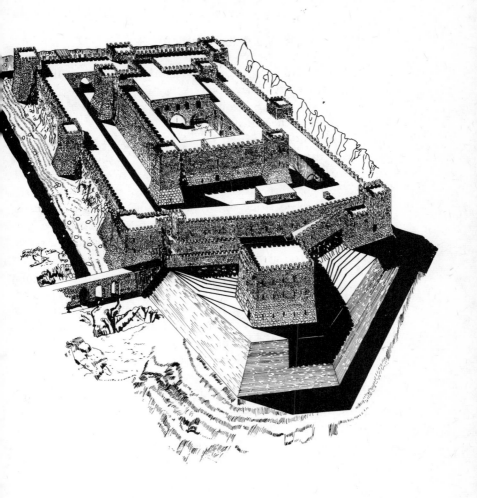

encompassing walls is a long and narrow (4m × 10m × c. 3.5m) rectangle, which contained the stores, stables and service rooms of the castle. The kitchens were in the southern part, near the small postern. Three rather large open ovens may have been connected with an adjacent dining room. The cooks could draw their water from a cistern in the inner bailey.

The living quarters of the Knights of St John were probably above the ground floor. In the western part of the inner bailey a large building changed the symmetrical pattern of the courtyard. In the south-western corner a large room was added, whose beautifully finished stones indicate that this may have been the refectory or chapter house. Above, a two-storey structure supported by three arches spanned the whole width of the courtyard. The largest central arch led to the western tower over the main gate. An interior flight of stairs led from the courtyard to the upper floor. Here were probably the main offices of the castle and perhaps the castellan's lodgings. The remnants of a church or chapel were found here, as was the lovely bas-relief of St Matthew and parts of what looked like the arch of a sumptuous portal.

The inner castle, with its unique gate and single postern, showed no other apertures but the narrow loopholes on the ground and upper floors. The windows of lodgings and store-rooms open into the courtyard eastern-fashion. Once outside the inner castle we step into the outer bailey, the open rectangular space (c. 14m to 16m wide) between the inner castle and the long, vaulted store-rooms and other utility structures, which were part of the outer fortifications. Whereas the inner bailey was paved with larger stone flags, the outer bailey does not seem to have been paved. On each side, except the east, three large arched gates opened into the vaulted store-rooms which run along the outer line of defences.

The outer shell of the castle was a pentagon, since its eastern wall is composed of two equal intersecting parts. The salient angle is even more thrust forward by the great eastern tower. The curtain has quadrangular towers at each corner and an additional tower in the centre of each side. The rock from which the wall rises is revetted in many places by mediocre masonry. Revetment is the rule in the *glacis* of all the towers, where excellent stonework was used. Three (in the south and west) of the seven towers have hidden posterns leading from the fosse through an 'L'-shaped staircase to the level of the store-rooms. Their construction is excellent: narrow openings hidden by the *glacis*, whose shadow perfectly masks the entrance. These sally-ports face that part of the plateau from which siege engines could have been used against the castle. The defenders could thus seize an occasion to sally forth and destroy them.

The *glacis* of the towers comes up to the ground level of the outer fortifications. From here curtain and tower rise perpendicularly. The fosse is 10 to 12 metres deep and some 12 metres must be added for the height of the walls, i.e. a stone wall more than 20 metres high rises from the bottom of the fosse to the battlements of the curtain, with an additional 2 to 4 metres for the top and parapet of the flanking towers.

The outer walls and their towers overlook the dry fosse of the castle, 10 to 12 metres deep and almost 20 metres wide. The plateau of basaltic rock was excavated, an important engineering feat in itself, and its stones partly used as building material for the castle. The counterscarp of the fosse clearly shows the work of the builders. The fosse could only be crossed in two places, both admirably defended. In the west a bridge spanned the fosse, near the centre of the south-western corner tower and the tower in the middle of the western curtain. In all probability the bridge was not a permanent structure, but built of beams which could be burned or removed in case of danger. As the fosse here is almost 20 metres wide, there was obviously a pillar or similar structure in its centre to support the bridge. The bridge was easily defended from both flanking towers and loopholes on both sides of the bridge. On the side of the castle the bridge led directly through a narrow gate into the vaulted rooms of the outer curtain and hence into the outer bailey.

The third unit was the 'Great Tower' in the eastern-most part of the castle. This was naturally the strongest point of the castle which overlooked the steep slope and the Jordan valley some 450 metres below. The eastern edge of the plateau was selected by the crusaders as the strongest part of their fortifications. This seems strange, until we realize that the function of this tower, hardly accessible by nature and sealed off from the surroundings by an artificial and mighty *glacis*, was that of a last stand and refuge. The Great Tower could withstand prolonged siege, even if all other parts of the castle were taken. Functionally one may regard it as a *donjon* moved from the traditional place at the centre of the castle or its weakest point beyond the line of the outer walls; one could almost compare this tower with a latter-day *redoute*, loosely connected with the outer fortifications. Unfortunately this part of the fortifications is almost completely destroyed and one can only guess at the original structure. To correctly appreciate its military functions we have to trace the connection of the Great Tower with the eastern fortifications of the castle. Although such a connection obviously exists, the Great Tower is an almost autonomous unit of defence. Whereas breaking through the outer walls of the castle brought an attacker directly before the inner castle, the fall of the outer and inner castle left the Great Tower intact. On the other hand it is impossible to see any role the Great Tower might have played in the defence of the castle. The roof of the Great Tower was lower than the walls of the castle and though the projectiles of catapult and mangonel could have reached the castle, this was an extremely dubious procedure. Thus the *redoute* should not be regarded as a structure destined to strengthen the weakest point of the castle, but rather to assure that the last refuge should be able to take care of itself even if the castle were captured.

The whole eastern part of the castle was built on a kind of natural *glacis* provided by the slope, but levelled at its top to form a space at its centre for the tower. The huge tower, a massive, quadrangular box (30m × 18m) showed a blank face on the main front to the east, but with loopholes on each floor. A small postern in its southern part led to the open space around it. Its connection with the main castle was at the north-eastern corner, where an 'L'-shaped staircase led through a vaulted passage between walls to the north-eastern corner and its twin towers. This passage could have been easily blocked or cut in times of danger, thus completely isolating the tower.

The ground floor of the Great Tower, more than 500 metres square of space, was a huge hall divided into two naves by a row of square columns. We could possibly envisage a two-storey building of which the lower floor was twice as high as the upper one. The loopholes of the floors were certainly of less importance than the roof of the tower with its battlements, which left ample space for archers and artillery. An enemy camp located at the foot of the slope would have been a good target for crusader projectiles, whereas the area around the tower and the eastern entrances into the castle (less than 40 metres away) were easily in range.

On this eastern side we find a most elaborate system of entrances into the castle. On the south-eastern side, one arm of the pentagon was defended by a rising triple line of fortifications. The exterior was a blank wall, followed at equal distances (c. 5m) by two parallel lines of loopholed walls, connected in the south with an entrance and the strong corner tower. From here a path led to a small well, some 500 metres to the south of the castle. In all probability this path also led to the Jordan valley below and to Jebel 'Awf across the Jordan. The fosse was bridged here just below the strong tower of the south-west angle. A short staircase and the typical 'L'-angle turn brought one within an arched gate. The gate was closed by double doors (the holes for the pivots and the opening for the bolt are well preserved), but the whole aperture was also closed by an iron portcullis which descended in grooves from a square turret above the gate. The gate led into the vaulted rooms within the castle walls or into a space connected with the outer bailey. A parallel and, it seems, not less elaborate entrance was at the north-eastern corner of the walls. A postern or a small gate and 'Z'-shaped staircase led into the interior of the castle between twin towers. At this point, we hesitate to assign a specific function to this entrance unless we presume the existence of another bridge across the fosse or a road leading from the Jordan valley to the castle. If the latter applies, the main entrance to the castle could be presumed here rather than on the opposite side. Gates and the roads leading to them were usually located so that anyone entering would have the castle on his right (a good example: Monfort) since this would handicap the right hand of the attacker.

MONFORT

Monfort[33] is an excellent representative of the type of fortification where nature has contributed more than man to the strength of the castle. If the architect of Belvoir was free in deciding the plan, shape and even size of the castle, this was certainly not the case for the castle of the Teutonic Knights at Monfort. We have already stated that its location was not chosen for its strategic importance, nor could it hold a large garrison, or sustain a prolonged siege.[34] Its simultaneous proximity to and isolation from Acre, and its central position among the many fiefs and manors acquired by the order in this area near a small fortified manor house at M'iliya (*Château du Roi*) were decisive in choosing the general location. Finally, the lie of the land determined the plan of the castle.

From the deep valley at the foot of the castle, one seems to be facing a gigantic ship's prow cutting through the green hills of Galilee. The steep slope rises from the bed of the Qurein river to some 180 metres above sea level and at the narrow western end of the valley two wadis intersect, enclosing the mountain spur on the north and south. On this ridge the Teutonic Knights began laying the foundations of the castle between 1226–9.

The architect had to cope with the extremely difficult problem of providing space for his buildings on the narrow mountain crest. Capital or manpower seems not to have been abundant. There are few crusader buildings with such poor stone-work and where lime has been used to cover the coarse masonry of the interior so frequently as in Monfort. Even the re-adapting of an earlier plan to new exigencies was rather slapdash, in a very un-Germanic manner. The feeling of limited possibilities is all the more striking compared

[33] The first scholarly description followed excavations in 1926 by the Metropolitan Museum of New York. See: *A Crusader Fortress in Palestine*. A report of explorations made by the Metropolitan Museum of Art, 1926. *Bull. of the Metrop. Mus.*, N.Y., 1927. There is now a better plan provided by the National Parks Dept. of the Government of Israel. The most recent description is that of W. Hubatsch, *Monfort und die Bildung des Deutschordensstaates im Heiligen Lande*, see cap. XIII, n. 32.

[34] See above, p. 293.

The refectory of the Order of St John in Acre, showing the underground passage to the building complex of the order

Aerial view of Acre from the south. The remains of the crusader port can be seen in the foreground

A view of Pilgrim's Castle from the west, showing the inside of the northern tower (13th century)

Aerial view of Caesarea from the west. The main gate to the city is
in the east, the ruins of a church are in the south and the crusader port
and ruins of a castle are in the foreground
Remains of St Louis's fortifications in Caesarea (mid-13th century)

overleaf Façade of the Church of the Holy Sepulchre in Jerusalem
(*c.* 1130–49) with the Chapel of Calvary on the right

Aerial view of the medieval citadel of Jerusalem (foreground). The mosque on the right is a later addition, and the glacis in the foreground indicated the location of the ditch

The church of the Convent of St Anne in Jerusalem (mid-12th century), which was restored to Christian hands in the second half of the 19th century

The main nave of the Church of the Nativity, Bethlehem, showing crusader paintings on the columns and crusader and Byzantine mosaics on the walls of the sanctuary to the magnificent 'Pilgrim's Castle', a contemporary of Monfort. Nevertheless, some parts of the castle have excellent stonework, e.g. the keep on the extreme east and parts of the revetment on the southern slope. The builders may have run out of money, or the more representative and vulnerable sections were treated differently than the rest of the structure.

The site of the castle was separated from the mountain-spur to the east by a deep and wide ditch cut into the rock. The crest thus isolated is elongated and slightly curved, about 110 metres long and nowhere more than 20 metres to 30 metres wide. The knights did not entirely level the top of the ridge and this made the erection of buildings rather awkward.

The defence of the place was thus mainly based on its natural advantages. The prodigious ditch below the keep took care of the eastern part of the castle. In addition, a tremendous amount of work went into strengthening the southern and northern slopes of the hill. A good type of masonry was used for their revetment; some of the stones are of great dimensions and convex to hamper ascent. Some stones were land in an extraordinary manner, the way roof-tiles overlap, to make escalation extremely difficult. Halfway down the slope there are remnants of a wall, but it is doubtful if it encompassed the whole hill and its defensive functions are not clear. We are inclined to think that the defences of the castle depended on its own curtain of walls.

The floor of the keep is some metres higher than the ground floor of the castle and the entrance was reached from the interior via a short winding staircase. Though picturesque, with its elegant stones and pointed windows, the only military function of the keep could have been to guard a drawbridge over the artificial fosse. It could hardly have had defensive importance. Once the castle was taken, the garrison of the keep, crowded into the narrow space of the tower (13m × 10m), could easily have been starved out.

Besides the keep, the building has three main parts – four, if we add the upper storey which certainly existed – as proven by the remnants of a staircase. In all probability this second floor was used for the lodgings and offices of the garrison. Moving from west to east, that is to say from the precipice to the keep, we encounter

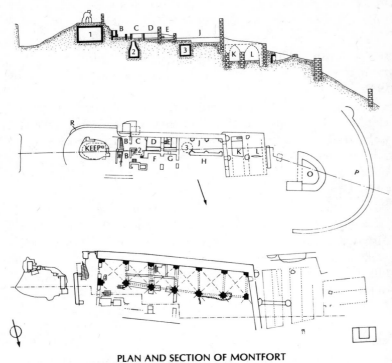

PLAN AND SECTION OF MONTFORT

R – WALLS OF KEEP   B – PASSAGE FROM CASTLE TO CITADEL   C – KITCHEN   F–G – WORKSHOPS
K–L – STABLES   J – CHURCH   O – GUARD ROOM   P – OUTER WALL   NUMBERS DENOTE CISTERNS

first the 'Great Hall', the most important part of the castle. As the ridge slants downhill at this point a strong substructure was needed: two rather ugly vaulted rooms, whose roofs form the ground floor of the hall. The latter was the most beautiful part of the castle, high and spacious (17m × 17m) with a remarkable centre piece, an octagonal 3m-high column. From here the pointed ribs and arches sprouted, intersecting at their apex (18m) and descending to three columns in the corners and in the middle of each wall. The lofty hall, the monumental octagon in the centre and the web of ribbed groins must have been truly impressive, a worthy architectural counterpart to the Wadi Qurein. A door in the eastern wall of the Great Hall led into the next room, probably used as a chapel. This spacious oratory (some 21m long and 15m wide) was a double nave, divided by a single line of cruciform pillars. Even here the work is not of the best quality; the half-pillar of the dividing line of columns is not inserted into the wall but stands free in a strange way, so as to use the supporting wall of the lower floors, neither are the eastern and western walls parallel. Consequently, the chapel has a slightly trapezoid form.

The third part of the castle seems to have been planned as one unit identical with the chapel, but subsequently divided into small and rather ungainly rooms. The original plan used the southern wall of the castle as the inner wall of the rooms and a parallel wall was built to the north. The roof of this quadrangle (23m × 7m) rested on pointed arches and stringers based on four cuneiform columns in the middle of the floor, with the same number of inserted half-columns along the walls. Thus three bays were created, to be partitioned later, no doubt on grounds of economy. The bays were closed by walls and stone partitions cut two of them into five small rooms which served as lodgings. The eastern most room was left at its original size and probably used as a kitchen. The northern part of the whole area, in addition to providing west–east communication, served everyday functions. This is proved by the well preserved double tank of an olive-press. On the kitchen side, excavations point to a forge and workshop.

Beyond this area a kind of paved vestibule connected with a staircase to the keep. The southern end of this vestibule has traces

of a gate which led to the southern slope and probably to the path
which descended from the castle to the valley below.

PILGRIM'S CASTLE

Ten years before the Teutonic Knights began work at Monfort,
the Templars – aided by important contingents from Europe –
started to build at 'Athlit, the only notable promontory between
Haifa and Jaffa. Here they erected one of the greatest castles ever
built in the Near East, the 'Pilgrim's Castle' (Chastel Pèlerin) as it
was named upon completion.[35] The building of the castle falls into
the period when growing Moslem pressure along the tenuous
frontiers of the Second Kingdom made its existence more and more
dependent on the fortified cities of the coast. By 1250 St Louis tried
to strengthen the sea-board by fortifying every city and castle,
from Sidon in the north to Jaffa in the south, a veritable belt of
stone armour.

The solution of the architectural and military problems at
'Pilgrim's Castle' show crusader talent at its best. The magnificent ruins – which are a landmark of the Sharon – survive as a
testimony to supreme skill and ingenuity, seldom equalled and
never surpassed. The Templars' great castle at Saphet, built a
generation later, could probably be compared with 'Pilgrim's
Castle'. But, alas, Saphet is hidden by later structures and the little
that has been excavated permits comparison only between the
physical remains of the former and the literary descriptions of the
latter.

The feature which determined the whole structure of 'Pilgrim's Castle' was the existence of a natural, square promontory
enclosed on all sides by the sea, except in the east, and dominated
by a low knoll at its centre. The promontory was 280 metres long
and 168 metres wide (maximum dimensions) and the knoll some

---

[35] The excavations of Chastel Pèlerin were directed by C.N. Johns who
published a series of excellent studies in the *Quarterly of the Dept. of Antiquities in
Palestine*, vols I-VI. The final results were summarized in his *Guide to 'Atlit*,
Jerusalem, 1947.

16 metres high. The whole area (c. 12 acres) was built up in the second half of the thirteenth century, though apparently in the beginning no more than a quarter or a third was envisaged for construction. It seems doubtful if the original plan provided for a double *enceinte*. The second line of defences (except for the east front) was erected later, not so much for military reasons, as because of the need for additional living space. This became urgent with the shrinking of the kingdom's territory around 1250. By then living and safety were so synonymous that both problems had to be solved simultaneously.

The defensive system of the castle can be discussed under three aspects: the defence of the most exposed eastern part, the inner ward and finally, the additional structures around the outlying baileys of the castle.

As could have been expected, the whole skill and ingenuity of the Templar architects was concentrated on the eastern part of the castle. Here the flat land does not rise above the level of the nearby sea. Thus the major military problem was to seal off the promontory from the surrounding area. Obviously a simple ditch was not adequate, since the open plain beyond furnished excellent positions for enemy artillery – though a good ditch could and did prevent direct attack of the walls by battering rams. Consequently, the defences were worked out as a combination of ditch, strong walls and a curtain and tower line which enabled the defenders to use the whole long front (c. 200m) as a double, multi-tiered fire base. Thus the second line of walls of the eastern front had a double task: to support and strengthen the fire of the first line and to become the main bulwark of defence if the first line were taken.

Enclosed between a revetted counterscarp and the first wall, the fosse ran from the north to the south beach, a distance of almost 200 metres. The counterscarp entered the sea at both ends, thus preventing enemy troops from wading through the shallows and approaching the main line of fortifications unhindered. Two arched gates in the counterscarp led through a narrow passage into the small city which grew at the foot of the castle.

The fosse, 18 metres wide and certainly dry (although in a similar situation in Tyre and possibly Caesarea, sea-water could have been

Plan of the Pilgrim's Castle

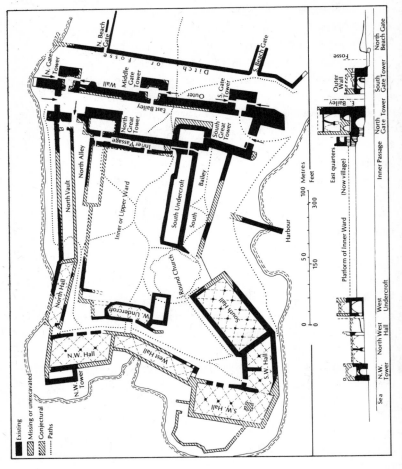

used to flood the ditch), extended to the wall-curtain and the towers rose directly from its base. Neither wall nor tower had a *glacis*, a rather unfamiliar feature in crusader fortifications. Since 'Pilgrim's Castle' was built on flat land near the sea, enemy sapping would have struck sea-water immediately. Thus a *glacis* was superfluous and the tremendous weight of the outer walls and towers sufficed to dissuade undermining.

There was no bridge across the fosse and one moved into and out of it on ramps under the eyes of the guards, into one of the three double gates of the towers in the outer wall. This wall was built of beautifully drafted stones – some of gigantic proportions like the Herodian temple masonry in Jerusalem – and ran along the whole length of the land neck. Three towers, each 16 metres high, were symmetrically spaced along the *enceinte*, and like the walls turned blank fronts to the enemy. The double entrances were in the side walls of the quadrangular and salient towers. Their only frontal openings were elaborate loopholes, twenty on each of the two superimposed galleries. Their embrasures could hold two men, which allowed one to discharge his bolt or arrow while the other made ready. Thus forty archers could shoot simultaneously from the double line of walls and towers. The distance between the central and side-towers was some 46m, ensuring effective cross-fire from loopholes in the sides of the towers and from their battlements. The pointed gates of the towers were heavily defended. Double doors and an iron portcullis lowered by windlasses from the second storey barred the entrance, and the dead ground just in front of the gates was covered by loopholes on the first floor, sometimes in the form of corbelled machicolations. It is difficult not to be impressed by this array, with almost every trick known to the architects of the period.

From the side gate of the tower, after a sharp 'L'-turn, one emerged into the outer bailey, a long and spacious alley (18m wide; 10m opposite the great towers) across the whole neck of land. Facing it was the second wall and its tremendous twin towers. The second line of walls was slightly shorter than the first, because of the narrowing promontory. Conversely, the central part of the wall between the great towers was thicker than the outer wall, and a passage in the interior of the walls allowed the free movement of a mounted knight through a long, barrel-vaulted tunnel.

The vast twin towers were an integral part of the castle's defences, but also served as keeps and seigniorial lodgings. The outside of the ground floor was blank and the first floor pierced by loopholes covering the outer bailey. The second storey begins at the height of the outer wall, with a gigantic superstructure. From here the walls rise another 16 metres and their flat top was supported by ribbed vaults springing from a mighty pillar in the centre of the room. The ribs of the vaults and the stringers rested on consoles in the walls. Those preserved in the great northern tower are carved with single heads on the sides and three in the middle. These magnificent rooms were certainly used for ceremonies and receptions. Above them was the parapet, with crenellated battlements to protect the archers and artillery men. As the top of the towers and the connecting wall (in all 34m) are 16 metres higher than the first or outer wall, the defenders of the second wall could shoot freely above the heads of the defenders of the first wall. Moreover, the great towers were staggered between the three gate towers, which ensured perfect covering fire over the area before the castle.

Behind these elaborate defences lay the slightly rising hill (c. 16m), acting as the inner ward of the castle. As high as the first floor of the great towers, it was a spacious quadrangle, twice as long as it was wide (128m × 62m). Originally it also had a line of walls enclosing the three remaining sides and possibly corner towers. But wall and towers became superfluous when additional buildings were erected beyond the inner ward. Nevertheless the old wall was not entirely destroyed and in some places it was integrated as the outer wall of the long and large underground tunnels on the northern and southern edges of the inner ward, which served as store-rooms. These were entered by a descending flight of stairs from the ground floor of the great towers. These undercrofts, almost 16 metres high, 10 metres wide and 67 metres long, could have stored almost inexhaustible provisions. Through openings in their barrel-vaulted ceilings the stores were raised from the underground vaults to the inner ward.

A smaller undercroft is to be found at the western end of the inner ward. This longish and curved structure is built in a rather negligent manner, as the north and west walls are not straight but shaped like badly fitting sides of a triangle. This was caused by the use of an existing wall clumsily integrated and badly adapted to the new requirements. The ribs of the intersecting groins met in flower-sculptured key-stones and descended into pot-like brackets of the type found in contemporary Acre. This must have been a small assembly room.

The only remarkable structure in the inner ward is the polygonal church. The pattern itself bears the imprint of the Templars, whose churches in the Holy Land and abroad imitate their erstwhile sanctuary, the Mosque of Omar in Jerusalem.

As already mentioned, the original defences became superfluous with the addition of new buildings some time around the middle of the thirteenth century. In a semicircle from south through west to north, eight large structures were erected – which gave the impression of an additional and concentric line of defence. The fortifications were thus pushed to the outer edge of the land on the sea-shore. Due to the rocky nature of the coast, military considerations could hardly have been decisive, and the expanding population of the castle probably prompted this development. In this connection we should bear in mind that a small city grew up at the foot of the castle approximately at the same time, catering to the needs of the castle and housing some of its labourers and livestock.

Additional buildings created a number of outer baileys divided by lanes and squares, hedged in by the inner ward and the new buildings. For example, an alley near the north vault probably served as an open shed and stable for horses. A similar area (though it might have existed earlier) was near an undercroft at the southern end of the promontory. Here a bailey was directly connected with the jetty of the castle's small harbour. The harbour area was closed from the inside by the wall of one of the new large buildings – the 'South Hall' – a huge quadrangle (58m × 32m) divided by two rows of columns into three equal naves. This might have served as the chapter house and the nearby buildings in the west and south could have been refectories. Two round and huge ovens nearby probably served the kitchens.

To facilitate communications between the new buildings and the inner ward, some metres higher than the flat base ground, bridges spanned the first floor and the inner ward of some of these buildings, usually at the narrowest point.

Chastel Pèlerin was never taken by storm, but abandoned by its garrison who escaped to Cyprus when Acre fell in 1291.

3   City Fortifications

Nineteenth-century romantics visualized the crusader knights against a background of lofty mountain castles, high as eagles' nests. This picturesque image did not correspond to reality. The Holy Land had few inaccessible mountains and crusader castles were more often located in plains and valleys, where even a slight hillock gave them strategic importance.

This is even more true of the crusader cities. The latter were never pure burgess cities, but the normal abode of nobles, burgesses and Italian or Provençal merchants. They were certainly important centres of commerce, but also the main reservoir of manpower, militarily not less important than the castles. The inherent military value of the city – important as it was in the twelfth century – became paramount in the thirteenth when the mountainous and hilly hinterland was lost and crusader dominion limited to a narrow coastal strip.

It was therefore natural that the crusaders endeavoured to fortify their cities. The task was all the easier, since the coastal cities had always been fortified since the late Roman period. In the interior – with the exception of Jerusalem – only a few places were fortified, like Nablus in Samaria and Tiberias. Their defences seem not to have been very strong. In contrast, all the coastal cities were heavily fortified. Today, with the exception of Jaffa and Gaza – the last remnants of whose fortifications disappeared in the last century – the whole coast from Ascalon in the south to Beirut in the north is dotted with crusader fortifications.

A detailed description of crusader city fortifications[36] is beyond the scope of this study. We shall thus concentrate on some characteristic features.

The flat land and the proximity of the sea were one of the decisive factors in shaping the defences. In a few places there is a knoll or ridge overlooking the sea. For example, Arsuf, the classical Apollonia, is built on a ridge some 65 feet above sea level. Ascalon, Jaffa, Caesarea, Acre, Tyre, Sidon and Beirut, to mention the major centres only, were on the flat coastal plain.

Their maritime location prescribed the pattern. The main defences faced landward, with very few towards the sea. Only the jetties with their walls and towers bearing huge suspended 'chains' (*catenae*) closed the fortified port entrances. Such were the port defences in Acre and in the small harbour of Arsuf, where wall remnants can still be seen on the now submerged jetties. The latter city was exceptional in being fortified both landward and seaward. The whole slope of the hilly ridge on which the city stood was used as a natural *glacis* and revetted with excellent masonry. The city walls rose from this natural-artificial *glacis*. Where the crusader architect struck rock along the slope there was naturally no need for additional revetting.

All cities were composed of two defensive units: the walled perimeter and the inner citadel. Most cities had only one line of walls, whose form depended on the terrain. Ascalon used parts of a hilly ridge and enclosed itself by a bow-shaped line of walls, with the coast forming the string of the bow. Where the terrain did not prescribe the shape of fortifications, the form was trapezoid as in Caesarea or quadrangular as in twelfth-century Acre. In Tyre the ancient island was firmly linked to the mainland, since Alexander the Great had built a causeway fourteen centuries earlier. The accumulating sands formed an isthmus and the shape of the island prescribed that of the city walls. According

[36] There is no special study of the problem. The monumental studies of C. Enlart and P. Deschamps give some descriptions of city fortifications. Worth consulting is a short essay written by P. Deschamps, 'L'architecture militaire en Terre Sainte' in C. Enlart, *Manuel d'archéologie française*, II, 2, Paris, 1932, 636–53.

to our sources the city boasted a double line of walls seaward and a a triple one landward.[37] At the end of the twelfth century, Acre's line of walls changes and to the original quadrangle in the south a wall was added, connecting a corner of the earlier fortifications with the coast, creating the characteristic triangular perimeter of Montmusard, the new suburb.

The technique of city defences differed only in scope from that of the crusader castles. The main features were a protected fosse outside the city walls, the *glacis* and the salient, almost always quadrangular towers.[38] The fosse or ditch had a strengthened counterscarp, a revetted slope, an upright wall (Caesarea), or a natural counterscarp if the terrain was rocky. There was seldom an *escape* proper, because the *glacis* of the walls performed that duty. The fosse, some 15 to 20m wide and of varying but suitable depth, was always (as in the castles) dry. The bottom of the fosse was not paved, so that rain water could drain into the sandy ground. The fosse of 'Pilgrim's Castle' might have been flooded by sea water, though not that of the city. The only exception seems to have been Tyre, where the fosse across the isthmus could have been filled with sea water.[39]

The walls of the city rose from the *glacis*, their line broken by salient towers and the projecting *glacis*. The towers were closely spaced so that bolts or arrows from adjacent towers could cover the ditch area before them. The towers seem not to have been or were only slightly higher than the walls. Thus the battlements of towers and walls formed one continuous line.

The general pattern was different when a city had more than one line of walls. This was the case in mid-thirteenth-century Acre and in Tyre. Since the remnants are few we can only conjecture on the

[37] William of Tyre, XIII, 5, According to Burchard of Mount Sion, the landward walls were 25 feet thick and were equipped with twelve towers, *PPTS*, XII, 11.

[38] Round towers are known in the late walls (second half of 13th century) of Acre. They were so exceptional that they are singled out by their name, as *turris rotunda*, Marino Sanudo, p. 230. It was a relatively new tower and thus indicated as *la tour neuve que l'on disait la tour d'ou roy*. Templier de Tyr, par. 494.

[39] Ibn al-Athir, *RHC*, *Hist. Orientaux* I, 707.

basis of literary sources, and assume that city fortifications followed the pattern of the castles. A double wall meant that the inner one would be higher than the outer, with a certain distance between the two lines. Such problems were already solved by the Byzantines, where the distance between two walls was generally about a quarter of the higher, i.e. inner wall. Thus walls about 98 feet high would have a distance of some 26 feet between them. Additionally, the inner walls were (if we may use the proportions of 'Pilgrim's Castle') twice as high as the outer ones (in the last example 34m to 16m). Finally, towers would be staggered, with the towerless sections of the outer wall covered by the towers of the second line.

It would be difficult to prove that this pattern was followed by the crusaders in all its details. A slightly different pattern is known from the excellent maps of thirteenth-century Acre. The reasons are obvious. The second line of walls around the old city was added as an external line of defence and had to be adapted by the architects to existing conditions. Only in the new suburb of Montmusard could an entirely new complex of fortifications be built without regard to earlier works.

In Acre the distance between the two walls resembled a narrow inner bailey, enclosed on both sides by the walls of the city. Roads, leading from the towers of the inner to those of the outer walls, traversed the bailey. In all probability there was also a circular road between the two lines of walls along the whole perimeter.

When safety and not comfort was the dominant factor, cities obviously reduced the number of their gates, though not beyond a given limit. Ascalon, a rather large city, had three gates; Jerusalem had four or five and an additional number of posterns; Caesarea does not seem to have had more than three, whereas Tyre had one gate only. The gates always had the most elaborate defences.[40]

To reach the gates an enemy had to cross the fosse, which could have a number of outer defences apart from the counterscarp, like palisades or barbicans (mentioned during the siege of Acre in 1291 as 'barbacanes'). After passing these outer defences one crossed the

---

[40] P. Deschamps, 'Les entrées des châteaux des croisés et leurs défenses', *Syria*, 13 (1932), 369–87.

ditch over a bridge. These bridges, known in Acre and with well preserved remnants in Caesarea, were entirely or partially of wood, issuing from corbel-like projections in the *glacis*. Half-way across the ditch they were supported by arches or rested on a strong stone pillar at the centre of the ditch. From here a bridge of wooden planks – easily destroyed in case of attack – reached the gate proper.

The gates were almost always 'L'-shaped as in Arab fortifications, and thus not to be crossed directly. In Tyre three walls, each with its own gate, formed a real maze. One had to pass the 'L'-shaped gate of one wall, cross a bailey to enter another gate and repeat the process when coming to the third wall. [41]

Crusader cities had huge double gates, turning on pivots at each end and closed by a vast beam which entered a socket on each side of the wall. Grooves on both sides of the door-frame indicate the use of a portcullis operated by a windlass from the second storey. The main gate of Caesarea had a second storey with an arched gallery facing the gate from the inside and could have been defended even if the enemy broke down the outer gate.

The gate was flanked by towers on both sides which seem to have been higher than the rest of the walls. Crusader seals usually depict two high towers flanking the gate.

Acre seems to have had many gates, and it was remarked by a Moslem chronicler that during the last siege the crusaders kept their gates open. [42] Since they could not be forced by a surprise attack the open gates had their logic, because they obliged the besieger to guard the whole city perimeter, as he could not foresee from which gate a possible sortie might come. Two such sorties were executed; the first failed when the crusader horses got entangled in the ropes of the Moslem tents; the other, in a moonless night, failed when the Moslems lighted fires in their camps. [43]

Some of the city fortifications, like those of Ascalon or the recently excavated Caesarea, struck the observer as much by the

---

[41] Descriptions of gates in Tyre. Ibn Jubair, *Voyage* in *RHC, Hist. Orientaux*, III, 452; Burchard of Mt Sion in *PPTS*, XII, 1, p. 11.

[42] Abu'l Fida in *RHC, Hist. Orientaux*, I, 164.

[43] *Templier de Tyr*, par. 491, in *Gestes des Chiprois*, ed. G. Raynaud, Geneva, 1887.

beauty of their work as by a feeling of inadequacy. The line of walls was simply too long to be effectively defended for a long time. We miss the feeling of compactness encountered in crusader castles. It was therefore natural that the cities envisaged a second unit of defence: the citadel. The citadel was a castle in itself, and should be visualized on these lines. Its position differed from city to city, e.g. the castle of Acre – once in the centre of the most exposed northern section of the wall – found itself almost at the centre of the interior line when the new fortifications of Montmusard were added. In Jerusalem, the citadel used one of the old Herodian towers known from the Middle Ages to our days as the 'Tower of David'.[44]

It was a rule, that the citadel – often the seat of the ruler, and not merely occupied by the local garrison – should be militarily independent of the city. Its location could thus be compared to that of the 'keep' in a castle. Nevertheless, most citadels were not built by the crusaders, but, like the cities themselves, were a legacy of the Jewish, Roman, Byzantine and Arab periods.

In Jerusalem the citadel, with its adjacent royal palace dominated the town for a thousand years before the crusaders took over and assigned to it the same functions. The citadel[45] was an irregular polygon ($750m^2$) flanked by six towers, three or four storeys high (that is $c.$ 35m), which enclosed a roomy courtyard divided by an earlier wall dating to the Herodian period. A solid two-storey wall seems to have separated the citadel from the city, but its main strength lay in the huge towers which faced the outside – especially to the north – where it overlooked one of the main gates of Jerusalem, the Jaffa gate. The citadel was encompassed by a dry fosse and connected to the city by a bridge. It can be assumed that a passage of some kind connected the citadel with the royal palace to the south. The sloped *glacis* of cyclopean stones, the remains of the 'Tower of Phasael', Herodian in origin, rose from the ditch.

[44] Properly speaking the name 'Tower of David' should be applied to the northernmost tower which directly overlooks the Jaffa gate.

[45] C. N. Johns, *A Guide to the Citadel of Jerusalem*, Jerusalem, 1944. *Id*, 'The Citadel of Jerusalem. A summary of work since 1934'. *QDAP*, 14 (1950), 121–90.

This was surmounted by walls and towers to the height of some 25 metres. Walls and towers were topped by platforms and breast-high battlements. The top of the towers, allegedly reached by two hundred steps,[46] could accommodate catapults and mangonels. The crusaders certainly repaired the citadel, and their characteristic masonry is evident among the Herodian stones. Crusader masonry was of two types: smoothly and diagonally drafted, and small, square stones with a narrow, flat margin and a protruding boss (best examples in St Louis's Caesarea).

We know from different sources that the stones were not only joined with a strong mortar, but by iron cramps or molten lead,[47] making it almost impossible to breach the tower (indeed the 'Tower of David' was never taken by storm).

In addition to the royal garrison under the castellan (sometimes called the 'Castellan of the Tower of David'), the place also served as a fortified storehouse for the garrison and probably also the city. It housed part of the royal administration, responsible for the gate tolls payable when entering the city.[48]

A different type of citadel is found in Caesarea, which occupies the best defended part of the city – the port – on its southern jetty. The location made it independent of the city proper; moreover it allowed evacuation by sea in case of danger. The few remnants of the crusader citadel do not allow full reconstruction, but contemporary descriptions convey a general outline of the defences. Under the crusaders the port of Caesarea was of secondary importance, hardly comparable to its Herodian grandeur – when Josephus Flavius described it as larger than Piraeus, the port of Athens. The northern jetty is one of the strangest structures to be found anywhere, sixty huge granite columns of Herodian origin were laid into the shallow water. The southern jetty used similar

---

[46] The citadel had five iron gates and 200 steps led to the top of the tower, according to the Russian pilgrim Daniel who visited it in 1106–7. *Itinéraires russes en Orient*, ed. B. de Khitrovo, Geneva, 1889, 17.

[47] Fulk of Chartres, *RHC, Hist. Occidentaux*, III, 356. A. M. Ben-Dov found similar joints in Belvoir.

[48] Large stores of grain mentioned by Daniel, see above, n. 46. Custom duties in the 'Tower of David', *Cartulaire du Saint Sépulcre*, ed. Rozière, 83–5.

foundations, but paved over. On this the citadel was built. A ditch cut off the citadel from the city and seems to have been filled with sea-water (or at least the sea could be let in through flood gates) turning the citadel into a small island. A strong wall flanked by two huge towers barred the entrance behind the flooded ditch. Nowhere (with the possible exception of Jerusalem) is crusader masonry more solid than in Caesarea's citadel. Herodian blocks and excellent crusader masonry formed the outer shell of the sloping foundations and walls, filled with a vast mass of rubble, stones and mortar. Additionally, short Herodian columns of porphyry and granite were inserted cross-wise into the foundations and walls, making the walls impregnable. [49]

The citadel of Arsuf is especially interesting. [50] The city was located on a steep ridge which dominated the coast. Consequently, there was no place for a citadel on the coast proper, neither was it practical to build one landward in the eastern part of the city where no natural defences were available. The crusaders thus built the citadel to the north of the city on the same ridge, but used a natural ravine which traversed the ridge as a ditch between city and citadel. The ravine, descending from the ridge to sea level, goes down some 30 metres and was widened to safeguard the citadel. From this ravine east and north of the citadel, the crusaders excavated a quadrangular fosse, behind which were the walls and the citadel proper. A long staircase, cut into the rock, led behind the walls of the citadel to the little port on the coast.

In Acre, as previously mentioned, the citadel lay in the inner part of the city during the thirteenth century. The peculiarity of Acre was not the accidental location of the citadel – which ultimately lost its proper fosse, [51] but the fact that, due to the internal history of the kingdom, the city came to have more than one citadel. We do not refer to the many fortified palaces and towers in the quarters of the privileged communities, but to real fortresses, like that of the

[49] As a matter of fact the citadel of Caesarea was stormed by scaling the walls and not by sapping their foundations.

[50] See plan of Arsuf in *Survey of Western Palestine*, II, 137.

[51] *Templier de Tyr*, par. 503, in *Les Gestes des Chiprois*, ed. G. Raynaud, Geneva, 1887.

Order of St John, whose refectory is a marvel of architecture. We can envisage such a building from a description of the fortified palace of the Templars by a member of the order:

> The *Temple* was the strongest place of the city, and took up a large stretch on the coast as a fortress. At its entrance was a stronghold very high and strong and its walls were very thick, a block of 28 feet. On each side of the fortress was a small tower and on each a *lion passant* as big as a fattened oxen, all covered with gold. The price of the four lions, in material and work, was 1,500 Saracene besants. It was marvellous to behold. On the other side, towards the Pisan quarter, was another tower; nearby above the street of St Anne was the palace of the master. Nearby, above the monastery of the nuns of St Anne, was another huge tower with bells and a marvellous and very high church. In addition there was a tower on the beach. This was an ancient tower, a hundred years old, built by command of Saladin. Here the Templars guarded their treasury. This tower was so near the beach that the sea waves washed it. And many other beautiful abodes were in the *Temple*, which I will forgo mentioning. [52]

B   Crusader Armies

Throughout history armies have been a function of society, reflecting its demographic features, stratification, ethos and attitude to warfare. Mediaeval European and Moslem armies were no exception. They reflected their particular political, social and ethnic traditions and preserved a remarkable traditionalism in their concepts of warfare throughout two hundred years of almost permanent confrontation. This resulted as much from a technological standstill, as from the fact that up to the end of the twelfth century few armies were professional and permanent. The system of education was bent on perpetuating a pattern of behaviour basically opposed to innovations. Changes occurred, but they were relatively few and slow – usually in response to an exterior chal-

---

[52] *Templier de Tyr,* par. 501.

lenge – like a different type of arms and armour or an unexpected way of fighting.

The military tradition of the Latin kingdom was European and remained thus as long as the kingdom existed, though local circumstance exerted influence on certain aspects of warfare.

The permanence of European-type armour was not necessarily the outcome of deeply ingrained traditionalism, but also the result of additional factors: the adequacy and skilful adaptation of European warfare to local challenges and the permanent relationship with the European military nobility, which participated in the great Crusades.

Crusader society and the pattern of its domination in the geopolitical framework of the Near East were the decisive factors which shaped the structure of crusader armies. Social structure postulated the existence of a class of hereditary warriors – the noble knights – and the pattern of domination imposed the double task of expansion and defence, based on strongholds and a mobile army. Finally, different ethnic traditions of warfare created practical challenges in strategy and tactics to which the crusaders had to find an effective response.

The backbone of the crusader army was the feudal host composed of knights owing military service in return for land-grants of the Crown. A list, fortunately preserved in the great book of crusader jurisprudence by Jean d'Ibelin,[53] count of Jaffa, reviews the situation around 1170. This inventory of services lists a total of 647 to 675 knights as the military force of the kingdom.[54] By modern standards this seems rather small. Nevertheless, famous battles were fought in Europe at that time with smaller numbers. Some of the great crusader expeditions, like one of the invasions of Egypt, were no larger.

The disparity between the mediaeval and modern approach to the size of armies is not only the result of a revolutionary population growth, but is also based on a different assessment of the fighting-man's role. We are so used to notions of disciplined units and to an

[53] Jean d'Ibelin, cap. 271–2, in *Lois* I, 422–6.
[54] R. C. Smail, *op. cit.*, 89, no. 3.

entire army performing as one group, that it takes some effort to visualize a situation in which the fighting-man is a military unit by himself. The heavily armoured mediaeval knight fought as a member of a unit only in the opening stages of a battle; after the first encounter he fought for himself and the battlefield split up into duels of fighting knights. Comparing the armoured knight to a modern tank could convey a better grasp of mediaeval realities.

The actual feudal host was probably greater than that listed in the above-mentioned inventory of services. The situation was analogous to that of Europe, where royal inventories list the services due to the Crown only. Each grand feudatory had at his disposal a number of knights, squires or armed retainers for his own purposes. Normally, these baronial knights would not serve the Crown, but in times of need they would take the field with their liege lord.

Moreover, a constant feature of crusader armies was the existence of hired soldiers. This expression is preferable to the technical term 'mercenaries', since there is no proof of the existence of a professional body of fighters, unemployed in times of peace. The bulk of hired fighters usually came from the crowds of pilgrims who, once their pilgrimage was accomplished, might stay on in the country. In the thirteenth century – when the means of livelihood were drastically cut by the shrinking frontiers of the kingdom – the great maritime cities like Acre and Tyre furnished a quantity of men willing to enter military service. The enlargement of the host by hired fighters depended on the financial resources of the Crown and the baronage. These were never too abundant and usually we hear about the recruitment of hired warriors in connection with special gifts sent to the East by European sovereigns or popes. A famous example is that of Henry II of England, another Philip II Augustus of France, and later on St Louis. At the Second Council of Lyon (1274) it was even envisaged that European sovereigns should keep on their payrolls fixed quotas of knights in the Holy Land.[55] Naturally, the recruitment of an army which

[55] H. Finke, 'Die *Constitutiones pro zelo fidei* des Papstes Gregor X auf dem Lyoner Konzil', *Konzilienstudien z. Gesch. d. 13ten Jahrhunderts*, Münster, 1891, 113–17.

depended on occasional donations from abroad could never have been a satisfactory solution. But since some of the money came from the papacy – which permanently taxed Christian Europe – crusader rulers could rely on a more or less steady income from foreign sources.

The feudal host consisted mainly of mounted warriors, which included many of the hired fighters. In addition, the kingdom disposed of a considerable infantry contingent and of mounted warriors who were not noble. The availability of infantry was of major importance in the crusader armies. What might be called light cavalry and infantry is usually described in crusader sources by the expression *serjant* (*serviens*). The expression *serjant à cheval* makes it clear that there were also mounted warriors of non-noble origin, but the name *serjant* alone does not point clearly to a specific way of fighting.

The *serjants*, on foot or mounted, were mobilized on a feudal basis, though we are in the dark as to the mechanism of their recruitment. The already mentioned inventory of Jean d'Ibelin lists the sizeable number of 5,025 *serjants* whose services are due to the Crown from ecclesiastical establishments and cities in the kingdom.[56] Strangely enough, no crusader charter ever mentions this type of obligation and one is inclined to presume that it was customary, based on an assessment of financial resources. This would fit the ecclesiastical institutions, the patriarch, bishops and abbots. They generally held their property 'in alms', i.e. as a non-military tenure. We do not find any satisfactory legal explanation in regard to city lords.

Finally, the kingdom disposed of an additional source of man-power in the *arrière-ban*, the general call to arms issued by the Crown in times of imminent danger. On such occasions all vassals, even those whose services were not due to the king, as being outside the obligatory contingents of the tenants-in-chief, would appear in the host. The same was also true for every able-bodied Frank in the kingdom. Naturally, the fighting power of the *arrière-ban* was not of the highest quality. But in times of danger it

[56] Jean d'Ibelin in *Lois* I, 426–7.

could play an important role, especially as a city militia when the garrison left to muster and give battle.

In this context we must return to the military orders discussed earlier.[57] Since the '30s of the twelfth century both Templars and Hospitallers played an ever increasing military role in the kingdom. The growing reliance on the military orders as defenders of the marches and especially as lords of castles – responsible for their garrisons and supplies – made them an important factor in the kingdom. Finally, their ability to supply troops at short notice and to make good their losses by drawing on financial and human resources in Europe made them indispensable.

It is not easy to estimate the military manpower of the orders. On a major occasion, like Amalric's expedition to Egypt, we hear that the Hospitallers alone were willing to put into the field 500 knights and 500 *turcoples;*[58] roughly as many as the kingdom could mobilize from all its feudal resources. This was an exceptional case and the normal manpower of an order could be put at some 300 knights. We shall probably not go wrong by assessing the combined manpower of both orders as equal to that of the kingdom.

The fighting men of the orders cannot be simply classified as the kingdom's warriors, since ultimately their grand masters and chapters decided policy. But we should not go to extremes by supposing that the orders refused service to the Crown. Rather, their power would sometimes permit them to dictate policy or force the Crown to accept their advice, even as the voice of a seasoned veteran carries weight in the councils of war.

The total strength of the kingdom, some 1,200 knights and more than 10,000 *serjants,* was not inadequate either for defence or expansion. Not military weakness, but demographic shortcomings put a stop to expansion and fixed the pattern of defence. Conquests were feasible – as proven time and again – not merely in nearby Transjordan or Damascus, but even in Egypt, across the vast Sinai peninsula. These conquests were ephemeral, since there was not enough manpower to maintain military domination for longer

[57] See above cap. XIV.
[58] Delaville le Roulx, *Cartulaire,* nos 402 and 409.

periods, let alone attempt colonization of the conquered country.

The problem looks different from the point of defence. The expression 'defence' in its narrow and exact meaning hardly covers the situation. 'Defence' meant not only the protection of a frontier – a difficult task in the open spaces of Transjordan – but also the rule and administration of inner territories.

The crusader forces had to prevent Moslem invasions. Even if they did not lead to a major battle, they were accompanied by the destruction of crops and property and undermined the material basis of crusader existence. Conversely, an invasion could lead to a major battle.

In both cases, the castles and fortified cities played a major role in crusader military thinking. A successful Moslem invasion – even if it devastated large areas – did not threaten crusader domination. As long as the invaders could not get a firm hold on the country by the capture of castles and cities, they would sooner or later have to retreat. Though the land would be devastated and the financial losses painful, crusader rule continued, since the centres of domination remained intact.

These factors shaped the military doctrine of the crusaders. To oppose an invading army the Franks had to drain their castles and cities of every able-bodied male. Often not even a token garrison could be spared. In case of defeat, there was literally nobody left to defend the strongholds. Hittin is the classical example. The disaster was followed by Saladin's military parade, when castles and cities unable to defend themselves opened their gates to the victor.

Hence, in the face of invasion the crusaders often vacillated between an adventurous campaign and more cautious inaction. This does not indicate a lack of planning or a volatile policy, passing from one extreme to the other, but on the contrary, an evaluation of the possible risks and opportunities. This took into account local circumstances, the type of opposing Moslem armies and their particular tactics.

Regardless of Moslem numerical superiority, the crusaders had several great advantages. To start with, the crusader army was a local and compact force, whereas the Moslem armies were heterogeneous and mobilized either in Egypt or Damascus. In the latter case they usually comprised, in addition to the Damascene contingents, elements from northern Syria (Aleppo, Homs) and even Mesopotamia. Their cohesion was always (up to the middle of the thirteenth century under the Mameluk sultan Baibars) weak and only in exceptional cases were they kept in the field for more than a few months. The normal campaigning season was between early and late summer, i.e. between sowing and harvesting. Indeed, a Moslem campaign rarely lasted more than a few weeks, unless the going was good and rich spoils were in view. Crusader warfare adapted itself to this pattern. Whenever numerical superiority was clearly with the opponent, the crusaders evaded battle and waited for the Moslem army to disintegrate. A classical example was the campaign which followed the crusader defeat at the battle of Sinn al-Nabra in June 1113. The crusader army barely escaped to the mountain ridge which overlooks Tiberias, where it was surrounded by a large Moslem army, composed of contingents from Damascus, Mosul and Mardin. It looked like the ultimate disaster, since at the same time the Palestinian countryside revolted against the Franks. For twenty-six days the crusaders remained in their precarious position; the Moslems did not dare a direct attack, but devastated the countryside and dispersed after three weeks. Similar tactics could have prevented the battle of Hittin. This was advocated on the eve of battle by Raymond of Tripoli – accepted by Guy de Lusignan – and then changed under the pressure of a contending faction.

It took almost four generations of fighting till the Moslem armies realized that only the destruction of strongholds and walled cities would put an end to crusader rule. Saladin seems to have first elaborated the new military doctrine, but one of his successors – al-Malik al-Mo'azzam, ruler of Damascus – systematically pursued this strategy. During the preliminaries to the peace talks with Richard Lionheart in Ramleh (1192), Saladin envisaged the razing of crusader strong-points which loomed as a future threat.[59] This

---

[59] *L'Estoire se la Guerre Sainte par Ambroise*, ed. G. Paris, v. 11775 ff; *Itinerarium Ricardi I*, ed. W. Stubbs, VI, 27.

policy, methodically continued for another generation, brought the crusaders to their knees. Victorious crusader campaigns and battles were ineffective, since there was not enough money and manpower to rebuild, repopulate and re-garrison the destroyed castles. The crusaders had just enough strength to entrench themselves in the coastal cities. St Louis spent a fortune on their fortifications (1250–54), but the Mameluk Baibars systematically isolated the maritime cities and captured them one by one. Baibars put into gear the machinery of destruction, razing the fortifications of the cities, despite the obvious and immediate material loss he suffered by devastating the coastal plain. There is no doubt that his major aim was to prevent any possible return of the crusaders and the use of the maritime cities as bridgeheads for a new conquest.

This major change in Moslem strategy brought about a total reversal of crusader policy in the thirteenth century. Changing the direction of the Crusades from the Holy Land to Egypt was not caused by an upsurge of 'jingoism' or imperialism, but constituted a dire necessity, a last minute effort to save the establishment by a new military doctrine. The aim was to bring Egypt to its knees and recover the Holy Land on the battlefields of Damietta and Cairo. A victory over Egypt was to break Moslem power in the Holy Land. By controlling Egypt the crusaders wanted to gain time to implant themselves anew in the Holy Land and guarantee their security. A combination of bad generalship and even worse diplomacy robbed the crusaders of their remarkable victories in the two great Egyptian campaigns, the so-called Fifth Crusade (1217–21) and the Crusade of St Louis (1248–50).

After the failure of the latter Crusade the Latin kingdom never regained the military or diplomatic initiative. The best it could do was to defend itself. The poor remnants of a kingdom along the coastal strip deepened their ditches and strengthened their walls. Entrenched in the face of a mobile enemy, the crusaders awaited a major Moslem onslaught shut up in their isolated cities. The Moslems did not need a new Hittin, since they could tackle each city by itself. They fell one after another following short sieges. Only the last stand of Acre (1291) could claim a place in the glorious past of the kingdom.

C   Arms and Armour

The arms and armour of the crusaders were essentially European. Too much has been read into the fact that Tancred appears on one of his coins wearing a kind of *kefiyah*, i.e. cloth over his helmet. This does not prove orientalization, but may simply indicate that Tancred, with typically Norman practicality adopted Moslem headgear to combat the hot sun of the East (and he may even have met with it in southern Italy or Sicily).

We have few crusader descriptions of their arms and armour. But we can get a good idea of the equipment used by the knights of the First Crusade because they were almost contemporary with the knights of William the Conqueror, eternalized in the Bayeux Tapestry. Subsequent changes in crusader arms can be followed through European sources. The most detailed and best study of European arms is based on the engravings of contemporary seals, a large number of which belonged to European nobles who were actual participants in the Crusades of the twelfth and thirteenth centuries.[60] In addition, actual crusader seals depict the arms and armour of the nobility.[61] To some extent we can also use illuminated crusader manuscripts which, even when dealing with biblical subjects, depict contemporary body armour and weapons.[62]

Taking the Bayeux Tapestry as the basic model, we can see that armour was strictly functional. Uncomfortable and far from elegant, it had to protect the wearer against a whole range of weapons: arrow, lance (sometimes hurled), axe, mace, sword and dagger.[63] At the same time it had to allow the wearer to take the offensive and use his own weapons.

The basic parts of body armour were the helmet and a garment which covered as much of the body as possible without impeding

[60] G. Demay, 'Le Costume de guerre et l'apparat d'après les sceaux du moyen-âge', *Mém. de la soc. nat. des antiquaires de France*, IV, 5 (1874), 120–71.

[61] G. Schlumberger, F. Chalandon, A. Blanchet, *Sigillographie de l'Orient latin*, Paris, 1943.

[62] H. Buchthal, *Miniature Painting in the Latin Kingdom of Jerusalem*, Oxford, 1957 (quoted below as Buchthal).

[63] E. Maclagan, *The Bayeux Tapestry*, 1953.

the knight. Over a light, long shirt, the knight wore a quilted or multi-layered tunic of cloth or leather which formed the under-garment for a coat of sewn-on or riveted metal lamellae.[64] This long and outer coat of lamellae armour reached below the knees and was called *broigne* or byrnie. It was slit at the front and back to enable the knight to mount his horse. Very often the legs were protected by hose made of the same material. The effectiveness of the byrnie depended on the density or quality of the metal lamellae or links.

A variation of the *broigne*, first used by magnates but later ex-tended to all knights, was the *hauberk* (originally *hals-berc*, 'pro-tecting the neck'), where the metal lamellae were replaced by mail – hand-wrought and individually riveted interlaced rings – which finally became a separate item from the leather or cloth undertunic. A quilted garment was worn underneath called the *gambeson*. In the thirteenth century the *hauberk* had sleeves ending in long protective mittens for arms and hands.

Due to their weight and, as in the case of leather, the stiffness of the garment, neither *broigne* nor *hauberk* were made for perfect comfort. Though mail was far more flexible, the *broigne* and *hauberk* became exceedingly hot under a strong sun. So a light long tunic of white cloth, the surcoat or *cotte d'armes* was worn over the *hauberk*. During the thirteenth century this bore the heraldic arms of the knight.[65] The blazon would be repeated on the trappings of his horse.[66]

The other main item of armour was the helmet whose design was substantially modified between the First Crusade and the fall

---

[64] Buchthal, A.D. 1131/43. pl. 8a.

[65] Buchthal, A.D. 1250/75, pl. 86 *c;* 112 *c.* Quilted jerkins as well as surcoats were also worn by Moslems. See Usama ibn Munqidh, 74, 88.

[66] The seal of Jean de Montfort and Balian d'Ibelin of Arsuf in Schlumberger, *op. cit.*, pl. XVIII, 7 and XVII, 1. The first has a *lion rampant*, the latter the cross of the Ibelins (*Or à une croiz de gueules patée*, Joinville, XXXIV) Buchthal, A.D. 1250/75, pl. 63, 80, 104 a, 104 c, 105 a, 105 b. Some crusader seals show a kind of a short jacket not unlike the pourpoint (or perhaps the *gambeson?*), e.g. the seal of Jean d'Ibelin of Arsuf, Garcia Alvarez, Amaury, viscount of Nablus. Schlum-berger, *op. cit.*, pl. XVII, 2; XVII, 5; XVIII, 6 and again Buchthal, A.D. 1250/75, pl. 86 *c.*

of Acre. The knights of the First Crusade wore an iron, conical helmet set on a round base. Bands of metal passed upwards from the
top. Leather thongs covered the neck. A fairly common addition to
this type of helmet was a nose-piece, providing the only cover for
the knight's face.[67] In the East it was not unusual for the crusaders
to drape a white cloth mantle over the helmet.[68]

In the last quarter of the twelfth century the helmet lost its
conical shape and became more cylindrical with a rounded or flat
top. This was now the great helm which continued well into the
thirteenth century, though in the middle of the century the top
of the cylinder was enlarged, forming a more bulbous shape. The
nose-piece, obviously insufficient protection for the face, was
replaced by a visor with two lines of apertures for breathing. In its
final form the helmet was known as *grand heaume, casque de St
Louis* or *casque de Croisades*.[69] The weight of such a *heaume* made it
impractical to wear until the last moment. A knight would thus
often wear a smaller helmet, called *chapeau de fer*, a round cap with a
large, curving brim.[70]

The body armour was completed by the shield. The knights
of the First Crusade carried great kite-shaped shields, rounded at
the top and pointed at the bottom, familiar from the Bayeux
Tapestry. This was a heavy affair made of wood, padded inside
and covered on the outside with leather. The design resembled a
sun with its rays, and metal bands strengthened the shield and
converged at the centre in a boss.[71]

---

[67] Balian II of Nablus, Amaury, viscount of Nablus, Pons of Tripoli. Schlumberger, *op. cit.*, pl. XIX, 8; XVII, 6; XVIII, 5.

[68] Seals of Hugh Granier, Baldwin of Mirabel. Schlumberger, *op.cit.* pl,
XVIII, 2; XVIII, 4.

[69] Seals of Garcia Alvarez of Haifa, Balian d'Ibelin of Arsuf. Schlumberger,
op.cit., pl. XVII, 5; XVII, 1. The best example is that on the seal of Jean de
Montfort, *ibid.*, XVIII, 7. Buchthal, A.D. 1250/75, pl. 104 a, 104 c, 105 a, 105 b.
A very elaborate example, pl. 105 c.

[70] Bohemond III of Antioch, Jean d'Ibelin of Arsuf, Hugh II de Puiset.
Schlumberger, *op.cit.*, pl. XVI, 6; XVII, 2; XIX, 1. Buchthal, pl. 111, 115 c, 119 c.

[71] To be seen on almost all early crusader seals, e.g. Bohemond III of Antioch,
Hugh II de Puiset, Baldwin of Ramle, Guillaume de Bures. Schumberger,
op.cit., pl. XVI, 6; XIX, 1; XIX, 3; XIX, 4.

This heavy, early shield was suspended from the shoulder by a leather band when riding and held to the left. When upright it covered a standing knight from neck to foot and gave excellent protection at a time when body armour was not very adequate.

During the First Crusade the Franks came across the round shield of the Orient, light and practical, excellent for riding, but insufficient for fighting on foot. The crusaders may have been somewhat influenced by this oriental shield very early. In any case European developments in armour were to lead in the same direction, though the round shield never became concave.

In the second half of the twelfth century, with the development of linked-mail mesh, the old shield became obsolete. Its successor was short, just covering the breast and abdomen of the rider and leaving him more freedom of movement. Round or a squat triangle in shape, this form continued during the thirteenth century. With the development of heraldry, the blazon was painted on the shield,[72] thus creating a repetitive pattern on shield, surcoat and horse trappings.

The basic arms of the knight were the lance, sword, mace and battle axe. The former, with the addition of a small pennon, the *gonfanon*, became the distinguishing mark of the knight. The lance rested on the right arm when riding and was normally used as a thrusting weapon, but could also be thrown. Its shaft was usually of ash tipped with an iron point which varied in shape. When obliged to fight on foot the knight could use it as a pike, though it was not really strong enough for this purpose.[73]

Finally there was the sword. In the twelfth century the dominant type of sword was short, not unlike the Roman one. It had a straight double-edged blade ending in a triangular point; another type,

[72] Seals of Jean d'Ibelin of Arsuf, Jean de Montfort, Balian d'Ibelin-Arsuf. Schlumberger, *op. cit.*, pl. XVII, 2; XVIII, 7; XVII, 1.

[73] Lances appear on almost all crusader seals, because their normal type is that of a galloping knight. Swords are rarer. See seals of Jean d'Ibelin of Arsuf, Balian II of Nablus. Schlumberger, *op. cit.*, pl. XVII, 2; XIX, 8; XVIII, 6. Usama ibn Munqidh mentions the use of a compound lance, which was 18–20 cubits long (p. 131). This type of lance is perhaps represented on the seal of Pons of Tripoli, *ibid.*, pl. XVIII, 5.

more elegant, narrowed from hilt to point. The pommel was usually round and flattened, though other shapes were fairly common. The sword was worn in a leather scabbard[74] strengthened by a chape and other metal fittings and hung from the neck or shoulder, later from the waist.[75] During the thirteenth century the sword became longer, heavier and stronger, so as to be effective against the more highly developed body armour. In addition we sometimes hear of maces[76] and axes[77] as part of a knight's armament. The cost of equipping a knight was very high. The Hospitallers assessed it in the thirteenth century at 1,500 to 2,000 silver deniers of Tours,[78] a major item of expenditure being of course the horse.[79]

The equipment of a foot-soldier was much more simple. It is doubtful if one can envisage a standard of armament like that described by the 'Assize of Arms' under Henry II of England.[80] The chroniclers of the Crusades usually describe the infantry as being less well armed than the knights. A well-equipped foot-soldier is described by the Norman troubadour Ambroise[81] during the Third Crusade: *Armez de coife e de hauberc e de parpoint a meint bel merc*, an expanded version is given in the Latin: 'He was armed quite well according to the custom of the foot, his head was protected by an iron cover; a hauberk and a linen tunic padded many times and difficult to penetrate, ingeniously worked with needle

[74] Buchthal, A.D. 1250/75, pl. 65.
[75] *Ibid.*, pl. 119 c.
[76] *Ibid.*, pl. 109 c.
[77] *Ibid.*, pl. 107 c.
[78] J. Riley-Smith, *op. cit.*, p. 244.
[79] *Ibid.*, 245.
[80] The Assize of Arms (1181) fixes the following armament. For a knight: shirt of mail (*lorica*), helmet (*cassis*), shield (*clypeus*), lance (*lancea*). Poorer free layman, that is serving on foot: hauberk (*aubergel*), iron cap (*capellet ferri*), lance (*lancea*). Burgesses and freemen: gambeson (*wambais*), iron cap (*capellet ferri*), lance (*lancea*). Stubbs, *Select Charters*, Oxford, 1890[7], 153 ff. A hundred years later Edward's I Statute of Winchester (1285) enumerates the following: For the wealthy: hauberk, iron cap (*chapel de feer*), sword (*espe*), knife (*cutel*) and horse. For the less monied: the same without horse. For the common people: pourpoint, iron cap, sword, knife, bow and arrows. *Ibid.*, 470.
[81] *L'Estoire de la Guerre Sainte par Ambroise*, vv. 3567/8.

and consequently called in the vernacular a pourpoint.'[82] Normally the protective clothing and armour would be less elaborate, an
iron cap, a leather or quilted linen breast-guard, a pike, bow – sometimes a crossbow,[83] and a dagger.

D   Warfare

Once in the field the crusaders had to deal with armies unknown
to the Western world, although quite familiar to the Byzantines.
In the twelfth century there was a noticeable difference between
the armies of Egypt and those of Syria and Iraq. The Egyptian
cavalry fought with sword and lance, not unlike the crusaders,
though the armour was lighter. Egypt was not an unknown quantity. The danger came from the Moslem armies of the north. Here,
the Seljuq conquest had grafted on to the Moslem cavalry, which
continued the Arab military tradition, a new type of warrior and
new tactics: the mounted archer fighting *à la turque*.

The bow and crossbow were not new weapons either in the
West or East. Yet in Europe the bow had been outmoded long
before the twelfth century and was looked down upon by the
cavalry. It had been virtually degraded and relegated to the non-
noble. Noblemen used the bow in hunting, but the shooting of
arrows or bolts in battle was definitely considered a vulgar form of
fighting. A parallel development seems to have taken place in the
Moslem armies, where, for example, the archers of the Egyptian
army were infantrymen recruited from among the black Sudanese.

This changed with the advent of the Turks. From their nomadic
life in Central Asia they brought with them the technique of
fighting with mounted, swift-moving archers. The bow became
the decisive weapon in the opening stages of the battle (and sometimes even the instrument of victory), followed up by the direct
encounter with lance, sword, mace, axe and dagger. The advantages of these tactics against an enemy unfamiliar with this type
of fighting are obvious.

[82] *Interarium Ricardi* I, ed. W. Stubbs, I, 48 (p. 99).
[83] Buchthal, pl. 65, 107 c, 113 c, 115c.

The crucial factor was the relative mobility of the armies. The difference in the weight of armour compelled the crusaders to use stronger and heavier horses, which were naturally slower. A crusader army on the march was thus always at a disadvantage. Many descriptions of battles present the same picture: squadrons of Moslem mounted archers approach a crusader column at tremendous speed, to some 50m to 80m, discharge flights of arrows and disappear as quickly as they came, to return shortly for another assault. Naturally, such attacks were primarily directed against the flanks and rear of the column. They are graphically described by contemporary chroniclers, who compare the enemy to bees circling around the crusader armies.

This method of fighting left the mail-clad crusader at a considerable disadvantage. Neither sword, lance nor javelin was effective against the mounted archer who attacked well beyond their range. The heavy armour did afford protection since it could apparently withstand arrows. Our chroniclers sometimes describe crusader shields and coats after an archers' attack as looking like porcupines! But if the mail failed the knight was vulnerable. Moreover, the Moslems profited by the fact that during the twelfth and thirteenth centuries horses were not protected. Consequently, it was sometimes easier to unseat a knight by killing his horse. A dismounted knight was of limited use and could hardly withstand the assault of a mounted warrior.

Turkish warfare represented a challenge to Westerners. They came up with two solutions: a new type of warrior, the *turcoples*, and the development of their own techniques to counter the danger. The *turcoples* are often regarded as squadrons fighting *à la turque*, but closer scrutiny of the texts indicates that the issue is more complicated. The name itself means 'sons of Turks', and crusader chronicles describe them as troops composed of native half-breeds, descendants of a Turkish or Arab father and Greek mother.[84] They were recruited within the kingdom itself, although some may have been recent immigrants from the north. In time the ethnic composition of these troops changed, and the

---

[84] Alb. Aqa., V, 3; Raim. d'Aguilers, cap. 7.

name 'turcople' was applied to this particular type of soldier[85] regardless of racial origin.

From an anecdote told by the troubadour Ambroise, a participant in the Third Crusade, it is clear that they had to be specially dressed and ordered to keep silent so as not to reveal that they were not Arabs.[86] Later on they may have been recruited from among the native population. The turcoples are described as knights (or horsemen) with light armour, though there is no proof that they fought exclusively as mounted archers. Obviously some of them might have used the bow, but as a whole they did not become the crusader counterpart of the Seljuq mounted archers.[87] They probably remained light troops even during the thirteenth century when armour became progressively heavier. They could thus use swifter horses than the knights and were used as vanguard, reconnaissance, and foraging units. The turcoples became an integral part of the crusader armies, commanded by the marshal of the kingdom,[88] and the military orders had a special commander, the turcoplier, who was responsible for them.

The turcoples were at best only a partial answer to the Turkish challenge. The crusaders themselves did not adapt their cavalry to the Turkish way of fighting, since this would have required a great deal of retraining in new tactics. The crusader answer was to use archers and crossbowmen on foot. The European infantry of peasant origin had never abandoned the bow which, often combined with pike and shield, remained its main weapon. In Europe yeoman archers were not important until the advent of the long bow in the thirteenth and fourteenth centuries. Things evolved differently in the East and the crusaders found that infantry bowmen were the answer to the Turkish threat. Units of bowmen were

---

[85] William of Tyre, XXII, 17, *Idem*, XIX, 25: *equites levis armaturaé, quos Turcopulos vacant (ce sont sergent legierement armé)*.

[86] *L'Estoire de la Guerre Sainte par Ambroise*, ed. P. Paris, vv. 10340–56; cf. *Itinerarium Ricardi* I, VI, 4.

[87] The name was known to the Arabs and Usama ibn Munqidh, p. 79 defined the 'Turkubuli' as the archers of the Franks. The text deals with the northern country of Tripoli. Cf. R. C. Smail, *op. cit.*, 112 ff.

[88] *Le Livre au roi*, IX.

posted before the squadrons of mounted knights. Their crossbow bolts and arrows kept the enemy's mounted archers at a suitable distance from the main army and protected the crusader cavalry. This exchange of missiles between crusader archer and crossbowmen and the Seljuq mounted archers could go on for a long time while the cavalry waited. Then at the right moment the ranks of the infantry opened and the crusader cavalry would hurl itself upon the enemy with superior weight and momentum.

The advantages of using foot-archers were obvious, but there were also some drawbacks. Such tactics were far better suited to pitched battles than to skirmishing on the move. The pace of advance was then prescribed by the slowly moving infantry, thus holding back the speedier cavalry. This explains why the Turks are always described as circling around the crusader army. Again, when the campaign was a combination of advances and halts, the safety of the crusader army depended on the cohesion of the whole body, which was not easy to preserve. In addition, compact units were a conspicuous and easy target for the Turks if they succeeded in approaching a crusader army to within missile range. Thus Saladin's troops, moving on a hilly ridge on the left flank of the crusaders when King Richard marched from Acre to Jaffa, harassed the army for days whilst sustaining virtually no losses themselves.

The success of the crusader army largely depended on its internal discipline, particularly in preventing knights from taking the initiative and breaking through their own infantry, which offered protection. Young bloods in every army present similar problems, but in the Middle Ages when individual combat was the highest test of a knight and with an army which (in the Third Crusade) had come all the way from Europe to fight the Infidel, such niceties of tactics could have appeared as unchivalrous procrastination. In this light it becomes clear why a stratagem of the mounted nomads – Scythian, Turk or Mongol – namely, simulated flight followed by a sudden turn, succeeded so well against the crusaders. Pursuing a fleeing enemy the whole crusader army disintegrated; more important, the mounted knight became separated from the foot-bowmen and exposed to the Moslem mounted archer, whom neither lance nor sword could reach. What happened to individual squadrons in pursuit of an enemy simulating flight, could happen to the whole army if the enemy succeeded in separating the knights from the infantry. This actually occurred at the battle of Hittin.[89]

The process is clearly described by James, bishop of Acre at the siege of Damietta:

> The Egyptians captured from among our knights and turcoples after they wounded their horses, who for some reason, whether for bringing in wood or collecting grain, ever rode farther away from the army; but they never dared to wait for an engagement when ours were assembled and massed together. Sometimes they would capture some of ours who without discipline pursued them when they simulated a flight.[90]

And later on:

> Because the Saracens were more cautious and more prompt to flight and they did not dare to wait for ours unless they were more numerous and had an obvious superiority, therefore they had in chains, as it is said, more than 3,000 of our people, whereas we hardly had more than 1,000 of them in our captivity.[91]

The difference in arms and tactics also had far-reaching effects on the choice of terrain by the two adversaries. For the Moslems it was extremely important to choose broken and open land, which would put to advantage their agility and mobility. Moreover, broken ground hampered the most dreaded of crusader tactics: direct, frontal assault by heavy cavalry reaching the full weight of their charge on flat ground without obstacles.

If mobility and missile attack from a distance were the major advantages of Moslem armies, shock power constituted the main strength of the crusaders. The mounted charge at the gallop by a mass of mailed knights on heavier horses – lances thrust forward and shielded from neck to thigh – gained momentum until the decisive moment of impact. Its purpose was to break up the enemy's formation, ride down and crush his lighter cavalry and gain a

[89] Cf. J. Prawer, 'La battaille de Hittin', *Israel Exploration Journal*, XIV (1964), 160–79.

[90] *Lettres de Jacques de Vitry*, ed. R.B.C. Huygens, ep. VII, 76–81.

[91] *Ibid.*, 105–9.

decision. If the first clash was not decisive, the enemy could employ his wings to attack from the flank – if his centre was the aim of attack – or have time enough to bring up his reserves and throw them into battle. Thus the force and correct timing of the first charge played a major role in the encounter. To be successful it was not enough to strike hard and fast, since the crusaders had to manoeuvre so as to bring the main body of the enemy within range of their charge. This meant to manoeuvre the enemy into a compact front on flat ground backed by hills or another obstacle to prevent his dispersion at the moment of being charged. In the latter case the battle might be won, though the enemy could usually reorganize some time later.

The Moslem answer, which proved itself time and again, was to open the ranks at the moment of onslaught. Just before the impact, the Moslems would open their ranks and let the crusaders tear through like a hurricane. The most famous of such charges was that by Raymond of Tripoli at the battle of Hittin. The Moslems opened their ranks and let his knights move from the plain through a narrow gorge to the village of Hittin and then through a valley to Lake Tiberias. His detachment saved itself but did not damage the enemy. Guy de Lusignan remained with a weakened army which found temporary refuge – followed by disaster – on the saddle-like hill of the 'Horns of Hittin'.

E   Siegecraft

Although sieges were no novelty in the West, the encounter with the military architecture of the Near East confronted the crusaders with new problems.[92] The fact that oriental cities and castles were built of stone, the use of which was hardly general in contemporary Europe, proved to have a far-reaching impact. The dimensions

[92] A detailed study of the subject remains a *desideratum*. A large amount of material is to be found in the studies of P. Deschamps, C. Enlart and in the monumental E. Viollet-le-Duc, *Dictionnaire raisonné de l'architecture française du XIe au XVIe siècle*, Bance, 1858. See now J.–F. Fino, *Fortresses de la France médiévale*, Paris, 1967, which has special chapters on siegecraft, (*l'art poliorcétique*).

of these fortresses transcended everything in Western experience. The two factors: solid building materials and great size, had long before produced a corps of expert pioneers in the Byzantine and Moslem armies for use in siege operations. No similar body was to be found in the armies of the First Crusade. The cities and castles they besieged were taken by the only two means known in Europe: close siege, which cut off a stronghold from supplies and ultimately starved out the garrison, or direct assault on the walls by scaling ladders or moving towers with drawbridges to grapple the battlements. An episode from the siege of Jerusalem in 1099 describes the situation. The siege of the great city became prolonged, as attempts to storm it failed. An important contribution to victory was the arrival of a Genoese fleet in Jaffa. The sailors dismantled their ships and brought across Philistia and Judaea the masts and timber, as well as cords, hooks and axes which were most helpful in building 'belfries' (movable towers) which facilitated the capture of the city. The crusader armies definitely lacked engineers and pioneers.

There is little doubt that in siegecraft the crusaders learnt from Moslem and Byzantine. When some years after the First Crusade we hear of new techniques employed by the crusaders, we can safely assume that they were acquired through friendly contacts with Byzantines and Armenians or from encounters with the Moslem enemy. The new techniques did not entirely supersede ancient traditions. Crusader siegecraft never became an *art savant*; old and new mingled and each was used according to need.

Siegecraft meant the employment of all means to capture a stronghold, whether by storm, mining, starvation or stratagem. To starve out oriental cities or even castles was not easy, since some stored provisions enough to hold out for years. Except in very special circumstances no crusader army could conduct a long siege. Starvation was thus hardly a suitable means of capturing a city. Moreover, the vast perimeter of some cities prevented close siege by the small crusader armies. In the Third Crusade the comparatively small city of Acre was virtually sealed off by the besieging forces.

This left only one choice: to capture the city by storm. Since small arms were naturally of no avail mechanical devices were employed. The relevant technology is very ancient and partially derived from Greek, Roman and Byzantine experience – themselves influenced by Assyria, Egypt, Babylon and Persia. This was adapted by the Islamic nations and incorporated influences from as far as China.

Three systems were used against the walls of strongholds: scaling by ladders; use of 'belfries' which not merely discharged missiles but were moved towards the walls and lowered drawbridges over the battlements; finally, breaching the walls or towers by bombardment, battering rams or mining of their foundations.

Each of these systems had first to tackle the crossing of the moat 15–22 yards wide. Filling of ditches is often mentioned in crusader warfare. Infantry were naturally preferred for this task, but in an emergency the knights also participated in this menial task. One can understand the feelings of the knights who declared in the '*Assise of Bilbeis*' that a knight is not obliged to descend from his horse, even in times of siege.[93]

Filling ditches was not only back-breaking, but also dangerous. The whole array of a stronghold's defences was aimed to dominate the area just across the ditch where the enemy concentrated and the ditch itself. The rain of arrows and other projectiles was aimed at the pioneers and the protection of shields was not adequate, since they hampered work and did not stop the more powerful missiles. The besiegers usually tried to sweep the archers from the walls, and used movable mantlets to protect soldiers filling the ditches. Once a passage was made over the ditch the besiegers prepared for direct assault on the walls. Enterprising individuals tried to scale the wall by using cords with grapnels; in one case we hear that they used parts of a horse's harness to scale the walls.[94] Once the battlements were reached, rope ladders were thrown down for the climbing parties or scaling ladders raised from outside. The assault force then made directly for the gates to throw them open for the

---

[93] On the *assise of Bilbeis*, see *Lois* I, 455 and J. Richard, *Le royanne latin de Jérusalem*, Paris, 1947, 78.

[94] During the siege of Caesarea by Baibars in 1265.

rest of the army. The besieged poured boiling water, oil, pitch and molten wax on the climbing parties. Luck and great daring were essential, though often treason from within helped to take a city by direct assault.

Major sieges saw the extensive use of machinery by the attackers. The most important device was the movable tower called a 'belfry'. This was several storeys high with stations for archers and crossbowmen on each floor. Some platforms were large enough to accommodate mangonels or catapults, the artillery of the attackers. The uppermost platform was higher than the walls, so that a drawbridge could be lowered to the battlements and an attacking party storm the city walls. The 'belfry' moved on rollers, tree trunks or sometimes wheels.

The besieged tried to destroy the 'belfry' by casting huge stones, setting it afire or overturning it. Sorties by the besieged destroyed many a 'belfry' and its covering party. Combustible projectiles were launched from the city: fire arrows, red-hot bolts, burning faggots and the famous 'Greek fire'. This was a mixture of resin, sulphur, pitch, naphtha and oil[95] (sometimes containing pinewood charcoal and incense) in breakable pottery containers;[96] it could not be extinguished by water. There is a famous description of its effect by Joinville, the chronicler of St Louis's expedition to Egypt:

This Greek fire, in appearance, was like a large tun of verjuice and its burning tail was of the length of a long sword. It made in coming such a noise like thunder; and it seemed a dragon flying through air. It gave so great a light, that you could see our camp as in broad day. [97]

Such projectiles were launched from *ballistae*, engines or, for small incendiary heads, by crossbows. To counter such incendiary pro-

---

[95] Different sources mention also pitch, gum, bitumen etc.

[96] Some of these smaller pottery containers were found in Jerusalem on Mt Sion. See J. Germer-Durant, 'Glanes épigraphiques', *Échos d'Orient*, IX (1906), 133; id., 'Cruches de Syrie', *Jérusalem* (periodical), I, 337.

[97] Joinville, *Histoire de Saint Louis*, ed. Natalis de Wailly, Paris, 1883, par. 206.

jectiles, the 'belfries' were covered with hides of freshly slaughtered animals or with felt etc. soaked in vinegar or even urine.[98]

'Belfries' were not always feasible[99] and the besiegers had to use the slower procedure of breaching the walls. Again we can safely assume that the crusaders learnt from their oriental allies and enemies. Contemporary polyorcetics were largely based on late Roman and Byzantine practices developed by the Moslem armies. Though Arab sources call some of these devices 'Turkish' or 'Persian', their true origin reaches back to antiquity.

The war engines of the period can be divided into two types according to their kinetic principles: swing and torsion machinery. The first used the weighted pendulum and the second the principle of tension. One of the major contrivances which used the pendulum motion was the battering ram. This was the classical *aries*, which crusader sources call *bellier*, *mouton* and *eue* (ram, mutton, sheep – respectively).[100] We have an excellent description of such an engine constructed by order of the bishop of Besançon during the Third Crusade:[101]

> It is usually called ram (*aries*), because it destroys the solid fortifications of the walls like the ram by repeated and rapid blows. The bishop ordered to apply the ram, which was strongly covered all sides with pieces of iron, to destroy the walls. . . . He brought the ram, which resembled a vaulted house, to breach the walls. Inside was a huge mast whose head was fitted with iron. The ram, pushed by many hands against the wall, was swinging back only to strike again with a greater force. And so they tried by repeated blows to hollow out the side of the wall or breach it. And those who swung the ram and struck it continuously were well protected inside from any possible damage from above.

[98] Jacobus de Vitriaco, *Hist. Orientalis*, in Bongars, *Gesta Dei per Francos*, 1611, p. 1098.

[99] An ingenious 'belfry' built by people from Flanders on two jointed ships is described during the siege of Damietta by Jacques de Vitry, *Lettres*, ed. R.B.C. Huygens, Leiden, 1960, IV, 127 ss, and see the parallel text of Oliverus Scholasticus quoted in a note. The cost of this belfry was enormous, 2,000 marks of silver.

[100] Ambroise, *L'Estoire de la Guerre Sainte*, vv. 3825, 4768.

[101] *Itinerarium Ricardi*, ed. W. Stubbs, I, 59, pp. 111–12.

This crusader battering ram is called in the Arabic sources 'kabsh', which means 'ram'. An Arabic description of a crusader ram depicts it as having two iron horns, as long as lances and as thick as columns.[102] The swinging beam was suspended from a wooden framework by cords or iron chains. Against the blows of such engines the crusaders used iron cramps or lead to strengthen the joints and fittings of their masonry.

To protect the soldiers working it against the projectiles of the defenders, the ram was covered by a more or less solid structure, a 'house' as it impressed the above-quoted chrinicler. These moving sheds were called 'tortoises' (testudo) and had sharp gable roofs to deflect missiles with ease. The Arabic name was 'dababa', probably a creeper. These moving houses are sometimes called 'cats' (cattes, chat) and an Arab chronicler calls them 'sanura' (cat) and describes them as fitted with a ploughshare-like roof. Some were very elaborate, like those built by St Louis at Mansurah. They had towers at their ends and were called 'chats-châteaux'.[103]

A variation of the battering ram was a device with an inclined iron head, which attacked the wall foundations by hollowing. It was called the 'sow' (truie) and 'rostrated boar' (sus rostrata), an instrument found in the Near East from antiquity.

The second type of war engines were the projectors for every type of missile. Their generic name was petrariae or pierrières, that is stone-throwing catapults. The vocabulary is rather loose and a clear distinction must be made between the two types. The catapults for shooting javelins used the tension of a mechanically drawn cord like a bow, which, when released, propelled the javelin along its grooved runner. The mangonel (from manganon) consisted of a beam with cup-like hollow at one end bearing a stone or other missile (sometimes the heads of decapitated captives). Drawn back mechanically or balanced by counterweights the vertical beam when released, threw the stone in a high elliptical orbit against the walls or into the interior of the besieged stronghold.[104]

[102] Immad al-Din quoted by Abu Shama in *RHC, Hist. Orientaux*, IV, 486.
[103] Joinville, *Histoire de Saint Louis*, ed. Natalis de Wailly, Paris, 1883, par. 192.
[104] An interesting description of siege engines from the pen of an Arab engineer, contemporary of the Third Crusade, was publ. by Cl. Cahen, 'Un

The counterpart to surface activities was the sapping of the walls. When the crusaders appeared in the East, the art of sapping and undermining was a long-established part of local siegecraft. Local corps of specialists, like those of Aleppo, were so highly renowned that the crusaders greatly prized captives from that city.

Walls were sapped by tunnelling. When the supporting timbers were fired or pulled by ropes, the section of wall or tower collapsed into the sap. Some castles on high eminences were almost entirely beyond the reach of this method, and the same was true of fortresses near the coast. Tunnelling in the sandy dunes to any depth would almost immediately cause ground water to flood the excavation. The system was effective in dry places inland, in hilly country or on mountainous ridges, even near the coast.

The normal technique was to open a shaft some distance from the stronghold beyond the ditch, and then excavate a tunnel towards the walls. It would have been best to start work beyond the effective reach of enemy projectiles, i.e. some 100 to 200m from the walls, but this would have involved protracted tunnelling. On the other hand, if tunnelling began nearer the walls the sappers were exposed to enemy fire. They were usually protected by wooden mantlets or wicker work screens and baskets, which stopped the smaller projectiles. A different technique was often used. The excavated earth was heaped into a mound or bank which hid the sappers from the enemy. This technique was used if the sappers decided to tunnel near the ditch and to use it as a shaft of the tunnel.[105] In this case the tunnel would be some 20 to 30m long and about 20m deep. The tunnel props were then collapsed as previously mentioned.[106] Theoretically, the besiegers would then storm through the breach.

Tunnelling and sapping were countered by special techniques of architecture and defence. Sapping was made dangerous and

manuel d'armurerie composé pour Saladin', *Bull. d'études orientales de l'Inst. français de Damas*, 12 (1948), 143 ff. and 159 ff.

[105] Maqrizi, *Histoire des sultans Mamelouks*, ed. Quatremère, Paris, II, 8–10.

[106] A detailed and clear description of tunnelling in Usama ibn Munqidh, p. 102. Contemporary Moslem siege machines are described by C. E. Bosworth and D. Ayalon in *Enc. of Islam* (new edit.), *s. v. Hisar*.

difficult by the profuse employment of *glacis* and sloped bases found in crusader fortifications. The pyramid-like *glacis*, leaning obliquely on the upright line of walls, rested its broad base on the bottom of the moat and exerted a tremendous pressure on the surface.[107] To effect this the *glacis* was filled with heavy stones between the wall and the exterior revetment. Thus any tunnel had to cope with heavy static pressure from above even before reaching the walls. The walls themselves were not an easy task, since in crusader fortifications they are about 10 to 17 feet thick. They were not always built of cyclopean stones, and often the same technique was used as for the *glacis*. Namely, two lines of good masonry on the outside, filled with rubble, broken pottery (beautiful *terracotta*, e.g. in Caesarea), earth and mortar. This not only added artificially to the thickness of the walls but increased their weight. Obviously, higher walls with deeper foundations and heavier pressures make tunnelling more difficult.

Counter-tunnelling was also used. The besieged would open a shaft inside their stronghold and tunnel in the direction of the besiegers' sap. Once the tunnels met, the garrison would try to fight the sappers and destroy their work. A collapse in part of the tunnel would seal it off and make its future problematical.

In some sieges the besieged anticipated the sapping of their walls by building a second makeshift wall behind the threatened section at very short notice.

[107] Moreover the slanted line of the *glacis* made the use of ladders more difficult.

XVI

ECONOMIC LIFE AND COMMERCE

Introduction

The crusader conquest and the Latin establishments on the Mediterranean not only cut off the Moslem countries from their sea outlets to the West, but also interrupted the normal flow of commerce on the north-south land-route which linked Mesopotamia and Syria with the great urban centres along the Nile and its delta. Simultaneously, a new economic entity came into being in the crusader states which stretched along the coast of the eastern Mediterranean from Lesser Armenia to the gulf of 'Aqaba.

Despite the unrelenting hostility of their neighbours, the new Western colonies were not thrown back upon a primitive autarchy. Not only did the hostile frontiers remain partly open for commerce, but the coastal cities continued to fulfil their earlier function as maritime outlets for their Moslem hinterland. Moreover, a new network of commercial links with Europe intensified economic activity in the Holy Land to a degree unknown since Byzantine times. The link with the ports of southern Europe was followed by the opening of the Moslem hinterland to European penetration and inversely by a flow of Eastern wares to the European marts and fairs across the Alps. The Moslem, Syrian and Jewish middlemen of the early Middle Ages, squeezed out from international commerce by the Christian merchant, were pushed back to the Eastern centres of production. The flow of precious metal from the West to the East grew in volume as imports from the Orient reached an unprecedented volume at a time when European exports were just getting a foothold in the East.

Intensified commercial relations with the Byzantine and Moslem East in the twelfth and thirteenth centuries was not an exclusive function of the Crusades, but accompanied the general awakening of Europe: demographic growth, increasing riches, new social strata of consumers for its new city-centred products, as well as for Eastern imports. It is often argued that this evolution would have taken place even without the Crusades; that the internal development of Europe was an irresistible process which inevitably led to the establishment of commercial links across the Mediterranean. This may be so, yet even if the Crusades were only partially responsible for Europe's economic evolution, there can be little doubt about their role in initiating, enlarging and consolidating Europe's awareness of the East. This psychological element should not be overlooked when dealing with economic phenomena. The fact that the crusader states were lesser emporia than those of the Moslem and Byzantine Orient does not minimize their role in East-West commerce. Economic factors did indeed influence the realities of international commerce, but their inception and entry into the range of interest of the European nations owes much to the Crusades. Furthermore, such phenomena as the growth of European fleets, new types of vessels and improved navigation cannot be regarded independent of the Crusades. Many a vessel going to the East had no other cargoes but gold or silver ingots and fare-paying pilgrims, which balanced the profitability of the voyage. All this might have developed on its own but at an unknown date. It occurred in the twelfth century precisely because of the psychological and material impact of the Crusades.

The dominant feature of economic life in the kingdom was the special relation between economic function and social status. Some aspects almost appear as those of a caste system. Four basic strata of society roughly corresponded to the four great divisions of the economy, with no or very little functional or social mobility. Men were born into their class and occupation. Legislation prevented social mobility in some cases though more often tradition created almost unbridgeable obstacles, or political agreements created *de facto* monopolies. All in all, the frozen social structure turned economic functions into an inalienable attribute of social status.

The population of the kingdom as a whole can be envisaged as participating in a type of complementary economy. Each stratum of society fulfilled given economic tasks, which complemented each other and formed a harmonious, though not always a viable whole. That basic structure illuminates the privileged position of some strata in crusader society and the limitations imposed on others.

Agriculture largely remained the sphere of native Moslems and Christians. The vigorous agricultural activity of the crusaders in the twelfth century (negligible in the thirteenth) did not change the general pattern of the economy. Agriculture meant production by the natives, as much as living on its revenues characterized the privileged standing of the crusader nobility.

Moving from agriculture to great commerce and international exchange: shipping, import, export, transit and banking, we reach an entirely different social *milieu*. These were monopolized *de facto* by the merchants of Italy, but also Provençals and Catalans. The local Frankish population was not legally barred from these lucrative occupations. Yet the privileged position of the communes, with their customs exemptions or reductions made competition entirely futile. The privileged position of the communes was enhanced by the ready outlets for their goods in their mother cities. The latter even legislated to bar foreign participation in importing goods from the Levant.

Between the two poles of agriculture and commerce lay the often combined sphere of local crafts and trade, the meeting place of the native and the colonist. Moslem, Jew, oriental Christian and Frankish burgess vied with each other in the *souks* and stalls of the cities in the excellence of their production and salesmanship. Competition was not always on an equal basis, often enough it was regulated in favour of the Frankish burgess.

Above these three main divisions of the economy, agriculture, international commerce, crafts and local trade, towered the Frankish lay nobility and its ecclesiastical institutions, drawing most of their income from the produce of their estates, from city and market tolls and taxes on international commerce.

A   Agriculture

The Kingdom of Jerusalem was established in one of the most ancient habitations of mankind. The population had advanced from nomadism to settled tillage long before the Hebrew tribes entered Canaan in the second millennium before the Common Era. Conquerors and rulers came and went. New plants and techniques changed the pattern of agriculture, governments influenced the population distribution, tax systems or crops, but the quality of the soil, the sun and the rain were immutable. Following the ravages of the destruction of the Second Commonwealth (in the first century CE), another economic and demographic catastrophe was caused by the Arab conquest of the country from the Byzantines. Even a cursory comparison of a map of the Holy Land during the Talmudic, i.e. Byzantine, period (c. 330–638) with the later Arabic (638–1099) and crusader (1099–1291) periods proves a major change in the pattern of settlement and soil exploitation.[1] The most striking phenomenon is the utter desolation of the semi-arid areas in the southern part of the country. South of a line running approximately from Gaza in the west, through Hebron in the centre and to the northern tip of the Dead Sea in the east – the land became a desert. Once it was densely settled along military and commercial highways, villages existed near springs and wells, and human skill and industry compensated for nature's parsimony by building marvellous water-conserving installations which made life possible under these conditions. Now dunes covered the ancient settlements and sand filled the wells and irrigation channels, which the spade of the modern archaeologist uncovers to the amazement of the scholar and visitor.[2] Only today a new, enthusiastic population is once again reclaiming the desert and redeeming the wilderness.

---

[1] A series of historical maps of the Holy Land was published in *Atlas Israel*. See especially the maps of M. Avi-Yonah for the Byzantine period, U. Ben-Horin for the Arab and Mameluk periods and M. Benvenisti and J. Prawer for the crusader period. *Atlas Israeok* part IX, sheets X–XIII.

[2] Excellent examples of large and prosperous settlements in a desert zone are the newly excavated Nabatean cities of 'Abdath and Sbeita in the Negev.

The retreat of life to the north created a natural desert frontier in the south: a barrier with few water resources along the caravan routes and no settlements. The abandonment of the south, although the major change in the pattern of settlement between the Byzantine and crusader periods, was not the only one. The southern part of the country – ancient Philistia on the coast and Judea inland – was less densely settled than in the Byzantine period. Galilee and the coastal plains of the Sharon and Phoenicia remained well-settled, though they but faintly evoked the glory of ancient times. It seems that the interior of the country, the mountainous regions of northern Judea and Samaria and the eastern parts of Galilee were emptier than the coast, the narrow plain and the hilly country to the east. It is difficult to assign a precise date to this change, but this desolation seems to represent the accumulated results of Roman destruction and Arab conquest.

This general picture of the country is in some measure a reflection of the documents at our disposal. The Italian communes had no interest in agricultural estates beyond the radius of the cities in which they had their quarters. Church property on the other hand was more frequent around ecclesiastical centres, which coincided with the traditional holy places, like Jerusalem, Mount Tabor, and Bethlehem. Consequently, the pattern of agricultural settlements in the Holy Land under the crusaders is better known near the coastal towns and ecclesiastical centres. This may, as we have said, influence our picture, but the margin of error should not be exaggerated.

Calculations from surviving data have established the existence of some 1,200 villages in the Latin kingdom during the twelfth and thirteenth centuries. Through topographical studies, students of the period have succeeded in identifying some 900 place-names, proving that on the whole the picture of the occupied areas as reconstructed by modern scholarship is fairly accurate.[3] The

[3] The evaluation of 1,200 villages is that of Cl. Cahen (see general bibliography of this chapter). The identification of about 900 villages was done by M. Benvenisti and J. Prawer in the index to their map of *Palestine under the Crusaders*, part IX, sheet XII.

number of villages in the twelfth and thirteenth centuries significantly enough recalls the number of settlements captured and destroyed by Hadrian during the Bar-Kochba uprising at the beginning of the second century. According to Dio Cassius, the Romans destroyed 50 large settlements and 985 villages, a number closely approaching that of the crusader period.[4] This should not lead us to conclude that there was an agricultural renaissance of the country, neither does the possibility of identifying crusader placenames with modern ones indicate uninterrupted development of the country. As we shall point out below, crusader toponymy is a clear indictment of a ruined countryside.

Almost a thousand names dot the map of the Holy Land under the crusaders. At first sight they seem to be French. Some are, but the overwhelming majority are of Semitic origin: ancient Canaanite, Hebrew or Aramaic names. Some of the more recent ones, usually denoting a specific physical feature of the area, are of Arabic origin. All the names whatever their origin bore an Arabic form in spelling and pronunciation under the crusaders. Arabic toponymy was the dominant feature of Palestinian rural settlement, as the Arabic language was the one normally spoken at this time by all natives, Moslem, Christian, Jewish or Samaritan. The apparently French toponymy is the result of the crusader administration, which registered native names in written Latin. In the process a good number were metamorphosed beyond recognition and others acquired a French sound so as to be taken for genuine French names. When a beautiful fortress overlooking the Jordanian valley is called Belvoir, its marvellous setting merited this name. The same place is also called *Coquet* or *Coquetum*, but this is not a more daring French name for Belvoir; it is the deformed first part of its Arabic name 'Kaukab al-Hawa' ('The Star of the Winds') or the more ancient Hebrew or Aramaic 'Kokhava'. Alien nomenclature – in this case French and Latin – was imposed on the old Semitic toponymy of the country and disappeared with its ephemeral conquerors. This is a recurrent phenom-

---

[4] Dio Cassius, 69, 14, 1, who refers particularly to Judea.

enon in the long history of the Holy Land. In a few places only, and these are usually fortified sites or castles, do we find really French names. Their presence symbolizes crusader domination of the country as much as their absence in the countryside is proof of the fact that this was never really colonized.

As today, the Holy Land shared three major agricultural products with the whole Mediterranean world: wheat, olives and grapes. The biblical blessings of Canaan still applied under the Crusaders: 'a land of wheat and barley, and vines and fig trees and pomegranates, a land of oil, olive and honey' (Deut. 9, 8). To a northern traveller or pilgrim of the period more used to rye and black bread, wine, and dairy products, the wheaten loaves of the East, the fresh grapes, olives and olive oil of the Holy Land seemed undeniable proof of the biblical promise. In countless *Itineraria* was the Holy Land called the 'Land of Milk and Honey', marvellously preserved to console and edify. Only a very shrewd observer or very sober pilgrim would refrain from filling his account with biblical connotations. The author of one of the most detailed and best descriptions of the Holy Land, Burchard of Mount Zion (1280), introduces the chapter on the flora and fauna by saying:

> Now you must know, that, as a matter of fact, the whole of the Holy Land was, and is at this day, the best of all lands, albeit some who have not carefully regarded it say the contrary. It is very fertile in corn, which is tilled and grown with scarce any labour.[5]

Small wonder if as late as the eighteenth century scholars seriously debated the problem of a bunch of grapes so heavy that two people could hardly bear it on their shoulders . . . . Should we then censor the naive Russian abbot Daniel (1106–7) who wrote: 'By sowing one bushel (of wheat) ninety or a hundred are reaped. Does not God's blessing rest upon this hallowed land?'[6]

Most notable to a European newcomer was undoubtedly the white bread eaten in the Holy Land, whether baked as loaves by the European settlers or in the native oven (*furn*) as flat cakes, the *pitta*.

---

[5] Burchard of Mt Sion in *PPTS*, XII, 99.
[6] Abbot Daniel in *PPTS*, IV, 26.

This was bread baked of wheat, the chief cereal of the Near East. Although the best wheat is now grown in the heavier soils of the coast, the Valley of Jezreel and the Jordan depression, the crusader corn belt was elsewhere.

The great granaries of the crusader kingdom and of Moslem Damascus were the lands east of the Jordan and north-east of Lake Tiberias; in the north, al-Sawad ('black land'), called by the crusaders *Terre de Sueth* just across the lake; in ancient Gaulan and more to the east in Hauran. These were also the classical pasture-lands of the country. The great production centres of this area were around Nawa to the east and near the strategically important and fertile valleys of Banyas in the west, extending into the western valleys of Galilee around Tibnin (Toron).

The western part of the country also had extensive corn fields. The best corn was grown in the historical Shefela, the hilly lowland between the coastal plain and the central ranges of Judea, Samaria and Galilee. The southern part of this belt was praised for its excellent wheat. The wheat area began at the western entrance to the Valley of Jezreel, at the height of Caesarea on the coast and continued southward to Ramleh on the crossroad to Jerusalem, and even more to the south through 'Akir to Beit-Jibrin. Caesarea, Ramleh, and 'Akir were famous for their white bread. In the coastal plain proper, wheat was grown around Ascalon and more to the south around Gaza up to the sands of Darum (Deir al-Balah). From this southern area corn was exported to Jerusalem before the arrival of the crusaders, but after their victory the whole area was devastated.[7] Beit-Jibrin and Tel al-Safi (Blanchegarde) were only settled around 1140 and fifteen years later Ascalon became Christian. Crusader chronicles remark on the extraordinary fertility of the Ascalon plain, which had not been tilled in some fifty years of warfare and now brought rich harvests to the new settlers.[8] Though wheat was the common and favourite cereal, some areas grew the less-demanding barley. Particularly around Hebron, from where the barley belt extended to the outlying villages of

---

[7] See Le Strange, *op. cit.*, under the names of these localities.
[8] William of Tyre, XVIII, 1.

Curmul and Samo'a on the edge of the great southern desert and to the north towards Bethlehem.[9]

From Bethlehem to Jerusalem and Ramallah the Judean mountains became settled under the crusaders. Despite the lack of springs and irrigation, crops were so rich that the aforementioned Russian pilgrim Daniel waxed ecstatic over God's blessing. In the middle of the twelfth century we hear that land was extremely difficult or very expensive to buy in this area.[10] This was undoubtedly the outcome of crusader colonization. From Bethlehem northward to el–Bira (Mahomeria) and Ramallah – on the main road to Samaria – the royal domain, the military orders, churches and monasteries all vied for land, though their main interest was not in corn, but vineyards.

The many villagers in the Judean mountains tilled the narrow valleys and mountain plateaux. Agriculture was never easy in this area, where ancient terraces on the slopes attested to the human effort required. An Arab geographer, Yakut, at the beginning of the thirteenth century, even remarks that because of the mountainous configuration of the area, beasts cannot be used for ploughing and the peasants break up the soil with hoes.[11]

Besides wheat and barley, which are the basic cereals, we also find millet (*dura*), oats, and spelt grown for human and animal consumption. An interesting crusader document from the middle of the thirteenth century mentions '*mais*' among the cereals grown in Galilee, which seems to be maize or Indian corn.[12] If our translation is correct, this is additional proof for the Asiatic (and not American) origin of corn.

An important addition to the cereals was leguminous plants and vegetables. Beans are mentioned among the former, important to humans and as fodder not to mention their value as a nitrate-producing and soil-enriching vegetation. Beans even gave their

[9] Nasir-I-Khusrau, *PPTS*, IV, 57; Theodoricus, *PPTS*, V, 53.

[10] Delaville le Roulx, I, 309.

[11] Noted by Arab geographers around Jerusalem.

[12] See details in the study of J. Prawer in the general bibliography of the chapter.

name to al-Fula in the Valley of Jezreel, or '*Castrum Fabae*'. In addition we hear of peas, lentils and chick-peas.[13]

Cucumbers and red and yellow melons (water and sugar melons) are also mentioned. We do not know if the famous Palestinian onions from Ascalon (shallots) were still cultivated, but onions, garlic and mustard were probably found on crusader tables. Other plants used as condiments were grown without being specially cultivated. Among those specifically mentioned are fennel, sage and rue – also used for medicinal purposes – and probably the cultivated mallow. Rue was the speciality of a Judean village, Kiriat al-'Anab, a few miles from Jerusalem.[14]

Since antiquity the great pride of the country has been its trees and fruits, the olive being the most important among them. The olive was ubiquitous and could be found anywhere in the mountains, plains and valleys, but its main area seems to have been in the southern part of the country. In Samaria, an early twelfth-century Christian pilgrim found olive trees planted in forest-like groves and the olives in the same area were praised a hundred years earlier by a Moslem geographer. The mountains of Judea, as far south as Hebron, boasted luscious olive trees. Before the Crusades their oil was even exported to neighbouring countries.[15] The vicinities of Hebron, Jerusalem and Nablus were great centres of olive cultivation. Strangely enough, olive trees are seldom mentioned in Galilee. This might be an accident, or could reflect mediaeval reality. On the other hand, all coastal cities, from Ascalon in the south, through Jaffa, Arsuf, Caesarea and Acre up to Tyre were surrounded by olive groves. The detailed descriptions of crusader sieges never fail to mention the olive groves and luscious orchards around the city concerned. In the vicinity of Tyre olive groves were exploited on a commercial basis.[16] As olive oil was pressed in every village, the *massara* or olive presses are to be found wherever a village existed in the Middle Ages, although many of these presses – worked by man or beast – probably reach deep into antiquity.

[13] See below n. 39.
[14] Nasir-I-Khusrau in *PPTS*, IV, 22.
[15] Le Strange, *op. cit.*, 309 ff.
[16] Tafel-Thomas, I, 383.

Another source of vegetable oil was the sesame plant sown in summer, balancing the crops and assisting in their rotation. Sesame furnishes an aromatic oil greatly appreciated in the Near East.

The outstanding fruit grown was naturally the grape, in the form of table grapes and for wine-making. For the Russian abbot Daniel grapes were: 'The best of all the fruits of the earth . . . comparable to the fruit of heaven'. [17] It seems logical to suppose that vineyards and wine-making were one of the few, if not the only, agricultural activities which felt the impact of the crusader conquest. Moslem law prohibited the consumption of alcohol and limited the cultivators to the growing of table grapes, although wine was produced under Moslem rule by the Christian communities. The demand for wine by the crusader landlords and city dwellers created a flourishing market and boosted viticulture. Vineyards surrounded almost all cities on the coast, but in the hilly and mountainous country inland, they were found in profusion. Vineyards were planted to the north of Sidon on the coast, in Galilee around Tiberias and Nazareth, but even more along the road from Samaria to Jerusalem, around Nablus, Ramallah, Jerusalem, Bethlehem, as far as Hebron in the south. At the end of the tenth century two kinds of grapes grew around Jerusalem: *duri* and *'ainuni*, which were famous enough to be exported to neighbouring countries. [18] As could be expected, crusader ecclesiastical establishments which acquired landed property took great care of vineyards. In the villages settled by the monks of the Holy Sepulchre on the road from Jerusalem to Ramallah, vineyards are prominent. [19] In other areas we hear that the administration of the military orders transformed cornfields to vineyards. This might have been done for the needs of the order, but there is no doubt that vineyards were far more profitable than cornfields.

Besides the three basic and characteristic products: wheat, olives and grapes, the Holy Land was also famous for its excellent fruit. While the northerner missed his homely apples, pears, nuts,

[17] Daniel in *PPTS*, IV.
[18] Mukaddasi in *PPTS*, III, 69.
[19] See details in J. Prawer, 'Colonisation activities' (below n. 48), 1098ff.

and cherries, he found a profusion of new, exotic and strange-tasting fruits. Apples could be found around Jerusalem, at Zo'ar to the south of the Dead Sea and in Beisan, and small quantities of nuts in Samaria. The Northerner marvelled at the juicy and sweetish fruit of the date palms. These grew in the semitropical areas around Beisan, along the Jordan valley and as far north as the swamps of the Huleh, in the famous oases of Jericho and at the southern tip of the Dead Sea in Zo'ar – called by the crusaders, as by the ancients, 'City of the Palms' (*Palmarea*). The saffron-coloured dates of this region called '*inkila*' were exported in the Arab period.[20] Date palms were also found around the coastal cities, adding colour and majesty to the surroundings. A famous palm grove between Haifa and Acre gave its name to a newly founded crusader village 'Palmarea'.[21] The dates were eaten fresh or dried and pressed into cakes. In addition they yielded a sweetish juice, the 'honey' of biblical fame ('milk and honey' – the second noun refers in all probability to 'honey' from dates).

Beisan lies where the Valley of Jezreel passes into the Jordan depression. With its heavy tropical heat, extreme humidity and semi-marshy conditions the area has water in quantities unknown in other parts of the country and was a natural hothouse for tropical fruits and plants, equalled only by Jericho. Some of these fruits could also be found in the Jordan valley near Lake Tiberias and in the marshy lands around the Huleh. Around Huleh, and even more Beisan, rice was grown before the crusader conquest. Crusader documents mention it rarely[22] and its production may have declined, since the Frankish population apparently did not take to it. Under the Mameluks rice is again mentioned near Banyas.

Besides the date palm, another exotic plant aroused extra-ordinary interest, and the rapturous descriptions make it seem of almost heavenly origin. This was the sugar-cane. The tall, sweetish and juicy canes were sucked and munched as delicacies by children and grown-ups alike.[23] Centres of sugar-cane growing existed be-

[20] Ibn Haukal in Le Strange, 289.
[21] Rozière, *Cartulaire du Saint Sépulcre*, no. 127.
[22] Mukaddasi in *PPTS*, III, 29 and *Regesta*, no. 1085.
[23] Heyd, *Histoire du commerce du Levant*, II, 680ff.

fore the Crusades around Sidon, in the Galilean village of Kabul, in the Jordan valley at Karawa, but mainly around Tyre. The crusaders seized on the importance of this plant for Europe, which used honey and fruit juices as its main sweeteners. They consequently preserved the older centres of production and expanded the industry elsewhere. The main centre remained in the vicinity of Tyre, where the copious waters of Ras el-'Ain irrigated mile-long sugar plantations.[24] On the coast more to the north, sugar-cane was grown in Sidon and Acre, where a great sugar refinery was erected.[25] As abundant water was one of the main factors in sugar-cane cultivation, we find this plant in water-rich areas, e.g. near Tiberias from where the Hospitallers drew their sugar supplies,[26] in the valley of Jericho with its many springs, near Nablus and near the seigniorial seat of Manueth in Galilee, where an elaborate system of water conservation and irrigation facilitated the growth of this luxurious plant.

No less marvellous to the European newcomer was the citrus fruit of the country. The lemon and the orange (called by its Arabic name *narange*) with its acidulous sweetness and strong fragrance captivated the Europeans. Sweet and bitter lemons were used directly, but they were most important as a novel condiment. The delicacies composed of citrus fruits, condiments and spicy sauces added to poultry and fish – especially remarked in a Frankish source – were all a part of the New World's marvels. Citrus fruit was found on the coast near Caesarea, inland around the castle of Monfort and in the north near Banyas. No less exotic was the banana, accurately described by crusader pilgrims and known to them as the 'apple of Paradise', in Arabic and Hebrew *moz*. They were grown all along the Jordan in the flat and humid valleys of its left bank. Another type of fruit very much appreciated was the several species of figs, rivalling those of Damascus in quality, and eaten fresh or dried and pressed into cakes. The fig tree seems to have been more common in the inland mountains. From Hebron

---

[24] See details J. Prawer, in *Byzantion*, 22 (1952), 30ff.
[25] Abu Shama in *RHC, Hist. Orientaux*, IV, 294ff.
[26] Rules of the Hospitallers of 1182. Delaville le Roulx, *Cartulaire*, I, 427.

to Samaria figs are mentioned by crusader pilgrims, and also at Ramleh, Yabneh and Caesarea, but for some reason there is no mention of them in Galilee.

Pomegranates, the former pride of the country and ornament of ancient monuments, seals and coins are seldom mentioned. We do hear of pomegranates in Jericho, near Nablus and in Transjordan, but on the whole they seem to have been neglected.

Less frequent and less tasty than the figs were the fig-like fruits of the sycamore tree. Sycamore wood was once used for building purposes and the small fruit which curiously sprout from the tree trunk are mentioned around Ascalon and Hebron. This tree, once important in the economy of the country, did not play a similar role under the crusaders.

In times of dire need the carob-tree came into its own. Mentioned as present in the mountainous country of Judea and Samaria, it also served as a staple food for the armies of the Third Crusade besieging Acre. The complete list of fruit trees and plants which grew in the Holy Land is long. A native geographer and great local patriot, the Jerusalem-born Moslem Mukaddasi (tenth century) recorded some four dozen species. These include quinces, pine-kernels, black currants, and certain kinds of nuts, almonds, asparagus, artichokes and lettuce. [27]

The variety of crops grown in such a relatively small area, along the narrow strip of land between the Mediterranean and the desert is remarkable. Agriculture seemed to be flourishing and this struck the mediaeval pilgrim, as it does the modern reader. The glowing contemporary descriptions, even if in some measure exaggerated, cannot be entirely untrue. But the variety of agricultural products is in itself a very fragile index of the rural economy. Fertile oases are no proof of the productivity of the desert. Crusader agriculture can only be seen in the right perspective against the agricultural background of the country as a whole.

---

[27] Mukaddasi in *PPTS*, III, 69ff. From among the Western descriptions of the flora of the Holy Land, the most detailed and reliable is that of Burchard of Mt Sion (1280). *Buchardi de Monte Sion Descriptio Terrae Sanctae* in J.C.M. Laurent, *Peregrinatores Medii Aevi Quatour*, Leipzig, 1864, 19 ff.

What did agricultural Palestine look like seven hundred years ago? What was the pattern of the agricultural settlement? The reconstruction comes to us through European eyes, via Latin and French terms, and is very seldom supplemented by data in the local (mainly Arabic) sources. This vocabulary was created under different skies and was now applied, not always happily, to Palestinian realities.

The basic living unit was the Palestinian village of origins immemorial. Palestinian French usage of the twelfth century termed it *ville*, as the 'villa' of Roman antiquity had not yet come to denote a city. But as a rule, a village was called, in Latinized French, *casale* (L. pl. *casalia;* Fr. pl. *casiaux*). This name came into being in Europe in the early Middle Ages and originally meant a rural estate, stressing the element of *casa*, an inhabited house or farm. The *casale* is thus an agglomeration of houses characteristic of the countryside.

Village houses were often of stone, more easily available and cheaper in the Holy Land than timber. Many houses were however built even more cheaply of a mixture of dry mud and straw. The buildings were one-storey with flat open roofs, often used for agricultural work or storage, and as sleeping quarters during the hot summer. The small windows assured a degree of coolness and protection against the fiery sun, and age-long experience had taught builders the art of capturing the cool breezes of evening. The floors of the houses were seldom paved and usually consisted of beaten earth, which conserved coolness and humidity in the summer but made the house rather chilly in the rainy season.

The village was usually a compact agglomeration, and isolated farms or homesteads were almost unknown. The only exception was temporarily occupied land outside the normal boundaries of the villages. The houses with their small windows faced the courtyard; the blank facades, broken by a single door, looked out on to the dirt paths winding between the houses. Some houses had underground cellars for grain storage. An oven was usually attached to the house, heated by dried dung, branches or thistles, gathered by the women. The village well – often some distance from the actual village – remained, as it has since biblical times, the centre of village evening gossip. Water from the well filled tall, porous jars, which assured a cool drink to the peasant family.

Stone building were certainly the rule. Quarries were found in many areas of the country, but building material was easily available from the numerous ruins of earlier cities and villages which dotted the countryside. Marble columns, capitals, window-embrasures, sad remnants of past glories were transported to the villages and re-used in the simpler homes of the fellahin. Some of the ancient urban centres became the ready-made quarries of the period. Herodian Ascalon and Caesarea were thus exploited almost up to our own times. Their beautiful monuments were used to build little crusader Caesarea, or the new city of Acre, as late as the end of the eighteenth and the beginning of the nineteenth century.

One or two among the village houses would be larger and more commodious, belonging to the local *rais* or headman. More often than not he would be the head of the largest clan in the village, a *hamula*, which might even be the only one, though sometimes two or more families lived in one village. The status of the *rais* was sanctioned by the crusader overlord, and his house would also furnish accommodation where a traveller or stranger would be welcome. Sometimes a special large room (the *madfaa*) served the same purpose.

The *rais* or *raicius*, as he is called in crusader documents, was not only the traditional leader of the village, but also its official representative and responsible to the authorities for local security and, primarily, tax collection. This was gathered in kind and transported to the administrative centre of the seigniory. In most cases these were in the cities on the coast, or in a castle or fortified tower inland. Normally, a village had one *rais*, but in some places we have two or even three headmen,[28] all duly confirmed by the Frankish overlord. This probably depended on the number of its important families.

Supported by tradition and by the sanction of his overlord, the *rais* would participate in certain official acts, such as the conveyance of his native village.[29] For reasons of convenience or due to feudal

---

[28] *Regesta*, no. 1237.
[29] *Regesta*, no. 1220.

ways of thinking, the *rais* was often regarded as a kind of inferior vassal,[30] or representative of a collective vassal, i.e. the peasants of his village. On one occasion we hear that the Hospitallers 'conceded to the *raicius* Abet a number of villages to hold, till and guard as long as it will please the master and brothers of the order'.[31] This case was not exceptional.

The *rais* and the village elders were obliged to affirm their dependence on the Frankish lord whenever he visited by supplying him with food. Symbolically, in a procedure so dear to the hearts of mediaeval men, they would welcome him on his visit with a few silver coins, some grains of wheat, and olives. When a village changed hands the former lord would order the *rais* and the elders to swear adherence to the new owner. This oath was, curiously enough, couched in feudal terms used between lord and vassal:

> Over a naked sword, they swore according to their custom an oath prescribed to them by the interpreter and they made fealty and homage to the master, who received it for himself and the brothers of the house (order).[32]

Whereas the *rais* appears constantly in crusader deeds and in treatises of jurisprudence, in some cases we find other officials fulfilling the same or similar tasks. The Teutonic Knights appointed a *baiulus* or bailiff to safeguard their rights in the Galilean village of 'Araba. An official bearing the same title is to be found in the administration of the archbishop of Nazareth (although in this case '*nostre bais de Saphorie*' might be a misreading for '*nostre rais de Saphorie*'). Some of these officials bear oriental names like Johan Semes (i.e. Shams) and his son Botros (Peter) who also entered the archbishop's administration.[33] These men were probably natives of the place, but it is not impossible, that like the Venetian *gastaldio* near Tyre, they were a kind of village supervisor while also acting as *rais*.

---

[30] *Regesta*, no. 1239, and below n. 32.
[31] *Regesta*, no. 1237.
[32] Delaville le Roulx II, 764–6, 786–7.
[33] Delaville le Roulx, II, 784–5.

Two other officials were connected with the supervision of rural estates, the *drugoman* and the possessor of a *scribanagium*. The expressions in themselves mean simply 'the interpreter' and 'the scribe', but it is clear that their later functions had very little in common with their original titles. The *drugoman* probably began his career as an interpreter between the Arabic-speaking natives and the Frankish overlord, and became an important official with a high income. We learn that in Galilee the rights of *drugomanagia* for three large Hospitaller villages were as follows:

> Every villein of these villages will pay to you [to the *drugoman*] from each *carruca* [a unit of holding] one *modius* [*c.* 190 litres] of wheat and one of barley; in addition you will have from the common crop of lord and villeins from each *carruca* two *manipuli* of wheat and two of barley. Besides, should you be in one of those villages, the villeins will provide you and your mount with food . . . In addition, when the lord and the villeins will have in common 100 *modii* of crops, then you will receive from them in common 6 *modii* and from less in proportion thereof.

The office even became hereditary and was sold like a fief in the royal court for the sizeable sum of 250 besants.[34] We are in no position to estimate the difference between the *scribanagium* and the *drugemanagium*.[35] Both must have developed from the practical needs of administration and by a process inherent in the feudal system slowly reached the status of prebends or fiefs, and their holders that of vassals, if not always noble. It seems doubtful if at this point a *drugoman* of Frankish origin who became the hereditary possessor of the office still functioned as an 'interpreter'. A Syrian Christian who acquired French in one of the cities was more suited to the technical task, leaving to the *drugoman* the administration of the village.

During harvest time, the village's threshing floor was not only a centre of busy activity, but also of assiduous haggling over taxes. His lordship, or the steward, would supervise the threshing to make certain of the lord's share, and usually of his own. The assessment

---

[34] Delaville le Roulx, I, 330–1.
[35] In one document at least they are juxtaposed. Strehlke, *op. cit.*, no. 16.

of a tax-in-kind was very often complicated by the fact that the villages did not always belong in their entirety to one seigniory, but were often split between two or more fiefs. We should not imagine any kind of boundary between fiefs. It seems there were two procedures in cases of divided property. One was derived from the peasant's villein status. The peasant and his family were assigned to a given lordship and this meant that their services and payments due would be collected by their Frankish overlord. In other cases no such assignment existed. If a village belonged to three different fiefs, each claiming a part, the crop was assessed on the threshing floor and divided between the respective Frankish over-lords. It is tempting to suppose that assessment of the entire crop is proof for the non-existence of private holdings, certifying the existence of common property – such as we find later in Palestine in the so-called *mush'a* land and in similar forms found elsewhere (as with the *zadruga* of Slavonic origin). These data should not be thus misconstrued. There was common village property (see below) but the cultivated area belonged to individual peasant families. Collective taxation was a matter of convenience and was followed by a proportionate allocation of payments among the village families. This was supervised by the *rais*, who fixed the quotas according to the land and crops of each peasant. The representatives of the different lords would then work out between them the quotas due to their masters.

The arable area of a village was measured in units called *carrucae* in Latin and *charrués* in French. The European unit in its native land denoted the amount of area which could be worked by a wheeled plough in one season. On Palestinian soil this was certainly a misnomer, exemplifying the indiscriminate transfer of European terms to entirely different conditions. The Palestinian plough of the Middle Ages, like the Arab plough of today, was never wheeled. It consisted of a wooden frame, handle and iron knife, which hardly turns the earth. The main purpose is to cut the upper crust and prepare the soil for sowing. This plough is admirably suited to light soils and to the conservation of their scarce humidity. This simple type, drawn by an ox, appears in the middle of the thirteenth century on a vignette of Matthew Paris's map of Acre.[36] Nevertheless *carruca* was retained by the conservative 'colonial spirit', which imposed its notions on entirely different realities.

Besides the *carruca*, we find other units of cultivated land. Often we hear of an *aratrum*, a plough, used as a measure, as in the expressions 'land of one plough' or 'land sufficient for two ploughs'. This notion does not basically differ from the *carruca*, for the Near-Eastern plough could be more properly described as an *aratrum*, the type of plough used in classical antiquity. Another system measured land in relation to beasts needed for cultivation, like 'land worked in one day by a pair of oxen'. In the county of Tripoli we again find European land units, like the *parilliata* of Provençal or Catalan origin. In Tripoli we also find a unit called *caballaria*, another misnomer (if it does not denote a type of Sicilian-Norman fief) coming from southern Europe. As might be expected, the principality of Antioch also used a measure called 'the Greek *carruca*'. Finally, land was also measured by the amount of grain needed for sowing, a very practical procedure which took into consideration the local soil and its fertility.

The normal meaning of *charrué*, a unit of ploughed land, might be described as that of a family holding. This means an area of private land and a corresponding amount of common land or rights in common land sufficient to sustain a family and to be cultivated by one. Thus the notion of a *carruca* is equivalent to that of a European *mansus* and, indeed, a crusader document explicitly states: 'a *carruca* which we call *massus*'.[37]

The *charrué* was a unit corresponding to the real needs of peasant life. Its size would differ from place to place according to the fertility of soil and its produce. Thus the Arab *faddan* of the plain is twice as large as that in mountainous Jerusalem. But for administrative reasons a common unit had to be invented. This was the kingdom's official *carruca*, kept in the *Secrète* or treasury and fixed

---

[36] An excellent reproduction of the map from a ms of Matthew Paris is printed in *Atlas Israel*, part I, sheet 4. See also R. Vaugham, *Matthew Paris*, Cambridge 1958, pl. XVI.

[37] Tafel-Thomas, II, 368.

by a special legislative act, an *Assise*. It was described as being: '24 cords long and 16 wide; and a cord has to have 17 *toises* of an average man.'[38] Thus counting 6 Roman feet to the *toise* we can calculate the *carruca* at some 35 hectares. As this was an administrative unit, each village was assessed at a given number of these official *carrucae* and paid taxes accordingly.

The agricultural year began just before the rainy season, so often disappointing in the Holy Land, around mid-November. The basic cultures were the winter crops. Usually the whole arable area was ploughed, partly to prepare it for winter sowing and partly for summer sowing. The land prepared for winter crops was then sown with wheat and following that with barley. Another part was reserved for leguminous plants: peas, lentils, '*ers*', gesces, vetches. A third part, called in crusader sources *garet*, remained fallow until next year's spring sowing. The land sown with winter crops bore no additional cultures during the current agricultural year, as its harvest came later than the spring-sowing of the summer crops.[39]

Land ploughed and left fallow in the autumn was ploughed again in the spring and then sown with summer crops. These spring activities are described in crusader sources of Italian origin as *maggiatica*, i.e. worked in May, although actually performed in March and the misnomer comes from the Italian agricultural calendar. The summer crops were economically not very important, but were badly needed for the conservation of the soil, accumulation of humidity and uprooting of wild grasses. The main crop was sesame seed, but probably also chick-peas and two kinds of millet (*beda* and *safra*), i.e. sorghum. The abundance of land made it possible to farm in a more extensive way by leaving large tracts entirely fallow and thus assuring higher productivity. As a matter of fact, crusader deeds sometimes describe the measure of land as 'a *charrué* of 4 *gareles* (= 12 *modii*) of sown grain and 4 for

[38] Strehlke, *Tabulae Ordinis Theutonici*, no. 31.

[39] The agricultural calendar is explained in detail in J. Prawer, *op. cit.*, 43ff (gen. bibl. of this chapter).

garet' or 'four *carrucae* of land for sowing and for *garet*'. Unfortunately it is difficult to establish the regular proportion of actual cultivated land to fallow land.

ROTATION OF CROPS

Year	Season	Field 1	Field 2
1st	Winter	Winter crops	Leguminous plants
	Spring-Summer	Fallow	Fallow. Summer crops
2nd	Winter	Leguminous plants	Winter crops
	Spring-Summer	Fallow. Summer crops	Fallow

The harvest was not bountiful. For some 33 kg of wheat or 26 kg of barley sown to the hectare the peasant harvested at a ratio of 1 : 5 or 1 : 7 for wheat and 1 : 10 or 1 : 13 for barley. The total harvest per hectare would thus be around 200 kg or 150 kg of wheat or barley respectively.

The large size of the 'official' *carruca* and the fact that families possessed more than one such unit (usually one and a half or even two), indicates one basic problem of the country's economy: there was no lack of land but there was a shortage of labour. The low population density also explains another feature of rural settlement under the crusaders: the great number of localities connected with agriculture described in our sources not as *casalia* but as *gastinae*. The hundreds of documents at our disposal communicate a definite pattern. Almost every *casale* is surrounded by a number of *gastinae*, around the central *casale*. The *gastinae*, which bear proper names, very often indicating a given type of culture or crop, are almost always mentioned among the appurtenances of the *casale*, such as pasture lands, wells or groves. The *gastina* of crusader vocabulary, or *wastina* more common in Europe, basically denotes a 'waste', a non-inhabited area. It corresponds in Arabic toponymy to *khirbet* (ruin), an area formerly inhabited but now abandoned. The extraordinarily large number of these *gastinae* is an outward sign of the desolate countryside, in comparison with its more prosperous periods. The *gastinae* were normally used for pasture but quite often also for temporary cultivation and then left fallow. Their legal standing corresponded to the European notion of *Almende* or 'commons' of undivided property in use by the whole village community.

The economic situation of the Palestinian peasantry was in all probability far better than that of their European contemporaries and their counterparts in the Moslem countries of the Near East. As to the latter, we have the unbiased testimony of Ibn Jubair, a Moslem traveller from Spain in the second half of the twelfth century, who points out that taxes paid to the crusaders by the local population are far lower than those paid by the fellahin in Moslem Syria. Once the taxes were paid, there was no Frankish inter-ference in the life of the village. [40]

The conspicuous absence of the *corvée* made the lot of the local peasant better than that of his counterpart in Western Christendom. Lacking the will or ability to do more than rule and live off the fat of the land, the crusaders did not establish a system of manorial economy. The familiar division of land between the sei-gniorial domain and the peasants' tenures, the first directly exploited by the lord of the manor and worked by manpower obligatorily furnished by the serfs of the estate, was unknown in the kingdom. The crusader feudal lord did not keep any land for his direct exploitation and all the village land was tilled by the peasants. Consequently, there was no need for forced labour to cultivate the demesne, and thus the most odious aspect of a manorial economy, the *corvée*, was hardly ever exacted. The peasant was not forced to give three days in the week, or 'boon-work' during the peak seasons (sowing, tilling and harvesting).

Here and there *corvées* are mentioned, but their use is very rarely concerned with actual labour in the fields. If exacted by a Frankish overlord the *corvée* was used in the most profitable way possible, i.e. in cultivating sugar-cane, olive groves or vineyards. In some cases we hear of the commutation of services for money and the amount is so small that the *corvées* must have been negligible.

[40] Ibn Djobeir in *RHC, Historiens Orientaux*, III, 448.

The basic payment due from the holding was a tax called *terraticum*, originally exacted in kind from land newly brought under tillage. In crusader sources the *terraticum* or *terrage* denotes the normal tribute exacted from land. Under cover of the Latin name, we suspect an earlier Moslem tax, the *kharaj*, once exacted from non-believers but later from lands which had once belonged to them, although in the meantime their holders were Moslems. At least in one crusader document we read that the tithe should be paid 'from the *kharaj* of the villeins'.

The *terrage* generally exacted from the peasants was one-third of the crops. This was not too heavy a burden compared with contemporary European payments or even with modern taxation. However, the *terrage* was often augmented by additional payments. By certain grants, for example, from King Amalric, the Teutonic Knights annually received from every *carruca* in the royal domain of Judea and Samaria 'one *robba* of wheat and one of barley from the share of the villeins'.[41] In addition, payments were collected under the general name of *xenia* or *exenia*, an unhappy Greek term, meaning originally presents or gifts, but in reality including payments connected with religious feasts or with the agricultural calendar. Despite their occasional incidence they represented a steady income and as such the clergy claimed and received them. King Baldwin IV confirmed to William, archbishop of Tyre: 'the tithe of *exenia*, i.e. from all gifts, which we shall have from the seigniory of Toron (Tibnin) on Christmas, Shrovetide (before Lent) and Easter, namely in fowl, eggs, cheese and wood'.[42] Or again we find an enumeration of 'gifts' connected with the Teutonic Knights: 'fowl, eggs, cheese'. In another document of Venetian origin the 'gifts' are marked as 'personal payments' but are paid: 'from each *carruca* a fowl, ten eggs, half a rotl of cheese and twelve besants for a load of wood'.[43]

In addition to taxes on arable land there were special taxes on fruit trees, the most important being on the olive. The tax was

[41] Strehlke, no. 6.
[42] Strehlke, no. 15.
[43] Tafel-Thomas, II, 383.

normally one third of the oil extracted. However, in olive groves, like one near Tyre, which had over two thousand trees, in vineyards and in sugar-cane plantations the Frankish lords did use the *corvée* due from the peasants. As there was no manorial domain, compulsory labour could have been directed and concentrated on these plantations. [44]

Among other charges on villeins we should mention the '*portagium*', the obligation to transport grain to granaries or threshing floors, a tax on bees and honey and taxes on livestock (sheep, oxen and buffaloes). In places where the Frankish lord possessed forests or scrub land there were also payments for pasture rights, for collecting wood used in heating and building, and branches used as poles (*paxilla*) in vineyards.

A remarkable feature of arable land was areas described as 'free *carruca*' (*carruca libera* or *carruca francesia*). So far there is no satisfactory explanation for the 'free *carruca*'. [45] It is obviously an area not paying taxes, in all probability free from the *terrage*. But we cannot say whether the franchise was traditional and connected with the earlier history of the land, or created by an enactment of the conquerors.

Though disposing of rather large tracts of land the actual villages of the crusader period seem to have been very small indeed. In the vicinity of Tyre, where documentation is rich, the average village numbered some 20 families. To judge by the amount of land found in other villages the situation was not much different elsewhere. On the basis of hearsay, a Venetian official in Tyre wrote to the metropolis: 'It is said that in the district of Ascalon there are 72 *casalia*, and even in the smallest you will find 200 families, beside smaller *casalia* which have more or less 20 families.' [46] The second figure seems to represent the average number of families in a village. Moreover, as far as can be ascertained the native family was not very large. There were three or four per family, including children living with their parents. The available demographic data confirm

[44] Tafel-Thomas, II, 375.
[45] On the different types of *carruca* see *Byzantion*, 22 (1952), 27 and 23 (1954), 157.
[46] Tafel-Thomas, II, 398.

our views on the pattern of rural settlement given earlier. The land as a whole was underpopulated.

This explains another interesting feature of crusader agriculture. Besides several attempts to colonize the countryside by settling Frankish peasants, the Frankish lords, lay and ecclesiastical, tried to develop their own landed property by using Frankish or native labour. This usually comes to light in connection with the payment or rather non-payment of tithes. As a rule, the tithe was paid by the whole Frankish population, but not by native non-Christians. The lord paid it from his income and, as early as 1120, a church council held in Nablus in the presence of King Baldwin II made it obligatory for the whole kingdom. [47] Exemptions existed, especially for the military orders concerning the *novales*, newly reclaimed land and land directly exploited by church establishments. In this connection quarrels arose between the regular clergy and the exempted institutions. It was bad enough if an estate in Frankish possession which paid the tithe was acquired by a military order, but it was even worse when a military order put it to the plough for its own profit. As long as the order received part of the crop from its villeins, income was taxable and the order could have been compelled to pay tithes, but in the case of direct exploitation matters were different and the order refused to pay the tithe. How did the order and other church establishments manage to acquire a labour-force to work such land? One possibility was to use the non-military and non-clerical members. In some orders, lay-brothers could have been employed in reclaiming land, but the usual procedure was to use the European system of *champart* or *complant*. This meant that the colonizing agent would put up the capital (land, seed corn, plants, equipment) and the peasants provided the labour. The crops would be divided in a given proportion (usually one-third to two-thirds) between the two. [48] The church felt that it was short-changed on such deals and claimed its tithes whereas the colonizers felt that this infringed on their exemptions. To give an

---

[47] Mansi, *Concilia*, XXI, 261–6.
[48] J. Prawer, 'Colonisation activities in the Latin Kingdom of Jerusalem', *Revue belge de philologie et d'histoire*, 29 (1951), 1063ff.

illustration we follow a quarrel between the bishop of Acre and the Teutonic Knights. The bishop claimed:

> that the master and the brothers (of the order) should compel their villeins and peasants, to whom they committed the cultivation of their possessions and lands located in the Diocese of Acre, to pay the tithe integrally . . . from that part of the fruits which the peasants and villeins have and retain for their work (*pro agricultura*) or for any other reason.

The order, on the other hand, not only refused but claimed an enormous refund of 24,000 besants:

> for tithes, which – they said – they paid unduly to the church of Acre through ignorance for lands and possessions, exploited by their own labour and at their own expense, and for *novales* (newly reclaimed land) and fodder for beasts and for orchards in money and in other things.

After long bickering it was agreed that the order would pay 'a fifteenth of the tithe on all their cultures, whether they work them themselves or made it to be worked by others'.[49]

The case itself (and there are many of this type) proves that paid workers, or share-croppers from among the villeins, were used to reclaim land and especially in planting the lucrative vineyards.

The data at our disposal do not enable us to evaluate the income of a peasant family. But we can get some idea as to incomes derived from agriculture. From a large number of cases it seems that an average village was worth between 3,000 and 5,000 besants. Naturally some villages were valued far higher either because of their size and specialized products or because of their proximity to urban centres. A village boasting the romantic name of 'Casal Damor', in reality Damur, was sold for 12,000 besants and the famous Kafr Kana (Cana of Galilee) for 24,000 besants.[50] The average annual income from a village was estimated at 500 besants. Significantly enough, the latter sum roughly corresponds to the income of a knightly fief, assuring the military service of one knight. On the other hand,

49 Strehlke, *op. cit*, no. 112.
50 *Regesta*, nos 1210 and 1217.

it shows the relative value of investment in agriculture. It should be calculated as assuring a ten to twelve per cent return, a small fraction of a corresponding investment in commerce. Only special crops like sugar-cane or vineyards approached an income-level usual in commerce.

Information about agriculture and the rural organization of the Latin kingdom allows us to draw several conclusions as to economic conditions and the characteristics of crusader domination. There can be no doubt that in the twelfth and thirteenth centuries the country was less prosperous than under Byzantine rule. The intervening four hundred years of Arab domination witnessed a sharp decline in the number of settlements and brought about a concentration of activity in the more fertile parts of the country. The decline was not, however, so sharp as one might assume from the sources of the Arab period only.[51] Hundreds of villages un-documented in the Arab period are recorded in the crusader period. It is impossible to accept that these villages were all new founda-tions, so we have to assume their continuous existence since Roman and Byzantine times. Crusader toponymy, when compared with the succeeding Mameluk period, does not show any marked dif-ferences. The main change was in the size and standing of cities, rather than villages. The cities, all of them fortified, were system-atically destroyed or dismantled by the Moslems during the thirteenth century, to prevent any possible crusader *reconquista*. This did not affect the rural pattern of settlement. We can only surmise a contraction of agricultural production because of reduced urban markets. The countryside became autarchic. It is even doubtful if rural demography was markedly influenced in the Mameluk period, though a notable worsening of the situation seems to be discernible during the four hundred years of Ottoman rule.

Whereas the general pattern of settlement seems to have been fixed, marked changes can be detected in the demographic pattern. It is apparent that all the *gastinae* found in almost every village tell

---

[51] Cf. the map of *Palestine under the Arabs*, ed. U. Ben-Horin in *Atlas Israel*, part IX, sheet XI.

a tale of abandoned dwellings. The same is also indicated by the large amount of land attributed to each family unit. The crusader conquest itself may have played some role in depopulating the countryside. We know of Moslem refugees from Palestine who settled in Egypt and Syria. It is impossible to be certain whether they came from the captured cities or villages. But even allowing for crusader influence, one cannot attribute such far-reaching changes solely to the conquest. For one thing, the period of conquest was relatively short, some ten years in all. Moreover, it was in the invaders' interest to preserve the villages and their peasant population, as their own existence would depend on them. It seems then, that we have to reckon with changes in rural demography which were slowly etched in over the long period which preceded crusader domination.

The crusaders did not strike roots in the countryside. Attempts at colonization, including new systems of settlement, were developed but their scope was small and should be regarded as an exception. The colonizing effort certainly did not change the ethnic structure of the peasantry. Not merely the Frankish peasant was conspicuously absent from the rural scene, the same applied to the Frankish landowner. His normal place of residence was the city, and exceptionally the local castle. The reasons have been discussed before. This fact in itself had far-reaching economic and and sociological repercussions on the crusader society.

Living in his palace or city house or often even outside the lordship, as for example in Acre, the crusader is an early example of an absentee landlord. There were no direct links between him and the land. The relationship was that of an exploiter to his regular source of income. This regularly prevented '*Raubwirtschaft*', as the Germans term the merciless exploitation of landed resources, because it was in his interest to safeguard land and people for his future profit. On the other hand, there was little trace of a squire-tenant relationship, where exploitation was mitigated by common interests, regular neighbourly contacts and by traditionally sanctioned paternalism. The absentee lord was first and foremostly a *rentier*, his absenteeism even more obvious and resented because he belonged to the conquerors. To many, he was oppressor, exploiter and Infidel at one time. Though a Moslem geographer like Ibn Jubair stresses that the economic situation of the Palestinian fellahin under the crusaders was better than that of their counterparts under Moslem domination, this was not enough to endear a crusader landlord to the peasantry.

This position of *rentier* also explains the most important feature of crusader rural organization, namely the absence of manorial exploitation, with its demesne land and *corvées*. Demesne land could hardly be profitably administered without direct and permanent supervision. A Slavonic proverb states that 'the eye of the owner fattens the horse'. An absentee landlord, given a lack of administrative infrastructures, could not do well in the direct exploitation of his domain. The crusaders drew the logical conclusion and resigned themselves to forgo the profits of a manorial system.[52] The one-third of basic crops and the quotas of fruits, vegetables and dairy products more than met the needs of a noble crusader's family. His urban possessions and commercial revenues provided additional income. The agricultural surplus of the great landowners was stored in the citadel or castle, and often used as a part of the fief for his knightly and non-knightly retainers. Thus non-manorial exploitation ultimately created a fairly satisfactory economic relationship between crusader landowner and Moslem peasant. The former was assured of an income which might vary from year to year depending on the season; the peasant was freer and less exploited than under Moslem rule, and certainly less than his Christian counterpart in the West.

Agriculture was the economic and physical basis of crusader existence and the rural organization introduced by the conquerors determined the character of crusader colonial society. Its most typical feature is the class of *rentiers* and absentee landlords, deepening the abyss between conqueror and conquered.

[52] The manorial system was not the rule in the foregoing period, though there were apparent tendencies in this direction. See Cl. Cahen, *op. cit.* (gen. bibl. to this chapter). A wholesale introduction of the system by the crusaders would have caused a deep-reaching revolution in agrarian relations. Still a similar experiment took place two generations earlier in Anglo-Saxon England conquered by the Normans.

B Money

During the Middle Ages and far into modern times the word 'Levant' conjured up the image of great Eastern bazaars, teeming oriental *souks* and busy ports. This is a tempting preconceived image of the Latin establishments in the East. On the crossroads of Europe, Asia and Africa, the Latin kingdom and its crusader neighbours seemed to have been destined for a major role in international traffic. The picture of teeming bazaars is certainly true and many an itinerary to the Holy Land cites ample evidence. Nevertheless, the place of the crusader establishments in the commercial relations between East and West requires more precise definition.

The international commerce of the declining Roman Empire and the early Middle Ages was dominated by one coin, the Byzantine *nomisma* or *hyperperon*, a gold piece of excellent quality and relatively great stability. An instrument of exchange in the Mediterranean and an important commodity hoarded in barbarian Europe as far north as Scandinavia, this gold coin was recently termed the 'mediaeval dollar'. When the monopoly was broken at the end of the seventh century and the Moslem gold *dinar* poured into the atrophied arteries of international commerce, the world around *mare nostrum* accepted both monetary units, backed as they were by the potential of two major empires whose economic activities extended across Europe to the North Sea and via the Indian Ocean and the Eurasian steppes to the Far East.

The establishment of the crusader colonies on the confines of Byzantium and Islam produced a third money unit, struck by the crusaders: the *besant*. Many hopes and beliefs that the *besant* could become the third coin of international commerce must have accompanied the decision to strike this golden coin. Based on European gold supply and commerce and on the nearness of the Eastern markets it appeared to have an excellent chance. But the crusader *besant* at its best never fulfilled these expectations. Seeking to penetrate between the *nomisma* and the *dinar*, the *besant* attempted a symbolic fusion. The name itself commemorated the fact that the first gold coins encountered by the crusaders were those of Byzantium; while its Arabic inscriptions were those of the Fatimid *dinar* of Egypt, until religious sensitivity added a cross and replaced the praise of Allah and his Prophet by that of the Trinity, still written in Arabic. No propensity to 'orientalization' prepared Arabic dies or moulds in the royal mint, but sober commercial considerations aimed at making crusader money acceptable in the East. Failure or partial failure resulted because the coins, though used, could hardly be regarded on a par with their Byzantine or Moslem counterpart. Nevertheless the *besant* has the honour of being the first Christian gold coin in wide circulation, struck a hundred years before the *florins* and *ducats* of Italy.

Even more than the northern Christian principalities, the Kingdom of Jerusalem must have been swamped by a variety of currencies.[53] Whereas plurality of coinage was common in all great European emporia, some limits were set by the fact that larger sums could be paid in the scarce gold coinage, ingots or by the exchange of goods. Additionally, the bulk of business was transacted with a relatively small number of other centres, whose currency would thus be in common use. The situation differed in the crusader East, since the influx of money did not merely follow the merchant, but came with the many pilgrims converging from the four corners of Christendom. During the First Crusade we hear that the host used coins from Poitou, Chartres, Le Mans, Lucca, Valence and Melgueil. A hoard of money, some 3,500 silver and *billon* pieces buried in Tripoli some time after 1221, was composed almost equally of 1,700 crusader and 1,800 French coins, from two dozen different places.[54] The most recent excavations beneath the Templars' compound in Jerusalem yielded a treasure of twelfth-century coins from Chartres.[55] This mass of Western coinage was

[53] Raymond d'Aguilers, 278. A study of weights and measures of the Latin kingdom remains an urgent *desideratum*. There are some important observations of C. Desimoni (see gen. bibl.). Valuable information is to be found in the recently published *Zibaldone de Canal*, ed. A. Stussi, Venice, 1967.

[54] D. H. Cox, The Tripolis Hoard of French Seigniorial and Crusader's Coins, *Numismatic Notes and Monographs*, no. 59, N.Y., 1933.

[55] To be published by B. Mazar.

augmented by all the currencies of the Near East, introduced by oriental merchants, as well as Moslem, Christian and Jewish pilgrims. This explains the importance of the money changers, for whom special streets or *piazzas* were reserved in Tyre, Acre and Jerusalem. In the capital two streets bracketing the main bazaars from south and north were occupied by Syrian and Latin money changers, respectively. Although this division could be connected with different taxation, essentially it must have been the result of specialization.

Local currency was of gold, silver and copper.[56] The minting of coins was a royal monopoly, and as late as the reign of Baldwin II, but probably even under Baldwin III, the nobility was barred from this privilege under pain of fief confiscation.[57] The royal prerogative was never officially abolished, neither was the privilege of minting accorded to any vassal of the kingdom. Based on existing finds we would suggest that seigniorial coinage made its appearance very late, certainly after the battle of Hittin. Even then its use was limited, and though possibly lucrative to the feudal lord who struck coins, it seems doubtful if minting had purely economic reasons. The coins were of small denominations and poor alloy. Their chief purpose seems to have been as an announcement of political independence.

Foreign gold coins were the most important currency in the kingdom. The earliest were the Byzantine *hyperperon* or *Michelois* (coins struck by Emperor Michael VII of Paphlagonia). These were common in Antioch.[58] In the south, at Tripoli and Jerusalem, the earliest gold currency was the Fatimid *dinar*. With time, crusader currency made an appearance, and it seems to have been struck

---

[56] A new find of a matrix for the preparation of lead jetons was discovered in Acre. Although coins could have been struck from the jetons, it is plausible to suggest that these are small weights as there is no proof of crusader lead coins. See Y. Meshorer, *The Production of coins in the Ancient World*, Israel Museum, no. 70. Jerusalem 1970, pl. XIV.

[57] See J. Prawer, 'Droit de confiscation et droit d'exhérédation', *Rev. hist. de droit français et étranger*, 1962, 29 ff.

[58] William of Tyre, XI, 470. Cf. Ph. Grierson, 'From *Solidus* to *Hyperperon*: The names of Byzantine gold coins', *Numismatic Circular*, 74 (1966), 123–4.

earlier in the north. The normal procedure was to impress crusader names and symbols on existing Byzantine pieces. The crusaders struck their own money only later, at an unspecified date during the twelfth century. Payments in *bisantini* are mentioned very early,[59] but there is no way of knowing whether this refers to genuine or imitated Fatimid *dinars*. The *bisantini sarracenati* appeared in the '60s of the twelfth century and seemed to be a novelty.[60] The appearance of crusader gold coins did not withdraw the Fatimid *dinars* from circulation. Moslem and crusader gold was used and the distribution of the currency was determined by patterns of economic activity.

Compared with the ancient *dinar* containing 4.25 g of almost pure gold,[61] the later Fatimid *dinar*, imitated by the crusaders, was lighter and of a cheaper alloy, but still surpassed in weight and gold content the crusader imitation called *bisantinus sarracenatus*. Ordinarily the latter was 22 to 23 mm in diameter and weighed some 3.5 to 3.7 g (maximum variation: 3.15 g and 4.02 g).[62] The alloy contains 65.5% to 75% of gold.[63] It is a most peculiar and clumsy imitation. These early crusader coins have the outward appearance of Arab coins, but anyone even faintly familiar with Arabic easily perceives that the inscription is meaningless and that, with few exceptions, the letters are not even Arabic, but simply a collection of vertical strokes, circles and the like. This could hardly have been done on purpose. We are obviously dealing with occidental minters working in the East, but ignorant of the native language. The phenomenon is all the more interesting, since the

---

[59] Prebends in besants are mentioned as early as 1103. Rozière, no. 36, p. 71–2, but they refer in all probability to Byzantine or Moslem gold coins.

[60] *Bisantinus sarracenatus* appears in 1168, Strehlke, *op. cit.*, no. 4 (pp. 5–6) and might refer to crusader money. A Venetian contract mentions in 1161: 'bisancios aureos sarracenatos de moneta regis'. Morozzo della Rocca, *op. cit.*, I, 152 (no. 154) quoted by J. Yvon in *Museum Notes*, IX, 298. It is safe to suppose that it is at this period only that crusader besants identifiable as such were struck.

[61] See P. Balog and J. Yvon in *Revue numismatique*, 1958, 138 ff.

[62] See the latest find of 3.15 g and the average of 3.78 g, J. Yvon in *Museum Notes*, IX, 295.

[63] A. Ehrenkreuz, 'The Standard Fineness of Gold Coins circulated in Egypt at the time of the Crusades', *Jour. Amer. Oriental Soc.*, 74 (1954), 163.

Fatimid mint at Tyre was still active a year or so before the city was captured by the crusaders (1124) and the conquerors seem even to have continued to strike Fatimid dinars, using existing dies. The local personnel, Moslems or native Christians, must have been dismissed or a different mint established – perhaps in Jerusalem – which struck these poor imitations.

In time various crusader imitations of the *dinar* reached a point where several letters or words, like dates and the place of minting, became readable and some coins bore a small cross and the Latin letters 'B' and 'T', which might denote one of the Bohemonds (or Bertrand of Tripolis) and Tancred, or indicate the mint at Tripoli, Tyre, Antioch or Acre.[64] A new imitation of the *dinar* appeared later, though it did not replace the earlier one. The new coin imitated the Ayyubid *dinar*. Since only one gold example of this type was discovered it is difficult to estimate its importance. It is 22 mm in diameter and slightly lighter (3.31 g) than the preceding Fatimid imitation. Part of the inscription is well copied, though the *kufic* lettering is not too well reproduced; another part of the inscription does not make sense and the minter obviously knew no Arabic.

A major change took place in crusader coinage only in 1250. The papal legate, Eudes de Châteauroux, was scandalized 'that on besants and drachmas struck by Christians in Acre and Tripoli, the name of Muhammed as well as the date of his birth is impressed'[65] and Pope Innocent IV banned crusader coinage with Moslem inscriptions. The crusader authorities complied with the demand in a particular way: on their new coins the inscriptions remained in Arabic, but their contents became Christian. Gold coins of that type were struck for at least eight years (1251–7), whereas the more common silver coins which imitated the Ayyubid *dirhem* (21

---

[64] See the discussion in P. Balog (n. 61) p. 139–40. It is worthwhile to note that this eminent specialist envisages the possibility that some of the Fatimid imitations were not struck by the crusaders but by mints in southern Europe. There is no tangible proof of this thesis.

[65] Quoted by G. Schlumberger, *op. cit.*, 139–40. The date referred naturally to the *Hegira* and not to Muhammed's birth-date. See now Ph. Grierson in American Numismatic Society, *Museum Notes*, VI, 169 ff.

mm–23 mm; 2.12 g–2.88 g) had a shorter run, and slowly but steadily circumvented the papal orders.[66] The new gold 'Christian' *besant* externally imitated the Fatimid *dinar* with its concentric inscription (instead of the square Ayyubid type), but the letters were in the *nashky* script used by the mints of the later Ayyubites. A prominent cross in the centre and the inscriptions proclaimed Christian origin. The Arabic read: *Daraba bi' aka sana alf wa-maitayin wahad wa-hamsin litajasad; al-ab wa al-ibnu wa al-ruh al quds*, that is 'struck in Acre in the year 1251 of the Incarnation; Father, Son and the Holy Ghost'. In the centre: *Allah wahad*, 'God is One'. The reverse read: *Naftathar bi-Salib rabana Yasu'a al-masih al-ladhi bihai salamatana wa-tahayatana wa-qiyamatana wa-bihu tahalasana wa-'afyana* (= We are proud of the Cross of our Lord Jesus Christ, in whom our Salvation and Resurrection and our Existence, and in Him our Safety and Forgiveness).

These gold coins were some 23 mm in diameter, but varied in weight from 2.80 g to 3.63 g and there is a smaller half-*dinar* of 19 mm with a relatively higher weight at 3.12 g. An anonymous crusader gold coin whose centre bears an *Agnus Dei* and the circular inscription *Agnus Dei qui tollit peccata mundi* and on the reverse *Christus vincit, Christus regnat, Christus imperat* seems to belong to the same period. This specimen (*c.* 20.5 mm–21 mm) is of a base alloy and weighs between 3.31 g and 3.62 g.[67]

Gold coins were used in international exchange and to pay larger sums of money. Everyday commerce used silver and copper coins. Whereas the crusaders did not strike gold coins with the effigy of their rulers, identifying symbols or Latin and French inscriptions, this became the rule for silver. But since international commerce used gold and silver currency, the crusaders also struck imitation silver coins. This could have been for the benefit of the native Moslems, Christians and Jews. The first imitations were made immediately after the conquest, when the local population sabotaged settlement and went so far as to refuse to till the soil, so as

[66] P. Balog in *Bull. de l'Inst. d'Egypte*, 34, 45–8.
[67] Ph. Grierson, 'A rare Crusader Bezant with the *Christus Vincit* legend', American Numismatic Society, *Museum Notes*, VI, 169–78.

to withhold food from the crusaders. The natives still expected the Egyptians or Damascenes to invade the kingdom and throw the invaders and their currency into the sea. Such an attitude could have caused a certain reluctance to accept money of unknown type and uncertain fate.

The silver imitations are not dated and we thus know little of their issue. Even in the thirteenth century when crusader silver was an established currency, new silver imitations continued to be struck, possibly because by then they had become traditional. Some silver imitations of Moslem coins are so strange as to merit special attention. A hoard of coins from Fayyum in Egypt had several crusader coins among its real Ayyubid silver *dirhems*, the former with Christian inscriptions in Arabic. But there is also a special hybrid coinage. The Arabic inscriptions proclaim that the coins were minted in Damascus during the caliphate of al-Mustansir billah and the reign of sultan Saleh Ismail in the year (Christian era!) 1253 (or during the '50s of the thirteenth century as the last digit is often missing). The date gives away its crusader origin. We also remark that the shortened invocation: 'In the name of Allah the merciful and gracious' (skipping the name of the 'Prophet Muhammed') was so contrived as to be acceptable to Moslem and Christian alike. A better imitation of an Ayyubid silver *dirhem* with a complete invocation gives itself away by wrongly indicating the dates of the reigning caliph and sultan of Damascus, both by then already deceased.[68]

The proper silver crusader coin was the *denarius* or *denier* whose Moslem counterpart was the *dirham*. Crusader sources, even an official list of market tolls, use both names indiscriminately.[69] Despite large finds of royal *deniers* the chronology of the different issues has still not been conclusively established. This is largely due to the fact that five kings went by the name of Baldwin and coins with the name *BALDUINUS REX* (and variations) make matters

[68] P. Balog, *ibid.* (n. 66), 48–54.

[69] See the list of market-tolls in Acre. *Livre des Assises des Bourgeois*, cap. 224–5, *Lois* II, 179 ff. There is also a crusader coin called *Dragma Acconensis*. Schlumberger, *op. cit.*, Supplement 22, pl.XX, no. 3.

extremely difficult. Moreover, as new coin issues did not supersede earlier ones the whole problem is almost insoluble. This problem is more numismatic than economic, because there is little difference in size, weight and fine-silver content between the different coins. This may hint at some measure of monetary stability in the silver coinage. The royal silver *deniers* with the name of Baldwin struck in Tyre and Acre (and perhaps also in Jerusalem)[70] weighed some 0.90 g to 0.95 g, with about 34.7% silver content[71] (i.e. 0.285 g of fine silver).

There is a general tendency to assign the earliest royal coins to Baldwin II (1118–31) or Baldwin III (1143–63), which tallies well with legislation in regard to royal prerogatives.[72] If this is correct, neither Godfrey de Bouillon nor his direct successors Baldwin I, Baldwin II (perhaps) or Fulk of Anjou (no coins ever found) struck coins in their own name. Though this is not impossible, it seems rather peculiar that for some forty years after the conquest there was no royal coinage in circulation. Until numismatic finds reverse this hypothesis, we can only surmise that the Fatimid coins in circulation (large quantities of which came into Frankish coffers during the conquest and from payments by the native population) supplied the normal economic needs of the country. In addition Western currencies brought by pilgrims and immigrants remained in circulation. Crusader currency came into existence only during the period of greater stability in the middle of the twelfth century.

As far as numismatic finds can ascertain, the royal coinage of the thirteenth century shows a decline compared with that of the twelfth. The great crisis[73] seems to have been at the time of King

---

[70] Some of the coins have a figure of the 'Tower of David'. Though this is not a decisive proof of a Jerusalem emission, it seems that it might be surmised with safety that the capital had a royal mint.

[71] Cox, *op. cit.*, p. 57. One silver *denier* of Baldwin from that collection weighs 1.02 g and contains 0.35 g of fine silver (*c.* 34.7%). It is remarked that this corresponds to the continental *denier* of the first half of the 12th century, or one quarter of a sterling of 1.40 g.

[72] We follow J. Yvon in *Revue numismatique*, 8 (1966), 89–107 whose conclusions create a solid working hypothesis.

[73] There is a possibility that Conrad of Montferrat struck money in Tyre. Cf. G. Schlumberger, *op. cit.*, suppl., pp. 494–5. The pieces assigned to him are

Aimery (1194–7; Cyprus 1197–1205). The average weight of his *deniers* dropped by half, namely to 0.55 g (extreme variations: 0.290–0.721 g), and their silver content by a third to 20.3%, i.e., half of the fine silver per *denier* (from 0.2938 g in the coins of Amalric to 0.162 in Aimery's). It is argued, though inconclusively, that Aimery's *deniers* were struck for Cyprus. Better coinage is connected with Guy de Lusignan (coins possibly struck for Cyprus) and Jean de Brienne after the capture of Damietta. They weigh about 0.73–0.80 g, but their silver content was low: 0.157 to 0.163 g of fine silver per *denier* (20.3% and 22%).[74]

In addition to silver and bullion *deniers*, crusader currency had half-*deniers*, the *oboles* (13 mm–15 mm; 0.40 g–0.51 g) and smaller copper pieces (0.022 mm; 1 g 40), like the extremely rare *pugeoise* which Count Henry of Champagne struck at Acre.[75] In times of crisis and no acknowledged central government, anonymous pieces came into circulation. Though there is no direct evidence, they seem to belong to the time of the Third Crusade, bearing inscriptions like '*Moneta Regis*', '*Turris Davit*', '*Sepulchri Domini*', '*San Aerea*', '*Via Crucis*'.[76]

Crusader money does not appear to have been a well established coinage, and in a sense this reflects the economic situation of the country. Some seigniorial mints competed for prestige, if not value, with the royal mint. The date of their first appearance is obscure. They would have been unthinkable under the strong

16.5 mm in diameter and weigh 0.65 g. See recently N. Du Quesne Bird in *Numismatic Circular*, 73 (1965), 207 but cf. *ibid.*, 74 (1966), 152.

[74] Cox, *op. cit.*, pp. 56–60.

[75] A unique silver coin of Henry of Champagne with a curious oriental design on the reverse was discovered recently and needs further study. Data regarding the metal composition of crusader coinage are now being studied by A. Gordus (Ann Arbor), and M. Metcalf (Ashmolean Museum), who generously allowed us to use some of their data. The results based on a large collection of money and the new technique should be invaluable to crusader numismatics.

[76] These anonymous pieces were assigned to the First Crusade; to coinage struck by the patriarch, Schlumberger, *op. cit.*, pp. 89,91; to coinage struck by military orders, Seltman and N. Du Quesne Bird in *Numismatic Circular*, 74 (1966), 152–3. For our part we prefer to assign them to the Third Crusade. Cf. J. Prawer in *Rev. hist. de droit français et étranger*, 1951, 340–1, n. 1.

monarchs of the First Kingdom, since the infringement of these royal prerogatives was legally punished by the confiscation of fiefs without a judgement of the High Court.[77] Only after the dislocation of central power under Baldwin v and his successors did ambitious nobles begin to strike their own money, obviously a usurpation, since this was never accorded them in the laws or privileges of the kingdom. Archaeological finds prove the existence of such coinage for several lordships. This coinage, usually bullion or just copper, is attested: for Jaffa (perhaps Gautier de Brienne after 1205), for Sidon under Reginald (possibly after 1187) with the curious emblem of an arrow (*sagitta* pointing to the Arabic name of the city '*Saida*' or in Frankish '*Saiette*'), for Beirut under Jean, the *Vieux Sire de Baruth* (1205–36), for Toron (Humphrey iii) and Tyre under Philip de Montfort and Jean de Montfort, lords of Tyre and Toron (middle and second half of thirteenth century).

C   International Commerce

Like many other aspects of the Crusades, their commercial importance was extolled by some and decried by others. Whereas some scholars credit the Crusades with the great outburst of economic activity which marks the European twelfth and thirteenth centuries, others reason that sooner or later things would have developed as they did even without the Crusades. Our sources are unfortunately far from sufficient in regard to the volume of trade, on which economic studies must ultimately be based. Not many conclusions can thus be reached without controversy. Nevertheless some general lines of development can be drawn and the place of the kingdom in international commerce envisaged.

The Frankish colonies, though founded in prosperous lands, controlled no major economic centres. Latin domination never extended beyond the deep depression which divided the coastlands from the great cities of the Arab interior: Damascus, Aleppo and Baghdad. In the south, the Sinai peninsula was the frontier and

[77] See above n. 57.

apart from a brief interlude, the crusaders never dominated Cairo or Alexandria. The third great emporium of industry and trade, Constantinople, did come under Latin domination as the result of the Fourth Crusade, but this had little or no impact on the commercial position of the Latin kingdom. In the whole area dominated by the crusaders only three cities were important centres of production: Antioch, Tripoli and Tyre. Until the crusader conquest their economy was tuned to trade with the Moslem hinterland: Damascus and Baghdad in the east and with the ports of Egypt or along the land-routes, the ancient *via maris* or the caravan routes across Transjordan and Sinai.

The direct impact of the crusader conquest was the establishment of a new pattern of commercial relations, foreshadowed in the eleventh century by direct contacts with Europe, in which the merchants of Amalfi seem to have taken the lead. This does not mean that the crusader establishments radically changed the Near-Eastern economy. Egypt continued its relations with Syria and Mesopotamia via the Red Sea and the Persian Gulf. Even overland commerce did not disappear, but continued along the caravan routes. In times of peace a *modus vivendi* was created whereby the crusaders guaranteed the safety of Moslem caravans for a transit toll. Yet, despite the obvious interests of Christian and Moslem authorities, overland connections became sporadic and often precarious.

The direct and major result of the crusader conquest was the gearing of the commercial activities along the eastern coast of the Mediterranean to the needs and possibilities of Europe. Henceforth it played the double role of exporting its own products and – what was far more important – that of an outlet for the products of the Moslem hinterland (including Africa, Arabia and the Far East). Simultaneously, it became Asia's door to the West.

The 'needs' and 'possibilities' of Europe underwent extensive changes during the two hundred years of crusader domination. Growing riches enlarged the market for foreign imports and facilitated the acquisition of new tastes and views on decent or comfortable living. The new needs were qualified by the ability to pay in specie or products acceptable to the East.

The gearing of the Palestinian and Syrian economy to that of western Europe was thus the great innovation of the period. Existing industries looked more to Europe than to the Moslem hinterland. Non-industrial production – mainly food – described in such glowing terms by the Moslem geographer Muqaddasi in the tenth century,[78] lost in importance as an export, because of the dangers of transportation from Palestine to Syria and Egypt.

Strictly speaking, crusader exports depended on the production centres of the country. Handicrafts certainly flourished, crusader pottery is found in every archaeological excavation and their ironwork was famous. But these items were hardly basic elements of export. Export-oriented local production included textiles, glass, dyestuffs, sugar and its derivatives. The most important single item was textiles. Antioch and Tripoli inherited the late classical and Byzantine tradition of textile production, continued under Moslem domination and preserved by the crusaders. According to one source, Tripoli alone had some 4,000 weavers engaged in the manufacture of silk and camlot.[79] Silk production included the magnificent and costly brocades. 'Attire of Antioch' (*guimples et messares*) in silk and brocade is singled out in the customs tariff of Acre.[80] Not less famous was the white silk of Tyre, whose Syrian artisans were one source of revenue to the Venetian quarter of the city.[81] A less important centre was Beirut, which exported cotton fabrics and silks.[82] Later, mulberry trees were planted in its vicinity to cultivate the silk worm. A cheaper textile – cotton – was also exported from the country and seems to have been grown in the plains of Acre and Tiberias. Some woollen fabrics came from the Shefela, near Ramleh.[83]

[78] Mukaddasi in *PPTS*, IV, 68–72.

[79] Burchardus de Monte Sion, ed. J. C. M. Laurent, Leipzig, 1864, 28; cf. Heyd, I, 179.

[80] *Livre des Assises des Bourgeois*, ed. H. Kausler, cap. 238, p. 284; ed. Beugnot, cap. 243 *Lois* II, 179.

[81] Tafel-Thomas, *op. cit.*, II, 359.

[82] Tafel-Thomas, *op. cit.*, II, 233.

[83] Zibaldone da Canal, p. 63 (38 v. 6ff.): 'li marchanti che volleva andar fora d'Acre a cunprar banbaxio e per lo pllan d'Acre siò sì è per li chaxalli de intorno la tera infina Tabaria.' The manual was written in 1311 but this refers clearly to an earlier, namely crusader period. Cotton-wool and cotton thread

We are less informed about another export product of highest importance, namely dye-stuffs. The customs list of Acre cites a large number of dye-stuffs,[84] but only a few centres of production were located in the kingdom. Indigo was grown in the Jordan valley and madder in that of the Orontes, bitumen was collected near the Dead Sea and balsam still cultivated around Jericho. This makes it plausible to assume that as far as they were not consumed by local industries, these substances were exported.

Glassware was another article of export, whose manufacture was mainly centred on Tyre. This glass was famous in Europe and the manufacture of Venetian glass could have originated there. Two preserved examples of painted glasses are probably of Tyrian origin, and show excellent craftsmanship. Though the local glassmaker was probably a Jew, a Westerner later painted a Madonna scene on one with a Latin inscription.[85] Among ceramics, preserved slipware is of a common type and painted rather crudely.[86] It thus seems doubtful if local ceramics were exported. Indeed, we have evidence of ceramics being imported into the kingdom,[87] probably a better kind of pottery, since there was also an import of artistically painted vases.[88] As a curiosity, we cite turquoises of Tyre listed by Pegolotti, who also mentions the Tyrian purple of classical fame.

are mentioned as sold in Acre by Pegolotti, p. 63. Woollens are mentioned in Ramleh, *ibid.* 101. The best cotton-wool, we learn from Pegolotti, came from 'Amman in Transjordan, *ibid.* 366.

[84] *Livre des Assises des Bourgeois*, ed. Kausler, cap. 237–8; *Lois* II, ed. Beugnot, cap. 223–1. cf. Pegolotti, p. 63.

[85] William of Tyre, XIII, cap. 3, *RHC, Hist. Occidentaux*, I, 559; cf. Müller, *op. cit.*, p. 376. The painted glasses are in the British Museum. Reproduced in J. Prawer, *Histoire du royaume latin de Jérusalem*, Paris, 1969, I, 332. Pegolotti, p. 380 mentions *Cenere gravella di Soria*, which is a kind of potash used in the fabrication of soap and glass.

[86] C. N. Johns, 'Excavations at Pilgrims' Castle ('Atlit)', *QDAP*, I (1932), 129 (pl. LIII). Some good examples are to be seen in the Museum of Acre.

[87] *Livre des Assises des Bourgeois* ed. Kausler, cap. 238 mentions: 'les labors de poterie, si coume est escuelles et pignates et pos' to be taxed at the *fonde*, and again: 'labour de terre de poterie c'on aporte de paienime en Acre'.

[88] *Lois* II, 179, par. 7, 16.

Among comestibles of local origin which were probably exported, we may assume the excellent olives and sesame oil. The olive groves exploited by the Venetians around Tyre were certainly used for export. This was not new to a country which paid part of its taxes in oil under Moslem rule.[89] Perhaps more important was the wine, which received a great boost when the country fell into Christian hands. Supplying provisions to European ships in port was certainly the minimum outlet, but wines were possibly exported to the West.[90] According to Pegolotti, Syrian rice was also an article of commerce, but it is not clear to which part of Syria he refers.[91]

Whereas the export of oil and wine depended on their quality, since both products were abundant in southern Europe, the cultivation and processing of sugar-cane was almost an eastern monopoly. The plantations and sugar presses centred around Tyre, Tiberias (sugar from Kerak is mentioned by Pegolotti) and the Jordan valley, which supplied a wide market. The end product was exported in the form of syrup, crystal, powder or loaf sugar.[92] Some iron ore found near Beirut and mentioned in passing by our sources would hardly have been exported, seeing the need of the crusader establishments for arms and building materials.

A summary of the above from the economic point of view is hampered by the impossibility of quantitative evaluation. One of the great scholars who dealt with the problem, Wilhelm Heyd[93] concluded: 'From all that was said one can see how Syria was rich in articles of export', but we are frankly in the realm of speculation.

Despite the seemingly important list of products, the kingdom's place in international commerce was only partially dependent on its position as a producer. It had a far greater role as a transit and

[89] Le Strange, *Palestine under the Moslems*, 45.
[90] One is curious to know what happened to the wines of Gaza of Pirennean fame.
[91] Mukaddasi in *PPTS*, IV, 29 mentions Beisan as the great centre of rice growing.
[92] Heyd, *op. cit.*, II, Suppl. I, 680–93. Exports of sugar to Europe are also mentioned by Benjamin of Tudela, ed. Adler, p. 31.
[93] *Id.*, *op. cit.*, I, 180.

supply centre for industrial and other goods originating outside its boundaries and as an outlet for European wares consumed in the kingdom or re-exported to the Moslem East.

Viewed as a market for European products the kingdom was certainly of some importance. At their zenith the population of the Latin establishments reached some 250,000 inhabitants (for the Kingdom of Jerusalem proper *c.* 120,000 and for Tripoli, Antioch and Edessa together, approximately the same number). This was certainly a potential clientele for European products. Imported cloth and finished articles catered to traditional needs. This was certainly true for capes from Champagne or berets and the like, which hardly appealed to the Moslem market. Keeping up with European fashions was characteristic of this colonial society and created a steady market for some Western products.

European goods which reached the Levant could not have been solely destined for European inhabitants of the kingdom and the crusader principalities. A great part of the European imports continued eastward to the Moslem hinterland.

The inverse movement of Moslem merchandise was even less destined for local market. There can be little doubt that the merchants in the coastal cities shipped these articles to southern Europe and across the Alps. Moreover, already in the twelfth century the Italians and Provençals actually became intermediaries between the far-flung countries of Islam and they transported merchandise between Egypt, North Africa and Spain. In addition to their importance as a place of transit, the Latin colonies probably acted as a subsidiary financial centre for the inner circle of Near-Eastern trade, between Constantinople, Antioch, Acre and Alexandria.

Whatever their importance in international commerce, no one can deny that the Crusades radically changed the position along the eastern littoral of the Mediterranean compared to the foregoing Arab period. For two hundred years these lands reached prominence in international economy until a new Moslem conquest (that of the Mameluks followed two hundred years later by the Ottomans) brought slumber and obscurity until our own times.

The country's position as a centre of transit and finance, which regulated the flow of precious metals and currencies, was largely due to the Italian merchants. Their partial or total exemption from customs, market tolls and taxes turned the harbours of the kingdom into free ports. The privileges of the communes absorbed a goodly share of the potential revenues. But this had its compensations: Italian and (to a lesser degree) Provençal merchants were attracted by these privileges and by the security of Christian domination. Few products were unavailable in the ports of Egypt, Lesser Armenia or Byzantium. The goods of Damascus and Baghdad might even be more expensive in the kingdom because of additional transport costs. The most lucrative article of commerce, generally described as 'spices', came from southern and eastern Asia, via the Persian Gulf, Baghdad and Damascus, or from Cairo and Alexandria via the Red Sea. The crusader exemptions prevented a far larger concentration of European commerce in Egypt and the privileges of the communes thus assured the country a standing not warranted by its own resources or geographical position.

During the two hundred years of the kingdom's existence the international movement of trade underwent some important changes, both in extent and nature. Despite the activity of several European centres – Venice, Pisa, Genoa, Marseilles, Barcelona, to name the most important – their exports and imports give an impression of quasi-homogeneity. There might have been local nuances, but none of these cities catered to itself or to its nearest surroundings. They supplied the marts and fairs of Europe with identical products. Changes in ports of call, often caused by purely political reasons (Venetian influence in Constantinople after the Fourth Crusade; Genoese and Venetians alternately excluded from Acre and re-established in Tyre or Beirut) had little effect on the movement as a whole, because the clientele of the country and the eastern hinterland dictated the nature and volume of trade.

For the First Kingdom (1099–1187) our information depends largely on the privileges of the communes, the registers of the Genoese notary, Giovanni Scriba, and a relatively small number of other notarial registers.[94] They indicate that most transactions

---

[94] See gen. bibl. Cf. Bach, *op. cit.*, 14–15.

in the second half of the twelfth century involved a drain of precious metals from Europe to the Orient. The West had not yet reached the stage of an exporter whose goods could balance imports. Its position was that of a buyer who largely paid in hard currency. Yet what is true for the total exchange between East and West does not necessarily apply to the centres of Levantine commerce. Their income depended not only on direct trade with the East, but also on the transport of immigrants and pilgrims. Moreover, as previously mentioned, Italian fleets established connections between the different centres of Islam itself. Their imports were thus paid for by additional income.

Even payment in precious metal should not be exaggerated. Some European products were sold very early to the East. In the middle of the century, cheap textiles[95] (*fustanei, baldinelli* and *vogiae*) – but also the expensive green and scarlet cloth of northern origin – and the fur of hares, timber and lead were shipped from Europe to the ports of the Levant.[96] These products were not a novelty around 1150 and there is no reason to suppose that they were not exported a generation or more earlier, though no notarial register supports this hypothesis.

The scarcity of documentation led some scholars to assume a fixed pattern of commerce between Europe and Syria, where the exports were sold or precious metals exchanged for products and local currency and the realized capital then went to Egypt. This assumption is based on the fact that notarial registers cite exports to Syria but none to Egypt, whereas they attest considerable imports from Egypt.[97] This picture seems excessively one-sided. It does not explain why goods available in Syria should have been bought in Egypt (some Egyptian products were naturally cheaper and some, like cotton flax and high-quality alum, available only in Egypt). The solution to these puzzling notarial registers can probably be found in the fact, that exports to Egypt were largely classified as contraband, which offended against papal and often

---

[95] *Baldinelli* are explained as 'tessuto di tela estretto'. Zibaldone da Canal, 128.
[96] H. Schaube, *op. cit.*, 159–160 (based on Giovanni Scriba).
[97] *Ibid.* p. 165.

communal prohibitions, e.g. timber, iron, lead and pitch – all of them materials of war not to be found in Egypt and an absolute necessity for shipbuilding. Such transactions surely could not be recorded by a notary, though a relevant agreement was officially concluded between Pisa and Egypt.[98] Direct exports to Egypt thus made capital available to buy exclusively Egyptian products or imported spices. Crusader Syria was in a different position. The import of building materials, though attested,[99] was negligible and could not compare with that of European cloth and materials.

This can also be proved by comparing the data of the afore-mentioned Genoese notary, Giovanni Scriba. Out of 335 agreements (from a total of 1,300), 116 concern Italy and Sicily, 107 North Africa, southern France and Spain, 112 the Levant. The last item is divided as follows: Alexandria 58, Syria 34 and Byzantium 20 contracts. There were then almost twice as many voyages to Alexandria as to Syria,[100] but the investments show a completely different picture: Genoese £9,031 for Alexandria; G£10,075 for Syria and G£2,007 for Byzantium. The average investment per voyage was G£ 300 for Syria, G£ 156 for Alexandria and G£ 100 for Byzantium. Thus the apparent preponderance of Egyptian trade is misleading and the Syrian investments were twice as large as those of Egypt and higher than those of Egypt and Byzantium together. Crusader Syria is thus proven to have occupied a key position in European commerce with the Levant. The large number of voyages to Egypt could be explained by the fact, that the exports to Syria were high-priced goods of smaller volume, whereas those to Egypt were bulky and demanded more space, and tonnage. Consequently they necessitated more voyages without raising the total of capital investments.

Following later notarial registers (all of them from Genoa) we can state that the second half of the twelfth century did not mark any notable change in the nature of the Levant trade. As before, the crusader states largely imported cheap textiles. Occa-

---

[98] G. Müller, op. cit., 7; H. Schaube, op. cit., 149–50; Heyd, I, 392 ff.

[99] Decision of the Venetian Consiglio Maggiore to unload all iron and timber in crusader ports. See below, cap. XVIII, n. 56.

[100] E. H. Byrne, 'Genoese trade with Syria', AHR, 25 (1919–20), 202.

sionally we hear about cloth of Verona and the export of swords to Syria (despite the famous Damascene blades which must have been far more costly), in addition to silver and currency. There is also evidence that northern French textiles, hides, pearls and gold were exported to Syria.[101]

For 1184 the notarial register of Oberto Scriba de Mercato notes 18 contracts for Syria totalling £1,109. For 1186 the same notary registered 14 contracts for Syria totalling £3,056; for 1190 he registered 20 contracts with a total investment of G£2,091. A year later, no doubt in connection with the Third Crusade, the notary Guglielmo Cassinese registered 42 contracts with a total value of G£6,387.[102] The small sums in the contracts of 1190 (some of G£2–3), are noteworthy, although even in a year of heavy investments (sums above G£500, 600 and 700) we find small amounts of a few pounds only.

For the second quarter of the thirteenth century we have a better record of European imports from Syria. In 1233 Venice enacted a statute regarding shipments to Syria.[103] The volume and weight of merchandise was regulated according to the tonnage of vessels. Ships between 200 and 1,000 milliari could hold 120 to 1050 cantars. The imported products were divided according to weight and volume. The first category included: cotton, cotton yarn, wool for berets, liquorice, sugar-cane and lavender (spicum). The second: pepper, long pepper(?) (piper longum), melegete (also pepper), ginger, nutmeg, cloves, cubebs, rice, sugar, castor sugar, gum, gum-lac, myrrh, aloe, frankincense, cardamon, zedoary, camphor, sandalwood, myrobalan, galangal, simoniacum, orpiment, ammoniac; wax, indigo, alum, glass, vitriol, emery; raw silk, cloth of silk, buckram. The third class included: brazilwood, flax, cinammon, cummin, mace, anis and camlot.

Fifteen years later, a notary from Marseilles, Amalric,[104] reveals

---

[101] E. Bach, op. cit., 91–2.

[102] Based on the analytical tables of E. Bach, op. cit., Appendix.

[103] Maritime Statutes of Venice in Nuovo Archivio Veneto, N.S., IV, 285 ff.

[104] L. Blancard, Documents inédits sur la commerce de Marseille, 2 vols. Marsielle, 1884–5.

the opposite movement, namely that of European merchandise to Syria, which partly paid for the impressive list of Eastern products quoted above. Several ships left Marseilles in the spring of 1248. The clientele of one of them, the *Saint Esprit* – which belonged to one Raymond Suffren – used the services of the above Amalric the notary. His registers can be rightly described as the ship's inventory, though some other contracts for the same voyage may have been concluded before a different notary. During the fortnight preceding departure (14–31 March 1248) not less than 150 contracts were registered by Amalric involving almost 180 persons of whom one third embarked, the others (the capital investors) usually remained in Marseilles. The invested sums (money or merchandise) ranged on the average between £10–£50 of Marseilles currency (5 cases: below £10; 59 cases: £10–£50: 24 cases: £50–100; 30 cases: above £100). Among the travelling merchants one Pierre Bellaigue received in 13 contracts money and merchandise worth £1,323 (the investments ranged from 7s.8d. to £230). There was also a consignment of local, mixed and oriental currency, sometimes as sea loans, or to be used for buying Oriental wares. A large share consisted of miscellaneous articles (*in communibus implicitis*), but most involved textiles (*draparia*). Those specified by name came from Châlons (green, blue, white) and Reims, other varieties included cloth of Tarascon, of Narbonne, woollen cloth (*stamina*) of St Pons and Arras, cloth of Champagne, of Louvière, *vintain* (*in vintenis*), cloth from Cambrai, of St Quentin, black Stanford from England, linsey-woolsey of Chartres (*in Chartresio*), vermilion cloth, red cloth of Ypres, cloth of Basel; silk-cloth, cloth of Avignon, gold-thread (*aurum filatum*) of Genoa and Lucca, thread of Burgundy, brown cloth of Douai (*in runetis*), fustian, biffes of Paris, cloth from Germany. Other articles included: saffron, tin (*stagnum*), coral, quicksilver and fox furs. [105]

The list is impressive and even more so if we attempt to value the items. Goods and currency, the whole cargo of *Saint Esprit* was worth £11,100 of money current in Marseille, £1,110 of

---

[105] All these articles are mentioned in the cargo of the ship *Saint Esprit*.

Melgueil and 1,228 of Tour.[106] At the same time eight more ships left Marseilles in a short period following 1 April 1248.

The notarial cartularies of Genoa from the thirteenth century have only been partially edited. But some studies point to the fact, that Genoese investments in the Levant for the thirty years between 1233 and 1262 (with the exception of the fratricidal war of the communes in Acre, 1256–8) were very high. In 1253 they reached more than G£50,000 and constituted from 40 to 70% of all contracts preserved for Genoa's overseas commerce.[107]

For the middle of the thirteenth century a crusader document of Acre throws additional light on exports from this great emporium. Some of the articles listed as taxable seem to have been destined to provision ships and were not necessarily intended for Europe. For example, salt fish from Egypt or products of local fishing, chickens, turkeys, geese and also probably olives, asparagus, apples, pears, quinces – all to be had in Europe – appear in the customs tariff. Among manufactured articles we find silk, cotton, thread of Damascus, lac, linen, buckram, ivory, local pottery, beams and rafters (probably exported to Egypt) and in addition saddles and belts. Naturally enough, onions (perhaps the famous shallots of Ascalon), prickly pears (çabar – figues de Barbarie), dates, sesame, almonds and the like might have been exported or supplied to the ships sailing from Acre. The major part of the tariff deals with 'spices', perfumes and dyes. We find liquorice, alum, frankincense, cardamom, ammoniac, orpinent, root of camphor, cinnamon, emery, aloe, clove, nutmeg, musk, nuts, several types of sugar, lavender, myrobolan, ginger, aspic and clove (gillyflower).

All sources from the middle of the twelfth to the second half of the thirteenth century indicate that the place of the crusader kingdom in the web of international commerce should not be underestimated.

---

[106] £100 of Marseilles were usually counted as 250 besants, sarraccenats. This was undoubtedly not the real exchange rate, but represented loans with high interest.

[107] M. Balard, 'Les Génois en Romanie entre 1204 et 1261', Mélanges d'arch. et d'hist., École française de Rome, t. 78 (1966), 469–502, cf. Table 2. The author uses the name Ultramare only, without indicating the respective parts of Egypt and crusader Syria.

D   The Cathena

The commercial life of any large maritime city concentrated in two areas: the *cathena* and the *funda* – the port quarter and the markets. The *cathena*, the 'Street of the Chain', included the port installations, spaces for marketing, storage sheds, the customs office and probably the building which served as the 'Court of the Chain'. Cities which served as terminals of international overland roads also had *khans* or *caravanserais*, which fulfilled the same task as the *cathena*. Here customs were paid, baggage deposited and the foreign merchants would take up supervised lodgings. Arabic-speaking clerks, probably oriental Christians, were employed by the director of customs, who received the office from the lord of the city. [108]

Disembarkation was a complicated business. Unlike our customs controls, crusader officials had to pay attention not only to the merchandise, but also check the legal standing of the ship and of the individual merchant. Linen imported to Acre, for example, paid a different duty according to its quality and the privileged standing of the importer. Venetians, Pisans and Genoese paid different duties, which also differed from Jaffa to Acre, Beirut and Tyre. However, all these duties were far lower than those of a native or foreign merchant, not belonging to a privileged commune. Consequently the prices of the same item would differ according to its specific tax. Moreover, port dues paid by ships differed, which was again expressed in the final price of products.

Ships paid two major taxes: the *terciarium* and the *anchoragium*. [109] The first must have originally been the payment of one

---

[108] Ibn Jubair in Le Strange, *Palestine under the Moslems*, p. 331: 'And they brought us to the *Diwan*, which is a khan prepared as the halting place of caravans. Before the gate is a carpeted platform on which sit the secretaries of the *Diwan* on the part of the Christians, before desks of ebony ornamented with gold work. These write in Arabic and talk the language also, and their head is the *Sahib el-Diwan* [Chief of the Customs], and they take not of all that passes before them.'

[109] E.g. in the privilege granted by Jean d'Ibelin, Lord of Beirut, to Genoa in 1223: 'Omnia uasella ianuensium . . . magna et parua sunt liberi et immunes de terciaria et de ancoragia.' *Liber Iurium*, I, 687.

third, but it is not clear of what, possibly of the transportation costs. Though this seems rather high, we find the authorities of Marseilles collecting from ships' captains a third of the pilgrim fares to the Holy Land.[110] This tax is very often among the exemption rights of a commune.

The *terciarium* led to frequent quarrels between the city authorities and the privileged commune. The original agreement with the Venetians, the *Pactum Warmundi*, of 1123 stipulated that the Venetians would pay the tax on pilgrims coming to or leaving the country. They were recompensed by a yearly treasury grant of 300 besants from the market of Tyre, and later from that of Acre. Yet in 1244 the Venetians claimed that they should pay the tax for returning pilgrims only.[111] The same tax is found in Antioch as *tertienaria* and a privilege granted by Bohemond in 1200 to Pisa reduced it to a half of the normal payment. In Tripoli the Genoese were exempted from the payment, excluding the transport of pilgrims.[112]

Related to this tax on transport was the *anchoragium*, which as the name states was a port due.[113] Another tax whose meaning and purpose escapes us was called '*carates*' and it has been argued that this meant one twenty-fourth of the cargo's value.[114]

Only when the two major taxes were paid did the real customs haggling begin. A modern reader, perusing the privileges enjoyed in Acre by different nationals may wonder if anybody paid 'normal' taxes at the *cathena* or elsewhere. The situation is reminiscent of buying a railway ticket in modern Italy, Greece or even France. It is always a hilarious experience to see the local commuters approaching the counter with a small pile of documents claiming

---

[110] Statute of 1288, quoted by Ch. de la Roncière, *Histoire de la marine française*, 280, n. 5.

[111] Tafel-Thomas, I, 86; *ibid.*, 141; *ibid.*, II, 397.

[112] Müller, 80 and cf. the confirmation of 1216, *ibid.*, 90. See the privilege of Bertrand of Tripoli to Genoa in 1109, *Liber Iurium*, I, 18.

[113] Cf. the privilege granted by Jean d'Ibelin, Lord of Beirut, to Venice in 1221, Tafel-Thomas, II, 231; cf. the confirmation of 1222, *ibid.*, 232, where the tax is not mentioned.

[114] The privileges of Venice in Antioch, Tafel-Thomas, I, 102, 134, 148. Müller, 80: 'De quirato commercii' – payment of 2% of the value. Cf. *ibid.*, 90. and Cl. Cahen, *op. cit.*, 478, n.4. We doubt if Tafel I, 134, can mean *charroi*.

exemptions or reduced fares as soldiers, policemen, war invalids, heads of *famille nombreuse* not to count *aller et retour*, season and long distance tickets . . . . Yet this seems extremely simple compared with mediaeval taxation. Almost everybody claimed exemptions for something and those who could not, did everything to break into the exempted circle by oath, affiliation or simply by hook and crook. A cluster of cities around Genoa enjoyed the standing of the Genoese; people from Tuscany claimed to be Pisans; citizens of Provence claimed to be Marseillaises and the Catalonians were naturally Barcelonians. As identification papers were non-existent or rudimentary, sorting out people and collecting the right tax in all the currencies circulating in the Mediterranean must have been quite a feat. No wonder that the communes sent their representatives to the *cathena* to help out their nationals,[115] by proving their identity and taking care that they should not overpay at the customs. Some unfortunates paid full customs duties, as the tariffs of Acre speak about *coutume enterine*[116] a rather symptomatic name in itself. The 'normal' customs duty in Acre seems to have been about $11\frac{1}{2}\%$ of the total value.

Though the early exemptions became limited, the reductions still ranged from total exemption to one half of the normal dues. In Antioch the Venetians paid 5% customs duty on linen and silk cloth and 7% on other goods, but these were reduced in 1153 to 4% and 5% respectively.[117] Pisans at the same time (1154) paid half the usual customs as entrance, exit, sale and buying duties in Antioch, but enjoyed complete freedom in Tripoli (1187).[118] In the kingdom proper, Amalric, as count of Jaffa and Ascalon, reduced the Pisan customs duties in Jaffa to half and there was a similar reduction in Antioch.[119] A series of privileges for Genoa in

---

[115] In the privilege granted by Conrad of Montferrat to Pisa for Tyre 'ponant homines pro velle ad cathenam et fundam et portas civitatis Tyri qui habeant curam de omnibus Pisanis et de his qui Pisanorum nomine censentur aut de eorum avere ad katenam vel fundam vel portas civitatis intranto vel exeundo'. Müller, 26, cf. 28, 30.

[116] *Livre des Assises des Bourgeois, Lois*, II, cap. 242–3.

[117] Tafel-Thomas, I, 133.

[118] Müller, 6, cf. 16; *ibid.*, 25.

[119] *Ibid.*, 8, 80.

Tripoli, Gibelet, Tyre and Antioch proclaims they enjoyed complete freedom from taxes. [120] Yet whenever we have detailed privileges, the picture differs.

It must be borne in mind that exemptions at the *cathena* were merely the first stage of entry into the kingdom (for imports or transit) or the last for exports. To fully evaluate all customs duties on merchandise we have to add the toll often levied at the city gates and in the *funda* or market-place. In some cases the communes were exempted even from these payments and in others they paid, though reduced rates. A good example of total exemption is the Venetian privilege granted by Conrad of Montferrat in 1192 or that granted by Jean d'Ibelin of Beirut in 1229. [121] Here, in addition to the exemption at the *cathena*, it is explicitly stated that merchandise bought in the *funda* of Beirut will be exempted from payments. The goods listed include cotton, silk, cloth of silk, pepper, frankincense, sugar, all spices, indigo, *nerci*, wool, woollen cloth, linen cloth, pearls, precious stones, glass and soap. [122] A contemporary (1223) privilege for Genoa in the same city accords them total exemption from customs with the exception of ceramics (*opus poterie*), wine and oil. [123] On the other hand, Pisans (according to privileges of 1200 and 1216) paid roughly half the dues, personal and on merchandise in Antioch. [124] According to a privilege granted by Henry of Champagne, the Genoese in Tyre paid full dues for imports from Barbary, Egypt, the Moslem East and Constantinople, but merchandise in transit was duty-free. [125] Somewhat similar was the Venetian position in Tyre in the middle of the thirteenth century. Goods imported from Damascus or other Moslem centres paid about $9\frac{1}{3}\%$ and the same was due on Venetian imports. Merchandise in transit through Acre to Venice paid about

[120] *Liber Iurium*, 18, 230, 358, 364.

[121] *Ibid.*, 401, 412.

[122] Tafel-Thomas, I, 233. *Nerci* may possibly refer to bibl. *nerd* which the *Vulgata* translates: *Jasciculus myrrhae*. In the authorised version: spikenard (Cant, I, 12).

[123] *Liber Iurium*, 387.

[124] 'Half the tax called *de passagio* and half of what the Latins used to pay at the Iron-bridge'. Müller, 80, 90.

[125] *Liber Iurium*, I, 406.

$4\frac{1}{6}\%$ and slightly more than 5% if in transit from Venice to Damascus or another Moslem destination. [126]

Though one would presume that the *cathena* dealt only with imports and exports, we hear that Jean de Brienne exempted Syrians living in the royal quarter of Tyre from customs duties at the *cathena* – to the detriment of the Venetians – as the Syrians moved from their quarter to that of the king of Jerusalem. [127]

E   The *Funda* and the Local Market

The fourteenth-century author of the famous *Pratica della mercatura* or *Libro di divisamenti di paesi e di misure di mercatantie* (Book of Descriptions of Countries and of Commercial Measures), Francesco Balducci Pegolotti, found it worthwhile to introduce his subject by some didactic verses:

Mercato in Toscana, e
Piazza in più lingue.
Bazarra e raba in genovesco.
Fondaco in più lingue.
Fonda in Cipri.
Alla in fiammingo.
Sugo in saracinesco.
Fiera in Toscana e in più linguaggi.
Panichiero in grechesco. [128]

There is the feeling of the universal institution of the market whatever it was called in the languages of the merchant community. 'These names' – he continues – 'mean places where merchandise is being sold in cities and castles and towns. All manner of victuals and things needed for the life of men, and grain and beasts. Some of them function permanently, some at certain regulated times of the week or months of the year.' Though the institution is universal it does not function everywhere in the same way. The dividing

[126] Tafel-Thomas, II, 387–8.
[127] *Ibid.* 384–5.
[128] *Op. cit.*, 17.

line is that between permanent and seasonal markets. Pegolotti put his finger on one of the major characteristics of the crusader market, namely its permanency.

Every crusader city had a commercial centre serving foremost the needs of the local inhabitants. This was known as the *fonde* (L. *funda*) and the actual area was sometimes described as *plathea* or *ruga*, which corresponds to *piazza* and *rue* in modern languages. The former was a square of irregular shape bounded by buildings, the latter a narrow passage between houses whose lower floors were taken up by shops (*bothegae* or *stationes*) and stalls (*banci*) leaning against the walls. The upper floors served as living quarters and magazines (from Arab. *makhzan*) of the merchants and crafts-men.[129] Some of the narrow streets were vaulted against sun and rain, others had cloth awnings, to be used or removed according to season.

In common with European markets, those of the crusaders specialized in certain wares and products. One peculiarity was markets established according to the ethnic or religious origin of the merchants. Moreover, the political structure of the city was often responsible for a multiplication of commercial centres, according to the fiscal interests of different powers.

Most local commerce dealt in victuals and the products of local craftsmanship. Bulk comestibles, like cereals, oil, wine and vege-tables (probably because of their volume) often moved from the narrow streets of the bazaars to more open spaces. Thus Jerusalem had a large square immediately to the left of the main gate near the citadel, which served as the grain market of the city. Its location facilitated transport and the collection of tolls at the citadel.[130]

---

[129] A detailed description of the Venetian commercial centre in Acre is given by J. Prawer, 'I veneziani e la colonie veneziane nel regno latino di Geru-salemme', *Venezia e l'Oriente* (in press). The names of the different installations can be studied in the inventories of Marsiglio Ziorzi for Venetian Acre in Tafel-Thomas, II, 351–89, and in the Genoese inventories in *Archives de l'Orient latin*, II, 215–21.

[130] *La citez de Iherusalem*, 34: 'là ù on vent le blé'. Cf. *Cont. de Guillaume de Tyr*, 146 (*Itinéraires à Jérusalem et descriptions de la Terre Sainte*, ed. H. Michelant et G. Raynaud, Geneva, 1882). See the privilege of Baldwin II in 1120 abolishing customs on victuals, *Cartulaire du Saint Sépulcre*, ed. E. Rozière, 83–5.

The second and most picturesque commercial centre in Jerusalem was the bazaar. Fruit and spices, smaller in volume and more expensive per unit, had their special market in one of the three parallel and main divisions of the bazaar, in the vaulted *Rue des Herbes*. 'Here' – we are told – 'is sold all the fruit of the city and the herbs and spices.' The 'Street of Herbs' ran into the 'Fish Market' which then turned into a piazza, the 'Poultry Market', where one could buy poultry, eggs, cheese and birds.[131] The other divisions of the bazaar were taken up by the 'Street of the Cooks' (*Malcuisinat*) and textile vendors.[132] This second complex was located near the Church of the Holy Sepulchre at the crossing of the two main city streets (north-south and east-west). The third centre was near the Temple area, in the vicinity of the Wailing Wall. Here was the '*Boverie*' or 'Cattle Market' (which as always in the Near East had more sheep than oxen) and nearby the butcheries and tanneries of the city.

Jerusalem's commercial centres were not necessarily established by the crusaders and there is reason enough to suppose that they existed on the eve of the Crusades.[133] The oriental Christians may have preserved and transmitted the topographical traditions of the city to its new conquerors and colonizers. As the locations were convenient they were adopted by the crusaders, and some still exist to this day.[134]

[131] Above n. 130: 'une grandisme place là ù on vent les oes et les fromages et les poules et les anes'. One should obviously read *aves* which is to be found in one of the mss, *ibid.*, n.t.

[132] *Ibid.*, 43: 'A ces canges tiennent les iij. rues . . . dont l'une des iij. rues a à non la *Rue Couverte*. Là vendent li drapier Latin lor draperie. Et li autre a à non la *Rue des Herbes;* là vent on les espeses; et la tierce a à non de *Malquisinat*', cf. *ibid.* 151, 155. The best description of these markets (with an excellent plan) is that of F.–M. Abel, 'L'estat de la Cité de Jérusalem', Jerusalem, *Records of the Pro-Jerusalem Council*, ed. C. R. Ashbee, Jerusalem, 1918–20; cf. *Jérusalem nouvelle*, vol. 2. On these studies is based the map of C. N. Johns in *Palestine of the Crusaders*, Jerusalem, 1936.

[133] J. Richard, 'Sur un passage du *Pélerinage de Charlemagne:* le marché de Jérusalem', *RBPH*, 13 (1965), 552–5.

[134] The tripartite bazaar continues the crusader tradition almost without change.

Thus Jerusalem furnishes an example of commercial centres organized according to economic needs only. Though Syrian and Latin money-changers had their special stalls at both ends of the bazaar, it does not seem that ethnic division influenced marketing as a whole, though it is not impossible that different taxes were paid.

This was not the only type of market organization. Jerusalem was an inland city and consequently gate tolls and market dues were sufficient to control the whole volume of traffic. Not less important was the fact, that despite the existence of the autonomous patriarch's quarter, there were no exempted areas in the city. The markets and bazaars were royal. Ecclesiastical establishments owned properties, like shops[135] or stalls in the bazaars or the bakeries of the city. This assured rents to their owners but did not exempt the merchants from the normal payment of market dues to the lord of the city.

A similar situation existed also in Beirut. The Ibelin lords of the city did not accord territorial privileges to alien elements, though they were lavish in granting commercial ones. Here again we deal with a seigniorial market in which different goods had their own marketing areas. This was not only the result of the common social urge which everywhere brought together people of similar professions (in many cases the merchants were also the producers) but might have been connected with administrative supervision. This was exercised by the market inspector, the *mathesep* and his underlings.[136] One of their duties was the verification of weights and measures in the interest of public justice and the royal or seigniorial revenues. These seem to have involved two different types of payment: market tolls according to merchandise and merchant, and a fee for the use of measures and balances. In the nature of things, balances and, even more, liquid or capacity measures were only used for a specific type of merchandise. Consequently vendors

---

[135] Two shops in the bazaar of Jerusalem still have the letters 'SCA ANNA' chiselled at their entrance. They belonged in the twelfth century to the nuns of St Anne.

[136] The *mathesep* is specifically mentioned in Tyre. Tafel-Thomas, II, 359. The *cathena* had similar officials, the *baiuli cathene*, Müller, 96.

of such commodities would naturally group together. The weights and measures are a permanent feature of privileges regarding the *fonde* and are usually listed with other seigniorial monopolies or rights of *ban*. The *Pactum Warmundi* lists the Venetian privileges: 'oven, mill, bath, balance (*statera*), capacity measures (*modius*), measures of liquids (*buza*, 'wine skin') for wine, oil or honey'.[137] The right of *ban* which compelled merchants to use the seigniorial measures facilitated the supervision of honest standards, but also assured seigniorial income.

The measures were often farmed out for a global sum, as was customary for other seigniorial monopolies. Thus a detailed inventory from Tyre[138] shows that the balances were farmed out for the very high sum of 1,900 besants yearly and the liquid and dry capacity measures (grain, wine, olive oil) for 310 besants. At the same time we hear about a seigniorial monopoly on the sale of musical instruments: trumpets, flageolets (*zalamellae*), *vocini*, tambours and the like farmed out for 500 besants; *ban* rights on slaughterers and pork-butchers – 400 besants; on glass – 350 besants, sesame oil – 160 besants, fish – 70 besants, lime – 160 besants and wine and milk – 22 and 20 besants respectively.[139]

The use of seigniorial measures was connected with special payments and thus became an object of privilege. In Tyre the Venetians had the right to use their own measures when dealing with their own nationals or when selling, but had to use royal measures when buying from others.[140] A similar privilege was accorded to the Pisans in Tyre by Conrad of Montferrat in 1187.[141] In Beirut a Genoese privilege by Jean d'Ibelin fixed a payment of one *denier* for a jar of Beirut or for two *modii* of grain, but the pay-

---

[137] Tafel-Thomas, I, 85–6. The privilege of Baldwin II (above n. 130) mentions *merces modii consuetudinaria*. A privilege of 1175 mentions another measure instrument *rubus* or *ruba* which like the Spanish *arroba* might be of Arabic origin. Tafel-Thomas, II, 165.

[138] Tafel-Thomas, II, 385.

[139] Other monopolies included the sale of soap, candles, spices and meat, *ibid.* 367.

[140] Tafel-Thomas, I, 85–6.

[141] Müller, 26, 28.

ment was double if instead of borrowing the measures, weighing was done by the official *mensurator ville*.[142]

Economic and sociological factors were not alone in shaping the physiognomy of a crusader city. Not less important were the economic aspects of political privilege. Thus in the two largest cities of the kingdom, apart from the capital, the privileges of the communes and of other bodies created a different and far more complicated pattern of organization. In Tyre the existence of an autonomous Venetian quarter doubled the market area, since besides the royal (later seigniorial) market, there was a special *funda Venetorum*. Each market had its own balances and measures, supervisors and tolls. Each party exercised coercive *ban* rights over the inhabitants of its quarter. This explains the initiative of Jean de Brienne, who by exempting the local Syrians from paying customs caused their migration from the Venetian to the royal quarter.

The situation was even more complicated in the royal city of Acre. Though the *cathena* remained royal, the royal *funda* almost disappeared. In hundreds of documents dealing with Acre, only *one* mentions the royal *funda* and even then so vaguely that it is difficult to fix its location with any accuracy.[143] Obviously, this does not mean that the commercial centre of Acre was insignificant. For a city which counted some 30,000 inhabitants at the end of the twelfth century and probably twice that fifty years later one can assume the opposite. The relative unimportance of the royal *fonde* points to a remarkable evolution which dotted Acre with half a dozen independent *fondes*. Venice, Genoa and Pisa had their own market-places inside their quarters and were followed by the Provençals under the lead of Marseilles. It seems that the military orders also had their own market-places, since we know from Pegolotti that they used their own measures.[144] Naturally not all of these

[142] *Liber Iurium*, I, 687.

[143] Müller, no. 27 (p. 33). An attempt to locate the *funda* by J. Richard, *Moyen-Age*, 1953, 334–5. It was this *fonde* where the newly arrived pilgrims massacred the Moslem peasants in 1290. The place was near the *cambium* or *change*. Marino Sanudo, 230.

[144] Pegolotti, ed. A. Evans, 64: 'Grano e orzo e tutti biadi, e noce e castagne e nocelle, si vendono in Acri a moggio, ed è il *moggio del signore* e *della ruga di Pisa* e

market-places offered all the varieties of merchandise, so that functionally different markets did not disappear. But the administrative factor was strong enough to decentralize the economic life of the city. In that framework we must envisage the curious customs tariffs of Acre. Regardless of whether all the non-Latin inhabitants of Acre were compelled to live in a given quarter or only compelled to use a given market – it is clear that a royal *Assise* was proclaimed to assure income from non-Latin market dues, a procedure which parallels that of Jean de Brienne in the *cathena* of Tyre. [145]

The relations between the *cathena* and the *funda* are not always clear. One would assume that the *cathena*, certainly a market and not only customs-house, [146] catered to export only, and the *funda* to local commerce. This is not quite certain. If the Syrian weavers of Tyre were freed by royal decree from a fee at the *cathena* which they would otherwise have paid at the Venetian *fonde*, relations were more complicated than meets the eye.

The most characteristic feature of the local markets was their size and permanency. While this reflected an ancient oriental tradition and its money economy, it was also the result of demographic factors characteristic of crusader society, namely its highly urbanized structure. Not even the nobility drew its entire sustenance from landed possessions. This was partially true of its upper crust only and a relatively small number of lesser knights; others held money fiefs, though these sometimes included prebends in

della ruga di Vinegia tutto uno con quello delle *magione dello Spedale de Tempio*.' One wonders if it should not be 'dello Spedale e de Tempio', namely the Hospital and the Temple.

[145] The claim for the existance of a non-Latin ghetto in 13th-century Acre was advanced by J. Prawer who also drew attention to the legislative aspects of the customs-list. This was opposed by Cl. Cahen who, nevertheless, admits that there was a residential zone barred to non-Latins. This makes it a problem of semantics. J. Richard gave a different interpretation, which we follow here, namely of a market in the interests of the lord of the city, in which non-Latins were compelled to buy and sell their products. This interpretation does not exclude the limitation on the zones of habitation.

[146] E. G. Pegolotti, *op. cit.*, 63 mentions: 'il cantare della fonda e il cantare della catena'. If the buyer does not explicity mention the type of *cantare* it is understood that he means that of the *fonde*.

kind – like wheat, oil and wine. Consequently, the majority of crusader nobles bought their food in the city markets. This naturally applied even more to the burgesses and members of the communes who, with the exception of gardens or orchards, were legally prevented from possessing feudal estates. Thus, the Frankish population as a whole were consumers dependent on external supplies of food without direct command of its sources.

The permanent demand was met by the economic and administrative structure of the country's agriculture. The absence of a true manorial system and the money fiefs which prevented the distribution of agricultural estates created a surplus of agricultural products at the two poles of society. The upper ranks of the nobility and the peasantry were left (barring years of drought or over-abundant rains) with quantities of agricultural products above their direct needs. After filling their own granaries for the year's needs and next year's sowing, the Crown and the noble families with large estates disposed of a surplus, which found its way to the free market of the cities. Ecclesiastical establishments were in a similar position, since all were well endowed with landed estates. Their revenues and tithes covered household needs and filled the granaries, while the surplus went to market. One would hesitate to assume an excessive surplus for the military orders, as the castles were stocked with provisions for a year or more. It was even worthwhile to import custom-free grain from Europe to balance their needs.

The other source of supply was the peasants themselves. Once the rents were paid to their lords, two-thirds or even three-quarters of the crop remained with the peasant. Though not abundant in normal years this left a surplus beyond the direct needs of his household. If an agreement between Damascus and Jerusalem regarding the north-eastern 'Terre de Sueth' could stipulate that the Frankish lords and Damascus will each have one-third of the crops, the remaining third must have been sufficient to sustain the local peasantry. This is not more than circumstantial evidence, but it surely points to the fact that a peasant family which disposed of two-thirds could sell a sizeable amount. Naturally grain had to be hoarded for future sowing and bad years would bring peasants to the verge of bankruptcy and the need to borrow seed grain from their overlord. Thus the food supply of an urban populace was met by an almost free flow from the estates of the nobility from the non-manorial villages. This is the framework of the economic difficulties of the Second Kingdom. Except for short periods the kingdom was restricted to a narrow strip along the coast. This was not more than one-third or even less of the former state, without counting the Negev (beyond Hebron there was little if any agriculture) and the *Terre d'Oultre-Jourdain*. Even statistics do not sufficiently emphasize the problem of food supply. The territorial losses of the kingdom in the wake of Hittin were overwhelmingly agricultural areas, with only one great city, Jerusalem, and three smaller urban centres: Nablus, Tiberias and Nazareth. Though these were lost, part of their populations survived and migrated with Saladin's consent first to Tyre and then, after the Third Crusade, to other urban centres. Thus the cities on the coast did not lose their population. Moreover, immigration concentrated in these centres only. This further urbanized Frankish society and aggravated the position of a people depending for its food on a narrow strip of arable land along the coast. Demand remained constant while supply diminished almost catastrophically. Neither nobility, nor ecclesiastical establishments could market the products of their diminished estates, and there was much truth in the complaint of Jean, lord of Beirut, that he had to fortify his city from the income of his Cypriot estates.[147] The Frankish population in the cities of the coast, who could hardly supply their needs from the former territories of the kingdom, depended more than ever on the local peasantry in the eastern part of the country, now under Moslem domination. We are unable to determine the nature of the relations between the two parts of the former kingdom, but we can certainly assume that they were far more tenuous than during the First Kingdom. Clearly enough, the crusader cities had now often to rely on food imported from Cyprus, Armenia and Europe.[148]

---

[147] *Les Gestes des Chiprois*, 41–2.
[148] E.g. from Marseilles, 1244–9, Delaville le Roulx, *Cartulaire*, II, 615; from Pisa in 1202 (to Tripoli), Müller, 83.

XVII

THE ARTS

A   Ecclesiastical Architecture

A pilgrim from the West making his way from Acre to Jerusalem or towards Nazareth seven hundred years ago, might have felt the exotic nature of the land when passing Moslem villages. But upon approaching the cities, familiar features undoubtedly recalled home, despite the flat Eastern skyline broken only by glittering domes and the tall silhouettes of minarets. Strange indeed were the dry and staccato prayer calls of the oriental Christians and the mournful voice of the *muezzin*, but these alien sounds were diluted by the ringing of church bells. Though the walled cities, the mighty fortresses and citadels were cast in alien forms, churches, monasteries and chapels were reminiscent of Europe, familiar as the Latin clergy and the daily liturgy.

Until our time, there was never a period in the long history of the Holy Land that witnessed such a feverish outburst of building as in the crusader kingdom. Not even Herod built as much. The reasons for the tremendous urge to build were complex, but basically, the mass movement from the West determined the rhythm and scope of construction. There was little need to build private dwellings, since expulsion of the former inhabitants left the cities empty and the new conquerors could hardly manage to fill the void. Public buildings presented a different problem. Many mosques and palaces became churches and residences of the nobility, but more were needed, and the warriors, pilgrims and settlers re-created their former environment on a monumental scale. Churches, monasteries, citadels and fortresses provided an outer shell, while sculpture, painting and mosaics enhanced the functional and beautified the commonplace.

As mentioned elsewhere, fortifications constituted the most striking and conspicuous achievement of *Outremer*, but here we shall concentrate on non-military architecture.

The churches and monasteries built, restored or converted to ecclesiastical use reflected the spiritual needs of the new society.[1] There was first of all the demand for church services by a basically religious population. Every crusader settlement postulated a parish church. In addition the kingdom's hierarchy – too numerous for a relatively poor country – but bound by weight of tradition and history, distributed bishoprics and founded cathedral churches according to the ancient Byzantine divisions. Moreover, the military orders: Hospitallers, Templars, Teutonic Knights and the Knights of St Lazarus had their own churches or chapels. A similar position was enjoyed by the communes. Their quarters were enclaves in the parish administration administered by a national clergy appointed by their own metropolitan hierarchy. We have a long list of churches built according to the pattern of crusader settlements and a large number whose construction was based on the specific institutional organization of the kingdom. In addition, a great number of ecclesiastical buildings arose due to what we have called 'The Holy Geography of the Holy Land'. Connected with the traditions of the Old and New Testaments or of the Apocrypha, many locations were newly sanctified and boasted at least a chapel, if not a church, where pious pilgrims might pray and gather indulgences. Communities of regular clergy and of the monastic orders also established themselves in the Latin kingdom: Benedictines, Cluniacs and Premonstratensians among the older congregations; Franciscans and Dominicans

---

[1] The earliest modern study of ecclesiastical architecture is the old but still useful book by M. de Vogüe, *Les églises de la Terre Sainte*, Paris, 1860. The standard study of the subject is C. Enlart, *Les monuments des croisés dans le royaume de Jérusalem. Architecture religeuse et civile*, 2 vols, Paris, 1925–28. See also: T.S.R. Boase, 'The Arts in the Latin Kingdom of Jerusalem', *Journal of the Warburg Institute*, 2 (1938/9); P. Deschamps, *Terre Sainte romance*, Paris, 1960. F.M. Abel, *Jérusalem nouvelle*, Paris, 1926.

among the more recent; some new congregations like the Carmelites, the Order of the Holy Spirit, the Nuns (Repentant) of St Mary Magdalen etc.

It is clear that the number of churches in the crusader period far exceeded the needs of even a pious population. Although we cannot estimate the total number of ecclesiastical buildings, some data may provide a fair illustration of their profuseness. In the Latin kingdom proper there were about a hundred crusader settlements. This includes cities, villages, castles and smaller fortifications, as well as some isolated monasteries. In comparison, we know for certain that the city of Acre alone had some forty churches, Jerusalem thirty and Tyre sixteen. These numbers (not including chapels), taken from the acts and deeds of the period, certainly represent only a small fraction of the total.

The size and splendour of crusader churches in no way matches their numbers. With one or two exceptions, these churches were quite modest by contemporary European standards. Only the Church of the Holy Sepulchre and the church of the Nativity, the 'Temple of the Lord' and the 'Temple of Solomon' could be called magnificent; but of those cited, that in Bethlehem was Byzantine. The 'Temple of the Lord' and the 'Temple of Solomon' were the former mosques of 'Omar and al-Aqsa. The crusader-built churches of Tripoli and Tortosa were large, but located beyond the kingdom's boundaries. Perhaps the very proliferation of church buildings determined their proportions. The cathedral churches of Jerusalem, Nablus and Acre (the latter, the church the Holy Cross, disappeared entirely) were large and brilliant; but the same cities housed many small chapels serving parishes, monasteries or Italian communities. The desire to display status (as with the military orders) vied with the real needs of a congregation in determining the size and the sumptuousness of its church.

Most ecclesiastical crusader buildings belong to the twelfth century, i.e. to the First Kingdom. The thirteenth century saw a good number of repairs and restorations in the wake of re-establishment. Although the crusaders held all the maritime cities in the thirteenth century, they do not seem to have built new churches.

New churches may have been built in the capital, Acre, as for example in the new suburb of Montmusard beyond the old walls.

Yet, even in the twelfth century, the period of actual construction can be narrowed down to some fifty years. Except for castles and fortifications, little building took place before *c.* 1125, during a period of almost chronic warfare when the very poor young kingdom struggled for existence. Only in the second quarter of the century was there time and money to build, and this activity went on for some three generations up to the disaster of Hittin in 1187.

Ecclesiastical and civil architecture thus falls almost entirely into the Romanesque period. Early Gothic was already creating its marvels in Europe, but its influence on the Holy Land seems to have been slight. It certainly came into prominence in the thirteenth century, but by then the great period of crusader building was over, excepting fortresses. Crusader Gothic architecture is to be found in Cyprus rather than in the Holy Land.

The Romanesque style owes much to the genius of the East, deriving many of its features from Byzantium and its Moslem successors. Whether that influence crossed the Mediterranean or filtered through the Pyrenees, it converged upon France in the eleventh century and created a school of architecture whose major attributes transcended regional differences. How strange, then, that crusader monumental buildings, constructed in the immediate vicinity of Byzantine and Moslem architecture seldom seem to have been inspired by their style. Crusader Romanesque with its oriental motifs was directly imported from Europe, more specifically from Provence and Burgundy. Only the polygonal Mosque of 'Omar was genuinely imitated, though less for its artistic value than for the fact that it became the symbol of the Templars. As such, it was imitated both in the kingdom and in Europe. Wherever the order was ensconced, the polygonal or round church followed.

As a rule, crusader churches were some 35m long (from portal to apse) by 20m wide. The proportion of length to width often varied from that of an elongated quadrangle (2:1) to almost a square, although never completely square. They were usually

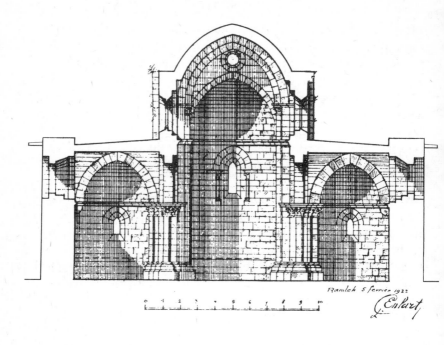

Ramleh 5 fevrier 1922

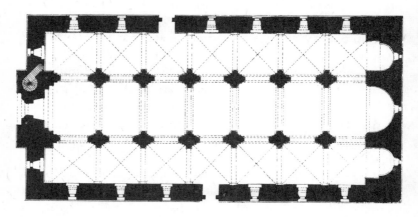

Main nave (above) and floor plan of the Crusader cathedral at Ramleh

of the tripartite basilica type, composed of a nave and two aisles; very seldom was there a nave only. All churches were 'oriented', i.e. facing the east, the nave closed at its eastern end by a round apse and flanked to the north and south by the apses of the aisles. In some places the lateral apses were as large as the main apses and ended on the same line; in others, the side apses are smaller and receding. The central apse, or a rectangle just in front of it, housed the main altar; additional altars were placed in the lateral apses.

Except for the Church of the Holy Sepulchre, no crusader church had an ambulatory. Indeed, one of the characteristic features of crusader churches was the straight wall to the east, the *chevet*, in which the apses are enclosed invisible from the outside. The nave was divided from the aisles by a row of piers, usually massive and cruciform pillars with inserted round half-columns. The piers which form a double arcade running from east to west on both sides of the nave, supported the arches of the nave and of the aisles on their capitals.

The main nave was usually barrel-vaulted and divided into bays by round or slightly pointed arches. Only a few naves had groin-vaulting. This was almost always the rule for the aisle bays. In the walls of the aisles, arches and groins (seldom ribbed) rested on consoles at the height of the pier capitals of the nave. The barrel-vaulted nave and the aisles were intersected by a transept. No crusader church had really projecting transepts. In the land of the Cross, cruciform church plans were hardly distinctive. Only a few churches had slightly accentuated projections and the choir at the crossing of transept and nave was often almost square. The dome at the intersection frequently rested on pendatives accommodating its round form to the rectangular opening beneath it. Sometimes a polygonal or round lantern supported the dome. To the east, the dome joined the half-dome of the main apse.

Church interiors were lit by narrow windows in the clerestory, at the height of the gallery in the aisles. The dome could also have openings and there was often a window in the half-dome of the apses, with a larger one (*oeil de boeuf* or 'lancet') above the main apse.

From outside, crusader churches looked square and squat, an impression enhanced by the fact that the eastern section of the church seldom offered a view of free-standing apses. The apses, imbedded in an obtuse square *chevet*, thus presented a straight wall joining the northern and southern walls at right angles. This squatness was sometimes accentuated by imbedding the dome of the choir in a polygonal drum and strengthening the side walls with vertical buttresses. Crusader churches seem to have been built for prayer and defence.

The severity and crude strength of the buildings is almost always compensated by the western façade, location of the main portal. With the exception of the Church of the Holy Sepulchre, no Romanesque crusader façade could be called sumptuous. But there is a disciplined and restrained use of external decorations, perfectly suited to the building and creating a sense of restrained elegance. In ecclesiastical building, the stones are almost always relatively small, although the lower course might consist of larger rectangular blocks. The material is usually a yellowish or light brown limestone, or a reddish sandstone, that gives warmth to the unbroken expanse of the walls. The plain and smooth dressing is of the finest. The diagonal and parallel lines left by the dressing hammer invariably identify crusader work of the twelfth and thirteenth centuries. The other characteristic type of crusader stone-dressing – square or slightly rectangular stones with a slim margin that places in relief the 'rustic boss' – is almost never used in ecclesiastical buildings, but belongs to the tougher order of military architecture.

A perfect example of a twelfth-century crusader church, and one of the most beautiful in the Romanesque style, is the Benedictine nunnery in Jerusalem, the church of St Anne. The western façade presents a central three-storey rectangular wall, with a slightly inclined and almost flat roof flanked to the north and south by two-storey laterals. The central part of the façade leading into the nave is separated from the walls closing the aisles by slim and slightly projecting perpendicular buttresses that reach the top of the second storey. The façade of excellent masonry is broken by the main portal. Three receding, half-square piers form its embrasure, arched over by graceful voussoirs. The receding arches are plain and only the extrados has a simple lozenge decoration. The tympanum (now harbouring Saladin's inscription which commemorates the conversion of the church into a '*madrassa*') beneath the voussoirs rests squarely on the imposts of the innermost piers.

Slightly less than one course above the portal, a straight cornice of four lines of 'billet' moulding topped by a line of 'egg and tongue' ornament, marks the second storey. Resting on the cornice is a lancet window, one of a continuous series that runs across the façade and the lateral walls. Three courses above it, towering over the façade, is an ornamental window. The bevelled stones of its inner embrasure are enclosed by two short columns, level but slightly detached from the outer walls, and end in capitals with floral ornaments. From the straight imposts above the capitals springs a moulded arch, and above it the slightly pointed sweep of an archivolt with an acanthus relief emphasizing the elegance and simplicity of the window decoration.

The interior of the basilica conveys quiet harmony. One moves from the main entrance into the column-flanked nave that leads the eye directly to the altar in the main apse. The three bays of the nave and of the aisles are divided by almost round arches resting on projecting shafts. The latter are a part of cruciform clusters of square piers, which support, on the level of the arches, the quadripartite groins of each bay. On the side, the arcades divide nave and aisles and the groins of the lower bays of the aisles. The transept is well marked but not projecting, and over the choir – resting on pendentives – is a polygonal lantern covered by a small dome. This is joined to the east by the half-domes of the apses. There is little ornament or decoration. Some corbels of the receding-step type, simple capitals with a geometric design or acanthus carving, make up the whole finery of the interior. This plainness is certainly deliberate as ornament should not detract from the main purpose, prayer and meditation. The lighting is excellent, although it could have been dimmer when stained glass filled the openings. The windows of the first floor let into the aisles the light that streams through the arcades into the nave. The choir has its own light coming from the windows of the lanterns in the dome. Finally, three windows light the apse of the main altar while single ones illuminate the lateral apses. The light falling from different directions, never glaring, always soft and discreet, creates a pattern of shadow on the cruciform piers, arcades and arches that accentuates the purity of design. One recalls, involuntarily, Péguy's remark about the purity of Chartres. This church does not invite mystical contemplation but prayer.

Entering the holy city through its main western gate, the 'Gate of David' (today's Jaffa gate), the mediaeval pilgrim passed the citadel on his right, with the adjoining royal palace. A sharp left turn brought him into the quarter of the patriarch and its great basilica, the Church of the Holy Sepulchre, the most venerated sanctuary in Christendom.[2] Today it takes good will and imagination to envisage the original splendour of the cathedral, one of the greatest built in the middle of the twelfth century. The dilapidated courtyard before the main portals, the ugly maze of adjoining buildings, the odd repairs in unmatching materials and mediocre workmanship, the baroque, nineteenth-century 'improvements' on the lovely Romanesque apses, the steel scaffolding to prevent collapse of the façade all make a venerable relic of a building once endowed with grandeur.[3] For this was what the Frankish architects aimed at when they built the Church of the Holy Sepulchre.

[2] L.H. Vincent, D. Baldi, L. Marangoni, A. Berluzzi, *Il Santo Sepolcro di Gerusalemme*, Bergamo, 1949; W. Harvey, *The Church of the Holy Sepulchre, Structural Survey*, London, 1935; G. Jeffery, *A Brief Description of the Holy Sepulchre*, London, 1919; F. M. Abel, *op. cit.*, in n. 1; K. Schmaltz, *Mater ecclesiarum. Die Grabeskirche in Jerusalem*, Strassburg, 1918.

[3] Since 1958 many things changed for the better. The plan for a common restoration, finally agreed to by Latins, Greeks and Armenians and essentially based on the plan of the mediaeval basilica, is being pursued vigorously. The diligent work of architects and masons revealed the original parts of Byzantine and Crusader architecture which, until recently, were covered by thick layers of plaster. The façade and the main nave are almost cleaned, repaired and restored. It is the central part of the Cathedral, the '*Anastasis*' together with the Holy Tomb, which presents the most difficult problems of restoration.

At the time of the crusader conquest there remained in the area around the Holy Sepulchre two Byzantine churches, repaired several times during Moslem rule (the last time following their destruction by the Fatimid ruler of Egypt, el-Hakim, in 1010). These were the ruins of the church of the Crucifixion and the round church of the Resurrection (*Anastasis*). Nearby was Calvary, the chapel of St Helena, and the grotto of the Invention of the Cross. The daring plan of a master architect combined all these buildings into a vast sanctuary to shelter under one roof the monuments erected to commemorate the Crucifixion, Burial and Resurrection of Christ. Additionally, there was the problem of housing the patriarch of Jerusalem and the clergy which, after the reform of 1114, became an Augustinian chapter. We do not know the names of the architects, nor do we know when the cornerstone was laid. It is presumed that the plans were ready by 1130, and that the whole complex was completed by 15 July 1149 – the day when the new basilica was consecrated and the fiftieth anniversary of the conquest of the city.

From the artistic point of view, the most important achievement was the new basilica of the Holy Sepulchre, although the palace of the patriarch to the west, as well as the cloisters, refectory, the chapter hall, and the dormitories of the Augustinian canons, did not lack artistic merit. The new basilica, erected just before the middle of the twelfth century, is thus a contemporary of Chartres and Vézelay. Although lacking their unity and inspiration, it occupies a place of honour. First and foremost, it was a monument in the very cradle of the faith, a historical repository to illustrate the vicissitudes of Christianity. The Jewish rock-cut tomb, the remains of the resplendent basilica of Constantine, the riches of the later Byzantine mosaics, and the crusader portals, naves and sculptures are the petrified evidence of history. The mere realization of an integral design had been a great challenge. It involved the merging of architectural plans drawn up in Constantinople in the fourth and sixth centuries with plans drafted by the Western newcomers – and executed by local masons and stone carvers. From the beginning this extraordinary potpourri was ill-destined to preserve any sort of artistic unity throughout the

Engraving (above) and plan of the Church of the Holy Sepulchre, Jerusalem

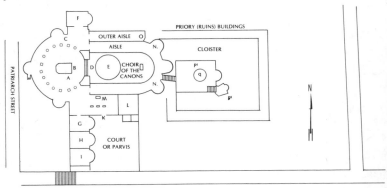

A Anastasis B Sepulchre C Ambulatory of Anastasis D Arch between Anastasis and Canons' Choir E Cupola over Canons' Choir F Chapel of St Mary the Virgin G Chapel of St John the Evangelist H Chapel of the Trinity I Chapel of St James K Great South Doorway L Golgotha M Stone of Anointing N Ambulatory of Choir, with apses O 'Prison of Christ' P¹ Crypt of St Helena P² Crypt of the Inventio Crucis Q Cupola over Crypt of St Helena

stages of planning and execution. Nevertheless, the attempt was made, though the results were far from dazzling.

A visitor from the West who ventured into the 'Palmers' Street' may have thought it strange that the main entrance to the sanctuary was not – as usual in European cathedrals – in the west, facing the main altar. The entrance was from the south, through an arcade resting on five Byzantine columns, and across the *parvis* (or courtyard) one faced the twin portals of the sanctuary. To the right, a separate side entrance led to the porch of the Calvary. The contemporary skyline was curious and resembled a cubist design. In the left foreground rose the high and square belfry with its faceted dome. Just behind to the right (east) was the strange roof above the Holy Sepulchre, in the form of a cone truncated just below the apex. This was the roof over the rotunda of the Byzantine *Anastasis*. More to the east was the dome over the choir of the new crusader cathedral, while at some distance the lantern and small dome of the chapel of St Helena were visible.

The highpoints along the lofty skyline marked the main parts of the basilica. Its western side was the Byzantine rotunda. On the ground floor there were eighteen piers and columns arranged in a circle, which supported a gallery along the entire length. At the centre of this circle was the small and square structure above the actual Sepulchre, with a low entrance to the Tomb proper, a projecting piece of rock covered with marble. Its small dome was open to the conical roof of the rotunda. Beyond the circular arcade led the round ambulatory from which three passages radiated to the west, north and south.

In order to join the ancient church of the Resurrection to the new assembly the crusaders had to destroy part of the elegant round arcade. They suppressed its eastern apse and replaced it rather clumsily with a triumphal arch which led to the new building. The inner circle of the rotunda led eastward into the rectangular nave, whereas the outer ambulatory was metamorphosed, on the north and on the south, into the quadrangles of the aisles flanking the main nave.

From this point to the east, the sanctuary became a Romanesque church. The nave and aisles were intersected by a non-projecting transept and, at the point of intersection, a dome spanned the choir. Here was the famous *Omphalos*, marked by a cross in the pavement – 'the Navel of the World' – according to the theological geography of the Middle Ages. The northern arm of the transept ended in a wall supported by huge piers with inserted semi-columns, whereas the southern, longer arm of the transept opened into the great portals of the sanctuary and the courtyard. The nave, tending to the east, ended in a half-circle sheltering the main altar, whereas the aisles resolved themselves into a new, eastern ambulatory with three radiating chapels.

The belfry seems not to have been included in the original plan of the building and was erected later. The square and massive tower was five storeys high and strengthened by non-salient buttresses, conveying the air of a mediaeval keep. Three pairs of double or triple windows on each floor, resting their slightly vaulted arches on clusters of slim and elegant colonettes, somewhat relieved its severity. This tower had a most peculiar roof. A slightly projecting square gallery with a crenellated parapet ran around the highest floor. From this gallery rose a faceted dome with accentuated ridges resting on a petal-like pattern of triangles. The top ended in a floral pompom.

Reminiscent of similar buildings in Provence and Spain, this odd tower seemed far more oriental than the rest of the buildings. Added as an afterthought, it was not integrated into the sanctuary and masked part of its southern transept, flanking its left (western) portal.

Taken as a whole, the ground plan of the basilica resembled a rectangle, closed at both ends by half-circles, of which the western was almost twice as large as the eastern. Both ends had three radiating apses each, those along the western side being larger than those of the new crusader cathedral. The eastern apses followed the usual Romanesque pattern: a half-circle with chapel and altar preceded by a quadrangle, with the entrance to the ambulatory through an arcade resting on four pillars.

The Church of the Holy Sepulchre is an exception to the normal pattern. Its size and form, with a combination of older buildings in a new assembly, created problems not encountered elsewhere.

The church of the Nativity in Bethlehem and the Temple of Solomon (al-Aqsa) in Jerusalem, were, after all, not the work of the crusaders, though they were partially restored and adapted to the needs of the crusader community. The basilica of the Holy Sepulchre was a unique achievement. The Byzantine element was imposed by reality, though the new was entirely Western. The vicissitudes of this influence have been summarized by a scholar of the Romanesque as follows:

> The masters of the Toulouse school of building drew the plan of the Latin church over the tomb of Christ, but Normandy rather than Languedoc was responsible for its execution. Toulouse gave the ground plan and the galleries of the aisles, but northern France contributed the alteration of the piers, the vaulting and the formation of the upper part of the choir. Then, due to the patriarch Fulk, the influence of Aquitaine replaced that of northern France. To him we owe the façade and the dome. Finally, northern France regained her influence, adding to the side of the Aquitaine façade a northern French belfry. It seems that no northern masons took part in the work, and while the schools of Toulouse are evident in the capitals and cornices, the façade seems to point exclusively to the hands of Provençal craftsmen. [4]

This very learned analysis is certainly exaggerated, though the idea of a mixture of European influences is probably basically correct. The conquerors needed a sense of belonging and this they achieved by re-creating their own environment, however inappropriate. There is much to the view expressed by a scholar:

> In ideal art, i.e. ecclesiastical architecture – the colonial art of the Latins in the East – it became a matter of pride to abstain from producing a possible hybrid and remain as faithful as possible to the art of the homeland. [5]

[4] Quoted from K. Schmaltz, *Mater ecclesiarum*, 238.
[5] G. G. Dehio and G. V. Bezold, *Die kirchliche Baukunst der Abendländer*, II, Berlin, 1887, 433. On the ornamental sculpture of the Holy Sepulchre, see below.

B   Sculpture

Although the ravages of time have bitten deeply into crusader walls and buildings, the destruction is slight in comparison with the almost total annihilation of crusader sculpture. Caved-in roofs, fallen ceilings, or razed buildings buried sculpture or destroyed it forever. That which escaped the hand of time fell victim to the iconoclastic fanaticism of the Orient. With rare exceptions, it is impossible today to find a representation of a human figure in painting or mosaic or a sculptured human figure that can boast a whole head on its shoulders.[6] Judging by the achievements of *Outremer* in those examples that remain, we may conclude that artists working in the East did not create an original school of sculpture; nevertheless, there did exist a lively centre of Romanesque art developed by individuals. Let us add immediately that the artists were hardly Eastern Franks. It is almost certain that they were Europeans, invited by local authorities or, perhaps, commissioned on the spot when they arrived as pilgrims in the Holy Land. Even prosaic work such as stone-dressing or the repetition of a floral pattern reveal art of high quality. The elaborately carved cornices, keystones, consoles and delicately carved capitals were unquestionably wrought by accomplished craftsmen. But one must behold the lintels over the portals of the Holy Sepulchre, the capitals in the church of the Annunciation at Nazareth, and above all the main cornice of the Holy Sepulchre, to realize that these are not only *chefs d'oeuvre* – but labours of love.

These particular sculptures had a providential fate. While the belfry of the Holy Sepulchre, a landmark too conspicuous to be tolerated in Moslem al-Quds, was destroyed, the cathedral was spared and the portals and their lintels preserved. In Nazareth a fortunate coincidence preserved the capitals. One is inclined to be

[6] Studies of crusader sculpture are dealt with in the books indicated above in n.1. In addition: P. Deschamps, 'La sculpture française en Palestine et en Syrie à l'époque des croisades', *Mém. de la Fondation Piot*, 31 (1930). See the recently published collection of studies by M. Barash, *Crusader Figural Sculpture in the Holy Land*, Jerusalem, 1971.

thankful to the twelfth-century bishop of Nazareth, who ordered the burial of the capitals of the unfinished cathedral on the eve of Saladin's invasion. This saved the capitals, which were recovered almost intact, seven hundred years later, at the beginning of this century. They are the finest of the crusader period. Smaller finds, fragments, now in the museums of Damascus, Constantinople, Jerusalem and in the Louvre, as well as some drawings made around eighty years ago of objects that are now lost, can only make us regret that so much is gone forever.[7]

In the following account we shall concentrate on three major creations of crusader sculpture: the two lintels over the portals of the basilica of the Holy Sepulchre and the series of sculptured capitals from the church of the Annunciation in Nazareth. In the case of the Holy Sepulchre we have the whole frame, namely, the façade at the end of the southern arm of the transept; in Nazareth we have only the capitals and must try to reconstruct their intended setting. Although description of the façade belongs to architecture, it is being treated here, justifiably, we believe, in the context of sculpture.

As previously mentioned, the main entrance to the cathedral was situated across the *parvis*, or courtyard, at the southern end of the transept, which ended in a two-storey façade with double portals at ground level and a double window on its second floor. Around these apertures the crusader architects, sculptors and stone-carvers displayed all their skill and ingenuity. The portals and the corresponding windows are almost of the same size when measured at the extrados of the archivolts. But whereas the actual gates take up all the space in between, the upper openings are almost lancet windows, descending from the inner arch to half the height of the

---

[7] About the more interesting fragments of crusader sculpture, see: Clermont-Ganneau, 'Monuments inédits des croisés. La présentation du Christ au temple d'après un chapiteau provenant de Jérusalem', *Revue archéologique*, 18 (1877). Some drawings of bas reliefs were reproduced by M. de Vogüe, *op. cit.* The beautifully sculptured capitals of the newly excavated Caesarea (middle thirteenth cent.) have not yet been studied. A remarkable figure of St Matthew and the comic heads discovered at the excavations of Belvoir (1168–87), publ. by M. Ben-Dov in *Qadmoniot*, 2 (1969), 22–47, were newly reproduced and studied by M. Barash, see n.6.

columns. Yet, the same outer frame of the archivolts, the strongly marked goudrons of the outer, slightly pointed arches, and the splayed gates and windows create a harmonious and imposing whole, divided into two halves by a cornice of sumptuous, near-baroque carving, on which the columns of the upper window rest.

The twin gates are separated by a cluster of five columns. Resting on a cruciform pedestal, the columns ascend to richly sculptured capitals. The outer column receives the goudron decorated arches of both gates, which join in a series of square cushions, whereas two inner columns receive the arches that frame the tympana of both gates. There may have been a trumeau between the two gates. According to a German pilgrim Theodorich (1172):

> Outside the gate of the church (covered with solid bronze), in the space between the two doors, stands the Lord Christ in a saintly garment, as though just risen from the dead, while Mary Magdalene lies prostrate at His feet, but not touching them. The Lord holds out towards her a scroll containing these verses (in Latin): 'Human, wherefore weeps't thou, kneeling unto Him thou seekest dead? / Touch Me not, behold Me living, worthy to be worshipped.'[8]

Whether this piece of statuary served as a trumeau or stood detached from the columns of the portals is difficult to ascertain.

Beginning at the capitals, the observer is well rewarded by the view of their sumptuous, carved foliage, acanthus leaves overhanging the columns and simpler scroll carvings at the top. Above the projecting square impost of delicately carved leaves and a line of 'bead and reel' pattern, the eye reaches the two marble lintels of the doors surmounted by the tympana, empty today, but once resplendent with mosaics. The two lintels[9] differ in style and subject in the most remarkable way. This dissonance, for which no explanation can be given, upsets the harmony of the common

---

[8] Theodorich in *PPTS*, V, 19.

[9] The lintels were removed for reasons of preservation and can be admired today in the Rockefeller Museum in Jerusalem. Cf. M. Piccirillo, 'Basilica del Santo Sepolcro e Lintelli medioevali del Portale', *Terra Santa*, 45 (1969), 106–17; A. Borg, 'Observations on the Historical Lintel of the Holy Sepulchre, Jerusalem', *Journal of the Warburg and Courtauld Institutes*, 32 (1962), 25–40.

sculptured decor of the portals.[10] Clearly, the artists who sculpted them treated entirely different subjects and belonged to two different schools. As the portals exist today, and as they existed in the crusader period, the difference is singularly disconcerting. One is almost tempted to ask: was not, perhaps, the original conception of the portals that of a triple, and not of a double, gate? In this case the lintels of the side gates could present the flowery arabesque decoration that so well accords with the sculpture of the capitals, the imposts and the archivolt, forming a naturally harmonious frame for the figured lintel of the central gate. Did the square, heavy tower of the belfry, which intrudes to the left of the façade, prevent the execution of this plan?

The two lintels cannot be dated precisely. Not being directly connected with the structure, they could have been executed any time between *c.* 1130 and the conquest of Saladin in 1187. As it happens, no crusader 'Itinerary' (i.e. description of the Holy Land), usually so preoccupied with the holy places and with their internal decorations, ever mentions the existence of the lintels.

The right lintel is a thin, quadrangular slab of marble, presenting a revolving scene sculpted with grace and harmony. The basic pattern is set just below the middle of the left-hand frame of the lintel: a thick tree-branch springs from a cluster of stylized date-leaves. This bough, decorated by a parallel line of tricusped and elongated leaves, evolves in half-circles over the whole length of the lintel. Thus it creates five distinct planes, three above and two below it. Each of the three compartments above the master branch is filled with a triple, ever-narrowing spiral described by a stylized branch spangled with squares flanked by a double line of small orifices. The spiral ends in a stem with an artichoke-like flower protruding from a cluster of four short leaves that holds, in its turn, an open bunch of foliage. Smaller stems and foliage branch off elaborately in every direction.

[10] Besides the studies of Abel, Enlart, and P. Deschamps, see also: C. Enlart, 'Sculptures de l'église du Saint Sépulcre à Jérusalem', *Bul. de la Soc. des Antiquaires de France*, 1923; A. Fabre, 'La sculpture provençale en Palestine au XIIe siècle', *Échos d'Orient*, 21 (1922).

Two vertical, boyish figures and one horizontal figure, their bodies interlaced in the main spiral, fill each of the three compartments. The naked boys hold on to the spiral as if setting it into a whirling motion, and in fact, the three units give the impression of slowly moving floral wheels.

While the first and last panels are symmetric, differing primarily in the direction of the wheel movement (the left one is anti-clockwise, the right clockwise), the middle panel represents several special features. In the frame of the same (clockwise) spiral liana, the vertical figure on the left resembles its counterparts in other panels, but the vertical figure on the right is different. It is a *centaur sagittarius* whose face is turned in a three-quarter profile. The human part of the body is badly fitted to the animal rump (the same peculiarity found in some crusader book illustrations); he holds an arrow and shoots at the siren figure at the bottom. The siren has a woman's head set on a large bird's body and reminds one of the *Kherubim* in some mediaeval illuminations.

The remaining semicircular panels follow the same pattern as that of the triple spiral. Instead of terminating in a down-hanging cluster of foliage and fruit, they swerve upward. The three balancing human figures on each of the preceding panels are replaced by birds. Each wheel has two birds at its upper parts and one at the bottom, pecking at the foliage. The space between the five medallions is filled by tree-branch spirals, each taking up the higher or lower half of the space.

It was pointed out that contemporary Toulousian sculpture and Coptic sculpture used the same type of decoration, which harks back to antiquity: lovers and birds grape-gathering among the vines. Whatever its antecedents, the lintel strikes one as being inspired by classical and pagan models. The boys' haircuts are Roman but strangely enough, the hair falls in a single plait on the neck and shoulders. And although the bodies are not always correct from the anatomical point of view (Babylonian-like gesture of the left hand of the first figure on the right; accentuated breasts of the right figure in the second group), the pose in movement is rendered gracefully as in classical art. It is also rather remarkable that the figures are nude, their manhood not only distinctly delineated

434

but, by coincidence or by intent, pointed out by the right hands of the vertical figures of the first and last panels.

As already mentioned, the left lintel over the portals differs in mood, style, and subject matter. Gone is the virtuosity of the artist of the right lintel. The grace, harmony and rhythm of movement, the exuberant yet disciplined whirling foliage, and the free pose of naked bodies is replaced by a frozen tableau which, generally speaking, shows, if not less skill, certainly less inspiration than that of the right lintel.

The lintel has six panels representing episodes from the life of Jesus, all directly connected with Jerusalem and its surroundings. The remaining story of the Gospels was enacted within the precincts of the sanctuary. The panels present a historical sequence – except for the first two which, inexplicably, are interchanged. The first describes the raising of Lazarus from the dead, the second, Mary and Martha imploring Jesus to perform the miracle. Artistically, these are the best panels; yet, it was the same master who carved the whole lintel, which has a unified style. Some of the figures in the first and last panels (the Last Supper) are almost identical.

The first panel, as mentioned, describes the raising of Lazarus. As the miracle took place inside a house, there is, on the left, a decorative frame of a column, which also marks the beginning of the panel. From the capital, which rests shakily on the column, springs a triple arcade, representing a city. The tops of the arcades have strange, pumpkin-like domes. The springers of the arcades are fitted with interesting buildings, a square two-storey tower on the left, a gate and a round tower, a dome and a top-knot (which strikingly resembles the turrets on the 'Tower of David' as engraved on the royal seals of Jerusalem).

The figures are arranged in three vertical groups corresponding to the bows of the triple arcade. Taking up the whole of the right arcade is the towering, bearded figure of Jesus. He wears a long robe and sandals on his feet; one hand holds an open book, while the other gives the Latin benediction. A crossed halo frames his head and an attendant peeps from behind his shoulder. On the opposite side, four figures fill the first arcade. Lazarus, raised from the dead, is already on his feet, wearing a hooded tunic and swathed in some kind of ligature that one of the attendants attempts to untie. Behind him are two other persons, one holding a kerchief to his nose and mouth; in front a man takes down the slab covering the tomb. Finally, in the middle arcade, are three persons: the highest holding his nose and mouth while his right hand clasps a knobbed stick; next is a person holding up his hand as if to express his wonder at the miracle performed before his eyes; last comes the most successfully carved figure, a stocky man holding his hand to his eyes. In front, a kneeling Martha implores or thanks Christ, while another person helps to move the slab of the tomb and the crutches of the dead man.

The composition as a whole is skilful: the ten figures in the panel are well-placed in three planes of depth and, although the carving leaves something to be desired, the whole tableau is impressive. The figures around Christ wear long robes with triangular or horizontal folds; their beards, either straight or undulating, argue respectability. More interesting figures are the two attendants who move the slab from the tomb. They are evidently servants, as their tunics do not fall to their feet; these are the short tunics of the working man, so often represented in early mediaeval sculpture and painting. They also wear shoes while the others wear sandals. The gestures of the imploring Martha and of the men holding their mouths and noses are well rendered. The usual explanation for the latter gesture is that the men ward off the stench coming from the body of Lazarus. This interpretation is not completely convincing. One person, at least, holds his fingers to his eyes, and it is not impossible that the gestures of all the figures really express grief. Similar nose-touching gestures, to be found in some illuminations and paintings assigned to the Latin kingdom, certainly express grief.

The next panel, chronologically inverted with the foregoing, depicts Mary at the feet of Jesus and Martha kneeling before Him and imploring Him to resurrect Lazarus. The towering figure of Christ in the middle of the panel divides it in two. The figure (the head is smashed) does not lack majesty, but does not fit very well into the tableau; Christ stands on a small globe and holds an open book at an impossible angle. It looks more like an Ascension

A painted glass, probably from Tyre, 13th century

A capital from Nazareth (12th century) depicting St Peter raising Tabitha

opposite Columns of the portal of the Church of the Holy Sepulchre, Jerusalem

A capital from Nazareth (12th century) showing demons threatening the believer, who is saved by the Queen of Faith

Right lintel above the entrance to the Church of the Holy Sepulchre

Left lintel above the entrance to the Church of the Holy Sepulchre

Ivory covers of Queen Melissande's Psalter (12th century)

The triumphal entrance to Jerusalem, from a crusader illuminated
manuscript of the second quarter of the 12th century

scene than anything else. To the left, against the background of city towers, are four persons connected with Bethany. All of them hold sticks to emphasize their journey from the city to welcome Jesus. The patriarchal figure with an Oriental turban might represent Simeon. Paralleling the four figures on the left are four figures on the right, no doubt the apostles, the two in front holding books.

The next three panels are damaged, but fortunately, this lost segment of the lintel was discovered and presented to the Louvre. The third panel on the left is divided horizontally into two: above, Jesus commissions St Peter and St John to find a place to celebrate Easter; below, in the frame of a seven-foil opening, the two apostles prepare the lamb of sacrifice. Then, in the next panel, comes the finding of the ass to be ridden by Jesus on his way to Jerusalem. The penultimate panel represents Jesus's entry into Jerusalem: the populace acclaims him, some climbing a palm tree, some seen among the branches or climbing on each other's shoulders to witness the scene. Above the gate leading into Jerusalem there is a strange decoration. It seems to represent a domed sanctuary with battlements around the cupola and two slender, round turrets ending in small cups surrounded by battlements.

The last scene represents the Last Supper. The triple arcades, as as in the first panel on the left with its city representation, end in an interesting column. A fluted socle rests on a square pedestal and a plaited column (to be found in the tombs of the crusader kings and in some of their buildings). The panel is horizontally divided by a semicircular, cloth-covered table, which clumsily rests directly on the knees of the apostles. They are ten in number, sitting on a kind of dais. A beardless St John is uncomfortably reclining before Christ; the apostles on the right are the same figures found in the resurrection of Lazarus. Judas appears on the other side of the table, his traditional location in mediaeval art. Artistically, the panel is not a great achievement.

There is only one other example of well-preserved crusader sculpture, the Romanesque capitals of Nazareth. If they are at all representative of the sculpture created in the last quarter of the twelfth century, one can conclude that the kingdom lacked neither artists nor masterpieces.[11]

Five magnificent capitals confront the visitor from behind the glass of a shabby cupboard in a dark and dingy room, in the museum attached to the church of the Annunciation. A brand new building in doubtful Italian Renaissance style is destined to become their permanent abode. The new building encompasses in its ample space the remains of the crusader cathedral which, but for the Holy Sepulchre, was the largest built in the Holy Land. It was a basilica to compete with European contemporaries, 248 feet long by 99 feet wide, with three apses enclosing the nave and the two aisles. More than sixty columns gave the cathedral a magnificence conspicuously absent in other crusader churches.

The five capitals belonged, in all probability, to the main, western portal which led to the altar at the eastern end of the church. The largest capital, higher by almost one third than the rest, seems to have adorned a central pier, and only three of its facets are sculptured. The other capitals, octagonal in shape, have two facets flattened to fit into columns which are inserted into walls, and six facets sculptured. Today, when the capitals are not on their columns, one has the strange impression of viewing a *maquette* for a marionette theatre. The stage is animated by a whole world of figures, no less than forty-eight of them, arrested in their movement, telling their tale to the living world.

The common and unifying feature of the capitals is an upper band of decorations. It is a line of arches decorated by square beads and supporting an arcade, which represents a city. The narrow and slim arcade recalls, with its pillars and round arches, a Roman aqueduct. Above the springing point of the arches, a roof, seen from above, throws into relief a corner building, and some superimposed arches hint at another corner building or tower above it. In the largest capital, the central arch is replaced by a double arch, whose springers end in horizontal imposts of a type that support, on both ends, two buildings with ridge and sloping roofs.

[11] The capitals were discovered and studied by R.P. Viaud, *Nazareth et ses deux églises de l'Annonciation et de l'Atelier de St. Joseph*, 1909.

The continuous line of identical arches running at the same height over columns and pillars unifies the composition. It could be an ingenious variation of the continuous cornice in the apses of crusader churches. But the strongest impression is that of the baldaquin-like top of each capital. Under this exquisitely ornate awning were holes drilled into arches, once brilliant in still visible reds and blues, where the artist put his tiny (some 8 in. high) sculptured figurines.

There is not much movement in the figures, but for two or three exceptions, where the sculptor expressly aimed at movement. This he achieved by the positioning of the feet, but more often by billowing the dresses, which appear to be swept by the wind rather than swayed by a moving body. But, as a rule, the figures are in frozen positions: the saints, venerable and thoughtful, their gestures expressively heavy. Flat, vertical haloes rise from their shoulders and tower behind their heads, like huge church plates. There is nothing serene about these sculptures and they hardly induce meditation. In each capital there is an inherent element of tension. The impression is that this was deliberately produced by endowing each capital with a double dissonant perspective which, taken together, creates an unreal situation. While the arcaded city, with hundreds of slim, arched-over columns and roofs is seen from above, exhibiting its sloping roofs and overhanging arcades, the figures are represented as they would seem to an observer looking up from below. Although heads, feet, and hands do not project from the façade of the sculptured stone block, one has, nevertheless, the impression that they lean out to the onlooker, an impression that must have been even stronger when the capitals were some $6\frac{1}{2}$ to 9 feet above ground. Various techniques created this impression: deep hollowing and undercutting of the space behind the heads while the lower part of the body adheres to its background; using smooth, slightly concave disks on a rugged background to represent the haloes of the saints; accentuating the depth of the circular openings at the bottoms of the dresses, which can only be seen from below by the spectator.

The subjects of the sculptures, the tale they wanted to tell to the man who came to pray, to the pious and to the pilgrims, are rather surprising. The major capital, which may have been destined to adorn the pillar between the two wings of the portal or a *trumeau* between gates, represents 'Faith' (or the church) as 'Queen' leading a saint or apostle. The minutely curved, floating dress of the queen with its multifarious folds is rounded about the breasts (alas, the male saints have the same drapery folding, although they boast only one rounded breast). She holds a cross-topped staff in her right hand, while her left clasps the right hand of the saint. The way of the queen is blocked by two elegantly sculptured demons, one drawing an arrow and one behind him armed with a triangular shield and lance. A corresponding pair of devils are behind the saint. One must add that the devils, half rid of their clothes and exhibiting a remarkably moulded musculature, are far more alive than the central, edifying figure. The worst fate befell the saint who, although prodded by two devils, seems very reluctant to follow the dominating queen.

This major capital, with its universal subject matter, could have fit well into the portal of this church or, for that matter, into any other church in Christendom. But the subject of the four other capitals conveys a very strange feeling. They deal consecutively with St Thomas and Jesus; St Peter, the miraculous draught, St Peter and Tabitha; the apocryphal mission of St Bartholomew to the Indies; the apocryphal mission of St Matthew to Ethiopia, and St James the Elder's denunciation and death. The main theme seems thus to be the apostles or the story of their mission, a rather strange choice given that the capitals were destined for the church of the Annunciation in its traditional location. Surely Christian missions did not preoccupy the crusaders to a degree that warranted their place on the portals of the great sanctuary in Nazareth. One can only conjecture that scenes connected with the Annunciation were sculpted, painted, or made in mosaic in lintels below the tympanum, or reserved for the interior of the cathedral.

A short description of the capitals might be useful. The two main figures in the first of the smaller capitals, directly facing the viewer, are Jesus and St Thomas, each in his own apse-like niche. Jesus, wearing a drapery covering his left shoulder and the lower part of his body, raises his right hand to show St Thomas the wound in his side. The raised hand projects across the dividing line of his niche. St Thomas stretches his left hand, which he supports with the right one, to touch the wound. The outstretched hand protrudes from an over-heavy drapery; the other hand holds the end of the gown (all saints seem strangely preoccupied in holding together their garments). His robe is richly carved, forming circles around joints (knees, elbows, shoulders), and ending in an ornate, lozenged collar on which falls, from behind, a soft ringlet of the saint's hair. Thanks to a mannerism of Romanesque sculptors, whereby the shinbone is shortened, the thighs are elongated, and drapery carved to stress the intervening knee – the pose of the figures, especially in movement, is rather clumsy, like that of wading in water. Eight apostles, paired in two niches on each side of two central figures, fill the remaining four facets.

The capital of St Peter represents two different episodes of his mission, each taking up three facets. Facing the viewer to the right is the story of the miraculous draught. The right-most facet represents a small, crescent-shaped sailboat manned by two apostles, one of whom holds a rounded rudder. The ribbon-waves beneath the boat overflow into the next compartment where St Peter is walking on the waves. The next figure is Jesus facing the apostles. The other three facets are taken up by the episode of St Peter resuscitating Tabitha in Jaffa. Tabitha, in a wooden bed (the side of the bed has arches of the aqueduct type to be found in the city above the figures), lies half-naked, trying to rise with the help of the supporting hand of a young man (possibly St John). The muscles of her right hand are strained to express the effort of rising. The breasts are very mediocre in execution. The apostles occupy the last facet of the capital.

Two stories share the next capital, although it is not very clear if each has three niches or one has two and the other four. The first shows the mission of St Bartholomew in the Indies where he resuscitates King Polyanius's son. The king's obsessed daughter is being led by a hairy devil, whose open mouth shows monstrous teeth. The lady in distress is looking to the saint for her liberation. The other facets describe the martyrdom of St James. He is denounced by the high priest Abiathar to King Herod Agrippa. Both of these personages wear ornate cloaks with round, studded and decorated collars. One wears an oddly shaped headgear with a double ribbon trailing behind. Next is the saint, who, on his way to death, baptizes the scribe Josia, although his hands are tied to his neck by a strong cord. Death follows when the executioner heaves his sword over the head of the kneeling saint. Some unidentified persons in the last niche are looking on or discussing the events. Strangely enough, it is the executioner, his legs bare to the knees, who is probably the best sculpted figure. His lifted sword is bent to fit the little vault of his niche, and his pose is more that of a graceful dancer or fencer.

The last capital represents the apocryphal legend of St. Matthew. It describes his mission to Ethiopia where the apostle restored the son of King Eglippus, to the consternation of the local magicians, Zaroes and Arphaxad. The king, his son and the magicians are charmingly composed. The theme then changes and the scene is taken up by King Hyrax wearing a fancy crown. Intent on marrying his niece, Iphigenia, he is opposed by St Matthew, and Iphigenia, on her knees, implores the blessing of the apostle. A group of four, two unidentified persons, one beardless, and two demons vanquished by the saint, fill the remaining two facets.

The sculptures of Nazareth were appreciated by such authorities as E. Enlart and P. Deschamps as examples of the most beautiful Romanesque. They seem influenced by Burgundian models and some of their decor has evident links with Berry. They were undoubtedly executed by a great sculptor, entirely Western in character. The figures that appear to represent Semitic types are found in the Burgundian school. There is nothing more curious than that sculptures for the Annunciation of Nazareth have only one accidental link with the Holy Land, the lake of Tiberias in the capital of St Peter. The roofed buildings above the columns of the city have neither flat, oriental roofs nor domes. One roof resembles a section of the sixth-century Madaba mosaic, but this is illusory. These are the gabled, sloping roofs of the north, above aqueduct-like Roman colonnades. This magnificent sculpture seems to be an imported product, both in conception and execution. Two generations of prosperity were not sufficient to create an artistic centre in the kingdom. In sculpture, and in almost every other branch of art the crusader kingdom remained a colony with a natural inclination to import or imitate the homeland.

C Miniatures and Illuminated Manuscripts

The Roman saying, '*habent sua fata libelli*' (books have a destiny of their own) accurately reflects the fate of crusader books. The majority of the works produced are gone, but happily, not all is lost. In the great libraries of the West, books written and illuminated in the Latin kingdom have been discovered. Consequently, we can now describe this type of art, whose existence was almost unsuspected ten years ago.

Twenty illuminated books have been identified and assigned to the Frankish East. Of these, fourteen are purely religious in content: psalters, sacramentaries, missals, pontificals and French translations of excerpts from the Old Testament; three are universal chronicles; and three are crusader chronicles of the thirteenth century. The preserved books can be related to two great centres of book-copying and book-illumination: the scriptorium of the Holy Sepulchre in Jerusalem and a thirteenth-century scriptorium in Acre. Surprisingly, Antioch, the richest crusader city, is not yet represented, though we continue to hope that works of Antioch, as well crusader Cyprus, will come to light.[12]

Almost all the preserved books are so luxuriously and lavishly illuminated that they must have been destined for an extremely rich clientele. The royal house of Jerusalem, and perhaps that of Cyprus, was in a position to commission such masterpieces, and it seems plausible that others were destined for equally noble houses in Europe. It seems probable that European ecclesiastical

[12] The major and only comprehensive study of the subject is the classical H. Buchthal, *Miniature Painting in the Latin Kingdom of Jerusalem*, Oxford, 1957. While this book was in press, a study appeared by J. Folda, 'A Crusader Ms. from Antioch', *Rendiconti della Pontificia Acad. Rom. di Archeol.*, 42, 1969–70, 283–98.

centres should possess such treasures, but until now none have been identified. A new possibility has now been opened by the discovery, in a most unlikely place, of paintings probably of crusader origin. We refer to a large collection of beautiful icons in the monastery of St Catherine in Sinai. Since only a preliminary study of these works of art has appeared, we have not included these icons in our discussion.[13]

The first impression conveyed by these illuminations, especially those of the twelfth century, is definitely Byzantine. The great historical scenes of the Gospels, connected with the Crucifixion and Ascension, seem to come directly from a Byzantine scriptorium. There are rich golden backgrounds, hieratic figures and Greek inscriptions. However, detailed analysis of the miniatures reveals a different origin. The Latin text of these psalters, sacramentaries and missals is written in a European hand; the ecclesiastical calendar is Western and the miniatures themselves show Westerners at work, diligently copying Byzantine models. The copying artists regarded their models as sacrosanct objects and were afraid to use their own inspiration and imagination. Moreover, their techniques were rather poor and not much can be said for their imagination. All changes made by copy artists in the model tended to lower the standard. Transposing figures in a tableau, changing a posture, pose or gesture, resulted usually in clumsy drawing and unsure painting. The best results were achieved when the artist slavishly followed the original.

One of the earliest products by the scriptorium of the Holy Sepulchre is 'Queen Melissande's Psalter', assigned to 1131–43. One of its beautiful miniatures depicts the Visitation, representing Mary and Elizabeth embracing each other. Their flowing robes, the sculpture-like modelled plaids of their tunics and overcoats, rich and full drapery and the well-rounded figures are impressive. Dramatic tension is conveyed by the movement of the bodies, in the kiss and the warm embrace. The light background sets off the dark robes to advantage, while the lighting of the painting

---

[13] K. Weitzmann, 'Icon Painting in the Crusader Kingdom', *Dumbarton Oaks Papers*, xx, 1966. We doubt whether the icons reached Sinai in the crusader period.

and the dark lines emphasize the spontaneous, almost whirling embrace.[14] But another miniature of the same psalter, that of the Presentation, is frozen and lifeless. The only good drawing is that of the Temple roof, an onion-shaped dome with a short drum resting on a round substructure. The high priest, handing Jesus back to Mary, is fairly well drawn. But Mary, as drawn by our artist, is almost unwilling to take back the child. The outstretched hands of Jesus meet a rather reluctant mother. Her right hand, thumb down, seems to be paralysed. St Joseph, with a sad face, almost treads on the right foot of the Virgin. The prophetess on the right, with the Greek scroll, is a lifeless figure. It has been explained that the artist departed from his model, in which Jesus is handed by Mary to the high priest. Reversing the roles and lacking a model to copy, the whole posture of Mary became distorted while her hands were simply displaced.

The painter of miniatures often used different models which he tried to combine in one tableau and the result was not always happy. Thus, in the raising of Lazarus almost everything is unnatural. The tomb looks like a house in whose doorway Lazarus is already on his feet presenting a rather healthy face. But the strangest part is in the foreground. Mary and Martha are drawn on a pygmy scale at the feet of the Saviour, the two servants are the same size; the badly balanced tomb-slab evidently does not fit the tomb and one of the servants seems to be running away in order to escape from the burden of the slab. The miniature is thus more grotesque than edifying. Evidently the artist copied figures from different models, but never succeeded in unifying them in one composition. At times, copying unwittingly created rather charming tableaux. The attempt to represent the Palm Sunday entry into Jerusalem resulted in a dream-like picture. People exit through the city gate, above rises a schematic picture of the Temple. A fan-like palm tree and a man climbing it are quite decorative. On the left, a fantastic hill represents the Mount of Olives, behind which stands a Roman temple with the statue of an idol! The striking figure is that of Jesus in the foreground. He sits sideways

---

[14] Buchthal, plates, I, 6.

on a donkey so that we can see him *en face*, but the donkey does not touch the ground. Floating in the air, he is rather more reminiscent of Mohammed's nocturnal voyage on his fabulous horse Buraq.

The artist who painted the miniatures for 'Queen Melissande's Psalter' signed his name in the miniature of the *Deesis*. Below the feet of Christ resting on a footstool we read: '*Basili(us) me fecit*'. Although Greek names could have been found among the crusaders, it is more plausible that the artist took a *nom de plume* in order to proclaim his Byzantine apprenticeship, which served him in the manner of a diploma. Or perhaps a common Frankish name like *Rex* or *Rei* was translated into Greek. But it does seem strange that the artist who worked in the Jerusalem scriptorium in the '30s and '40s of the twelfth century and his *confrère* who carved the left lintel of the Holy Sepulchre were entirely unaware of each other's activities. Some of the scenes, like the raising of Lazarus, the entry into Jerusalem and the Last Supper are represented by both, but there is not the slightest trace of any contact. Perhaps it was a case of professional jealousy, although it is also possible that the two artists were not really contemporary. It is however, clear that the miniature painter who worked in Jerusalem did not dare to introduce local colour into his Byzantine models. Except for the dome of the Temple – and even here the dome seems to have little in common with the *Templum Domini* or the Mosque of 'Omar – the background has no relation to the actual surroundings.

It is quite clear that the illuminations in 'Queen Melissande's Psalter' were done by several artists. A series of saints connected with the litany was executed by a different and less skilful hand. Here, again, the painter followed Byzantine models. Artistically, the miniatures are mediocre, a testimony to the superiority of the models and the inferiority of the copyist. But another artist was also at work on the psalter, the man who drew the *Incipit* pages of the liturgical divisions in the text. The initials appear in black on a luxurious gold background, while the text on the remainder of the page is wrought in gold letters on purple strips. Analysis established that these masterly initials derive their inspiration from several sources which, after passing through transitional stages, finally found their way into the Latin kingdom. Thus, a most beautifully drawn 'B' of the *Beatus* seems English in origin. The two half-shafts of the letter are inhabited by a shooting centaur-sagittarius in the upper part and a climbing dragon biting a flower in the lower part. A so-called Franco-Saxon interlace connects the top and bottom of the stem to the bows. These are all good Romanesque drawings of northern Europe, as is the floral scroll of the bows of the letter and the masque that connects them, with the vulture and bird-siren in the upper bow and the stately King David playing the harp. All can be traced back to twelfth-century England.[15] The English models were not the only, and certainly not the direct, source of inspiration. The exuberance of the Romanesque was channelled into a disciplined pattern, a classicizing spirit,[16] which ultimately connects Jerusalem with a scriptorium on Monte Cassino. Another instance of such composite influence is the initial 'D' of *Dominus illuminatio mea*.[17] There is a definite resemblance to Islamic models and, indeed, the two pairs of superimposed squares are found in Fatimid manuscripts from Egypt. But the model did not come directly from the Moslem East. The *hippocampus* (fabled sea-monster with the body of a horse, winged and fish-tailed) at the top left of the letter and the griffins (with body and legs of a lion, wings and beak of an eagle and listening ears) in similar initials come from southern Italy, in all probability through the influence of the Monte Cassino scriptorium. Some other illuminated manuscripts are assigned to the twelfth-century Jerusalem scriptorium, but their artistic merit falls below their historical importance as rare evidence of the art in crusader Jerusalem.

Almost a hundred years later, a magnificent bible was produced in the East. Preserved today in the Bibliothèque d'Arsenal in Paris, it is known as the Arsenal Bible. This beautiful book of excerpts, from a French translation of the Old Testament and the Apocrypha, has twenty full-page illuminations which serve as

[15] Buchthal, plates, 13a.
[16] *Ibid.*, p. 13.
[17] *Ibid.*, plates, 14a.

frontispieces to the different books of the Bible. Their splendour makes them comparable to the famous *Bible Moralisée* of Paris and to the Old Testament Picture Book in the Morgan Library. Internal evidence points to the Holy Land in the thirteenth century, and this magnificent volume could have been commissioned by St Louis during his stay in the Latin kingdom (1250–4). The luxurious execution is reminiscent of contemporary European bibles. Indeed, there is a direct connection. The artist of the Palestinian Bible – who must have worked in Acre – used the European bibles as his model. Single figures and entire scenes, which can ultimately be traced to Byzantine models, were not directly borrowed or copied, but taken from European and predominantly French models which modified Byzantine style.

Two examples convey the magnificence of the Arsenal Bible. The frontispiece to 'Exodus'[18] is composed of six scenes (some of the full-page miniatures have as many as twelve scenes) painted in round medallions that take up the whole page. They describe key stories in the Book of Exodus, beginning with the finding of Moses by Pharaoh's daughter. In front of the palace flow the teeming waters of the Nile, where the princess finds the floating basket containing the swaddled child. Her nude, curvaceous body is well drawn. There follows the scene of the burning bush. God, surrounded by a crown of laurels, appears in the bush on Mount Horeb. Moses, at the foot of the holy mountain, discards his sandals while his flock, represented by four sheep, nibbles at the grass. A striking scene is that of the Pharaoh's army drowning in the Red Sea. The waters are just breaking over the Egyptians, who wear crested helmets and plate armour with surcoats. In the foreground a chariot is drawn by two horses. The horses, one mounted by a warrior, are in full gallop. The whole is remarkably well drawn and was probably copied from a chariot race scene. However, as the racing chariot was copied from a special model, it is not well integrated in the whole scene. The harness is antiquated and does not resemble thirteenth-century equipment, while the horses seem to be floating in the air.

[18] *Ibid.*, plates, 63.

The next picture is that of Israelites crossing the Red Sea escaping from the pursuing Egyptians. Moses is in the lead, his tunic blown from behind by the wind. Next to him is Aaron, who holds a pyx-like box. Behind them come the whole people, men and women leading children by the hand or bearing them on their backs. They walk on dry land while the separated waters of the sea, with fish drawn in the foreground, portray the miraculous crossing. A charming drawing is the medallion at the bottom which depicts the giving of the Law, with Mount Sinai in the centre. God floats in the sky and hands the Tables of the Law to the elders of Israel. The Israelites wear curious headgear, resembling a Phrygian cap.

It seems rather early to evaluate the artistic importance of illuminations and miniatures created in the crusader East. Available material is fragmentary, while the links with Europe and the East need further study. Indeed, there might still be some doubt about assigning some of the manuscripts to crusader scriptoria. Nevertheless, a general picture can be outlined. The artists all seem to be Westerners. Some could have settled in the kingdom, others may have been pilgrims working in the twelfth-century scriptorium of the Holy Sepulchre or that of the cathedral church in Acre, *Sainte Croix*, in the thirteenth century. Style and technique reveal their respective homelands. Northern France, Norman England and Italy seem to be the lands of their origin and the cradles of their inspiration. In a new state born from the chaos of conquest with a rough society of warriors, the arts found patrons only among the better educated and wealthy church prelates and members of the ruling dynasties. The arts were thus influenced by the traditions of Europe, liturgical demands and by the wishes of their royal patron. Whereas Europe remained the major influence, artists coming to the East found themselves relying on Byzantine models. The illuminated manuscripts in our possession were probably the product of royal or princely patronage; and in the Latin East – despite the all-embracing French influence – royalty was represented by Byzantium. Hence the appeal of Byzantine models to European artists, above and beyond the undisputed excellence of their work. The possession of a sumptuous psalter with Byzantine miniatures was a status symbol. If the psalter was really commissioned by or for Queen Melissande (a half-Armenian) nothing could be more natural than to have it *à la byzantine*. The painter's calling himself Basilius might be a coincidence, but this could have been good publicity for a contemporary illuminator.[19] A special apprenticeship in Constantinople is not essential. The library of the Holy Sepulchre – Greek until the conquest – could offer some models, and Antioch remained Greek even after that event.

This fashion of imitating often produced awkward results, but changed later in the century, and even more during the Second Kingdom. Since some links in the chain are missing, we can only suppose that after the middle of the twelfth century, the glamour of Byzantium faded with the loss of political power. Byzantine models were still used, but in a more restrained manner and there is less servile copying. We would hesitate to assume that a native school of illumination was created and perpetuated in the kingdom. It seems more plausible to suppose that illuminators continued to come from abroad, bringing their native models with them. Byzantine and Moslem influences can be found in thirteenth-century illuminations, but analysis proves that they arrived via Europe. Copied and integrated in England, France and Italy, they eventually reached Acre. A specific or particular influence might be dominant in a certain manuscript, reflecting the wish of the patron who commissioned it. Despite all scholarly efforts, it is almost impossible to find much relation between the place of work and the illumination. It is really exceptional to find the belfry of the Holy Sepulchre in the thirteenth-century miniature. Sometimes the dome of the 'Temple' or the rotunda of the Anastasis are depicted. But the Eastern dress, armour and gestures are all phoney. Since Europe had a fixed image of the East, the painter could have catered to his audience. The illuminator was a better painter of exotic camels than of costumes, buildings and the natural surroundings. In this context we recall the peculiar miniatures in some of the French *codices* of the great crusader historian, William of Tyre. Born in the Holy Land and educated in

---

[19] See below, n. 25 and n. 26.

France, he knew Europe and Constantinople as well as his birth-
place. His chronicle is a mine of geographical information and his
descriptions are verbal drawings from nature. How do the miniatures compare with this wonderful chronicle, one of the best in
twelfth-century Christendom? Not only is any oriental element
hardly detectable, but nothing in the imagery points to the Latin
kingdom. The paintings are those of a France, which happens to be
located in *Outremer*. The stained glass windows once in St Denis,
as well as some twelfth-century European frescoes depicting battle
scenes between crusaders and Infidels are a far more reliable mirror
of the East than the miniatures painted in the Latin kingdom.

In the realm of illuminations we once again encounter the
phenomenon already observed in ecclesiastical architecture and
sculpture. The creative artist shut his eyes to his surroundings.
Free of the overwhelming Byzantine superiority, he followed in
the footsteps of his homeland. The Holy Land can hardly be said
to have developed an art that could easily be identified as local in
origin.

D   Mosaics, Paintings and
the Minor Arts

Time gnawed at crusader architecture and sculpture, accidents of
history scattered the illuminated manuscripts, but negligence,
fanaticism and sectarianism doomed the obviously rich artistic
heritage of murals and mosaics. What remains is proof enough
that Byzantium found a worthy heir for two hundred years.
By supplementing surviving examples with contemporary accounts, we can visualize the lost treasures. Nothing could be clearer
than a description (1212) by the German imperial envoy to the Latin
East, of the Ibelin palace at Beirut:

> In one of those towers, newly constructed (in the city walls) we saw
> a most beautifully decorated palace, which I intend, as far as I can, to
> describe to you briefly. It is strongly built in a well-chosen place. On
> one side there is the sea with its trafficking ships, and on the other

there are meadows, orchards and most pleasant surroundings. Its pavement is made of marble, which imitates water moved by a light breeze. And this is done so subtly that whoever treads on it feels as if he were wading, marvelling at not leaving any impression on the depicted sand. The walls are entirely covered by marble slabs in which ingenious work wrought various vases. The ceiling is so appropriately painted in the selfsame colour of the air that you seem to distinguish the floating clouds, here a zephyr breeze, there the sun, the year, the months, days, and weeks, hours and minutes moving in the zodiac. In all these, the Syrians, Saracens and Greeks take pride in the masterly art of an ever-changing marvellous work. In the interior of the palace, in the middle, there is a pool constructed of marble composed of pieces in various colours. . . . They represent a variety of innumerable flowers. When the onlooker tries to discern them, they dissolve and convey an illusion. In the middle there is a dragon, who seems to inhale the animals depicted. He ascends from a crystal clear fountain that splashes water so abundantly that it rises into the air which streams in through a beautifully ordered window and in time of heat makes the air humid and cool. The water that overflows on each side of the pool drains through small openings and brings, through its quiet whisper, repose to the lords who sit around.[20]

Alas, nothing remains today to evoke the luxury of a Frankish palace. The architectural remains of civil buildings are all of the functional type, small houses, streets and markets. In some of the monumental buildings, all of them churches, more of the inner decor has been preserved. But even here the remains are a poor reflection of a splendid original. The description of the German pilgrim Theodorich (*c.* 1172) conjures up the twelfth-century magnificence of the decorative arts in the Holy Sepulchre. The *édicule* of the Holy Sepulchre had:

a picture of mosaic work, that of Joseph and Nicodemus placing our Lord's body in the tomb, with our Lady, His mother, standing by and the three Marys . . . with jars of perfume and with the angel also sitting above the sepulchre and rolling away the stone.[21]

[20] Wilbrand von Oldenburg, 166/7.
[21] Theodoric in *PPTS*, V, 8.

In the Rotunda:

> the surface of the wall ... glows with mosaics of incomparable
> beauty. There, in front of the choir ... may be seen the boy Jesus
> wrought in the same mosaic, but of ancient workmanship, depicted
> in glowing colours as far as the navel, with a most beauteous face;
> on His left hand His mother and on His right the Archangel Gabriel
> pronouncing the well-known salutation: 'Hail Mary full of grace;
> the Lord is with thee, blessed among women and blessed the fruit
> of thy womb.' This salutation is written both in Latin and Greek
> round the Lord Christ Himself. Further on, to the right, the twelve
> apostles are depicted in a row of the same mosaic, each of them holding
> in his hands praises of Christ in words alluding to the holy mysteries.
> In the midst of them, in a recess slightly sunken into the wall, sits in
> royal splendour, wearing the *trabea* (robe of state), the Emperor
> Constantine. ... Also, beyond the apostles, the blessed Archangel
> Michael glitters in wondrous array. On the left follows a row of
> thirteen prophets, all of whom have their faces turned towards the
> beauteous boy, and reverently address Him, holding in their hands
> the prophecies with which He inspired them of old. In the midst of
> them, opposite to her son, sits the blessed Empress Helena, magni-
> ficently arrayed. [22]

Some of the mosaics are of Byzantine origin, although restored or
renewed under Frankish domination, as attested by Greek and
Latin inscriptions. Competing with them were the paintings of
the sanctuary. These are even less known than the mosaics. While
the latter adorned the Byzantine rotunda, the murals decorated
the arches on the eastern side of the cathedral, beyond the choir.
Again we quote from the pilgrim Theodorich:

> The high altar is dedicated to ... our Lord and Saviour, and behind it
> is placed the patriarch's seat, above which hangs from the arch of the
> sanctuary a very great and adorable picture of our Lady, a picture of
> St John the Baptist and also a third picture of the holy Gabriel, her
> bridesman. In the ceiling of the sanctuary itself, our Lord Jesus Christ
> is represented, holding his cross in His left hand, bearing Adam in his
> right, looking royally up towards heaven, with His left foot raised

[22] *PPTS*, V, 11–12.

in a gigantic stride, His right still resting on the earth as He enters heaven, while the following stand around – that is to say, His mother, St John the Baptist and all the apostles.[23]

No less sumptuously decorated was the chapel of the Calvary:

> Its pavement is beautifully composed of various kinds of marble and its vault or ceiling is most nobly decorated with the prophets – that is to say, David, Solomon, Isaiah and some others – bearing in their hands texts referring to Christ's Passion, wrought thereon so beautifully in mosaics that no work under heaven could be compared with it, if only it could be clearly seen; for this place is somewhat darkened by the buildings that stand around it.[24]

What remains of these lavish mosaics is mainly preserved in the church of the Nativity at Bethlehem.[25] (There is, though, a magnificent 'Christ in Glory' in the vault of the Calvary). The remnants in the naves and the choir salvaged from former mosaics – if not exactly the best products of the Byzantine school – are at least instructive in regard to the decorations in major crusader churches. Luckily, a Latin and a Greek inscription provide us with names and dates of patron and artists, as well as the period of their activity. The mosaic painter Ephraim, a Syrian Christian if not a Greek, eulogizes in his inscription the beneficence of Emperor Manuel Comnenus, the patronage of King Amalric and that of the Norman bishop of Bethlehem, Ralph, in whose time he executed the commissioned work. The year stated is 1169. The aforementioned names are, in themselves, revealing, and explain the style of the work and, to a large measure, its contents.

The mosaics in Bethlehem represented an abbreviated history of Christian dogma. They commemorate the great ecumenical councils and several provincial councils, depicting the cities in which they were held and their teachings succinctly stated. This main theme is inserted as a layer into a five-band horizontal

[23] PPTS, V, 13.

[24] PPTS, V, 19.

[25] F. M. Abel and L. H. Vincent, *Bethléem*, Paris. R. W. Hamilton, *Structural Survey of the Church of Nativity*, London 1935; Id., *A Guide to Bethlehem*, Jerusalem, 1939; B. Bagatti, *Gli antichi edifici sacri di Betlemme*, Jerusalem, 1952.

decoration. Facing each other on the north and south side of the nave, the lowest bands represent the two genealogies of Jesus, one according to St Matthew and the other to St Luke. Above them are the councils, topped by a foliage scroll. At this height the mosaics reached the windows, and the space between them was filled with angels. Finally, above them came another band of foliage. The mosaics did not stop at the naves. From contemporary and seventeenth-century descriptions we know that the west wall of the nave contained a 'Tree of Jesse', with heads of prophets in its branches and scrolls prophesying the coming of the Messiah. On the opposite side, the transept's columns preserved crusader paintings, and in the space above them, as also in the semi-domes of the apses, were mosaics, some of which are preserved. The mosaics in this part of the church dealt with scenes from the New Testament.

A description of some of these mosaics may help us to visualize their style and workmanship. The mosaics of the councils of: Nicaea I (325), Constantinople I (381), Ephesus (431), Chalcedon (451), Constantinople II (553), Constantinople III (680), and Nicaea II (787) take up one wall, while the opposite depicts the provincial councils at: Carthage (255), Laodicaea (c. 350), Gangrae (c. 345), Sardica (c. 343), Antioch (272) and Ancyra (314).

There is little beauty in these didactic pictures, but they show excellent workmanship. Possibly the subject was not sufficiently inspirational, since their purpose was to state the basic dogmas of the faith. Two types of pictures represent these councils. Each of the ecumenical councils on the south wall is represented by a double arcade resting on three columns. In each arcade there is an altar or lectern with the Gospels, and above is the text of the council's decisions, while the altar is flanked by candelabras or hanging censers. The provincial councils represented on the north wall are far more elaborate. The better preserved mosaics, representing the Council of Sardica, give us a general idea of the rest. Although the schematic outlines of churches or cities vary, essentially all follow the same pattern. A cross section of a three-naved church serves as an outer frame of the panel and four columns clearly indicate the parts of the building. The nave and aisles are closed in its semi-dome. Beneath the central apse is the text of the teachings, while the whole space of the aisles is filled with a rhomboidal pattern, which seems to be a part of a screen that divided the apses from the aisles. A dome on a scalloped drum flanked by two cross-crowned turrets surmounts the imaginary choir. In the upper part of the smaller semi-domes of the apses are candelabras and flat *ampullae* not unlike flat pilgrims' flasks. Above them, inside the narrow vaults of the ceiling, there are vases with clumsily attached flowers.

The representation of the other councils follows the same pattern, although details may vary. The space between the panels is filled with elaborate floral decorations. The basic pattern is a fantastic tree planted in a large vase, from which several tiers of horizontal branches, stylized leaves or *cornucopiae* rise. This floral centre is sometimes flanked by two slimmer, more vertical floral patterns composed of several vases with geometrical patterns of leaves. 'Wings', a remarkable feature of one of those patterns, replace leaves in the uppermost tier. They particularly remind one of ancient Mesopotamian motifs. Although the pattern of the mosaics on the northern and southern walls is similar, the superiority of the northern wall is unmistakable. Its decorations are more elaborate and richer; the artist even used iridescent mother-of-pearl to provide a glittering effect.

Some of the texts in this mosaic history of dogma have strange characteristics. While the texts of the councils are in Greek, one, that of Nicaea II (787), is in Latin. The reasons are probably the two anathematized Byzantine emperors and the anathematized patriarch of Constantinople. To save the sensibilities of the Greek population, the inscription was composed in a foreign tongue. But it must also be remembered that the decisions of this ecumenical council (the 7th) were not easily accepted in the West. In this sense, the Latin commemoration of the council might be regarded as an expression of the 'ecumenical spirit', which characterizes the Bethlehem mosaics as a whole. The double Greek and Latin inscriptions are a constant feature that appears in the genealogies of Jesus, the names of angels, saints, and apostles.

Another type of mosaic decoration in the basilica of Bethlehem, well enough preserved to give an idea of others that are lost, is that of the doubting Thomas in the northern arm of the basilica's transept. Although the composition as a whole is rather lax, the scene is very lively indeed. The central part is taken up by the figure of Christ with a nimbus, standing before double-winged and panelled portals. On both sides, triple arcades rest on capital-crowned columns of the crusader type with foliage, ornamented shafts, and round bases. Two groups of five persons each represent the apostles. Most remarkable is the graceful, almost classic pose of the apostle on the extreme right, in all probability the young, beardless St John. There is dramatic tension in the central scene where Christ bares his right side, grips the outstretched hand of St Thomas, and pushes it into his wound.

By coincidence, the basilica of the Nativity also guards the best examples of crusader wall paintings.[26] Only a few other specimens are known (Bethphage, Abu Gosh and Tripoli), meagre remnants of one of the arts which flourished in the Latin kingdom. The crusader paintings adorned the round columns of the basilica.[27] Today they are much deteriorated, but the work of restoration carried out some years ago skilfully re-creates their pristine image. The double row of columns that leads from the entrance to the transept, some of them with Byzantine, others with crusader capitals of the luxuriant foliage type, was covered with paintings of the saints. There are thirty-two paintings distributed in an odd fashion on the columns. Twenty-three paintings on eleven columns are on each side of the nave (the last column on the north has two), and eight more paintings are on the columns of the southern aisle (two columns have double paintings). One would expect the northern aisle to have had matching column paintings, but there are none.

[26] The paintings are dealt with in the studies indicated in n. 25. In addition: L. Dressaire, 'Les peintures executées au XIIe siècle sur les colonnes de la Basilique de Bethléem (with colour reproductions by T. Richter), *Jérusalem*, 27 (1932), 365–9; V. Juhász, 'Las pinturas de los Cruzados en la Basilica de Belén', *Terra Santa* (1950), 313–18; 349–53.

[27] See Abel-Vincent, *op. cit.*, pl. XIII.

above St Vincent
above, right St Canute
right Elijah the Prophet

Line representations of the paintings on the columns of the Church of the Nativity in Bethlehem

Below the golden mosaic background, the face of the monolithic columns of nave and transept are covered with paintings.
Beneath the capitals the dominant colour was a pale blue framed
in a red and white border, which served as a background for the
upper part of the saints' bodies. The lower extremities had a
different background, probably a darker red, which has disappeared. The colours preserved are done in oil. The saints are
identified by bilingual inscriptions in Greek and Latin, usually
near their haloes. Sometimes the names appear on scrolls held by
the saints, and occasionally at their feet.

A full list of saints or their detailed description would serve no
purpose. We shall therefore concentrate on figures of artistic or
historical interest. [28]

The long line of saints on the northern row of columns is
interrupted by an unexpected painting, Mary feeding the Child. [29]
There is no inscription, as the subject clearly needed no comments.
The Virgin wears a long, deep blue tunic and over it a rose shawl
that covers head and shoulders. She holds the haloed and swathed
Child in her left arm, while her right presses the bare left breast.
The drawing is mediocre, and the figure with its slightly inclined
head frozen. The folds of the drapery are badly done. The decorative elements are the cushion, the acanthus-decorated throne and
the carpet on which the black-shod feet of the Virgin rest.

Among the saints, Stephen is accorded a more elaborate treatment. There is a Latin inscription on both sides of his haloed head.
The Greek inscription, like all the others around the paintings of
the saints, is remarkable in that some of the letters ('A', 'S', 'E')
are not really Greek, but a copy of the corresponding Latin. The
latest student of the painting, P. Juhász, remarks that the head of
the saint is drawn in a special way. Seen from below, the saint
seems to be looking down, whereas from above, the head and gaze
are entirely frontal. The saint wears a very long tunic with a unique
collar. The ends of the fringed stole are seen above the sandals.

[28] Fullest reproduction in Bagatti, *op. cit.*, 96ff.
[29] *Ibid.*, 97, fig. 23 and V. P. S. Sandoli, 'Il piu antico tipo di Madonne allat-
tante della Palestina', *Terra Santa*, 25 (1950), 302–4.

Most visually commanding is the richly embroidered dalmatic. Its collar, hem and sleeves have a pearl-studded border with some larger precious stones. Two geometrically decorated strips emphasize the front of the dalmatic, which is lavishly decorated. Round medallions harbour white eagles with spread wings and little flowers in the quadrangular spaces between the medallions. The saint holds a floriated cross in his right hand, while his left, with the maniple, holds a richly bound book.

The painting of Elijah and the ravens[30] is a rather exceptional one in the series. The Greek inscription reads simply: 'St Elijah', while the Latin has a clumsy verse: 'Food each day brings the raven with its mate to Elijah.' Contrasting with the usually blank backgrounds, Elijah sits in a field with flowers near a river and a mountain is seen in the background. He wears a blue tunic and a rose mantle. His pose is that of meditation; his right hand rests on his knee and supports his head, which turns to the two ravens that come from the upper right with flat, crossed breads.

A painting of the Virgin with the Child and three praying figures is important for several reasons. A far better work than the Virgin feeding the Child, it represents the Virgin and the Child who embraces the Virgin's neck. The position of the Child is more natural, as is the softly folding drapery of the blue tunic and the rose mantle. On both sides of the Virgin are praying figures, a young man on the left, two girls on the right. Most intriguing are the Latin inscriptions. Above the head of the Virgin we read: 'Son, Thou who art God, I pray to have pity on those.' Then comes a very abbreviated indication of the date, which, when deciphered, reads: 'In the year 1130 of the Incarnation, 8th indiction, 15th of May', which means that this painting was done under Baldwin II, more than one generation before the mosaics, which belong to the period of King Amalric. At the bottom there is a Latin verse: 'Heavenly Virgin, confer solace on the sad.' And on both sides two mysterious letters, 'W-A', no doubt the signature of the painter.[31]

---

[30] Bagatti, *op. cit.*, 101, fig. 28.
[31] Hamilton, *op. cit.*, 79, fig. 14; Bagatti, *op. cit.*, pl. 36, fig. 62–3.

For their historical interest, we should also mention the two rather unexpected paintings of royal saints: King Olaf of Norway and King Canute of Denmark.[32] They wear round crowns and ample fur-lined mantles held together by a clasp on the breast. The left hand rests on an oblong, short shield with a jewelled cross in the centre, while the right holds a spear.

It is obvious that the column paintings of Bethlehem were never conceived as a series. The saints and madonnas were probably painted as commissioned by donors. The saints of East and West, Scandinavia and the Italo-Normans represent national preferences. The paintings can be safely assigned to the twelfth century, although in one case only is the date expressly stated (1130). The painters seem to be Westerners, but some of their technique is Byzantine, and it is possible that some were local Christians who followed Byzantine traditions in their paintings. Thus, both the artists and the subject matter of their paintings reflect a meeting of cultural currents.

Only a few examples testify to the quality of the minor arts in the Latin kingdom. Much has disappeared completely. Such was the fate of the goldsmith work, which to judge by the number of people who bore the title *aurifaber*, must have been abundant. The shock caused by the bejewelled Frankish prelates in the West conveys the inclination of the crusader nobility to adopt oriental extravagance. Other crafts, such as stone-carving, are fairly well represented. Surviving tombstones provide us with a convenient model.[33] Engraving is represented by the surviving seals of kings, nobles, institutions and private persons, not to mention the numerous coins. Whether we seek artistic merit or the skill of the craftsman, we find little that is worthy of comment. Funeral inscriptions, seals and money all follow Western patterns and, generally speaking, are of lower quality than those of contemporary Europe.

[32] Bagatti, *op. cit.*, 100, fig. 26.
[33] A good example of epitaph carving is an Acre tombstone of 1290, preserved in the city museum. It is in all probability the tombstone of the last bishop of Nazareth under the crusaders.

In minting – especially of the famous Saracen *besant* – gradual progress can be detected from clumsy and unintelligent imitation at the beginning of the twelfth century to the excellent execution of some pieces by the middle of the next century. But it is also possible that this progress was realized by using local, Moslem or Christian craftsmen, whom the crusaders originally eliminated from the lucrative art of minting.[34]

Crusader ceramics, interesting from the archaeological point of view, are not very attractive, to judge from the remaining examples. The technique and ornaments are those used by the local population and are hardly distinct from the preceding Arab and the following Mameluk periods. The same type can be found in Cyprus and Sicily, and in the Moslem centres of the East. Only specific Christian symbols, such as crosses or figures, point to a crusader origin of the well-glazed wares with their dominant greens and browns. But there are no *chefs d'oeuvre* – at least none were found – to compare with the exquisite beauty of contemporary Egyptian, Syrian or Persian ceramics.[35]

It would be instructive to know more about crusader glass-making and textiles. The latter were exported from Antioch while the former had their great centre in Tyre. There are two beautiful specimens of glasses in Edward VII's Gallery of the British Museum, probably thirteenth-century Tyrian. On the milkish-white glass a painted madonna with a Latin invocation shows excellent workmanship; the other glass bears an unidentified escutcheon.

Ivory carving is represented by the ivory covers of 'Queen Melissande's Psalter'.[36] As the covers are obviously contemporary

---

[34] See cap. XVI, Economic Life and Commerce: B.

[35] A good amount of crusader ceramics is exhibited in the museum of Acre. For a study of crusader ceramics from Château Pèlerin see: C. N. Johns, 'Excavations at Pilgrim's Castle', *Quart. of the Dept. of Antiquities in Palestine*, 1–6 (1931–36).

[36] On the covers of the Queen Melissande's Psalter, see: O. M. Dalton, *Catalogue of the Ivory Carvings of the Christian Era of the British Museum*, London, 1919, pl. XV–XVI and explanations in text.

with the text of the psalter, the carvings belong to the '30s of the twelfth century.

Inside a frame of foliage and geometrical decorations, the upper cover has six scenes from the story of King David. The frame itself presents an elaborate vine scroll. From two vases in its upper border spring two grape branches that meet at the centre in a geometrical interlacing pattern. On both sides there is a fish with a floriated tail and a bird pecking at the base of the vase. The vine stems extend to the corners in a stylized leaf pattern and descend in foliage scrolls, with two centred, geometrical interlacing patterns going to the bottom, where the scrolls end in a flowery design flanked by two symmetrical pecking birds. A rhomboid band on the inside and a beaded band on the outside border the frame of the cover.

The six scenes from the life of David are carved in six round medallions connected by a 'bead and reel' pattern with four flowery clasps. The two upper medallions represent David guarding his flock, killing a lion and chasing away a bear. David, with long hair, a flowing short tunic and a scrip over his right arm steps on the lion's claws and prises open his jaws (more reminiscent of Samson). A bear is running away and a lamb, David's entire flock, is saved. The names 'DAVID', 'LEO', 'URS(US)', 'AGN(US)' are incised in red letters on small tablets. There follows the anointing of David by Samuel. The latter, an elderly bearded man with long hair, wears a tunic and a mantle clasped below his neck; he holds the horn with sacred oil in his left hand and his right touches the head of the kneeling David. On the right side is a gate with the inscription: 'BETHLEHEM', and above it the hand of God touches the horn of anointment. The incised inscriptions read: 'UNGITUR DAVID' and 'SAMUEL'. In the middle row, the medallion on the left represents David and Goliath. They fight in an open field, represented by tree branches. Goliath, in a coat of mail, conical helmet and twelfth-century elongated shield, brandishes his spear over the head of David. In the next medallion, Abimelech the priest hands a sword to David. The lamp hanging from the ceiling, the altar and the show bread indicate the inside of the Temple. Behind Abimelech, who wears a tunic and a hooded mantle, there is another person with the label: 'DOEG'.

In the bottom row on the left the penitent David, now bearded, with royal crown and mantle, kneels before a flaming altar. The wall in the background probably represents Arannah's threshing floor. Above, an angel brandishes his sword. On the right hand, the prophet, labelled 'P(RO)PH(ETA) GAD', holds a scroll with the inscription: 'CONSTRUE ALTARE D(OMI)NO.' Over the head of David is the inscription: 'EGO PECCAVI'. The last medallion represents David the psalmist. He plays a dulcimer holding two sticks in his hands. On his shoulder is a pigeon, representing the Divine inspiration. The upper part of David's body is rendered frontally, the lower part sideways. On both sides are the royal musicians, duly labelled: 'ETAN', 'IDITUN', 'ASAPH', 'EMAN'. Two play differently shaped harps, one a guitar-fiddle, the other a treble viol. The setting is that of a palace with a trefoil ceiling and an arcaded dais at the bottom.

The spaces between the medallions are filled with representations of the 'combat between virtue and vice'. In the upper part are two women, labelled: 'BONITAS' and 'BENIGNITAS'. Between them, 'FIDES' mercilessly stones 'IDOLATRIA', represented by a woman holding a banner. In the lower range 'PUDICITIA' is cutting the throat of 'LIBIDO'. Both ladies have conical hats, fitting dresses with extremely ample and pendant sleeves and girdles above the hips. In the middle, a crowned 'HUMILITAS', helped by another figure, who holds the sheath, cuts the throat of 'SUPERBIA' with a naked sword. The latter is represented by a mail-coated warrior, with sword and round shield, who has fallen into a pit. To the right, 'PATIENCIA' stands by, while 'IRA' kills herself. In the lower range on the left, 'SOBRIETAS', with a banner, clumsily attacks 'LUXURIA'. In the middle a mail-coated 'FORTITUDO' spears 'AVARITIA', who holds on to her sack of money. To the right, 'CONCORDIA' drives a knife through the head of 'DISCORDIA'. Finally, in the lowest two, three non-violent virtues are found: 'BEATITUDO', 'LARGITAS', and 'LETICIA'.

The back cover of the psalter has the same general disposition, but the ornamental frame and the contents of the medallions differ. Although the basic motif of the frame is foliage, as in the upper cover, the pattern is set by two major branches. One creates a double trefoil pattern, two in the upper and lower frame of the cover, three on the right and four on the left side, while the second branch fills the interior of the trefoils, and the empty spaces are filled with leaves and grapes. Between the trefoils and foliage groups of two types there are vine leaves and a poppy-like design. As a rule, precious stones decorated these intervening spaces. At the corners a lyre-like foliage pattern is held together by round bands from which stem the main branches of the vine scrolls.

The six medallions, connected by cable bands, are covered with representation of the 'works of mercy' and the intervening spaces are occupied by animals. The works of mercy, all labelled in Latin, represent: 'Feeding the Hungry and Thirsty', 'Hospitality', 'Clothing the Needy', 'Visiting the Sick', 'Visiting Prisoners'. The man who dispenses all these charities is represented in four medallions as a royal personage wearing Byzantine imperial vestments. The needy man wears the loose tunic of the working man. Four birds on each side of the cover fill the side spaces. Two larger fighting animal scenes fill the spaces in the middle. A hare is at the bottom and a large bird with the label 'HERODIUS' in the upper part of the cover.

Besides ivory, the artist had recourse to precious stones. The eyes of the personages are of rubies and green stones, while the foliage of the borders glitters with turquoises, amethysts and some carbuncles.

Both covers were admirably suited for the presumed possessor of the psalter. King David was a recurring motif as far back as late antiquity, and was certain to have a special appeal in the Latin kingdom – often called the 'Kingdom of David' – indeed, one of its kings was crowned in Bethlehem rather than Jerusalem. The HERODIUS could be another name for FULCIA and represented those who follow or imitate Christ. At the same time it alluded to Fulk, king of Jerusalem, husband of Queen Melissande, the presumed owner of the psalter. The contents of the medallions generally follow well known art motifs, such as the struggle between virtue and vice, based on the fourth-century poem of Prudentius, the *Psychomachia*.

The identity of the artist is a mystery. The carving itself is hardly an indication of his origin, though the general arrangement seems Western. Unlike the fantastic dress and armour represented in the illuminated manuscripts, these psalter figures show Western costume and armour of the twelfth century, as it existed in Europe and in the Latin kingdom. The Byzantine emperor might be a reflection of reality or an expression of the previously mentioned inclination on the part of Jerusalem royalty to imitate the greatest Christian ruler. Not much can be learned from the genre of decoration, which, although of oriental design, was common to East and West by the twelfth century. A Westerner, possibly from southern Italy (i.e. in the sphere of Byzantine culture) possibly carved the covers of this psalter.

A review of the different arts practised in the Latin kingdom presents a picture of great variety, with different degrees of accomplishment. The few extant objects spaced over a period of two hundred years, make evaluation hazardous. Nevertheless, some general remarks seem warranted.

It is obvious that the Holy Land under the crusaders never became a centre of original creativity. It is even doubtful if the artists whose work is preserved were permanent inhabitants of the Holy Land. Brought up in Europe and nourished by its artistic heritage, they migrated to the East and practised their arts. We do not know if they remained or left later for their homelands. In either case we have no convincing proof that local schools of art were created. The assigning of illuminated manuscripts to Jerusalem or Acre rests basically on the establishment of their chronology (twelfth or thirteenth century) and far less on any characteristics which could identify their place of origin.

What is true of illumination and painting applies even more to sculpture and the decorative aspects of architecture. They cannot be attributed to a definite European centre. Languedoc and Provence, Burgundy and Champagne chiselled their influence in Palestinian stone or marble. At the same time, oriental masons perpetuated Byzantine traditions in the non-figurative branch of sculpture.[37]

___

[37] This will be successfully argued by N. Kenaan, 'Local Christian Art in Twelfth-Century Jerusalem', to be published soon.

It is thus difficult to assess the artistic creativity of the kingdom as a whole. The different *objets d'art* cannot be appraised in local terms, but only compared with contemporary European and Byzantine models. By this scale of comparison – with few exceptions (the capitals of Nazareth, the illuminations of Acre) – the artistic creations of the Holy Land do not reach the highest standards of contemporary art. The obvious conclusion is that the leading artists of the period did not migrate to the crusader kingdom.

In some spheres of artistic activity the Orient left its imprint on the crusaders. Mosaics were and remained an art of the orientals and as such continued ancient Byzantine and Moslem traditions. There is not enough material available to study a possible interchange between this art and the Occident. What is described by pilgrims and what remains is oriental in motif and execution.

Eastern influences can also be detected in such minor arts as ceramics and some aspects of the decorative elements in architecture. Crusader ceramics hardly differ from Arab or Mameluk work. Only in sites where archaeological and historical data permit exact chronology, or where the figures (clergymen, crosses and other Christian symbols) are explicitly connected with the crusaders can we with certainty assign a given artifact to the crusader period. This would point to the fact that ceramics continued to be produced by the local Christian and Moslem artisans, who exercised their craft in the traditional way, but catering to a new clientele, they responded by introducing additional figures and symbols.

If the oriental influence is felt in this lower order of art we also find it in some features of architectural decoration. These are not strong enough to impart an oriental appearance to buildings, but point to the fact that among the masons and foremen some were locals who used traditional techniques when working on crusader buildings designed by Westerners. The sculptured capitals and friezes of the Holy Sepulchre may have been by local Christians who continued the traditions of provincial Byzantium.

The existing artistic documentation proves a certain progress in the techniques of illuminators, but there is not enough material to evaluate sculpture, mosaics and architecture, which all seem to concentrate in a short span of some fifty years. The progress in itself is interesting, since it shows transition from clumsiness – even in copying – to a far freer style and less slavish following of models. At the same time sculpture and illumination alike illustrate a trait inherent in crusader society: indiscriminate catering to European tastes, despite the presence of excellent oriental models which could have provided some local colour. The sculptor of the beautiful capitals in Nazareth, chiselling into his stone scenes of the Orient, never thought of reproducing oriental sky-lines with their domes and flat roofs. His model is the accepted European image of cities and the traditional way of reproducing them. In book illuminations this phenomenon is even stronger. Depicting biblical scenes in the land of the Bible, it is extremely rare to see the artist attempting to reproduce scenery among which he lived, or even such obvious objects as local costumes. Whereas nineteenth-century artists will accept Arab dresses as befitting biblical personalities, the twelfth and thirteenth-century Palestinian artists went to great lengths in order to portray their personalities clad in some outlandish attire unknown in the Holy Land. The orientals of their creation wore Phrygian caps or even stranger headgear. This was how Europe imagined the Orient, and the crusader poised in the middle catered to preconceived tastes and ideas.

What was true for the artist was also so for the 'intellectuals'. No major European poet, theologian, scholar or historian ever migrated and settled in the crusader states. Some went on pilgrimage and their voyage was reflected in their literary production, in their poems concerned with the pilgrimage, the Holy Land and in a new imagery of motives imported from the East. Though the Crusade and the Holy Land became an important topic of contemporary European poetry, very often acquiring the position of a sublimated kind of *excitatoria* (i.e. exhortations to go to the Holy Land), the poet preachers seldom became practitioners.

XVIII

THE LEGACY OF AN EPOCH

A   The Crusades as a Colonial Movement

Europe came of age at the end of the eleventh century. The historical threads of the preceding half millennium met in a pattern in which the features of modern times can already be discerned. In another five hundred years a Europe bursting with energy would spread over the globe, diffusing its peoples, institutions and culture.

The Crusades were interposed between the break-down of the Roman Empire and the great Age of Discovery. Their tangible results were the first European colonies beyond the physical boundaries of the continent. In point of time, the Crusades are the opening chapter of European expansion and foreshadow all later colonial movements.

Colonization is not a modern phenomenon. Prehistory as well as classical antiquity furnish numerous examples. But migration and colonization must not be confused. A peaceful or war-like migration may or may not result in colonization. Only when the migrating element becomes the dominant factor in a newly created polity can one speak of colonization. The term is sometimes used subjectively as for the Germanic migrations of the early Middle Ages, known by the Germans as 'Völkerwanderung', but perceived inside the *limes* to be *invasions des Barbares* (in all Romance languages).

Until the Crusades, colonizing movements which left a lasting imprint upon civilization were essentially Mediterranean in origin, e.g. Phoenician, Greek and Roman. The expansion of Hellenic culture hugged the shores of the Mediterranean and the same applies to the republican phase of the Roman Empire. The ideal limits of colonial tradition in antiquity were geographically marked by *mare nostrum*. This is the European perspective, which perceived Judaism, Christianity, Hellenism and Roman civilization as basic ingredients of its culture. In contrast, the crusaders brought no common *Mediterranean* legacy to the East; by then they were already the bearers of the *common heritage of European culture*. They belonged to the Western branch of the Church, were brought up in the same traditions, lived in a world of identical concepts and attitudes, and their social stratification was based on the same ethical and ideological premises. It is no accident that to the Moslems, *al-Franj* meant Europeans, and to Christian chroniclers of the Crusades *Franci* denoted the European conquerors in the East.

If the Crusades are distinguished from the mediterranean expansion of classical antiquity by their role in an expanding *all-European* culture, the same notion forges links between them and the great Age of Discoveries. Whereas a millennial hiatus separates the colonizing movements of Greece and Rome from those of Europe in the eleventh century, there is continuity between the Crusades and the discovery of the Canaries and that of the Western hemisphere.

With the Crusades we partially leave the Mediterranean as a 'colonizing center' – since they bring northern Europe into the arena. Yet despite the preponderance of transalpine elements, the Mediterranean played a major role in the movement. Not only because it was directly affected, but because the colonial legacy of the Crusades would be mainly absorbed and treasured by the Mediterranean nations, to act as a stimulant and stepping stone in future colonial enterprises.

Viewed from the aspect of colonial history a basic distinction must be made between the First Crusade and all subsequent migrations, whether or not called Crusades. [1] We allude firstly to the *mass character* of the First Crusade, when tens of thousands left their native soil and moved to the new lands in the East. None of the following Crusades or peaceful migrations in between military expeditions ever had the same character. Not less striking is the fact that the First Crusade was almost entirely unprepared. No earlier attempts on a smaller scale preceded it. There was no test, pilot plan or adventurous pioneers to blaze the trail. To the amazed chroniclers, it looked like a general exodus from Europe and this seems the right expression in more than one sense for the great masses moved by religious exaltation. This does not exclude the fact that every one had his private little hope, a vision of riches or other form of satisfaction. Nevertheless, the First Crusade was not actuated by the sum total of such expectations and its ideology – which stirred hundreds of thousands – did not conceal an urge for material gains. So many would hardly abandon their normal – even if not over-abundant – sources of livelihood to plunge hazardously into the unknown. Future movements were substantially different. One knew, or, at least, thought that one knew something about the land of immigration, and possible risks could be weighed against potential advantages. Thus in its mass character, unpreparedness and motivation the First Crusade differs basically from any other movement of expansion and colonization.

Closely related is the question of the human element in the First Crusade. The relative insignificance of material factors influenced the human composition. The typical elements found in all colonial enterprises – namely the marginal people who play such a major role in the history of colonization – were hardly decisive in the First Crusade. We miss the maladjusted, the enterprising outcast destined to become a *conquistador*; we miss the adventurer, whether pirate, merchant or explorer, the missionary

---

[1] On the character of the first Crusade in general: P. Rousset, *Les origines et les caractères de la première Croisade*, Neuchâtel, 1945. M. Villey, *La Croisade. Essai sur la formation d'une théorie juridique*, Paris, 1942. Important in our context is A. Dupront, 'Croisade et eschatologie', *V. Convegno internacionale di studi umantistici*, Padova, 1960. See below: Colonial Society.

or the ostracized noble. Admittedly, the armies of the First Crusade were not a host of saints. They certainly comprised robbers, murderers, prostitutes and transgressors of every type, marginal people at variance with society. But their kind rarely make path-finders. They are hangers-on who seldom move by their own will. Though enterprising in their own fashion, they belong to the forced rather than to those willing to take the initiative of migration. The basic hosts of the First Crusade were part and parcel of a settled and stable society. The nobleman, knight, free man, cleric and serf who went to the East were not outcasts, but a cross-section of the established and existing order. Their leaders were not *conquistadors* out for boundless loot, but represented the most traditional part of the European establishment.

The great masses went to the East in the name of an idea, to liberate the Holy Sepulchre from the Infidels. Born amidst eschatological fervour this idea created a single-mindedness that left no room for any conscious political or economic plan. The abundant contemporary sources mention no scheme as to the future of the liberated Holy Sepulchre. The silence of all sources is in itself a witness to the unformulated political aims of the Crusade. Nothing was envisaged beyond the rescue of Eastern Christendom. Yet long before this aim was achieved, a major change took place in the behaviour and mood of the army. The journey to the East lasted for almost three years. It would have been humanly impossible for the Crusade to survive as such while maintaining religious fervour for three consecutive years. Some infringements can already be detected at the end of the march through Asia Minor, such as the conduct of Baldwin and Tancred in Cilicia and later in Edessa. But after the great victory at Antioch the new reality became evident: the Crusade was on the point of disbanding, each leader overrunning the countryside, capturing villages and cities on his own. The half year spent around Antioch marked the moral bankruptcy of the original claims and premises: Jerusalem and the Holy Sepulchre were relegated to the background; one was content with northern Syria without insisting on Canaan. Despite this explosion of greed, the leaders – with the possible exception of Bohemond, himself from a famous race of state-founders – did not yet think in clear terms of political organization. Spoils and booty were foremost in their minds. Nothing was more symptomatic than the 'Law of Conquest', which later became a part of the kingdom's legislation. According to the 'Law of Conquest', the man who put a particular sign on any object in conquered territory, like a house or village, thereby became its proprietor. Whatever the exact formula, which was obviously qualified by the hierarchical concepts of the period, a proprietary claim was established between the individual and real estate – in short a stake in the conquest. This seems to be symptomatic for the transition from the religious to the political phase.

The shift did not take place without opposition. Particular elements in the host, faithful to the original commitment, attempted to stem the new trend. They threatened to burn the conquered cities if the leaders did not immediately abandon northern Syria and march to Jerusalem. The threat was effective and the host moved southward. But this was only a momentary victory. A confrontation between radically opposed ideas was inevitable and it took place just before and immediately after the capture of Jerusalem. A party in the host, 'the poor', as they were defined, probably peasants and lower clergy – but possibly also simple knights – opposed the establishment of any kind of government! Nihilism? Hardly so. Theirs was the expectation of the Kingdom of Heaven destined to descend on Mount Zion and its social concomitant, the inauguration of a new world order. In this new order, the millenniel human dream of absolute justice would be realized: the *sans-avoir* would be acknowledged as the elect, first to enter 'Heavenly Jerusalem'. In comparison, the two other contending parties, the one demanding a lay ruler for the kingdom and the other a patriarch, did not proclaim revolutionary ideologies. Both represented the existing order, though they disagreed on which element was to be supreme.

Following this confrontation Godfrey de Bouillon was elected to safeguard the conquest. His election marks a decisive point in the history of the Crusade, as well as in its ideology: the decision to create a European kingdom and society in the Holy Land. However, the former ambiguity was not yet wholly overcome.

Godfrey's title: *Advocatus* or 'Defender of the Holy Sepulchre', not only pointed to the self-evident task, but also emphasized the claims of earlier ideas. He is not yet king, and the new political entity not yet a state, rather a treasure or deposit entrusted into his hands till a better and final decision can be taken. This allegiance to the past was acknowledged and asserted in earthly and realistic terms, when Godfrey recognized himself as the vassal of the patriarch and promised to relinquish to him Jerusalem and Jaffa. The obligations taken over by Godfrey de Bouillon were conceived in the traditional terms of reference known to Europe at the time. But they also expressed a current of ideas quite different from those usually conceived in the normal act of homage, namely the principle of other-worldliness couched in terms of subjection to the Church. The ideological mortgage was not yet entirely paid off.

This finally occurred at the end of 1100, one and a half years after the capture of Jerusalem. Baldwin I, brother and successor to Godfrey de Bouillon, let himself be crowned in the basilica of the Nativity at Bethlehem. Deliberately rejecting the ambiguous 'Advocate of the Holy Sepulchre' he called himself: 'King of the Kingdom of Jerusalem'. In the clash between ideology and reality, the latter won. The liberation of the Holy Sepulchre meant the establishment of a Christian kingdom in the Holy Land, the conquerors were the sinews of a new society and citizens of the new state. The idea of liberating the Holy Sepulchre – without plan for the day after – ended in creating a habitation for those who came and for those who would come in future to the new Christian and European state in the East.

The logic of this decision depended upon a realistic approach to human institutions and society, though it needed explanation and justification. The conquest had to be accorded legitimacy in tune with the ethico-religious premises of the period. This was already sketched out by Urban II, who justified the movement by the legitimate right of Christendom to hold the Promised Land, but we find it developed after the capture of Jerusalem. A good example is the imaginary dialogue between the patriarch of Jerusalem and the Moslem inhabitants of Caesarea during the siege (1101) of that city. The latter advance the biblical injunctions against bloodshed and the seizing of alien property. Challenged on his own ground, the patriarch replies:

> True that it is in our law not to rob or kill and we do not want to order it or to do it. But this city is not yours, but was St Peter's and should be his, and it is your ancestors who expelled him by force from the city. And if we, who are the vicars of St Peter, want to recover his land, then surely we do not rob you of your land.

Thus the conquest was legitimate and explained, or rather explained away. The conquest and the establishment of the kingdom were classified as a recovery, a restoring of property, to its rightful owners.[2]

The same trend of thought resorted to history in order to graft the new kingdom on an old tree. An ancient and venerable genealogy was constructed and the new establishment was not merely the 'Kingdom of Jerusalem' or 'of the Jerusalemites', but also the 'Kingdom of David'. This was not simply a biblical reminiscence, but a historical justification (for itself and others) of its existence. All the more convenient, since it thus paid tribute to the mediaeval *horror novi* and catered to the deeply ingrained traditionalism of the Middle Ages. The Crusade was thus not a movement of imperialism or colonization, since from its Christian perspective it was an act of *decolonization*!

Legitimized and supplied with a genealogy, the ruler of the new kingdom, Baldwin I, soon proclaimed its political programme by titling himself 'King of Babylon and of Egypt'. Belief in the magical power of words implies that their utterance conjures up reality. Four years later the same Baldwin I 'granted' to the Genoese one third of Cairo and rural estates in its vicinity.[3]

While the crusader kingdom came into being, two other Christian states arose on the ruins of former Moslem domination: Spain and Sicily. There is much in common between the Iberian peninsula, Sicily and the crusader establishments in the East, though

---

[2] Caffaro, cap. 15, *RHC, Hist. Occidentaux*, V, 62–5. Significantly enough, the same idea is also expressed by Dante, *Paradiso*, cant. XV.

[3] *Liber Iurium*, I, no. 8.

the differences are not inconsiderable. The facts of conquest and contemporaneity did not create the same patterns. The major differences do not appear in the sphere of motivation and ideology. The Spanish term *reconquista* points to the notion of recovery or 'decolonization', which we met in the Holy Land. The major difference is in the physical and historical circumstances.

The '*continental*' character of the conquest and colonization in Spain and Sicily seems to be the major distinguishing mark from the type of '*overseas*' colonization predominant in the crusader East. In type, the Sicilian and Spanish enterprises resembled the German colonization in the Slavonic and Baltic areas. In the Spanish and German examples we discern the centres from which the campaign of conquest was waged and which continued to play a major role in the process of colonization after the conquest was accomplished. Continental in character, the expansion postulated bridgeheads and a common frontier with the enemy. This determined the features of future conquest and domination, as it was decisive in moulding the new society in the recently acquired areas. There was a permanent hinterland, which assured a free flow of immigrants into the devastated and expanding frontier areas. Where victory annihilated the former population, new settlers took over; where land became desolate, it was brought under the plough by newcomers. Where the conquered population survived under Christian rule, its social cohesion was loosened or broken and it was made accessible to assimilation, i.e. conversion and integration. All this distinguished Sicily and Spain from the Holy Land. The fact that the crusaders did not move into adjoining areas while constantly advancing their frontiers – as was the case in the Iberian peninsula – became a paramount factor in shaping the crusader state and society. Perhaps in a different technological age, able to shorten distances or enlarge cargoes, this might have led to a somewhat different development; but at the turn of the eleventh century physical conditions were insurmountable obstacles which prescribed the mode and rhythm of evolution.

The time-span of conquest was not less decisive. To be successful the crusaders had to move swiftly, strike and establish their bases. Otherwise, their inevitably dwindling forces – unreplenished by a manpower reservoir across the frontier – would have disintegrated and disappeared. The bases once established, frontiers and bridge-heads were set up from which to forage, penetrate and occupy enemy territory. This type of conquest required military strength at the moment of onslaught. Indeed the hosts of the First Crusade were numerically superior to any other army the crusaders were ever able to put into the field. Whereas the conquest of Spain or the Baltic went on for generations, the crusader effort was not a process, but a very short, almost one-time event. The final frontiers of the kingdom took only slightly more than ten years to establish. Thus, contrary to Spain, the process of conquest in itself did not become a factor in shaping the destinies of future society. The character of the state was decided immediately after the conquest. The choice lay between the establishment of fortified points – mainly sea-ports – forming enclaves in foreign territory, to tap the outlets of commerce and serve as factories to distribute the products of the homeland, or state-like colonies dominated and possibly settled by an immigrant society. The decision was never in doubt. The crusader states were not created by commercial calculations and the idea of trading factories was meaningless within the framework of their ideological premises. It was thus a foregone conclusion that the future crusader colonies would not fall into the category of Phoenician or Carthaginian settlements, or resemble the later Portuguese, French and English efforts in India and the Far East. Indeed, they foreshadowed the English and Spanish colonies in the Western hemisphere.

Throughout history, colonization, whether of the trading or settler type, was facilitated by the activity of colonizing centres. The state, city or company mobilized manpower and capital, while providing the practical knowledge essential for success. A colonial enterprise may or may not begin with a grant of privileges or powers by the colonizing centre. In the case of a company, its own privileged position is assured by a political power and its own right to grant privileges is therefore of a secondary or derived nature. Whatever the case, the state power behind the successful enterprise will sooner or later move into the newly conquered or colonized territory, and make its presence felt and acknowledged by advancing a claim to sovereignty and to the potential revenues. Links of dependence, which *de iure* are never absent, will be institutionalized. The modes of intervention differ but the trend is common. In continental colonization, the possibilities of direct communication are likely to assure more control and a tighter grip on newly acquired territories than in overseas colonization. In the former, the state power behind the war-like or peaceful enterprise was just one step behind the colonists and conquerors. Independence, or partial autonomy, even if originally granted, was soon curtailed and a mechanism of controls, created at the colonizing centre, tended to integrate the colony within the political structure of the centre. This happened in the different kingdoms of the Iberian peninusula (Portugal, Castile, Aragon), in the Muscovite east and in Prussia of the Teutonic Knights. In overseas colonization, things were different, since real integration was never possible. Here we meet a dependent status, which becomes a source of tension and contention between centre and colony, until sooner or later the links are severed by the colonists. As long as links of dependence exist, the colony is supposed to be defended by the centre, while serving the needs of the homeland – primarily providing revenue. Later on, when colonies became pawns in international politics, colonial strategy and international prestige were no less important than revenue in the contests and bargains between colonial or colonizing powers.

Viewed from these aspects the Crusades as a colonial movement seem to be rather unique and acquire a special significance. Their uniqueness consists in the fact that there was no actual colonizing centre or homeland with political or economic claims to future conquests. A pan-Christian ideology and European participation – which despite national groupings, regarded itself as primarily Christian – barred *ab initio* any political or economic claims on the kingdom by any single element. In theory, the Papacy could have advanced such claims, but it is more than doubtful if patriarch Daimbert's demand for homage from Godfrey de Bouillon was inspired by the supreme pontiff, indeed no such claim was ever repeated. Thus the pervasive pan-Christian ideology – already dominant in the First Crusade – determined the future destinies of the conquests as independent political entities with no links to any colonizing centres. Kings of France or England, emperors of Germany, princes and dukes of Bavaria or Hungary never regarded their expeditions as 'national', although, according to mediaeval concepts, any expedition headed by the king was a 'state' affair. The moneys sent to the kingdom were part of the general European effort for the maintenance of the crusader establishments. European heads of state went on Crusades, fought for the kingdom and supported it in the full conviction that they fought for Christendom.

To this general pattern there were three exceptions, two of which could be specially meaningful, since they exemplify a different attitude and different concepts. During the Third Crusade there was an agreement between Philip II Augustus of France and Richard Lionheart of England to divide their future conquests.[4] At the same time, both rulers promised the Genoese territories in the lands to be conquered, if the latter did not formerly belong to the kingdom.[5] In practice, the conquests – limited to a fraction of the former kingdom – were handed over to the king of Jerusalem, but both European rulers had decisive votes in according the rights to the half-vacant Crown of Jerusalem.

The situation changed in 1225 when Frederick II Hohenstaufen married Isabel, heiress of the Latin kingdom, and daughter of Jean de Brienne. To his long list of titles the emperor added 'King of Jerusalem'. This personal union could have assumed international character if political circumstances had not prevented its free development. As it happened, Frederick II never revisited his Eastern kingdom and after a period of absentee lordship, the local nobility reverted to their native rulers, the Lusignans of Cyprus. But even during this short Hohenstaufen episode we can detect elements which were to be found in later colonial experience. Frederick II's Crusade (1228–9), precipitated a clash with the local nobility.

[4] *Itinerarium Ricardi I*, 1. II, cap. 9 (p. 150); II, cap. 18 (p. 166); *Ambroise*, vv. 365–70; *ibid.* 1045 ss.

[5] Richard I promises to Genoa: *Liber Iurium*, I, nos 381–2; Philip II privileges to Genoa, *ibid.* no. 384

In the ensuing confrontation, the 'War of the Lombards', the emperor tried to act according to the principles of imperial law, but was immediately checked by the local baronage, who haughtily replied that they were ruled by their own laws and customs.[6] This short episode in the confrontation between crusaders and a foreign power was thus enough to initiate an attempt to impose the customs of the 'homeland' on the acquired territories. It was too late for such an attempt, a homeland which had never been a colonizing centre was in no position to regulate the life of its dominion.

Only in the last years of the kingdom was an attempt made, which could have marked a new departure in colonial history, namely the creation of a particular type of link between the Latin establishments and the West. Its exponent was one of the more remarkable personalities in the thirteenth century, the Genoese Benedetto Zaccaria. In 1287, when the county of Tripoli was in open revolt against its ruler, Benedetto Zaccaria, the emissary of Genoa suggested an agreement by which the county should become part of the republic of Genoa. This was a momentous change from the customary autonomous quarters of the communes in the maritime cities of the kingdom, and would have meant a crusader state ruled by a high commissioner or governor, a *podestà* specially sent to the Orient. The idea was never put into practice and the imminent fall of Tripoli to the Moslems prevented its further pursuit.[7]

But for these few exceptions, the crusader establishments represent a particular case in colonial history, in that from beginning to end they existed as absolutely independent states. Their dependence on the papacy was moral, and despite economic dependence was never formulated in political terms. Though territorial domination was not alien to the Roman curia, such aspirations – if they existed at all – were never put into form or deed as far as the crusader kingdom was concerned. True, the papacy might be regarded as a 'colonizing centre' *sui generis:* it

---

[6] *Gestes des Chiprois*, par. 127, 41–2.
[7] See below: Colonizing the Colonist – the Italian Experiment.

formulated and elaborated crusader ideology, was its *spiritus movens*, the focus of mobilization and propaganda, and very often, even the treasury of the movement and state. Above all, the papacy represented the pan-Christian idea. Despite all that, it never acquired any sovereign status in the Latin establishments of the Levant.[8]

The political independence of these establishments is a remarkable fact in colonial history. It holds out a meaningful lesson. Independence means or may mean being left to one's own devices. In the formative age of a colony, the amount of support from the homeland is essential for its development; in later periods it may be of paramount importance for its survival if endangered by rivalry or threatened by alien powers. This, precisely, was the weakness of the Latin kingdom. Independent – it had first and foremost to rely on its own forces. The legitimacy of its claim on European support was a function of the strength and vitality of the pan-Christian idea, of which the kingdom was a tangible emanation. Thus in the absence of direct political links, the potential support of the crusader establishments had to rely on factors entirely beyond their scope of influence. These hinged on Europe's intellectual evolution.

Of the two categories of links which connected the kingdom and Christendom – material and ideological – the former depended in large measure upon the latter. Not merely did the financial participation of Europe depend upon the vitality and viability of pan-Christian sentiments, but even prosperity, migration and settlement in the Holy Land were directly linked to it. As long as Europe or Christendom felt that they had a stake in the kingdom, they could appeal to and set into motion masses towards the East.

[8] On the place of the papacy in the direction of the First Crusade, see J. Richard, 'La papauté et la direction de la première Croisade', *Journal des Savants*, 1960, 49–59. The nearest we come to any claim of 'sovereignty' is the equivalent of Peter's Penny demanded from the kingdom by the papacy. See: C. Daux, 'L'Orient latin censitaire du Saint-Siège', *Rev. de l'Orient Chrétien*, 10 (1905), 225–50. See also J. L. La Monte, 'La Papauté et les Croisades', *Renaissance*, t.2/3 (1944/5).

But after the Third Crusade and the failure of the Fourth, no great Crusade – though often envisaged – was ever put into motion, excepting that of St Louis. The troubadour Rutebeuf succinctly summarized the situation:

> Alas Antioch, alas Holy Land – here is their bitter complaint: there is no Godfrey in their midst, the fire of love is extinguished in the hearts of the Christians. Neither old nor young care any more for the war of God. [9]

It is beyond the scope of our study to explain the various factors which brought a decline of crusading activity. [10] What matters here is to point out, that the decline of the idea put an end to military expeditions as well as to peaceful migration. The papacy and it alone remained the staunchest supporter and ally of the kingdom. Of the two official representatives of the pan-Christian ideology, the Roman Empire forfeited its claims and international standing in the wake of the rising feudal monarchies; the papacy was weakening markedly by the middle of the thirteenth century and could hardly have commanded the support still feasible under Innocent III. The decline of its power at the very time when the crusaders had to face the new Mameluk unity of Islam, left the kingdom weakened and vulnerable. The diminishing power of the papacy meant the disappearance of the only factor on which the crusaders could rely in the West. Thus political independence was not the all-saving formula of the colonization enterprise.

B Colonizing the Colonists – the Italian Experiment

Following the conquest, the first generation of immigrants and colonizers laid the foundations of a new society, which with time

---

[9] Rutebeuf, 'La complainte d'Outremer (1265–6)', *Onze poèmes de Rutebeuf concernant la Croisade*, publ. by J. Bastin and E. Faral, Paris, 1946, 86–94.

[10] The basic study remains that of P. A. Throop, *Criticism of the Crusades*, Amsterdam, 1940. See now J. Prawer, *Histoire du Royaume latin de Jérusalem*, II, Paris, 1970, 375–97.

patterned its structure on models brought over from Europe. Later waves of immigration were integrated, without apparent difficulty, into the existing frames of social cohesion. But success in the sphere of social organization was not paralleled by institutional integration. The latter was never complete. Even such bodies as the military orders, with their well defined role in the kingdom, were never formally integrated. They were part of the colony, without institutionally defined standing or recognition of the kingdom's sovereignty (though not undermining it). No feudal bond tied them to the Crown of Jerusalem and they were not subjects of the kingdom in the accepted sense of the word. The situation thus remained unclarified, whereas in Antioch and Tripoli they were almost independent, state-like formations. The situation was different for the Italian communes, whose position was legally defined by treaties between the European mother-cities and the powers (Crown and later particular barons) of the kingdom.

The implantation of the Italian communes in the Latin East can be described as a parallel and superimposed process of colonization. In a way, a colonization of the crusader establishments. Its object was neither the conquest of Moslem territory, nor the domination of a native populace and its economic exploitation. When they occurred, such phenomena were purely derivative, the result of the grants given to the communes in city quarters and rural estates. The main aim of the Italian establishments after the earliest period of conquest was to use crusader territory as a political and economic base. The crusader kingdom exploited and ruled the country, whereas the Italians advanced their own, non-feudal purposes. Their rural estates and banality rights made them in some measure independent – though hardly autarchic. But these were secondary considerations. Of paramount importance was the congenial frame of the crusader kingdom and their commercial privileges throughout its territories and, partially through it, in the neighbouring countries.

The Italians used the kingdom as a base of operations, a market, for their merchandise and a market of primary and finished products to be exported elsewhere, wherever good roads, friendly winds and demand-supply relations promised profits. One peculiarity of the Crusades – seen as a colonial movement – was their existence on two levels, each with its own particular aims, methods, characteristics and achievements.

Though there was a similarity in their colonial enterprises, the activities of the big three – Venice, Genoa and Pisa – differed in many important aspects, especially at the beginning. Provençal and later Catalan communes which established themselves in the Holy Land added to the heterogeneity of the commercial quarters.

Little can be said about Italian motivation which would indicate a meaningful difference from the mainstream of the Crusades. It seems natural that a mercantile community might have somewhat more material motives than other large groups in the mass movement of the Crusades. This is born out by the fact that none of the sources originating in Venice, Genoa or Pisa hint at any Messianic expectations, so common in many Transalpine documents of the period. This does not prove the absence of religious motivation, but only indicates – always assuming the representative character of our sources – the non-existence of exaltation, which so often culminated in eschatological dreams. To judge by the narrative of the Genoese chronicler, Caffaro de Caschifeleone – a participant in the early expeditions to the Holy Land – there was an ambiguous balance between religious aspirations and cupidity. Perhaps we can say that it was a wonderful feeling to strive for earthly gains, while accumulating celestial credit. To another contemporary of the First Crusade from across the Alps – Albert of Aachen – all those Pisans, Genoese, Venetians and Amalfitans on the Crusade were people 'who used to fight and pillage, sailing as is the custom of robbers (or pirates)'.[11]

To understand the historical importance of the Italian colonization experiment, we have to analyse some of its most striking characteristics. We propose to do this under three headings: the organization of the earliest expeditions, the standing of the colonies in relation to their mother-cities and the elaboration of a system of administration and control by the metropolis over its colonies.

[11] Albertus Aquensis, X, 45.

The first question concerns the organization of the early expeditions. As maritime enterprises, their system of financing differed entirely from that of the mass Crusade. The noble from across the Alps collected as much money and provisions as he could, often mortgaging his estates in the process, and joined the great host. When his provisions and money ran out, he was often supported for the rest of the expedition by one of the great leaders. This happened even to a noble like Tancred and must have been the fate of the common knight. In the maritime cities the question of financing was basically that of ships and their equipment, that is an immense capital investment in an extremely hazardous venture. In less than ten years mighty fleets were built and launched, speedily and efficiently.

At this point we already detect the first differences between the Italian cities. Whereas the later fleets of all the cities were partly financed from the proceeds of successful piracy and looting in the East, the origins of the earliest fleets differ for Genoa, Pisa and Venice. Genoa launched its earliest fleets – which participated in the capture of Antioch and Jerusalem – as an enterprise of individuals with no official participation by the city authorities. In Pisa and Venice, city authorities or their equivalent intervened from the beginning.

Ten noblemen are identified by Caffaro as leaders of the first Genoese fleet. Together they equipped twelve galleys and one transport manned by some three or four thousand fighters and sailors.[12] We do not know if the men were paid; it is even possible that they (though not the professional sailors) contributed themselves to their expenses. Nevertheless, the launching of such a fleet meant a tremendous outlay of money. The leaders of the expedition were necessarily also its financiers, investing their own money and perhaps also funds from people who did not directly participate in the expedition. Most known by name were members of the 'viscountal' families or families holding

---

[12] This is the proportion of men and ships in the fleet of 1100 – see p. 486. In the fleet of Bertrand of Tripoli in 1109: 40 galleys with 4,000 men without counting sailors. *Liber Iurium*, I, 18.

the lucrative posts of church 'advocates'.[13] The accumulated income of their landed possessions must have been used earlier in commerce and business and this certainly included investments in shipbuilding. Although it is not impossible that the first dozen ships which went east were built between 1096 –when the call of Urban II reached the city – and 1097, the date of their departure to the East, this seems highly improbable. It seems likely that at least some of them were built earlier and now employed for the expeditions. Following that first expedition we hear again in 1097 of two Genoese galleys of the Embriaci brothers (future rulers of Gibelet) going to the East, followed in 1100 by twenty-four galleys and four transports with eight thousand men aboard of William Embriaco, and then in 1101: eight galleys, eight *golabi* and one transport. Even supposing that some of these ships were used repeatedly (some were dismantled in the Holy Land like the galleys of the Embriaci, who bought a new one for their return voyage), this still meant feverish shipbuilding and an unprecedented investment. This was partly financed by the quick and high turn-over of the initial investment, but also by drawing continuously upon fresh resources among the merchant class of Genoa. Judging by the pattern of Genoa's later commerce with the crusader East, it can be assumed that the investments were not numerous, but very high. The capitalists of the period invested great sums and expected a good return. Sailors and the men aboard hardly invested, but expected a share in the spoils of piracy and conquest.

From the organizational point of view we can regard these early Genoese expeditions as prototypes of the merchant company. They were financed by their own members, recruited their own men and sailors and expected returns on the investments. From the Genoese expedition of 1101 – which participated with Baldwin I in the capture of Caesarea – we learn some details on the division of spoils. After the capture of the city 10 percent (the tithe) was reserved for the church, 5 percent was put aside for the ships (that is reserved for the shipowners); the participants were then remunerated according to rank and standing and finally each

---

[13] R. S. Lopez, *Storia delle colonie Genovesi nel Mediterraneo*, 80.

participant received 48 sous of Poitou and 2 pounds of pepper.[14] With the division of spoils, which can be euphemistically described as the payment of dividends on investments, the original company of 1101 was dissolved. A new venture, as was the case in the commercial contracts of the period, required the creation of a new company. But we shall not be surprised to find the same people or families, repeatedly financing and commanding Genoese expeditions. After the conquest, this led to the *de facto* establishment of a commercial monopoly in the crusader Levant by a number of noble Genoese families, the so-called 'consular' families. In their home-town they occupied the key positions of consuls and represented the merchant-noble aristocracy of the city.

Pisa and Venice followed a different course. Daimbert's leadership of the Pisan expedition (summer of 1099) was more than that of an archbishop. Daimbert was not merely the most important man in Pisa because of his ecclesiastical office, but also because of his position in the newly organized republic. Fourteen years earlier, in 1085, Daimbert was instrumental in mediating a civil war. The warring factions comprised the Marquis of Tuscany (whose power was waning), the noble families who tried to substitute their own authority and the Marquis's representative in the city, the viscount, who went over to the popular party. Finally, the 'Charter of Peace' mediated by Daimbert transformed Pisa into an independent commune. Two years later (1087), the first consuls of the commune appeared. Daimbert then, leading a Pisan fleet of 120 ships as *rector et ductor*,[15] represented the commune in arms on its way to the East. Unlike that of Genoa, the Pisan fleet was sponsored by the commune. This does not mean that the commune financed the whole expedition. The 120 ships must have belonged to the great merchants, though some were probably built by the city or paid for by the rich bishopric. But the fleet embarked in the name of Pisa.

Things were similar in Venice, though possibly even more

---

[14] Caffaro, *De liberatione civitatum Orientis*, cap. 18. *RHC, Hist. Occidentaux*, V, 65.
[15] Bernardus Marangone, *MGH.SS*, XIX, 239.

official. Sponsorship was more formal, because at the time of the First Crusade Venice was an ancient state and its commercial links to the East – especially with Byzantium – dated back several centuries. The Venetian fleet reached the East when the First Crusade was already over and crusaders took root in Antioch and Jerusalem. We can follow a chronicler of this earliest Venetian expedition, which started in the summer of 1099. It reached the Holy Land in 1100 and captured the insignificant port of Haifa. The monk of Lido who accidentally wrote the story of this expedition, had as his main theme the *Translation of the relics of St Nicolas* from Myra to Venice, one of the pious robberies of the time. He recaptures something of the spirit of Caffaro for Genoa.[16] Nothing can better illustrate the situation than a direct quotation from his narrative.

> Three years after the beginning of the Crusade (says the monk of Lido) the Venetians, because of the position of their city, were using ships where others used horses. This nation, more exercised than any other in sea-warfare, and habituated to victory, prepared diligently and with great outlay a great quantity of ships for the service of the 'Road of God' (Crusade) and they equipped them sufficiently with men and military stores. As it was not yet plainly stated who should rule the fleet and who command the army, all unanimously made for the church of the Evangelist Marc and the clergy as well as the people, requested in one voice Henry, bishop of Castellana, as *rector et preceptor* and John, the son of Michiel the doge, they put at the head of the army and navy. And so Henry, bishop of Castellana, though unwilling, was overcome by the obedience due to the patriarch, by the order of the doge and by prayers of the clergy and populace.[17]

The first Venetian expedition to the crusader East was state-sponsored. The bishop of Castellana, Henry Contarenus, son of the doge Domenico Contarenus, belonged to the ruling patriciate of the city and like Daimbert, archbishop of Pisa, served as rector of the expedition. The direct command of the fleet and army was in

[16] Monachus Littorensis, *Historia de translatione Magni Nicolai*, *RHC*, *Hist. Occidentaux*, V, 253 ss. The story was written *c.* 1116 but probably based on an earlier source contemporary with the events.
[17] *Ibid.* cap. 2, 255.

the hands of Giovanni Michiel, son of the ruling doge Vitale Michiel. Moreover the expedition was organized by a formal command of the doge. A brief and victorious encounter with a Pisan fleet in Rhodes (autumn 1099), made the Venetians aware of the danger from Pisa and Genoa, newcomers to the eastern Mediterranean. The mixture of piety and greed which character- ized the Venetian expedition is fully attested by the conditions under which the captured Pisans were liberated: 'they will never again enter Romania (= Byzantium) for commercial purposes, they will never again fight Christians in any way, unless they will be crossing for the devotion of the Holy Sepulchre.'[18] The expedition ended – to quote the monk of Lido – with the triumph of the twin palms of pilgrimage and victory.[19]

The privileges and obligations of the Italian communes were not less important for the future of colonialism than the original organization of the expedition. Besides their material privileges, we are concerned with the creation of a status pattern – the elabora- tion of a particular concept of relations – which will play a major role in the history of Italian colonization. The privileges were not granted (not even to the Genoese) to the conquering group of Italians, the real participants in the expeditions, but all were assigned to a collective and to its descendants. Such privileges were normal for ecclesiastical institutions (like monasteries) or ethnic groups (like the Jews), but constituted an innovation among Christian laymen. The fact in itself marks the introduction of a new element in the juridical structure of the period. They were certainly copied from feudal models, but only by tacitly accepting the notion of collective vassalage. But the communes were never regarded as vassals of the kingdom. By trial and error, a new formula of lasting interest for the future was taking shape.

If the privileges had to be lasting, they could not be abolished when dissolving the association which organized the expedition. This was especially important for Genoa whose expeditions were

[18] *Ibid.*, cap. 7, 258–9.
[19] *Ibid.*, cap. 43, 278.

not state-sponsored. One apparent solution was a type of grant such as that accorded as late as 1188 to a Pisan corporation, known as *Societas Vermiliorum* ('Society of the Reds'), following the successful defence of Tyre. Conrad of Montferrat granted to them and their successors properties in Acre and Tyre. The charter states, that if they decide to divide this property given to them in common, the privilege will remain in force as long as the association continues. Moreover, the donation will remain valid even after the dissolution of the association and each member will freely possess his own share.[20] We do not know if this type of privilege was ever granted at an earlier period, though such a solution was theoretically possible. What really prevailed was the notion of collectivity or corporation. Thus the earliest Genoese privileges were accorded by Bohemond in 1098 to 'all the men of Genoa in the city of Antioch' and the phrase is enlarged in the Genoese oath to the prince of Antioch as taken by the 'good men of Genoa' and then 'to all men of Genoa, that is those whose names were mentioned and all the rest (or others), who will be in the city of Antioch or in such place (that is under Bohemond's dominion) where they will be able to take an oath'.[21] The link thus created between the Genoese and the prince includes *any* Genoese who might in future settle in his dominions. By 1104 Baldwin I accorded a privilege to 'the Genoese church of St Lawrence' and the cathedral church of San Lorenzo would henceforth play a major role in the history of the Genoese establishments in the East.[22]

Whereas the involvement of the Pisan and Venetian cathedral churches is self-evident due to the role played by their prelates in the earliest expeditions, the case of Genoa warrants some elucidation. The Genoese merchant-nobles of the earliest expeditions were looking for a title to whom the newly acquired privileges could be granted. A single individual was out of the question. It had to be a collective privilege and the cathedral church was a plausible grantee.[23] A donation to an ecclesiastical institution had some

[20] Müller, *op. cit.*, nos 27–8, pp. 33–4.
[21] Hagenmeyer, *Epistolae*, XIII, 155–6.
[22] *Liber Iurium*, I, no. 8, p. 16, and so again in Tripoli in 1109. *Ibid.*, no. 11.
[23] In this connection see the interesting study of Sleesarev.

obvious advantages, e.g. support of the hierarchy and its power of censure to assure the fulfilment of promises. It must also be kept in mind, that the earliest Genoese expedition almost coincided with the revolution which created the commune.[24] In all probability, the bishop of the city was instrumental in the movement. In a period when the commune was still a new-born institution, it seemed wise to name the church as the grantee.

The collective character of the privilege posed a problem which the leaders of the Crusade could hardly have faced in their former experience, namely the definition of duties and obligations by the contracting parties. In the Genoese privilege the agreement is called *securitas* (security) and in the Pisan *convenientia et pactum* (covenant and pact).[25] No oath of homage and fealty is rendered, but in the former case both parties took a mutual and identical oath: not to take life or limb; not to make each other prisoners; not to seize property. This was as far a cry from an agreement between states as it was from the knightly spirit.[26] As late as 1156 Baldwin IV and the Pisans promised to abstain from mutual acts of violence. With time the oath underwent a change and became more chivalrous, at least by stressing positive obligations. So in 1169 the Genoese swore to Bohemond of Antioch:

> They will help me and will cherish my honour and augment it; they will defend to the best of their ability my men and their possessions and all that is mine. They will guard and maintain them against all people.[27]

[24] It seems impossible to agree with E. Bach, *La cité de Gênes au XIIe siècle*, Copenhagen, 1955, 13, that the commune was created in order to build a fleet and to safeguard the newly acquired possessions in the Orient.

[25] The privileges for Genoa of Baldwin I in 1104–5 and Bertrand of Tripoli in 1109. *Liber Iurium*, nos 8, 10, 11. The privileges for Pisa granted by Tancred for Antioch in 1108 and Baldwin IV for the kingdom in 1156. Müller, *op. cit.*, nos 1, 5.

[26] This type of oath might have been common in southern France. See J. H. Hill and L. L. Hill, 'The Convention of Alexius Comnenus and Raymond de St Gilles', *American Historical Review*, 58 (1952–3), 322–7. Rather baffling is the presence of similar wording in the obligations of the abbots of Sta Maria latina and of *Templum Domini* to the patriarch of Jerusalem! Rozière, *op. cit.*, nos. 1, 3.

[27] *Liber Iurium*, no. 276, pp. 249–50.

Still some of the early roughness can be found (explained by times of tension) as late as 1193 when Henry, count of Champagne, the ruler of the kingdom, requested the consuls and nationals of Pisa to swear that 'as long as they stay in my land and dominion – to preserve my life and my honour and my land against all people'.[28]

The particularity of the early agreements is also apparent in the way they attempted to establish special rules for disputes between the communes and the Crown. Obviously it was impossible to rely on the existing feudal rules and more fitting arrangements were needed. Thus Baldwin I (1104) obliged himself to satisfy Genoese complaints thirty days after their claim; Bertrand of Tripoli (1109) promised the same with a delay of fifteen days only.[29] Though no procedure is mentioned, it is hardly possible that ordinary jurisdiction was envisaged. Perhaps it was more in the nature of arbitration than judgment. Later crusader authorities tried to fit such cases into normal *formulae*. Thus Bohemond's privilege to the Genoese for Antioch (1169) promised the redress of grievances forty days after the complaint (which is the normal delay in feudal jurisdiction), in case of an *impedimentum* (obstacles corresponding to the crusader *'essoin'*) another delay of fifteen days was allowed, and then the procedure to be followed was to be 'according to the use and institutions of my court'.

The novelty of the situation, a collective privilege on one hand and a kingdom just coming into being on the other, explain the agreements. They are part of the new colonial experience, a first encounter where the parties take cognizance of each other, none being very clear about its own potential profit and the counter-demands of the confronting party. All the major privileges were accorded to the communes in the first quarter of the twelfth century i.e. they coincide with the primary expansion and establishment. Hence, we reach a new stage of development whose major theme was to define the position of their acquisitions vis-à-vis the kingdom and their standing vis-à-vis their mother-cities.

[28] Müller, *op. cit.*, no. 37.
[29] *Liber Iurium*, nos 8, 11.

What was the interest of the metropolis in its colonies? The expectation of direct income or indirect advantages from their possession? The communes had quarters in the major maritime cities of the kingdom. This included real property and sometimes fixed income from different sources.[30] The documents do not reveal if any of the income from these sources went to the mother-cities. Members of the commune and others who lived in their quarter paid rent for their lodgings or a *'cens'* (a token payment) for their possessions which were the commune's property. Some houses were put aside for specific purposes, such as renting to the nationals of the commune during the *passagium*. Establishments of common utility, like ovens, butcheries, baths were not only exempted from the seigniorial ban, but became monopolies of the commune. Then there was income from rural estates. Additional revenues were drawn from jurisdiction over nationals and in specific cases over all inhabitants of a quarter.

Together these sums must have been rather important. Part of the revenue naturally went to cover the expenses of local adminis-tration, which included not only the salaries of the officials,[31] but also the expenses of the parish churches. Money was often needed to assure the good will of the local powers. Sometimes money in the local treasury was even used to defray external expenses. In Venice, for example, the *Maggiore Consiglio* ordered its representatives in the Holy Land to send money to its officials in Armenia.[32] During the thirteenth century, when the fratricidal strife of the communes necessitated the building of walls around their quarters, costly military equipment and the hiring of men for defence, much money was needed, certainly more than local revenue could cover. In view of the rather large local expenses we

---

[30] Income from real property is enumerated, e.g. in the Genoese and Venetian inventories of their possessions in Tyre and Acre. 'Quatre titres des propriétés des Génois à Acre et à Tyre', *Archives de l'Orient latin*, II, 213–30. Tafel-Thomas, II, 215–21, 351–98. Fixed revenue from the city, port or *catena*, see, e.g., *Liber Iurium*, nos. 8, 374, 401, 405 and above n. 29.

[31] See below, n. 51.

[32] Decision taken in 1282. Cessi, *op. cit.*, III, 3. See below n. 47.

doubt if any significant sums were sent to the metropolis.[33]

It seems plausible to assume that the major interest of the metropolis was not in the direct income derived from its colonies, but in the possibilities which they opened to its nationals in trade and banking. The true income of the metropolis was derived from the rich merchant class at home, whose business flourished owing, *inter alia*, to the existence of colonies.

The relations between metropolis and colonies, despite different starting points, developed everywhere on similar lines. As a rule, this meant institutionalizing the relations by creating a state-machinery of supervision, a phenomenon of far-reaching importance in the history of colonization. The Italian colonies in the kingdom 'belonged' to the mother-city. But 'belonging' had different degrees and meanings. Thus the city of Gibelet, which belonged to Genoa until the metropolis lost control in the middle of the twelfth century, was on the verge of becoming a part of what might be called 'Genoa Overseas'. Again, the Venetian third of the city of Tyre had not only considerable 'autonomy' but so high a political standing in the kingdom that the Venetians could regard their section of Tyre as part of Venice. This was less applicable to the communal quarters of Genoa and Pisa elsewhere. It would not be exaggerated to say that with time, the general trend of development might have raised the Italian colonies to a significant position, not merely autonomous enclaves in the crusader kingdom, but separate entities in the body politic of their own metropolis.

We do not know how the mother-cities took over the acquisitions of their nationals abroad. Such questions may have been non-existent for Pisa and Venice, because their expeditions were state-sponsored from the beginning. This was different for Genoa. There is, however, no reason to suppose that metropolitan intervention was resented or opposed either by the crusader powers or the Italian colonists. The former were surely interested in establishing

---

[33] A possible exception was revenues assigned to the cathedral churches, e.g. income from the Pisan colony in Constantinople is assigned (1160) for building the cathedral in the mother-city. Müller, *op. cit.*, no. 7.

direct relations with the Italian metropolis – the source of power and potential support – and the latter could only gain by the protection of their powerful mother-country.

To assure the existence and development of its colonies the metropolis soon took over their administration. The first half of the twelfth century was a period of experimentation, characterized on the whole by two trends: the use of well-known forms of feudal administration, like enfeoffment, and the introduction of bureaucracy into overseas administration. The lead in the experimental period seems to have been taken by the enterprising Genoese.

The first officials appointed by Genoa to safeguard its newly acquired possessions and privileges were simply 'guardians' and one of the earliest known was the parish priest of the Genoese church of St Lawrence.[34] What followed was an attempt to use feudal machinery for administration. One of the earliest possessions received by the Genoese in the crusader states was the biblical city of Gebal (the Greek Byblos), called by the crusaders 'Gibelet'. The first privilege accorded them a third, but by 1109 the grant was enlarged to include the whole city.[35] This was the first and only occasion on which a non-feudal owner became the possessor of a whole crusader city. Genoa enfeoffed the city to the noble Embriaco, who thus became a vassal of the commune and also of the count of Tripoli. Legally, the count of Tripoli was the feudal suzerain of the Embriaci, but the latter – lords of Gibelet – were at the same time vassals of the commune or of its cathedral. This cannot be interpreted as a relation of liege homage to the count and simple homage to the commune. *Sui generis* the Embriaci had, theoretically, to take two feudal oaths to two different suzerains for *the same* fief. The enfeoffment of Gibelet and of other Genoese possessions in Palestine and Syria was on extremely advantageous terms. We do not know the conditions before the middle of the twelfth century, but in 1154 – a year of crisis which followed Genoese failures in the western Mediterranean – the commune farmed out all its possessions in Antioch to the Embriaci for the

[34] See below n. 41.
[35] Privilege of Bertrand de Saint-Gilles in *Liber Iurium*, no. II.

span of the next twenty-eight years, for £80 of Genoa, those in Gibelet and Laodicea in Tripoli for 270 besants and a *pallium* worth 10 besants for the altar of St Lawrence, and the possessions in Acre for £50 of Genoa (for the next four years: £100). Investiture with Gibelet was formal. William Embriaco 'in full parliament received from the commune of Genoa the silk banner as investiture of the aforenamed places until the end of that term'.[36] The Genoese regarded the enfeoffment as limited, requiring the renewal of investiture at the end of the term. William Embriaco promised accordingly, that 'he will stay at the will and order of the consuls as to the above places, when the term will come to its end'. It seems that the agreed payments continued up to 1168, but by 1179 the Embriaci evaded oath and payments and in 1186 Pope Urban III threatened them with excommunication and the confiscation of the fief, but to no avail.[37] Gibelet was definitely lost to Genoa and became a family fief of the Embriaci, who owed for it feudal service to the count of Tripoli. Yet some links with Genoa remained even as late as the thirteenth century, possibly because of the Genoese colonists in the city, but no formal ties were re-established. The emancipation of the Embriaci from their feudal tie to the mother-city did not entail all Genoese possessions. During the Third Crusade and the massive help offered for the defence of Tyre and the transport of crusader armies (the latter for a large consideration), the commune recovered its privileges and possessions outside Gibelet.[38]

The experiment to safeguard colonial privileges and possessions through feudal administration ended in disaster. The lesson was learnt and never repeated in the crusader kingdom. Pisa does not seem to have ever tried the system, whereas Venice used it partially and wisely. When the *Pactum Warmundi* (1123), which accorded to Venice one third of the city and lordship of Tyre was confirmed by Baldwin II (1125), it was stipulated that the commune will

[36] *Liber Iurium*, nos. 196, 197, 198. Quotation from no. 197.

[37] *Ibid.*, no. 353. Alexander III letter following the complaint of the archbishop and chapter of Genoa, *ibid.*, no. 321. For Urban III, *ibid.*, nos. 351, 352, 354, 359.

[38] *Ibid.*, nos 363, 374, 401.

contribute three knights to the royal host.[39] The Venetians then enfeoffed part of their possessions to the Venetian noble Rolandus Contarenus and made him responsible for the military duties. The possessions enfeoffed were incredibly large in proportion to the military service: 10 or 12 entire villages (out of 21) and one third in 4 or 6 villages (from a total of 51), in which the commune had property. Another noble family, that of Pantaleone was also enfeoffed by the commune (services unknown). Thus almost half of the rural possessions were enfeoffed. The Venetians now also experienced the risks of administration through feudal institutions. The widow of Rolandus Contarenus, the Lady Guide, commended herself and her possessions directly to the king (after 1164) who then entered partially into the feudal succession.[40]

The distance between colony and mother-city made supervision of feudal relations and controls of the nobility difficult. The obvious interests of the counts of Tripoli or the kings of Jerusalem to infringe upon privileges once lavishly granted, made administration through feudal channels risky. It was hence logical to develop another type of administration, based on bureaucratic premises. The nucleus of an administration was indeed organized almost immediately after the first grants to the communes, when the participants of the expeditions returned to their homelands. The title of the earliest known official is not clear;[41] later it was 'viscount' (*vicecomes*), which raises several questions as to its origin. With the exception of Venice, this title is found in all the commercial colonies of the East. But this was also a title in the administrative machinery of the kingdom. In the latter, it was a non-hereditary governorship, first in royal and later in seigniorial

[39] Tafel-Thomas, *op. cit.*, I, pp. 90–4.

[40] *Ibid.*, II, 387, 375, 389. Cf. J. Prawer in *Byzantion*, XXII (1952), 14–16.

[41] The title *vicecomes* appears for the first time in the county of Tripoli. After the capture of Gibelet, the count kept for himself two thirds of the city: 'et *vicecomitem* suum ibi posuit et Januenses in tertia parte Ansaldum Corsum pro guardia posuerunt'. Caffaro, *RHC, Hist. Occidentaux*, V, 70. Ansaldo still guarded the one-third of the city in 1109 when the whole city was granted to the Genoese, *ibid.* 73. In Acre, already in 1105, a canon of San Lorenzo is called: '*viceomes Siguembaldus*', *ibid.*, 72.

cities. The viscount presided over the court of burgesses. Should we then assign the title an Italian origin or assume that the Italians took it over from the crusader administration? Unfortunately our sources are not explicit. Whatever the case, in Genoa the title *vicecomes* still had at that time a very definite and recent feudal connotation. The viscount was the great feudal lord in the city and in the *contado*. The members of the *Visconti* family (descending from a tenth-century viscount Ydo) remained up to the end of the twelfth century a great power in the city, and a large number of the early consuls of the commune came from the different branches of that family,[42] though the ancient feudal office was not re-established. With the establishment of the commune its leading officials became the consuls. If then the overseas title 'viscount' was of Genoese origin, we encounter a strange phenomenon, the transfer of a Genoese institution to the East when it was declining and disappearing in the mother city. Curious as this seems, we shall find a similar phenomenon in the later evolution of Genoese overseas administration.[43]

Whatever the origin of the Italian overseas *vicecomes* (later taken over by Provençals and Catalans), at the end of the third quarter of the century, first Pisa[44] (1179) and then the other communes introduced into their overseas administration a new official, the *consul*. The viscount became a subordinate official, though sometimes the title remained coupled with that of the new consul. The change in the title was not fortuitous and points to the growing importance of the colonies in the eyes of the metropolis. It corresponded to the title of the highest officers in the republic. Only Venice shunned that title, but its own concern for colonial possessions is evident in the appointment of a special official, the *baiulus* or *baiulo*.

During the Second Kingdom (1187–1291) the colonies were

[42] E. Bach, *op. cit.*, 34.

[43] The Genoese will appoint 'consuls' overseas at the time that office was supplanted by the *podestà* regime in the metropolis. It was R. Lopez, *Storia delle colonie Genovesi nel Mediterraneo*, Bologne, 1938, 92, who drew attention to that curious phenomenon.

[44] Müller, *op. cit.*, 159.

better supervised, or perhaps more regimented. All communes attempted to create a central representation for Syria and Palestine, normally located in Acre or Tyre. Thus Venice had a *baiulo*, a Venetian high commissioner for Syria, who had under him local representatives, also called *baiuli* and often a lower official called *vicecomes*. Genoa and Pisa created an interesting collegiate system, the former having two consul generals, sometimes with the title 'consuls and viscounts in Syria' and lower officials bearing the same title but limited in competence by the qualifying name of their city of residence (of Acre, Tyre, Beirut). Pisa started out with two consuls (1192) like Genoa but then switched to three and then one again, 'consul of the commune of the Pisans in Acre and the whole of Syria'.[45] The introduction of the collegiate system might have been prompted by efficiency but more probably, as everywhere else, it was a system of mutual control. As a curiosity one should mention the federation of Provençal and Catalan communes in Tyre with six or seven consuls but one common court, presided over by a viscount whereas Marseilles and Montpellier had their own consuls in Acre.[46] The procedure of appointments and the competences of overseas officials were strictly regulated and their activities minutely supervised. Thus the Venetian *Maggior Consiglio* goes into the smallest details of the election, competences and activities of its *baiuli*.[47] The Venetian *baiulo* and his counsellors (*consiliarii*) were elected in Venice and on leaving for their respective posts (remarkably called *signoria*)[48] received a special brief (*commissio*), to which the *Maggior Consiglio* added from time to time

[45] The earliest general *baiulo* of Venice appears *c.* 1192–8. Cf. W. Heyd, *op. cit.*, I, 331. For Genoa and Pisa, *ibid.*, 332–3.

[46] *Ibid.*, 334.

[47] The following section on Venice is based on the *Deliberazioni del Maggior Consiglio di Venezia*, II, publ. by R. Cessi, Bologne, 1931. One of its divisions is: *Septima rubrica continens in se consilia omnibus et singulis Rectoribus de Ultramare et Tunixio pertinentia, ibid.* 352 ff. Cf. G. M. Thomas, 'Die ältesten Verordnungen der Venezianer für auswartige Angelegenheiten', *Abhandlungen d. könig. Akad. d. Wissenschaften*, I Classe, t. XIII, 99–145.

[48] Order of 1249. *Liber officorum* in *Deliberazioni*, II, 350: 'De Potestates Constantinopolis, Duche Cretensis, Baiuli Accon, Tyri et Negropontis et Castellani Corone et Motone qui modo iverint in dictis signoriis.'

particular decisions sent to them overseas. The *baiulo* had at his direct disposal a sergeant and a squire (*scutiferus*) in addition to an official notary (*tabellio*).[49] He and his counsellors represented the mother-city in relations with its colonists and the colony before the crusader authorities. The mother-city ruled its colony through them, very often with surprisingly detailed orders. On the other hand a famous *baiulo*, like the Venetian Marsiglio Ziorzi, had a rather free hand in dealing with important political problems in the kingdom,[50] though probably within the framework of a brief from the *Maggior Consiglio*. As officials of the commune, the *baiulo*, his counsellors and notary were quite well salaried,[51] and even had a generous expense account.[52] They were helped in the administration of the communal property by at least two subordinate officials called chamberlains (*camerarii*). They were responsible for renting property, collecting payments to the treasury (*casella communis*) and keeping accounts (*quaterna*). Once a month the *baiulo* and counsellors checked accounts and visited the communal property.[53] Not less important were the competences of the *baiulo* as head of the autonomous Venetian court, in which a part of the public jurisdiction of the kingdom was vested. The Venetian court often held jurisdiction over all (including non-Venetian) inhabitants of the quarter. Closely related to jurisdiction were the competences connected with the registration of all commercial contracts by Venetians. Registration was effected before the *baiulo*, and the counsellors served as witnesses.[54] The

---

[49] *Septima rubrica*, I, 8, cf. I, 3.

[50] Tafel-Thomas, *op. cit.*, II, 354 ff.

[51] The *baiulo* had a yearly salary of 1,400 besants, that is roughly 3 single knight's fiefs; the sergeant received 25 besants and two vestments – according to a decision of 1270. *Septima rubrica*, I, par. 3. In 1276 it is stated that the latter will receive 12 besants yearly and 3 besants for expenses, *ibid.*, par. 8. They were also paid transport expenses: the *baiulo* received 40 *denarii grossi* of Venice and 10 *den. grossi* for transport of his horse. The *camerarii*, half that sum for their transport and the same amount for their horses. *Liber officiorum, Deliberazioni*, II, 350.

[52] The *baiulo* received 100 besants for expenses *in conviviis et corredis, ibid.*, I, 1.

[53] Decisions of 1273, *ibid.*, II, 1–3.

[54] Decision of 1272, *ibid.*, II, 109–10.

supervision of the *baiulo* himself was rather strict. He was prohibited from carrying merchandise when going to the Levant, though it is not clear if he was barred from engaging in trade when in office. To prevent favouritism, the *baiulo* was not allowed to alienate communal property to any member of his family.[55] It is remarkable how the *Maggior Consiglio* sitting in Venice intervened in the everyday business of its colony, though some of the orders were part of a general overseas policy. E.g. in 1272 the mother-city ordered that 'twenty of the most important of our burgesses who live or stay in Acre' should stay at least for a year inside the walls and gates of the Venetian quarter. A year earlier (1271) the council goes back on its decision and orders that the Jews (probably former inhabitants of the Venetian quarter and as such under Venetian jurisdiction) have to live inside the quarter. To assure Venetian interests, its nationals are ordered not to rent houses in Acre unless all the homes and shops of the commune are occupied. At the same time orders of a political or commercial nature are sent to the *baiulo* for execution, e.g. all Venetian cargoes of iron and timber have to be unloaded in Tyre or Acre and cannot be re-exported without the permission of the *baiulo*,[56] clearly to prevent the smuggling of materials for shipbuilding to Moslem countries. In another decision the Venetian authorities prohibit import from overseas unless it is Venetian property.

Parallel legislation is to be found in Pisa.[57] The 'consul of Acre and of the whole of Syria' as well as his two counsellors and the notary were elected in a secret ballot by the *Maggior Consiglio* in the presence of two Fransciscans and two Dominicans in the cathedral of the city. Men could be elected to these offices only once in a lifetime and the election was to all the offices at the same time, which meant that each new consul brought over with him a completely new administrative personnel. All offices were salaried and the salaries (called 'fiefs'), probably paid from local revenue.

---

[55] *Septima rubrica*, I, 3, 5.

[56] *Ibid.*, I, 12; *Liber officiorum*, VII, 402; *Septima rubrica*, I, 16; *Ibid.* 15.

[57] The following is based on the Pisan statute: *De consule Accon et totius Syrie*, publ. by Bonaini, *Statuti Pisani*, I, 333–5 and Müller, *op. cit.*, 380–1.

It is interesting to note that of the two counsellors, one had to be a lawyer (*iuris peritus*) and one a known merchant (*publicus mercator*). The regulations stress the importance of guarding Pisan monopoly privileges. Thus the consul will be very heavily fined if he allows a non-Pisan to enjoy the customs privileges at the *catena* of the city.

For the sake of comparison it seems worthwhile to analyse similar legislation in Marseilles,[58] important not only because it deals with a non-Italian commune, but, because Marseilles as a latecomer, had few privileges. Thus the organization of its overseas commune represented a more primitive stage, which might have existed in the Italian communes a hundred years earlier. Where there is no consul – say the municipal statutes of Marseilles – if there are ten or twenty nationals of the city, they will elect from among themselves a consul who will have all the competences of the office. For larger places the consul and his counsellors are elected by the municipal authorities of Marseilles: the rector, syndics and heads of guilds. The elected consul, although an official of Marseilles, had a different standing from his Pisan or Venetian colleagues. He is primarily a merchant in the Levant trade[59] – the type of man whom Venice barred from holding office. But even Marseilles bars from office a man who personally enjoys a privileged position in Syria, as well as shipowners and ships' captains.[60] A man elected to the consulate who refuses to take office is heavily fined. Besides safeguarding the privileges of the commune, the major business of consul and counsellors was the exercise of jurisdiction and the registration of commercial deeds. His coercive powers included fining his nationals, but the rector of Marseilles could cancel the fine upon appeal. The consuls were responsible for the register and archives of the court (*cartularium*) kept by a notary, or in his absence by the scribe of the ship. Upon returning to Marseilles the *cartularium* was deposited in court.[61] The officials seem not to have

[58] The following is based on the Marseilles statute: *De consulibus extra Massiliam constituendis* in *Les Status municipaux de Marseille*, publ. by R. Pernoud, Monaco-Paris, 1949, 29–31.

[59] *Ibid.*, par. 4, 1.

[60] *Ibid.*, par. 7: *qui majori libertate vel franquesia gaudeat vel utatur in Syria.*

[61] *Ibid.*, par. 5, 8.

been salaried, but shared half the fines, with the authorities of Marseilles.[62] An important position in the overseas administration was held by the manager of the *fondaco* (*fundegarius fundici*) and his associate, called *nabetinus*. These men seem to have been permanent residents of the colony, and although possibly under the jurisdiction of the consul, they held office as a concession directly from the rector of Marseilles, to whom they took their oath of office.[63]

C   Colonial Society

The conquests of the First Crusade created the physical shell filled by subsequent waves of Europeans, mainly French. States were founded and a new society came into being, Whereas the actual conquest was a very short process the moulds of political and social organization took almost two generations to harden. Evolution was haphazard, nor were social structures and modes of cohesion envisaged beforehand. Nevertheless, neither state nor society started with a *tabula rasa*. The European legacy was strong enough to overcome potential friction between the components. The new population tended to concentrate according to the larger sub-divisions of its ethnic and cultural origin, Normans in Antioch and Provençals in Tripoli. The Kingdom of Jerusalem had a more mixed population, but the northern French established themselves as the dominant element. This inner concentration facilitated cohesion and integration, though the process levelled and annihilated some smaller cultural or ethnic entities.[64]

In a new society immigrants bring their cultural traditions to new surroundings. Whatever social elements settled after the First Crusade and later, they ultimately recreated the pattern of European society. The social mobility which usually characterizes countries of immigration, upgraded the ranks and filled the gaps among the

---

[62] *Ibid.*, par. 3, 19. In cases dealing with more than 10 besants, the consul will have 1/10 from the loser; from less than 10 besants – 1/3 from the loser.

[63] *De consulibus*, par. 2, 8, 9. The origin of the name '*nabetinus*' is not clear. Perhaps from *nabulum* (= freight).

[64] See above, cap. XIV: The Military Orders.

settlers. In one important aspect social structure differed from that of the old country: crusader society was the only feudal, European society which had no serfdom and *a fortiori* no slavery[65] in its own ranks, nor any type of legal or economic dependence. Though hierarchic, it was a society of free men, where even the poorest and most destitute were not only free, but enjoyed a higher legal standing than the richest among the conquered native population. Social theories did not create this remarkable difference; this was based on the ideological premises of the Crusade, whereby any man who joined the host became legally free.[66] A serf who succeeded in reaching the kingdom automatically became a free man and could not be degraded to a non-existent serfdom or slavery. The new settlers thus created their own society and dispensed with the institution of serfdom. In a milder form of villeinage this was supplied by the conquered population.

The new society had to create a pattern of co-existence with the local population. Theoretically, there were three possible solutions: a purely Latin Christian society, an eventual mixed Roman and oriental-Christian society, or a mixed European and oriental (Moslem and Christian) society. The first possibility meant the displacement and expulsion of the native population, its replacement by immigrant colonists and the creation of a viable society where all economic tasks and social functions would be performed by the newcomers, i.e. peasant, craftsman, merchant and official – the ruler and the ruled – would be from among the colonizing European population. The other solutions – a mixed European and oriental society – meant the preservation and

---

[65] Slavery was absolutely non-existent among Franks and very rare in the country. It existed only in the sense that prisoners of war were degraded by the crusaders to the rank of slaves and economically exploited in fortifications and similar work. The military orders used them more rationally as craftsmen, cf. *Le Templier de Tyr.*, par. 318 in *Gestes des Chiprois*, 167. As far as we know they were not used in agriculture, though sometimes as domestics. Crusader sources often confuse them with simple serfs. Cf. *Livre des Assises des Bourgeois*, cap. 144. See also *ibid.*, cap. 16, 34, 144, 203, 208, 210, 235.

[66] Cf. the important studies of J. A. Brundage, *Medieval Canon Law and the Crusader*, Madison, 1969.

subjugation of the local population, treating it as a source of income by using the new political and military power. A specific legal and social standing had then to be assigned to the native population or its different parts (Christians, Moslems) in the new polity.

The choice between these two alternatives was determined by reality and reality was demographic. It has been estimated that at the siege of Jerusalem (June–July 1099) the crusader host numbered some twenty thousand. This was a sizeable army and could have become an important factor in settling the Holy Land. Yet a few months later – at the end of 1099 – they had dwindled perilously to several hundred families, knights and commoners. The land which had to be settled was neither empty nor sparsely populated. Hence the expulsion of the natives (as was done in the cities captured before 1110) was practical only if future waves of migration were assured and if the new settlers were psychologically ready to strike roots in the country as farmers. None of these conditions applied to the crusaders, neither at their moment of establishment nor at any time in the future. Palestine was populated, its agriculture established and its population numerous, especially around the cities. Bedouin nomads existed only along the fringes. On the other hand, the mounted warriors of the crusader host did not envisage their future as peasants in the Holy Land. Their former life prepared them for fighting, while living off the rents and *corvées* in a farming society. The non-noble – though mostly of peasant stock – did not propose to become an exploited serf, even if he wished to continue his traditional occupation. Indeed, he was not even willing to be an exploited tenant farmer. Moreover, demographic and security considerations forced most immigrants to concentrate in the cities. Though the native population could be expelled from the cities, it was impossible to dispense with them in the countryside.

This dictated a clear pattern of co-existence: the crusaders never intended to be producers of primary foods or any other type of wealth, since they saw themselves as rulers, economically exploiting the local population. The latter were relegated to the role of suppliers by political and military pressure. Thus from the beginning the new society was composed of conquerors and conquered, exploiters and exploited.

Such a situation was not unique in the conquered areas of contemporary Europe. What makes the crusader kingdom 'colonial' is the fact, that concepts and realities created in the immediate aftermath of conquest remained permanent for the next two hundred years of the kingdom's existence. The 'colonial situation' was created by the fateful intent of the conquerors to perpetuate this frame of co-existence. The basis of the economy, it also became a tenet of its socio-religious ideology. Hence the repression of any effort to assimilate and integrate.

The crusaders were destined to exist as a dual society. The use of the terms, 'conquerors' and 'conquered', 'exploiters' and 'exploited' is certainly fitting, but to realize their actual meaning it is necessary to advance beyond their purely economic connotations. Crusader exploitation was in all probability less harsh than that in the former period of Moslem domination or in the neighbouring Moslem countries. Many a native peasant had long ago lost his proprietary rights and became the tenant of a Moslem landowner, city-merchant or religious institution (*waqf*). He was economically exploited before and, as said, often more than under the crusaders. Except for occasional hardships connected with war or the arbitrariness of a local Frankish lord,[67] the new regime was not more oppressive. But for the crusaders the role of exploiter and conqueror combined to create an entirely new frame of relations. Under the harshest Moslem rule, the exploited was part of the same religious community – an extremely important tenet of Islamic society – moreover he belonged to the same cultural entity as his exploiter. He might have fatalistically accepted his lot as preordained, as the European serf did, or regarded exploitation and arbitrary exactions as impious acts to be punished in this or in the next world. Though current social thought and the teachings of religion condemned harsh landlords and impious rulers, there was no feeling of humilia-

[67] To the judicious remark of Cl. Cahen (below n. 74) we should now add the important study of E. Sivan, 'Réfugiés syro-palestiniens à l'époque des Croisades', *Revue des études islamiques*, 25 (1967), 135–47.

tion and degradation other than social and economic, mingled with a resentment of injustice. With the crusaders the same exploitation meant something different. Resentment became imbued with non-economic emotions. There was a feeling of humiliation because of being conquered by the unbeliever, a thing clearly against the will of Allah. The exploiter was an alien, an enemy of religion, a destroyer of the faithful. This created an unbridgeable chasm, which could never have been filled by more lenient treatment.

Thus on both sides an ideology and practice of non-acceptance was created. No integration, or even *rapprochement* was possible, both sides rejected each other. The permanence of this 'colonial situation' is of paramount importance. Why permanence? Why no change, or almost none in the long span of two hundred years? The most obvious reason was the economic dependence of the conquerors on the conquered for their daily existence. This in itself postulated far more than political domination, since it dictated a policy whose major tenet was to reject any *rapprochement* or integration, which could have undermined the existing order. Theoretically integration was possible. The ideological distinction between Franks and non-Franks was religion and conquest. But this did not necessarily create an immutable situation. Only the human element compelled permanency. Not merely the original conquerors, but also their descendants, and all future waves of migration participated in the fruits of conquest. Their participation was based on their share in a Christian heritage, and in a strictly crusader view, in the heritage of Latin denomination.

This reasoning could lead to the assumption that any local Moslem converted to the Latin creed, would *eo ipso* become a fully fledged citizen. This was indeed, the law of the kingdom.[68] But it never worked for any meaningful section of the conquered, though individual conversions certainly took place. Conversion was tantamount to assimilation. The neophyte not merely cut himself off from his former religion and co-religionists but accepted the normal languages of his new environment (French)

---

[68] Converted Moslem becomes free citizen, *Assises des Bourgeois*, cap. 204–12 and see n. 69.

and religion (Latin), as well as integration into a particular social class (noble or burgess). This was possible only if the absorbing society regarded conversion and assimilation as a worthwhile aim or value, declaring itself missionary in character, whether religious, cultural or both. The peculiarity of the Latin kingdom resided precisely in the fact that it *never* became a missionary society and never declared itself to be one. In particular instances its dominant factors opposed missionary efforts. One has to read the bitter indictment of Jacques de Vitry, bishop of Acre, in the first quarter of the thirteenth century, to visualize the opposition. Nothing seemed more fitting and noble to the European prelate than to preach the saving doctrine to schismatics, heretics and Moslems. To his greatest astonishment he found opposition – and by no means ambivalent – among the Franks of the country![69] They were ready to fight and die for their religion, but not ready to convert even the willing!

Theoretically we could envisage a different situation. Was it impossible to preserve the existing economic and social order even after conversion? After all, a European serf was as much a Christian as his overlord; there existed then a model which could have been imitated. Yet the possibility of conversion without change of social status was purely academic. In such circumstances conversion lacked the material incentive of assimilation.

In this context the position of the oriental Christians was of utmost importance and puts into relief the 'colonial situation'. Here we deal not with an enemy, but with sects of the same religion. Moreover, the ideology of the First Crusade was to 'liberate' these Christians from the yoke of Islam. Here was a large Christian community, which in some places even preserved its territorial compactness. Even without conversion – as in the case of Moslems – the whole block could have been integrated into the body politic of the conquering Europeans. This never happened and the local

[69] *Lettres de Jacques de Vitry*, ed. R. B. C. Huygens, II, 206–10: 'Christiani servis suis Sarracenis baptismum negabant, licet ipsi Sarraceni instanter et cum lacrimis postularent. Dicebant enim domini eorum: "si isti Christiani fuerunt, non ita pro voluntate nostra eos angariare poterimus".' Cf. above n. 65 and cap. XII, n. 22.

Christian communities were left beyond the pale of the victorious Franks.

In the thirteenth century the mendicant orders made serious efforts to bring about conversion, in the sense of church unification. At one time or another agreement was reached with almost every Christian sect: Maronites, Armenians, Jacobites and Nestorians. Yet, with the exception of the Maronites[70] nothing was accomplished. The oriental Churches were split up on a territorial basis and their communities pursued separate policies. Often they opposed their official heads for reasons of expediency, just as their prelates tried from time to time to reach an agreement with Rome on similar grounds.[71]

But the opposition of the crusader clergy to the new policy of the Roman curia was not less significant. The twelfth century attempted to impose the Latin hierarchy on the native Churches, which deprived the Greeks of their bishops and made the higher prelates of other Churches suffragans of the Latin prelates. This was practically a failure. By the thirteenth century new ideas were current in Rome, i.e. established dogmatic formulas acceptable – at least on a verbal basis – to the oriental Christians and recognition of papal supremacy, alongside an acceptance of the autonomy of the native Churches. This meant 'to remove, in the name of an ethnic and not a dogmatic principle, the Greek believers from obedience to the Latin clergy of Syria'. All attempts failed, beginning with the Armenian Church in the twelfth century, followed by the Greek, Jacobite and Melkite Churches.[72] Whatever the general policy of the pontiffs, the crusader clergy was not ready for any union at the summit which would maintain separate existence at the base. If there was to be union – the religious counterpart of lay integration – it had to mean complete fusion and the undisputed domination of the Latin clergy.

---

[70] The ambivalent attitude of the Maronites to the crusaders, or possibly the change of attitude at different periods remains rather puzzling. Cf. K. S. Salibi, 'The Maronites of Lebanon under Frankish and Mamluk Rule (1099–1516)', *Arabica*, IV (1957), 288–303.

[71] Cl. Cahen, *La Syrie du Nord*, 680.

[72] *Ibid.*, 689 ff.

Ecclesiastical integration thus never took place, since the crusader clergy was ready to accept it only on their own terms. Thus oriental Christendom was rejected on the ecclesiastical level, and even more so in the frame of state and society. Native Christians were treated no better than Moslems, Jews or Samaritans. Though in practice they may have been favoured, the kingdom's legislation – on principle – did not grant them any standing different from that of the conquered, alien and inimical Moslem population. Thus the fact that the kingdom did not conceive itself as having a missionary destiny (the mediaeval equivalent of the 'white man's burden'), deprived it of any spiritual basis of existence, except as the *de facto* guardian of the holy places. There was no religious dimension to its existence, unless conceived of as another territory, which recognized itself as belonging to the Roman church. The position of the Holy Land as a legitimate part of the Christian inheritance simply meant territorial possession. The crusaders did not make the country Christian, but implanted a Christian population to live in Palestine as its dominant factor. In a sense this can be regarded as the bankruptcy of the ideological claim to the Holy Land. The crusaders neither expelled the former Moslem population nor integrated the oriental Christians. In its laicized outlook this was just another earthly kingdom, with no special standing apart from the fact that it was founded by conquest in the land of the holy places. From that standpoint all Crusades after the first great expedition only sought to assure the physical survival of the kingdom. No wonder that Bernard of Clairvaux saw the religious importance of the Crusades not in their aims, but in the conscious decision of a repentant sinner to join the Crusade as a part of the sacrament of penance.

We have discussed the problems of creating an integrated society from the standpoint of the conquerors. In this context 'integration' may mean many things, from conversion and total assimilation to the graded acceptance of the conquered into the framework of state and society. Obviously, this could not only depend on the absorbers, but also upon the readiness of those to be absorbed, i.e. their willingness to abandon their own cultural heritage. In a non-pluralistic society no real integration is possible, without such an abandonment, though elements of the discarded tradition might survive to influence the new. Apart from the will and clearly formulated policy of the integrating element, two main factors seem almost indispensable for successful assimilation and integration: the belief of the conquered in the general superiority of the conquerors' culture, civilization and institutions, and the break-up of native culture – preceded by the loss of its social cohesion and mode of life. Nothing of the kind took place or could have taken place for the native Palestinian population. This was a solid block rooted in the land, not sparsely scattered tribes or marginal nomads whose social cohesion might be looser and more exposed to external influences. The conquerors largely left the natives to their own devices, as long as they paid their taxes. The non-introduction of the manorial system and the preservation of the village community with its traditional chieftains meant a policy of non-intervention in the existing social framework. No attempt was made to break up the traditional forms of social life.

Conversely, though hatred was seemingly the uppermost feeling of the conquered, a certain feeling of contempt for the conqueror was even more significant in our context. The memoirs of a twelfth-century Arab noble – like Usama ibn Munqidh,[73] who frequented and knew Frankish courts and the Franks – reflect neither fear nor hatred, rather contempt colours his attitude to the Franks. This is not equivalent to a total rejection of all things Frankish. There is appreciation of their military valour and even some jealousy regarding the code of Frankish chivalry. This does not mitigate the fact that essentially he looks down on them as illiterate barbarians, for whom physical force is a supreme virtue, their religion is a despised polytheism, their medicine a collection of superstitions and their judicial procedure – with its formalities and duels – an array of antics and irrational vagaries. This representative

---

[73] *An Arab-Syrian Gentleman and Warrior in the Period of the Crusades. Memoirs of Usamah ibn Munquidh*, transl. by Ph. K. Hitti, New York, 1929, 93 and *passim*.

of the refined Arab aristocracy can hardly be compared to a Palestinian fellah. Nevertheless, what he has to say about the Franks would have found a ready response – though less sophisticated – among the lower strata of the native population. Far from feeling inferior to the conqueror, the conquered regarded himself not only his equal, but by far his superior.

Without totally subscribing to Ibn Munqidh's subjective criticism, there is no doubt that in the beginning of the twelfth century the encounter of West and East was that of a culture in its earliest phases of development – far from its achievements two hundred years later – with a highly developed, refined and sophisticated Moslem civilization, a far more worthy heir to classical antiquity than its Romano-Germanic successor. In the realm of thought, literature, art, architecture, material culture, technological achievements, medical knowledge, or geographical experience – let alone the refined style of living at a Moslem court – the West was inferior, hardly able to grasp the advantages of the Orient. Culturally the crusader could offer little to the East; while Moslem society – despite its flimsy political framework – had a solid structure, not easily dissolved under foreign impact, even supposing that such an impact was ever intended.

Political and social non-integration could not and did not remain confined to these two realms. Their sociological and psychological counterpart was a refractory attitude to the Oriental environment. Much has been written about the 'orientalization' or 'Levantinization' of crusader society.[74] It is difficult to escape the feeling that many of these conclusions were highly coloured by ultra-liberal or romantic scholars. In some cases this was wishful thinking, a deliberate attempt to prove the viability of contemporary colonial situations in North Africa and the Near East.

[74] From among the extensive bibliography – very often purely publicistic – attention should be paid to J. L. La Monte, 'The Significance of the Crusaders' States in Medieval History', *Byzantion*, 1940–1, 300–15; Cl. Cahen, 'Indigènes et Croisés', *Syria*, t. 15, 351–60. A typical romantic view is presented by F. Duncalf, 'Some Influences of Oriental Environment in the Kingdom of Jerusalem', *Annual Report of the American Hist. Assoc.*, I (1914), 137–45.

In two hundred years (in human terms some ten generations) of physical co-existence, the Oriental environment undoubtedly influenced the European colonies in the East. But the facts must be visualized in their proper setting. The expression 'orientalization' applied to the crusaders, is as much opposed to the modern expression 'going native', as to 'Levantinization'. For a twelfth-century European there was objectively nothing derogatory in being 'orientalized'. On the contrary, it meant to aspire to and to emulate a degree of civilization and a level of culture far higher than his own. Refinement against coarseness, comfort and luxury against uncouthness, an urge for empirical and speculative knowledge and a breadth of views fitting the immense areas of Moslem domination as against ignorance and parochialism, a study of nature based on the Bible and the Fathers as against intellectual curiosity – this was objectively the 'threat' of being orientalized.

We alluded to the objective meaning of the term, arrived at by detachment in time and space, but diametrically opposed to the evaluation of contemporary Europeans, wielding a different yardstick. Theirs was a scale of values based on belief in one's own religious and ethical superiority, let alone in an elevated position in the order of things. Thinking in such terms it was easy to discern effeminacy, the sin of luxury, the lack of dignity, the belief in ridiculous speculations and connivance with the dark powers to master nature, as against the revealed truths of the Gospels. Many a text could be cited to illustrate this attitude. The most famous is the collection of diatribes by Jaques de Vitry, bishop of Acre, and he is far from being a lonely witness.[75] As to 'Levantinism' in its modern pejorative sense the Latin establishments were well fitted to be its breeding place. Such tendencies were apparently a class

---

[75] There was also the possibility of completely ignoring the oriental. From the best two 'Itineraries' of the Holy Land in the 12th century, that of the pilgrim Theodorich (*PPTS*, V) describes (*c.* 1172) in detail all places of pilgrimage without so much as mentioning the native population. John of Würzburg (*ibid.*) a few years earlier adds in his last chapter the following: 'I have omitted many of the chapels and smaller churches which are maintained there by men of various nations and languages (*follows a long list*) and very many others, it would take long to tell. So with this let us make an end of this little work.' (p. 69).

attribute, rather than a general propensity and were limited to the lower strata of crusader society.

'Orientalization' – despite its obvious virtues and an environment which fostered the process – was balanced and qualified by a basic refractory attitude. The accumulation of texts alluding to contacts between the crusader and his environment distort the picture. Meaningful classification is possible, if the spheres of opposition, autonomy and interaction could be followed up in terms of social participation or involvement.

The most obvious and inevitable level of contact was in the sphere of material culture. Whatever image the crusader colonist might have had of himself in relation to the native, it could hardly have survived the test of extended confrontation. The superiority of comfort and adaptation to local needs was self-evident. Even a zealot could not have denied the excellence of oriental lodgings, unless he was bent on living as a hermit. What could a European – especially from across the Alps – oppose to

> those streets (of Acre) which were exceedingly neat, all the walls of the house being of the same height and all alike built of hewn stone, wondrously adorned with glass windows and paintings, while all the palaces and houses in the city were not built merely to meet the needs of those who dwelt therein but to minister to human luxury and pleasure, each one as far as possible excelling all others in its glazing, painting, pavilions and the other ornaments with which it was furnished within and beautified without.[76]

On solemn occasions the streets of that city were carpeted with cloth of gold and silk.[77] One has to remember the six-storey buildings of Tyre[78] or the previously described palace of the lords

[76] Ludoph von Suchem in *PPTS*, XII, 50–3. The German description was written more than a generation after the fall of Acre. The description of the physical structure of the destroyed city was based on observation of the ruins. What he has to say about the inhabitants of Acre is in part pure fantasy. This description of Acre was plagiarized in the 15th century by Hermann Corner (*Eccardi Corpus Historiorum Medii Aevi*, II, 941 ff.) and transmitted to the historians of the last century, who used it indiscriminately.

[77] Joinville, cap. 102, describing the visit of the sultan of Homs in 1252.

[78] Nasir-I-Khursrau, *Diary of a Journey through Syria and Palestine*, *PPTS*, IV, 11.

of Beirut[79] to understand that the crusaders willingly accepted the oriental life style. They accepted the flat roofs of the houses, economically and socially useful in the Orient; the narrow windows and the novelty of glass panes in common dwellings, and houses built of stone, an excellent insulation against heat and cold. Here the revolution seems to have been almost complete although the statement should be qualified. It has been previously mentioned that for reasons which had nothing to do with the Orient, but on grounds of security, the crusaders were predominantly city-dwelling. Yet the cities were not built by them. With the exception of Acre – where an entirely new and spacious suburb was added – the crusaders simply lodged themselves in the former Moslem houses after expelling the native inhabitants. Thus a crusader city with its layout, markets and houses was physically Moslem, if not of earlier origin. If any new houses were built for the common people, it can be assumed that they imitated the local pattern.

Moving from house to palace – if the latter was not already the former seat of a local potentate – we find a conscious imitation of the oriental, which, as in Beirut might have fused Moslem and Byzantine elements. When comparing a twelfth-century European *donjon* with a contemporary Moslem building no additional explanation is needed. The crusader gave up his traditional concept of human dwellings fitting a knight and noble without much of a fight. The technological, artistic and human advantages of the Orient were so great that only irrational fanatics could have resisted them.

But the victorious march of oriental influence was halted when it came to religious and military architecture. The dome crowned pre-crusader churches or converted mosques, but was very seldom used in new buildings. The later Crusader churches proper were Romanesque in plan and appearance. Oriental decor may appear on a frieze or capital, testimony to the fact that local masons participated in the construction. The slavish imitation of late Byzantine, Corinthian capitals could have been the last flicker of a native art which had survived among the Christians of Syria.

[79] See above, cap XVII, The Arts: A.

Perhaps a minaret could easily be turned into a belfry, but when the crusaders built belfries, as in the Holy Sepulchre, they brought their model from southern France. Native, local loans did not make a crusader church or monastery oriental, nor even a fusion of East and West. The West dictated the style and figurative art, and where the Occident could furnish no models, it deigned to accept local elements which seemed suitable. Military architecture probably absorbed far more oriental elements, often as a response to the Moslem challenge. But the surviving examples of crusader interiors are thoroughly European in concept and style of execution,[80] e.g., the crypt of St John in Acre (probably the refectory of the Hospitallers), or the nearby remnants of the same establishment; the interior of the great hall at Chastel Pèlerin, the rooms in Monfort of the Teutonic Knights, those of the Hospitallers in Beit-Jibrin, the gate room in Caesarea. Today they make a more European impression than when they were still inhabited and oriental carpets covered walls and floors. The orders were not averse to pomp in their reception rooms and were willing to use oriental decor, backed by a solid Romanesque or Gothic model.

The same applied in large measure to the realm of food and dress. The culinary art of the Orient opened a whole new world of smells and tastes to the colonists: unknown fruits, condiments and spices. Palestine and Syria did not, however, add much to the crusader table in the way of meat or venison. The country's fauna was infinitely poorer than that of Europe. The Orient invaded the colonies via the culinary art. Inter-marriage with Byzantines and Armenians on the royal and princely level, or lower down with Armenians, Syrians and converted Moslems, was probably directly responsible for this pleasant infiltration of the crusader kitchen. Not less important was the institution of public cooking-stalls in the cities, especially Jerusalem. They existed before the Crusades, but now catered to the large pilgrim trade, no different from modern tourists. To obtain 'a European impression' we follow the pilgrim Thietmar (1217) into an Eastern *souk* or bazaar:

---

[80] The description of the palace of the Templars in Acre makes the impression of an Italian *palazzo*. Cf. *Templier de Tyre*, par. 501.

The people (of Damascus) are as delectable as their place. They have
as many delicacies and varieties of food as a human mind can conceive,
and even more. Twenty varieties of bread and more, I saw them and
tasted some. It is very rarely that anyone prepares his food at home,
because it is customary that such things are prepared in the public
market and these things are carried around the city for sale. [81]

In Jerusalem and Acre – and probably also in Tyre – the principal
mediators were the native Christians, for the simple reason that
the Moslem population was exterminated during the conquest,
and in Jerusalem was legally barred from re-settling in the city.
Here the European colonist had his first fill of spices and condiments. Sugar, a medicine for many generations to come (because
of its benign taste as well as its price), was consumed directly by
sucking the marvellous *cana mellis* (sugar-cane) or as syrup. Fulk
of Chartres during the First Crusade does not find words to describe
the marvels of this unknown plant[82] when he encountered it for
the first time. More marvels were to come. As today, the local
flora was extensively used for condiments, and spices from far
away lands were easily and cheaply obtainable. For Joinville, who
was certainly not a yokel, these spices come directly from Paradise.

Before this river (Nile) enters Egypt, there are expert men, who throw
of an evening their nets into the river and let them lie outspread.
When morning comes they find in their nets such things as are sold
by weight in this land, namely, ginger, rhubarb, aloes and cinnamon.
It is said in the country that these things come from the earthly
paradise, and that the wind strikes down the trees in paradise as it
does dry branches in our forests and what falls into the river the water
carries and the merchants collect it and sell it to us by weight. [83]

---

[81] One of the *souks* of Jerusalem was called *Malquisinat* – 'Street of bad
cooking': 'On this street meat is cooked for pilgrims which is being sold to them.'
Itinéraires à Jérusalem, publ. by H. Michelant and G. Raynaud, Geneva, 1882,
150–1, cf. 38. On Damascus: *Mag. Thietmari Peregrinatio*, ed. Laurent, Hamburg,
1852, 21–2.
[82] Fulco Carnotensis, I, cap. 33.
[83] Joinville, cap. 40.

This was written in the second half of the thirteenth century when Italian and Provençal commerce certainly penetrated the seneschal's native Champagne and spices were no novelty.

It was difficult not to accept the amenities of this cuisine. The syrup of sugar or honey of sugar (by-product of sugar) being used as a honey-drink or for flavouring Eastern cakes. The citrus fruit, oranges, lemons, Adam's apples, were used by 'the natives for pickles to eat with fowls, fish and other food, and they make food very palatable'. The preserves of peaches and citrus, the bananas which are 'sweet, like fine butter and honey from the comb'[84] all added to the simple and heavy Northern menu. The basic kitchen fat changed from butter or lard to olive oil. By-products of oil production were the famous eastern sweets. The crusaders themselves revived the ancient glory of the country, its grapes and wines, which had suffered under Islam. Figs and pomegranates, olives, rice, corn and the chick-pea (prepared as the delicious *hummus*), marvellous fruit from Damascus at all seasons and snow from Mount Hermon, which chilled sherbets (from Arab. *sharaba* – 'drink') – all this was new and tantalizing, revealing the Orient at its best. Here and there oriental influence overcame European custom. Although tables and chairs were normally used, native-born knights learned the art of squatting during meals.[85] The dishes of the Orient were far more suited to the climate than Western foods[86] and one had to learn to eat less. The gargantuan appetites of the North were not compatible with the new climate. Mortality was high and what happened to the colonists before adjustment remained the common lot of all new crusaders for two hundred years. The Palestinian climate was decimating and felled hundreds and thousands.[87]

As the crusaders adopted oriental food so they could have picked

[84] Burchard of Mount Sion, *PPTS*, XII, 100–1.

[85] Joinville, cap. 98.

[86] Usama ibn Munqidh tells the story of a crusader old-timer whose *cuisine* is purely Egyptian, ed. Hitti, p. 169.

[87] Jacques de Vitry stresses the continence of the Italians in food, cap. 67. Cf. e.g. *Freidanks Bescheidenheit*, ed. Pannier, Leipzig, 1878, 126; Joinville, cap. 81.

up habits of oriental attire. Tancred's *kefiyeh* (a cloth used for headgear) which appears on one of his coins received much attention, but to regard this as 'orientalization' seems exaggerated. Tancred spoke Arabic,[88] which he could have learned in southern Italy – as did his compatriot Richard de Principatu and this could also apply to the *kefiyeh*. Whatever the case, it was practical to cover an iron helmet with cloth in the hot climate of Syria. There is no doubt that silk was much used by the Frankish nobility and patriciate, as were the expensive brocades of the East on solemn occasions. It is here that Joinville bought camlet cloth for Queen Margaret and the latter kneeled, taking it for holy relics.[89] The crusader states served as stepping stones for the march of Eastern textiles to Europe, conquering nobility and church alike. The Byzantine monopoly over the export of expensive cloth was bypassed by direct contact with Egypt, Damascus and Baghdad, as well as with some local industries in Syria.[90] The oriental wives of the princely houses may well have taken the lead in this trans-formation. They also mediated the use of perfumes and toilet accessories, which were not shunned by Frankish nobles and even ecclesiastics. Though in the spheres of food and dress the adoption of local habits must have been widespread, strong barriers existed, and the refractory attitude found earlier in architecture can be detected again.

The crusader kingdom has the doubtful privilege of being the first Christian state to enforce dress regulations. As early as 1120 the Council of Nablus threatened that any Moslem wearing Frankish dress would be at the mercy of the king.[91] This was a one-way prohibition, since there was obviously no need to prohibit Franks from wearing Moslem dress. The aim was to prevent any possible mixing of Franks and natives. As far as the Franks were concerned the wearing of native dress would mean degradation. Thus the Frankish adoption of oriental textiles does not mean that

[88] *RHC, Hist. Occidentaux*, III, 198.

[89] Joinville, cap. 118.

[90] See above cap. XVI: Economic Life and Commerce.

[91] Mansi, *Concilia*, XXI, col. 264: 'Si Sarracenus aut Sarracena Francigeno more se induant – infiscentur.'

they accepted Moslem dress. From the silence of Western sources, so prompt to criticize the crusaders especially when suspected of imitating the Orientals, it can be safely deduced that the crusaders followed European fashions. It was deemed degrading that the Syrian Christians wore the same attire as Moslems, except for a distinct type of woollen girdle (later, post-crusader sources, called them 'Christians of the girdle' – *Chrétiens de ceinture*).[92] Very often Syrian Christians were taken for Moslems and killed because of their beards and attire. Judging by clothes there could be no doubt who was and who was not a Frank. Frankish women, for example, never accepted trousers as part of their dress,[93] though we are told that some husbands, certainly of the lower classes, imposed on them the wearing of veils. The most expensive type of oriental clothing often came into the possession of the Frankish nobility as gifts from Moslem rulers.[94] But public opinion was decidedly against 'going oriental'. Henry of Champagne who tried to establish friendly relations with Saladin sends the following message: 'You know that the use of the tunic and tarbush (turban) is among us a dishonour. I will wear it for friendship to you'.[95]

Since fashion is directly connected with general appearance we shall not be surprised to find the Franks following European tradition. The warriors of the First Crusade were bearded. Indeed, Baldwin I in dire need of money effectively threatened his Armenian father-in-law with the loss of his beard unless he paid his debts.[96] However, beards disappeared by the middle of the twelfth century and names like *cum barba* which appear in our sources point to the exceptions. By the end of the century a Moslem chronicler remarks about a Frankish nobleman: 'He was really handsome, but clean shaven, according to the fashion of his nation'.[97]

[92] Burchard of Mount Sion, *PPTS*, XII, 104.

[93] *Magistri Thietmari Peregrinatio*, ed. Laurent, p. 19.

[94] E.g. Baldwin II when liberated from Moslem captivity. *RHC, Hist. Orientaux*, III, 644: A gift from Saladin to Bohemond, *ibid.* II, 67.

[95] Ibn al-Athir, *ibid.* 59.

[96] William of Tyre, XI, 11.

[97] Beha ed-Din, *RHC, Hist. Orientaux*, III, 266–7.

In matters of dress the obvious barriers were the monastic congregations, the clergy and the military orders. No conclusions should be drawn from this fact, as we deal here with formal regulations common to Europe and the Christian East. The white woollen mantles of the military orders might have been influenced by some Eastern garment, like the Moslem *abbaya* or burnous, which in modern times influenced the dress of the *pères blancs* of North Africa and the French spahis. Its practicibility in the hot climate was undisputed.

The third sphere of contact, or rather a symptom of proximity, was the language of the country. Words of Arabic origin in European languages are often pointed to as a sign of orientalization.[98] Some historians even ventured to conclude that the Franks knew Arabic. Our sources prove the contrary. All the Arabic in crusader sources proper amounted to some three dozen nouns, one third of them applying to Moslem objects, whose use was simply inevitable, e.g. *qadi, rais, mameluk, turgeman, faqi, mahomeria* (a neologism deriving from 'Muhammed'), but also *mesged* and *masquida, halifa* (= khalif) and *Baffumet* (= Muhammed). The *turgeman* – finally transformed into a Frankish office and type of fief or tenure – the *dragomanagium*, points to the necessity for an interpreter in a land where lord and peasant did not speak the same language. Some other words derive from commerce or agriculture, e.g. *massera* – for wine and oil press; *jarra* – jar, a receptacle and measure of liquid, *quintar* and *rotulus* – *rutl*, weights current in the Near East as well as *ghirara*[99]; money units like *robuinus, robba* – a quart and *carrubla;* customs and taxes like *kharaj* and *tuazo,* the customs office *duana* (= diwân), the money unit *daremus* (= dirhem); the market inspector *motasep* (= motaheseb), *rabbatium* (= ribât) – a merchants' halting place, *sochelbes* (= sûk al-bezz) – textile market, *soguedic* (= suk el-dik) – poultry market, *funeidec* – a small market[100].

[98] Naturally any inquiry into this difficult problem has to ascertain if a given word entered a European language through the crusader kingdom or via Sicily or Spain.

[99] On these measures, see J. Prawer, 'Le muid royal de Saint-Jean d'Acre et les mesures arabes contemporaines', *Byzantion,* XXII (1952), 58 ff.

[100] For measures, cf., e.g., Strehlke, *Tab. ord. Theutonici,* no. 34; *Regesta.* p. 243.

Other words denote objects of native origin like: *sussiman* – sesame, *zuccarum* – sugar; fabrics like *samit* – samite, *baudequin* – baldachin, *taffeta*, damask, camlet and muslin; musical instruments: *nacare*, *cassaria* and *zalamella;* weapons like: *casigans*, *targe* – shield.[101] More often appear nouns like *berquile* – for water reservoirs, *caravan* – for the seasonal transport ship and *arsenal* (dar al-sana) for a dock or place of ship repairs.

The appearance of some lonely Arabic words is more surprising, like the Persian *izeq* (= iazaq) for a military unit, *calige* (= khalige) – canal, *karaque* – a small boat or *tabout* – coffin, *muzâr* – tomb and the rather surprising *mesquine* (= poor) in the sense of an arab prostitute.[102]

Geographical names were normally accepted in their oriental version, like *Kefar* – village, *Beit* – house, *'Ain* – source, sometimes *Jebal* – mountain, though a *Kefar* will often become *casale* if connected with the name of a Frankish proprietor, like *casale Roberti*, *casale episcopi* etc. We find also *oedi* (= wâdi)[103] though it is normally rendered by *vallis*.

The few loans from arabic over a period of two hundred years hardly prove a major impact of the local language on the crusaders. Compared with Spanish or Italian, few Arabic words entered the crusader vocabulary. Though it seems probable that more words were in current use in the *souks* of Jerusalem, Acre and Tyre, they did not find their way into the written sources.

A knowledge of Arabic does not seem then to have been very common. Not only was there a need for official interpreters, but the special attention in the sources, Western and Eastern, to men who spoke Arabic is symptomatic. If in 1146 a crusader emissary,

169. For money units: *Regesta*, pp. 120, 363 Strehlke, no. 34. For taxes: Strehlke, no. 112; *Regesta*, p. 290. *Tuazo* is thought by Röhricht to be an Arabic word, might be Italian or French. For market designations: *Regesta*, pp. 135, 158, 325, 223. For customs: *Regesta*, pp. 48, 226, 243.

101 For plants: Regesta, p. 102; textiles: William of Tyre, IX, 29, Cont. of William of Tyre, p. 587; musical instruments: *Gestes des Chiprois*, p. 212, *Regesta*, p. 294; weapons: *Itinerarium Ricardi I*, p. 390, *Gestes*, p. 245.

102 Respectively: *Gestes*, p. 165, Cont. of William of Tyre, p. 356, *Gestes*, p. 133, *Gestes*, p. 217, *Regesta*, p. 288, William of Tyre, IV, 22.

103 E.g., Oedi el-Hammen in *Regesta*, p. 330.

already suspected of connivance with the Moslems, is sent again on a mission because of his knowledge of the Moslems and their language, [104] it seems difficult to argue that such knowledge was common. Indeed, the early crusader imitations of Arab money prove their total ignorance of the enemy's language. [105]

For different reasons some of the Franks learned Arabic. Among the lower classes it might have been an everyday need or at least the casual acquisition of a language spoken in the market-place, whereas a different attitude could have prevailed among some of the upper classes. William of Tyre in the middle of the twelfth century, the great and only luminary of the kingdom, was able to read and probably speak Arabic. He also wrote the earliest Latin history of Islam, a work unfortunately lost to posterity. In the third quarter of the thirteenth century, William of Tripoli, of whose origins we know nothing, knew the language well and wrote for missionary purposes a short description of the propagation of Islam.[106] A similar purpose in learning the language guided the Dominican, Yve le Breton.[107] A subordinate commander (possibly of Syrian origin) of the Templars, Lion Cazalier of Saphet (1266), was sent to Baibars because he knew Arabic. The language is spoken by a member of the crusader patriciate, Nicholas of Acre, by a knight, Philip Mainebeuf of Acre,[108] but also by members of the highest native-born aristocracy like Humphrey, who interpreted for Richard Lionheart and al-Malik al-'Adil at Arsuf and Baldwin d'Ibelin.[109] Some of that knowledge could have been acquired by frequenting Moslem society, which although not unknown was rare. There was some opposition to this kind of fraternization. It is enough to remember the attitude

[104] William of Tyre, XVI, 12.

[105] See above, cap. XVI: Economic Life and Commerce.

[106] The *Tractatus de statu Saracenorum et de Mahomete pseudopropheta et eorum lege et fide* by William of Tripoli, then a Dominican in Acre was finished in 1273; published by H. Prutz, *Kulturgeschichte der Kreuzzüge*, 575–98. Cf. P. A. Throop, *Criticism of the Crusade*, Amsterdam, 1940, 115 ff.

[107] Joinville, cap. XXIX.

[108] *Gestes des Chiprois*, par. 347; Joinville, cap. LXXI, *Gestes*, par. 485.

[109] Beha ed-Din, *RHC, Hist. Orientaux*, III, 266–7; Abu Shama, *ibid*, IV, 396–400; Joinville, cap. LXX.

of the Franks to Emperor Frederick II (though the circumstances were rather exceptional), but it is not unknown elsewhere. There is the story of the friendship between Reginald Mansuer, son of the constable of Antioch and lord of Bulunyas and Marakiyeh, who would spend days with his Moslem friends in the orchards of the city and then invite them to his castle. But finally this idyll was interrupted by a zealot or suspicious Frank who expelled the Moslems.[110]

Non-integration, or more exactly *Apartheid*, had deep-reaching influences and not merely in the social and political domain where it was specifically envisaged. It was also reflected in a particular attitude, a mental disposition to erect barriers even in spheres where proximity created contacts and co-existence exerted mutual influence. This was probably one of the major factors responsible for the failure of the crusader kingdom to become an intermediary between the Moslem East and Christian Europe. The almost permanent state of war may have handicapped the kingdom from playing that role, yet we cannot fully subscribe to the opinion which puts all the blame on the martial character of the colonies. Crusaders eager to study Arabic, Moslem culture and religion could and did do so, as witnessed by William, bishop of Tyre, or some less known scholars, like the Pisan Stephen of Antioch, a graduate of Salerno and the translator (1127) of the medical works of Ali ben Abbas (tenth century), who also envisaged the translation of Arab philosophy. There was Philip of Tripoli, a canon under Guy de Valence, presumably the bishop of Tripoli, who translated (*ca.* 1250) the popular book of all-round wisdom and knowledge attributed to Aristotle, the *Secretum Secretorum*.[111] Then again Amalric, a Spaniard, archdeacon of Antioch, who in the middle of the twelfth century wrote a Spanish translation of part of the Old Testament interpolated by an 'Itinerary' of the

---

[110] Caffaro, *RHC, Hist. Occidentaux*, V, 67. One of the chief complaints of Jacques de Vitry against the *poulains* is their nearness to the Moslems.

[111] Cf. H. Haskins, *Studies in the History of Mediaeval Science*, N. Y., 1927 (reprint 1960), 130 ff.

Holy Land and dedicated it to Raymond, archbishop of Toledo, the founder of the great school of translators in that city. Amalric's knowledge of biblical Hebrew and perhaps even Aramaic is remarkable. His translation, the earliest Spanish version of the Old Testament is based in preference on the Hebrew original, rather than the Vulgate.[112] The question remains why so few and so little. Even stranger, why did not the superior geographical knowledge of Islam enter the crusader heritage.[113] In some cities, like Antioch or Jerusalem, the treasures of oriental knowledge could undoubtedly be had for the asking. William of Tyre received from king Amalric the Arabic sources for his lost *Deeds of the Oriental Princes*,[114] among them the chronicle of Eutychius of Alexandria (Sa'id ibn Batriq). Frederick II's 'philosopher' Theodorus was an Arab of Antioch. Syrian and Jewish physicians, natives of the kingdom or of neighbouring countries, attended crusader princes. A book of oriental astrology was dedicated to King Amalric.[115] The question then was not of availability, but the degree of receptiveness by crusader society to the intellectual treasures of the East. To this the answer is negative.

Could the martial and commercial character of the crusader establishments be the root of a certain insensitivity to the intellectual and spiritual achievements of the Orient? We do not believe that this is an entirely satisfactory answer. If arguments are needed it can be pointed out that there were intervals of peace and that even during war caravans moved over the commercial routes. Moslems scholars visited Syria and Palestine and the oriental Christians frequented crusader cities.[116] Decidedly, there were ample possibilities of contact, even under existing circumstances – though less than in Sicily or in not always peaceful Spain. Some

---

[112] Cf. Almerich, *La Fazienda de Ultra Mar. Biblia romanceada et Itinéraire biblique en prose castillane du XII siècle*, publ. by M. Lazar, Salamanca, 1965.

[113] Cf. J. K. Wright, *The Geographical Lore of the Time of the Crusaders*, N.Y., 1965, 109.

[114] William of Tyre in his *Prologus*, *RHC, Hist. Occidentaux*, I, 5: *ipso Arabica exemplaria ministrante*.

[115] See above n. 111.

[116] Cl. Cahen, *La Syrie du Nord*, 577–8.

oriental knowledge was brought from here to Europe, some topics transposed and absorbed into the literature of the West. But only the *Chansons des Chétifs* might actually have been written in Antioch.[117] The crusaders did not mediate such transmissions. European visitors to the East gathered local material and once safely back in the West, spun their oriental yarns. In the nature of things some behaved like modern tourists. A pilgrim like Thietmar (1217) says with more assurance than real modesty: 'I was in Damascus for six days and I learned *quedam* of the teachings and life of the Saracens.' What he learned was that the vice of homosexuality would menace the future of Islam, were it not for the *muezzins* whose call from the minarets wakes the Moslems to perform their marital duties! No wonder that he concludes: 'Their life is uncouth and their law corrupted.'[118]

A basic condition of receptivity is a certain appreciation for the utility, importance or intrinsic value of the achievements of an opponent. A utilitarian factor (like material well-being where the crusaders were surely receptive) can also be envisaged in the non-material sphere. For example, the urge to study the Quran, Moslem theology and philosophy did not start out as an act of scholarly or human curiosity, but to forge weapons for religious disputation and ultimately Christian mission. Such developments though current in the West were bypassed in the crusader establishments. The crusaders had an eye for the military valour and often chivalry of the Moslems despite the recurrent label of *gens maudits*. Yet not much else is noted, let alone recommended. It was only when the kingdom was nearing its end that an appreciation of Moslem religion, *mores* and character came to the fore, but even then it did not come from the crusader *milieu* proper, but from European missionaries, who came for a closer look at their opponents.

---

[117] A. Hatem, *Les poèmes épiques des Croisades*, Paris, 1932; S. Duparc – Quioc, *Le cycle de la Croisade*, Paris, 1955. To the literature on East-West contacts recently, G. Schreiber, 'Christliches Orient und mittelaterliches Abendland', *Oriens Christianus*, t. 38 (1958), 96–112; t. 39 (1959), 66–78, who has little to say on the crusader period.

[118] *Mag. Thietmari Peregrinatio*, ed. Laurent, p. 22.

William of Tripoli is still occupied with Moslem religion and how to use some of its tenets to propagate Christianity, but a generation later Riccoldo de Monte Croce will give a sympathetic account of Islam and of the Moslems.[119] But the crusader *milieu* proper remained non-receptive.

This was certainly not the result of zealotry or bigotry. Of whatever vice the crusaders might have been accused, they were anything but zealots. Not only did mosques remain in their cities, and freedom of religion a part of the political structure, but their liberalism in matters of religious tolerance caused much disapproval, until the image of double-tongued, perfidious or even perjured colonist entered some European literature. The German *Minnesinger* Freidank, a participant in the Crusade of Frederick II, speaking about Acre, puts it succinctly: 'Take my word for it, no difference is there between Christian and pagan. . . . Old and young speak a pagan language. For them a pagan is worth more than two Christians and some.'[120] In summary, without denying the possible influence of adverse political circumstances, other factors have to be taken into consideration to explain the non-receptiveness of crusader culture and, consequently, the negligible role it played as an intermediary between East and West.

---

[119] William of Tripoli (above n. 106) advises the missionary to use some of the Christian tenets accepted by Islam to open the way to the hearts of the Infidels. Riccoldo de Monte Croce, ed. J. C. M. Laurent, *Peregrinatores Medii Aevi Quatuor*, Leipzig, 1864, 100–41, has a favourable account of the oriental Christian sects and a warm appreciation of the Moslems. He introduces a lengthy description of their *mores* by the following: 'they received us (in Baghdad) as we were God's angels in their schools, colleges, monasteries, in their churches or synagogues or their houses and we learned assiduously their teachings and their actions. We were absolutely overwhelmed how one could find actions of such perfection in such perfidious teachings. We refer here briefly to the acts of perfections of the Saracens more for the confusion of Christians than recommendation of Saracens. Who will not be overwhelmed if he diligently considers the Saracens' solicitude for study, devotion in prayer, charity to the poor, reverence for the name of God, prophets and holy places, altruism in behaviour (possibly: gravity – *gratuitas in moribus*), affability to strangers, friendship to strangers, friendship and love to their own people', *ibid.*, cap. XXI–XXII.

[120] *Freidanks Bescheidenheit*, ed. Pannier, Leipzig, 1878, 126.

Although the lack of a programme, the rapid conquest and the overseas character of the Crusades do not have much in common, some of their results converged to create a particular situation, which was responsible for the cultural character of the colonies. We refer to the notion of 'frontier', as it existed in Spain, Sicily and the Muscovite east. In all these 'continental' colonial movements, the 'frontier' played a major role in the future of the different colonies. The 'frontier' is not only a military march, but also an area of confrontation between the contending parties and a sphere of prolonged contacts between peoples and cultures. Cognizance of the enemy across the frontier over decades plays a paramount role in expansion, and even more so in the future of colonization. The virtues and weakness of the opponents are assessed and challenge meets response. In the 'frontier' area a kind of osmosis takes place, percolation and finally inter-mixture of both cultures. In such areas a particular receptiveness is thus moulded even if checked and balanced by inherent refractory attitudes. Subsequent expansion and colonization, carry with them the knowledge already acquired, but also receptiveness for a different social order and culture. Moreover, the culture of the colonizer is by then partly influenced by that of his opponent, and a certain levelling of the difference enhances an open-minded approach. Such 'frontier' areas move with expansion and what was previously enemy territory becomes in its turn a 'frontier' area. If the former population is not exterminated or expelled, the chances are that the newly conquered area will even more efficiently facilitate the exchange of mutual influence. Its role as 'frontier' will largely depend on the interval preceding renewed expansion. In overseas colonization, where there was no former common 'frontier' the first establishment, the erstwhile bridgehead, could fulfil the functions of a 'frontier'.

The First Crusade and the resulting European colonies lacked any of the conditions alluded to. There was no former common 'frontier' and contact zone, no knowledge of the opponent or of his culture. If anything there was a completely erroneous image of the enemy, his characteristics, modes of life, religion, scholarship and science, often relegated to the realm of sorcery and witchcraft.[121] Thus the First Crusade, in addition to its religious zeal and fanaticism, brought with it a refractory attitude. The conquest itself was short, too short to turn the Western bridgeheads into a 'frontier' in the previously described sense. The cities, the main centres of Islamic culture, were systematically looted during the first generation of conquest and the bearers of this culture expelled or exterminated. The Moslem intellectual élite (as well as that of the oriental Christians) was never re-established in the kingdom. Thus East-West contacts took place on the material level; commerce spread them into the neighbouring countries but contacts which could have become decisive on the level of intellectual intercourse were rare. Pilgrimages or visits to adjacent Moslem areas could not fill this gap. Later missionaries with an appreciative ear were not Syrian-born *poulains*, but like Riccolus de Monte Croce, of European origin. At that time Europe had already been influenced via Spain and Sicily.

Furthermore, the cultural level of the kingdom itself is important in explaining why the colonies never became a cultural exchange centre. It is certainly wrong to suppose that the colonies remained permanently bent on war and that the clash of swords silenced all other voices. But the kingdom[122] never became a centre of intellectual activity, and remained an extension of European culture, provincial and marginal. Schools there certainly were, parochial, monastic and cathedral – none left any traces of importance. No college of translators, no university was ever created in an age of university founding. Whatever a crusader generation had and thought worthwhile to transmit to its successors was sufficiently taken care of by everyday life, by imitating the older generation in their chivalrous code of behaviour and techniques of commercial intercourse. Not by chance did the study

---

[121] Cf. R. W. Southern, *Western Views of Islam in the Middle Ages*, Cambridge, Mass, 1962, cap. I: The Age of Ignorance. This interesting essay does not take into account crusader sources.

[122] See above cap. XIX.

[122] A lonely witness to intellectual activity: 'magister Leonius qui legebat de theologia in civitate Acconensi', Jacques de Vitry. *Lettres*. p. 110. Other *magistri* appear sporadically in documents.

of law, oral and customary, become the great playground of the crusader aristocracy. In addition to being the cornerstone of class privilege, the law was by nature the most traditional and conservative element. With all that is common to Europe and its Eastern colonies, no European country ever used and abused legal precedent to the utmost as in the Latin East. *Silbenstecher* (= hairsplitters) is the name fittingly given to crusader jurists by one of the greatest scholars of mediaeval law.[123] This was the only important aspect of intellectual life created in the kingdom.

The absence of any school in the mediaeval sense of the word is not only a symptom of the intellectual level, but played a decisive role in our context. The transmission of culture can very rarely be assured by the activity of a lonely individual. The potential diffusion of one man's knowledge is limited and his time-span relatively short. Though an intellectual centre, college, university or a particular school cannot permanently assure a high level, it does become a repository of culture. The fact that no Salerno or Toledo was ever established in the kingdom could explain the absence of any mechanism for the preservation and transmission of oriental culture which might have been acquired by a previous generation.

Finally there were the Crusades themselves, repeating the initial pattern. The constant stream of immigrants during the twelfth century, and especially the great military expeditions, acted as a spiritual solvent upon any potential intermixture of East and West. The colonies did not create a cultural web strong enough to absorb and assimilate the waves of newcomers. Every new Crusade or wave of migration strengthened the Western element and assured the permanence of its values. This could explain why in the thirteenth century we hear new and appreciative voices in regard to Islam. In that century the waves of migration abated until their almost complete cessation and the great Crusades also disappear.

---

[123] H. Brunner, 'Wort und Form im altfranzösischen Prozess', *Forsch. zur Gesch. des deutschen u. französischen Rechts*, Stuttgart, 1894, 274.

societies. As demonstrated, influences – even in areas of natural and obvious contact – were sifted by an array of intellectual and emotional filters. Particular social classes reacted differently to the enticements of a higher and more developed alien culture.

Even this selective process of partial assimilation seemed degenerate to many a European newcomer, and to some modern historians. It is true that other historians saw this trend in a positive light, the beginnings of fusion and merger, a phenomenon which really never took place and was certainly not envisaged by the crusaders. There is a good deal of truth and acute observation in the saying of a cultured Moslem: 'The Franks are an accursed race, who do not assimilate with any but their own kin.'[124] As might be expected, this attitude of rejection was stronger among newcomers – participants in the great Crusades, pilgrims or simple immigrants – than among those living in the country. To quote the same Moslem author: 'Among the Franks some have become acclimatized and have associated long with the Moslems. These are much better than the newcomers from the Frankish lands. But they constitute the exception and cannot be treated as a rule.'[125] The first two phrases are obvious but this is more than could be said for the last one. Taken literally, it means that there was in the country a permanent majority of newcomers, which will be difficult to prove or disprove. It is not, however, impossible to assume that during the twelfth century, a period of continuous immigration, this was really the case. One way or another, to the Moslem observer the crusader society which he frequented seemed on the whole non-assimilative.

Some areas were consciously and jealously guarded from any admixture of or influence by the native culture and remained exclusively European. They represented the entire spectrum of social institutions, political rule and administration, social stratification and codes of behaviour for the different classes of crusader

[124] Usama ibn Munqidh, transl, by Ph. K. Hitti, p. 159.
[125] Usama ibn Munqidh, p. 169. A stimulating study on conditions of cultural receptiveness from a different point of view was written by H. A. R. Gibb, 'The Influence of Islamic Culture on Medieval Europe', *Changes in Medieval Society*, ed. S. L. Thrupp, New York, 1964, 155–68.

society. The legal institutions and procedures were European and were meant to create and perpetuate a European society. Although some aspects of material culture changed, the realms of the spiritual, intellectual, artistic, social and political were not influenced, or were hardly scratched, by two centuries of co-existence. The line of demarcation between areas open or closed to influence coincided with the self-image of the crusaders. All characteristics and features regarded as essential in preserving the crusader view of their own identity were barred to alien influence.

The deliberate creation and maintenance of such barriers might have had even more far-reaching results. Could it not have influenced in some measure the crusaders' relationship to their own heritage? All their political and social institutions, their military organization and some aspects of their artistic creativity were imbued with a strong sense of traditionalism. Despite permanent contacts with Europe, perhaps even a feeling of being a part thereof, the crusaders were reluctant followers or at best latecomers in moving with European developments. They appear to have cherished an anachronistic image of Europe, characteristic of that continent at the turn of the eleventh century. This deeply ingrained traditionalism was probably the result of several factors. First and foremost, this was the feeling of being a younger offspring, common to many colonial societies, which tends to create a sentiment of inadequacy and the need to follow an existing order, to accept and bow to the *mores* of ancestors and homeland. A reversal of such an attitude could take place if an overwhelming or forceful alien element were to become dominant and supplant the existing emotional ties by another set of allegiances and pieties. Such a change could also be effected by an élite, in some measure intellectual, with a less despondent outlook and a more daring approach, willing to cut loose from existing links and strike out on its own. None of these factors ever existed in the crusader kingdom. From beginning to end the French element was the decisive social and cultural factor, strong enough to absorb and dominate all other elements in an immigrant society. Finally, we already stressed the almost total absence of an intellectual élite in the kingdom. Against this background the attitude to oriental society might have played an important role, if not creating then at least putting into relief already existing features. A society which raises barriers against the new and the alien tends to entrench itself ever more deeply in its own heritage. The latter becomes sacrosanct as much in its essential as in its non-essential components. Resentment against alien innovations fossilizes the perspective of one's own heritage, which is perceived as perfect at the earliest stage of transfer. This is followed by wholesale apotheosis of the past. The same, though not total rejection which dominates the attitude to an alien culture, is expressed by looking askance at new developments in the original home of one's own heritage. Apotheosis of the past and the link with tradition, important at a certain state of growth in a new society, turn into a dead weight of anachronistic postulates.

BIBLIOGRAPHY

I   On the Eve of the First Crusade

No attempt is made here to give a full bibliography on the Crusades as the book deals primarily with the crusader kingdom. The best bibliography of the Crusades and of the Latin establishments in the East in the Middle Ages is the monumental work of:

H. E. Mayer, *Bibliographie zur Geschichte der Kreuzzüge*, Hanover 1962 (new edition in preparation). Now supplemented by the same author 'Literaturbericht über die Geschichte der Kreuzzüge', *Historische Zeitschrift*, Sonderheft 3, 1969, pp. 641–736.

Almost all current publications regarding the Holy Land are listed by:

P. Thomsen, *Die Palästina-Literatur*, 1908 ff. and *Kiryath Sefer* publ. by the Jewish National and University Library, 1924 ff.

Major works dealing with the Crusades and the history of the Latin kingdom:

H. Prutz, *Kulturgeschichte der Kreuzzüge*, Berlin, 1883.

R. Röhricht, *Geschichte des Königreichs Jerusalem*, Innsbruck, 1898.

W. B. Stevenson, *The Crusaders in the East*, London, 1907.

L. Bréhier, *L'église et l'Orient au moyen-âge: les Croisades*, Paris, 1928.

R. Grousset, *Histoire des Croisades et du royaume franc de Jérusalem*, 3 vols, Paris, 1934–6.

S. Runciman, *A History of the Crusades*, 3 vols, London, 1952–4.

J. Richard, *Le royaume latin de Jérusalem*, Paris, 1953.

A History of the Crusades, ed. K. M. Setton and M. W. Baldwin (in progress), 2 vols appeared since 1955, 1969.

H. E. Mayer, *Geschichte der Kreuzzüge*, Stuttgart, 1965.

J. Prawer, *Histoire du royaume latin de Jérusalem*, 2 vols, Paris, 1969–71.

II The Crusade

Major works dealing with the formation of the ideology of the Crusades:

C. Erdmann, *Die Entstehung des Kreuzzugsgedankens*, Stuttgart, 1935.

P. Alphandéry et A. Dupront, *La chrétienté et l'idée de croisade*, 2 vols, Paris, 1954–9.

E. Delaruelle, 'Essai sur la formation de l'idée de croisade', *Bulletin de la littérature ecclésiastique*, 42, 45, 54/5 (1941, 1944, 1953/4). See also bibl. to cap XVIII.

Specifically for the First Crusade:

F. Chalandon, *Histoire de la première croisade jusqu'à l'élection de Godefroi de Bouillon*, Paris, 1924.

R. Röhricht, *Geschichte des ersten Kreuzzuges*, Innsbruck, 1901.

A. C. Krey, *The First Crusade. The Accounts of Eye Witnesses and Participants*, Princeton, 1921.

H. Hagenmeyer, *Peter der Eremit*, Leipzig, 1879.

On the Peasants' Crusade and the persecution of the Jews:

F. Duncalf, 'The Peasants' Crusade', *Amer. Hist. Rev.*, 26 (1920/1), 440–53.

T. Wolff, *Die Bauernkreuzzüge des Jahres 1096*, Tübingen, 1892.

W. Porges, 'The Clergy, the Poor and the Non-Combatants in the First Crusade', *Speculum*, 21 (1946), 1–24.

J. Baer, 'Gzeroth Tatnu' (Heb.), *Sefer Assaf*, Jerusalem, 1953, 126–41.

Hebräische Berichte über die Judenverfolgungen während der Kreuzzüge, ed. A. Neubauer and H. Stern, Berlin, 1892.

Sefer Gzeroth Ashkenaz ve-Sarfath (Heb.), ed. A. M. Habermann with an introduction by J. Baer, Jerusalem, 1946.

S. Baron, *A Social and Religious History of the Jews*, vol. 4, N.Y., 1957.

III Conquest and Establishment

Descriptions of the conquest will be found in all the general histories of the kingdom. The geopolitical factors which influenced crusader policy were elaborated in detail by:

J. Prawer, *Histoire du royaume latin de Jérusalem*, 2 vols, Paris, 1969–71. For the history of the northern principalities:

H. F. Tournebize, *Histoire politique et religieuse de l'Arménie depuis les origines des Arméniens jusqu'à la mort de leur dernier roi*, Paris, 1910.

D. Ter-Gregorian Iskenderian, *Die Kreuzfahrer und ihre Beziehungen zu den armenischen Nachbarfürsten bis zum Untergange der Grafschaft Edessa*, Leipzig, 1915.

Cl. Cahen, *La Syrie du nord à l'époque des Croisades et la principauté franque d'Antioche*, Paris, 1940.

J. Richard, *Le comté de Tripoli sous la dynastie toulousaine, 1102–1187*, Paris, 1945.

On the maritime Italian powers, see below, cap. XVI and cap. XVIII. For geographical data of the crusader expansion, see below, cap. V and cap. IX.

IV The Kingdom of Jerusalem

The earliest phase of state organization was studied by:

H. Hampel, *Untersuchungen über das lateinische Patriarchat von Jerusalem von der Eroberung des heiligen Landes bis zum Tode des Patriarchen Arnulf, 1099–1118*, Breslau, 1899.

B. Kugler, *Boemund und Tankred Fürsten von Antiochien*, Tübingen, 1862.

R. B. Yewdale, *Bohemond I, Prince of Antioch*, Princeton, 1912.

J. Prawer, 'Les premiers temps de la féodalité dans le royaume latin de Jérusalem', *Revue d'histoire du droit*, 22 (1954), 401–24.

Cl. Cahen, 'La féodalité et les institutions politiques de l'Orient latin', *XII Conv. Volta. Accad. Naz. dei Lincei*, Rome, 1959, 167–94.

V The Conquered Lands and Their People

See the studies on the historical geography in cap. IV, note 5. In addition:

C. Ritter, *Die Sinai-Halbinsel, Palästina und Syrien*, 3 vols, Berlin, 1852–5.

M. Gaudefroy-Demombynes, *La Syrie à l'époque des mamelouks d'après les auteurs arabes. Déscription géographiques, économiques et administratives*, Paris, 1923.

F.-M. Abel, *Géographie de la Palestine*, 2 vols, Paris, 1933–8.

M. Benvenisti, *The Crusaders in the Holy Land*, Jerusalem, 1970.

G. A. Smith, *The Historical Geography of the Holy Land*, N.Y. and London, 1932.

Encyclopedia Hebraica, vol. VI, *Eretz Israel* (Heb.)

There are no general studies of Palestinian population at this period. Christian communities, see below, bibliography to cap. XII. On the Jews, see below, bibliography to cap. XIII.

VI   The Conquerors – Classes of Society

A   NOBILITY

Many studies deal with the European nobility of the Crusades, but very few with that ultimately established in the Latin kingdom. Besides chapters in the general histories of H. Prutz, E. Rey and J. Richard, see:

J. Prawer, 'Les prémiers temps de la féodalité dans le royaume latin de Jérusalem', *Revue d'histoire du droit*, 22 (1954), 401–24.

——, 'La noblesse et le régime féodal du royaume latin de Jérusalem'. *Le Moyen Age*, 1959, 41–74 (Engl. transl. by F. L. Cheyette, *Lordship and Community in Mediaeval Europe*, 1968, 156–79).

S. Runciman, 'The Families of Outremer: The Feudal Nobility of the Crusader Kingdom of Jerusalem', *Creighton Lecture*, London, 1959.

J. Richard, 'Pairie d'Orient latin: Les quatre baronies du royaume de Jérusalem et de Chypre', *Rev. hist. de droit français et étranger*, 28 (1950), 67–89. Cf. also: Cl. Cahen, 'La féodalité et les institutions politiques de l'Orient latin', *XII Conv. Volta. Accad. Naz. dei Lincei*, Rome, 1959, 167–94.

B   BURGESSES

The most important source regarding the burgesses is the anonymous mid-13th century legal treatise: *Livre des Assises des Bourgeois*, ed. Beugnot, *Lois* II, Paris, 1842. As to its origin and connection with the Provençal law treatise, the so-called *Lo Codi*, see J. Prawer, 'Étude préliminaire sur les sources et la composition du *Livre des Assises des Bourgeois*', *Rev. hist. de droit français et étranger*, 1954, 198–227, 358–82. Rich additional data are to be found in the legal and commercial deeds of the period. There is no special study of the burgesses as a class, though there are good descriptions of the court of burgesses.

A chapter on the burgesses by J. Prawer is scheduled for *A History of the Crusades*, vol. IV, ed. K. M. Setton. Particular aspects are studied by J. Prawer, 'Estates, Communities and the Constitution of the Latin Kingdom', *Proc. Israel Academy of Sciences and Humanities*, II (1966), No. 6.

C NATIONAL COMMUNES

Major data regarding the communes are to be found in the collections of privileges of the respective communes.

For Venice:

G. L. F. Tafel and G. M. Thomas, *Urkunden zur älteren Handels-und Staatsgeschichte Venedigs*, 3 vols, Vienna, 1856–7.

For Genoa:

Liber iurium rei publicae Ianuensis. Historiae Patriae Monumenta, vols VII–IX, Turin, 1854–7.

C. Imperiale di Sant Angelo, *Codice diplomatico della republica di Genova dell 1163 al 1190*, 3 vols, Rome, 1936–42.

For Pisa:

G. Müller, *Documenti sulle relazioni delle città Toscane coll'Oriente*, Firenze, 1879.

F. dal Borgo, *Raccolta di scelti diplomi Pisani*, Pisa, 1765.

For Marseilles:

L. Mery and F. Guindon, *Histoire analytique et chronologique des actes et des déliberations du corps et du conseil de la municipalité de Marseille*, I, Marseilles, 1841.

These major collections of official documents should be supplemented by the rich sources regarding commerce. See below bibliography to cap. XVI:D.

There is no special study of the nationals of the communes abroad, but material might be found in the works of Heyd, Schaube, Lopez and others indicated below in cap. XVI.

For Venice:

J. Prawer, 'Gli Veneziani e il colonie Veneziane nell regno latino de Gerusalemme', *Venezia e Levante*, ed. Fondazione Cini (in press).

VII The Crown

Our major primary sources are the detailed law treatises of the crusader jurists and the royal charters. Among the former the most important are the works of Philip of Novara, *Livre de forme de plait* in *Lois* I, 469–571, and a more elaborate treatise by the great feudal jurist Jean d'Ibelin, publ. as *Le livre de Jean d'Ibelin* in *Lois* I, 7–432. These should be confronted and checked with a curious treatise, written, it seems, at the turn of the twelfth century by an anonymous jurist and published as *Le Livre au Roi* in *Lois* I, 601–44. The latter draws a different picture of the competences of the Crown and reflects an earlier stage of evolution, deliberately omitted by the aristocratic jurists of the thirteenth century.

As the royal archives are lost we have to look for extant royal charters in the surviving collections of the ecclesiastical establishments and mercantile communes. The publication of the extant original royal charters is being prepared by H. E. Mayer. A new edition of Philip of Novara is being prepared by J. Richard.

G. Dodu, *Hist. des institutions monarchiques du royaume Latin de Jérusalem*, Paris, 1894, and J. L. La Monte, *The Feudal Monarchy in the Latin Kingdom of Jerusalem, 1100–1291*, Cambridge, Mass., 1932; new studies entirely changed our view of the position and evolution of the Crown and of the High Court, and to a lesser degree of the working of the kingdom's central administration.

J. Richard, *Le royaume latin de Jérusalem*, Paris, 1953, was a pioneering work in the field and pointed the direction of new research.

J. Prawer, 'Les prémiers temps de la féodalité dans le royaume latin de Jérusalem', *Revue d'histoire du droit*, 22 (1954), 401–24.

For the understanding and use of the law treatises, see: M. Grandclaude, *Etude critique sur les Livres des Assises de Jérusalem*, Paris, 1923. Some of his conclusions regarding the *Livre des Assises des Bourgeois* and probably *Le Livre au Roi* have to be revised.

Royal legislation needs a thorough study to follow up and complete M. Grandclaude, 'Liste d'Assises remontant au premier royaume de Jérusalem', *Mélanges Paul Fournier*, Paris, 1929, 329 ff.

All extant charters are indicated in the monumental *Regesta Regni Hierosolymitani*, ed. R. Röhricht, Innsbruck, 1893–1904.

VIII   The Machinery of Government

The sources are the same as in the foregoing chapter.

There are no monographic studies of the central administration. Chapters dealing with the problem will be found in:

G. Dodu, *Histoire des institutions monarchiques dans le royaume latin de Jérusalem, 1099–1291*, Paris, 1894.

J.L. LeMonte, *Feudal Monarchy in the Latin Kingdom of Jerusalem, 1100–1291*, Cambridge, Mass., 1932.

H. H. Delaborde, *Chartes de la Terre Sainte provenant de l'abbaye de Notre Dame de Josaphat*, Paris, 1880, introduction.

On the position of institutional studies, see:

Cl. Cahen, 'La féodalité et les institutions politiques de l'Orient latin', *XII Conv. Volta. Accad. Naz. dei Lincei*, Rome 1959, 167–94.

H. E. Mayer, 'Probleme moderner Kreuzzungs forschung', *Vierteljahreschrift für Sozial-und Wirtschaftsgeschichte*, 50 (1964), 505–13.

J. A. Brundage, 'Recent Crusade Historiography', *Catholic Hist. Rev.*, 49 (1964), 493–507.

IX   The Lordships – Government at the Local Level

No particular sources can be indicated for this chapter.

The process of emergence of a seigniorial class can be studied by following the history of the different noble families of the kingdom.

An original list of dynasties was compiled in the fourteenth century and largely supplemented by Ch. du Fresne Du Cange, *Les familles d'Outremer*, ed. E. G. Rey, Paris, 1869. Additional supplements were published by E. G. Rey as *Sommaire du supplément aux Familles d'Outremer*, Chartres, 1881, and by R. Röhricht, *Zusätze und Verbesserungen zu Du Cange*, Berlin, 1886.

Rich additional material was collected by L. de Mas Latrie and remains in MSS in the Bibliothèque Nationale, Paris: Ms. fr. n.a. 6793–803. Some of it was used in later published studies.

H. Pirie-Gordon, 'The Reigning Princes of Galilee', *Engl. Hist. Rev.*, 27 (1912), 445–61.

A. Giry 'Les châtelains de St Omer', *Bibl. de l'École des Chartes*, 35 (1874), 325–55.

L. de Mas Latrie, 'Les comtes de Jaffe et d'Ascalon', *Rev. des questions historiques*, 26 (1879), 181–200.

——'La Terre-au-delà-du-Jourdain et ses premiers seigneurs', *Bibl. de l'Ecole des Chartes*, 39 (1878), 416–20, 588.

——'Les seigneurs du Crac du Montréal', *Archivio Veneto*, 25 (1883)

E. G. Rey, 'Les seigneurs de Montréal et de la Terre d'Outre-le-Jourdain', *Rev. de l'Orient latin*, 4 (1896), 19–24.

J. L. La Monte, 'The Lords of Caesarea in the Period of the Crusades', *Speculum*, 22 (1947), 145 ff.

——'The Lords of Sidon in the 12th and 13th centuries'. *Byzantion*, 17 (1944/5), 183 ff.

M. E. Nickerson, 'The seigneurie of Beirut in the 12th century and the Brisebarre family of Beirut-Blanchegarde', *Byzantion*, 19 (1949), 747 ff.

L. de Mas Latrie, 'Les seigneurs d'Arsuf en Terre Sainte', *Rev. des questions hist.*, 55 (1894), 585–97.

E. G. Rey, 'Les seigneurs de Giblet', *Rev. de l'Orient latin*, 3 (1895).

J. L. La Monte. 'The lords of Le Puisset on the Crusades', *Speculum*, 17 (1942), 100ff.

E. G. Rey, 'Note sur le fief du comte Josselin, sénéchal de Jérusalem', *Bull. de la Soc. Nat. des Antiquaires de France*, 1880.

L. de Mas Latrie, 'Le fief de la Chamberlaine et les Chambellans de Jérusalem', *Bibl. de l'Ecole des Chartes*, 43 (1882), 647–52.

E. G. Rey, 'Note sur la vicomté du Merle (Tantaurah) en Palestine', *Bull. de la Soc. Nat. des Antiquaires de France*, 1874.

——'Note sur le fief de St. George de Labaene en Syrie', *ibid.*, 1878.

J. Richard, 'Les listes des seigneuries dans le Livre de Jean d'Ibelin. Recherches sur l'Assebèbe et Mimars', *Rev. hist. de droit français et étranger*, series 4, 32 (1954), 565–77.

L. de Mas Latrie, 'De quelques seigneuries de Terre Sainte oubliées par Ducange dans les Familles d'Outremer: les seigneurs de St. Georges, du Bouquiau et de Saor', *Rev. historique*, 8 (1878), 107–20.

J. L. La Monte. 'John d'Ibelin, the Old Lord of Beirut, 1177–1236', *Byzantion*, 12 (1937), 417–48.

J. Richard, 'Un évêque d'Orient latin au XIVe siècle: Guy d'Ibelin, évêque de Limassol', *Bull. de correspondance hellénique*, 74 (1950), 98–133.

H. H. Rüdt-Collenberg, 'Les premiers Ibelins', *Moyen-âge*, 1965, 433–74.
See also:

J. L. La Monte. 'Chronologie de l'orient latin. Enquête de la commission de chronologie', *Bull. of the International Committee of Historical Sciences*, XII, 2, Paris, 1943, 141–202.
Basic for the study of the problem:

J. Richard, 'Pairie d'Orient latin. Les quatres baronnies des royaumes de Jérusalem et de Chypre', *Rev. hist. de droit français et étranger*, series 4, 28 (1950), 67–88.

Cl. Cahen, 'La féodalité et les institutions politiques de l'Orient latin', *XII Conv. Volta. Accad. Naz. dei Lincei*, Rome, 1959, 167–95.

Maps:

C. J. Johns, *Palestine of the Crusaders*, Jerusalem, 1946.

J. Prawer and M. Benvenisti, *Crusader Palestine. Atlas of Israel*, Sheet 12/ix, Jerusalem, 1960, and new ed., 1972.
Studies of particular areas:

J. Riley-Smith, *The Knights of St John in Jerusalem and Cyprus*, London, 1967.

G. Beyer, 'Das Gebiet der Kreuzfahrer-schaft Caesarea siedlungs und territorialgeschichtlich untersucht', *ZDPV*, LIX (1936). 'Neapolis (Nablus) und sein Gebiet in der Kreuzfahrerzeit. Eine topographische und historischgeographische Studie', *ZDPV*, LXIII (1940). 'Die Kreuzfahrergebiete von Jerusalem und S. Abraham (Hebron)', *ZDPV*, LXV (1942). 'Die Kreuzfahrergebiete Akko und Galilaea', *ZDPV*, LXVII (1944/5), 183–260. 'Die Kreuzfahrergebiete Südwestpalästinas', *ZDPV*, LXVIII (1946/51).

R. Röhricht, 'Studien zur mittelalterlichen Geographie und Topographie Syriens', *ZDPV*, X (1887), 195–320; XI (1888), 139–49; XII (1889), 33–4; XVIII (1895), 82–7; XIX (1896), 60–2.

F. M. Abel, *Géographie de la Palestine*, 2 vols, Paris, 1934–9.

P. Deschamps, *Les châteaux des Croisés en Terre Sainte, II: La défense du royaume de Jérusalem*, Paris, 1939.

R. Dussaud, *Topographie historique de la Syrie antique et médiévale*, Paris, 1927.

X   The Church

The main sources of ecclesiastical history are the archives of the ecclesiastical establishments. Among the chronicles the most important in this regard are those written by William, bishop of Tyre, Jacques, bishop of Acre and the chronicle of the Venetian Marino Sanudo. Occasionally additional material can be found in the different 'Itineraries', that is descriptions of the Holy Land written by pilgrims of the crusader period.

Chronicles:

Wilelmus Tyrensis, *Historia rerum in partibus transmarinis gestarum*. '*Recueil des Historiens des Croisades*', *Historiens Occidentaux*, I, 1–2. A new edition by H. E. Mayer and R. B. C. Huggens in preparation.

Jacobus de Vitriaco, *Historia Orientalis*, ed. Bongars, *Gesta Dei per Francos*, Hanover, 1611, 1076–85. The description of church organization is also to be found in his *Letters*, ed. R.B.C. Huygens, Leiden, 1960.

Marino Sanudo, *Liber Secretorum Fidelium Crucis*, ed. Bongars, *Gesta Dei per Francos*, Hanover, 1611, 175–9. Reprint with introduction by J. Prawer publ. by Toronto Univ. Press, 1972.

Collections of sources (excluding sources on the military orders listed in bibliography to cap. XIV):

E. de Rozière, *Cartulaire de l'église du Saint-Sépulcre de Jérusalem*, Paris, 1849 (also in Migne, *Patrologia latina*, 155). New edition by Mlle G. Bautier in preparation.

H. F. Delaborde, *Chartes de la Terre Sainte provenant de l'abbaye de Notre-Dame de Josaphat*, Paris, 1880.

Ch. Kohler, 'Chartes de l'abbaye de Notre Dame de Josaphat en Terre Sainte, 1108–1291. Analyse et extraits', *Rev. de l'Orient latin*, VII (1899) – complements Delaborde.

Delaville le Roulx, *Cartulaire du Mont Tabor* in *Cartulaire générale de l'Ordre des Hospitaliers de Saint Jean de Jérusalem*, vol. 1 (at end).

E. G. Rey, 'Chartes de l'abbaye du Mont Sion', *Mem. de la Soc. Nat. des Antiquaires de France*, 8 (1887), 31–56.

J. Richard, 'Le chartier de Ste Maria Latine et l'établissement de Raymond de St-Gilles à Mont Pèlerin', *Mélanges Louis Halphen*, Paris, 1951.

——'Quelques textes sur les premiers temps de l'église latine de *Jérusalem*', *Rec. des travaux offerts à C. Brunel*, Paris, 1955, 420 ff.

H. E. Mayer, 'Sankt Samuel auf dem Freudenberge und sein Besitz nach einem unbekannten Diplom König Balduins V', *Quellen und Forschungen aus italienischen Archiven und Bibliotheken*, 44 (1964), 35–71.

The sources regarding the Franciscans are conveniently indicated in:

G. Golubovich, *Biblioteca Bio-bibliographica della Terra Santa e dell' Oriente Francescano*, I, Quaracchi, 1906.

The following studies deal directly with the history and organization of the Latin Church in the Holy Land under crusader domination:

W. Hotzelt, 'Kirchengeschichte Palästinas im Zeitalter der Kreuzzüge', *Palästinahefte des Deutschen Vereins vom Heiligen Lande*, 29–32 (1940).

——, 'Kirchliche Organisation und religiöses Leben in Palästina während der Kreuzzugszeit', 24–7.

R. Röhricht, 'Syria Sacra', *Zeit d. deut Palästinavereins*, 10 (1887), 1–48, and 11(1888), 139–42.

Special chapters are devoted to the subject in the works of G. Dodu, J. L. La Monte, J. Richard, and H. E. Mayer.

XI   Pilgrims, Pilgrimages and the 'Holy Geography' of the Holy Land

The main sources for the chapter are the 'Itineraries' of Western pilgrims listed below and in the bibliography to cap. XVI. In addition there are commercial contracts of Italian and Provençal merchants and the maritime regulations of the communes indicated in the bibliography to the same chapter.

On pilgrimages see especially:

B. Kötting, *Peregrinatio religiosa. Die Wallfahrten in der Antike und das Pilgerwesen in der alten Kirche*, Münster, 1950.

E. van Cauwenbergh, *Les pèlerinages expiatoires et judiciaires dans le droit communal Belgique au moyen-âge*, Louvain, 1922.

A. Baumstark, *Abendländische Palästinapilger des ersten Jahrtausends und ihre Berichte*, Köln, 1906.

E. Labande, 'Recherches sur les pèlerins dans l'Europe des XIe et XIIe siècles', *Cahiers de civilisation médiévale*, I (1958) 159–69, 339–49. The full list of sources is indicated in:

R. Röhricht, *Bibl. geographica Palaestinae*, Berlin, 1890 (suppl. in *Zeit. d. deut. Palästinavereins*, 14 (1891), 113–34; 16 (1893), 269–96). Reprinted with suppl., Jerusalem, 1963.

M. Villey, *La Croisade. Essai sur la formation d'une théorie juridique*, Paris, 1942.

P. Rousset, *Les origines et les caractères de la première Croisade*, Neuchâtel, 1945.

On the relation between pilgrimage and Crusade:

P. Alphandéry, *La Chrétienté et l'idée de Croisade*, 2 vols, ed. A. Dupront, Paris, 1954–9.

J. A. Brundage, *Medieval Canon Law and the Crusader*, Univ. Wisconsin Press, 1969, 3–30.

The major sources were published:

Itinera Hierosolymitana et descriptiones Terrae Sanctae bellis sacris anteriora et latina lingua exarata, ed. T. Tobler and A. Molinier, I, 1–2 vols, Geneva, 1872; vol. II, ed. A. Molinier and Ch. Kohler, Geneva, 1885.

T. Tobler, *Descriptiones Terrae Sanctae ex saec.*, VIII, IX, XII, XV. Leipzig, 1874.

J. C. M. Laurent, *Peregrinatores medii aevi quattuor*, Leipzig, 1873.

M. Michelant and G. Raynaud, *Itinéraires à Jérusalem et descriptions de Terre Sainte rédigés en français aux XIè et XIIIè siècles*. Geneva, 1882.

XII   The Oriental Churches

There is no monograph on the subject but the problem is treated in almost all studies of the Latin kingdom. The approach is unfortunately very often biased by preconceived ideas or apologestic tendencies of the historians.

Our sources comprise, besides the juridical treatises, the legal documents, the 'Itineraries' and the Western chronicles of the kingdom, also several chronicles written by the oriental Christians themselves.

The point of view of the Jacobites is represented by:

Michel le Syrien, *Chronique*, ed. and transl. J.-B. Chabot, 4 vols, Paris, 1899–1924.

Barhebraeus (Gregoire Abu'l-Faraj), *Chronicon Ecclesiasticum*, ed. J. B. Abbeloos and Th. J. Lamy, 3 vols, Louvain, 1872–7.

Barhebraeus, *Chronography*, ed. and transl. E. A. Budge, 2 vols, Oxford, 1932.

Syrian Anonymous Chronicle of 1234. Text ed. Chabot in *Corpus Scriptorum Christianorum Orientalium. Scriptores Syri.*, Ser. III, vols 14–15. Partially transl. by A. S. Tritton in *Journal of Royal Asiatic Society*, 1933, 69–100; 273–305. A good summary by A. Rücker in *Oriens Christianus*, 32 (1935), 124–39.

Armenian chroniclers, but for Matthew of Edessa, deal very rarely with the Latin kingdom proper. The chronicles are published with Fr. transl. in *Recueil des historiens des Croisades. Historiens Arméniens*, 2 vols, Paris, 1896–1906.

See also E. Dulaurier, *Bibliothèque historique arménienne ou choix des principaux historiens arméniens*, Paris, 1858.

The Coptic point of view is represented by the compilation known as the *History of the Patriarchs of the Egyptian Church* by Sawirus ibn al-Mukaffa, ed. and Engl. transl. by A. S. Atiya, Y. Abd al-Massih and O. H. E. Khs. Burmester (last volume, Cairo, 1959, brings the narrative to AD 1106). Transl. and summaries in Latin by E. Renaudot, *Historia patriarcharum Alexandrinorum Jacobitarum a D. Marco usque ad finem saeculi, XIII*, Paris, 1713.

There is nothing comparable in Greek sources dealing directly with the Holy Land. But for general Byzantine chronicles the following 'Itineraries' are of greatest importance:

Vie et pélerinage de Daniel, hégoumène russe 1106–1107, Itinéraires russes en Orient, vol. I, transl. B. de Khitrovo, Geneva, 1889 (Engl. transl. by A. Stewart in *PPTS*, IV).

Johannes Phocas, *A brief description of the Holy Land, 1185, PPTS*, V, 1–36.

General studies:

D. Attwater, *The Christian Churches of the East*, vol. 2, Milwaukee, 1961.

R. Janin, *Les églises orientales et les rites orientaux*, Paris, 1926.

A. S. Atiya. *A History of Eastern Christianity*, London, 1968.

The most important studies:

E. Honigman, *Le couvent Barsauma et le patriarcat jacobite d'Antioche et de Syrie, Corpus Scriptorum Christianorum Orientalium, Subsidia*, vol. 7, Louvain, 1954.

C. Karalevskij, 'Antioche', *Dict d'hist. et géog. ecclésiastique*, 3 (1924), 566–703.

P. Kawerau, *Die jakobitische Kirche im Zeitaler der syrichen Renaissance. Idee und Wirklichkeit*, Berlin, 1955.

B. Spuler, '*Die westsyrische (monophysitische) Kirche unter dem Islam*', *Saeculum*, 9 (1958), 322–44.

I. Ziade, 'Syrienne (église)', *Dict. de théologie catholique*, 14, 3017–88.

F. Rey, 'Les conditions des indigènes dans les colonies italiennes de Syrie et de Chypre au moyen-âge, *Rev. hist. de droit français et étranger*, 23 (1899), 225–47.

G. Every, 'Syrian Christians in Palestine in the Middle Ages', *Eastern Churches Quarterly*, 6 (1945/6).
    See recently: E. S. Sivan, 'Notes sur la situation des chrétiens à l'époque ayyubide', *Rev. de l'hist. des religions* 1965, 8–130.

E. Cerulli, *Etiopi in Palestina. Storia delle communita etiopica di Gerusalemme*, 2 vols, Rome, 1943–7.

D. F. Meinardus, *The Copts in Jerusalem*, Cairo, 1960.

H. Duensing, 'Die Abessinier in Jerusalem', *ZDPV*, 39 (1916), 98–115.

R. Janin, 'Les Géorgiens à Jérusalem', *Echos d'Orient*, 16 (1913), 32–8, 211–19.

G. Peradze. 'An account of the Georgian monks and monasteries in Palestine as revealed in the writings of non-Georgian pilgrims', *Georgica* (1937), 181–246.

A. Zagarelli, 'Historische Skizze der Beziehungen Grusiens zum Heiligen Lande und zum Sinai' (transl. from Russ. by A. Anders), *ZDPV*, 12 (1889), 353 ff.

K. S. Salibi, 'The Maronites of the Lebanon under Frankish and Mamluk rule, 1099–1516', *Arabica*, 4 (1957), 288–303.

S. Vailhé, 'Les origines religieuses des Maronites', *Echos d'Orient*, 4 (1900), 96–102, 154–62.

A. Catoire, 'L'église maronite et le Saint-Siège, 1213–1911', *Echos d'Orient*, 15 (1912), 28–38.

G. Khouri-Sarkis, 'Introduction aux Églises de langue syriaque', *L'Orient Syrien*, 1 (1956), 3–30.

T. E. Dowling, *The Orthodox Greek Patriarchate of Jerusalem*, N.Y., 1913.

F. Macler, 'Les Arméniens en Syrie et en Palestine', *Congrès français de la Syrie*, Marseilles, 1919.

——, 'Notes latines sur les Nestoriens, Maronites, Arméniens, Georgiens, Mozarabes', *Rev. de l'hist. des religions*, 1918, 243–60.

See also the monumental work of G. Graf, *Geschichte der christlichen arabischen Literatur*, 4 vols, Vatican, 1944–53.

A. Baumstark and A. Rucker, *Die syrische Literatur. Hdb. der Orientalistik*, ed. B. Spuler, vols 2–3, Leiden, 1954.

W. Hotzelt, 'Kirchliche Organisation und religiöses Leben in Palästina während der Kreuzzugszeit', *Das Heilige Land in Vergangenheit und Gegenwart*, 24–7 (1940), 43–107.

XIII   The Jews

The sources of the history of the Jews in Palestine under crusader and Mameluk rule will be published in *Sefer ha-Yishuv*, vol. 3, ed. J. Baer, J. Prawer and H. Ben-Sasson.

An excellent collection of sources is that of B. Dinur, *Israel ba-Gola*, vols II–III new (enlarged) edition in print. This enlarges and supplements the great collection of the Cairo Geniza material published by: J. Mann, *The Jews in Egypt and in Palestine under the Fatimid Caliphs*, 2 vols, Oxford, 1920–2; *Id.*, *Texts and Studies in Jewish History and Literature*, 2 vols, 1931–5.

See also: E. Ashtor, *History of the Jews in Egypt and Syria under the Mameluks* (Hebrew), 3 vols, Jerusalem, 1951–70.

Additional material was published by S. D. Goitein in a large number of articles. See *Speculum*, 1964, 741–5.

Very important are the 'Itineraries' of the Jewish travellers, among them the famous description of Benjamin of Tudela. The 'Itineraries' and contemporary letters were conveniently edited by A. Ya'ari, *Masa'oth Eretz Israel*, Tel-Aviv, 1946, and *Iggroth Eretz-Israel*, Tel-Aviv, 1953.

Special studies:

J. Prawer, 'The Jews in the Latin Kingdom of Jerusalem' (Heb. with short Engl. summary), *Zion Quart. Rev.*, XI (1946), 38–82.

B. Kedar, 'Remarks on the History of the Jews in Jerusalem in the thirteenth century' (Heb.), *Zion Quarterly Rev.* 41, 1972, 82–94.

Z. Ankori, *The Karaites in Byzantium*, N. Y., 1953.

XIV   The Military Orders

The archives of the military orders were moved to Europe before the fall of the Latin Kingdom and escaped destruction. The archives of the Templars were to be handed over to the Hospitallers at the dissolution of the order, but local (royal, princely and feudal) interests often prevented—especially in France—the execution of this arrangement and only poor remnants have come down to our time.

Major collections of sources:

J. Delaville le Roulx, *Cartulaire général de l'ordre des Hospitaliers de St. Jean de Jérusalem, 1110–1310*, 4 vols, Paris, 1894–1906 (replaces all earlier publications including S. Paoli, 2 vols, Lucca, 1733–7) contains also the rules and statutes of the order.

Marquis d'Albon, *Cartulaire général de l'ordre de Temple* (1119?–50). *Recueil des chartes et de bulles relatives à l'Ordre de Temple*, Paris, 1913. Suppl. by Fournier, Paris, 1922.

La Règle de Temple, ed. H. de Curzon, Paris, 1880.

G. Schnürer, *Die ursprüngliche Templerregel*, Freiburg im Breisgau, 1903.

E. Strehlke, *Tabulae ordinis Theutonici*, Berlin, 1869.

M. Perlbach, *Die Statuten des deutschen Ordens*, Halle, 1890.

A. de Marsy, 'Fragment d'un cartulaire de l'Ordre de St. Lazare en Terre Sainte', *Arch. de l'Orient latin*, II (1884), 121–58.

Most studies dealing with the military orders usually include the Orient and the Christian West. The best documented and most comprehensive study of the military orders is H. Prutz, *Die geistlichen Ritterorden. Ihre Stellung zur kirchlichen, politischen, gesellschaftlichen und wirtchaftlichen Entwicklung des Mittelalters*, Berlin, 1908.

There is no special study of the Templars in the East. Among the general histories of the Templars:

G. A. Campbell, *The Knights Templars*, London, 1937.

H. Prutz, *Entwicklung und Untergang des Tempelherrenordens*, Berlin, 1888. See also: H. Neu, *Bibliographie des Templer-Ordens, 1927–65*, Bonn, 1965.

The older studies of J. Delaville le Roulx, *Les Hospitaliers en Terre Sainte et à Chypre*, 1904, and E. J. King, *The Knights Hospitallers in the Holy Land*, 1931, have been dated, by a thorough study of J. Riley-Smith,

The Knights of St. John in Jerusalem and Cyprus, c. 1050–1310, London, 1967.

See also:

H. Prutz, 'Die finanziellen Operationen der Hospitaliter', *Sitzungsberichte d.-philog. und phil. -hist. Klasse d. Bayerischen Akad. d. Wissenschaften*, Munich, 1906.

E. Wickersheimer, 'Organisation et legislation sanitaires au Royaume franc de Jérusalem', *Arch. internat. d'histoire des sciences*, vol. 4 (1951).

J. Piquet, *Les banquiers au Moyen Age: Les Templiers*, Paris, 1939.

M. Melville, *La vie des Templiers*, Paris, 1951.

M. L. Bulst-Thiele, 'Zur Geschichte der Ritterorden und d. Königreichs Jerusalem im XIIIten Jahrhundert (bis 1244)', *Deutsches Archiv f. Erforschung d. Mittelalters*, 22 (1966).

For the Teutonic Order see n. 32.

XV   Warfare and Fortifications

A   FORTIFICATIONS

The best studies of crusader fortifications are the monumental works of:

C. Enlart, *Les monuments des Croisés dans le royaume de Jérusalem: Architecture religieuse et civile*, 2 vols, Paris, 1928.

P. Deschamps, *Les châteaux des Croisés en Terre Sainte:* I. Le Crac des Chevaliers, Paris, 1934. II. La défense du royaume de Jérusalem, Paris, 1939. Parallel studies of the County of Tripoli and Principality of Antioch in preparation. These replace the pioneer work, excellent for its time, of E. Rey, *Étude sur les monuments de l'architecture militaire des Croisés en Syrie et dans l'Ile de Chypre*, Paris, 1871.

In addition, many plans are to be found in:

W. Müller-Wiener, *Castles of the Crusaders*, London, 1966.

T. S. R. Boase, *Castles and Churches of the Crusading Kingdom*, Oxford, 1967.

For a more popular treatment of the subject see:

R. Fedden and J. Thomson, *Crusader Castles*, London, 1957.

For an inventory of plans:

R. B. C. Huygens, 'Monuments de l'époque des Croisades. Réflexions a propos de quelques livres récents', *Bibliotheca Orientalis*, XXV (1968) 4–9.

An excellent guide to Crusader antiquities:

M. Benvenisti, *The Crusaders in the Holy Land*, Jerusalem, 1970, esp. 273 ff.

The general treatment of the subject since E. Rey and especially H. Prutz, *Kulturgeschichte der Kreuzzüge*, Berlin 1883, 181–213, and partially P. Deschamps, *op. cit.*, was reviewed and criticized in the excellent study of R. C. Smail, *Crusading Warfare, 1097–1193*, Cambridge, 1956, 204–51.

B   CRUSADER ARMIES

A large number of studies deal with crusader armies and warfare in the framework of the military history of the Middle Ages.

The classical studies are:

Ch. Oman. *A History of the Art of War in the Middle Ages*, 2 vols, London, 1924.

H. Delbrück, *Geschichte der Kriegskunst im Rahmen der politischen Geschichte*, vol. 3, Berlin, 1907.

O. Heermann, *Die Gefechtsführung abendländischer Heere im Orient in der Epoche des ersten Kreuzzuges*, Marburg, 1888.

G. Köhler, *Die Entwicklung des Kriegswesens und der Kriegführung in der Ritterzeit*, vol. 3, Breslau, 1886–90.

H. Delpech, *La Tactique au XIIIe siècle*, Paris, 1886.

F. Lot, *L'Art militaire et les armées au moyen-âge*, 2 vols, Paris, 1946.

H. Prutz, *Kulturgeschichte der Kreuzzüge*, 181–213.

J. L. La Monte, *op. cit.*, 138–66.

The whole subject was renewed by R. C. Smail, *Crusading Warfare, 1057–1193*, Cambridge, 1956. A study of the subject in the 13th century remains a *desideratum*.

XVI   *Economic Life and Commerce*

A   INTRODUCTION

The main sources for this chapter are the collections of documents of the different crusader institutions. They are listed in detail in chapters: The Church, The Military Orders, The Conquerors. In addition rich data, especially in regard to the fauna and flora of the kingdom, are to be found in contemporary descriptions of the Holy Land. A large number of (esp. Western) descriptions are translated into English in the series: *Palestine Pilgrims' Text Society*, 13 vols, London, 1890–7.

The Arabic descriptions were published by M. J. de Goeje, *Bibl. geographorum arabicorum*, 8 vols, Leiden, 1870–94. English summaries and translations were edited by G. Le Strange, *Palestine under the Moslems*, Boston, N.Y., 1890. German translations by Gildenmeister in *Zeitschrift des deutschen Palästinavereins*, vol. 4, 6–8, and *Zeitschrift der deutschen Morgenländischen Gesellschaft*, vol. 36. Fr. transl. by A.-S. Marmadji, *Textes géographiques arabes sur la Palestine*, Paris, 1951.

The Hebrew descriptions were edited by A. Ya'ari, *Masa'oth Eretz Israel*, Jerusalem, 1943. *Id.*, *Iggroth Eretz Israel*, Jerusalem, 1946.

B   AGRICULTURE

Near Eastern agriculture in the Middle Ages is a largely unexplored subject. There is too much of a tendency to project later data into earlier periods, and not enough direct studies of the earlier periods.

Chapters on agriculture and the rural economy can be found in the studies of Count Beugnot in his introductions to the two volumes of *Lois*, as also in the study of E. G. Rey. In addition: Count Beugnot, 'Mémoire sur le régime des terres dans les principautés fondées en Syrie par les Francs à la suite des Croisades', *Bibl. de l'École des chartes*, 14–15 (1853–4), which is antiquated.

More reliable is the chapter on agriculture in H. Prutz, *Kulturgeschichte der Kreuzzüge*, 313–34.

H. G. Preston, *Rural conditions in the Latin Kingdom of Jerusalem during the 12th and 13th Centuries*, Philadelphia, 1903, projects European institutions into the crusader establishments.

From among modern studies: Cl. Cahen, 'Notes sur l'histoire des croisades et de l'Orient latin: le régime rural syrien au temps de la domination franques', *Bullet. de la Faculté des Lettres de l'Université de Strasbourg*, 29 (1950/1). For the time being the only detailed study of agricultural demography and techniques: J. Prawer, 'Étude de quelques problèmes agraires et sociaux d'une seigneurie croisée au XIIIe siècle', *Byzantion*, 22/3 (1952–3).

C   MONEY

General:

C. M. Cipolla, *Money, Prices and Civilization in the Mediterranean World*, Princeton, 1956.

A. Dopsch, *Naturalwirtschaft und Geldwirtschaft in der Weltgeschichte*, Vienna, 1930.

M. Bloch, 'Économie nature ou économie argent', *Annales d'hist. sociale*, I (1939), 7–16.

Van Werveke, 'Économie nature et économie argent', *Annales*, 3 (1931), 428–35.

M. Bloch, 'Le problème de l'or au Moyen-âge', *Annales*, 5 (1933), 1–34.

R. S. Lopez, 'The Dollar of the Middle Ages', *Journal of Economic History*, II (1951), 209–34.

——, 'Il dollaro dell'alto medioevo', *Misc. in onore di Roberto Cessi*, Rome, I, 1958, 111–19.

——, 'Il ritorno all'oro nell'Occidente ducentesco', *Riv. storica italiana*, 65 (1953), 161–98.

N. Rodolico, 'Il sistema monetario e le classi sociali nel Medioevo', *Rivista Italiana di Sociologia*, 8 (1904), 462–9.

R. S. Lopez, 'Back to gold, 1252', *Econ. Hist. Rev.*, 9 (1956–7), 227 ff.
Crusader numismatics:

G. Schlumberger, *Numismatique de l'Orient latin*, Paris, 1954[2].

D. H. Cox, 'The Tripolis Hoard of French Seigniorial and Crusaders' Coins', *Numismatic Notes and Monographs*, no. 59, N.Y., 1933.

H. Longuet, 'La trouvaille de Kessab en Orient latin', *Rev. numismatique*, 38 (1935).

C. Desimoni, 'Observations sur les monnaies, les poids et les mesures cités dans les actes du notaire génois Lamberto di Sambuceto', *Revue de l'Orient Latin*, 3 (1895), 1–25.

J. Yvon, 'France, Italie et l'Orient latin', *A Survey of Numismatic Research, 1960–1965*, II: Medieval and Oriental Numismatics, ed. K. Skaare and G. C. Miles, Copenhagen, 1967, 216–56.

——'Deux Trésors de Monnaie d'Or des Croisés', *Museum Notes*, II, 295–302, pl. 48.

——'Monnaies et sceaux de l'Orient latin', *Revue numismatique*, 8 (1966), 89–107. pl. III.

Ph. Grierson, 'A Rare Crusader Bezant with the *Christus Vincit* Legend', *American Numismatic Society, Museum Notes*, VI, 169–78.

P. Balog, 'La trouvaille du Fayoum: dirhems ayoubites du premier roi Memelouk Aybek et d'imitation arabe des Croisés', *Bull. de l'Inst. d'Egypte*, 34 (1951–5), 17–55.

A. Ehrenkreuz, 'The Standard Fineness of Gold Coins circulating in Egypt at the time of the Crusades', *Jour. Amer. Oriental Soc.*, 74 (1954), 162–6.

Shirley Fox, 'Diemaking in the Twelfth Century', *Brit. Num. Journal*, VI (1909), 191–6.

A new thorough study of Crusader money by M. Melcalf and A. Gordus is in press.

D   INTERNATIONAL COMMERCE

The sources for the study of commerce can be roughly divided into collections of international treaties which regulated the standing of the different communes, sources of private origin, namely commercial contracts of companies or individual merchants, and commercial manuals. The treaties are indicated in the bibliography to cap. VI:C.

For bibliographical guidance see the excellent résumé of R.-H. Bautier, 'Les sources de l'histoire du commerce international en Méditeraneé (XII–XVe s.)', *Les sources de l'histoire maritime en Europe du Moyenâge au XVIIIe siècle*, ed. M. Mollat, 1962, 137–81.

The richest collection of contracts comes from the notaries of Genoa. A list of notaries was published by the Italian Direction of Archives: *Archivio di Stato di Genova. Cartolari notarili. Inventario*, I, 1 a, Rome, 1956.

From among the individual notaries were published:

Il cartolare di Giovanni Scriba, ed. M. Moresco and M. Chiaudano, 2 vols, Turin, 1935.

Oberto Scriba de Mercato, 1186, ed. M. Chiaudano, Genoa, 1940.

Oberto Scriba de Mercato, 1190, ed. M. Chiaudano and R. Morozzo della Rocca, Genoa, 1938.

Guglielmo Cassinese, 1190–2, ed., M. W. Hall, H. C. Krueger and R. L. Reynolds, Genoa, 1938.

Bonvillano, 1198, ed. J. E. Eierman, H. C. Krueger and R. L. Reynolds, Genoa, 1939.

For Venice:

R. Morozzo della Rocca and A. Lombardo, *Documenti del commercio veneziano nei secoli XI-XIII*, 2 vols, Turin, 1940.

——, *Nuovi documenti del commercio veneto*. Venice, 1953.

For Pisa:

Some contracts were published by G. Müller, op. cit., pp. 109–111.

R. S. Lopez, 'The unexplored wealth of the notarial archives of Pisa and Lucca', *Mélanges L. Halphen*, 417–32.

For Marseilles:

L. Blancard, *Documents inédits sur le commerce de Marseille au Moyen-âge*, 2 vols, Marseilles, 1884–5.

Special studies:

R. S. Lopez, 'The Trade of Medieval Europe: The South', *CEH*, II, 257–355 (with extensive bibliography).

A. Schaube, *Handelsgeschichte der romanischen Völker des Mittelmeergebiets bis zum Ende der Kreuzzüge*, München-Berlin, 1906.

G. Heyd, *Histoire du commerce du Levant au Moyen-Âge*, 2 vols. Amsterdam, 1967 (reprint).

R. S. Lopez and I. W. Raymond, *Medieval Trade in the Mediterranean World. Illustrative Documents*, N. Y., 1955.

S. Y. Labib, *Handelsgeschichte Ägyptens im Spätmittelalter (1171–1517)*. *Viert. f. Sozial u. Wirtschaftsgeschichte*, Beiheft, 1965.

E. Ashtor, *Histoire des prix et des salaires dans l'Orient médiéval*, Paris, 1969, esp. 231–67.

Commercial manuals:

S. F. B. Pegolotti, *La Pratica della mercatura*, ed. A. Evans, Cambridge, Mass., 1936.

Zibaldone da Canal. Manoscritto mercantile del sec. XIV, ed. A. Stussi, Venice, 1967.

In addition:

E. H. Byrne, *Genoese Shipping in the 12th and 13th centuries*, Cambridge, Mass., 1930.

Cl. Cahen, 'Orient latin et commerce du Levant', *Bullet. Fac. Lettres de Strasbourg*, 29 (1950/1).

E. Bach, *La cité de Gênes au XIIe siècle*, Copenhagen, 1955.

E. H. Byrne, 'The Genoese Colonies in Syria', *The Crusades and other Historical Essays presented to Dana C. Munro*, ed. L. J. Paetow, N.Y., 1928.

——, 'Commercial Contracts of the Genoese in the Syrian Trade of the 12th Century', *Quarterly Journal of Economics*, 31 (1916/17).

——, 'Genoese Trade with Syria in the 12th Century, *American Historical Rev.*, 25 (1919/20), 191–219.

G. Luzzatto, 'Relazioni economiche fra Oriente ed Occidente dal secolo X al XV', *Oriente ed Occidente nel Medio Evo*, Rome, 1957.

——, *Studi di storia economica veneziana*, Padua, 1954.

——, 'Capitale e lavoro nel commercio veneziano dei sec. XI e XII', *Rivista di storia economica*, 1941.

R. -H. Bautier, 'Les relations economiques des occidentaux avec les pays d'Orient an moyen-âge'. *Sociétés et compagnies du commerce en Orient et dans l'Océan Indien*, ed. M. Mollat, Paris, 1971, 263–331.

A. E. Sayous, 'Le rôle du capital dans la vie locale et le commerce extérieur de Venise entre 1050 et 1150', *Revue belge de philologie et d'histoire*, 13 (1934).

——, 'Les mandats de St. Louis sur son trésor et le mouvement international des capitaux pendant la septième croisade (1248–1254)', *Revue historique*, (1931), 254–304.

R. Pernoud, *Essai sur l'histoire du port de Marseille des origines à la fin du XIIIe siècle*, Marseilles, 1935.

There is little about the mercantile laws of the kingdom besides the dated introduction of Beugnot to his edition of the *Lois*. See also: H. Mitteis, 'Zum Schuld- und Handelsrecht der Kreuzfahrerstaaten', *Beiträge zum Wirtschaftsrecht*, I (1931), 229–88.

E   THE *FUNDA* AND THE LOCAL MARKET

Some of the problems connected with the *funda* were studied by J. Richard, 'Colonies marchandes privilégiées et marché seigneurial. La fonda d'Acre et ses *droitures*', *Moyen-Age*, 1953, 325–39. Additionally J. Prawer, 'L'établissement des coutûmes du marché à Saint Jean d'Acre', *Rev. hist. de droit français et étranger*, 1951, 329–51, and Cl. Cahen, 'A propos de coutûmes du marché d'Acre'. *Ibid.*, 1963, 287–90. Cf. n. 144.

XVII   The Arts

There is no study which deals with the arts of the Latin Kingdom as a whole. A general study of the subject by T. R. S. Boase is scheduled for the fourth volume of *A History of Crusades*, ed. by K. M. Setton. Studies of the different arts of the Kingdom are indicated in the notes of this chapter.

XVIII   The Legacy of an Epoch

There is no bibliography properly speaking which deals directly with the subject, since the Crusades were seldom analysed as a colonial movement in the sense emphasized here. Studies which attempt to place mediaeval colonial history into the general frame of colonial movements are more relevant. A stimulating essay was written by H. Lüthy, 'Die Epochen der Kolonisation und die Erschliessung der Erde: Versuch einer Interpretation des europäischen Zeitalters', *In Gegenwart der Geschichte*, 1967, 174–271 (parts publ. earlier in 1963 and 1966). See also H. Kohn, 'Reflections on colonialism', *The Idea of Colonialism*, ed. R. Strausz-Hupé and H. W. Hazard, N.Y., 1958, 1–16.

On the need for comparative studies: M. Jensen and R. Reynolds, 'European colonial experience. A plea for comparative studies', *Studi in onore de Gino Luzzatto*, IV, Milan, 1950, 75–90.

The most recent attempt to describe mediaeval expansion deals with the Latin kingdom in a cursory way and covers the 13th century only: P. Chaunu, *L'expansion européenne du XIIIe au XVe siècle*, Nouvelle Clio, Paris, 1969.

Special attention should be paid to the studies of Ch. Verliden: 'Précédents medievaux de la colonie en Amerique', *Comision Panamericana de Historia. Homenaje à José Marti*, Mexico, 1954, 7–61. 'Les origines coloniales de la civilisation atlantique. Antécèdents et types de structure', *Cahiers d'histoire mondiale*, 1 (1953), 378–98. 'Le problème de la continuité en histoire coloniale. De la colonisation médiévale à la colonisation moderne.' *Revista de Indias*, Madrid, 1951, 219–36.

'Les influences médiévales dans la colonisation de l'Amérique', *Revista de historia de America*, Mexico, 1950, 440 ss.

'Modernità e medioevalismo nell'economia e nella società coloniale americana', *Univ. de Napoli, Istituto di storia economica e sociale*, Annali IV (1965), 3–62.

INDEX